The Wiley Handbook of What Works in Child Maltreatment

The Wiley Handbook of What Works in Child Maltreatment

An Evidence-Based Approach to Assessment and Intervention in Child Protection

Edited by

Louise Dixon
Victoria University of Wellington, NZ

Daniel F. Perkins
Pennsylvania State University, US

Catherine Hamilton-Giachritsis
University of Bath, UK

Leam A. Craig
Forensic Psychology Practice Ltd
University of Birmingham, UK

WILEY Blackwell

This edition first published 2017
© 2017 John Wiley & Sons Ltd

All rights reserved. No part of this publication may be reproduced, stored in a retrieval system, or transmitted, in any form or by any means, electronic, mechanical, photocopying, recording or otherwise, except as permitted by law. Advice on how to obtain permission to reuse material from this title is available at http://www.wiley.com/go/permissions.

The right of Dr Louise Dixon, Prof. Daniel F. Perkins, Dr Catherine Hamilton-Giachritsis and Dr Leam A. Craig to be identified as the authors of the editorial material in this work has been asserted in accordance with law.

Registered Offices
John Wiley & Sons, Inc., 111 River Street, Hoboken, NJ 07030, USA
John Wiley & Sons Ltd, The Atrium, Southern Gate, Chichester, West Sussex, PO19 8SQ, UK

Editorial Office
The Atrium, Southern Gate, Chichester, West Sussex, PO19 8SQ, UK

For details of our global editorial offices, customer services, and more information about Wiley products visit us at www.wiley.com.

Wiley also publishes its books in a variety of electronic formats and by print-on-demand. Some content that appears in standard print versions of this book may not be available in other formats.

Limit of Liability/Disclaimer of Warranty
While the publisher and author have used their best efforts in preparing this book, they make no representations or warranties with respect to the accuracy or completeness of the contents of this book and specifically disclaim any implied warranties of merchantability or fitness for a particular purpose. It is sold on the understanding that the publisher is not engaged in rendering professional services and neither the publisher nor the authors shall be liable for damages arising herefrom. If professional advice or other expert assistance is required, the services of a competent professional should be sought.

Library of Congress Cataloging-in-Publication Data

Names: Dixon, Louise (Lecturer in psychology) author. | Perkins, Daniel, author.
Title: The wiley handbook of what works in child maltreatment: an evidence-based approach to
   assessment and intervention in child protection / Louise Dixon, Daniel F Perkins,
   Catherine Hamilton-Giachritsis, Leam A Craig.
Description: Hoboken: Wiley-Blackwell, 2017. | Includes index.
Identifiers: LCCN 2016051174| ISBN 9781118976173 (hardback) |
   ISBN 9781118976142 (Adobe PDF) | ISBN 9781118976104 (epub)
Subjects: LCSH: Child abuse–Diagnosis. | Abused children–Services for. |
   BISAC: PSYCHOLOGY / Forensic Psychology.
Classification: LCC HV6626.5 .D59 2017 | DDC 362.76–dc23
LC record available at https://lccn.loc.gov/2016051174

Cover Design: Wiley
Cover Image: © helgy716/Gettyimages

Set in 10/12.5pt Galliard by SPi Global, Pondicherry, India

10 9 8 7 6 5 4 3 2 1

LOUISE DIXON: To James, the most wonderful father any child could ever wish for. I love you, always.

DANIEL F. PERKINS: To Kiera, Brighid and Colman, you inspire me to work towards a better place.

CATHERINE HAMILTON-GIACHRITSIS: To my family – you mean the world to me and are the reason for everything.
Σας λατρεύω.

LEAM A. CRAIG: To Hazel and Tony for my loving childhood and the never-ending support to pursue my dreams.

LOUISE DIXON: To James, the most wonderful father any child could ever wish for. I love you, always.

DANIEL F. PERKINS: To Kiera, Brighid and Colman, you inspire me to work towards a better place.

CATHERINE HAMILTON-GIACHRITSIS: To my family – you mean the world to me and are the reason for everything.
Σας λατρεύω.

LEAM A. CRAIG: To Hazel and Tony for my loving childhood and the never-ending support to pursue my dreams.

Contents

About the Editors — x
Notes on Contributors — xiii
Foreword — xxiii
Acknowledgements — xxv

1 Overview and Structure of the Book — 1
Louise Dixon, Daniel F. Perkins, Catherine Hamilton-Giachritsis and Leam A. Craig

Part I   Research and Theoretical Perspectives — 13

2 Child Abuse and Neglect: Prevalence and Incidence — 15
Lorraine Radford

3 Child Abuse and Neglect: Ecological Perspectives — 29
Catherine Hamilton-Giachritsis and Alberto Pellai

4 Fatal Child Maltreatment — 48
Peter Sidebotham

5 Psychological, Economic and Physical Health Consequences of Child Maltreatment — 71
Sarah A. Font

6 The Neurobiology and Genetics of Childhood Maltreatment — 85
Eamon McCrory, Amy Palmer and Vanessa Puetz

7 Intimate Partner Violence and Child Maltreatment — 97
Louise Dixon and Amy M. Smith Slep

Part II   Children's Services and Public Health Approaches to Prevention — 111

8 Implications of Children's Services Policy on Child Abuse and Neglect in England — 113
Jenny Gray

9 Children's Services: Toward Effective Child Protection — 131
Chris Goddard, Karen Broadley and Susan Hunt

10 Using the Formal Pre-Proceedings Process to Prevent or Prepare
    for Care Proceedings in the UK   150
    Judith Masson

11 The Prevention of Child Maltreatment: The Case for a Public Health Approach
    to Behavioural Parenting Intervention   163
    Matthew R. Sanders and John A. Pickering

12 What Works to Prevent the Sexual Exploitation of Children and Youth   176
    Sandy K. Wurtele and Cindy Miller-Perrin

Part III Assessment   199

13 Evidence-Based Assessments of Children and Families: Safeguarding Children
    Assessment and Analysis Framework   201
    Stephen Pizzey, Arnon Bentovim, Liza Bingley Miller and Antony Cox

14 Utilising an Attachment Perspective in Parenting Assessment   222
    Carol George

15 Evidence-Based and Developmentally Appropriate Forensic
    Interviewing of Children   239
    Annabelle Nicol, David La Rooy and Michael E. Lamb

16 Considering Parental Risk in Parenting (Child Custody) Evaluation Cases
    Involving Child Sexual Exploitation Material   258
    Hannah L. Merdian, David M. Gresswell and Leam A. Craig

17 Assessments in Child Care Proceedings: Observations in Practice   278
    Martin C. Calder

Part IV Interventions with Children and Families   295

18 Evidence-Based Approaches to Empower Children and Families at Risk for Child
    Physical Abuse to Overcome Abuse and Violence   297
    Melissa K. Runyon, Stephanie Cruthirds and Esther Deblinger

19 Effective Therapies for Children and Non-offending Caregivers
    in the Aftermath of Child Sexual Abuse or Other Traumas   313
    Esther Deblinger, Elisabeth Pollio and Melissa K. Runyon

20 Effectiveness of Cognitive and Behavioural Group-Based Parenting Programmes
    to Enhance Child Protective Factors and Reduce Risk Factors for Maltreatment 328
    Tracey Bywater

21 Critical Factors in the Successful Implementation of Evidence-Based Parenting
    Programmes: Fidelity, Adaptation and Promoting Quality   349
    *Nick Axford, Tracey Bywater, Sarah Blower, Vashti Berry, Victoria Baker and
    Louise Morpeth*

22 School-Based Prevention of and Intervention in Child Maltreatment:
    Current Practice in the United States and Future Directions   367
    Cristin M. Hall, Megan C. Runion and Daniel F. Perkins

23 Using Assessment of Attachment in Child Care Proceedings to Guide Intervention 385
Patricia McKinsey Crittenden and Clark Baim

Part V Novel Interventions with Families **403**

24 Working Systemically with Families with Intimate Partner Violence 405
Arlene Vetere

25 Working with Non-Offending Parents in Cases of Child Sexual Abuse 415
Isabelle V. Daignault, Mireille Cyr and Martine Hébert

26 Working with Parents with Intellectual Disabilities in Child Care Proceedings 433
Beth Tarleton

27 Working with Parents with a Diagnosis of Personality Disorder 452
Tanya Garrett

28 Working with Parents Who Misuse Alcohol and Drugs 466
Rebecca L. Sanford, Stephanie Haynes Ratliff and Michele Staton-Tindall

Index 493

About the Editors

Louise Dixon, PhD, CPsychol is a Reader of Forensic Psychology at Victoria University of Wellington, New Zealand where she is the Director of the Forensic Programme. She is a Registered Forensic Psychologist with the UK Health and Care Professions Council (HCPC) and a New Zealand Registered Psychologist. Louise enjoys an active international research profile in the prevention of interpersonal and family aggression. Primarily, her research has centred on the study of intimate partner violence and abuse and the overlap with child maltreatment in the family. Louise aims to understand how and why people are aggressive in intimate relationships and the wider family, with a view to developing effective assessment, intervention programmes and policy. Louise's research has influenced practice and policy in correctional settings, policing and psychological, health and political areas. She is currently co-investigating a number of funded research projects in this area, including an Economic and Social Research Council-funded project *Understanding and improving risk assessment on domestic abuse cases*. She is a series editor to the *What Works in Offender Rehabilitation* Wiley-Blackwell book series, having published her first co-edited book in the series, *What Works in Offender Rehabilitation: An Evidence-Based Approach to Assessment and Treatment*, in 2013. She is a Fellow of the International Society for Research on Aggression (ISRA) and sits on the editorial board of international journals *Partner Abuse*, *Child Maltreatment* and *Aggressive Behavior*.

Daniel F. Perkins, PhD is a Professor of Family and Youth Resiliency and Policy at the Pennsylvania State University. He is Director of an applied research centre, the Clearinghouse for Military Family Readiness at Penn State (http://www.militaryfamilies.psu.edu/). In addition, he is also an affiliate faculty member of the Prevention Research Center for the Promotion of Human Development. Dr Perkins' scholarship involves the integration of practice and research into three major foci: (1) Positive Youth Development – decrease risks and increase skills and competencies of youth through evidence-based programmes; (2) Healthy Family Development – increase resiliency through evidence-based, strength-based educational programming; and (3) Community Collaboration – promote strategies for mobilising communities in support of children, youth and families. Dr Perkins has been designing and evaluating strengths-based family and youth development programmes in 4-H and Cooperative Extension, and leading complex projects within the field of prevention science, for more than 20 years. In particular, Dr Perkins examines Type II translational research, that is, examining the transitioning of evidence-based programmes tested in tightly controlled environments to their large-scale expansion into real-world settings. He is currently investigating the utilisation of technical assistance and the role of other contextual factors in contributing to long-term implementation quality and sustainability of evidence-based programmes. This current research, the PROSPER project (Spoth, Greenberg, Bierman & Redmond, 2004), is a large-scale randomised trial of a university–community partnership model for delivery, dissemination and sustainability of evidence-based preventative interventions. The Clearinghouse that he directs is an interactive, knowledge-based platform for helping professionals supporting military families to support their programme implementation and assessment activities. The Clearinghouse is specifically designed to promote and support: (1) the use of research-based decision-making; (2) the selection, dissemination and implementation of evidence-based programmes and practices; (3) the evaluation (process and outcome) of programmes and the identification or creation of measures and metrics; and (4) the continued education of professionals assisting military families.

Catherine Hamilton-Giachritsis, PhD, CPsychol, AFBPsS is registered with the UK Health and Care Professions Council as both a Forensic and Clinical Psychologist. She is currently a Reader in Clinical Psychology at the University of Bath, UK, having previously been Assistant Director of the Centre for Forensic and Criminological Psychology at the University of Birmingham, UK. Catherine has varied experience in both clinical practice and academic settings. She spent several years working in child and family services undertaking child/parenting assessments and providing expert witness testimony in child protection cases. Catherine also has an extensive body of research published in peer-reviewed journals, as well as by national and international organisations. Her work focuses on child maltreatment, trauma and risk assessment, considering both victims (e.g., prediction, prevention and impact of abuse and neglect) and offenders (e.g., harmful sexual behaviour; online grooming) and always has an applied element, impacting on individuals, organisations and policy-making. Catherine has undertaken international consultancy and led European and nationally funded research. She has worked collaboratively with a variety of NGOs and other organisations, such as the World Health Organization (WHO), the British Council, the National Society for the Prevention of Cruelty to Children (NSPCC), Escaping Victimhood, the Child Exploitation and Online Protection Centre (CEOP) and the regional police. Her work on the early institutionalisation of young children across Europe was considered at international level and led to training in multiple European countries. Current projects are focused on online abuse, homicidal bereavement and institutional care.

Leam A. Craig, PhD, MAE, CSci, CPsychol, FBPsS, FAcSS, EuroPsy is a Consultant Forensic and Clinical Psychologist and Partner at Forensic Psychology Practice Ltd. He is Professor (Hon) of Forensic Psychology, the Centre for Forensic and Criminological Psychology, University of Birmingham, and Visiting Professor of Forensic Clinical Psychology, School of Social Sciences, Birmingham City University, UK. He is a Chartered and Registered [Forensic and Clinical] Psychologist, a Chartered Scientist and holder of the European Certificate in Psychology. He is an Accredited Member of the Academy of Experts. In 2013 he was appointed Fellow of the British Psychological Society and the same year he was the recipient of the Senior Academic Award by the Division of Forensic Psychology for distinguished contributions to academic knowledge in forensic psychology. He has previously worked in forensic psychiatric secure services, learning disability hospitals and consultancy to prison and probation services throughout England, Wales and Northern Ireland, specialising in high-risk, complex cases. He is currently a Consultant to the National Probation Service on working with offenders with personality disorders. He has previously been instructed by the Catholic and Church of England Dioceses, South African Police Service and the United States Air Force as an expert witness. He acts as an expert witness to civil and criminal courts in the assessment of sexual and violent offenders and in matters of child protection. In 2015 he co-authored a Ministry of Justice research report into the use of expert witnesses in family law. In 2016 he was appointed as Chair of the British Psychological Society Expert Witness Advisory Group and awarded Fellowship of the Academy of Social Sciences. He sits on the editorial boards of several international journals. He has published over 80 articles and chapters in a range of research and professional journals. He has authored and edited ten books focusing on the assessment and treatment of sexual and violent offenders, offenders with intellectual disabilities and What Works in offender rehabilitation. He is a series editor for the *What Works in Offender Rehabilitation* book series for Wiley-Blackwell. His research interests include sexual and violent offenders, personality disorder and forensic risk assessment and the use of expert witnesses in civil and criminal courts.

Notes on Contributors

Nick Axford, PhD is Senior Researcher and Head of What Works at the Dartington Social Research Unit. He leads a team that focuses on identifying effective interventions to improve child well-being through evidence reviews and evaluations. Nick is a member of the Early Intervention Foundation Evidence Panel and an Advisor to the Board of the European Society for Prevention Research, and was co-editor of the *Journal of Children's Services* (2006–2015). He tweets about evidence-based prevention and early intervention @nick_axford.

Clark Baim, MEd (BPA, UKCP) is a Senior Trainer in Psychodrama Psychotherapy and Co-Director of Change Point Ltd. Clark has worked as a psychotherapist, group facilitator and trainer in prisons, probation centres, forensic hospitals and therapist training programmes in 15 countries. He was the lead national trainer for the sexual offending treatment programmes run by the probation service in England and Wales (2000–2012). He publishes in the fields of attachment, psychodrama psychotherapy, co-working, working with survivors of trauma, offender rehabilitation and theatre-based approaches with offenders and youth at risk. Clark is the co-author of *Attachment-based Practice with Adults* (2011) and is a fellow of the Berry Street Childhood Institute in Melbourne, Australia.

Victoria Baker, MA is an Associate of the Dartington Social Research Unit. She specialises in children's services research and theory of change development, and has trained practitioners and commissioners in evidence-based service design and how to promote implementation fidelity. Victoria is studying for a PhD on the experiences of young people who instigate parent abuse, and is a member of the Connect Centre for International Research on Interpersonal Violence and Harm at the University of Central Lancashire.

Dr Arnon Bentovim, FRCPsych, FRCPCH is a Child and Family Psychiatrist, Director and co-founder of Child and Family Training, and Visiting Professor, Royal Holloway University of London. He trained as a psychoanalyst and family therapist, and worked at Great Ormond Street Children's Hospital and the Tavistock Clinic. At Great Ormond Street he shared responsibility for Child Protection, and helped to initiate services (e.g., the first Sexual Abuse Assessment and Treatment Service in the UK; Child Care Consultation Service).

Vashti Berry, PhD is a Senior Research Fellow at the University of Exeter Medical School, within the South West Peninsula's Collaboration for Leadership in Applied Health Research and Care (PenCLAHRC). Her research interests are intervention development and evaluation, specifically around improving children's mental health and enhancing parenting support. Vashti is an expert reviewer for the NIHR, and is on the Early Intervention Foundation's evidence review panel. Vashti tweets about issues in the application of evidence @vashtilou.

Liza Bingley Miller, MSc is a co-founder of Child and Family Training. She was National Training Coordinator and a Director until retiring in December 2013. Liza currently chairs adoption panels for North Yorkshire's children and family care service. Liza is a social worker and family therapist by training, working for many years at Great Ormond Street Children's Hospital, London, including as a Leverhulme Research Fellow, and as a Lecturer in social work at the University of York.

Sarah Blower, PhD is a Research Fellow in the Department of Health Sciences at the University of York. Her research interests and expertise are in the design, implementation and evaluation of services designed to improve the well-being of children and families. Sarah is currently part of the Healthy Children Healthy Families Theme of the NIHR CLAHRC Yorkshire and Humber, and also manages the ESEE trial – an evaluation of parent programmes delivered using a proportionate universalism approach. Sarah tweets about service design, implementation and evaluation @sarah_blower.

Karen Broadley, MSocSci, BA has more than 20 years' experience working in child welfare. She has held a number of roles within the child protection system, including high-risk infant specialist and adolescent consultant. Karen has researched in various areas of child welfare, including a critique of the public health model; intervening to protect children from chronic maltreatment; risk assessment; and child protection decision-making. Karen is currently completing a PhD at Monash University studying prevention of child sexual abuse.

Tracey Bywater, PhD is Professor of Family Wellbeing in the Department of Health Sciences at the University of York. Her work focuses on enhancing parent and child outcomes, particularly around social–emotional well-being, behaviour and health. Tracey's work has involved randomised controlled trials of complex parent, teacher and child programmes. She is currently part of the Healthy Children Healthy Families Theme of the NIHR CLAHRC Yorkshire and Humber, and also leads on the social emotional development workstream for Better Start Bradford, and leads the ESEE trial – an evaluation of parent programmes delivered using a proportionate universalism approach. For information on research projects please see: www.york.ac.uk/healthsciences/ourstaff/tracey-bywater/#research. For publications see/www.york.ac.uk/healthsciences/our-staff/tracey-bywater/#publications.

Martin C. Calder, MA, CQSW established his own company in 2005, having managed the child protection and domestic abuse services for a decade. He has written extensively about developing and disseminating assessment tools to help frontline staff. He has done significant work with managers to ensure the local environment is conducive to safe, evidence-based assessment practice coupled with effective supervision. He works with a number of authorities to reshape frontline assessment processes, systems and assessments. He is an Honorary Senior Lecturer, Queens University, Belfast.

Antony Cox, FRCPsych is Emeritus Professor of Child and Adolescent Psychiatry at Guy's, King's and St Thomas' School of Medicine. He was formerly Professor of Child and Adolescent Psychiatry at Liverpool University Medical School. Research interests included epidemiology and aspects of parenting (e.g., cultural differences, the impact of parental mental illness, parent–child interactions) and interventions (e.g., for children with autism). Recent work has focused on developing training on standardised assessments for workers in health and social services.

Leam A. Craig, PhD, MAE, CSci, CPsychol, FBPsS, FAcSS, EuroPsy is a Consultant Forensic and Clinical Psychologist. He is Professor (Hon) of Forensic Psychology, University of Birmingham, and Visiting Professor of Forensic and Clinical Psychology, Birmingham City University. He is a Fellow of the British Psychological Society, a Fellow of the Academy of Social Sciences and recipient of the Senior Academic Award by the Division of Forensic Psychology. He acts as an expert witness to civil and criminal courts in the assessment of sexual and violent offenders and in matters of child protection and currently Chair of the British Psychological Society Expert Witness Advisory Group. He has over 80 publications including ten books and he is a series editor to the *What Works in Offender Rehabilitation* book series for Wiley-Blackwell. (See About the Editors section.)

Patricia McKinsey Crittenden, PhD is a developmental psychopathologist who worked with Mary Ainsworth at the University of Virginia to develop the Dynamic-Maturational Model of Attachment and Adaptation (DMM). She pioneered video-feedback with maltreating mothers, ran a family support centre, trained as a behavioural and family systems therapist, was the Director of the Miami Child Protection Team, and consulted to family courts in several countries. She has developed a lifespan series of assessments of attachment and has served on faculties in several countries. In 2004, she was given a Career Achievement Award by the European Family Therapy Association. She has published more than 100 empirical papers and chapters, as well as several books including: Crittenden (2015), *Raising Parents: Attachment, Representation, and Treatment*; Crittenden, Dallos, Landini & Kozlowska (2014), *Attachment and Family Systems Therapy*; Crittenden & Landini (2011), *Assessing Adult Attachment: A Dynamic-Maturational Model*.

Stephanie Cruthirds, LCSW is a mental health clinician at the Child Abuse Education and Service (CARES) Institute. She provides CPC-CBT and Trauma-Focused Cognitive Behavioural Therapy (TF-CBT), as well as training in CPC-CBT and consultation to professionals in Trauma-Focused Cognitive Behavioural Therapy (TF-CBT).

Mireille Cyr, PhD has been a full-time faculty member of the Psychology Department of University of Montreal for 25 years. She is the scientific director of the Centre for Interdisciplinary Research on Domestic Violence and Sexual Abuse and co-holder of the Marie-Vincent Inter-university Research Chair for sexual abuse on children. Her research focuses on the effects of child sexual abuse, parental support as a determinant of child's adaptation, and on investigative interviews of alleged young victims.

Isabelle V. Daignault, PhD is Professor at the School of Criminology of University of Montreal. She is also a practising psychologist with children and families exposed to trauma. Her research explores the impact and efficacy of therapeutic and judicial interventions for sexually abused children. She is a member of the *Violence sexuelle et santé* research team and co-researcher of the Marie-Vincent Inter-university Research Chair for sexual abuse on children affiliated to a Child Advocacy Centre.

Esther Deblinger, PhD is Co-Founder and Co-Director of the Child Abuse Research Education and Service (CARES) Institute and Professor of Psychiatry at Rowan University School of Osteopathic Medicine. Her funded research examines the efficacy and dissemination of treatment for families impacted by child sexual and physical abuse as well as other trauma(s). In collaboration with Drs Judith Cohen and Anthony Mannarino, she developed and extensively tested Trauma-Focused Cognitive Behavioural Therapy (TF-CBT). In collaboration with Dr Melissa Runyon she has developed the Combined Parent Child Cognitive Behavioural Therapy (CPC-CBT) for families at risk for physical abuse. Esther has co-authored numerous scientific publications and several widely acclaimed professional books, as well as a number of children's books about body safety.

Louise Dixon, PhD, CPsychol is a Reader of Forensic Psychology at Victoria University of Wellington, a UK-registered Forensic Psychologist and a New Zealand Registered Psychologist. She specialises in the prevention of interpersonal and family aggression. Primarily, her research has centred on the study of intimate partner violence and abuse, and the overlap with child maltreatment in the family. Louise has received funding from prestigious UK research councils such as the Economic and Social Research Council, Higher Education Funding Council for England and Police Knowledge fund. She is a series editor to the *What Works in Offender Rehabilitation* book series for Wiley-Blackwell (See About Editors Section).

Sarah A. Font, PhD is an Assistant Professor in the Department of Sociology and Criminology at Pennsylvania State University. She holds a PhD in Social Welfare from the University of Wisconsin-Madison and is a formal investigator for a state child protective services agency. Her research focuses on causes and consequences of child maltreatment and the functioning and effectiveness of child protection policies and practices.

Tanya Garrett, PhD is a Chartered Psychologist, Chartered Scientist and a registered Clinical and Forensic Psychologist. After over 20 years of working in both adult and child psychology in the NHS, Tanya now works in independent clinical practice. She is an Honorary Senior Lecturer at the University of Birmingham and has served on the British Psychological Society's Investigatory Committee. Her research relates to sexual violations in therapy and clinical psychology training. She co-edited *Sex Offender Treatment: A Case Study Approach to Issues & Interventions* (2014), Wiley.

Carol George, PhD is Professor of Psychology at Mills College, Oakland, CA. She received her doctorate in developmental psychology from UC Berkeley in 1984. Dr George is considered an international expert in attachment across the lifespan. She has authored numerous publications on adult and child attachment, including *Disorganized Attachment and Caregiving* (2011) and *The Adult Attachment Projective Picture System* (2012). Dr George consults on the application of attachment assessment in research and clinical settings.

Jenny Gray joined the Social Services Inspectorate, Department of Health in 1991 and led the development of the new inspection methodologies. In 1995, she was appointed as the professional adviser to the British government on safeguarding children, firstly in the

Department of Health and then in the Department for Education. She became a social work consultant in September 2012. Jenny has a particular interest in utilising evidence from research and practice to develop effective national child protection systems in collaboration with governments and key stakeholders; international multidisciplinary training resources; and good-quality national child protection data collection systems.

Chris Goddard, PhD, MSocWk(R), Dip App Soc Stud, CQSW, BA (Hons) has worked in child protection in the UK and Australia. His research career started at the Royal Children's Hospital, Melbourne, where he undertook some of the earliest work connecting child abuse and intimate partner violence. Professor Goddard has published widely on child abuse, child protection and children's rights in books, journal articles and the broader media. He is Visiting Professor in Social Work at the University of Hertfordshire and Adjunct Professor in Education, Arts and Social Sciences at the University of South Australia.

David M. Gresswell, DClinPsych is Co-Director of the Trent Clinical Psychology Training Programme at the Universities of Lincoln and Nottingham and has a part-time appointment as a Consultant Clinical and Forensic Psychologist in the NHS. He has a long-standing interest in the assessment of offenders, and has published on clinical case formulation and behavioural functional analysis.

Cristin M. Hall, PhD is an Assistant Professor at the Pennsylvania State University. She received her MA in Clinical Psychology from the University of Colorado and her PhD in Psychology from Penn State University. Cristin has worked with children and adults in various settings including public schools, in- and out-patient mental health settings, and community corrections. Her current research interests include social and emotional development, technology-assisted delivery of interventions, military families, diagnostic interviewing and clinical interventions.

Catherine Hamilton-Giachritsis, PhD, CPsychol, AFBPsS is HCPC-registered as both a Forensic and Clinical Psychologist, and is Reader in Clinical Psychology at the University of Bath, UK. She is widely published in the field of child maltreatment/family violence, including on outcomes and resilience. Her work on the early institutionalisation of young children across Europe was considered at international level and led to training in multiple countries. Current projects with West Midlands police, CEOP and NSPCC are focused on online abuse (See About Editors Section).

Stephanie Haynes Ratliff, MSW, CSW has practised as a social worker for over 20 years and currently serves as Clinical Faculty and Director of the Credit for Learning Program at the University of Kentucky College of Social Work. She collaborates with child welfare agency partners and universities in Kentucky to facilitate child safety, permanency and well-being by enhancing the professional expertise of child welfare personnel through graduate social work education.

Martine Hébert, PhD (psychology) is the Tier 1 Canada Research Chair in Interpersonal Traumas and Resilience and Professor in the Department of Sexology, Université du Québec à Montréal (UQAM). Her research explores the diversity of profiles in sexually abused youths and pathways to resilient outcomes. She is also involved in evaluative studies of both intervention (TF-CBT) and prevention programmes. She is director of the Violence sexuelle et santé research team and the CIHR Team on Interpersonal Traumas, co-holder of the Marie-Vincent Inter-university Research Chair in child sexual abuse, and member of the Centre for Interdisciplinary Research on Domestic Violence and Sexual Abuse.

Susan Hunt, BSc (Hons) completed her honours degree in developmental psychology at the University of Melbourne. She began her research career at the Murdoch Institute, and was then employed by the National Ageing Research Institute developing public health education resources. Following this, she conducted research at Monash University into physical and mental health, and child protection issues. Susan is currently a lecturer at Central Queensland University. Her research involves parental violence, supervision in child protection, the experiences of children in out-of-home care, and the education that professionals receive regarding child abuse and child protection.

Michael E. Lamb, PhD is Professor of Psychology at the University of Cambridge and was, until July 2016, a Member of the Scottish National Child Abuse Inquiry Panel. He is President of Division 7 (Developmental Psychology) of the American Psychological Association and Editor of the journal Psychology, Public Policy and Law. His research has focused on improving the quality of investigative interviews with alleged victims worldwide and has also sought to change the ways in which children are questioned in court. He has been honoured by many international organisations and Universities for his contributions to science and policy.

Judith Masson, MA, PhD, FAcSS is Professor of Socio-legal Studies at the University of Bristol and teaches child and family law. Throughout her career, Judith has researched the interface between children's social work and the civil justice system in England and Wales with studies of step-parent adoption, children's representation, emergency intervention and care proceedings. She has served on the Judicial Studies Board and the Family Justice Council, and has been a specialist adviser to House of Commons Committees.

Eamon McCrory, PhD is Professor of Developmental Neuroscience and Psychopathology at University College London and Director of the Developmental Risk and Resilience Unit. His research uses brain imaging and psychological approaches to investigate the impact of maltreatment on children's emotional development and their risk of future mental health problems. He is also a Consultant Clinical Psychologist at the Anna Freud Centre and Director of the UCL MRes in Developmental Neuroscience and Psychopathology.

Hannah L. Merdian, PhD is a Senior Lecturer in Clinical and Forensic Psychology at the University of Lincoln. She is co-founder of onlinePROTECT, a research programme addressing the safety of children and young people by targeting the individuals who engage in online sex offences against minors. She developed the Integrated Model for the Classification, Assessment, and Treatment of Users of Child Sexual Exploitation Material and provides consultation and training for offender management and child protection services.

Louise Morpeth, PhD is Co-Director of the Dartington Social Research Unit and oversees the day-to-day running of the charity. She has a particular interest in advocating for the greater use of evidence-based programmes, practices, processes and policies in children's services and has worked at the interface of research, policy and practice throughout her career. Louise has played a leading role in developing large investment strategies with statutory and voluntary children's services providers, and leads the Unit's work on place-based reform.

Annabelle Nicol, PhD focuses her research on the training of investigative interviewers of children and assessing the quality of role-play training interviews with adult actors as well as field interviews. She has completed an NICHD training course on coding forensic interviews and works closely with some police jurisdictions in Scotland, delivering inputs to their investigative interviewers' training courses on conducting appropriate child investigative interviews and participating in their role-play training interviews.

Amy Palmer, PhD is a Research Psychologist at an Operational Stress Injury Clinic for Veterans Affairs Canada. Her main focus is examining the impact of evidence-based treatments for patients with PTSD. Also, following on from her postdoctoral work at the Developmental Risk and Resilience Unit, which examined the cognitive impact of early life adversity, Amy works with the Royal Canadian Mounted Police and other governmental agencies to improve access to mental health services for youths across Canada.

Alberto Pellai, MD, PhD works as a Researcher in Public Health at Milano State University and as a Psychotherapist in private practice. He has created the child sexual abuse prevention programme 'Le parole non dette', the most popular Italian school-based child sexual abuse primary prevention programme, replicated in five different European countries. He is author of many books for teachers, parents and children. In 2004 the Italian Ministry of Health awarded him the Silver Medal for Public Health.

Daniel F. Perkins, PhD is Professor of Family and Youth Resiliency and Policy and Director of an applied research centre, the Clearinghouse for Military Family Readiness at Penn State (http://www.militaryfamilies.psu.edu/). He has been designing and evaluating strengths-based family and youth programmes for more than 20 years. Currently, he is examining the transitioning of evidence-based programmes from tightly controlled environments to real-world settings. Since 2006, he has been consulting with several prevention and early intervention projects in Ireland (See About Editors Section).

Cindy Miller-Perrin, PhD is Distinguished Professor of Psychology at Pepperdine University. She has authored numerous journal articles and book chapters covering a range of topics, including child maltreatment, family violence and positive psychology. She has co-authored four books, including *Why Faith Matters: A Positive Psychology Perspective* (2015), *Family Violence Across the Lifespan* (2011), *Child Maltreatment* (2013) and *Child Sexual Abuse: Sharing the Responsibility* (1992). She is a Fellow of the American Psychological Association and is currently President of Division 37's Society for Child and Family Policy and Practice of APA.

John A. Pickering, PhD is a Behavioural Scientist at the University of Queensland with a background in the development and evaluation of evidence-based interventions. His research interests focus on how innovation in programme design can bring behavioural scientists together with other scientists and industry collaborators to develop behaviour change interventions in areas such as public health and the environment.

Stephen Pizzey, MA is the Chair of the Board of Directors of Child and Family Training. Stephen was Head of the Social Work Department at Great Ormond Street Hospital for Children and shared responsibility for child protection at the hospital. Previously, he was the Independent Chair of an Area Child Protection Committee, a guardian ad litem and part-time lecturer in social work. Currently, Stephen is an expert witness in actions against local authorities, including cases of historical abuse, and prepares Serious Case Reviews.

Elisabeth Pollio, PhD is a member of the faculty at the Child Abuse Research Education and Service (CARES) Institute, Rowan University School of Osteopathic Medicine. She is the Mental Health Director of the Institute's foster care programme, which provides mental health screenings and medical evaluations to children entering foster care. Elisabeth is also the coordinator of the Institute's postdoctoral fellowship programme. She has provided and supervised assessments of children who have experienced trauma, as well as Trauma-Focused Cognitive Behavioural Therapy (TF-CBT).

Vanessa Puetz, PhD Vanessa Puetz conducted her doctoral research on the impact of early-caregiver separation on children's psychosocial, endocrine and neural development. She joined the Developmental Risk and Resilience Unit (DRRU) at University College London (UCL) as a postdoctoral research associate where she continues to investigate the neural and behavioural underpinnings of maltreatment and resilience in looked-after children and children in need with Professor Eamon McCrory.

Lorraine Radford, PhD is Professor of Social Policy and Social Work at the University of Central Lancashire, UK and Co-Director of the Connect Centre for Research on Interpersonal Violence. She has previously also worked in children's organisations and in government. Her research and publications include work on childhood victimisation, prevention of domestic and sexual violence and the overlapping aspects of abuse.

David La Rooy, PhD is a Lecturer in Psychology in the school of law at Royal Holloway University. While completing a Postdoctoral Research Fellowship at the National Institutes of Health he received specialist police training on child forensic interviewing, as well as training in the assessment of the quality of investigative interviews conducted with children alleging abuse. He provides specialist training to various professionals involved in investigative interviewing of children and received the Academic Excellence Award from the iIIRG in 2014.

Megan C. Runion, BA is a graduate student in the School of Psychology programme at the Pennsylvania State University and a graduate research assistant at the Clearinghouse for Military Family Readiness at Penn State. She graduated in 2012 from the University of Maryland with a BA in Psychology. Megan's work experience has primarily involved programme evaluation and technical assistance on issues of implementation, evaluation and sustainability. Research interests include prevention and early intervention programming, social and emotional development, and resiliency.

Melissa K. Runyon, PhD is sole member, consultant and licensed psychologist at Melissa Runyon, PhD, PLLC in Prospect, KY. She previously served as treatment services director of the Child Abuse Education and Service (CARES) Institute for nearly 16 years and was

Professor of Psychiatry at Rowan University School of Osteopathic Medicine. She received funding from the National Institute of Mental Health, Substance Abuse and Mental Health Administration, and the Swedish Children's Welfare League to evaluate and disseminate Combined Parent Child-Cognitive Behavioural Therapy (CPC-CBT). She provides national and international training and consultation to professionals in CPC-CBT and Trauma-Focused Cognitive Behavioural Therapy (TF-CBT) and has co-authored therapist guides related to both of these evidence-based models.

Matthew R. Sanders, PhD is Professor of Clinical Psychology at the University of Queensland and the Founder of the Triple P–Positive Parenting Program. Professor Sanders is an expert in the development, implementation, evaluation and dissemination of population-based approaches to parenting and family interventions.

Rebecca L. Sanford, PhD, MSSA, LCSW is a Lecturer at Thompson Rivers University School of Social Work and Human Service in Kamloops, British Columbia. She has nearly 15 years of experience as a clinical social worker, researcher and educator, with specialisation in the areas of child and adolescent mental health, working with youth and their families, child welfare, and workforce development for public child welfare.

Peter Sidebotham, PhD is a Consultant Paediatrician and Associate Professor of Child Health at Warwick Medical School. He is a member of the Warwickshire Local Safeguarding Children Board and Child Death Overview Panel. His research interests include child maltreatment, sudden infant death syndrome, child death review and fatal maltreatment. He is the author/editor of three books and several book chapters and has published extensively on child abuse and child death review.

Amy M. Smith Slep, PhD completed her doctorate at SUNY Stony Brook in 1995. She is the co-director of the Family Translational Research Group. Her work focuses on anger, conflict and aggression in families, including understanding of (a) interconnections between parent-to-child and partner violence, (b) mechanisms of intra- and interpersonal anger regulation during conflict, and (c) the implications of family conflict and aggression for children and their development. She has incorporated this basic work into effective family-focused prevention initiatives. Her work on definitions of maltreatment and effective approaches to reliable case-substantiation decisions has been disseminated across the United States Department of Defense. She has reported her work in over 100 publications and has received over 45 federal research grants and contracts.

Julie Taylor, PhD, FRCN, RN, MSc, BSc (Hons) is a nurse scientist specialising in child maltreatment. She is Professor of Child Protection in the Institute of Clinical Sciences at the University of Birmingham, in partnership with Birmingham Children's Hospital NHS Foundation Trust. Julie's work is at the leading edge nationally and internationally in reframing child maltreatment as a public health concern. Her research programme is concentrated at the interface between health and social care and is largely underpinned by the discourse of cumulative harm and the exponential effects of living with multiple adversities.

Michele Staton-Tindall, PhD, MSW is an Associate Professor in the College of Medicine, Department of Behavioral Science and a Faculty Associate of the Center on Drug and Alcohol

Research at the University of Kentucky. Dr Staton-Tindall is the PI for an ongoing study funded by the National Institutes of Health/National Institute on Drug Abuse to study drug abuse, risky sexual behaviour and HIV/HCV among rural women in the Appalachian area of eastern Kentucky. She has published in the areas of substance abuse treatment, rural service delivery, and substance-using caregivers and child trauma.

Beth Tarleton, MPhil is a Senior Research Fellow at the Norah Fry Research Centre, University of Bristol. Beth co-ordinates the Working Together with Parents Network, which is a free network for professionals working with parents with learning difficulties/disabilities: wtpn.co.uk. She has undertaken a number of studies around positive support for parents with learning difficulties over the last ten years.

Arlene Vetere, PhD, DipClinPsychol is Professor of Family Therapy and Systemic Practice at VID Specialized University, Oslo, Norway, and Visiting Professor of Clinical Psychology at Universita Degli Studi di Bergamo, Italy, since her retirement as Professor of Clinical Psychology at Surrey University, UK. Arlene co-directs Reading Safer Families, a family violence intervention service based in Reading, UK.

Sandy K. Wurtele, PhD is a Psychologist and Professor in the Department of Psychology at the University of Colorado at Colorado Springs. Sandy currently serves as the Child Protection Consultant for the Catholic Diocese of Wilmington (DE) along with the USA Swimming *Safe Sport* Committee. She has authored or co-authored numerous scholarly articles and chapters, has written books for parents on CSA prevention (*Off Limits*; *Out of Harm's Way*; *Safe Connections*), and co-authored the 1992 book for professionals, *Child Sexual Abuse: Sharing the Responsibility*. Her evidenced-based personal safety programme for children, *Body Safety Training*, is available in different teaching formats and languages. Sandy has received funding for research on CSA prevention, including a FIRST Award from the National Institute of Mental Health. She is the recipient of the 2009 William Friedrich Memorial Child Sexual Abuse Award.

Foreword

The current (2016) rapid spread of the Zika virus in Latin America and the Caribbean, and now more than 50 countries, has led the Federal agency for the Department of Health and Human Services in the USA, the Center for Disease Control and Prevention (CDC), to focus national attention on the issue. While those affected are most usually asymptomatic, transmission from pregnant women to their unborn foetus can lead in some cases to microcephaly, other severe brain malformations and birth defects. In the last year this appears to have affected around 3500 children (CDC, 2016). While this is shocking and must be controlled, affected numbers at population level are miniscule. Imagine then the scale of media hype and international response if one in four children worldwide were affected by a disease that had devastating short- and long-term health, social and developmental consequences, with regular fatalities and transmission into subsequent generations. It would be catastrophic and of immediate worldwide concern. However, it is of no surprise to readers of this book to hear that we do have that disease: child maltreatment. We have long argued that this is a global public health issue for which we have not yet mobilised a co-ordinated, efficient and effective response (Daniel, Taylor & Scott, 2011; WHO, 2016a).

The 2014/2015 outbreak of Ebola shocked the world and rightly demanded a concerted global response. The key features for containing Ebola were centred on community engagement and early supportive care (WHO, 2016b). Having tackled the outbreak effectively, current efforts have three objectives: to interrupt remaining chains of Ebola transmission; to respond to the consequences of residual risks; and to work on systems recovery (WHO, 2016c). This book, focused on an evidence-based approach to assessment and intervention in care proceedings, refreshingly takes a similar public health approach to maltreatment. First, tackling the disease is addressed in programmes described in Part I, where epidemiological approaches, treatment, rehabilitation and therapeutic approaches are described. Second, interrupting chains of intergenerational transmission is crucial and is well described through ecological approaches, where we know that multiple risk factors are important (Taylor & Lazenbatt, 2014). Third, responding to the consequences of maltreatment is key and is addressed in relation to decision-making and responding to children, not to just preparing children for court. Fourth, systems-wide approaches are needed and are described in relation to primary prevention measures and novel innovations.

We are probably a long way off eradicating child abuse and neglect, but our direction of travel is systemically and comprehensively laid out in the following chapters. Preventing and responding to child maltreatment needs a bold, global, multidisciplinary public health response that is not afraid to be innovative and challenging. Dixon, Perkins, Hamilton Giachritsis and

Craig have set out both challenges and solutions in assessment and intervention in care proceedings, framed within the worldwide scourge of child maltreatment. This is a comprehensive and authoritative text from a truly multidisciplinary international team.

Julie Taylor
Professor of Child Protection, University of Birmingham, UK

References

Center for Disease Control and Prevention (2016). Zika virus, www.cdc.gov/zika/ (accessed 1 October 2016).

Daniel, B., Taylor, J.S. & Scott, J. (2011). *Recognizing and Helping the Neglected Child: Evidence-Based Practice for Assessment and Intervention.* London: Jessica Kingsley.

Taylor, J. & Lazenbatt, A. (2014). *Child Maltreatment and High Risk Families.* London: Dunedin Academic Press.

World Health Organization (2016a) *Preventing child maltreatment. A guide to taking action and generating evidence.* Geneva: WHO/ISPCAN.

World Health Organization (2016b) Ebola virus disease [online], www.who.int/mediacentre/factsheets/fs103/en/ (accessed 1 October 2016).

World Health Organization (2016c) Ebola outbreak 2014–2015 [online], www.who.int/csr/disease/ebola/en/ (accessed 1 October 2016).

Acknowledgements

Thank you to the authors. We are grateful for your contribution and commitment to this volume. Without your desire to understand child protection issues and improve the life of children, this book would not have been possible. Thank you for finding the time to share your expertise.

We would also like to extend our thanks to those at Wiley-Blackwell who have worked on this volume. Thank you for believing in the need to share the evidence and improve research and practice in child protection.

1

Overview and Structure of the Book

Louise Dixon[1], Daniel F. Perkins[2], Catherine Hamilton-Giachritsis[3] and Leam A. Craig[4]

[1] Victoria University of Wellington, New Zealand
[2] The Pennsylvania State University, USA
[3] University of Bath, UK
[4] Forensic Psychology Practice Ltd, UK
[4] University of Birmingham, UK
[4] Birmingham City University, UK

Introduction

The idea that 'something' works in offender rehabilitation suffered a devastating blow in the 1970s following reviews that 'nothing worked' (Martinson, 1974). This conclusion was later attributed to the poor methodology and research designs of studies investigating this issue (Lipton, Martinson & Wilks, 1975), rather than an inability to rehabilitate behaviour. However, the concept of 'nothing works' led to a body of research that investigated which practices are effective in the rehabilitation of people who offend, often referred to as the What Works literature (Craig, Dixon & Gannon, 2013). The What Works literature is based on an overarching principle that highlights the need for empirically rigorous evidence-based practice. Several systems have been developed to aid the evaluation of the quality of evidence on the efficacy of particular therapeutic techniques and their use with particular groups of people. The work has been subsumed under the category 'What Works in the treatment and management of offenders to reduce crime'.

The three main systems of empirical evaluation used to examine the quality of outcome studies that are most often referred to in the literature are: (i) the American Psychological Association (APA) Chambless and colleagues' system (Chambless & Hollon, 1998; Chambless, Baker, Baucom et al., 1998; Chambless & Ollendick, 2001); (ii) Sherman, Gottfredson, MacKenzie et al.'s (1997) 'levels' system for reviewing the quality of evidence and intervention; and (iii) the Cochrane System (Higgins & Green, 2006/2008/2011). In brief, the APA system examines the quality of evidence from outcome studies on the effectiveness of psychological therapy. Sherman, Gottfredson, MacKenzie et al.'s (1997) report to the US Congress described a 'levels' system for reviewing the quality of evidence supporting any given intervention in the field of criminal behaviour.

They developed and employed the Maryland Scale of Scientific Methods, ranking each study from Level I (weakest) to Level V (strongest) on overall internal validity. The Cochrane System has been influential in categorising evidence on the effectiveness of psychological and pharmaceutical interventions from different studies and remains the most exacting of review systems for clinical evidence.

Although such methods of empirical evaluation exist to inform crime reduction, some domains of practice remain better informed by the evidence than others. Family violence and child maltreatment are two areas that can arguably benefit from further understanding. This is a crucial area of investigation considering that family violence and child maltreatment is a serious and international public health concern (Pinheiro, 2006; Krug, Dahlberg, Mercy et al., 2002). For example, in England, recent statistics show that there were 635,600 referrals of children made to children's social care in 2015. On 31 March 2015, 391,000 children were assessed as being in need of some family support and 49,700 children were the subject of a child protection plan, providing population rates of 337.1 and 42.9 per 10,000 children aged under 18 respectively (Department for Education [DfE], 2015). In England and Wales, 12,781 families were referred to the Children and Family Court Advisory and Support Service (CAFCASS) between April 2015 and March 2016 for care applications (CAFCASS, 2016).

Furthermore, despite official statistics notoriously underestimating child maltreatment deaths (e.g., Frederick, Goddard & Oxley, 2013), reported rates remain high. The 2002 *World report on violence and health* estimated that of children aged 0–14, 31,000 males and 26,000 females were victims of homicide, perpetrated both by family and non-family members (Krug, Dahlberg, Mercy et al., 2002). More recently, in 2012, an estimated 95,000 children and young people died as the result of homicide across the world, most of whom (85,000 or 90%) lived in low- and middle-income countries (UNICEF, 2014). There are also some indicators that rates may have fallen over the last few decades, particularly for younger children; for example, in England there has been a decline in infant mortality due to assault falling from 5.6 per 100,000 in 1974 to 0.7 in 2008 (Sidebotham, Atkins & Hutton, 2012). However, despite apparent improvements in mortality rates, they remain unacceptably high, emphasising the need for the use of evidence-based interventions with families.

The need to work with families is exemplified by the high levels of family re-referral to children's services (i.e., where the same family is referred again for a different child), which can be as high as 85% over a 10-year period (DePanfilis & Zuravin, 1998; Thompson & Wiley, 2009). Also worthy of note is the high rate of co-occurrence of child maltreatment with other forms of family violence (e.g., co-occurrence with intimate partner violence (IPV) has been estimated to occur in between 30–60% of cases (e.g., Cox, Kotch & Everson, 2003; Sousa, Herrenkohl, Moylan et al., 2011)). Indeed, in families where IPV and child maltreatment co-occur, there tend to be more previous referrals, more serious IPV and quicker re-referral to child protection services (Casanueva, Martin & Runyan, 2009). This demonstrates the potential risk posed to children through wider family violence issues and the need to assess and respond to risk of harm to the child in these situations. Arguably then, in a time of austerity where community resources are stretched, the need for empirically sound and efficacious interventions to child maltreatment and family violence has never been greater.

Despite this well-documented need, research into child protection practice has arguably been limited. Indeed, leading researchers in the field have suggested that evidence for child protection is scant. Nearly 20 years ago, Finkelhor (1999) stated:

First we need good epidemiological data to see the location and source of the child abuse problem, and also to be able to track and monitor its response to our efforts. This is something we currently do not have, at least at the level that would satisfy any even generous public health epidemiologist. Second, we need experimental studies to evaluate new and existing practices, so we can agree on what works…There is more experimental science in the toilet paper we use every day than in what we have to offer abused children or families at risk of abuse (p. 969).

Munro (2009, p. 1015) further stated that the evidence has not considerably progressed since that time, asserting that 'There is only limited knowledge about good practice and the major need is to increase this, to find out more about what methods are effective.'

Based on knowledge of what constitutes methodologically robust research, several countries have begun to introduce structured assessment and intervention programmes in a variety of areas of intervention, which include areas of childcare and family violence. In a time where other areas of violence and abuse prevention are being evidenced (e.g., Craig, Dixon & Gannon, 2013), this book aims to put the need to evidence child protection practice at the forefront. It sets out to provide a comprehensive overview of the current evidence in child and family assessment, intervention and service provision that promotes safeguarding and child well-being. It details the contemporary research and practice that informs theory, assessment, service provision, rehabilitation and therapeutic interventions for children and families undergoing child care proceedings. In doing so it provides an account of what we know works so far *and* what still needs to be accomplished. What follows is a collection of international knowledge from leading researchers and practitioners in the field who use the evidence to inform best practice. To reflect practice in this domain, the authors and their contributions are written from multidisciplinary perspectives.

Structure of the Book

The book is divided into five parts, each of which is described below.

Part I: Research and Theoretical Perspectives

This part of the book provides the reader with an overview of important theoretical and evidence-based arguments in the field of child and family maltreatment, beginning with issues on the prevalence and aetiology of child maltreatment and its fatal forms, through to the consequences and outcomes, before considering how child maltreatment may overlap with other forms of family violence. It begins with an overview of the prevalence and incidence literature by Lorraine Radford in Chapter 2. Before considering the prevalence and incidence of child maltreatment at an international level, Radford briefly reviews the conceptual and methodological challenges researchers, practitioners and policymakers face when wanting to make robust estimates of the extent of violence within the community. The chapter moves on to consider what is known about levels of violence from officially reported incidents of child abuse and neglect, as well as from self-report community-based surveys. Radford highlights that surveillance data and surveys show that violence against children, including child abuse and neglect, is prevalent across the world. Data from community surveys produce estimates of lifetime and past-year prevalence at least 4–16 times higher than estimates based upon recorded child protection cases. The chapter concludes by highlighting the implications for practice, arguing that knowledge about the extent and burden of violence against children can be used to improve prevention, identification and response as well as to inform provision, service monitoring and the measurement of outcomes for children.

Next, in Chapter 3, Catherine Hamilton-Giachritsis and Alberto Pellai provide a summary of the historical and current theoretical perspectives that enhance our understanding of the aetiology of child maltreatment. This chapter tracks the development from single-factor models focused on individual deficits in the perpetrator (e.g., psychopathology) or social factors (e.g., poverty) through to multi-factor models that acknowledge the complexity of the causes of child abuse and neglect. Such models, most notably the ecological model and its derivatives, attempt to encompass elements at individual, family, peer, social, community and cultural levels. Within the chapter, prior research identifying risk and protective factors at each level of the ecological model are explored. However, in order to demonstrate that each level is also interlinked, the authors use a case example throughout based on the added dimension arising from new technologies (a social-level factor). The most recent research on the role of adolescent neural systems in risk behaviour is outlined and discussion is made of how the knowledge gained through research has informed interventions at each level of the ecological system.

Peter Sidebotham goes on to discuss the extreme end of a spectrum of child maltreatment in Chapter 4. The chapter begins with a review of the incidence and heterogeneous nature of fatal child maltreatment. It is argued that prevention requires an in-depth understanding of the nature and causes of fatal maltreatment and the chapter goes on to present a conceptual model that details the spectrum of violent and maltreatment-related deaths in childhood, within and outside the family. The model further highlights the heterogeneity of fatal child maltreatment and that risk factors will likely differ between types. Although a number of recognised risk factors for fatal child maltreatment are identified from the published literature, it is concluded that the evidence is limited by poor quality data and it is not possible to predict those children most at risk of death with any certainty over and above those at risk of general harm. It is therefore argued that a strong public health approach is necessary to promote initiatives to prevent child maltreatment generally.

Next, in Chapter 5, Sarah Font presents a review of the potential psychological, economic and physical health consequences that may arise following child maltreatment. Alongside reviews of physical and sexual abuse, physical neglect (one of the least well-researched areas) is considered. Initial indicators suggest that physical neglect can affect cognitive development and internalising behaviour problems, as well as being linked with higher rates of a range of negative outcomes in adolescence (Hussey, Chang & Kotch, 2006). Furthermore there is a relatively new body of research demonstrating links between childhood victimisation and lower educational attainment and income. However, additional research is required to identify causal relationships between maltreatment and economic outcome, and whether other factors mediate this relationship. Overall, Font notes that there is strong evidence for increased likelihood of negative psychological consequences, but that the evidence base for physical health and economic outcomes is smaller and less conclusive. Therefore, this chapter also outlines the methodological difficulties inherent in research in this area that need to be considered when interpreting research findings.

In Chapter 6, Eamon McCrory, Amy Palmer and Vanessa Puetz provide an overview of important findings from neuroimaging research to explain ways in which maltreatment in childhood may heighten a person's vulnerability to psychopathology. First, a review of findings from neuroimaging studies of key brain structures involved in emotion processing, memory and regulation processes is provided. Second, how genetic factors may interact with environmental experience (such as child maltreatment) to influence maladaptive outcomes in psychological and emotional development is considered. A focus on structural and functional brain alterations is given. Finally, the clinical implications that follow from the research are discussed. It is concluded that the evidence demonstrates the importance of a 'reliable adult caregiver to help the child regulate stress', and that further clarification of the neurocognitive systems most associated with psychiatric risk may promote resilience.

Finally, in Chapter 7 Louise Dixon and Amy M. Smith Slep consider the child in the context of the family by providing an overview of the co-occurrence of physical intimate partner violence with child physical abuse. In the main, this chapter limits its discussion to physical violence, as this is what the majority of empirical research has investigated to date. They describe the high rates of overlap of child abuse and intimate partner violence and the effects on the child before noting the theoretical perspectives and risk and protective factors that may help explain its co-occurrence. It is proposed that the evidence suggests that research and practice should adopt a systemic view and explore and respond to patterns of family violence and abuse in research and practice. Although the majority of the evidence considers male-to-female physical violence and abuse in heterosexual relationships, the authors also note the need to expand this knowledge base to understand the spectrum of family aggression and its effects on parental care.

Part II: Children's Services and Public Health Approaches to Prevention

To place the assessment and treatment of parents and children in child care proceedings into context, Part II first reviews the situation in children's services, focusing on current processes and reforms in place to safeguard children, before moving on to consider prevention from a public health perspective using examples of behavioural parenting intervention and the sexual exploitation of children and young people to illustrate the point. Given the potential outcomes for children and young people, the role of protective services is crucial. In Chapter 8 Jenny Gray details the current situation with regard to children's services in England and their role with families in need, as well as child protection. Importantly, international and national legislation that underpins children's services in the UK are outlined, demonstrating how international law is filtered down to small localities but also how cultural contexts can have an impact on the attitude toward child abuse and neglect (e.g., the acceptability of certain behaviours). Internationally, the UN has called for children and young people to be able to grow up free from violence and, in this chapter, Gray outlines how a public health approach might provide a useful framework for this goal to be achieved.

Chapter 9, written by Chris Goddard, Karen Broadley and Susan Hunt, explores the challenges and complex nature of child protection practice in children's services. The authors focus on the need to recognise that in this field, there is a lack of empirical evidence and as such family preservation ideology can dominate decision-making and practice. This chapter highlights and evaluates the rarely debated challenges. Three primary challenges are presented and discussed in detail. These are: the lack of evidence for the efficacy of family support programmes; what criteria should be used to determine the removal of the child from parental care; and, working with 'uncooperative, hostile, threatening or violent parents' and the realities this entails. Practical solutions to these challenges are offered in this chapter, which tackles a rarely acknowledged phenomenon head on.

Next, Judith Masson in Chapter 10 focuses on what works in prevention where families are on the brink of care proceedings, specifically, the impact of legislative changes first introduced in 2008 in England, Wales and Northern Ireland, which set out the steps required before the issuing of care proceedings; these are known as pre-proceedings. Masson explains that pre-proceedings is a process by which local authorities are required to follow specific steps before issuing care proceedings, where there is sufficient time to do so and where this would not compromise the child's safety. Although the introduction of pre-proceedings was atheoretical, Masson provides the results of an empirical evaluation of the process which found that local authorities have made substantial use of the pre-proceedings process, using it in 43% to 73% of cases considered by their lawyers to meet the threshold for care proceedings. The impact of pre-proceedings is helpfully illustrated by three case examples in the chapter. While Masson argues that the reformed care proceedings provide a stronger impetus to use the pre-proceedings process as a tool to support case management, she cautions that there is a real danger that work becomes focused on preparing for court, rather than supporting families to avoid court.

Moving to consider a broader (including pre-maltreatment) perspective, in Chapter 11 Matthew Sanders and John Pickering present the case for preventing child maltreatment using a public health approach to behavioural parenting intervention. The authors note that improving parenting is a basic element within the prevention of child abuse and neglect, and that adopting an approach that encompasses the whole population will ultimately allow a more comprehensive means of reducing the occurrence of maltreatment. This chapter provides an overview of the Positive Parenting Programme, otherwise known as 'Triple P', focusing specifically on one variant – Pathways Triple P – that is designed for families at risk of child abuse and neglect. Sanders and Pickering review the 35-year evidence base associated with Triple P and the more recent research demonstrating the effectiveness of Pathways. In conclusion, Sanders and Pickering discuss the necessary elements for parenting interventions, such as they are non-stigmatising, have flexible delivery formats and, ideally, adopt a public health approach.

Also taking a public health perspective, Sandy Wurtele and Cindy Miller-Perrin discuss what works to address the public health problem of sexual exploitation of children and young people in Chapter 12. They first present the magnitude of the global problem before arguing that tertiary prevention strategies, such as treatment of victims and punishment of offenders, are insufficient. Rather, they suggest, a problem of this complex nature requires primary prevention efforts. The chapter goes on to review primary prevention strategies that have been adopted internationally targeting children, parents/caretakers, youth-serving organisations, society and cyberspace. They use an ecological framework to review the various strategies and go on to suggest direction for future preventative initiatives.

Part III: Assessment

When parents fail to provide their children with a good enough and safe standard of care, or where there is evidence that a child has been subjected to physical, sexual or emotional abuse, the State is obliged to intervene. Current professional practice associated with family proceedings is founded on the core principles that the interests of the child are paramount; that delay in determining the questions concerning a child's upbringing is likely to prejudice the welfare of the child; and that non-intervention is preferred, except in cases where it can be demonstrated that a court order would be better for a child than no order. These principles are based on practitioners having a thorough understanding of the developmental needs of children; the capacities of parents to respond appropriately to those needs; and the impact of wider family and environmental factors on parenting capacity and children. This section of the book focuses on different aspects of assessing parents and children in child care proceedings. It begins with the structuring of assessments, commenting on the role of evidence-based tools and the utility of specific theoretical approaches, then considers the developmentally appropriate forensic interviewing of children as part of the assessment process, moves on to consider a special issue that may need to be addressed in an assessment and concludes with practitioner perspectives on frontline practice.

This section begins with Chapter 13 where Stephen Pizzey, Arnon Bentovim, Liza Bingley Miller and Antony Cox report on the development and use of an evidence-based assessment tool – the Safeguarding children Assessment and Analysis Framework (SAAF). SAAF is designed for those working in child protection services and is complementary with the Framework for Assessment. It has seven stages, considering assessment, analysis, planning and implementation of intervention, with structured guidance on how to complete each step. Important elements are the inclusion of a means of assessing capacity to change but also how to evaluate what success 'looks like'. This type of structured decision-making tool, providing guidance and enabling multidisciplinary work, embodies the concept of taking research findings and developing tools that are of daily, practical use for practitioners. A randomised control trial (Macdonald, Lewis, Macdonald et al., 2014) is currently underway to evaluate the programme demonstrating the authors' commitment to evidence-based practice in child protection.

Carol George then provides a comprehensive account of how to utilise an attachment theory perspective to assess parenting, in Chapter 14. First, an overview of 'what is attachment' is provided, with George presenting the well-recognised secure, organised-insecure and disorganised/dysregulated model of children's attachment and the parenting patterns associated with them. The chapter then goes on to discuss the developmental accomplishments and risks associated with each of these parenting patterns. Emphasis is placed on using validated assessments of parenting using an attachment perspective. It is argued that the attachment model has withstood over 40 years of empirical scrutiny and that valid attachment assessments used systemically with parents can help to identify how best to support parents by promoting their strengths and 'breaking traumatic parenting cycles'.

Next, in Chapter 15, Annabelle Nicol, David La Rooy and Michael Lamb review the evidence base for developmentally appropriate forensic interviewing of children as part of the assessment process. They highlight that inappropriate interview techniques are still in use, but argue that by utilising techniques suited to the developmental (rather than chronological) age of the child, a fuller, more informative picture can be achieved. To enable a greater understanding of the importance of adapting interview techniques for developmental age, the authors first outline memory, language, salience and suggestibility in children, emphasising how this knowledge can be used to inform better practice. Interviewing strategies include introductions (rapport building), free-recall narrative using open prompts (to access recall memory), focused questions or recognition prompts (to tap into recognition memory processes), and closure. The chapter concludes with a discussion about training approaches that not only allow interviewers to learn these techniques in the short term but enable them to utilise them over the longer term in practice situations.

In Chapter 16, Hannah Merdian, David Gresswell and Leam A. Craig comment on the assessment of parental risk, usually in relation to the father, of those involved in child care proceedings who have been convicted of being in possession of and/or have engaged in the distribution, trading and/or production of Child Sexual Exploitation Material (CSEM). The authors note that court evaluations for parental risk in CSEM cases are more frequently requested, especially concerning a risk of crossover to contact sexual offences. However, the authors also caution that the psychological research on CSEM is still developing, providing the assessor with very little empirical and theoretical guidance in the decision-making process. In this chapter the authors offer some guidance for formulating custody cases by providing systemic and reflective insight into the current legal and psychological context of CSEM, by reviewing the evidence concerning the link between CSEM and contact sexual offences against minors, and by reflecting on the function and contextualised assessment of this offending behaviour.

This section concludes with Chapter 17 where Martin C. Calder offers professional observations of frontline practice from a social worker's perspective. With frontline practitioners frequently operating in the gaps between theory and research, Calder argues that they are in danger of losing sight of the child amid legislative and bureaucratic challenges. Calder suggests that while many practitioners recognise the need for evidence-based practice in assessments and recommendations to court, many frontline staff lack the opportunity for reflective practice or time to read and digest research findings. In attempting to overcome these difficulties, Calder offers practice-based suggestions and elucidates a risk-formulation framework for structuring risk-related information with the aim of keeping children the priority within child care proceedings.

Part IV: Interventions with Children and Families

Having discussed various theoretical perspectives and issues to do with assessments, the next two parts of the book move on to consider interventions. Part IV focuses on interventions with children and families, considering abuse-specific type interventions followed by parenting programmes and school-based interventions and finally moving to reflect on work with parents within a specific theoretical model of attachment. It begins with Chapter 18 by Melissa Runyon, Stephanie Cruthirds and Esther Deblinger, who present the need for evidenced approaches to empower children and families at high risk for physical abuse to help them overcome their abusive and violent experiences. The authors argue that child physical abuse is a public health problem that affects many domains of a child's functioning, yet evidence-based therapies to assist children and caregivers are in their infancy. They describe five evidence-based therapies that have been used with the child physical abuse population and meet a priori criteria, a majority of which are based on cognitive behavioural theory and include both parents and children. It is concluded that although there is a need for further understanding and research, the evidence shows that early evidence-based interventions address the therapeutic needs of families at risk for child physical abuse.

In Chapter 19, Esther Deblinger, Elisabeth Pollio and Melissa Runyon go on to detail effective therapies for children and non-offending caregivers in the aftermath of child sexual abuse and other traumatic experiences. This chapter briefly reviews the research that has demonstrated the negative effects of sexual abuse and other violence and adversity in childhood. It then provides an overview of the following evidence-based interventions that help children and their non-offending caregivers to cope with the effects of such abuse and trauma: Child Parent Psychotherapy, Eye Movement Desensitisation and Reprocessing for Children and Adolescents, Prolonged Exposure for Adolescents and Trauma-Focused Cognitive Behavioural Therapy. A particular focus is given to Trauma-Focused Cognitive Behavioural Therapy because, the authors argue, the evidence for this approach is strong. It is concluded that the interventions described show positive impact in addressing the immediate and long-term impact of trauma, however, further research is needed to reduce incidence and prevalence rates of abuse, children's resilience and their responsiveness to treatment when trauma is experienced.

Moving away from abuse-type specific interventions, Tracey Bywater then considers the efficacy of cognitive behavioural group based parenting programmes to promote child protective factors and reduce risk factors for any form of child maltreatment in Chapter 20. First whole system approaches such as *Communities that Care* and *Evidence2Success* are reviewed, whereby level of need in a geographical area is identified and a variety of commissioners (e.g., local authority, charities, community leaders) collaborate to provide services to meet those needs. Evidence from the USA has shown that such an approach can have significant impacts on reducing health and behaviour problems in adolescents. At a different level, other programmes focus on working with parents, with Bywater noting that evidence suggests this is the most effective means of working to reduce risk. Overall, however, there is considerable evidence that parenting programmes are a useful way of increasing protective factors and reducing risk.

Having identified the evidence base for the use of parenting programmes, in Chapter 20, Nick Axford, Tracey Bywater, Sarah Blower, Vashti Berry, Victoria Baker and Louise Morpeth consider the critical factors in the successful *implementation* of such programmes, focusing on issues of fidelity, adaptation and quality. The potential of programme fidelity to moderate the intended outcomes of interventions is highlighted, before acknowledging that, in practice, adaptations are a reality. A summary of research is then provided about whether adaptations increase or reduce programme effectiveness and sustainability. The authors go on to outline solutions to resolve the tension and methods for promoting fidelity before concluding with future research recommendations.

In Chapter 22, Cristin M. Hall, Megan C. Runion and Daniel F. Perkins consider school-based prevention and interventions in cases of child maltreatment in operation in the United States. They point out that schools are important contexts for the detection, reporting, prevention and intervention of child maltreatment and as a result school personnel in the United States are bound by mandated reporting laws. However, they note that despite mandated reporting being codified into US law current efforts at detecting, preventing and intervening in cases of child maltreatment continue to fall short. The authors discuss the use of the IOM Protractor, a conceptual framework tiered-service delivery model adopted from public health, and review the empirical support for the three main pillars of the model, prevention, treatment and maintenance within school settings. While the majority of programmes discussed have some empirical support, the authors note there continues to be gaps in the literature with research focusing on prevention models (developing participant knowledge and skills tied to educational programme content) with little research in the areas of treatment for victims of maltreatment. They conclude by arguing that schools that move toward a public health approach to the prevention and treatment of child maltreatment could better serve children and they encourage school personnel to use resources in a more impactful way while collaborating with community resources specifically targeted to serve victims of maltreatment.

Finally, this part concludes by looking at an alternative model to working with parents. Specifically, in Chapter 23, Patricia Crittenden and Clark Baim demonstrate how the assessment of attachment in child care proceedings can be used to guide intervention with families. The chapter reports on the IASA (International Association for the Study of Attachment) Family Attachment Court Protocol, which is based on the Dynamic-Maturational model of attachment (DMM). The DMM takes a life-span approach to attachment and maladaptation; originally devised by Ainsworth, it was expanded by Crittenden in collaboration with

Ainsworth, and includes a strengths-based focus. The Protocol presented in this chapter is a model of assessment, formulation and treatment planning that can be used with families engaged in child care proceedings. A case study highlights how this can be applied in practice.

Part V: Novel Interventions with Families

This final section of the book contains chapters that cover key and novel areas in interventions with parents where child maltreatment is an issue. It provides a focus on interventions for parents with unique clinical or forensic presentations. Arlene Vetere begins this part of the book with Chapter 24, which describes a systematic approach to working with families that present with intimate partner violence. The chapter describes an approach to safe relationship therapy with couples and families, used in the UK based 'Reading Safer Families' family violence intervention project. The literature on the efficacy of systemic approaches with a wide range of client groups is noted before providing a description of the safety methodology used in the programme. It addresses further violence risk management, risk assessment of further violence, taking responsibility for safety and for behaviour that harms others, and collaborative practices. The use of a safety plan that is developed to help predict and prevent violent interactions, and to help family members repair relationships where possible is also outlined, along with the need for therapists to look after themselves.

In Chapter 25, Isabelle Daignault, Mireille Cyr and Martine Hébert consider working effectively with non-offending parents in cases of child sexual abuse. The authors begin by recognising the numerous challenges parents face in attempting to provide support to their child following disclosure as well as the challenges in the aftermath of disclosure. They describe in detail some of the support and advocacy services available for parents and children in the United States and Canada and report positive research findings for the use Child Advocacy Centers (CACs). They go on to consider the physical and psychological impact of child sexual abuse on the non-offending parent before outlining strategies and therapeutic models such as Trauma-Focused Cognitive Behavioural Therapy (TF-CBT) in supporting non-offending parents while focusing on the recovery of the child. They argue that parents need to be well supported by therapists and other professionals involved who should nourish the therapeutic relationship with the parent.

Next, in Chapter 26, Beth Tarleton presents an account of working with parents with intellectual disabilities (ID) in child care proceedings. Tarleton begins by introducing parents with ID and the issues and difficulties they might face related to their impairment, as well as barriers related to their often poor socio-economic status and lack of community support. Tarleton discusses the issues relating to engaging parents with ID and reviews the literature on the efficacy of intervention and supportive parenting programmes for this client group from studies in the United States, Canada, Europe and Australia. While Tarleton notes that a substantial amount of best practice has been developed around working with parents with ID, in many areas pro-active support is not available and a 'paradigm shift' is required in order to ensure that these vulnerable parents are provided with support that is tailored to their needs that reduces the likelihood of poorer outcomes for and concerns about the welfare of their children.

In Chapter 27, Tanya Garrett considers working with parents with a diagnosis of personality disorder as part of child care proceedings. Garrett begins by discussing definitions of personality disorder and diagnostic systems before considering the wider prevalence and co-morbidity of personality disorder. This is followed by a discussion on the impact of parents with personality disorders and how key difficulties such as attachment styles, behaviours, problematic emotions and interpersonal difficulties in the parent can impact on the child. Garrett highlights research indicating that the aggregation of all of these concerns points to an increased risk of the child of a parent with personality disorder developing the same problems. Garrett considers interventions such as schema therapy, cognitive therapy and Dialectical Behaviour Therapy (DBT) as the most commonly used interventions within the UK. While community resources and service provisions are limited, Garrett reports the results of an Early Years Parenting Unit (EYPU) in London, UK, which focuses on the parent's own problems and mental health, their parenting and the child's developmental problems. A working case example is described of a parent with a narcissistic personality disorder and strategies to overcome common therapeutic stumbling blocks are provided. In conclusion, Garret reiterates that in addition to therapies for personality dysfunction, parents with personality disorders need interventions that can address their relationships with their children and their parenting skills.

Finally, in Chapter 28, Rebecca Sanford, Stephanie Ratliff and Michele Staton-Tindall consider the well-established impact of caregiver substance misuse on child welfare outcomes and highlight the need to work with caregivers who use alcohol and drugs in the child protection system. The professional practice and policy issues required to make this work possible, and ensure its efficacy, are highlighted. These include: better understanding of the prevalence of substance abuse in system and the impact of substance addiction; establishing collaboration and consensus between professionals on the issue; accurate identification of substance use among caregivers; better systems for collecting, reporting, and disseminating the data; and more practical education for professionals regarding effective work with substance abusing caregivers. The authors emphasise the need to implement programmes that demonstrate efficacy, and for further research to continue in terms of evaluative practice in the area.

References

Casanueva, C., Martin, S.L. & Runyan, D.K. (2009). Repeated reports for child maltreatment among intimate partner violence victims: Findings from the National Survey of Child and Adolescent Well-Being. *Child Abuse & Neglect*, 33, 84–93.

Chambless, D.L. & Hollon, S.D. (1998). Defining empirically supported therapies. *Journal of Consulting and Clinical Psychology*, 66, 7–18.

Chambless, D. & Ollendick, T. (2001). Empirically supported psychological interventions: Controversies and evidence. *Annual Review of Psychology*, 52, 685–716.

Chambless, D.L., Baker, M., Baucom, D.H. et al. (1998). Update on empirically validated therapies, II. *The Clinical Psychologist*, 51, 3–16.

Children and Family Court Advisory and Support Service (CAFCASS) 2016. Care Applications 2016, https://www.cafcass.gov.uk/leaflets-resources/organisational-material/care-and-private-law-demand-statistics/care-demand-statistics.aspx (accessed 24 August 2016).

Cox, C.E., Kotch, J.B. & Everson, M.D. (2003). A longitudinal study of modifying influences in the relationship between domestic violence and child maltreatment. *Journal of Family Violence*, 18, 5–17.

Craig, L.A., Dixon, L. & Gannon, T.A. (2013). *What Works in Offender Rehabilitation: An Evidence-Based Approach to Assessment and Treatment*. Chichester: Wiley-Blackwell.

DePanfilis, D. & Zuravin, S.J. (1998). Rates, patterns and frequency of child maltreatment recurrences among families known to CPS. *Child Maltreatment*, 3, 27–42.

Department for Education (2015). *Characteristics of children in need 2014–2015, SFR 41/2015*. London: Department for Education, www.gov.uk/government/collections/statistics-children-in-need (accessed 6 November 2015).

Finkelhor, D. (1999). The science. *Child Abuse & Neglect*, 23, 969 – 974.

Frederick, J., Goddard, C. & Oxley, J. (2013). What is the 'dark figure' of child homicide and how can it be addressed in Australia? *International Journal of Injury Control and Safety Promotion*, 20, 209–217.

Higgins, J.P.T. & Green, S. (2006). *Cochrane Handbook for Systematic Reviews of Interventions 4.2.6* [updated September 2006]. In: The Cochrane Library. Chichester: John Wiley & Sons, Ltd, http://community-archive.cochrane.org/sites/default/files/uploads/Handbook4.2.6Sep2006.pdf (accessed 24 August 2016).

Higgins, J.P.T. & Green, S. (2008). *Cochrane Handbook for Systematic Reviews of Interventions 5.0.0*. In: The Cochrane Library. Chichester: John Wiley & Sons, Ltd.

Higgins, J.P.T. & Green, S. (2011). *Cochrane Handbook for Systematic Reviews of Interventions 5.1.0* [updated March 2011]. In: The Cochrane Library. Chichester: John Wiley & Sons, Ltd, http://handbook.cochrane.org/ (accessed 24 August 2016).

Hussey, J.M., Chang, J.J. & Kotch, J.B. (2006). Child maltreatment in the United States: Prevalence, risk factors, and adolescent health consequences. *Pediatrics*, 118, 933–942.

Krug, E.G., Dahlberg, L.L., Mercy, J.A. et al. (2002). *World report on violence and health*. Geneva: World Health Organization.

Lipton, D.S., Martinson, R. & Wilks, J. (1975). *The Effectiveness of Correctional Treatment: A Survey of Treatment Evaluation Studies*. New York: Praeger.

Macdonald, G., Lewis, J., Macdonald, K. et al. (2014). The SAAF Study: Evaluation of the Safeguarding Children Assessment and Analysis Framework (SAAF), compared with management as usual, for improving outcomes for children and young people who have experienced, or are at risk of, maltreatment: Study protocol for a randomised controlled trial. *Trials*, 15, 453.

Martinson, R. (1974). What works? – Questions and answers about prison reform. *Public Interest*, 10, 22–54.

Munro, E. (2009). Managing societal and institutional risk in child protection. *Risk Analysis*, 29, 1015–1023.

Pinheiro, P. (2006). *World report on violence against children*. Geneva: United Nations.

Sherman, L.W., Gottfredson, D., MacKenzie, D.L. et al. (1997). *Preventing crime: What works, what doesn't, what's promising*. Washington, DC: US Department of Justice, National Institute of Justice, https://www.ncjrs.gov/pdffiles/171676.PDF (accessed January 2012).

Sidebotham, P., Atkins, B. & Hutton, J.L. (2012). Changes in rates of violent child deaths in England and Wales between 1974 and 2008: An analysis of national mortality data. *Archives of Disease in Childhood*, 97, 193–199.

Sousa, C., Herrenkohl, T.I., Moylan, C.A. et al. (2011). Longitudinal study on the effects of child abuse and children's exposure to domestic violence, parent–child attachments, and anti-social behaviour in adolescence. *Journal of Interpersonal Violence*, 26, 111–136.

Thompson, R. & Wiley, T.R. (2009). Predictors of re-referral to child protective services: A longitudinal follow-up of an urban cohort maltreated as infants. *Child Maltreatment*, 14, 89–99.

UNICEF (2014). *Hidden in plain sight: A statistical analysis of violence against children*. New York: UNICEF.

Part I
Research and Theoretical Perspectives

2

Child Abuse and Neglect
Prevalence and Incidence

Lorraine Radford
University of Central Lancashire

Introduction

Violence against children, including child abuse and neglect, is prevalent across the world and the burden on children's health and well-being is considerable (Gilbert, Spatz Widom, Browne, K. et al., 2008a; Pinheiro, 2006). There are, however, problems in getting accurate estimates of the extent and, although knowledge has improved, it is generally accepted that current figures are underestimates. This chapter will begin by briefly reviewing the conceptual and methodological challenges researchers, practitioners and policy makers face when wanting to make robust estimates of the extent of violence within the community. Next we will consider what is known about levels of violence from incidents of child abuse and neglect reported to services such as the police, health care sectors and child protection agencies. Findings from the growing number of community-based surveys on violence against children will be reviewed, as well as key conclusions about developmental risks, the overlapping and accumulating nature of victimisation and poly-victimisation experiences. This chapter will consider research on trends in violence and the question as to whether violence against children is increasing or decreasing. The chapter will conclude by highlighting the implications for practice, arguing that knowledge about the extent and burden of violence against children can be used to improve prevention, identification and response as well as to inform provision, service monitoring and the measurement of outcomes for children.

Conceptual and Methodological Challenges

In any society, what is considered to be 'violent' has a normative or 'socially acceptable' element. In the UK for example, violence toward children that was in earlier times deemed to be 'acceptable', such as using corporal punishment in education settings, is now condemned. Children are less likely to be openly beaten by adults 'for their own good' than they were in the past. Children and young people in the UK, however, still lack the right enjoyed by adults to equal protection from violence because the State condones parental use of physical violence towards children as 'reasonable punishment'. Different societies have varied views about what levels of violence towards children can be tolerated. In 46 countries of the world, all forms of physical punishment of children, including in the home, are outlawed (Global Initiative, 2015). In many other parts of the world though, parents and other adults, such as teachers, penal staff or care staff, are still able to use physical violence to chastise children and young people (Pinheiro, 2006). Legal definitions and social norms about 'acceptable' and 'unacceptable' violence will influence what is counted and recorded. Historically, as recognition of the different aspects of child abuse and neglect has grown, definitions have expanded (Radford, 2012).

The World Health Organization has defined child maltreatment as:

> All forms of physical and/or emotional ill-treatment, sexual abuse, neglect or negligent treatment or commercial or other exploitation, resulting in actual or potential harm to the child's health, survival, development or dignity in the context of a relationship of responsibility, trust or power.
> (Krug, Dahlberg, Mercy et al., 2002)

This broad definition does not necessarily match the concepts of child abuse and neglect operationalised in research or used in policies guiding everyday child protection practice. The narrowest estimates of the extent of child abuse and neglect typically come from research based on *known* cases, reported to agencies such as the police, child welfare or health services. What gets reported, recorded and counted is highly dependent on what law and policy says should be reported, the ability of individuals to recognise child abuse and neglect, and their willingness to take action. There are barriers that can prevent child victims telling anybody about their experiences. Reasons why a child or young person may not disclose experiences of maltreatment include:

- The child not recognising the behaviour as abuse. Children who live with abuse and neglect, particularly younger children, may believe that what they experience is 'normal'. Younger children may be aware of problems but may be less likely than older children to understand what is happening and why. For example, 'I didn't quite understand it when I was so young, because...I just got used to it, when he used to hit me and my little brother and then my mum. I just got used to it' (Marilyn aged 15, p. 98, McGee, 2000).
- Fear of the consequences, especially getting their family or themselves into 'trouble'.
- Thinking, or being told, they are to blame for the abuse.
- Feeling ashamed.
- Attachment to the abuser.
- Being 'groomed' or frightened by the abuser into silence.
  (Howe, 2005; Kendall-Tackett, 2008; McGee, 2000).

Few maltreated children come to the attention of child protection agencies in any country. In a review of the research literature on professional responses to child abuse and neglect, Gilbert, Spatz Widom, Browne et al. 2008a found typically between 1.5% and 5% of the child population in the UK, USA, Australia and Canada are reported to child protection services each year. Just 1% of the child population are recognised as 'substantiated' cases of child abuse and neglect yet self-report community surveys in these countries estimate levels of prevalence to be between 4 and 16 times higher. There is growing evidence indicating a failure of professionals to recognise, report and investigate in order to substantiate cases. Reasons for professionals not reporting included: not knowing what to do, the belief that reporting will not help the child, concern that reporting might adversely affect the relationship between the professional (such as a teacher or GP) and the family or will have other negative consequences (Gilbert, Kemp, Thoburn et al., 2008b).

Self-report surveys drawing representative samples from the population are regarded as providing more reliable estimates of the extent of the problem. Many research studies have collected information on the lifetime prevalence of child maltreatment via retrospective research with adults (Cawson, Wattam, Brooker & Kelly, 2000; MacMillan, Fleming, Trocmé et al., 1997). However, a number of research reviews have since questioned the relevance of retrospective reports based on adult memories of childhood maltreatment. For example, Hardt and Rutter (2004) reviewed 18 longitudinal studies that compared adults' retrospective recall against officially documented cases of abuse (10–30 years previous to the interview) and found that a third or more of the participants across the studies failed to report the adverse event, even when they were specifically asked about it, which may reflect recall or non-disclosure issues. Research based on adult memories of past childhood abuse can only measure lifetime experiences and cannot tell us about rates of violence experienced by children at the present time. Crime and victimisation surveys conventionally ask about current rates of violence by asking respondents about events within the last 12 months (or an even shorter referent period). Direct research with children and young people themselves is now far more common than previously was the case as it allows us to gather this information on recent experiences.

Within the self-report survey research literature on child maltreatment there are considerable variations in the severity, types of violence and types of offenders included by researchers when measuring prevalence. Many studies of child abuse and neglect focus on caregiver or parent to child abuse or neglect, typically in the home or family environment. At the narrowest level there are studies that assess just one type of violent experience, such as physical violence from parents excluding parental 'discipline' (Stoltenborgh, Bakermans-Kranenburg, Kranenburg et al., 2013), or child sexual abuse (Andrews, Corry, Slade et al., 2004; Pereda, Guilera, Forns & Gómez-Benito, 2009; Stoltenborgh, van IJzendoorn, Euser & Bakermans-Kranenburg, 2011) but seldom including child sexual exploitation. More often researchers include all the different types of child abuse and neglect (physical, sexual and emotional abuse, plus neglect, as defined by the World Health Organization; Cawson, Wattam, Brooker & Kelly 2000). In low-resource settings though, neglect is often excluded because of the difficulties in measurement when absolute poverty levels are high (Stoltenborgh, Bakermans-Kranenburg & von IJzendoorn, 2013; UNICEF, 2011, 2012). At the broadest level, researchers have included measures of child abuse and neglect within questions about a range of victimisation experiences, covering the continuum from common or 'everyday' victimisation through to severe violence. These also cover the range of different perpetrators (peers, siblings, non-resident adults, intimate partners, caregivers) and the varied settings where violence happens including the home, school and community (Burton, Ward, Artz & Leoshut, 2015; Finkelhor, Turner, Ormrod & Hamby, 2009a).

Victimisation surveys typically give higher estimates for levels of violence against children. This is due to a significant amount of child victimisation, including sexual abuse and violence in the home, being perpetrated by peers (Averdijk, Mueller-Johnson & Eisner, 2011; Finkelhor, Turner, Shattuck & Hamby, 2013; UNICEF, 2014). Victimisation researchers argue that violence perpetrated by other young people is not necessarily less harmful than that perpetrated by adults. While common acts of childhood physical violence such as sibling violence, are often assumed not to be harmful and part of a young person's developmental process (Kiselica & Morill-Richards, 2007), this is not the case for all sibling violence and certainly not for a lot of peer abuse (Barter & Berridge, 2011; Finkelhor, Ormrod & Turner, 2006).

School-based peer abuse or 'bullying' is one of the most common reasons prompting children to call ChildLine (ChildLine, 2011) and it can have devastating consequences for the mental health and well-being of young people. The adverse consequences for mental health can be identified even in very young children (Arseneault, Walsh, Trzesniewski et al., 2006). Experiences of violence often have overlapping and accumulative impacts and it is important for prevention to study and understand these and how they influence children's vulnerabilities (Finkelhor, Ormrod & Turner, 2009b; Hamby, Finkelhor, Turner & Ormrod, 2010).

How a survey asks about violence has an influence on what is reported. Generally the more questions asked about sensitive topics such as sexual abuse, the higher the rates reported (Andrews, Corry, Slade et al., 2004; Stoltenborgh, Bakermans-Kranenburg, Kranenburg et al., 2013). Safe and private methods to ask about experiences of victimisation are especially important. Higher rates of violence tend to be reported when participants are asked using Computer Assisted Self Interviewing (CASI) or Audio CASI methods, compared with being asked directly in a face-to-face interview. CASI interviews involve the interviewer handing over a laptop computer to the interviewee so that the interviewee can read sensitive questions (or hear via headphones if using audio CASI) and respond to the questions directly themselves by entering their answers onscreen. A national survey of children and violence in South Africa tested different methods to interview 9,730 young people aged 15 to 17, 5,635 in households and 4,095 in schools, using an administered interview and a self-completion (CASI) interview. Highest rates of reporting were found in the self-completion surveys, especially as regards those completed in schools (Burton, Ward, Artz & Leoshut, 2015).

Who is Missing from the Prevalence Research?

Community surveys may not give details about the prevalence of abuse and neglect among some groups of children and young people who are thought to be particularly vulnerable. There is a considerable gap regards younger children's experiences of violence as most community surveys have relied on parental reports on behalf of their younger children or on older children's retrospective accounts of their experiences. Surveys which use household samples or telephone landline sampling methods will often exclude children and young people who do not have a secure household base such as those who are homeless, migrant, in state residential care or in detention centres. School-based surveys tend to miss out children and young people who do not attend school. Some studies have tried to address this issue by targeting these groups of vulnerable children. For example, research in nine Balkan countries using a school-based study of children recruited an additional sample of those excluded from school (Nikolaidis, 2013). Children with disabilities or with learning difficulties may also often be excluded, as different methods may be needed to enable their participation. The most severely disabled children with limited communication ability will have particular vulnerabilities, but research on their experiences of abuse is methodologically challenging. The few studies which have considered disabled children's experiences have found them to be more vulnerable to all forms of victimisation (Averdijk, Mueller-Johnson & Eisner, 2011; Jones, Bellis, Wood et al., 2012). Children with depression and mental health problems are at greater risk of both victimisation and perpetration of violence (Andrews, Corry, Slade et al., 2004; Cuevas, Finkelhor, Turner & Ormrod, 2007).

These methodological and conceptual differences found across research studies and data surveillance systems have a profound impact on the conclusions and comparisons that can be drawn about the global, regional and even national levels of child abuse and neglect, making accurate cross-national comparisons difficult (Stoltenborgh, Bakermans-Kranenburg

& von IJzendoorn, 2013). There are variations in prevalence estimates across and within global regions and within countries (Ji, Finkelhor & Dunne, 2013; Stoltenborgh, Bakermans-Kranenburg & von IJzendoorn, 2013). There is however evidence that low-income areas have higher rates of violence (Sethi, Bellis, Hughes et al., 2013; UNICEF, 2014).

Cases Known to Services

It would be expected that child deaths resulting from intentional injuries, severe neglect or homicides would be the cases most likely to be known to agencies such as the police, health and welfare services. The recording of non-accidental child deaths however varies considerably from country to country and it is likely that such deaths are under-counted. Due to varied practices in detection, recording and prosecution, it has been estimated, for example, that across the World Health Organization (WHO) European region only 33% of child maltreatment deaths are classified as homicides (Sethi, Bellis, Hughes et al., 2013). A survey of global progress on preventing child maltreatment by the WHO found that while 88% of the 133 countries responding had police data on homicides, 9% had no police or vital registration data on homicides (WHO, 2014). In 2012, an estimated 95,000 children and young people died as the result of homicide across the world. Most of the victims (85,000 or 90%) lived in low- and middle-income countries. Child homicides are relatively rare in high-income countries (UNICEF, 2014; Table 2.1).

Globally, rates of child homicides are highest in Latin America and the Caribbean (27 homicides per 100,000 population in El Salvador) and lowest in high-income regions such as Europe (<0 homicides per 100,000 population in UK and most countries in Western Europe), North America (4 homicides per 100,000 population in the USA), Australia and New Zealand (1 homicide per 100,000 population) and Japan (<0 homicides per 100,000 population). Lower rates of child homicide co-exist with lower rates of adult homicides, and vice versa.

Most homicide victims are adults; typically men under 25 years of age (Sethi, Bellis, Hughes et al., 2013). For children, the risk of dying as a result of homicide varies according to age and gender. There are typically two age categories in childhood where homicide rates are higher – in infancy and early childhood (i.e., under the age of four years), where the majority of victims are killed by a parent or carer, and in later adolescence, where many of the victims are killed by

Table 2.1 Child homicide rates 2012 per 100,000 child population aged 0–19 years by region and within region highest and lowest rate countries.

Region	Rate per 100,000 pop^n	Highest country rate		Lowest country rate	
C & E Europe	1	Turkmenistan	4	Croatia	0
East Asia & Pacific	1	Myanmar	7	Brunei Darussalam	0
Eastern & Southern Africa	6	Lesotho	18	Mauritius	1
West & Central Africa	10	Democratic Republic Congo	14	Cabo Verde	1
Middle East & North Africa	2	Sudan	6	Qatar	0
South Asia	2	Afghanistan	8	Nepal	1
Latin America & Caribbean	12	El Salvador	27	Suriname	0
Countries outside these regions	2	USA	4	UK	0

Note: WHO mortality data groups the rates into age categories for late adolescence from ages 15 through to 19 years, including young adults aged 19, so under-18 rates for child homicides cannot be shown.

peers (UNICEF, 2014). Infants under age one year are more likely to die as a result of violence and in high-income countries have rates of homicide higher than the rest of the population. In England and Wales, for example, there were three homicides per 100,000 population of babies aged under 12 months in 2012–2013 compared with 0.97 homicides among all ages and 1.4 per 100,000 of the population among adults aged 30–49 years (ONS, 2014). As infants, both boys and girls in England and Wales are equally vulnerable to homicide and this is the case across most countries in Western Europe. Boys aged 15–19 years are vulnerable to peer violence and in many countries across the world show highest increases in homicide rates between these ages. In Venezuela, for example, the homicide rate in 2012 for children between ages 10 and 19 years was 39 per 100,000 of the population, but the rate for boys in this age group was 74 per 100,000 of the population compared with 3 per 100,000 for girls (UNICEF, 2014).

The WHO has estimated that for every *recorded* child fatality resulting from peer violence, there are another 20–40 hospital admissions for peer violence-related injuries (Sethi, Bellis, Hughes et al., 2010). Hospital data, usually in the form of emergency attendance, admissions and discharge records, provide another source of information on child abuse and neglect although recording practices vary. Research into hospital data in England found the highest rates in hospital attendance for maltreatment and violence-related injuries among children from 2005 to 2011 were for infants and for adolescents. Mirroring the findings on child homicides, maltreatment and violence-related injuries were estimated as being 86.9 injuries per 100,000 of the population aged under one year, 18.8 injuries per 100,000 of the population aged 1–10 years and 118.4 injuries per 100,000 of the population aged 11–18 years (Gonzalez-Izquierdo, Cortina-Borja, Woodman et al., 2014). Adolescent boys have higher rates of hospital-recorded injury resulting from violence. There is evidence to suggest that some children have repeated injuries recorded, as 21.1% of girls and 24.2% of boys tracked through the hospital episode data had readmissions for multiple types of adversity related injury (i.e., recorded as violence, self-harm, drug or alcohol misuse; Herbert, Gilbert, Gonzalez-Isquierdo & Li, 2015).

Many countries, including those in the UK, keep official statistics on cases of child protection recorded by welfare services. As previously said, recording practices vary as many countries do not have mandatory child abuse reporting laws, and definitions and practices in identification and reporting vary. The most recent statistics for England show that there were 635,600 referrals of children made to children's social care in 2015. Following initial investigation or assessment, over one-third of these referrals (36.8%) resulted in no further action being taken and 24% were re-referrals of children within the last 12 months (Department for Education [DfE], 2015a). There were 391,000 children assessed as being in need of some family support on 31 March 2015, a population rate of 3,373 per 100,000 children aged under 18. More males (52.5%) than females (45.5%) were children in need, 30.7% were children and young people aged 10–15 years, 25.3% were children aged less than 5 years (DfE, 2015a). Smaller numbers of children are assessed as requiring child protection. The most common reasons for a child needing to be looked after by child protection services is child abuse and neglect, with 61% of the children subject to a new care order for this reason in 2015. Neglect and then emotional abuse are the most frequently recorded types of maltreatment in care orders, with physical violence and sexual abuse less commonly recorded. There has been a steady increase in the numbers of looked-after children in England since 1994 (DfE, 2015b). In March 2015, 69,540 children were looked after, 600 children per 100,000 of the population (0.6%). The highest numbers of looked-after children are in areas with highest population density, London and Inner London, but rates per 100,000 of the population vary by local authority area from 1,580 per 100,000 of the child population in Blackpool and 1,350 in Wolverhampton to 220 in Richmond Upon Thames and 200 in Wokingham (DfE, 2015b). Variations from area to area are generally thought to reflect differing practices, particularly on determining the thresholds for child protection (DfE, 2015b).

Some countries have taken steps to calculate national incidence rates from a range of agencies in contact with children so that services can be planned and commissioned efficiently. The American (Sedlak, Mettenburg, Basena et al., 2010), Dutch (Euser, Van IJzendoorn, Prinzie & Bakermans-Kranenburg, 2010) and Canadian (Trocmé, Fallon, MacLaurin et al., 2005) incidence studies are designed to do this. They take similar approaches in order to collect data on a regular basis using sentinel reporters, who are usually based in children's services and trained to record, in a standardised way, cases of child maltreatment, including those that may not appear in child protection agency records (Sedlak, Mettenburg, Basena et al., 2010). Data collected from reporters in this way provides higher estimates of the prevalence of child maltreatment than are reflected in child protection statistics, and allows some comparison of trends in case reports over time. However, they are still limited to cases that come to the attention of some children's service.

Community Prevalence Surveys

Surveys of violence conducted with community-based samples of children and young people have increased in number in recent years. However, a survey of global progress on preventing child maltreatment by the WHO found that less than half the 133 countries responding had conducted nationally representative prevalence surveys (WHO, 2014). Surveys on child sexual abuse are more prevalent than surveys of child maltreatment in general. A number of systematic reviews and meta-analyses of the global prevalence research have been undertaken (for example, Barth, Bermetz, Hein et al., 2012; Stoltenborgh, van IJzendoorn, Euser & Bakermans-Kranenburg, 2011; Stoltenborgh, Bakermans-Kranenburg, Kranenburg et al., 2013; UNICEF, 2014) and although these highlight considerable challenges in making comparisons, all confirm high prevalence rates for child abuse and neglect. A combined analysis of self-report surveys across Europe for example found that 13.4% of girls and 5.7% of boys had experienced childhood sexual abuse, 22.9% of both sexes had experienced physical violence, 29.1% had experienced emotional abuse and 16.3% had experienced physical neglect (Sethi, Bellis, Hughes et al., 2013). Typically these surveys provide estimates of the extent of child abuse and neglect that are at least five to sixteen times greater than those gained from child protection, hospital or prosecution records. A meta-analysis of 111 research studies on child physical abuse found rates of self-report from community surveys were 75 times greater (affecting 22.6% of children, 22,600 per 100,000 of the population) than rates estimated by informants (covering 0.3% of children, 300 per 100,000 of the population), for lifetime experiences (Stoltenborgh, Bakermans-Kranenburg & von IJzendoorn, 2013).

Findings from one country study, a UK-wide nationally representative survey with 6,196 participants (2,160 parents/carers of children aged 0–10 years, 2,275 children and young people aged 11–17 years, 1,761 young adults aged 18–24 years; Radford, Corral, Bradley & Fisher, 2013), can be used to show some of the common features of the prevalence of child abuse and neglect across the age range and in the context of other victimisation types. Table 2.2 presents the prevalence rates of past-year and lifetime victimisation by age group, child's gender and perpetrator type. As can be seen, a minority of children and young people reported no victimisations at all. Victimisation by peers and by siblings was the most common victimisation reported. Apart from sibling victimisation, highest rates for most types of lifetime victimisation were reported by young adults, most likely because victimisation experiences tend to accumulate over time, as shown by the greater mean number of victimisations at ages 18–24 years.

Table 2.2 Prevalence of lifetime (LT) and past-year (PY) childhood victimisation by victimisation type, victim age group and gender (95% confidence intervals, weighted data).

Victimisation type	Under 11						11–17s						18–24s		
	LT			PY			LT			PY			LT		
	All	Male	Female	All	Male	Female	All	Male	Female	All	Male	Female	All	Male	Female
No victimisation	46.4% (1194) +/−1.2	45.5% (598)	47.5% (596)	58.6% (1443)	57.5% (725)	59.7% (718)	16.3% (281)	12.2% (108)	20.6% (173)	42.9% (680)	38.5% (322)	47.7% (358)	12.7% (241)	11.1% (108)	14.3% (133)
Mean number of victimisations	1.78	1.91	1.63	1.01	1.14	0.88	5.18	5.57	4.71	1.77	1.92	1.61	6.32	6.88	5.74
Parent or guardian maltreated child[a]	8.9% (229) +/−1.2	9% (118)	8.8% (111)	2.5% (63) +/−0.7	2.5% (33)	2.5% (31)	21.9% (379) +/−1.7	22.7% (201)	21.2% (178)	6.0% (103) +/−1	5.7% (51)	6.2% (52)	24.5% (465) +/−2	22.7% (219)	26.5% (246)
Neglect	5% (130) +/−0.9	4.9% (65)	5.2% (65)	—	—	—	13.3% (229) +/−1.4	14.8% (131)	11.8% (99)	—	—	—	16% (303) +/−1.7	15.6% (151)	16.4% (152)
Emotional abuse by parent/guardian	3.6% (74) +/−0.8	3.7% (40)	3.4% (34)	1.8% (38) +/−0.6	1.7% (18)	2% (20)	6.8% (116) +/−1	5.5% (49)	8% (68)	3% (52) +/−0.7	2% (18)	4% (34)	6.9% (131) +/−1.2	4.3% (42)	9.6% (89)
Physical violence from parent/guardian	1.3% (34) +/−0.7	1.4% (18)	1.3% (16)	0.7% (19) +/−0.4	1.1% (14)	0.4% (5)	6.9% (119) +/−1	6.8% (61)	6.9% (58)	2.4% (41) 0.6	2.2% (20)	2.6% (922)	8.4% (159) +/−1.3	7% (67)	9.9% (92)
Sexual abuse by parent/guardian	0.1% (2) +/−0.1	0% (0)	0.1% (2)	0% (0)	0% (0)	0% (0)	0.1% (2) +/−0.1	0% (0)	0.3% (2)	0% (0)	0% (0)	0% (0)	0.6% (6) +/−0.4	1.5% (14)	1% (20)
Exposure to domestic violence	12% (308) +/−1.4	10.9% (143)	13.1% (165)	3.2% (82) +/−0.7	3.8% (50)	2.6% (32)	17.5% (302) +/−1.1	16.4% (145)	18.7% (157)	2.5% (43) +/−0.6	2.1% (19)	2.9% (25)	23.7% (449) +/−2	19.5% (188)	28% (260)
Sexual victimisation by any adult/peer perpetrator	1.2% (30) +/−0.5	1% (13)	1.3% (17)	0.6% (15) +/−0.3	0.7% (10)	0.5% (6)	16.5% (285) +/−1.5	12.5% (111)	20.8% (175)	9.4% (163) +/−1.2	6.8% (60)	12.2% (102)	24.1% (456) +/−2	17.4% (168)	31% (288)

	C1	C2	C3	C4	C5	C6	C7	C8	C9	C10	C11	C12	C13	C14	C15
Contact sexual abuse by any adult/peer	0.5% (11) +/-0.3	0.3% (3)	0.7% (8)	0.2% (4) +/-0.2	0	0.4% (4)	5.1% (115) +/-0.9	2.8% (32)	7.2% (83)	2.1% (48) +/-0.6	1.3% (15)	2.9% (33)	12.5% (219) +/-1.5	5.3% (43)	18.6% (176)
Intimate partner victimisation[b]	—	—	—	—	—	—	7.9% (137) +/-1.1	7% (62)	8.9% (74)	5.0% (86) +/-0.9	4.2% (37)	5.8% (49)	13.4% (254) +/-1.6	10.7% (103)	16.2% (150)
Sibling victimisation[c]	28.4% (731) +/-1.9	28% (369)	28.8% (362)	23.7% (608) +/-1.8	23.3% (306)	24.1% (302)	31.8% (550) +/-1.9	29.3% (259)	34.6% (290)	16% (275) +/-1.5	15.8% (140)	16.1% (135)	25.2% (478) +/-2	23.4% (225)	27.2% (253)
Peer victimisation[d]	28.0% (721) +/-1.9	30.5% (401)	25.5% (320)	20.2% (519) +/-1.7	23% (303)	17.2% (216)	59.5% (1,028) +/-2	66% (585)	52.7% (443)	35.3% (609) +/-2	41.2% (365)	29.1% (244)	63.2% (1198) +/-2.3	69.6% (671)	56.6% (526)
Physical violence from non-caregiver (adult or peer)	33% (713) +/-2	34.7% (365)	31.5% (348)	25.8% (557) +/-1.9	27.2% (286)	24.5% (271)	565 (1274) +/-2	62.8% (706)	49.4% (568)	28.2% (642) +/-1.9	34.4% (387)	22.2% (255)	55.5% (972) +/-2.3	64.8% (528)	47% (444)
Exposure to community violence	11.3% (2910) +/-1.3	11.1% (146)	11.5% (145)	4.8% (122) +/-0.9	5.1% (68)	4.3% (55)	61.4% (1060) +/-2	67.9% (601)	54.6% (459)	31.2% (539) +/-1.9	34% (301)	28.3% (238)	66.5% (1259) +/-2.2	73% (705)	59.7% (555)

[a] Any physical, sexual, emotional abuse or neglect of child by parent or guardian, excluding exposure to parental domestic violence.
[b] Any physical violence, sexual victimisation or emotional abuse of young person aged over 11 by their adult or peer intimate partner.
[c] Any physical violence, sexual victimisation or emotional abuse of child by sibling.
[d] Any physical violence, sexual victimisation or emotional abuse of child by another person under age 18, excluding victimisation by young person's intimate partner and siblings.

Note. All percentages are the (weighted) percentage of children and young people in the age group who experienced this type of victimisation. Bracketed figures are the percentages as expressed in numbers.

A sizeable minority reported abuse or neglect by a parent or caregiver across all three age categories (for example, 21.9%, one in five of participants aged 11–17; Radford, Corral, Bradley & Fisher, 2013). Parental neglect was the most commonly reported type of abuse in the family, affecting 13.3% of children and young people aged 11–17 at some time in their lives. For those aged 11–17 other types of abuse and neglect in the family had reported lifetime rates of 6.9% for physical violence (excluding parental physical discipline), 6.8% for emotional abuse and 17.5% for exposure to parental domestic violence. The rate of reported sexual abuse by parents was low across all age groups, possibly because the conduct of the survey in households may have influenced reporting rates. Sexual victimisation by any adult or peer, however, was more common and showed gender differences in self-reporting for those aged 11–17 and 18–24 years, with girls reporting lifetime rates around twice the level of those reported by boys (20.8% of girls sexually victimised in age group 11–17 compared with 12.5% of boys; 31% of girls victimised by age 18 in age group 18–24 compared with 17.4% of boys).

Contact sexual abuse, ranging from sexual touching to penetrative rape, was less frequently reported, with 7.2% of girls in age group 11–17 reporting this compared with 2.8% of boys, 18.6% of girls having this experience before the age of 18 in age group 18–24 compared with 5.3% of boys. Being female is a significant risk factor for sexual abuse and sexual exploitation in most parts of the world and is linked to the gender-based power inequalities that persist globally, although it is important to recognise that boys can also be sexually abused and exploited and can be stigmatised and deliberately targeted because of their gender. Most adult perpetrators of sexual and domestic violence are male (WHO, 2013), although this does not mean we should ignore abuse by women.

Findings from this UK study, alongside similar studies (Averdijk, Mueller-Johnson & Eisner, 2011; Finkelhor, Turner, Shattuck & Hamby, 2013; UNICEF Tanzania, 2011), support the developmental victimology view (Finkelhor, 2008) that risks of victimisation vary across the life course. Risks in childhood are dependency related and vary with the age, vulnerability and dependency status of the child. Infants and young children are especially vulnerable to harm resulting from any abuse or neglect and are at greatest risk of harm from a parent or caregiver. Typically older children and young people report more victimisation experiences and from a wider range of perpetrators, including those outside the immediate family such as intimate partners (boyfriends/girlfriends), peers and adults in the community. School-age children and adolescents will be exposed to additional risks outside the immediate family as they spend more time in settings outside the home. Interestingly though, both the USA and UK national studies found higher rates of physical violence, emotional abuse (excluding exposure to parental domestic violence) and neglect from a parent or carer reported by older adolescents (Finkelhor, Turner, Shattuck & Hamby, 2013; Radford, Corral, Bradley & Fisher, 2013). There is now mounting evidence that older adolescents are not only more likely to report higher rates of lifetime victimisation than younger children but also are more likely to experience multiple types of victimisation (poly-victimisation), so that the child or young person abused and neglected at home is more likely to be also experiencing victimisation from peers or adults in school and in the community (Finkelhor, Ormrod & Turner, 2009b; Radford, Corral, Bradley & Fisher, 2013). A number of research studies have found an overlap between domestic violence between adults, most commonly from males to females, and direct abuse and neglect of the child (Dixon, Browne, Hamilton-Giachritsis & Ostapuik, 2010; Hamby, Finkelhor, Turner & Ormrod, 2010). In the UK study children exposed to domestic violence were over eight times more likely than children not so exposed to have experienced physical violence from a caregiver and more than four times more likely to have been maltreated (Radford, Corral, Bradley et al., 2011).

Trends in violence

Finkelhor and Jones (2006) present evidence from a variety of sources, including self-report victimisation studies, to support their view that the prevalence of some types of child abuse, especially sexual abuse, has declined in high-income countries such as the USA. They argue there is cause for some modest optimism about child protection, as awareness has grown, behaviour may have changed and interventions are working. Comparing self-report victimisation survey data regarding children and young people aged 2–17 from 2003, 2008 and 2013, Finkelhor and colleagues found lower reports of physical violence, sexual assaults, physical bullying, peer and sibling victimisation, as well as lower reports of psychological and emotional abuse from parents or caregivers. Physical violence and neglect from a caregiver however had not declined (Finkelhor, Shattuck, Turner & Hamby, 2014). The UK prevalence research included a limited number of questions in the 2009 study that were the same as those asked of the 18- to 24-year-olds interviewed in the research completed in 1998–1999. This found significant reductions in reports of some types of abuse in 2009 compared with 1998–1999. Like the USA self-report studies, no decline was found for neglect. But the findings do not negate the view that there may also be some increases in things that were not measured among young adults in 1998–1999 – cyberabuse and partner abuse for example (Radford, Corral, Bradley et al., 2011).

Gilbert, Fluke, O'Donnell et al. (2011) draw on a careful cross-national analysis of official data including data on child deaths, child protection cases and hospital admissions in Sweden, England, New Zealand, Western Australia, Manitoba (Canada), and the USA, and conclude that there is no consistent evidence for a decrease or increase in all types of indicators of child maltreatment across the six countries or states studied, despite several policy initiatives over many years designed to achieve a reduction. Interestingly, lower levels of maltreatment indices in Sweden than in the USA were said to be consistent with lower rates of child poverty and parent risk factors, and policies providing higher levels of *universal* support for parenting in Sweden.

A third possibility, also noted by Gilbert, Fluke, O'Donnell et al. (2011), is that growing awareness and expanded definitions of child abuse have brought more cases to the attention of child protection agencies, and possibly brought forward more children in need of support earlier on at the same time. So child abuse has increased because of expanded definition, but declined because of better awareness and possibly changes in attitudes and behaviour.

Implications for Practice

Child abuse and neglect is prevalent in most countries across the world but is often 'hidden' and not identified early on. All adults need to be aware of the prevalence and nature of violence against children and be alert to indicators that a child may be vulnerable. Knowledge about the different developmental and gender-related risks could be used to inform prevention and response. It is especially important to keep sight of the accumulating and overlapping nature of different types of victimisation so that where one type of victimisation is identified the possibility of the co-occurrence of other types can be sensitively and safely explored. While there is clearly still a lot of work to be done to improve the research and surveillance data on children's experiences of violence to allow tracking of trends over time and across different countries, monitoring change with robust epidemiological data will greatly help us to build knowledge about what are effective policies.

References

Andrews, G., Corry, J., Slade, T. et al. (2004). Child sexual abuse. In: M. Ezzati, A.D. Lopez, A. Rodgers and C.J.L. Murray (eds), *Comparative Quantification of Health Risks Global and Regional Burden of Disease Attributable to Selected Major Risk Factors*, vol. 2. Geneva. World Health Organization, 1851–1940.

Arseneault, L., Walsh, E., Trzesniewski, K. et al. (2006). Bullying victimisation uniquely contributes to adjustment problems in young children: A nationally representative cohort study. *Pediatrics*, 118, 130–138.

Averdijk, M., Mueller-Johnson, K. & Eisner, M. (2011). *Sexual Victimisation among Adolescents in Switzerland*. Geneva: UBS Optimus Foundation.

Barter, C. & Berridge, D. (2011). *Children Behaving Badly: Peer Violence Between Children and Young People*. London: Wiley-Blackwell.

Barth, J., Bermetz, L., Hein, E. et al. (2012). The current prevalence of child sexual abuse worldwide: A systematic review and meta-analysis. *International Journal of Public Health*, 58, 469–483.

Burton, P., Ward, C., Artz, L. & Leoshut, L. (2015). *Research Bulletin: The Optimus Study on Child Abuse, Violence and Neglect in South Africa*. UBS Optimus Foundation, http://www.cjcp.org.za/uploads/2/7/8/4/27845461/cjcp_ubs_web.pdf.

Cawson, P., Wattam, C., Brooker, S. & Kelly, G. (2000). *Child Maltreatment in the United Kingdom*. London: NSPCC.

ChildLine (2011). *Data on counselling calls 2005–2011*. London: ChildLine.

Cuevas, C.A., Finkelhor, D., Turner, H.A. & Ormrod, R.K. (2007). Juvenile delinquency and victimisation: A theoretical typology. *Journal of Interpersonal Violence*, 22, 1581–1602.

Department of Education (2015a). *Characteristics of children in need: 2014 to 2015, SFR 41/2015*. London: Department for Education, www.gov.uk/government/collections/statistics-children-in-need (accessed 6 November 2015).

Department of Education (2015b). *Children looked after in England (including adoption and care leavers) year ending 31 March 2015*. London: Department for Education.

Dixon, L., Browne, K.D., Hamilton-Giachritsis, C. & Ostapuik, E. (2010). Differentiating patterns of violence in the family. *Journal of Aggression, Conflict and Peace Research*, 2, 32–44.

Euser, E.M., Van IJzendoorn, M.H., Prinzie, P. & Bakermans-Kranenburg, M.J. (2010). Prevalence of child maltreatment in the Netherlands. *Child Maltreatment*, 15, 5–17.

Finkelhor, D. (2008). *Childhood Victimisation: Violence, Crime, and Abuse in the Lives of Young People*. Oxford: Oxford University Press.

Finkelhor, D. & Jones, L. (2006). Why have child maltreatment and child victimisation declined? *Journal of Social Issues*, 62, 685–716.

Finkelhor, D., Ormrod, R. & Turner, H. (2006). Kid's stuff: The nature and impact of peer and sibling violence in younger and older children. *Child Abuse & Neglect*, 30, 1401–1442.

Finkelhor, D., Turner, H., Ormrod, R. & Hamby, S. (2009a). Violence, abuse and crime exposure in a national sample of children and youth. *Pediatrics*, 124, 1411–1423.

Finkelhor, D., Ormrod, R.K. & Turner, H.A. (2009b). Lifetime assessment of poly-victimisation in a national sample of children and youth. *Child Abuse & Neglect*, 33, 403–411.

Finkelhor, D., Shattuck, A., Turner, H. & Hamby, S. (2014). Trends in children's exposure to violence 2003 to 2011. *JAMA Pediatrics* online, April.

Finkelhor, D., Turner, H., Shattuck, A. & Hamby, S. (2013). Violence, crime and abuse exposure in a national sample of children and youth: an update. *JAMA Pediatrics*, 167, 615–621.

Gilbert, R., Fluke, J., O'Donnell, M. et al. (2011). Child maltreatment: Variation in trends and policies in six developed countries. thelancet.com.

Gilbert, R., Kemp, A., Thoburn, J. et al. (2008b). Recognising and responding to child maltreatment. *The Lancet*, 373, 9658, 167–180.

Gilbert, R., Spatz Widom, C., Browne, K. et al. (2008a). Burden and consequences of child maltreatment in high-income countries. *The Lancet*, 373, 9657, 7–20.

Global Initiative (2015). Countdown to universal prohibition, Global Initiative to End all Corporal Punishment of Children, www.endcorporalpunishment.org/progress/countdown.html (accessed 6 November 2015).

Gonzalez-Izquierdo, A., Cortina-Borja, M., Woodman, J. et al. (2014). Maltreatment or violence-related injury in children and adolescents admitted to the NHS: Comparison of trends in England and Scotland between 2005–2011. *BMJ Open* 4: e004474.

Hamby, S., Finkelhor, D., Turner, H. & Ormrod, R. (2010). The overlap of witnessing partner violence with child maltreatment and other victimisations in a nationally representative sample of youth. *Child Abuse & Neglect*, 34, 734–741.

Hardt, J. & Rutter, M. (2004). Validity of adult retrospective reports of adverse childhood experiences: Review of the evidence. *Journal of Child Psychology and Psychiatry*, 45, 260–273.

Herbert, A., Gilbert, R., Gonzalez-Isquierdo, A. & Li, L. (2015). Violence, self-harm and drug or alcohol misuse in adolescents admitted to hospitals in England for injury: A retrospective cohort study. *BMJ Open* 5: e00607.

Howe, D. (2005). *Child Abuse and Neglect: Attachment, Development and Intervention*. London: Palgrave Macmillan.

Ji, K., Finkelhor, D. & Dunne, M. (2013). Child sexual abuse in China: A meta-analysis of 27 studies. *Child Abuse & Neglect*, 37, 613–622.

Jones, L., Bellis, M., Wood, S. et al. (2012). Prevalence and risk of violence against children with disabilities: A systematic review and meta-analysis of observational studies. *The Lancet*, published online 12 July.

Kendall-Tackett, K. (2008). Developmental impact. In: D. Finkelhor (ed), *Childhood Victimisation: Violence, Crime, and Abuse in the Lives of Young People*. Oxford: Oxford University Press.

Kiselica, M. & Morill-Richards, M. (2007). Sibling maltreatment: The forgotten abuse. *Journal of Counselling and Development, Spring*, 85, 148–160.

Krug, E., Dahlberg, L., Mercy, J. et al. (2002). *World report on violence and health*. Geneva: World Health Organization.

MacMillan, H.L., Fleming, J.E., Trocmé, N. et al. (1997). Prevalence of child physical and sexual abuse in the community. *Journal of the American Medical Association*, 278, 131–135.

McGee, C. (2000) *Childhood Experiences of Domestic Violence*. London: Jessica Kingsley.

Nikolaidis, G. (2013) *Balkan epidemiological study on child abuse and neglect: Project final report*. BECAN, www.becan.eu.

ONS (2014) *Violent crime and sexual offences*. London: Office of National Statistics, http://www.ons.gov.uk/peoplepopulationandcommunity/crimeandjustice/compendium/focusonviolentcrimeandsexualoffences/2015-02-12/chapter2violentcrimeandsexualoffenceshomicide (accessed 2 December 2016).

Pereda, N., Guilera, G., Forns, M. & Gómez-Benito, J. (2009). The prevalence of child sexual abuse in community and student samples: A meta-analysis. *Clinical Psychology Review*, 29, 328–338.

Pinheiro, P. (2006). *World report on violence against children*. Geneva: United Nations.

Radford, L. (2012). *Re-Thinking Children, Violence and Safeguarding*. London: Bloomsbury.

Radford, L., Corral, S., Bradley, C. & Fisher, H. (2013). The prevalence and impact of child maltreatment and other types of victimisation in the UK: Findings from a population survey of caregivers, children and young people and young adults. *Child Abuse & Neglect*, 37, 801–813.

Radford, L., Corral, S., Bradley, C. et al. (2011). *Child abuse and neglect in the UK today*. London: NSPCC, www.nspcc.org.uk/childstudy (accessed 2 December 2016).

Sedlak, A., Mettenburg, J., Basena, M. et al. (2010). *Fourth national incidence study of child abuse & neglect (NIS-4): Report to Congress*. Washington, DC: Administration for Children and Families, US Department of Health and Human Services.

Sethi, D., Bellis, M., Hughes, K. et al. (2010). *European report on preventing violence and knife crime among young people.* Copenhagen: WHO Regional Office for Europe, http://www.euro.who.int/__data/assets/pdf_file/0012/121314/E94277.pdf (accessed 6 November 2015).

Sethi, D., Bellis, M., Hughes, K. et al. (2013). *European report on preventing child maltreatment.* Copenhagen: World Health Organization Regional Office for Europe.

Stoltenborgh, M., Bakermans-Kranenburg, M. & von IJzendoorn, M. (2013). The neglect of neglect: A meta-analytic review of the prevalence of neglect. *Social Psychiatry and Psychiatric Epidemiology*, 48, 345–355.

Stoltenborgh, M., van IJzendoorn, M., Euser, E. & Bakermans-Kranenburg, M. (2011). A global perspective on child sexual abuse: Meta analysis of prevalence around the world. *Child Maltreatment*, 16, 79–101.

Stoltenborgh, M., Bakermans-Kranenburg, M., Kranenburg, M. et al. (2013). Cultural-geographical differences in the occurrence of child physical abuse? A meta-analysis of global prevalence. *International Journal of Psychology*, 48, 81–94.

Trocmé, N., Fallon, B., MacLaurin, B. et al. (2005). *Canadian incidence study of reported child abuse and neglect – 2003: major findings.* Minister of Public Works and Government Services, Canada.

UNICEF Tanzania (2011). *Violence against children in Tanzania: Findings from a national survey 2009.* UNICEF, US Centers for Disease Control and Muhimbili University of Health and Allied Sciences, Dar es Salaam, Tanzania.

UNICEF (2012). *Violence against children in Kenya: Findings from a 2010 national survey –Summary report on the prevalence of sexual, physical and emotional violence, context of sexual violence, and health and behavioral consequences of violence experienced in childhood.* UNICEF Kenya Country Office, Division of Violence Prevention, National Center for Injury Prevention and Control, US Centers for Disease Control and Prevention and Kenya National Bureau of Statistics, Nairobi, Kenya.

UNICEF (2014). *Hidden in plain sight: A statistical analysis of violence against children.* New York: UNICEF.

WHO (2013). *Global and regional estimates of violence against women: Prevalence and health effects of intimate partner violence and non-partner sexual violence.* Geneva: World Health Organization.

WHO (2014). *Global status report on violence prevention.* Geneva: World Health Organization.

3

Child Abuse and Neglect
Ecological Perspectives

Catherine Hamilton-Giachritsis[1] and Alberto Pellai[2]

[1] University of Bath, UK
[2] Milano State University, Italy

Child Abuse and Neglect: Ecological Perspectives

There are large bodies of work looking at both the rate of occurrence of child maltreatment and potential outcomes. In this edited book, the current state of knowledge about incidence and prevalence of child abuse and neglect, as well as the methodological difficulties obtaining accurate estimates, are outlined in Chapter 2 by Lorraine Radford. Similarly, Sarah Font in Chapter 5 overviews the outcomes that may follow child abuse and neglect, including the increased risk of negative outcomes for victims in childhood (Barnes, Noll, Putnam & Trickett, 2009; Cicchetti & Toth, 1995; Johnson, Kotch, Catellier et al., 2004), adolescence (Hussey, Chang & Kotch, 2006) and into adulthood (Hillberg, Hamilton-Giachritsis & Dixon, 2011). However, how and why does child maltreatment occur? This chapter aims to provide a summary of the theoretical perspectives behind the aetiology of child abuse and neglect, including historical perspectives. In particular, the most commonly considered approach is outlined: the ecological theory of child maltreatment. This latter perspective argues that child abuse and neglect must be seen within the broader context of a child, their family, immediate environment (school, peers, community) and the wider social and cultural context. For example, in recent years there has been a very substantial and notable social change, i.e., the increased use of and dependence on technology. This has both positive and negative outcomes: alongside increased channels by which potential offenders can access children, there are also increased opportunities for positive interventions following abuse and neglect. Hence this will be used as an example throughout the chapter.

Historical Single-Factor Approaches

Early theories of child maltreatment focused on single-factor causes, such as psychopathology/mental illness. In the 1970s, the concept of victim to offender became popular, whereby it was argued that offenders had generally experienced victimisation themselves (Fontana, 1973;

Steele, 1976). This was also known as the intergenerational cycle of maltreatment (ICM); that is, abuse is passed down through families where the abused child becomes the abusing parent (e.g., Kaufman & Zigler, 1987). However, later research clearly showed that, while both psychopathology and experiencing prior abuse were present in the risk factors for some abusers, neither approach could explain all incidents of child maltreatment. For example, in terms of ICM, even the Kaufman and Zigler (1987) research with high-risk parents only found a rate of 30% (+/− 5%) ICM, while cohort studies have found it to be much lower (e.g., 6.7%; Dixon, Browne & Hamilton-Giachritsis, 2005; Dixon, Hamilton-Giachritsis & Browne, 2005). Most recently, a 30-year longitudinal study following abused children found that, as parents themselves, 21.4% were referred to children's services compared to 11.7% of the non-abused parents (Widom, Czaja & DuMont, 2015). That is approximately one in five. Clearly, therefore, early experience of abuse and neglect is a risk factor for later abuse of one's own children. However, the concept of ICM is often referred to as though it is almost an inevitable outcome, as opposed to an increase in risk, and professionals should be cautious in over-generalising.

Later theories of child maltreatment included evolutionary theory (Daly & Wilson, 1985) and the social–biological or social–cultural models (Gelles, 1983; Gil, 1970). Wilson and Daly (1988) proposed that child maltreatment was more likely to be perpetrated by an individual who was not biologically related to the child, such as a stepfather. If this were the case, with the rise in rates of children living with a non-biological parent in the last few decades, it would be expected that this phenomenon would be more apparent. Indeed, other research has shown that the rate of abuse by fathers and stepfathers is similar when the proportion of children *living* in those environments was taken into account. For example, in a sample of 400 children referred to child protection units, 59% of children *living* with their biological father were abused by him compared to 53% of children *living* with a stepfather (Hamilton & Browne, 1999).

Thus, it became apparent that single-cause explanations for child maltreatment are too simplistic and do not allow for the heterogeneous pathways into maltreatment (Belsky, 1980; Wolfe, 1985). While one factor may account for some of the outcomes, none accounted for significant amounts of the variance overall (Sameroff, Bartko, Baldwin et al., 1998). Other approaches have considered parent–child interactions and child vulnerabilities.

Developmental Theories

Social learning theory (Bandura, 1977) and social cognitive models (Crick & Dodge, 1994) focused on the role of learning in developing abusive behaviour, with children learning though observing their parents. In contrast, trauma-focused theories state that trauma is seen as affecting normal development processes, with different impacts of abuse occurring at different points in time. It should be noted that the term 'trauma' in these instances is used to define incidents more broadly than child maltreatment. For example, research in this field has mainly been in terms of post-traumatic stress disorder following other forms of trauma, such as accidents or witnessing a natural disaster (PTSD; Sullivan, Fehon, Andres-Hyman et al., 2006; Widom, 1999). Less is currently known about *parents* experiencing PTSD and the impact of this on their relationship with their children (even the child maltreatment literature focuses relatively little on PTSD in parents following early childhood abuse). However, some authors (e.g., Milot, St-Laurent, & Éthier, 2016) have argued that theories of complex trauma should look beyond solely PTSD, to include other outcomes such as insecure or disorganised attachment. It is these outcomes that then increase (or not) the risk of abusing or neglecting one's own child.

There is a vast literature on attachment theory (Bowlby, 1980) and the role of attachment in adaptive and dysfunctional parenting (Egeland, Bosquet & Chung, 2002). Attachment theory is often used as a means of evaluating or intervening in a parent–child relationship. In Chapter 14 of this book, Carol George considers how attachment can be used for assessing parenting, outlining the biological, evolutionary basis for attachment theory, in that attachment behaviours are viewed as a 'protection strategy' to elicit caregiving in the presence of threat. Then, in Chapter 23, Patricia Crittenden and Clark Baim report on the IASA Family Attachment Court Protocol and how this can help inform assessments to guide interventions with families in child care proceedings. In brief, attachment theory proposes that secure attachment is developed through the provision of consistent, sensitive parenting, while inconsistent, insensitive or frightening parenting can lead to insecure or dysfunctional attachment in children. Insecure attachment can impact on risk of victimisation for the child and an adult with an insecure attachment style may also be at increased risk of being a maltreating parent. However, on the other hand, it has been argued that, in the presence of risk factors, a secure attachment can be a buffer between maltreatment occurring or not (Browne, 1988). However, taking a buffering perspective is moving beyond a single-factor model (i.e., attachment) into multi-factor models, where attachment is seen as either a risk or a protective factor.

Moving beyond child maltreatment that occurs only within the family, Finkelhor proposed a model of why some children may be more vulnerable to victimisation. Termed 'developmental victimology' (Finkelhor, 1995), this perspective argued that the risk of victimisation differs across the lifespan, based on factors such as age, developmental stage and interruption of key developmental tasks or transition. According to developmental victimology, babies and young children are very vulnerable as they are most dependent and have fewest other sources of support. Indeed, data from child protection services in the UK and the USA does indeed show that young children are more likely to be deemed in need of protection and more likely to be the victims of fatal maltreatment (Kleevens & Lieb, 2010; Sidebotham, Bailey, Belderson & Brandon, 2011). However, looking at children on the UK Child Protection Plans (register), there is a fairly even split between age groups 1–4, 5–9 and 10–15 years (28.5%, 29.7% and 26.1% respectively), with 10.5% under 1 year, 3.1% 16+ years and 2.1% unborn babies (Department for Education, 2015). Risks to older children come from different sources: physical violence may be more likely to occur in disputes about boundaries, but other risks will come from peers and adults in the wider community given that the young person will have more time outside the home.

One factor that is impacting greatly on this level of age-related risk is the rise in social media. With increased access by younger children, this is raising the risk from external peers and adults beyond what was previously possible (Tokunaga, 2010). Thus, although Finkelhor and colleagues have noted higher rates of *offline* victimisation in teenagers across a wide variety of sources including peer bullying (Turner, Finkelhor & Ormrod, 2010) and this is supported by other research (Radford, Corral, Bradley & Fisher, 2013), rates of *online* victimisation have also risen (Whittle, Hamilton-Giachritsis, Beech & Collings, 2013a). While it is possible to consider the potential vulnerabilities of children and young people to victimisation in the online environment (e.g., Whittle, Hamilton-Giachritsis, Beech & Collings, 2013b; Whittle, Hamilton-Giachritsis & Beech, 2014a,b), this only explains why some children are more likely to experience victimisation, not the reasons why some individuals offend against children, either within or outside of the family home.

Overall, therefore, although interaction and vulnerability models can provide partial explanations, they do not provide a full picture. Thus, multi-factorial models of child abuse and neglect are required to fully consider the complexity of risk.

The Multi-Factor (Ecological) Model

Thus, the development of multi-model approaches arose in part from the recognition that there are numerous risk factors for child abuse and neglect, and the necessity to move beyond single-factor models (Appleyard, Egeland, van Dulmen & Sroufe, 2005; Jaffee, Caspi, Moffitt et al., 2007). A variety of chapters in this edited volume will review risk for different types of maltreatment, including fatal CAN (Sidebotham, Chapter 4). However, these risk factors can occur at many levels; child-, family- and school-related are more commonly considered in the literature, but social policy also impacts (see Gray, Chapter 8) as does culture. Thus, it is not just the presence of one or more risk factors that seems to be relevant, but a complex interplay between them.

Ecological model

The most commonly adopted model in the child abuse and neglect literature is the ecological model. This is also utilised in models of intimate partner violence (e.g., Heise, 1998). The ecological models all view child maltreatment as a multi-factorial, dynamic and complex process, proposing that it is the interplay between an individual (the child), their relationships with others, the community in which they live and the wider society/culture that is important in determining risk. First proposed by Bronfenbrenner (1979; see Figure 3.1), the ecological model was initially adapted by Belsky (developmental–ecological model; 1980, 1993). However, Cicchetti and colleagues later developed the 'transactional' approach (Cicchetti & Rizley, 1981) and then the 'ecological–transactional model' (Cicchetti & Lynch, 1993; see Figure 3.2).

Bronfenbrenner's model had five levels:

(a) Individual (i.e., child's characteristics, such as developmental stage, gender, disability, that may increase the likelihood of maltreatment occurring)
(b) Microsystem – groups that directly impact on the child (i.e., the family environment, school, neighbourhood and peers)
(c) Mesosystem – interactions between the different microsystems, such as the parents and teachers
(d) Exosystem – systems that have indirect influences on the child, such as a parental working environment
(e) Macrosystem (i.e., beliefs and values within the society and culture).

Thus, the child is based within broader contexts, both immediate (e.g., family, friends) and more widely (social influences, legal perspectives). Some have argued that it is the *accumulation* of risk factors that is most important (Thornberry, Matsuda, Greenman et al., 2014), but the ecological model would argue that it is the interaction of factors that is most important (Cicchetti & Lynch, 1993). Indeed, the relevance of trying to separate out situational factors (i.e., family and environment) from vulnerability factors in the child has been questioned. Furthermore, ecological models also purport that proximal factors (family, peers, school) will have a more direct effect than distal factors (society and culture; Bronfenbrenner & Ceci, 1994).

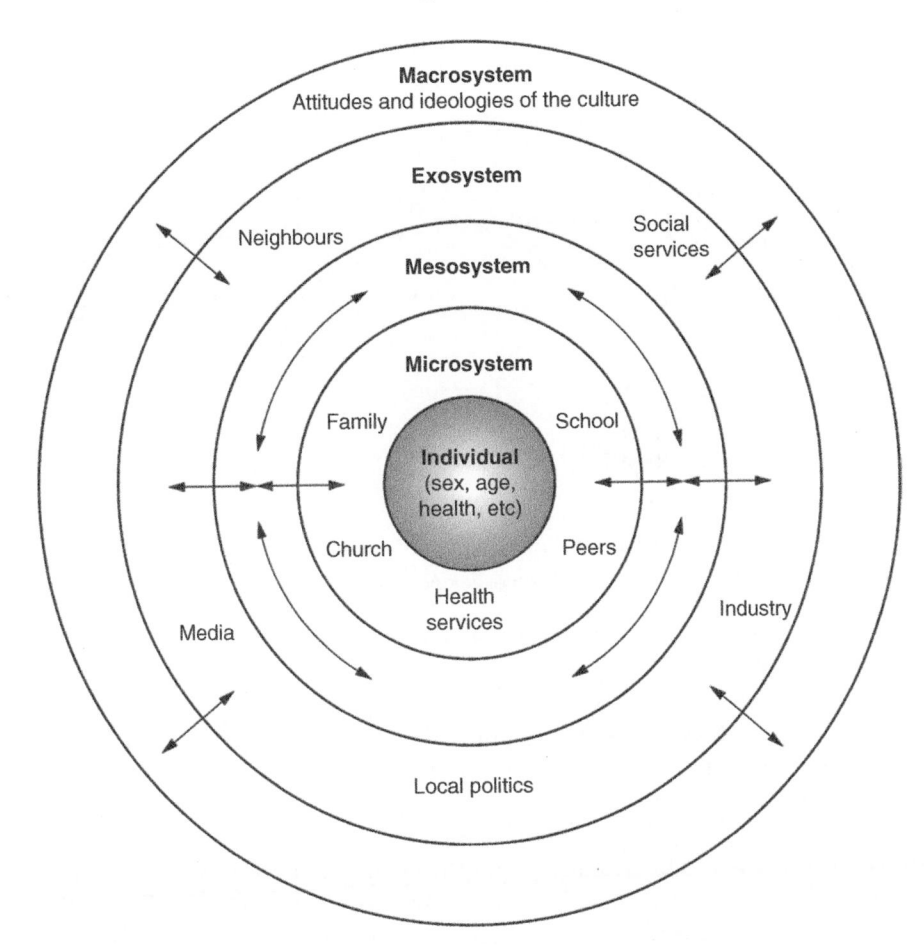

Child Abuse and Neglect: Ecological Perspectives

Figure 3.1 Bronfenbrenner's Ecological Systems model (1979). Source: https://en.wikipedia.org/wiki/File:Bronfenbrenner%27s_Ecological_Theory_of_Development.jpg#filelinks. Used under CC-BY-SA 4.0 https://creativecommons.org/licenses/by-sa/4.0/deed.en.

Ecological–transactional model

According to the ecological–transactional model (Cicchetti & Rizley, 1981; Cicchetti & Lynch, 1993; Cicchetti, Toth & Maughan, 2000), there are potentiating and compensatory factors at every level. Specifically, Cicchetti and Rizley noted four levels affecting risk:

(a) *'Potentiating' factors that cause ongoing vulnerability:* long-term factors or conditions, such as parental, child or environmental factors that may be biological, historical (e.g., prior history of abuse), psychological or sociological.
(b) *'Transient challengers' within the environment that may temporarily increase risk*: short-term conditions or stressors, or temporary triggers. These can include factors affecting the adult (e.g., unemployment, illness, marital difficulties) or the child (e.g., new developmental phase, behavioural problems).
(c) *Enduring protective factors*: long-term or relatively permanent factors, e.g., no parental history of childhood abuse, positive co-parental relationship.

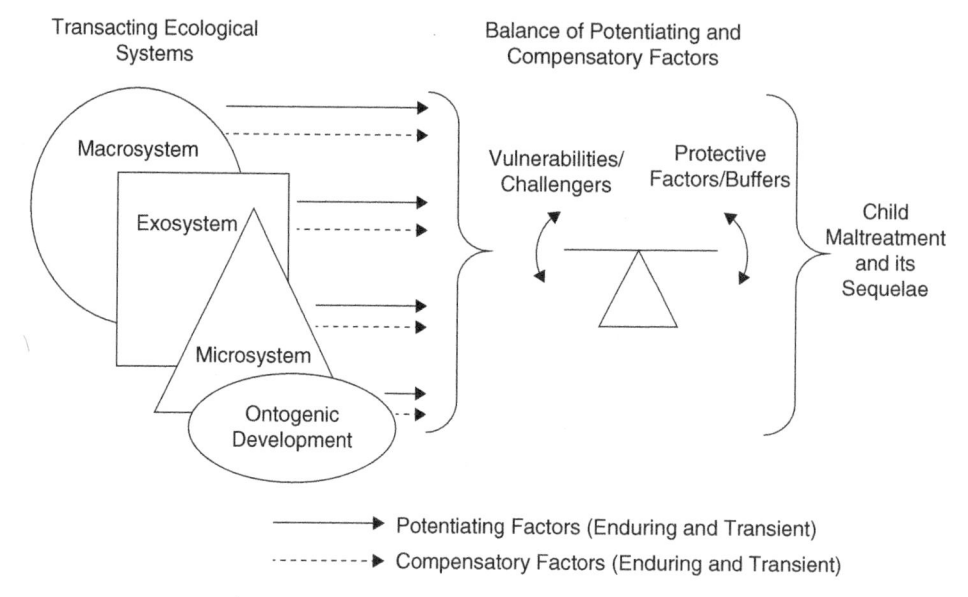

Figure 3.2 An ecological–transactional model of child maltreatment. Source: Cicchetti 2000. Reproduced with permission of Springer.

(d) *Transient buffers*: these are more temporary but will still decrease risk of maltreatment, such as new job, improved marital relationships and child moving into a different developmental phase.

The first two levels relate to increasing risk but the latter two decrease risk of violence. Using this model, it is possible for two families with the same risk factors to have different likelihoods of abuse because they have different protective factors (Cicchetti & Lynch, 1993). For example, having a child in the family with an enduring vulnerability factor (e.g., Asperger's syndrome) combined with a 'transient challenger' (e.g., parental unemployment in the short term) increases the stressors in the family and therefore the likelihood of abuse. However, if these factors occurred alongside enduring protective factors (e.g., positive parenting style) and buffers (e.g., secure attachment), it would be expected that the likelihood of abuse occurring was lower than if the child was in a family with risk factors but few protective factors or buffers. Overall, it is the 'balance of stressors and supports' that is important (Belsky & Stratton, 2002, p. 95). Indeed, one 13-month follow-up of new parents found that it was the presence or absence of protective factors (specifically social support and financial security) that distinguished between abused children going on to abuse their own children (Maintainers) or not (Cycle Breakers; Dixon, Hamilton-Giachritsis & Browne, 2009).

Resilience model

In a useful development from the original ecological model, Kumpfer (1999) also specifically incorporated resilience factors (see Figure 3.3). In this model the stressors impact on the environment that is defined by the risk and protective factors at all levels (i.e., the original ecological model), but there is an interaction between that environment and the balance of risks/stressors associated with an individual's personal internal resiliency (in terms of cognitive, emotional, spiritual, physical and behavioural). Internal resilience factors include perception, reframing and

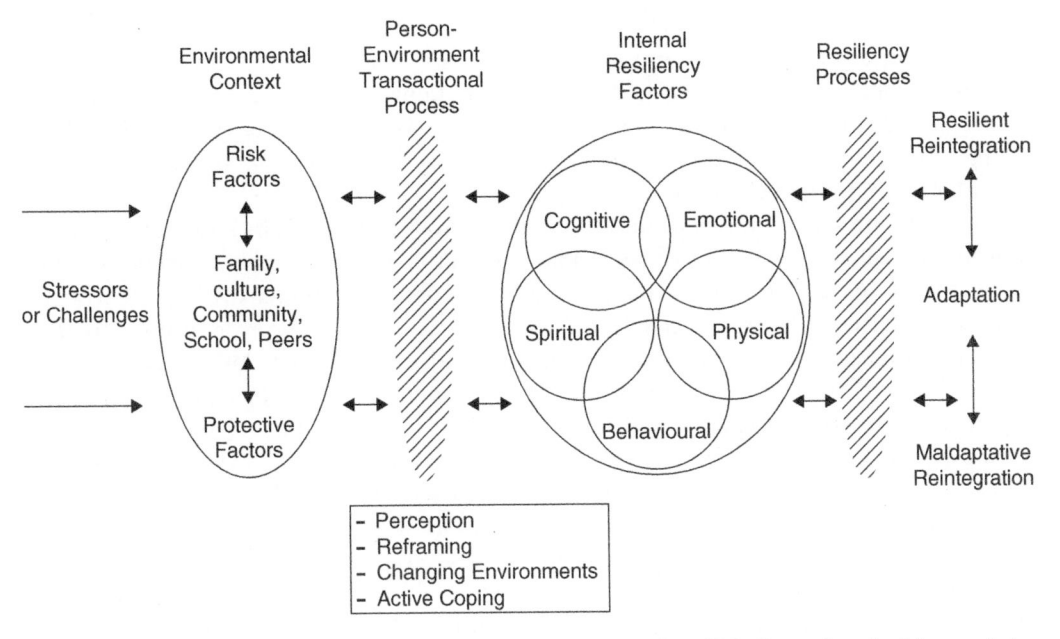

Figure 3.3 Resilience-based ecological model. Source: Kumpfer 1999. Reproduced with permission of Springer.

active coping (all forms of cognitive appraisal). Cognitive appraisal and coping styles are increasingly recognised as important in resilient outcomes, including not repeating childhood experiences of maltreatment with one's own children. Luthar and Cicchetti (2000) assert that this developmental psychopathology approach of finding vulnerability and protective factors at all levels of the ecological model can increase understanding of what makes an individual maltreat children, but also allows for positive interventions that impact on outcome following maltreatment. For example, parental warmth and positive attributions of children's behaviours mitigate risk of developing conduct disorder and/or violent acts following witnessing of domestic violence, thus potentially impacting in the long term on likely rate of ICM (Pinna, 2016).

Risk and Protective Factors

To fully explore the ecological model of child abuse and neglect, risk and protective factors at each level will be considered.

Interpersonal variables

Factors that may make a child vulnerable to maltreatment include age (stage of development), gender, disability and difficulties at birth (Gilbert, Spatz-Widom & Browne, 2009; Leventhal, 1996). In the US, France and the UK, most fatalities occur in children under the age of five years and particularly in infants under one year old; head injury, physical battering and/or severe neglect are the most common causes of death (Kleevens & Lieb, 2010; Makhlouf & Rambaud, 2014; Scarcella, Bess, Zielewski & Green, 2011). Infant and toddler boys are more at risk of death due to physical abuse, with severe neglect affecting infant/toddler girls to a greater extent (Scarcella, Bess, Zielewski & Green, 2011).

In terms of maltreatment more broadly, risk of sexual abuse increases with age and is more common for (but not exclusive to) girls, with boys more likely to experience harsh physical abuse (Krug, Dahlberg, Mercy et al., 2002). This may be linked to the behaviour of the child. One early proponent of interactionist models (Wolfe, 1991, 1993) noted that behavioural difficulties in children increased the risk of maltreatment, but that this is cyclical. Parents with risk factors for maltreating behaviour and who experience stress from other sources will have fewer coping resources to deal with a difficult child, hence increasing the likelihood of an aversive cycle of interaction leading to abuse.

Child ill-health has also been identified as a risk factor (Iwaniec, 2004). One study of children and siblings within an abusive household found little evidence for child illness contributing to scapegoating a particular child; rather it appeared that the stress impacted on the parenting generally and increased risk for all (Hamilton-Giachritsis & Browne, 2005). However, a recent meta-analysis on 17 studies found that deaf and/or disabled children and young people are three to four times more likely to be abused than their non-disabled peers, as well as to experience more types, greater frequency and greater severity of abuse (Jones, Bellis, Wood et al., 2012; Stalker, Taylor, Fry & Stewart, 2015). This increased risk, however, also includes abuse by peers and in institutional settings (Biehal & Parry, 2010; Sullivan, 2009).

Looking at the online world, Whittle, Hamilton-Giachritsis & Beech (2014a) found risk and protective factors for online sexual abuse at several levels of the ecological model (Table 3.1). Notably, three groups were identified, two of which mimicked the Cicchetti & Lynch model of long- and short-term vulnerabilities. One group of young people were vulnerable to online grooming due to long-term risk factors and the other group due to short-term risk factors (triggers). However, a further mechanism of what appeared to be engagement in risky behaviour characterised the third group (e.g., talking to unknown others or sexting; Whittle, Hamilton-Giachritsis & Beech, 2014b).

Some researchers have argued that this engagement in risky behaviour can be explained through neural systems. It has been stated that child and adolescent brains have difficulty integrating messages from the limbic system (which develops earlier) and the pre-frontal cortex (which only develops in late adolescence and early adulthood; Jensen & Nutt, 2016). The former is sensitive to social and emotional stimuli (excitement, fear and arousal), while higher functioning cognitive processes needed to assess risk and prevent it (e.g., decision-making, problem-solving and critical thinking) are located in the pre-frontal cortex. At puberty, there can be an increased focus on reward seeking (particularly influenced by peers), while later adolescence is based more on self-regulatory competence, which occurs gradually and is not complete until the mid-20s (Steinberg, 2008). Thus, the less-developed cognitive skills (including problem-solving) do not compensate for the more emotional responses of excitement and fear, leading children and young people to show a heightened vulnerability to display risky and reckless behaviour. As Dahl notes:

> For some adolescents, this tendency to activate strong emotions and this affinity for excitement can be subtle and easily managed. In others these inclinations toward high-intensity feelings can lead to emotionally-charged and reckless adolescent behaviors and at times to impulsive decisions by (seemingly) intelligent youth that are completely outrageous. (Dahl, 2004, pp1–22)

In terms of protective factors noted in the model, some children do well despite adverse early experiences (Goldstein & Brooks, 2005; Layne, Beck, Rimmasch et al., 2009) and there is a large body of work looking at resilience and protective factors. Protective factors within the child include temperament, good health, above-average intellectual functioning and positive self-esteem, but seemingly the most important factors for outcome relate to cognitive appraisal (e.g., perceived internal control), emotional regulation and good relationships with significant (non-abusing) others

Table 3.1 Risk and protective factors at different ecological levels for online sexual grooming and abuse.

Risk Factors Relating to Self	% of Interviews Mentioned
Low self-esteem	75
Loneliness	63
Hit a low point in life	50

Risk Factors Relating to Family	% of Interviews Mentioned
Reconstituted family	75
Fights at home	75
Parents separated	75
Distant from family	63
Illness within the family	63
No parent discussion of online safety	63
Family bereavement	50
Low-income family	38
No internet restrictions at home	38
Parents working a lot	38
Pet death	38
Unhappy childhood	38
History of crime in the family	25
Parents lack internet understanding	25

Protective Factors Relating to Family	% of Interviews Mentioned
Parents steps toward online protection	63
Close to wider family	50
Close to parent	38
Close to sibling	38
Happy family	25
Parents together	25
Would tell parents about online concerns	25

Risk Factors Relating to Friends	% of Interviews Mentioned
Victim being bullied	38
Fights with friends	25

Protective Factors Relating to Friends	% of Interviews Mentioned
Good close friend(s)	100
Hobbies & extra curricula activities	100
Friends are important	88
No experience of bullying	63
Consistent friends	25
Other social support	25

Risk Factors Relating to School	% of Interviews Mentioned
Little or no internet safety education	88
Dislikes school	38
Naughty at school	25
Stressed by school work	25

(*Continued*)

Table 3.1 (cont'd)

Protective Factors Relating to School	% of Interviews Mentioned
School is good	75
Had sex education	75
Supportive school	38
Some general internet safety education	38

Risk Factors Relating to Living Area	% of Interviews Mentioned
Bored in living environment	75
Dislike of and problems with local area	63

Protective Factors Relating to Living Area	% of Interviews Mentioned
Happy in living environment	50
Good neighbours	50

Risk Factors Relating to Internet Use	% of Interviews Mentioned
Spoke to strangers online	100
Had own internet-enabled device	75
Spent a long time online	75
Used internet in bedroom	75
Felt status of more online contacts	63
Sometimes shared personal information online	38
Has an open profile	25
Close online relationship with another (not offender)	25

Protective Factors Relating to Internet Use	% of Interviews Mentioned
Rarely shared photos or webcam with strangers	88
Speaking to strangers was rare	75
Steps to protecting personal information online	63
Access included a shared family computer	50
Access included computer in a family room	50
Used privacy settings	38

Source: Whittle, http://www.hrpub.org/journals/article_info.php?aid=240. Used under CC-By 3.0 https://creativecommons.org/licenses/by/3.0/.

(Alik, Cicchetti, Kim & Rogosch, 2009; Bolger & Patterson, 2001; Flores, Cicchetti & Rogosch, 2005). Thus, these are key areas to target both for post-maltreatment interventions but also in targeted early interventions to reduce vulnerability.

Parent and family variables

Negative parental behaviours, attributions and interactions have long been recognised as risk factors for child abuse and neglect (Crittenden, 2002; Sagy & Doton, 2001). A wide range of variables have been indicated as relevant, some of which are summarised below.

Within the parenting domain, in addition to prior experience of childhood abuse outlined above (ICM, Egeland, Bosquet & Chung, 2002), other factors have been shown to include: young age at onset of parenting (Putnam-Hornstein & Needell, 2011; Putnam-Hornstein, Needell & Rhodes, 2013), being a single parent (National Research Council, 1993; Olds, Henderson & Eckenrode, 2002; Straus, Hamby, Finkelhor et al., 1998), unwanted pregnancy

(Browne & Herbert, 1997), substance abuse (Berger, Slack, Waldfogel & Bruch, 2010) and mental health difficulties (Conron, Beardslee, Koenen et al., 2009; Denholm, Power, Thomas & Li, 2010). Similarly, parental poor impulse control (Klevens, Bayon & Sierra, 2000; Sidebotham & Golding, 2001), hostile or controlling behaviour (Bardi & Borgognini-Tari, 2001), negative parenting styles or attributions (Crittenden, 2002; Dixon, Hamilton-Giachritsis & Browne, 2005) and relationship difficulties (Stith, Liu, Davies et al., 2009) also relate to increased risk. Factors relating to the family more broadly have included larger or unstable families (Belsky, 1993; Dubowitz & Black, 2001; Hamilton-Giachritsis & Browne, 2005) and lack of social support (Brown, Cohen, Johnson & Salzinger, 1998), but generally relate to socio-economic factors, such as poverty and unemployment (Font, Chapter 5; Sledjeski, Dierke, Bird & Canino, 2009). Hence, the association of child maltreatment with higher stress (Browne & Herbert, 1997) is most likely to be reflective of the wider difficulties within the family that are the *source* of stress for parents. For example, in a national US study, compared to children who were maltreated but survived, younger children living with both parents were more likely to be fatally maltreated when there was also greater financial and housing difficulty in the family (Douglas & Mohn, 2014).

Of these factors, intimate partner violence (IPV), mental health difficulties and substance misuse have repeatedly been identified as significantly increasing risk to a child. Research has consistently shown an overlap of approximately 40–50% between IPV and child maltreatment (Cox, Kotch & Everson, 2003), with such families often seen as higher risk and in greater need of support (Beeman, Hagemeister & Edleson, 2001). However, as noted above, the cumulative effect is important. Thornberry, Matsuda, Greenman et al. (2014) considered risk across ten domains occurring in adolescence (e.g., exposure to violence, family difficulties, education, peer relationships); when no risk domains were present, only 3% were investigated as adults for child maltreatment compared to 45% of those who had risk in nine domains in adolescence. However, it should be noted that 55% of those with risk in nine domains were *not* involved in child maltreatment. Thus, not all individuals who experience early child abuse and neglect go on to show negative outcomes, and it is in these cases that protective factors play an important role.

Family protective factors include consistent sensitive parenting (Sagy & Doton, 2001), high parental education, consistent parental employment and middle to higher socio-economic status (Browne, Hanks, Stratton & Hamilton, 2002). As noted above, social support and lack of financial difficulties have been shown to protect families from the ICM (Dixon, Hamilton-Giachritsis & Browne, 2009; Ertem, Leventhal & Dobbs, 2000). Parental warmth and support are increasingly recognised as vital factors in both protection and for recovery; their importance can be seen in the rising trend for post-maltreatment intervention programmes for young people to encompass specific modules to work with parents on appropriate support and reaction post-disclosure (e.g., Hiller, Springer, Misurell et al., 2016; Pinna, 2016).

Peers and community variables

The role of peers and the community in risk of maltreatment has been emphasised in recent years by Finkelhor, Ormrod, Turner, & Holt (2009) in their discussion of poly-victimisation, with increased recognition that maltreatment by a wider group should be considered. For example, alongside abuse or neglect within the family, Finkelhor, Ormrod, Turner & Holt (2009) have included other forms of maltreatment, such as witnessing crime in the community, witnessing violence toward another, being bullied, etc. Risk factors in this domain may include a violent neighbourhood, absence of community services and low social cohesion. In contrast, protective factors include supportive relationships with other adults, such as teachers and friend's parents.

Looking more specifically at peer relationships, the rise in online interactions has been accompanied by a rise in peer violence. For example, three cross-sectional, representative telephone surveys in the USA of 4,561 10–17 year olds in 2000, 2005 and 2010 showed an increase in youth online harassment from 6% in 2000 to 11% in 2010 (the Youth Internet Safety Surveys; Jones, Mitchell & Finkelhor, 2012). Mainly, young people reported an increase in 'indirect' harassment, i.e., posts or comments made about them by one person to another user. In 2010, 69% of victims were girls compared with 48% in 2000. Furthermore, over this ten-year period there was an increase in incidents of harassment from school friends or acquaintances on social-networking sites.

Communities can have an important role to play in child maltreatment. While this might initially be hard to conceptualise, it is notable that social networks and strong communities with good social cohesion have been shown to be protective factors (Krug, Dahlberg, Mercy et al., 2002).

Societal and cultural variables

At this level, beliefs and values are particularly important in understanding the causes of child maltreatment. This can include attitudes and ideologies, history, culture, social conditions, the economic system and legislation. Specifically, media portrayals of 'violence as acceptable', social policies related to child abuse and neglect (e.g., female genital mutilation), and legislation (that both defines what is child abuse and neglect, but also provides the framework within which statutory services work) are important factors. Social factors can create environments where violence against children is either more or less acceptable, as well as setting the tone as to the value placed on children and child care, e.g., maternity and paternity care (Krug, Dahlberg, Mercy et al., 2002).

Cultural norms and practices may create some debate – at what point is something that is acceptable within one culture not only unacceptable within another but also actually seen as a form of child abuse and neglect? These range from more extreme examples (e.g., female genital mutilation, forced marriage, use of witchcraft to drive out possession by the devil), to less extreme but still controversial examples (e.g., smacking, physical chastisement). While being respectful of cultural norms, the United Nations Convention on the Rights of the Child (UNCRC) can provide a framework within which to consider this question, providing a baseline of fundamental rights for children against which different behaviours can be evaluated.

Looking more broadly at societal influences, the different messages being provided to young people through the new media is a useful example of how values can change. The internet is as an area in which young people might look for information about sex and sexuality in what is seen as a safe forum. This can be very positive for young people, enabling them to access information about topics they might feel uncomfortable asking about more directly. However, it has also increased access to inappropriate sexual material and porn (Horvath, Llian, Massey et al., 2013), as well providing a socio-cultural context that has increased sexual messages targeting young people and decreased young people's alertness to the dangers. It is important therefore to consider young people's online behaviours in light of appropriate sexual development and exploration of sexuality. For example, young people may develop relationships with others online, feeling it is safe and appropriate to do so. When things go wrong (e.g., the 'boyfriend' is an online abuser), the focus is often on the lack of technology education for young people and the need to provide better net safety education programmes. However, an alternative way of viewing this would be to see it in the context of the sexual dis-education among young people that is reinforced by new media. Thus, young people need to be educated about both the benefits and risks of online use, but also to be given broader sexual education that enables them to show age-developmentally appropriate sexual curiosity safely, both in real life and online. Alongside that, society needs to consider the messages inherent to young people in mainstream culture, such as the role of pop music and videos. Adults (parents, teachers, educators) need to move beyond the sometimes naive stance that focuses only on the positives of newer technology, to enable young people to benefit from all the positive elements in a safe way.

Ecological Approaches to Prevention

The areas outlined above make it clear that families where maltreatment has occurred have multiple risks to be addressed and these can be conceptualised using an ecological model. Similarly, an ecological approach can be utilised to address these risks at different levels and to inform interventions (Cicchetti & Valentino, 2006). For example, the ecological–transactional model's four levels allows for risks to be identified and strengths to be targeted at each of the ecological levels. Examples of levels of prevention for all forms of child maltreatment include parenting programmes to promote positive parenting skills; friendship groups for children in schools to reduce social isolation; and policies that promote strong training standards for child protection professionals and those working with young people in other settings.

From a public health perspective, interventions can occur universally for all (primary prevention), individually for families seen as high risk (targeted, secondary prevention), and with those families where maltreatment has already occurred to reduce risk of recurrence (tertiary prevention). Primary prevention is needed by all children all over the world and must become a universal practice, without cultural, religious or political limits. Taking the social network and internet example that has run through this chapter, preventative education can take place with young people (child and peers), alongside work with parents, adults around the child and the community.

However, young people can benefit from approaches that go beyond providing factual information to also include a series of activities that lead to the acquisition of concrete skills to be used when experiencing high-risk situations and when in need of self-protection (Pellai, 2013; World Health Organization, 2004). The aim is to develop knowledge, attitudes and skills using a variety of learning experiences, with an emphasis on participatory methods to enable adaptive and positive behaviour (Mangrulkar, Whitman & Posner, 2001; World Health Organization, 2004). This approach can be adapted for all developmental ages and levels, and allow young people to engage in learning experiences that help them prevent situations and risks that can put their physical, social and emotional well-being in danger. For example, the 'Words Not Said' programme (Pellai, 2013) has team games, circle time and role play elements, as well as ending with relaxation time. Developed in Italy and translated for use in four other countries (including the UK), at the current time several evaluation projects have been undertaken (as yet unpublished). Hence, it will be of interest to see the impact of this approach on keeping young people safe.

This educational model can also be adapted for parents, teachers and other adults holding positions of authority within the community (e.g., religious leaders, child care providers, club leaders) to enable them to provide children and young people with help, skills and support. One example programme is run by the organisation 'Stop It Now', established in 1992 to help communities by keeping children safe. The main concepts of the model are:

- Adults are responsible for prevention, not children.
- All adults have a part to play in preventing child maltreatment, not just parents.

- Safe environments need to be created for children, rather than having a reliance on identifying risky individuals.
- Treating potential abusers or admitting actual ones to care is of fundamental importance for the prevention of new cases of abuse.

Thus, the emphasis is on the community working together to keep children safe. However, this will likely have a stronger impact if it is supported by changes in societal approaches to the online world (e.g., ease of access to inappropriate sexual material online).

Future Directions

In conclusion, the effects of child abuse and neglect on children and young people can occur in childhood, adolescence and into adulthood, including an increased risk of maltreatment of one's own children. In addition, alongside the many costs to victims and their families, child maltreatment also costs societies financially. For example, in the US, child welfare costs were estimated at $23.3 billion in 2005 (Scarcella, Bess, Zielewski & Green, 2006) and $80 billion in 2012 (Gelles & Perlman, 2012), with lifetime costs in 2008 estimated at $124–$585 billion (Fang, Brown, Florence & Mercy, 2012). Thus, for a multiplicity of reasons, there is an urgent need to predict and prevent child maltreatment. A starting point is to understand the origins and causes of child abuse and neglect.

While much research has occurred in this area and progressed the field in many ways, ongoing research is required to identify what works and, conversely, what is not effective, particularly in the area of newer technologies and how to keep young people safe in online environments (including smart phones, other mobile devices, gaming platforms, etc.). One positive development is that databases from different services (e.g., child protection systems, health systems, education) can now be linked; this allows for more methodologically sound sources of data including longitudinal studies and will enable broader analysis of the interaction between risk and protective factors (Putnam-Hornstein, Needell & Rhodes, 2013).

As has been outlined in this chapter, the aetiology of child maltreatment is complex and heterogeneous and single-cause approaches are not sufficient. The ecological model provides a framework to consider risk and protective factors at many levels of a child's life and is seen by many as the most useful model currently available. This systemic approach can feed into universal intervention programmes, but also targeted interventions (many of which are highlighted in this edited volume). Thus, it can be very beneficial to hold an ecological model in mind when formulating ideas about the aetiology of child maltreatment and identifying the best ways to intervene, both to prevent maltreatment occurring and to mitigate the impact on the child, family and wider society once it has occurred.

References

Alik, L.R.A., Cicchetti, D., Kim, J. & Rogosch, F.A. (2009). Mediating and moderating processes in the relation between maltreatment and psychopathology: Mother-child relationship quality and emotion regulation. *Journal Abnormal Child Psychology*, 37, 831–843.

Appleyard, K., Egeland, B., van Dulmen, M.H.M. & Alan Sroufe, L. (2005). When more is not better: The role of cumulative risk in child behavior outcomes. *Journal of Child Psychology and Psychiatry*, 46, 235–245.

Bandura, A. (1977). *Social Learning Theory*. New York: General Learning Press.
Bardi, M. & Borgognini-Tari, S.M. (2001). A survey of parent–child conflict resolution: Intrafamily violence in Italy. *Child Abuse & Neglect*, 25, 839–853.
Barnes, J.E., Noll, J.G., Putnam, F.W. & Trickett, P.K. (2009). Sexual and physical revictimization among victims of severe childhood sexual abuse. *Child Abuse & Neglect*, 33, 412–420.
Beeman, S.K., Hagemeister, A.K. & Edleson, J.L. (2001). Case assessment and service receipt in families experiencing both child maltreatment and woman battering. *Journal of Interpersonal Violence*, 16, 437–458.
Belsky, J. (1980). Child maltreatment. An ecological integration. *American Psychologist*, 35, 320–335.
Belsky, J. (1993). The etiology of child maltreatment: A developmental–ecological analysis. *Psychological Bulletin*, 114, 413–434.
Belsky, J. & Stratton, P. (2002). An ecological analysis of the etiology of child maltreatment. In: K.D. Browne, H. Hanks, P. Stratton and C.E. Hamilton (eds), *The Early Prediction and Prevention of Child Abuse: A Handbook*. Chichester: John Wiley & Sons, Ltd.
Berger, L.M., Slack, K.S., Waldfogel, J. & Bruch, S.K. (2010). Caseworker-perceived caregiver substance abuse and child protective services outcomes. *Child Maltreatment*, 15, 199–210.
Biehal, N. & Parry, E. (2010). *Maltreatment and allegations of maltreatment in foster care: A review of the evidence*. York: Social Policy Research Unit, University of York.
Bolger, K. & Patterson, C.L. (2001). Pathways from child abuse to internalizing problems: Perceptions of control as mediators and moderators. *Development and Psychopathology*, 13, 913–940.
Bowlby, J. (1980). *Attachment and Loss: Volume III: Loss, Sadness and Depression*. The International Psycho-Analytical Library, 109, 1–462. London: The Hogarth Press and the Institute of Psycho-Analysis.
Bronfenbrenner, U. (1979). *The Ecology of Human Development*. Cambridge, MA: Harvard University Press.
Bronfenbrenner, U. & Ceci, S.J. (1994). Nature-nurture reconceptualized in developmental perspective: a bioecological model. *Psychological Review*, 101, 568–586.
Brown, J., Cohen, P., Johnson, J.G. & Salzinger, S. (1998). A longitudinal analysis of risk factors for child maltreatment: Findings of a 17-year prospective study of officially recorded and self-reported child abuse and neglect. *Child Abuse & Neglect*, 22, 1065–1078.
Browne, K.D. (1988). The nature of child abuse and neglect: An overview. In: K.D. Browne, C. Davies & P. Stratton (eds), *Early Prediction & Prevention of Child Abuse*. Chichester: John Wiley & Sons, 15–30.
Browne, K.D. & Herbert, M. (1997). *Preventing Family Violence*. Chichester: John Wiley & Sons, Ltd.
Browne, K.D., H. Hanks, P. Stratton & C.E. Hamilton (2002). *Early Prediction and Prevention of Child Abuse: A Handbook*. Chichester: John Wiley & Sons.
Cicchetti, D. & Lynch, M. (1993). Toward an ecological/transactional model of community violence and child maltreatment: Consequences for children's development. *Psychiatry*, 56, 118.
Cicchetti, D. & Rizley, R. (1981). Developmental perspectives on the etiology, intergenerational transmission and sequelae of child maltreatment. *New Directions for Child Development*, 11, 31–55.
Cicchetti, D. & Toth, S.L. (1995). A developmental psychopathology perspective on child abuse and neglect. *Journal of the American Academy of Child and Adolescent Psychiatry*, 34, 541–563.
Cicchetti, D. & Valentino, K. (2006). An ecological–transactional perspective on child maltreatment: Failure of the average expectable environmental and its influence in child development. In: D. Cicchetti and D.J. Cohen (eds), *Developmental Psychopathology*, 2nd edn, vol. 3. Hoboken: John Wiley & Sons Inc, 129–199.
Cicchetti, D., Toth, S.L. & Maughan, A. (2000). An ecological–transactional model of child maltreatment. In: A. Sameroff, M. Lewis and S. Miller (eds), *Handbook of Developmental Psychopathology*, 2nd edn. New York: Kluwer Academic/Plenum Publishers, 689–722.
Conron, K.J., Beardslee, W., Koenen, K.C., et al. (2009). A longitudinal study of maternal depression and child maltreatment in a national sample of families investigated by child protective services. *Archives of Pediatric and Adolescent Medicine*, 163, 922–930.

Cox, C.E., Kotch, J.B. & Everson, M.A. (2003). Longitudinal study of modifying influences in the relationship between domestic violence and child abuse. *Journal of Family Violence*, 18, 5–17.

Crick, N.R. & Dodge, K.A. (1994). A review and reformulation of social information-processing mechanisms in children's social adjustment. *Psychological Bulletin*, 115, 74–101.

Crittenden, P.M. (2002). If I knew then what I know now: Integrity and fragmentation in the treatment of child abuse and neglect. In: K.D. Browne, H. Hanks, P. Stratton and C.E. Hamilton (eds), *The Early Prediction and Prevention of Child Abuse: A Handbook*. Chichester: John Wiley & Sons, Ltd, 111–126.

Dahl, R. (2004). Adolescent brain development: A period of vulnerabilities and opportunities. *Annals of the New York Academy of Sciences*, 1021, 1–22.

Daly, M. & Wilson, M. (1985). Child abuse and other risks of not living with both parents. *Ethology and Sociobiology*, 6, 197–210.

Denholm, R., Power, C., Thomas, C. & Li, L. (2010). Child abuse co-occurrence and associations with household dysfunction: Evidence from the 1958 British birth cohort. *Journal of Epidemiological Community Health*, 64(1).

Department for Education (2015). *Characteristics of children in need: 2014 to 2015*. London: National Statistics Office.

Dixon, L., Browne, K.D. & Hamilton-Giachritsis, C.E. (2005). Risk factors of parents' abused as children: A mediational analysis of the intergenerational continuity of child maltreatment (Part I). *Journal of Child Psychology and Psychiatry*, 46, 47–57.

Dixon, L., Hamilton-Giachritsis, C.E. & Browne, K.D. (2005). Behavioural measures of parents' abused as children: A mediational analysis of the intergenerational continuity of child maltreatment (Part II). *Journal of Child Psychology and Psychiatry*, 46, 58–68.

Dixon, L., Hamilton-Giachritsis, C.E. & Browne, K.D. (2009). Patterns of risk and protective factors in the intergenerational cycle of maltreatment. *Journal of Family Violence*, 24, 111–122.

Douglas, E.M. & Mohn, B.L. (2014). Fatal and non-fatal child maltreatment in the US: An analysis of child, caregiver, and service utilization with the National Child Abuse and Neglect Data Set. *Child Abuse & Neglect*, 38, 42–51.

Dubowitz, H. & Black, M.B. (2001). Child neglect. In: R.M. Reece and S. Ludwig (eds), *Child Abuse: Medical Diagnosis and Management*, 2nd edn. Philadelphia, PA: Lippincott.

Egeland, B., Bosquet, M. & Chung, A.L. (2002). Continuities and discontinuities in the intergenerational transmission of child maltreatment: Implications for breaking the cycle of abuse. In: K.D. Browne, H. Hanks, P. Stratton, C.E. Hamilton (eds), *Early Prediction and Prevention of Child Abuse: A Handbook*. Chichester: John Wiley & Sons, Ltd, 217–232.

Ertem, I.O., Leventhal, J.M. & Dobbs, S. (2000). Intergenerational continuity of child physical abuse: How good is the evidence? *The Lancet*, 356(9232), 814–819.

Fang, X., Brown, D.S., Florence, C.S. & Mercy, J.A. (2012). The economic burden of child maltreatment in the United States and implications for prevention. *Child Abuse & Neglect*, 36, 156–165.

Finkelhor, D. (1995). The victimization of children in a developmental perspective. *American Journal of Orthopsychiatry*, 65, 177–193.

Finkelhor, D., Ormrod, R., Turner, H. & Holt, M. (2009). Pathways to poly-victimization. *Child Maltreatment*, 14, 316–329.

Flores, E., Cicchetti, D. & Rogosch, F.A. (2005). Predictors of resilience in maltreated and nonmaltreated Latino children. *Developmental Psychology*, 41, 338–351.

Font, S. (2017). Psychological, economic and physical health consequences of child maltreatment. In: L. Dixon (ed), *What Works in Child Protection*. Chichester: John Wiley & Sons, Ltd (this volume).

Fontana, V. (1973). *Somewhere a Child is Crying. Maltreatment Causes and Prevention*. New York: Macmillan.

Gelles, R.J. (1983). An exchange/social control theory. In: D. Finkelhor, R.J. Gelles, G.T. Hotaling & M.A. Straus (eds), *The Dark Side of Families: Current Family Violence Research*. Beverly Hills, CA: Sage, 151–165.

Gelles, R.J. & Perlman, S. (2012). *Estimated Annual Cost of Child Abuse & Neglect*. Chicago, IL: Prevent Child Abuse America.

Gil, D.C. (1970). *Violence against Children: Physical Abuse in the United States*. Cambridge, MA: Harvard University Press.

Gilbert, R., Spatz-Widom, C., Browne, K.D. et al. (2009). Burden and consequences of child maltreatment in high-income countries. *The Lancet*, 373, 68–81.

Goldstein, S. & Brooks, R.B. (2005). *Handbook of Resilience in Children*. NY: Kluwer Academic/Plenum Publishers.

Hamilton, C.E. & Browne, K.D. (1999). Recurrent maltreatment during childhood. A survey of referrals to police child protection units in England. *Child Maltreatment*, 4, 275–286.

Hamilton-Giachritsis, C.E. & Browne, K.D. (2005). Risk to siblings in an abusive household: A retrospective study of children referred to police child protection units. *Journal of Family Psychology, Special Issue on Sibling Relationship Contributions to Individual and Family Well-being*, 19, 619–624.

Heise, L.L. (1998). Violence against women: An integrated ecological framework. *Violence Against Women*, 4, 262–290.

Hillberg, T., Hamilton-Giachritsis, C.E. & Dixon, L. (2011). Review of meta-analyses on the association between child sexual abuse and adult mental health difficulties: A systematic approach. *Trauma, Violence & Abuse*, 12, 38–49.

Hiller, A., Springer, C., Misurell, J. et al. (2016). Predictors of group treatment outcomes for child sexual abuse: An investigation of the role of demographic and abuse characteristics. *Child Abuse Review*, 25, 102–114.

Horvath, M.A.H., Llian, A., Massey, K. et al. (2013). *Basically ... porn is everywhere: A rapid evidence assessment on the effects that access and exposure to pornography has on children and young people*. Project report: Office of the Children's Commissioner. Middlesex University's Research Repository at http://eprints.mdx.ac.uk/10692/.

Hussey, J.M., Chang, J.J. & Kotch, J.B. (2006). Child maltreatment in the United States: Prevalence, risk factors, and adolescent health consequences. *Pediatrics*, 118, 933–942.

Iwaniec, D. (2004). *Failure to Thrive*. Chichester: John Wiley & Sons, Ltd.

Jaffee, S.R., Caspi, A., Moffitt, T.E. et al. (2007). Individual, family, and neighborhood factors distinguish resilient from non-resilient maltreated children: A cumulative stressors model. *Child Abuse & Neglect*, 31, 231–253.

Jensen, F.E. & Nutt, A.E. (2016). *The Teenage Brain: A Neuroscientist's Survival Guide to Raising Adolescents and Young*. USA: Harper Paperbacks.

Johnson, R.M., Kotch, J.B., Catellier, D.J. et al. (2004). Adverse behavioural and emotional outcomes from child abuse and witnessed violence. *Child Maltreatment*, 7, 179–186.

Jones, L.M., Mitchell, K.J. & Finkelhor, D. (2012). Trends in youth internet victimization: Findings from three youth internet safety surveys 2000–2010. *Journal of Adolescent Health*, 50, 179–186.

Jones, L., Bellis, M.A., Wood, S. et al. (2012). Prevalence and risk of violence against children with disabilities: A systematic review and meta-analysis of observational studies. *The Lancet*, 380(9845), 899–907.

Kaufman, J. & Zigler, E. (1987). Do abused children become abusive parents? *American Journal of Orthopsychiatry*, 57, 186–192.

Kleevens, J. & Lieb, R. (2010). Child maltreatment fatalities in children under 5: Findings from the National Violence Death Reporting System. *Child Abuse & Neglect*, 34, 262–266.

Klevens, J., Bayon, M.C. & Sierra, M. (2000). Risk factors and the context of men who physically abuse in Bogota, Colombia. *Child Abuse & Neglect*, 24, 323–332.

Krug, E.G., Dahlberg, L.L., Mercy, J.A. et al. (2002). *World Health Report*. Geneva: World Health Organization.

Kumpfer, K.L (1999). Factors and processes contributing to resilience. In: M.D. Glantz and J.L. Johnson (eds), *Resilience and Development: Positive Life Adaptations*. New York: Kluwer Academic/Plenum, 179–244.

Layne, C.M., Beck, C.J., Rimmasch, H. et al. (2009). Promoting 'resilient' posttraumatic adjustment in childhood and beyond. 'Unpacking' life events, adjustment trajectories, resources, and interventions.

In D. Brom, R. Pat-Horenczyk and J.D. Ford (eds), *Treating Traumatized Children: Risk, Resilience and Recovery.* East Sussex: Routledge.

Leventhal, J.M. (1996). Twenty years later: We do know how to prevent child abuse and neglect. *Child Abuse & Neglect*, 20, 647–653.

Luthar, S. & Cicchetti, D. (2000). The construct of resilience: Implications for interventions and social policies. *Development and Psychopathology*, 12, 857–885.

Makhlouf, F. & Rambaud, C. (2014). Child homicide and neglect in France: 1991–2008. *Child Abuse & Neglect*, 38, 37–41.

Mangrulkar, L., Whitman, V.C. & Posner, M. (2001). *Life skills approach to child and adolescent healthy human development.* Washington, DC: Pan American Health Organization.

Milot, T., St-Laurent, D., Éthier, L.S. (2016). Intervening with severely and chronically neglected children and their families: The contribution of trauma-informed approaches. *Child Abuse Review*, 25(2).

National Research Council (1993). *Understanding Child Abuse and Neglect.* Washington, DC: National Academy of Sciences Press.

Olds, D., Henderson, C. & Eckenrode, J. (2002). Preventing child abuse and neglect with parental and infancy home visiting by nurses. In: K.D. Browne, H. Hanks, P. Stratton and C.E. Hamilton (eds), *Early Prediction and Prevention of Child Abuse: A Handbook.* Chichester: John Wiley & Sons, Ltd, 165–182.

Pellai, A. (2013). *Le Parole non Dette.* Trento: Centro Studi Erickson. https://issuu.com/eljadiepenbrock/docs/porcospini_erickson_completo__final.

Pinna, K.L.M. (2016). Interrupting the intergenerational transmission of violence. *Child Abuse Review*, 25(2).

Putnam-Hornstein, E. & Needell, B. (2011). Predictors of child protection service contact between birth and age five: An examination of California's 2002 birth cohort. *Children and Youth Services Review*, 33, 2400–2407.

Putnam-Hornstein, E., Needell, B. & Rhodes, A.E. (2013). Understanding risk and protective factors for child maltreatment: The value of integrated, population-based data. *Child Abuse & Neglect*, 37, 116–119.

Radford, L., Corral, S., Bradley, C. & Fisher, H. (2013). The prevalence and impact of child maltreatment and other types of victimization in the UK: Findings from a population survey of caregivers, children and young people and young adults. *Child Abuse & Neglect*, 37, 801–813.

Sagy, S. & Doton N. (2001). Coping resources of abused children in the family: A salutogenic approach. *Child Abuse & Neglect*, 25, 1463–1480.

Sameroff, A.J., Bartko, W.T., Baldwin, A. et al. (1998). Family and social influences on the development of child competence. In: M. Lewis & C. Feiring (eds), *Families, Risk, and Competence.* Mahwah, NJ: Lawrence Erlbaum Associates, 161–186.

Scarcella, C.A., Bess, R., Zielewski, R.H. & Green, R. (2006). *The Cost of Protecting Vulnerable Children V: Understanding State Variation in Child Welfare Financing.* Washington, DC: Urban Institute.

Sidebotham, P. & Golding, J. (2001). Child maltreatment in the 'Children of the Nineties': A longitudinal study of parental risk factors. *Child Abuse & Neglect*, 25, 1177–1200.

Sidebotham, P., Bailey, S.E., Belderson, P. & Brandon, M. (2011). Fatal child maltreatment in England, 2005–2009. *Child Abuse & Neglect*, 35, 299–306.

Sledjeski, E.M., Dierke, L.C., Bird, H.R. & Canino, G.C. (2009). Predicting child abuse among Puerto Rican children from migrant and non-migrant families. *Child Abuse & Neglect*, 33, 382–392.

Stalker, K., Taylor, J., Fry, D., & Stewart, A. (2015). A Study of Disabled Children and Child Protection in Scotland - a hidden group? *Children and Youth Services Review*, 56, 126–134.

Steele, B. (1976). Violence within the family. In: C.H. Kempe and A.E. Helfer (eds), *Child Abuse and Neglect: The Family and the Community.* Cambridge, MA: Ballinger, 3–24.

Steinberg, L. (2008). A social neuroscience perspective on adolescent risk taking. *Developmental Review*, 28, 78–106.

Stith, S.M., Liu, T., Davies, L.C. et al. (2009). Risk factors in child maltreatment: A meta-analytic review of the literature. *Aggression and Violent Behavior*, 14, 13–29.

Straus, M.A., Hamby, S.L., Finkelhor, D. et al. (1998). Identification of child maltreatment with the Parent–Child Conflict Tactics Scales: Development and psychometric data for a national sample of American parents. *Child Abuse & Neglect*, 22, 249–270.

Sullivan, P. (2009). Violence exposure among children with disabilities. *Clinical Child and Family Psychology Review*, 12, 196–216.

Sullivan, T.P., Fehon, D.C., Andres-Hyman, R.C. et al. (2006). Differential relationships of childhood abuse and neglect subtypes to PTSD symptom clusters among adolescent inpatients. *Journal of Traumatic Stress*, 19, 229–239.

Thornberry, T.P., Matsuda, M., Greenman, S.J. et al. (2014). Adolescent risk factors for child maltreatment. *Child Abuse & Neglect*, 38, 706–722.

Tokunaga, R.S. (2010). Following you home from school: A critical review and synthesis of research on cyberbullying victimisation. *Computers in Human Behavior*, 26, 277–287.

Turner, H.A., Finkelhor, D. & Ormrod, R. (2010). Poly-victimization in a national sample of children and youth. *American Journal of Preventive Medicine*, 38, 323–330.

Whittle, H., Hamilton-Giachritsis, C.E. & Beech, A. (2014a). In their own words: An exploration of young people's vulnerabilities to being victimized and abused online. *PSYCHOLOGY*, 5, 1185–1196.

Whittle, H., Hamilton-Giachritsis, C.E. & Beech, A. (2014b). Victims' voices: The impact of online grooming and sexual abuse. *Universal Journal of Psychology*, 1(2), 59–71.

Whittle, H., Hamilton-Giachritsis, C.E., Beech, A. & Collings, G. (2013a). Online grooming: characteristics and concerns. *Aggression and Violent Behavior*, 18, 62–70.

Whittle, H., Hamilton-Giachritsis, C., Beech, A. & Collings, G. (2013b). A review of young people's vulnerabilities to online grooming. *Aggression and Violent Behavior*, 18, 135–146.

Widom, C.S. (1999). Posttraumatic stress disorder in abused and neglected children grown up. *American Journal of Psychiatry*, 156, 1223–1229.

Widom, C.S., Czaja, S.J. & DuMont, K.A. (2015). Intergenerational transmission of child abuse and neglect: Real or detection bias? *Science*, 347, 1480–1485.

Wilson, M. & Daly, M. (1988). Evolutionary social psychology and family homicide. *Science*, 242, 519–524.

Wolfe, D.A. (1985). Prevention of child abuse through the development of parent and child competencies. In: R.J. McMahon & R. Peters (eds), *Childhood Disorders: Behavioral-Developmental Approaches*. New York: Brunner/Mazel, 195–217.

Wolfe, D. (1991). *Preventing Physical and Emotional Abuse of Children*. New York: Guildford Press.

Wolfe, D. (1993). Child abuse prevention: blending research and practice. *Child Abuse Review*, 2, 153–165.

World Health Organization (2004). *Life skills-based education. Skills for health: An important entry-point for health promoting/child-friendly schools*. Geneva: WHO.

4

Fatal Child Maltreatment

Peter Sidebotham
University of Warwick, UK

Fatal child maltreatment is a global problem that has persisted throughout history and into the twenty-first century. Research over recent decades has emphasised that fatal maltreatment is a heterogeneous phenomenon. In this chapter I review international data on the incidence and nature of fatal maltreatment, drawing on previous work to present a model for understanding the different types of violent and maltreatment-related child deaths. Six categories of deaths are described. The literature is reviewed in relation to what is known about risk factors in the child, the parents and carers, and the wider family and environment. Lessons learnt from case reviews are presented as a background to deeper understanding of preventative measures within a broader public health framework.

Incidence of Fatal Child Maltreatment

The 2002 World Report on Violence and Health estimated that globally 31,000 males and 26,000 females aged 0–14 died as a result of homicide (Krug, 2002). Pinheiro, in a subsequent UN report on violence against children, estimated age-standardised homicide rates for 0–17 years to be 2.44 per 100,000 per year (Pinheiro, 2006). Rates vary by gender and age, are lowest in the 5–9 age group and highest in infancy and in the 15–17 age group, particularly among adolescent males. There is considerable evidence that rates vary between countries, with one recent analysis demonstrating at least a five-fold variation in child homicide rates between six high-income countries (Gilbert, Fluke, O'Donnell et al., 2012). The UN report concluded that rates in low-income countries (2.58 per 100,000) are more than twice those in high-income countries (1.21 per 100,000) (Pinheiro, 2006). In contrast, an earlier report indicated that mortality rates from inflicted injury in infancy are similar in developed and developing countries, suggesting that this is an issue which is relatively independent of culture (Christoffel, Liu & Stamler, 1981).

It is well recognised that official statistics, particularly those based on death registration, tend to underestimate the number of child maltreatment fatalities (Crume, DiGuiseppi,

Byers et al. 2002; Frederick, Goddard & Oxley, 2013; Herman-Giddens, Brown, Verbiest et al., 1999; Jenny & Isaac, 2006; Klevens & Leeb, 2010; Palusci, Wirtz & Covington, 2010; Riggs & Hobbs, 2011; Schnitzer, Gulino & Yuan, 2013). A number of factors influence this under-ascertainment, including difficulties in distinguishing non-accidental from accidental deaths; failure to recognise neglect-related or other less obvious forms of fatal maltreatment; and variations in protocols for investigation, reporting and coding of deaths. While direct physical abuse fatalities may be reasonably well captured in official statistics, neglect-related and other less obvious forms of fatal maltreatment may be particularly prone to under-ascertainment (Palusci, Wirtz & Covington, 2010; Schnitzer, Gulino & Yuan, 2013).

While caution should be applied in interpreting data on child maltreatment fatalities and in comparing rates between countries and over time, there is evidence that rates have fallen over time in some countries, at least within the youngest age groups. Our analysis of death registration and police homicide data in England and Wales showed that death rates from assault in infants fell from 5.6 per 100,000 in 1974 to 0.7 in 2008, and in children from 0.6 to 0.2 per 100,000 over the same period, though with no change in rates among adolescents (Sidebotham, Atkins & Hutton, 2012).

The Nature of Fatal Child Maltreatment

A substantial body of research has identified heterogeneity in types of maltreatment fatalities (Christoffel & Liu, 1983; Fujiwara, Barber, Schaechter & Hemenway, 2009; Reder, Duncan & Gray, 1993; Sidebotham, Bailey, Belderson & Brandon, 2011). Child maltreatment deaths vary in the manner of death; characteristics of the incident, the child victim and the perpetrator; the context of the case; provision of public and other services; and the motivations behind the event (Table 4.1). This is important, as different types of death are likely to have different victim and perpetrator profiles and different risk factors, which we need to understand if we are to effectively identify and act to modify relevant risks. It is unlikely that one size will fit all in seeking to prevent fatal maltreatment.

Some of the earliest attempts to understand filicide stemmed from the seminal work of Resnick in the 1960s. Resnick (1969) proposed a classification encompassing altruism, acute psychosis, the unwanted child, accidental filicide and spousal revenge. This typology has subsequently been developed by others, providing a much more nuanced understanding of the heterogeneous nature of filicide, the characteristics of perpetrators and some of their underlying motives (e.g., Bourget & Gagne, 2002, 2005). Alongside this others have gone on to consider filicide from the perspective of the child victim and the circumstances of the death (e.g., Christoffel, 1984; Fujiwara, Barber, Schaechter & Hemenway, 2009; Reder, Duncan & Gray, 1993; Wilczynski, 1994, 1997).

Bringing these two strands of thinking together, I propose a model that encompasses both violent and maltreatment deaths in childhood, taking account of the nature and circumstances of each death, the characteristics and behaviour of the perpetrator(s), and the broader context within which the death has occurred (Figure 4.1). This model considers the concept of control as an observable behaviour in the perpetrator(s), and potentially allows us to classify these deaths in a way that facilitates a deeper understanding and identification of possibilities for prevention. The model is built on two overlapping circles: of maltreatment deaths, perpetrated by the parent(s) or primary carer(s), and violent deaths, perpetrated by violent means, both within and without the family.

Table 4.1 Factors to include in an understanding of fatal child maltreatment.

Domain	Factors to consider
Nature and circumstances of the death	Mode of death Use of overt violence or other means Involvement of others (including other family members, pets, and attempted or actual perpetrator suicide)
Child characteristics	Gender Age Development Factors such as disability or temperament that may interact with the parents' care of the child
Perpetrator characteristics	Gender Relationship to the child Mental and physical health Background history, including domestic violence and alcohol/substance misuse Possible motives for the killing; notions of control or lack of control
Family and environmental circumstances	Family structure and functioning Parental separation or divorce Any precipitating or moderating events Social support structures
Service provision and need	Public and other service provision Any unmet needs of the child or family Response of agencies to any recognised risks or concerns

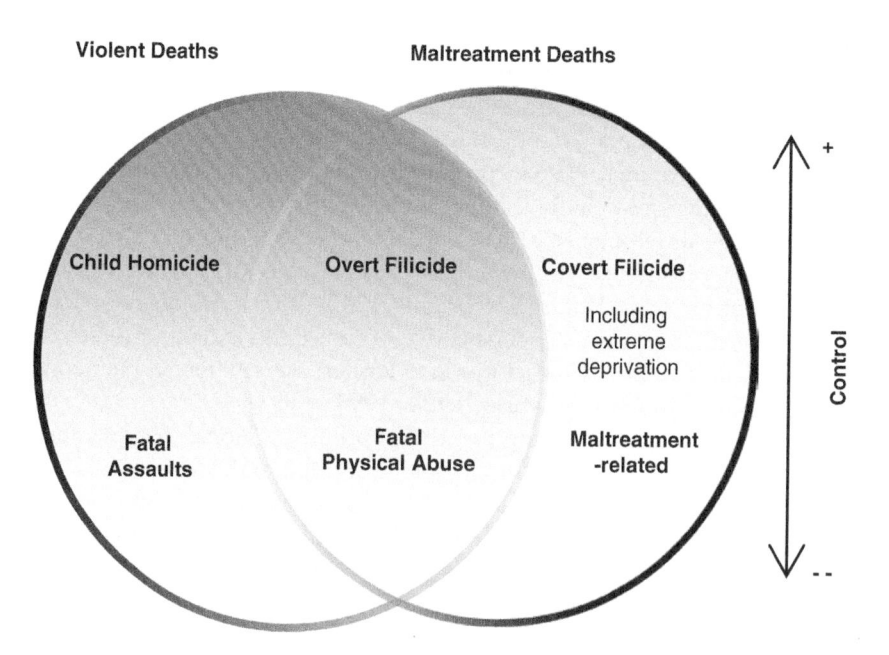

Figure 4.1 The spectrum of violent and maltreatment deaths in childhood. Source: Sidebotham 2013. Reproduced with permission of John Wiley & Sons.

This model classifies violent and maltreatment deaths in six primary categories: 'overt filicide', 'covert filicide', 'child homicide', 'fatal physical abuse', 'fatal assaults' and 'maltreatment-related deaths' (see Table 4.2 for a summary). These categories are described below, incorporating findings from a study of English Serious Case Reviews (SCR) (Sidebotham, Bailey, Belderson & Brandon, 2011) and other literature.

Overt filicides These cases occur across the age spectrum, although the highest risks are in younger children and there was a male predominance of 67% in the 2011 SCR study (Sidebotham, Bailey, Belderson & Brandon, 2011). The perpetrator is most commonly a father or father figure, although in the 2011 SCR cohort the mother was the perpetrator in 39% of cases. In these cases there is evidence pointing toward excessive or disordered control, with apparent intent to kill or harm the child, or some evidence of premeditation.

The fact of homicide is usually immediately apparent. They include deaths by stabbings or using other implements. In the UK, firearms are uncommonly used, although they are far more common in the USA and other countries with more lax gun control legislation (Richardson & Hemenway, 2011). Other cases involve asphyxia, poisoning, burns and drowning, and some deaths result from severe physical assault in which there appears to have been some intent to deliberately harm or kill the child. This category includes deaths in house fires with evidence of arson and intent to kill.

A striking subgroup among these deaths are those in which more than one family member is killed, including other siblings or the other parent, and some in which a family pet is also killed (Liem & Koenraadt, 2008; Liem, Levin, Holland & Fox, 2013; Sachmann & Harris Johnson, 2014). In a number the perpetrator takes or attempts to take his/her own life.

A number of theories have been put forward to explain these overt filicides (Bourget & Gagne, 2002, 2005; Fujiwara, Barber, Schaechter & Hemenway, 2009; Resnick, 1969; Wilczynski, 1997). Many of the homicides perpetrated by fathers appear to fit a model of revenge or control. This may involve an estranged father seeking to hurt his ex-partner, often with a background of domestic violence including psychological violence and control. In contrast, cases perpetrated by mothers more typically are categorised as altruistic. These often occur in the context of maternal mental ill-health and seem to arise out of a desire to spare the child further suffering. Other cases may involve distorted belief systems about the child, including extreme religious beliefs around evil or demon possession.

Covert filicides

These deaths typically occur in younger children and infants. They are similar to the more overt homicides, in that they occur in situations where there appears to have been some intent to kill the child. In the majority of cases the perpetrator is the mother, with or without involvement of her partner. Typically the perpetrator uses less-overtly violent means, such as smothering, abandonment or poisoning, and often the cause of death is not immediately apparent. Also included within this category are cases of extreme neglect or 'deprivational abuse' where there has been severe deprivation of a child's basic needs, whether for oxygen, food, warmth and shelter or other needs.

The motivation for these covert filicides is often unclear, but may involve distorted beliefs about the child as in the more overt homicides discussed above, or an apparent denial of the child's existence. In some cases there may be evidence of parental mental ill-health, although

Table 4.2 Classification of fatal maltreatment.

Category	Description
1. Overt filicide	Deaths perpetrated by one or more parents or parent figures using overtly violent means. These include deaths caused by stabbings and firearms, and severe beatings where there appears to be an intent to kill. In all cases there appear to be elements of excessive or disordered control by the perpetrator. It may include situations of domestic violence where the filicide is part of the perpetrator's attempts to control their partner. These include cases of killings of multiple family members or of multiple killings with subsequent suicide or attempted suicide of the perpetrator ('extended suicides'). This may include deaths from house fires with evidence of arson.
2. Covert filicide (including extreme neglect/deprivational abuse)	Deaths perpetrated by one or more parents or parent figures using less-overtly violent means. Typically these involve some kind of disordered control within the perpetrator, including situations where mental illness in the perpetrator leads to disordered perceptions of their need to kill the child. The victims are often very young infants or vulnerable children and often the cause of death is not immediately apparent. This category includes deaths as a result of exposure, asphyxiation, drowning, strangulation or poisoning where there is some indication that there was some intent to kill or harm the child (as distinct from accidental deaths from these causes). Also includes deaths following concealment of pregnancy where there was suspicion that the mother may have killed the child. This category includes cases where the direct cause of death is extreme neglect or deprivation of the child's needs, e.g., through starvation or exposure, or where there is evidence of deliberate failure to respond to medical needs of the child. Some cases of fabricated or induced illness will fall within this category.
3. Fatal physical abuse	Includes cases of severe physical violence with or without associated neglect perpetrated by a parent or primary carer in situations of loss of control, typically as an impulsive act in response to some exogenous stressor. The mode of death in these cases is typically a violent assault, most commonly an inflicted head injury, including shaking and shaking-impact injuries, but also multiple injuries and abdominal injuries. Other deaths may include the use of firearms, beatings, stabbings and strangulation, where there was some evidence of impulsivity without necessarily any intent to kill the child.
4. Child homicide	Deaths perpetrated, typically using violent means, by someone other than a parent or parent figure, including other family members, people known to the child and strangers. This may include homicides with associated sexual assaults or in circumstances of child sexual exploitation or other exploitation. In older young people, it may include peer homicides (including some gang violence) and intimate partner homicides.
5. Fatal assaults	Cases of severe physical violence perpetrated by those outside the family. Typically these will be in older children and young people, and the perpetrators are often peers known to the young person. May include deaths within the context of impulsive violence and situations of uncontrolled gang violence.

Table 4.2 (cont'd)

Category	Description
6. Deaths related to but not directly caused by maltreatment	Deaths considered to be related to maltreatment, but in which the maltreatment cannot be considered a direct cause of death. This will include: • sudden unexpected deaths in infancy with clear concerns around parental care, but not sufficient to label as extreme or persistent neglect; • fatal accidents where there may be issues around parental supervision and care, including accidental ingestion of drugs or other household substances; drownings; falls; electrocution; gunshot wounds; and fires; • those children dying of natural causes whose parents may not have sought medical intervention early enough; • deaths of older children with previous maltreatment, but where the maltreatment did not directly lead to the death, e.g., death from an overwhelming chest infection in a child severely disabled by a non-accidental head injury; suicide or risk-taking behaviours including substance abuse in young people with a past history of abuse.

Source: Adapted from Sidebotham 2013 and Sidebotham 2011.

this is not universal, and few cases meet the legal criteria for a charge of infanticide, dependent on proving that the balance of the mother's mind is 'disturbed by reason of her not having fully recovered from the effect of giving birth to the child or by reason of the effect of lactation consequent upon the birth of the child' (Infanticide Act 1938). This concept has its difficulties, and the charge is rarely used in practice.

In those cases of extreme deprivational abuse, there is typically evidence of long-standing neglect, sometimes with an acute event or exacerbation of the neglect precipitating the death. Some also have evidence of concurrent physical abuse and in some cases a severe assault may be the final cause of death in a child who has experienced severe ongoing neglect. In these cases there seems to be a deliberate intent to withhold food and other basic needs from the child. This distinguishes these cases from cases of neglect due to parental incompetence (e.g., through substance misuse, mental ill-health, or learning difficulties), lack of resources, or family stress, which are rarely fatal.

Fatal physical abuse

Severe physical assaults are the most common direct cause of fatal maltreatment. These occur predominantly among infants and young children, with a slight male preponderance. The most common cause of death in this category is a severe non-accidental head injury, including skull fractures and subdural haemorrhages. A high proportion of these have other associated injuries, including rib and limb fractures, bruises and other injuries. Other children die as a result of abdominal injuries, or of other severe and multiple injuries.

Most perpetrators are male, the majority (56%) in the 2011 SCR study being the father or the mother's partner (Sidebotham, Bailey, Belderson & Brandon, 2011). In a small number of cases, the perpetrator is another adult known to the family, including babysitters in rare cases. A high proportion of these cases will have some evidence of previous maltreatment, particularly prior physical abuse, although in some cases this is only apparent after the event, through the identification of old injuries.

It is postulated that these fatalities occur in situations of extreme stress, sometimes precipitated by inconsolable crying. Such incidents may occur when an isolated, vulnerable parent, with poor anger control and a low tolerance of stress loses their temper and lashes out at the child in an uncontrolled burst of anger. Such incidents may occur without prior indications that this is a likely scenario, although in many cases there may have been previous less severe episodes. Severe physical assaults may also arise in the context of physical discipline taken to extremes, in which the disciplining parent does not control and limit the discipline, which then escalates, becoming more and more violent and abusive. In these cases the perpetrator often seeks assistance immediately after the event, typically showing some remorse, though also attempting to conceal the true cause of the infant's condition, and in some cases with a delay in presentation (Wilson & Smith, 2015). The non-abusive parent may be unaware of the incident, or may attempt to conceal the true nature to protect their partner.

Child homicides and fatal assaults

Although not typically considered fatal child maltreatment, there are considerable overlaps between intra- and extra-familial homicides and fatal assaults. In both scenarios, children suffer harm, and our professional responses and efforts geared toward prevention should be no less vigilant for harm that originates in the wider community. It is notable that, in a review of violent child deaths in England and Wales since the 1970s, while rates in infants and children have fallen, deaths among adolescents have remained static or even risen (Sidebotham, Atkins & Hutton, 2012). This suggests that we are doing less well at preventing these community deaths than those occurring within families.

Among older children and young people, more homicides are perpetrated by non-family members, although in the majority of circumstances the perpetrator will be someone known to the child. Stranger homicides are uncommon, but may rarely occur in the context of child abduction and/or sexual assault. In the Home Office recording of homicides in England and Wales, of 722 homicides recorded in young people under 16 years of age from 1999–2010, 450 (62%) were perpetrated by a parent; a further 95 (13%) by another family member, friend or acquaintance; and just 96 (13%) by a stranger (Smith, Coleman, Eder & Hall, 2011).

Child and young person homicides outside the family include homicides in the context of gang violence, and intimate partner homicides involving young people. Homicides in the context of peer violence typically involve young offenders killing young victims who are the same age or younger than them (Carcach, 1997).

Deaths related to but not directly caused by maltreatment

While children may die as a direct consequence of maltreatment, many more children die in circumstances where abuse and/or neglect are contributory factors but not the immediate cause of death. In the English SCR study, of 246 deaths for which a category could be assigned, 44% were considered a direct result of abuse or neglect, with the remaining 56% being related to but not directly caused by the maltreatment (Sidebotham, Bailey, Belderson & Brandon, 2011).

There are a range of circumstances in which neglect may contribute to children's deaths (Brandon, Bailey, Belderson & Larsson, 2013). These include poor supervision of young children leading to risks from accidents, including drowning, road traffic accidents, home accidents and ingestion of prescribed or non-prescribed medications and household products. Neglect of a child's medical needs has been highlighted as a significant issue, particularly in children with chronic illness or disability, but also in response to acute illness and injury (Jenny, 2007).

In infancy, a number of unexpected deaths may present with factors suggesting maltreatment as a contributory, though not necessarily causal, factor. Given that we do not fully understand the causes of sudden infant death syndrome (SIDS), and that there are no definitive pathological markers for asphyxia, it is recognised that within those deaths labelled as SIDS, there will be some that result from accidental asphyxia, and others that are covert homicides. It is estimated that as many as 5% of sudden unexpected deaths in infancy may be related to maltreatment, either through poor parental care and neglect, or through more deliberate covert homicide (Bajanowski, Vennemann, Bohnert et al., 2005).

Among teenagers, deaths from suicide or self-harm and risk-taking behaviours, including alcohol or substance misuse, may be related to prior maltreatment. Earlier maltreatment, particularly physical and sexual abuse, is a recognised risk factor for suicidal behaviour, as is peer bullying (Evans, Hawton & Rodham, 2004; Grossman, Milligan & Deyo, 1991; Maniglio, 2011; Meltzer, Vostanis, Ford et al., 2011; Rey Gex, Narring, Ferron & Michaud, 1998; Seguin, Renaud, Lesage et al., 2011). Risk of suicidal behaviour in relation to prior sexual abuse appears to be stronger in boys than in girls (Borowsky, Resnick, Ireland & Blum, 1999; Choquet, Darves-Bornoz, Ledoux et al., 1997). Such risks need to be appreciated within the context of a complex interplay between genetic, biological, psychiatric, psychological, social and cultural factors (Hawton, Saunders & O'Connor, 2012).

Risk Factors for Fatal Child Maltreatment

While a lot is already known about risk factors for child maltreatment in general, the picture around specific risks of fatal child maltreatment is far less clear. Most published data on child maltreatment fatalities consist of uncontrolled observational studies, typically small, retrospective case series. While these are helpful in highlighting common findings, they typically do not provide comparator data to enable potentially fatal cases to be distinguished from other cases with lower risk of fatality. Most studies rely on retrospective reviews of case notes, and are therefore dependent on data collected by practitioners involved in the case, rather than systemically collecting comprehensive epidemiological data. This brings the potential for bias and for substantial gaps in information. Given the heterogeneity of types of fatal maltreatment outlined above, it is unlikely that the same risk factors will apply to all forms. Few studies are large enough to be able to distinguish between different types of fatal maltreatment and delineate risk factors pertinent to these different forms. In spite of these limitations, it is possible to draw some tentative conclusions on risk factors, drawing on themes which are consistently identified in the literature.

Child characteristics

Age and gender   Most studies on fatal child maltreatment show a clear age gradient with the highest risks in infancy accompanied by a steady decrease during the early preschool years to very low levels during middle childhood, before rising again slightly in the teenage years. This

Table 4.3 Rates of children subject to a child protection plan and child maltreatment fatalities, England, 2005–2010.

	Children subject to a child protection plan: Rate per 100,000		Child maltreatment fatalities: Rate per 100,000		Ratio – children subject to a child protection plan: child maltreatment fatalities	
	Female	Male	Female	Male	Female	Male
<1 year	564	568	3.95	5.32	143:1	107:1
1–4 years	379	391	0.46	0.73	818:1	539:1
5–9 years	289	302	0.17	0.23	1725:1	1335:1
10–17 years	180	171	0.36	0.35	501:1	491:1

gradient mirrors and is perhaps more pronounced than that for non-fatal physical abuse and neglect. The strong risks in infancy and early childhood are particularly marked for fatal physical abuse, for extreme neglect or deprivational abuse, and for the more covert forms of homicide. In contrast, overt homicide appears to occur across the age spectrum, without a clear gradient. A second peak in deaths in adolescence relates particularly to deaths from suicides and self-harming or other risk-taking behaviours to which prior maltreatment may have contributed.

Using those children subject to a child protection plan as a proxy for non-fatal maltreatment, the risks of non-fatal maltreatment are highest in infancy, then drop steadily with each successive age group to around 30% by 10–17 years (Table 4.3). There is an excess male risk in all age groups below 10. While the overall maltreatment mortality rate is around $1/400^{th}$ of the non-fatal maltreatment rate, the male:female ratio and the age gradient are both more marked. Thus, not only are infants and younger children more at risk of maltreatment generally, but beyond that, the risks of fatal maltreatment are even higher and increase substantially the younger the child.

The implications of these findings are that we need to recognise that infants and preschool children are particularly vulnerable to fatal maltreatment, and we need to focus our protection efforts on these age groups. However, we should not neglect the longer-term impact of all forms of maltreatment on older children and young people, and the ongoing risks of death related to such maltreatment. These groups of young people require additional support and rehabilitation to mitigate the effects of maltreatment and build resilience.

Most epidemiological studies of child maltreatment show an excess of males for all forms apart from sexual abuse. This slight gender bias is mirrored in most studies of fatal maltreatment (Bennett, Hall, Frazier et al., 2006; Mathews, Abrahams, Jewkes et al., 2013). Analysis of English SCRs from 2005–2010 gave an overall mortality rate of 0.70 per 100,000 males aged 0–17, compared to 0.55 per 100,000 females (Brandon, Sidebotham, Bailey et al., 2013). One contrary finding is the presence in some countries, notably in Asia, for an excess of neonatal and early infant deaths in girls, where concerns are raised that this may reflect a lower societal value placed on female offspring (Sahni, Verma, Narula et al., 2008).

Temperament and behaviour It has been postulated that infant crying is an important trigger for fatal child maltreatment, particularly through shaking injuries. The evidence for this is limited, but, at least anecdotally, crying has been reported to be a trigger for parental shaking of infants in up to 28% of cases (Adamsbaum, Grabar, Mejean & Rey-Salmon, 2010; Lee, Barr, Catherine & Wicks, 2007). For example, a French study of 112 convicted perpetrators of abusive head trauma explored in detail the statements of 29 perpetrators (26%) who had confessed to violence toward their child (Adamsbaum, Grabar, Mejean & Rey-Salmon, 2010). The authors comment, 'all of the perpetrators who confessed described a violent and inappropriate attack that resulted from fatigue and irritation connected with the infant's crying' (ibid., p. 553).

In a population study of parental responses to infant crying in the Netherlands, Reijneveld, van der Wal, Brugman et al. (2004) found that nearly 6% of parents reported having used smothering, slapping or shaking to stop their infant crying in the first six months of life, emphasising that these behaviours are used and have the potential to harm infants. These researchers identified that use of potentially harmful behaviours seemed more related to parental perceptions of crying, rather than more objective measures of the amount of infant crying, and that other background factors including family composition, ethnicity and unemployment also influenced the risks. While there are limitations to the interpretation of self-reporting of shaking incidents by presumed perpetrators, it is plausible to postulate that crying serves as a trigger in at least a proportion of such fatalities. The management of persistent crying in babies, and parental education and support for coping with infant crying, may therefore be important preventative strategies for this subgroup of maltreatment fatalities.

Disability In spite of limitations posed by the paucity and quality of research, there is now substantial evidence that disabled children are at higher risk of maltreatment and other forms of violence than their non-disabled peers (Govindshenoy & Spencer, 2007; Jones, Bellis, Wood et al., 2012; Stalker & McArthur, 2012; Sullivan & Knutson, 2000; Sullivan, 2009). The extent of fatal maltreatment among disabled children is not, however, known. Data from a review of 178 English Serious Case Reviews from 2009–2011 (118 deaths, 60 serious injuries) identified 21 cases (12%) with recorded disability (Brandon, Sidebotham, Bailey et al., 2013). There has been one published study of filicide–suicide involving disabled children (Coorg & Tournay, 2013). This study was based on a review of news articles from the USA between 1982 and 2010, and identified 21 cases involving 22 children. The authors postulate a number of factors which may put disabled children at higher risk, particularly those with autism. These include the feelings of stress or hopelessness engendered by having a disabled child; risks posed by behavioural difficulties in the child; and more general parenting and psychological stress. The absence of any rigorous population-based studies of child maltreatment fatalities in disabled children highlights an important area for research.

Previous maltreatment The extent to which previous maltreatment increases the risk of fatal maltreatment is clearly important as this has a bearing on secondary prevention in children identified as having suffered abuse or neglect. Data from England consistently show that around 20–30% of children subject to a Serious Case Review were either currently, or had previously been, on a child protection plan (Brandon, Bailey, Belderson et al., 2009; Brandon, Sidebotham, et al., 2013). These proportions are in keeping with those found elsewhere; for example, a case records review in Kansas found 32% of cases had evidence of prior child protection services involvement for the child or a sibling (Kajese, Nguyen, Pham et al., 2011).

There is some evidence that children who have been identified as having been maltreated are at greater risk of death, and particularly of fatal maltreatment; the evidence, however, is not consistent. There are at least four longitudinal studies which suggest an increased mortality risk in those with prior identified maltreatment (Table 4.4 provides a summary of their findings)

Table 4.4 Longitudinal studies of mortality risk in populations of maltreated children.

Study	Population	Overall mortality risk	Fatal maltreatment risk
Barth & Blackwell, 1998	233,000 children in foster care in California, 1988–1994. Death rates for 690 children who died while in foster care; 321 former foster care children and general child population	Deaths from natural causes: Foster care = 46.0 per 100,000 (95% CI, 39.9–52.1) Control = 18.7 (18.3–19.0) Deaths from accidents: Foster care = 15.6 (12.1–19.1) Control = 15.8 (15.5–16.2) Deaths from SIDS/ill-defined: Foster care = 31.6 (26.6–36.7) Control = 9.2 (9.0–9.5)	Violent deaths: Foster care = 16.6 per 100,000 (95% CI, 13.0–20.3) Controls = 9.5 (9.2–9.8)
Jonson-Reid, Chance & Drake, 2007	7,433 children in receipt of Aid to Families with Dependent Children, 1993–1994. Children reported for maltreatment matched with control children. 29 deaths in subsequent 7.5 years, or to age 18	Overall mortality = 0.51% in maltreated group; 0.27% in non-maltreated	Insufficient numbers to draw conclusions
Putnam-Hornstein, 2011; Putnam-Hornstein, Cleves, Licht & Needell, 2013	Record linkage study of 4,317,321 live births, California, 1999–2006. 514,232 children referred to CPS for maltreatment before age 5. 1,917 injury deaths (392 in the maltreatment group) controlled for socio-demographic variables	Hazard ratio for injury deaths 2.59 (95% CI, 2.27–2.97) Higher risks of unintentional injury in children previously referred for neglect	Hazard ratio for intentional injury deaths 5.86 (95% CI, 4.39–7.81) Higher risks of intentional injury for children previously referred for physical abuse
Sabotta & Davies, 1992	11,085 children reported to Washington State child abuse registry from 1973–1986, matched population of non-abused children. Identified deaths up to age 18. 61 deaths in abused cohort; 63 deaths in controls	Fatality rate for abused children = 9.1 deaths per 100,000 years of risk; control population = 3.1; relative risk = 2.9, 95% CI, 2.1–4.1 Higher risks for physical abuse compared to neglect or sexual abuse	Relative risk 18.0 (95% CI, 4.0–80.6)
White & Widom, 2003	908 abused/neglected children from 1967–1971 compared to 667 matched controls; followed to 1994 (52 deaths)	No significant differences in overall mortality (3.5% maltreated group; 3.0% controls) Relative risk = 1.17 (95% CI, 0.26–5.31)	No significant difference in violent deaths (RR = 0.44; 95% CI, 0.11–1.84)

(Barth & Blackwell, 1998; Jonson-Reid, Chance & Drake, 2007; Putnam-Hornstein, 2011; Putnam-Hornstein, Cleves, Licht & Needell, 2013; Sabotta & Davis, 1992). In contrast, one longitudinal study by White and Widom (2003) did not show any increased risk. Overall, these studies suggest there is an increased risk of fatality from all causes, particularly injury deaths and fatal maltreatment, but that the mortality rates remain low even in this high-risk group. There is currently little robust evidence from which to draw conclusions about what features within the previously maltreated group increase their risk, and what interventions with this group might help prevent subsequent fatalities.

Parent/carer characteristics

Three parental factors stand out in studies of fatal maltreatment: mental ill-health; alcohol/ substance misuse; and domestic violence. Of 72 fatal cases of child maltreatment in England from 2009–2011, 64% had evidence of parental mental health problems; 49% alcohol or substance misuse; and 64% domestic violence (Brandon, Sidebotham, Bailey et al., 2013). Co-morbidity plays a role for some: 92% had at least one of these factors present, with 43% having two or more and 25% all three (Figure 4.2).

One difficulty in interpreting data from observational studies is that there are rarely comparable control or population data to draw on to judge the likely impact of these factors. In a helpful summary of the research evidence around these three factors, Cleaver and colleagues draw on general population studies in the UK to provide some comparative data (Cleaver, Unell & Aldgate, 1999). Their estimates are summarised in Table 4.5, together with data from fatal maltreatment cases in Brandon's study of Serious Case Reviews (Brandon, Sidebotham, Bailey et al., 2013; Christoffel, Liu & Stamler, 1999). These data indicate that parental mental ill-health, alcohol or substance misuse and domestic violence are all more prevalent in families where there is evidence of child maltreatment, compared to the general population, and even more so in those where there is fatal maltreatment. This is an area where further research is needed to determine the extent of cumulative risks with all three factors and of how these interact with other risk or protective factors. One important rider on our interpretation of these data is that while each of these factors increases the risks of both non-fatal and fatal maltreatment, the majority of children living with parental mental ill-health or substance misuse issues do not experience maltreatment.

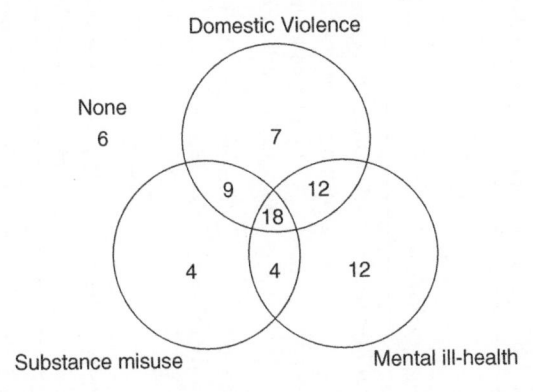

Figure 4.2 Parental characteristics of fatal maltreatment cases in England, 2009–2011 (N=72) (adapted from Brandon, Sidebotham, Bailey et al., 2013).

Table 4.5 Prevalence of parental mental ill-health, substance misuse and domestic violence and child protection concerns.

Parental problems	General population	Referral to children's social care	First enquiry or initial assessment	Child protection conference	Care proceedings	Fatal maltreatment
Mental ill-health	2.5–8.8% of the general adult population suffer from anxiety or depression 15.5% of couples living with children and 28% of lone parents suffer from neurotic disorders	10.4%	16.8%	25%	42%	64%
Alcohol or substance misuse	7% of men and 5% of women are considered higher-risk drinkers 22% of men and 15% of women binge drink 9% of adults have tried an illegal drug in the past year	5.8%	11.4%	25%	23%	49%
Domestic violence	7% of women and 4% of men report experiencing domestic violence within the past year	4.8%	16.7%	55%	51%	64%

Source: Adapted from Brandon 2013 and Cleaver 1999.

Mental ill-health may be a particular issue in the more deliberate overt and covert homicides, particularly for mothers (Friedman, Hrouda, Holden et al., 2005; Kauppi, Kumpulainen, Vanamo et al., 2008; Lewis & Bunce, 2003). While questions have been raised about the clinical utility of the concept of infanticide, there are risks to young infants of mothers who are suffering from severe depression or other mental illness, particularly where these are accompanied by suicidal ideation, psychotic thoughts or hallucinations (Friedman, Hrouda, Holden et al., 2005; Kauppi et al., 2008; Lewis & Bunce, 2003). One specific extension of this is a group of filicides characterised as 'altruistic filicides' (Resnick, 1969). A helpful qualitative study of seven women perpetrators identified that these women did not harbour malicious thoughts toward their children, but rather had distorted perceptions of mothering (Stanton, Simpson & Wouldes, 2000). Their findings suggest that, in the context of severe mental illness, the emotional investment of these women in their children may actually increase the risks, so that apparently strong attachments and good parenting are no longer protective factors.

Intergenerational cycles In 1983, Dr J.E. Oliver, a psychiatrist in England, reported on a cohort of 560 children from 147 families in which child maltreatment was known to have occurred over at least two generations (Oliver, 1983). Of these children, 513 were known to have suffered maltreatment and 41 had died before their eighth birthday. This paper and others in the 1970s and 1980s highlighted what has come to be known as the intergenerational cycle of maltreatment (Buchanan, 1996). Although not without controversy, there is considerable evidence that a proportion of parents who suffered maltreatment as children will go on to abuse or neglect their children (Egeland, 1993; Kaufman & Zigler, 1987, 1993).

It is difficult to ascertain from the literature what proportion of parents responsible for child maltreatment fatalities were themselves maltreated as children. Cavanagh, Dobash and Dobash (2007) found that 22% of 26 male perpetrators of child homicide had been physically abused in their childhood, while Lucas, Wezner, Milner et al. (2002) found a similar incidence (23%) in perpetrators of infant homicide, but lower rates in perpetrators of older child homicides. While retrospective studies suggest that a significant proportion of perpetrators of fatal child maltreatment will have experienced maltreatment in their own childhood, it is equally clear that the majority of those experiencing child maltreatment will not go on to perpetrate fatalities. It is likely that other risk factors in the personal histories, family and environment serve a more important role in compounding any effect of childhood abuse (Buchanan, 1996; Korbin, 1986).

Family and environmental characteristics

While child maltreatment occurs across all cultural and socio-economic groups, there is some suggestion of a socio-economic gradient (Rangel, Burd, Falcone & Multicenter Child Abuse Disparity, 2010). Surprisingly though, there has been very little epidemiological research taking account of socio-economic variables in relation to fatal maltreatment.

Studies from the USA have consistently shown higher rates in African-American and Hispanic families, a finding that is likely to be, at least in part, mediated by the lower socio-economic conditions of these communities (Bennett, Hall, Frazier et al., 2006; Klevens & Leeb, 2010; Lee & Lathrop, 2010; Lucas, Wezner, Milner et al., 2002). One study in nine paediatric trauma centres in the USA found that children admitted with abusive injuries had a

3.8 times greater odds of dying of their injuries if they did not have private insurance; those in the lower income quartiles had a higher fatality rate even after controlling for race, and race was not an independent predictor of mortality (Rangel, Burd, Falcone & Multicenter Child Abuse Disparity, 2010).

Other family and environmental factors have been identified frequently in studies of serious and fatal maltreatment, including young parental (particularly maternal) age and large family size (Brandon, Bailey & Belderson, 2010; Brandon, Sidebotham, Bailey et al., 2013; Luke & Brown, 2007). Cavanagh and colleagues, in a study of fathers convicted of murdering their children, concluded that these were predominantly undereducated and underemployed men with significant criminal histories (Cavanagh, Dobash & Dobash, 2007). Their findings may, however, only apply to a subgroup of fatal child maltreatment, those cases resulting from impulsive violent outbursts. In a comparison of fatal and non-fatal child maltreatment cases in the US, Douglas and Mohn (2014) found a high degree of financial and housing instability in the fatal group compared to the non-fatal cases. They also identified that the families of the fatal cases had received fewer social services than those whose children did not die.

A number of studies have identified that family stability offers some protection against fatal maltreatment, with a predominance in fatal cases of single parents, or prior family breakdown (Lucas, Wezner, Milner et al., 2002; Lyman, McGwin, Malone et al., 2003). Data from the Missouri child fatality review programme, however, suggest that children of single parents are not at greater risk, while those living in homes with non-related adults are (Schnitzer & Ewigman, 2005, 2008). In most of these cases, the perpetrator is the unrelated adult member of the household.

One consistent finding across all studies is that fatal child maltreatment is mainly perpetrated by parents or parental figures (Bennett, Hall, Frazier et al., 2006; Fujiwara, Barber, Schaechter, & Hemenway, 2009; Kajese, Nguyen, Pham et al., 2011; Klevens & Leeb, 2010; Lee & Lathrop, 2010; Lucas, Wezner, Milner et al., 2002; Lyman, McGwin, Malone et al., 2003; Makhlouf & Rambaud, 2014). There is a difference, however, in relation to the type of fatal maltreatment: deaths from abusive head trauma and other severe injuries most commonly occur at the hands of fathers or father figures; more deliberate overt or covert homicides may be perpetrated by mothers or fathers/father figures, with perhaps a greater frequency among mothers of very young infants; neglect-related deaths are mostly attributed to the mother, or jointly to both parents (Fujiwara, Barber, Schaechter & Hemenway, 2009; Klevens & Leeb, 2010; Knight & Collins, 2005; Makhlouf & Rambaud, 2014).

Learning from Child Maltreatment Fatalities

There has been a long history in the UK and elsewhere of reviewing child maltreatment fatalities in order to learn lessons for child protection practice (Brandon, Bailey & Belderson, 2010; Brandon, Belderson, Warren et al., 2008; Brandon, Sidebotham, Bailey et al., 2013; Reder & Duncan, 1999; Reder, Duncan & Gray, 1993; Rose, 2009; Rose & Barnes, 2008; Sinclair & Bullock, 2002). A number of themes relating to professional practice come up repeatedly in these Serious Case Reviews (Table 4.6). These highlight important learning, but should not be seen as being specific to the prevention of child maltreatment fatalities. The issues relate equally to all professional practice to safeguard children. The most consistent themes cluster around how we as professionals perceive and relate to children and families; inter-professional communication; and decision-making and reflective practice.

Numerous Serious Case Reviews have highlighted the apparent 'invisibility' of children. Professionals, perhaps not wanting to acknowledge the reality of the abuse children suffer, too often fail to consider what a child's life is really like. There is a danger of focusing too much

Table 4.6 Learning from Serious Case Reviews: Issues for professional practice.

Theme	Issues identified
The invisible child	Children are not seen or their voices not heard in assessment processes. Professionals fail to take account of the child's perspective.
Relations with families	Hostile and non-cooperative families are difficult to work with and professionals may avoid engagement with them. Disguised compliance – parents who appear to engage and cooperate, but hide ongoing harmful behaviours.
Exclusion of fathers	Limited assessment of the role or status of fathers in considering risks to children; most social care involvement centres around the mothers.
Inter-agency cooperation	Limited inter-agency cooperation and lack of service integration, especially between child and adult services. Individuals working within their own 'professional silos'. Failure of professionals to look at aspects of the children's needs outside of their own specific brief.
Thresholds	Different professionals and agencies may have different perceptions of the thresholds at which intervention is required; services may not be offered if a child or family is perceived not to reach a particular threshold.
Communication	Poor communication both between agencies and within agencies. Individual professionals failing to share with others information which may help to identify or understand risk. Different interpretation of language being a barrier to understanding or cooperation.
Interpretation and decision-making	Too high an emphasis on gathering information, with a failure to interpret or reflect on the information gathered. Lack of professional confidence; professional uncertainty in decision-making.
Recording	Poor recording of information and decision-making.
Taking responsibility	Each individual taking responsibility for protecting children; not 'passing the buck' or assuming others will take responsibility. Failure to challenge other professionals or escalate concerns.
Disjointed practice	Mirroring of behaviour in the family and in the agency responses – chaotic families with multiple problems, parents who feel overwhelmed, the child's needs get lost; this context is mirrored in the responses of professionals who also feel overwhelmed and respond in a chaotic, disordered way in which the child's needs get lost.
'Fixed thinking'	Previous assessments or categorisation of cases influencing professionals' decision-making about new findings; for example, through neglect being perceived as low-level, long-term risk and masking more acute risks to a child's immediate safety; or the concept of 'rough handling' downplaying risks to young infants. Failure to rethink a case if the findings do not fit previous theories.
'Start-again syndrome'	The tendency, when confronted with a new issue, to forget or ignore previous concerns, so underestimating cumulative risks of harm.
The 'rule of optimism'	Efforts not to be judgemental becoming failure to exercise professional judgement – professionals are typically reluctant to pass negative judgements on parents, but this can lead to a failure to then judge the situation and adequately appraise risk to the child.

Source: Sidebotham 2012. Reproduced with permission of BMJ Publishing Group Ltd.

on procedures, or in working to support families, while losing sight of the ongoing harm a child is suffering. This may be exacerbated when working with hostile or resistant families, where we, as professionals, may also feel intimidated (Tuck, 2013). In contrast, when parents appear to cooperate, even if this is only partial, our tendency is to think the best of them, and fail to recognise when change is not happening or unlikely to happen. Another issue that comes up repeatedly in these reviews is the invisibility of fathers and other adult males in case working. While it has been identified that in many fatalities it is a father or father figure who is the perpetrator, most work with families focuses on the mother, and often any partners are ignored.

Perhaps the most prominent issue is that of communication. Many professionals struggle with issues of consent and confidentiality when it comes to sharing information with others. Nevertheless, full and frank sharing of information is essential to building an understanding of the context of children's lives and possible harm they may be suffering. Numerous Serious Case Reviews identify instances where professionals have withheld information known to them and this has contributed to failures in adequately protecting children. Such inter-professional communication may be influenced by a lack of knowledge of the work of other professionals, mistrust of colleagues or of the system for protecting children, use of different language within different agencies, and different concepts of thresholds for intervention.

A final set of issues arising frequently in Serious Case Reviews is around professional decision-making and reflective practice. Child protection systems have been criticised for being bureaucratised, with professionals focusing too much on complying with procedures, gathering information and completing assessments, without stopping to process the information received, or to think about the case (Munro, 2010, 2011).

Preventing Child Maltreatment Fatalities

In light of what we understand about child maltreatment fatalities and the research literature on the nature and characteristics of these deaths, what can we learn in relation to prevention?

The limitations of the research base in this field mean that it is not possible, with any certainty, to predict those children who are most at risk of death, over and above those at more general risk of harm. Indeed, predictive tools for maltreatment risk generally have very poor accuracy (Barlow & Scott, 2010). Most of the risk factors for fatal maltreatment will apply equally to non-fatal maltreatment. This argues for a strong public health approach to preventing all child maltreatment: by taking steps to reduce harm to children at all levels, we are likely to shift the curve of severity of harm and therefore also reduce the numbers experiencing the most severe harm (Barlow & Calam, 2011).

In keeping with this public health approach, there is some limited evidence of specific interventions which have been shown to be effective in reducing harmful behaviours and, as such, may be effective in reducing fatalities.

Probably the most effective prevention campaigns have been those focused around reducing fatalities from shaken baby syndrome. There is some evidence that interventions such as the Period of PURPLE Crying Program can improve parental awareness of the dangers of shaking, and of strategies for dealing with infant crying (Barr, Barr, Fujiwara et al., 2009; Barr, Rivara, Barr et al., 2009; Fujiwara, Yamada, Okuyama et al., 2012). Time trend data from New York State before and after the introduction of a comprehensive regional parental education programme demonstrated a 47% decrease in the incidence of abusive head trauma (Dias, Smith, DeGuehery et al., 2005).

One preventative initiative aimed specifically at reducing maltreatment fatality that has been adopted widely in the US and elsewhere is the use of 'safe haven' laws, which allow parents to leave unwanted infants at a designated place without fear of criminal prosecution. It has been reported that by 2002, 42 states in the US had adopted such laws (Herman-Giddens, Smith, Mittal et al., 2003). Similar approaches have been adopted in Europe through 'anonymous delivery' and 'baby hatches' (Klier, Grylli, Amon et al., 2013). While these have been argued to provide an alternative to infant abandonment, there is limited evidence that they actually reduce infant mortality from abandonment, and their use has been subject to much debate (Asai & Ishimoto, 2013; Pruitt, 2008; Sanger, 2006).

In the absence of evidence to support any wider initiatives to specifically predict or prevent fatal maltreatment, the emphasis in prevention must surely be on a broader public health approach. Fatal child maltreatment represents the tip of a pyramid. While every effort must be made to learn lessons and prevent such fatalities, the numbers are small in comparison to those children who experience and live with the consequences of lower levels of maltreatment from day to day. The evidence on risk factors outlined above and an understanding of the different nature of different forms of fatal maltreatment provides a base for working with high-risk families. Much more could be done to support families, and to identify and intervene with those most at risk, but further research is needed to inform this, and in particular to evaluate programmes purporting to reduce the risks of fatal maltreatment.

References

Adamsbaum, C., Grabar, S., Mejean, N. & Rey-Salmon, C. (2010). Abusive head trauma: Judicial admissions highlight violent and repetitive shaking. *Pediatrics*, 126, 546–555.

Asai, A. & Ishimoto, H. (2013). Should we maintain baby hatches in our society? *BMC Med Ethics*, 14(9).

Bajanowski, T., Vennemann, M., Bohnert, M. et al. (2005). Unnatural causes of sudden unexpected deaths initially thought to be sudden infant death syndrome. *International Journal of Legal Medicine*, 119, 213–216.

Barlow, J. & Calam, R. (2011). A public health approach to safeguarding in the 21st century. *Child Abuse Review*, 20, 238–255.

Barlow, J. & Scott, J. (2010). *Safeguarding in the 21st century: Where to now*. Totnes: Research in Practice.

Barr, R.G., Barr, M., Fujiwara, T. et al. (2009). Do educational materials change knowledge and behaviour about crying and shaken baby syndrome? A randomized controlled trial. *CMAJ Canadian Medical Association Journal*, 180, 727–733.

Barr, R.G., Rivara, F.P., Barr, M. et al. (2009). Effectiveness of educational materials designed to change knowledge and behaviors regarding crying and shaken-baby syndrome in mothers of newborns: a randomized, controlled trial. *Pediatrics*, 123, 972–980.

Barth, R. & Blackwell, D. (1998). Death rates among California's foster care and former foster care populations. *Children and Youth Services Review*, 20, 577–604.

Bennett, M.D., Jr., Hall, J., Frazier, L. et al. (2006). Homicide of children aged 0–4 years, 2003–04: results from the National Violent Death Reporting System. *Injury Prevention*, 12 Suppl 2, ii39–ii43.

Borowsky, I.W., Resnick, M.D., Ireland, M. & Blum, R.W. (1999). Suicide attempts among American Indian and Alaska Native youth: risk and protective factors. *Archives of Pediatric and Adolescent Medicine*, 153, 573–580.

Bourget, D. & Gagne, P. (2002). Maternal filicide in Quebec. *Journal of the American Academy of Psychiatry and the Law*, 30, 345–351.

Bourget, D. & Gagne, P. (2005). Paternal filicide in Quebec. *Journal of the American Academy of Psychiatry and the Law*, 33, 354–360.

Brandon, M., Bailey, S. & Belderson, P. (2010). *Building on the learning from serious case reviews: A two-year analysis of child protection database notifications 2007–2009.* London: Department for Education.

Brandon, M., Bailey, S., Belderson, P. & Larsson, B. (2013). *Neglect and Serious Case Reviews.* London: NSPCC.

Brandon, M., Bailey, S., Belderson, P. et al. (2009). *Understanding serious case reviews and their impact. A biennial analysis of serious case reviews 2005–07.* London: Department for Children, Schools and Families.

Brandon, M., Belderson, P., Warren, C. et al. (2008). *Analysing child deaths and serious injury through abuse and neglect: What can we learn? A biennial analysis of serious case reviews 2003–2005.* London: Department for Children Schools and Families.

Brandon, M., Sidebotham, P., Bailey, S. et al. (2013). *New learning from serious case reviews: A two-year report for 2009–2011 (vol. DFE-RR226).* London: Department for Education.

Buchanan, A. (1996). *Cycles of child maltreatment: Facts, falacies and interventions.* Chichester: John Wiley & Sons, Ltd.

Carcach, C. (1997). *Youth as Victims and Offenders of Homicide* (vol. 73). Canberra, Australia: Australian Institute of Criminology.

Cavanagh, K., Dobash, R.E. & Dobash, R.P. (2007). The murder of children by fathers in the context of child abuse. *Child Abuse & Neglect*, 31, 731–746.

Choquet, M., Darves-Bornoz, J. M., Ledoux, S. et al. (1997). Self-reported health and behavioral problems among adolescent victims of rape in France: Results of a cross-sectional survey. *Child Abuse & Neglect*, 21, 823–832.

Christoffel, K.K. (1984). Homicide in childhood: A public health problem in need of attention. *American Journal of Public Health*, 74, 68–70.

Christoffel, K.K. & Liu, K. (1983). Homicide death rates in childhood in 23 developed countries: U.S. rates atypically high. *Child Abuse & Neglect*, 7, 339–345.

Christoffel, K.K., Liu, K. & Stamler, J. (1981). Epidemiology of fatal child abuse: International mortality data. *Journal of Chronic Diseases*, 34, 57–64.

Cleaver, H., Unell, J. & Aldgate, J. (1999). *Children's needs – parenting capacity: The impact of parental mental illness, problem alcohol and drug use, and domestic violence on children's development.* London: The Stationery Office.

Coorg, R. & Tournay, A. (2013). Filicide–suicide involving children with disabilities. *Journal of Child Neurology*, 28, 745–751.

Crume, T.L., DiGuiseppi, C., Byers, T. et al. (2002). Underascertainment of child maltreatment fatalities by death certificates, 1990–1998. *Pediatrics*, 110(2 Pt 1), e18.

Dias, M.S., Smith, K., DeGuehery, K. et al. (2005). Preventing abusive head trauma among infants and young children: A hospital-based parent education program. *Pediatrics*, 115, e470–477.

Douglas, E.M. & Mohn, B.L. (2014). Fatal and non-fatal child maltreatment in the US: An analysis of child, caregiver, and service utilization with the National Child Abuse & Neglect Data Set. *Child Abuse & Neglect*, 38, 42–51.

Egeland, B. (1993). A history of abuse is a major risk factor for abusing the next generation. In: R.J. Gelles & D. Loseke (eds), *Current Controversies on Family Violence.* Newbury Park, CA: Sage.

Evans, E., Hawton, K. & Rodham, K. (2004). Factors associated with suicidal phenomena in adolescents: A systematic review of population-based studies. *Clinical Psychology Review*, 24, 957–979.

Frederick, J., Goddard, C. & Oxley, J. (2013). What is the 'dark figure' of child homicide and how can it be addressed in Australia? *International Journal of Injury Control & Safety Promotion*, 20, 209–217.

Friedman, S.H., Hrouda, D.R., Holden, C.E. et al. (2005). Child murder committed by severely mentally ill mothers: An examination of mothers found not guilty by reason of insanity. 2005 Honorable

Mention/Richard Rosner Award for the best paper by a fellow in forensic psychiatry or forensic psychology. *Journal of Forensic Sciences*, 50, 1466–1471.

Fujiwara, T., Barber, C., Schaechter, J. & Hemenway, D. (2009). Characteristics of infant homicides: Findings from a U.S. multisite reporting system. *Pediatrics*, 124, e210–217.

Fujiwara, T., Yamada, F., Okuyama, M. et al. (2012). Effectiveness of educational materials designed to change knowledge and behavior about crying and shaken baby syndrome: A replication of a randomized controlled trial in Japan. *Child Abuse & Neglect*, 36, 613–620.

Gilbert, R., Fluke, J., O'Donnell, M. et al. (2012). Child maltreatment: variation in trends and policies in six developed countries. *The Lancet*, 379(9817), 758–772.

Govindshenoy, M. & Spencer, N. (2007). Abuse of the disabled child: A systematic review of population-based studies. *Child: Care, Health and Development*, 33, 552–558.

Grossman, D.C., Milligan, B.C. & Deyo, R.A. (1991). Risk factors for suicide attempts among Navajo adolescents. *American Journal of Public Health*, 81, 870–874.

Hawton, K., Saunders, K.E. & O'Connor, R.C. (2012). Self-harm and suicide in adolescents. *The Lancet*, 379(9834), 2373–2382.

Herman-Giddens, M.E., Brown, G., Verbiest, S. et al. (1999). Underascertainment of child abuse mortality in the United States. *JAMA*, 282, 463–467.

Herman-Giddens, M.E., Smith, J.B., Mittal, M. et al. (2003). Newborns killed or left to die by a parent: A population-based study. *JAMA*, 289, 1425–1429.

Jenny, C. (2007). Recognizing and responding to medical neglect. *Pediatrics*, 120(6), 1385–1389.

Jenny, C. & Isaac, R. (2006). The relation between child death and child maltreatment. *Archives of Disease in Childhood*, 91, 265–269.

Jones, L., Bellis, M. A., Wood, S. et al. (2012). Prevalence and risk of violence against children with disabilities: A systematic review and meta-analysis of observational studies. *The Lancet*, 380(9845), 899–907.

Jonson-Reid, M., Chance, T. & Drake, B. (2007). Risk of death among children reported for nonfatal maltreatment. [Erratum appears in *Child Maltreatment* 2007 May;12(2):199]. *Child Maltreatment*, 12, 86–95.

Kajese, T.M., Nguyen, L.T., Pham, G.Q. et al. (2011). Characteristics of child abuse homicides in the state of Kansas from 1994 to 2007. *Child Abuse & Neglect*, 35, 147–154.

Kaufman, J. & Zigler, E. (1987). Do abused children become abusive parents? *American Journal of Orthopsychiatry*, 57, 186–192.

Kaufman, J. & Zigler, E. (1993). The intergenerational transmission of abuse is overstated. In R.J. Gelles & D. Loseke (eds), *Current Controversies on Family Violence* (209–221). Newbury Park, CA: Sage.

Kauppi, A., Kumpulainen, K., Vanamo, T. et al. (2008). Maternal depression and filicide–Case study of ten mothers. *Archives of Women's Mental Health*, 11, 201–206.

Klevens, J. & Leeb, R.T. (2010). Child maltreatment fatalities in children under 5: Findings from the National Violence Death Reporting System. *Child Abuse & Neglect*, 34, 262–266.

Klier, C., Grylli, C., Amon, S. et al. (2013). Is the introduction of anonymous delivery associated with a reduction of high neonaticide rates in Austria? Authors' reply. *BJOG: An International Journal of Obstetrics & Gynaecology*, 120, 1028–1029.

Knight, L.D. & Collins, K.A. (2005). A 25-year retrospective review of deaths due to pediatric neglect. *American Journal of Forensic Medicine & Pathology*, 26, 221–228.

Korbin, J. (1986). Childhood histories of women imprisoned for fatal child maltreatment. *Child Abuse & Neglect*, 10, 331–338.

Krug, E.G. (2002). *World report on violence and health*. Geneva: World Health Organization.

Lee, C.K. & Lathrop, S.L. (2010). Child abuse-related homicides in New Mexico: A 6-year retrospective review. *Journal of Forensic Sciences*, 55, 100–103.

Lee, C., Barr, R.G., Catherine, N. & Wicks, A. (2007). Age-related incidence of publicly reported shaken baby syndrome cases: Is crying a trigger for shaking? *Journal of Developmental & Behavioural Pediatrics*, 28, 288–293.

Lewis, C.F. & Bunce, S.C. (2003). Filicidal mothers and the impact of psychosis on maternal filicide. *Journal of the American Academy of Psychiatry & the Law*, 31, 459–470.

Liem, M. & Koenraadt, F. (2008). Familicide: A comparison with spousal and child homicide by mentally disordered perpetrators. *Criminal Behaviour and Mental Health*, 18, 306–318.

Liem, M., Levin, J., Holland, C. & Fox, J. (2013). The nature and prevalence of familicide in the United States, 2000–2009. *Journal of Family Violence*.

Lucas, D.R., Wezner, K.C., Milner, J.S. et al. (2002). Victim, perpetrator, family, and incident characteristics of infant and child homicide in the United States Air Force. *Child Abuse & Neglect*, 26, 167–186.

Luke, B. & Brown, M.B. (2007). Maternal risk factors for potential maltreatment deaths among healthy singleton and twin infants. *Twin Research & Human Genetics: The Official Journal of the International Society for Twin Studies*, 10, 778–785.

Lyman, J.M., McGwin, G., Jr., Malone, D.E. et al. (2003). Epidemiology of child homicide in Jefferson County, Alabama. *Child Abuse & Neglect*, 27, 1063–1073.

Makhlouf, F. & Rambaud, C. (2014). Child homicide and neglect in France: 1991–2008. *Child Abuse & Neglect*, 38, 37–41.

Maniglio, R. (2011). The role of child sexual abuse in the etiology of suicide and non-suicidal self-injury. *Acta Psychiatrica Scandinavica*, 124, 30–41.

Mathews, S., Abrahams, N., Jewkes, R. et al. (2013). The epidemiology of child homicides in South Africa. *Bulletin of the World Health Organization*, 91, 562–568.

Meltzer, H., Vostanis, P., Ford, T. et al. (2011). Victims of bullying in childhood and suicide attempts in adulthood. *European Psychiatry*, 26, 498–503.

Munro, E. (2010). *The Munro review of child protection part one: A systems analysis*. London: Department for Education.

Munro, E. (2011). *The Munro review of child protection: Final report – a child-centred system*. London: Department for Education.

Oliver, J. (1983). Dead children from problem families in NE Wiltshire. *BMJ*, 286, 115–117.

Palusci, V.J., Wirtz, S.J. & Covington, T.M. (2010). Using capture-recapture methods to better ascertain the incidence of fatal child maltreatment. *Child Abuse & Neglect*, 34, 396–402.

Pinheiro, P. (2006). *World report on violence against children*. Geneva: United Nations.

Pruitt, S.L. (2008). The number of illegally abandoned and legally surrendered newborns in the state of Texas, estimated from news stories, 1996–2006. *Child Maltreatment*, 13, 89–93.

Putnam-Hornstein, E. (2011). Report of maltreatment as a risk factor for injury death: A prospective birth cohort study. *Child Maltreatment*, 16, 163–174.

Putnam-Hornstein, E., Cleves, M.A., Licht, R. & Needell, B. (2013). Risk of fatal injury in young children following abuse allegations: Evidence from a prospective, population-based study. *American Journal of Public Health*, 103(10), e39–44.

Rangel, E.L., Burd, R.S., Falcone, R.A., Jr. & Multicenter Child Abuse Disparity, G. (2010). Socioeconomic disparities in infant mortality after nonaccidental trauma: A multicenter study. *Journal of Trauma-Injury Infection & Critical Care*, 69, 20–25.

Reder, P. & Duncan, S. (1999). *Lost Innocents: A Follow-Up Study of Fatal Child Abuse*. London: Routledge.

Reder, P., Duncan, S. & Gray, M. (1993). *Beyond Blame: Child Abuse Tragedies Revisited*. London: Routledge.

Reijneveld, S.A., van der Wal, M.F., Brugman, E. et al. (2004). Infant crying and abuse. *The Lancet*, 364(9442), 1340–1342.

Resnick, P.J. (1969). Child murder by parents: A psychiatric review of filicide. *American Journal of Psychiatry*, 126, 325–334.

Rey Gex, C., Narring, F., Ferron, C. & Michaud, P.A. (1998). Suicide attempts among adolescents in Switzerland: Prevalence, associated factors and comorbidity. *Acta Psychiatrica Scandinavica*, 98, 28–33.

Richardson, E.G. & Hemenway, D. (2011). Homicide, suicide, and unintentional firearm fatality: comparing the United States with other high-income countries, 2003. *Journal of Trauma-Injury Infection & Critical Care*, 70, 238–243.

Riggs, J.E. & Hobbs, G.R. (2011). Infant homicide and accidental death in the United States, 1940–2005: Ethics and epidemiological classification. *Journal of Medical Ethics*, 37, 445–448.

Rose, W. (2009). *Improving practice to protect children in Wales: An examination of the role of serious case reviews*. Care and Social Services Inspectorate, Wales.

Rose, W. & Barnes, J. (2008). *Improving safeguarding practice: Study of serious case reviews 2001–2003*. London: Department for Children, Schools and Families.

Sabotta, E.E. & Davis, R.L. (1992). Fatality after report to a child abuse registry in Washington State, 1973–1986. *Child Abuse & Neglect*, 16, 627–635.

Sachmann, M. & Harris Johnson, C.M. (2014). The relevance of long-term antecedents in assessing the risk of familicide-suicide following separation. *Child Abuse Review*, 23, 130–141.

Sahni, M., Verma, N., Narula, D. et al. (2008). Missing girls in India: Infanticide, feticide and made-to-order pregnancies? Insights from hospital-based sex-ratio-at-birth over the last century. *PLoS ONE* [Electronic Resource], 3(5), e2224.

Sanger, C. (2006). Infant safe haven laws: Legislating in the culture of life. *Columbia Law Review*, 106, 753–829.

Schnitzer, P.G. & Ewigman, B.G. (2005). Child deaths resulting from inflicted injuries: Household risk factors and perpetrator characteristics. *Pediatrics*, 116(5), e687–693.

Schnitzer, P.G. & Ewigman, B.G. (2008). Household composition and fatal unintentional injuries related to child maltreatment. *Journal of Nursing Scholarship*, 40, 91–97.

Schnitzer, P.G., Gulino, S.P. & Yuan, Y.Y. (2013). Advancing public health surveillance to estimate child maltreatment fatalities: Review and recommendations. *Child Welfare*, 92, 77–98.

Seguin, M., Renaud, J., Lesage, A. et al. (2011). Youth and young adult suicide: A study of life trajectory. *Journal of Psychiatric Research*, 45, 863–870.

Sidebotham, P. (2012). What do serious case reviews achieve? *Archives of Disease in Childhood*, 97, 189–192.

Sidebotham, P. (2013). Rethinking filicide. *Child Abuse Review*, 22, 305–310.

Sidebotham, P., Atkins, B. & Hutton, J.L. (2012). Changes in rates of violent child deaths in England and Wales between 1974 and 2008: An analysis of national mortality data. *Arch Dis Child*, 97, 193–199.

Sidebotham, P., Bailey, S., Belderson, P. & Brandon, M. (2011). Fatal child maltreatment in England, 2005–2009. *Child Abuse & Neglect*, 35, 299–306.

Sinclair, R. & Bullock, R. (2002). *Learning from past experience: A review of serious case reviews*. London: Department of Health.

Smith, K., Coleman, K., Eder, S. & Hall, P. (2011). *Homicides, Firearm Offences and Intimate Violence 2009/10. Supplementary Volume 2 to Crime in England and Wales 2009/10*, 2nd edn. London: Home Office.

Stalker, K. & McArthur, K. (2012). Child abuse, child protection and disabled children: A review of recent research. *Child Abuse Review*, 21, 24–40.

Stanton, J., Simpson, A. & Wouldes, T. (2000). A qualitative study of filicide by mentally ill mothers. *Child Abuse & Neglect*, 24, 1451–1460.

Sullivan, P.M. (2009). Violence exposure among children with disabilities. *Clinical Child and Family Psychology Review*, 12, 196–216.

Sullivan, P. & Knutson, J. (2000). Maltreatment and disabilities: a population-based epidemiological study. *Child Abuse & Neglect*, 24, 1257–1273.

Tuck, V. (2013). Resistant parents and child protection: Knowledge base, pointers for practice and implications for policy. *Child Abuse Review*, 22, 5–19.

White, H.R. & Widom, C.S. (2003). Does childhood victimization increase the risk of early death? A 25-year prospective study. *Child Abuse & Neglect*, 27, 841–853.

Wilczynski, A. (1994). The incidence of child homicide: How accurate are the official statistics? *Journal of Clinical Forensic Medicine*, 1, 61–66.

Wilczynski, A. (1997). *Child Homicide*. London: Greenwich Medical Media.

Wilson, B. & Smith, H. (2015). Histories in abusive childhood fractures: A case series. *Child Abuse Review*, 24, 16–27.

5

Psychological, Economic and Physical Health Consequences of Child Maltreatment

Sarah A. Font
Pennsylvania State University, USA

The goal of this chapter is to summarise and provide context for the large body of research on child maltreatment, focusing on the best evidence and, where possible, studies that differentiate among various types of abuse and neglect. The chapter first summarises the evidence linking maltreatment to psychological, economic and physical health outcomes and then provides a brief discussion of key issues in maltreatment research that limit scientific knowledge.

Given the varying language used by countries and states to define and categorise maltreatment, it is important to clarify terminology before delving into the research. The basic categories and definitions of maltreatment used in this chapter are summarised in Table 5.1. Although circumstances such as parental drug abuse and domestic violence are sometimes discussed separately from maltreatment, or categorised under a different maltreatment type, this review places such circumstances under the definition of supervision neglect. In addition, emotional abuse and emotional neglect are considered separate forms of maltreatment, whereas they are often combined in legal statutes and research definitions.

Psychological Health

Psychological health includes mental and behavioural well-being. This section includes research on the effects of maltreatment at all stages of life. Notably, the body of research on psychological effects of maltreatment is rather extensive; thus, this section is divided into subsections by maltreatment type.

The Wiley Handbook of What Works in Child Maltreatment: An Evidence-Based Approach to Assessment and Intervention in Child Protection, First Edition. Edited by Louise Dixon, Daniel F. Perkins, Catherine Hamilton-Giachritsis, and Leam A. Craig.
© 2017 John Wiley & Sons Ltd. Published 2017 by John Wiley & Sons Ltd.

Table 5.1 Definitions of maltreatment used in this chapter.

Type	Basic definition
Physical abuse	A non-accidental physical injury to a child.
Sexual abuse	Sexual contact with a minor, or the exploitation of a child through prostitution or child pornography.
Emotional abuse	Injury to the psychological capacity or emotional stability of a child. Also known as mental injury. Usually refers to verbally aggressive, threatening or degrading behaviour toward a child.
Physical neglect	Failure to provide for a child's basic needs, including medical care, food, shelter and clothing.
Supervision neglect	Failure to provide adequate supervision for a child such that a threat of harm is presented. Also includes circumstances where a child is exposed to situations or behaviours that are unsafe, immoral or otherwise inappropriate, such as parental drug abuse, domestic violence or criminal activity.
Emotional neglect	Deprivation of nurturance, stimulation; failure to attend to a child's emotional needs.

Physical abuse

Evidence on the near-term effects of physical abuse consistently suggests sizeable negative impacts on mood and behaviour across multiple countries and populations (Fakunmoju & Bammeke, 2015; Fergusson, Boden & Horwood, 2008; Kim & Cicchetti, 2006; Maas, Herrenkohl & Sousa, 2008; Yen, Yang, Chen et al., 2008). Similarly-sized effects are consistently identified even when including experiences that many would not consider abuse, including frequent or severe corporal punishment (Fergusson, Boden & Horwood, 2008; Font & Berger, 2015; Font, Pettit & Ansari, 2015; Gershoff, 2002). Meta-analyses have also identified relatively major, long-term effects of physical abuse on the risk of various psychological disorders, including anxiety disorders, suicidal behaviour, eating disorders and drug use (Lindert, von Ehrenstein, Grashow et al., 2014; Norman, Byambaa, De et al., 2012).

However, independent effects of physical abuse are difficult to discern because physical abuse often occurs in concert with emotional abuse (Font, Pettit & Ansari, 2015). Additionally, only a few studies have been able to separate possible effects of physical abuse from the effects of related genetic and environmental risk factors, primarily using twin studies or related research designs. Such studies found that associations of physical abuse with cannabis abuse and dependence (Duncan, Sartor, Scherrer et al., 2008), alcohol abuse (Young-Wolff, Kendler, Ericson & Prescott, 2011), problem gambling (Scherrer, Xian, Kapp et al., 2007), and borderline personality traits (Bornovalova, Huibregtse, Hicks et al., 2013) are primarily *not* causal in nature. That is, the associations were primarily explained by heredity or environmental conditions.

Sexual abuse

Evidence on the early effects of sexual abuse is neither as prevalent nor as robust as the evidence for long-term effects (Hillberg, Hamilton-Giachritsis & Dixon, 2011). However, a recent longitudinal study found associations between childhood sexual abuse and the development of depression, anxiety, post-traumatic stress and dissociative symptoms, as well as risky sexual behaviour and other behaviour problems (Trickett, Noll & Putnam, 2011).

Other studies have also indicated that sexual abuse is associated with sleep problems and hypersexualised behaviour in childhood and adolescence (Beitchman, Zucker, Hood et al., 1991; Noll, Trickett, Susman & Putnam, 2006).

Evidence of negative impacts of childhood sexual abuse on long-term functioning is strong. Twin studies, which provide robust evidence on causal effects of sexual abuse, have found that sexual abuse increases risks for depression, social anxiety, conduct disorders, re-victimisation, bulimia nervosa, and suicide attempts (Dinwiddie, Heath, Dunne et al., 2000; Kendler, Bulik, Silberg et al., 2000; Nelson, Heath, Madden et al., 2002), but not for the development of generalised anxiety disorders, or drug dependence (Kendler, Bulik, Silberg et al., 2000). Notably, twin studies have found little evidence of causal effects on personality, mood, or substance use disorders when non-intercourse sexual abuse is included (Berenz, Amstadter, Aggen et al., 2013; Bornovalova, Huibregtse, Hicks et al., 2013; Dinwiddie, Heath, Dunne et al., 2000; Kendler, Bulik, Silberg et al., 2000; Nelson, Heath, Madden et al., 2002).

Meta-analyses also suggest associations of sexual abuse with somatic disorders (Paras, Murad, Chen et al., 2009), post-traumatic stress, and eating and sleep disorders (Chen, Murad, Paras et al., 2010), though the evidence of causality is less established. Notably, however, the effects of sexual abuse may be non-specific–that is, sexual abuse is similarly associated with a range of mental disorders (Andrews, Corry, Slade et al., 2004). Some evidence also suggests associations between sexual abuse and perpetration of violent or criminal behaviour, though not necessarily to a greater extent than for other forms of maltreatment (McGrath, Nilsen & Kerley, 2011). Sexual abuse may specifically impact the risk of committing a sex offence, particularly among men; however, the majority of sexual abuse victims do not become perpetrators (Felson & Lane, 2009; Glasser, Kolvin, Campbell et al., 2001; McGrath, Nilsen & Kerley, 2011).

Effects of sexual abuse may vary by several factors. As previously noted, the degree of contact is an important factor, along with the duration of victimisation (Andrews, Corry, Slade et al., 2004). Additionally, although sexual abuse is associated with adverse psychological effects in men and women (Andrews, Corry, Slade et al., 2004; Dube, Anda, Whitfield et al., 2005), male victims may experience a weaker emotional response and less self-blame consequent to the abuse as compared with female victims (Ullman & Filipas, 2005). Lastly, negative reactions from others and poorly handled investigations by law enforcement or children's services following disclosure of sexual abuse may increase the probability of negative impacts (Ullman & Filipas, 2005; Pence & Wilson, 1994).

Emotional abuse

Maltreatment studies often fail to examine emotional abuse, especially those using child protection records. Nevertheless, emotional abuse has been linked with higher rates of a variety of psychiatric symptoms and behaviour problems in childhood and adolescence, many times to an equal or greater extent than has physical abuse (Font & Berger, 2015; Teicher, Samson, Polcari & McGreenery, 2006). A large-scale meta-analysis by Norman, Byambaa, De et al. (2012) found that, although there were far more studies on physical abuse, the estimated effects of emotional abuse were often equally large. Specifically, emotional abuse was associated with a 3-fold increase in the odds of depressive and anxiety disorders, whereas physical abuse predicted a 1.5-fold increase in the odds. Additionally, somewhat smaller, but significant, effects of emotional abuse were found for suicide attempts and drug use. Studies that have examined possible confounding factors or subgroup effects have found that the effects of emotional abuse were not explained by other maltreatment or trauma exposure, and were observed across age and gender groups (Spertus, Yehuda, Wong et al., 2003; Vissing, Straus, Gelles & Harrop, 1991).

Neglect

Research on neglect has lagged behind studies of physical and sexual abuse. This is due to perceptions that it is less serious or harmful than abuse, in addition to conflict and ambiguity around defining neglectful parenting (Dubowitz, 2007; McSherry, 2007). Neglected children appear to differ from abused children in some ways –they tend to exhibit more isolative and withdrawn behaviours and fewer aggressive and disruptive behaviours (Hildyard & Wolfe, 2002). In a meta-analysis, Norman, Byambaa, De et al. (2012) concluded that there is credible evidence that neglect is associated with depressive and anxiety disorders, suicide attempts, drug use and risky sexual behaviour. Their study found effect sizes similar to those for physical abuse, though they did not distinguish among types of neglect. For other conditions, such as eating disorders, behavioural or conduct disorders in childhood, or alcohol problems, there is not strong evidence for effects of neglect – this may reflect insufficient evidence or a true null effect. However, neglect encompasses a broad range of circumstances; thus, to say that neglect has or does not have harmful effects on a given outcome is not especially useful for crafting policies or interventions and may obscure effects of specific forms of neglect. The ensuing sections, therefore, focus exclusively on studies that distinguish among specific types of neglect.

Physical Neglect. Few studies specifically examine physical neglect and as a result, there is a lack of strong evidence on its effects. In particular, research has yet to fully grapple with the difficulty of measuring physical neglect in a way that clearly distinguishes it from poverty. Most studies on physical neglect do include income as a control variable in their statistical analyses. It is generally found that physical neglect most strongly impacts cognitive outcomes, such as language development and academic performance (Font & Berger, 2015; Manly, Lynch, Oshri et al., 2013). However, there is also some evidence linking physical neglect to social–emotional problems, including moderate effects on internalising behaviours (English, Upadhyaya, Litrownik et al., 2005; Font & Berger, 2015), social skills and relationships (Bolger, Patterson & Kupersmidt, 1998; English, Upadhyaya, Litrownik et al., 2005), and depressive symptoms (Kim & Cicchetti, 2006). Research findings are inconsistent on whether there are associations between physical neglect and externalising behaviour problems, such as aggression (Dubowitz, Papas, Black & Starr, 2002; English, Upadhyaya, Litrownik et al., 2005; Font & Berger, 2015). In part, variation in findings is likely to reflect the sample composition and time of observation. More importantly, inconsistencies in studies' findings are also likely to stem from inconsistencies in how physical neglect is measured and in the extent to which confounding factors – especially socio-economic characteristics – are controlled. In sum, there is limited, but fairly consistent, evidence of negative impacts of physical neglect on child and adolescent cognitive development and internalising behaviour problems. Evidence on the long-term effects of physical neglect is especially scarce. However, one large, nationally representative study of young adults found that those who experienced physical neglect in childhood were at higher risk of depression, drinking, drug use and violent behaviour (Hussey, Chang & Kotch, 2006).

Possible effects of physical neglect can also be informed by research on material deprivation, given that these are, to a large extent, definitional equivalents. Kiernan and Huerta (2008) found that economic deprivation in infancy was associated with children's developmental outcomes at age three after accounting for a range of other factors, including parenting behaviours. Specifically, material deprivation predicted a 0.1 standard deviation (SD) decrease in cognitive skills, and 0.2 and 0.1 SD increases in externalising and internalising behaviour problems, respectively, at age three. Additionally, specific forms of deprivation are associated with children's cognitive and behavioural development, including food insufficiency (Belsky, Moffitt, Arseneault et al. 2010; Benton, 2010; Liu & Raine, 2006), and substandard housing (Leventhal & Newman, 2010).

Supervision Neglect. It could be argued that supervision neglect is a catchall for parenting acts or omissions that are believed to be harmful to children but do not fall under any other category. As such, this section pays specific attention to how supervision neglect is measured across studies. First, Font and Berger (2015) included in their supervision neglect measure indicators of lack of supervision (child left home alone) as well as exposure to inappropriate environments (parental substance abuse, domestic violence and criminal activity). They found that supervision neglect at age three was associated with increased anxious and depressed symptomology at ages five and nine, at a magnitude of approximately 0.25 SD. Smaller and less consistent effects were also observed for withdrawn and aggressive behaviour. Second, Bolger, Patterson and Kupersmidt, (1998) used Child Protection Service (CPS)-substantiated lack of supervision, a fairly narrow standard, from birth onward to examine social outcomes among children in primary school. They found that lack of supervision predicted diminished self-esteem and conflict in friendships among children and adolescents, suggesting that unsupervised children are not being guided toward pro-social behaviour. In one of few studies linking supervision neglect to adult psychological well-being, Hussey, Chang and Kotch (2006) found that retrospectively reported experiences of being left home alone prior to beginning sixth grade – again, a quite narrow measure – predicted higher odds of depression and several risky or antisocial behaviours at a magnitude similar to that of physical neglect and abuse.

Other studies examined specific circumstances that could constitute an unsafe or inappropriate environment. The maltreatment category under which such behaviours may fall varies across and within countries, but, as noted in Table 5.1, this chapter includes circumstances that expose children to an inappropriate environment under the umbrella of supervision neglect, including situations of parental substance abuse and domestic violence in the home. Domestic violence falls under child maltreatment statutes in at least 23 states in the US (Child Welfare Information Gateway, 2012a) and in other countries, including the United Kingdom. A meta-analysis of 60 studies found moderate effects of witnessing domestic violence on internalising and externalising behaviour problems, and a larger effect on trauma symptomology (Evans, Davies & DiLillo, 2008). Holt, Buckley and Whelan (2008) suggest that domestic violence harms children when it inhibits the abused parent from providing consistent and attentive care and a structured routine, disrupts the formation of secure parent–child attachment, or results in a child identifying with the abusive parent, which can interfere with the development of empathy. Notably, studies often cannot account for the degree of exposure, and children exposed to domestic violence are also more likely to also experience other forms of maltreatment (Holt, Buckley & Whelan, 2008; Teicher, Samson, Polcari & McGreenery, 2006).

Parental substance abuse may also constitute supervision neglect in specific circumstances (Child Welfare Information Gateway, 2012b). Two notable studies report strong associations between parental substance abuse and children's psychological health. In a national birth cohort, Osborne and Berger (2009) found that, after accounting for prenatal substance exposure and demographic and socio-economic factors, parental substance abuse predicted a 0.29 SD increase in aggressive and oppositional defiant behaviour problems, and smaller increases in anxious and depressed behaviours (0.13 SD) and attention deficit/hyperactivity behaviours (0.23 SD). They relied on parental reports of their own substance abuse, which may be underreported; thus, associations may be biased downward. Additionally, in a retrospective study of adults, Green, McLaughlin, Berglund et al., (2010) identified potential long-term effects of parental substance abuse. Those with substance-abusing parents had 2.3 times greater odds of having a substance abuse disorder in adulthood, as well as significantly increased risks of mood, anxiety and disruptive behaviour disorders. As with domestic violence, however, children exposed to parental substance abuse have a substantially higher risk of experiencing other forms of maltreatment, especially when both parents abuse substances (Walsh, MacMillan & Jamieson, 2003).

Emotional Neglect. Emotional neglect is infrequently studied in the maltreatment literature, and when it is studied, it is sometimes combined with emotional abuse. However, one study found that, even in the context of high-risk, low-income preschoolers, emotional neglect was associated with increases in internalising and externalising behaviour problems, whereas other forms of neglect were not (Dubowitz, Papas, Black & Starr, 2002). Aside from that, some effects of emotional neglect on children can be inferred from studies of children reared in orphanages or other institutions. Institutions provide children with limited stimulation and inconsistent access to responsive caregivers, both of which are aspects of emotional neglect. Thus, the effects of being in an orphanage or similar institution should encompass the effects of severe emotional neglect. In a randomised control trial of Romanian children abandoned as infants, Nelson, Zeanah, Fox et al., (2007) found that children who were moved from an institution to a foster family experienced recovery to cognitive function, whereas children who remained institutionalised did not. However, later exits to foster family care predicted less cognitive recovery, suggesting accumulating effects of emotional deprivation. A wealth of evidence has confirmed negative impacts of the institutional environment on cognitive functioning, especially for children institutionalised long-term (see Bakermans-Kranenburg, van IJzendoorn & Juffer, 2008). Less attention has been paid to the psychological impacts of such deprivation; however, increased risk of insecure attachment or attachment disorders, as well as adverse social development, have been implicated in a number of studies (see Johnson, Browne & Hamilton-Giachritsis, 2006).

Economic Health

The body of research on economic impacts of child maltreatment is quite small. However, four recent studies help to provide an interesting, but incomplete, picture. Using Child Protection Service (CPS) and court records, maltreatment has been found to predict lower educational attainment and income, and less or lower quality employment (Currie & Widom, 2010; Mersky & Topitzes, 2010). In early adulthood, Mersky and Topitzes (2010) found that maltreatment predicts a 34% lower probability of earning $12,000 or more in the past year, and 18% and 70% lower likelihoods of high-school completion and college attendance respectively. Currie and Widom (2010) suggest a 14% lower probability of being employed in middle age, and over $5,000 lower earnings among those who experienced maltreatment as compared with those who did not. Using self-report data, Font and Maguire-Jack (2015a) found that two forms of maltreatment – exposure to domestic violence and sexual abuse – were associated with economic outcomes but that physical and emotional abuse were not. However, Covey, Menard, and Franzese (2013), also using self-report data, did find associations between physical abuse and multiple economic outcomes.

Although the body of evidence is small, it is logical to suspect that maltreatment has the potential to impact economic attainment, given fairly robust evidence that maltreatment impacts cognitive functioning, academic achievement, likelihood of incarceration, and other factors that diminish employment prospects or interfere with productivity or dependability at work. Effects may be especially strong for neglect, which has a stronger impact on cognitive, language and academic skills than do other maltreatment types (Font & Berger, 2015; Hildyard & Wolfe, 2002; Stone, 2007). At the same time, childhood poverty is a strong predictor of both maltreatment and adult poverty – thus, evidence of causality remains elusive.

Physical Health

Associations between maltreatment and physical health in childhood and adolescence are not well established empirically, though a few studies have suggested impacts on cardiovascular health and the number of health problems one develops (Graham-Bermann & Seng, 2005; Pretty, O'Leary, Cairney & Wade, 2013). However, other effects are probable. For example, inadequate provision of food should impact children's physical health – poor nutrition can lead to stunted growth, emaciation, or obesity, and may interfere with cognitive development. Lack of supervision may also present risk for unintentional injuries and injury-related deaths (Landen, Bauer & Kohn, 2003). Short-term health consequences of maltreatment require additional inquiry.

In adulthood, studies of maltreatment and physical health often use the Adverse Childhood Experiences (ACE; Felitti, Vincent, Anda et al., 1998) survey, which includes measures of physical, sexual and emotional abuse, and aspects of childhood neglect, such as witnessing domestic violence and residing with an adult who has an alcohol or substance abuse problem. (Notably, these studies have limited implications for understanding the effects of maltreatment specifically, because ACEs include parental divorce and other stressful but non-maltreatment events, and studies often calculate a count measure, thus obfuscating differential event effects.) The original study (Felitti et al., 1998, the results of which have been replicated elsewhere) suggested that the largest effects on physical health were observed when comparing those with no ACEs to those with four or more. Specifically, among those with four or more ACEs, they observed a 100% or larger increase in the odds of several disease conditions, including chronic bronchitis/emphysema, heart disease, jaundice/hepatitis, poor self-rated health, sexually transmitted infections, and a 60–90% increase in the odds of cancer, skeletal fractures, and severe obesity (Felitti, Vincent, Anda et al., 1998). The same study found relatively larger associations between the number of ACEs and a range of negative health behaviours, including physical inactivity, smoking, alcoholism and substance abuse.

Few studies have examined specific subtypes of maltreatment and physical health. Studies have reported effects in adulthood of physical abuse on a number of medical diagnoses and physical symptoms: obesity, malnutrition and poor glycaemic control (Hussey, Chang & Kotch 2006; Springer, Sheridan, Kuo & Carnes, 2007; Widom, Czaja, Bentley & Johnson, 2012); emotional maltreatment on somatic symptoms (Spertus, Yehuda, Wong et al., 2003); neglect on poor glycaemic control, oral health, vision problems and peak air flow; and sexual abuse on malnutrition and Hepatitis C (Widom, Czaja, Bentley & Johnson, 2012). Overall, however, evidence of associations between maltreatment and long-term physical health is limited (Norman, Byambaa, De et al., 2012). Moreover, to the extent that there is evidence that maltreatment negatively affects long-term physical health outcomes, the mechanisms are not well established.

Maltreatment Research in Perspective

A large body of research has examined possible consequences of maltreatment, yet much remains unclear. First, it is important to note that measurements of maltreatment vary widely. In part, this reflects a lack of consensus on what maltreatment is (i.e., what acts and omissions should be included). Often definitions of maltreatment are updated based on new evidence of the harmful effects of a specific parental act or omission – hence, the effects of maltreatment are built into the definition. For example, exposure to domestic violence was identified as a form of maltreatment after research demonstrated how children were negatively impacted.

However, the potential for harm is a necessary, but not sufficient, standard for maltreatment. Attribution of blame and social norms also factor into states' legal definitions. For example, in the United States, several states exempt corporal punishment from their definitions of physical abuse (Child Welfare Information Gateway, 2014), not because it is harmless, but because it is socially accepted. Measurements of maltreatment also vary due to ambiguity around the threshold at which substandard parenting crosses over into maltreatment. That is, maltreatment can be considered the extreme end of a distribution of parenting quality, rather than a separate concept in itself.

Results of research studies may also vary because researchers use several approaches to collecting maltreatment data: official records of investigated or substantiated maltreatment from CPS, adults' (retrospective) self-reports of maltreatment, parents' reports of their behaviour toward their children, or, less frequently, children's contemporaneous reports of parental maltreatment. Official records are biased for many reasons, including the following: (i) a substantial portion of maltreatment incidents are never investigated by CPS (Sedlak, Mettenburg, Basena et al., 2010); (ii) some forms of maltreatment, particularly emotional maltreatment, are underrepresented in official data because they are rarely the focus of CPS investigations (Chamberland, Fallon, Black & Trocmé, 2011); (iii) in many countries, the majority of CPS reports and assessments do not result in a substantiated case or child protection plan (Munro & Manful, 2010); (iv) factors unrelated to the veracity of an allegation often substantially impact case decision-making (Benbenishty, Davidson-Arad, López et al., in press; Font & Maguire-Jack, 2015b); (v) official determinations of maltreatment may be ineffective at distinguishing children most at risk of adverse impacts (Hussey, Marshall, English et al., 2005; Leiter, Myers & Zingraff, 1994); and (vi) laws and practices vary across states and, especially, across countries, and thus the meaning of investigated or substantiated maltreatment is inconsistent in multi-state or multi-country studies. However, other approaches to measuring maltreatment are also flawed. Retrospective self-reports risk false negatives, because memories may fade or become distorted over time (Hardt & Rutter, 2004). Child reports of maltreatment may underestimate incidence because children may fear getting the maltreating perpetrator into trouble or being punished for disclosing. Research on child sexual abuse shows that children may wait a long time to disclose abuse, may recant their accusations, or may never disclose (Summit, 1983). Lastly, maltreatment measured by parents' self-reported behaviours present concerns about social–desirability bias, wherein parents may be reluctant to admit maltreating their children because it violates legal and social expectations. Each approach to measurement has strengths and weaknesses, but it is not yet clear whether, or to what extent, the approach to measurement affects the results of studies.

Maltreatment research must consider how to account for severity and timing. Severity is sometimes measured by the number of instances or the number of types of maltreatment. Multiple incidents or multiple types of maltreatment (as compared with single incidence and single type respectively) may impact social–emotional and cognitive development to a greater extent (Arata, Langhinrichsen-Rohling, Bowers & O'Farrill-Swails, 2005; Bolger, Patterson & Kupersmidt, 1998; Éthier, Lemelin & Lacharité, 2004; Jaffee & Maikovich-Fong, 2011; Teicher, Samson, Polcari & McGreenery, 2006). Additionally, early experiences of maltreatment may have more adverse impacts than maltreatment experienced at an older age (Font & Berger, 2015; Hildyard & Wolfe, 2002; Jaffee & Maikovich-Fong, 2011). Younger child age may exacerbate maltreatment impacts because younger children are more dependent on their parents for routine needs and less able to seek help from others.

Aside from definitional issues, there are some reasons why maltreatment could be associated with, but not cause, adverse outcomes. First, given that maltreatment is an extreme version of substandard parenting, and substandard parenting and maltreatment often co-occur, it is likely that low-quality parenting would impact children even in the absence of acts or omissions that constitute maltreatment. In addition, estimated effects of maltreatment are likely confounded by childhood poverty. Poverty is consistently correlated with risks of maltreatment (Sedlak & Broadhurst, 1996) and especially child neglect (Slack, Holl, McDaniel et al., 2004), as well as with many negative psychological, social and economic outcomes, including behavioural problems and non-completion of high school (Magnuson & Duncan, 2002). Similarly, many psychological and physical health conditions are environmentally influenced, and the environmental characteristics linked to these adverse outcomes are likely also to increase the probability of experiencing maltreatment.

Genetics may also be important. Parental mental health is associated with increased risk of maltreatment (Stith, Liu, Davies et al., 2009) and many mental health conditions have some degree of heritability. Thus, children whose parents have mental health problems are more likely both to be maltreated and to suffer from a mental health condition. Twin studies have been used to address causality in some studies, but they are unable to address causal issues in neglect, which is most often a household-level phenomenon. In sum, separating the influence of maltreatment from the influence of other factors would require observing maltreatment in the absence of other family dysfunction, hardship, or genetic vulnerability, yet this is rarely, if ever, the context in which maltreatment occurs.

Moreover, associations between maltreatment and child development are likely bidirectional. Children's temperament, behaviour, and other characteristics impact the interactions they have with their caregivers (Belsky, 1978). Children with disabilities (particularly emotional or behavioural disabilities) are at higher risk of being maltreated than children without disabilities (Hershkowitz, Lamb & Horowitz, 2007; Jaudes & Mackey-Bilaver, 2008), perhaps because they are more difficult to provide with care and require more care (Ammerman, Lubetsky & Stubenbort, 2000). In addition, children with disabilities may face greater difficulty in disclosing maltreatment and being viewed as credible victims, thus heightening their vulnerability. However, children's developmental attributes appear to affect maltreatment risk to a lesser degree than maltreatment impacts later development (Font & Berger, 2015).

Conclusion

Research on the effects of all forms of maltreatment on psychological health consistently suggests negative associations with a variety of immediate and long-term mental health and substance abuse problems, though evidence on physical and sexual abuse is more prevalent than evidence on the effects of emotional abuse or the various forms of neglect. However, aside from a handful of twin studies examining the effects of physical or sexual abuse, conclusive causal evidence remains elusive.

Evidence on the effects of maltreatment on economic prospects is limited, though a few studies have identified negative associations between maltreatment and future earnings and employment. While the mechanisms through which maltreatment affects economic prospects are likely to involve cognitive functioning and educational attainment, among other things, this has yet to be clearly established in the research. Similarly, associations with physical health, particularly chronic disease, have not been studied as widely, and thus much remains to be learnt about how, and why, maltreatment could affect the development or course of a chronic illness. Lastly, future research should also focus on issues of measurement – particularly as it pertains to how substandard parenting is distinguished from maltreatment and whether the various behaviours and omissions that can constitute neglect are similarly or differently associated with children's short- and long-term outcomes.

References

Ammerman, R.T., Lubetsky, M.J. & Stubenbort, K.F. (2000). Maltreatment of children with disabilities. In: R.T. Ammerman & M. Hersen (eds), *Case Studies in Family Violence*. New York: Springer US, 231–258.

Andrews, G., Corry, J., Slade, T. et al. (2004). Child sexual abuse. In: *Comparative Quantification of Health Risks: Global and Regional Burden of Disease Attributable to Selected Major Risk Factors* (vol. 2). World Health Organization. Retrieved from http://158.232.12.119/publications/cra/chapters/volume2/1851-1940.pdf.

Arata, C.M., Langhinrichsen-Rohling, J., Bowers, D. & O'Farrill-Swails, L. (2005). Single versus multi-type maltreatment: An examination of the long-term effects of child abuse. *Journal of Aggression, Maltreatment & Trauma*, 11(4), 29–52.

Bakermans-Kranenburg, M.J., van IJzendoorn, M.H. & Juffer, F. (2008). Earlier is better: A meta-analysis of 70 years of intervention improving cognitive development in institutionalized children. *Monographs of the Society for Research in Child Development*, 73, 279–293.

Beitchman, J.H., Zucker, K.J., Hood, J.E. et al. (1991). A review of the short-term effects of child sexual abuse. *Child Abuse & Neglect*, 15, 537–556.

Belsky, D.W., Moffitt, T.E., Arseneault, L. et al. (2010). Context and sequelae of food insecurity in children's development. *American Journal of Epidemiology*, 172, 809–818.

Belsky, J. (1978). Three theoretical models of child abuse: A critical review. *Child Abuse & Neglect*, 2, 37–49.

Benbenishty, R., Davidson-Arad, B., López, M. et al. (in press). Decision making in child protection: An international comparative study on maltreatment substantiation, risk assessment and interventions recommendations, and the role of professionals' child welfare attitudes. *Child Abuse & Neglect*.

Benton, D. (2010). The influence of dietary status on the cognitive performance of children. *Molecular Nutrition & Food Research*, 54, 457–470.

Berenz, E.C., Amstadter, A.B., Aggen, S.H. et al. (2013). Childhood trauma and personality disorder criterion counts: A co-twin control analysis. *Journal of Abnormal Psychology*, 122, 1070.

Bolger, K.E., Patterson, C.J. & Kupersmidt, J.B. (1998). Peer relationships and self-esteem among children who have been maltreated. *Child Development*, 69, 1171–1197.

Bornovalova, M.A., Huibregtse, B.M., Hicks, B.M. et al. (2013). Tests of a direct effect of childhood abuse on adult borderline personality disorder traits: A longitudinal discordant twin design. *Journal of Abnormal Psychology*, 122, 180.

Chamberland, C., Fallon, B., Black, T. & Trocmé, N. (2011). Emotional maltreatment in Canada: Prevalence, reporting and child welfare responses (CIS2). *Child Abuse & Neglect*, 35, 841–854.

Chen, L.P., Murad, M.H., Paras, M.L. et al. (2010). Sexual abuse and lifetime diagnosis of psychiatric disorders: Systematic review and meta-analysis. In: *Mayo Clinic Proceedings* (vol. 85). Elsevier, 618–629.

Child Welfare Information Gateway (2012a). *Child Witnesses to Domestic Violence*. Washington, DC: US Children's Bureau.

Child Welfare Information Gateway (2012b). *Parental Drug Use as Child Abuse*. Washington, DC: US Children's Bureau.

Child Welfare Information Gateway (2014). *Definitions of Child Abuse and Neglect*. Washington, DC: US Children's Bureau.

Covey, H.C., Menard, S. & Franzese, R.J. (2013). Effects of adolescent physical abuse, exposure to neighborhood violence, and witnessing parental violence on adult socioeconomic status. *Child Maltreatment*, 18, 85–97.

Currie, J. & Widom, C.S. (2010). Long-term consequences of child abuse and neglect on adult economic well-being. *Child Maltreatment*, 15, 111–120.

Dinwiddie, S., Heath, A.C., Dunne, M.P. et al. (2000). Early sexual abuse and lifetime psychopathology: A co-twin-control study. *Psychological Medicine*, 30, 41–52.

Dube, S.R., Anda, R.F., Whitfield, C.L. et al. (2005). Long-term consequences of childhood sexual abuse by gender of victim. *American Journal of Preventive Medicine*, 28, 430–438.

Dubowitz, H. (2007). Understanding and addressing the 'neglect of neglect': Digging into the molehill. *Child Abuse & Neglect*, 31, 603–606.

Dubowitz, H., Papas, M.A., Black, M.M. & Starr, R.H. (2002). Child neglect: Outcomes in high-risk urban preschoolers. *Pediatrics*, 109, 1100–1107.

Duncan, A.E., Sartor, C.E., Scherrer, J.F. et al. (2008). The association between cannabis abuse and dependence and childhood physical and sexual abuse: Evidence from an offspring of twins design. *Addiction*, 103, 990–997.

English, D.J., Upadhyaya, M.P., Litrownik, A.J. et al. (2005). Maltreatment's wake: The relationship of maltreatment dimensions to child outcomes. *Child Abuse & Neglect*, 29, 597–619.

Éthier, L.S., Lemelin, J.-P. & Lacharité, C. (2004). A longitudinal study of the effects of chronic maltreatment on children's behavioral and emotional problems. *Child Abuse & Neglect*, 28, 1265–1278.

Evans, S.E., Davies, C. & DiLillo, D. (2008). Exposure to domestic violence: A meta-analysis of child and adolescent outcomes. *Aggression and Violent Behavior*, 13, 131–140.

Fakunmoju, S.B. & Bammeke, F.O. (2015). Anxiety disorders and depression among high school adolescents and youths in Nigeria: Understanding differential effects of physical abuse at home and school. *Journal of Adolescence*, 42, 1–10.

Felitti, M.D., Vincent, J., Anda, M.D. et al. (1998). Relationship of childhood abuse and household dysfunction to many of the leading causes of death in adults: The Adverse Childhood Experiences (ACE) Study. *American Journal of Preventive Medicine*, 14, 245–258.

Felson, R.B. & Lane, K.J. (2009). Social learning, sexual and physical abuse, and adult crime. *Aggressive Behavior*, 35, 489–501.

Fergusson, D.M., Boden, J.M. & Horwood, L.J. (2008). Exposure to childhood sexual and physical abuse and adjustment in early adulthood. *Child Abuse & Neglect*, 32, 607–619.

Font, S.A. & Berger, L.M. (2015). Child maltreatment and children's developmental trajectories in early to middle childhood. *Child Development*, 86, 536–556.

Font, S.A. & Maguire-Jack, K. (2015a). Adverse childhood experiences and health: The mediating role of socioeconomic status. *Child Abuse & Neglect*, in press.

Font, S.A. & Maguire-Jack, K. (2015b). Decision-making in child protective services: Influences at multiple levels of the social ecology. *Child Abuse & Neglect*, in press.

Font, S.A., Pettit, K & Ansari, A. (2015). *Parenting Quality and the Social–Emotional Development of At-Risk Children*. Austin, TX: University of Texas at Austin.

Gershoff, E.T. (2002). Corporal punishment by parents and associated child behaviors and experiences: A meta-analytic and theoretical review. *Psychological Bulletin*, 128, 539–579.

Glasser, M., Kolvin, I., Campbell, D. et al. (2001). Cycle of child sexual abuse: Links between being a victim and becoming a perpetrator. *The British Journal of Psychiatry*, 179, 482–494.

Graham-Bermann, S.A. & Seng, J. (2005). Violence exposure and traumatic stress symptoms as additional predictors of health problems in high-risk children. *Journal of Pediatrics*, 146, 349–354.

Green, J.G., McLaughlin, K.A., Berglund, P.A. et al. (2010). Childhood adversities and adult psychiatric disorders in the national comorbidity survey replication I: Associations with first onset of DSM-IV disorders. *Archives of General Psychiatry*, 67, 113–123.

Hardt, J. & Rutter, M. (2004). Validity of adult retrospective reports of adverse childhood experiences: Review of the evidence. *Journal of Child Psychology and Psychiatry*, 45, 260–273.

Hershkowitz, I., Lamb, M.E. & Horowitz, D. (2007). Victimization of children with disabilities. *American Journal of Orthopsychiatry*, 77, 629–635.

Hildyard, K.L. & Wolfe, D.A. (2002). Child neglect: Developmental issues and outcomes. *Child Abuse & Neglect*, 26(6–7), 679–695.

Hillberg, T., Hamilton-Giachritsis, C. & Dixon, L. (2011). Review of meta-analyses on the association between child sexual abuse and adult mental health difficulties: A systematic approach. *Trauma, Violence, & Abuse*, 12, 38–49.

Holt, S., Buckley, H. & Whelan, S. (2008). The impact of exposure to domestic violence on children and young people: A review of the literature. *Child Abuse & Neglect*, 32, 797–810.

Hussey, J.M., Chang, J.J. & Kotch, J.B. (2006). Child maltreatment in the United States: Prevalence, risk factors, and adolescent health consequences. *Pediatrics*, 118, 933–942.

Hussey, J.M., Marshall, J.M., English, D.J. et al. (2005). Defining maltreatment according to substantiation: Distinction without a difference? *Child Abuse & Neglect*, 29, 479–492.

Jaffee, S.R. & Maikovich-Fong, A.K. (2011). Effects of chronic maltreatment and maltreatment timing on children's behavior and cognitive abilities. *Journal of Child Psychology and Psychiatry*, 52, 184–194.

Jaudes, P.K. & Mackey-Bilaver, L. (2008). Do chronic conditions increase young children's risk of being maltreated? *Child Abuse & Neglect*, 32, 671–681.

Johnson, R., Browne, K. & Hamilton-Giachritsis, C. (2006). Young children in institutional care at risk of harm. *Trauma, Violence & Abuse*, 7, 34–60.

Kendler, K.S., Bulik, C.M., Silberg, J. et al. (2000). Childhood sexual abuse and adult psychiatric and substance use disorders in women: An epidemiological and cotwin control analysis. *Archives of General Psychiatry*, 57, 953–959.

Kiernan, K.E. & Huerta, M.C. (2008). Economic deprivation, maternal depression, parenting and children's cognitive and emotional development in early childhood. *British Journal of Sociology*, 59, 783–806.

Kim, J. & Cicchetti, D. (2006). Longitudinal trajectories of self-system processes and depressive symptoms among maltreated and nonmaltreated children. *Child Development*, 77, 624–639.

Landen, M.G., Bauer, U. & Kohn, M. (2003). Inadequate supervision as a cause of injury deaths among young children in Alaska and Louisiana. *Pediatrics*, 111, 328–331.

Leiter, J., Myers, K.A. & Zingraff, M.T. (1994). Substantiated and unsubstantiated cases of child maltreatment: Do their consequences differ? *Social Work Research*, 18, 67–82.

Leventhal, T. & Newman, S. (2010). Housing and child development. *Children and Youth Services Review*, 32, 1165–1174.

Lindert, J., von Ehrenstein, O.S., Grashow, R. et al. (2014). Sexual and physical abuse in childhood is associated with depression and anxiety over the life course: Systematic review and meta-analysis. *International Journal of Public Health*, 59, 359–372.

Liu, J. & Raine, A. (2006). The effect of childhood malnutrition on externalizing behavior. *Current Opinion in Pediatrics*, 18, 565–570.

Maas, C., Herrenkohl, T.I. & Sousa, C. (2008). Review of research on child maltreatment and violence in youth. *Trauma, Violence & Abuse*, 9, 56–67.

Magnuson, K. & Duncan, G.J. (2002). Parents in poverty. In: M. Bornstein (ed), *Handbook of Parenting*, 2nd edn. Mahwah, NJ: Lawrence Erlbaum Associates.

Manly, J.T., Lynch, M., Oshri, A. et al. (2013). The impact of neglect on initial adaptation to school. *Child Maltreatment*, 18, 155–170.

McGrath, S.A., Nilsen, A.A. & Kerley, K.R. (2011). Sexual victimization in childhood and the propensity for juvenile delinquency and adult criminal behavior: A systematic review. *Aggression and Violent Behavior*, 16, 485–492.

McSherry, D. (2007). Understanding and addressing the 'neglect of neglect': Why are we making a mole-hill out of a mountain? *Child Abuse & Neglect*, 31, 607–614.

Mersky, J.P. & Topitzes, J. (2010). Comparing early adult outcomes of maltreated and non-maltreated children: A prospective longitudinal investigation. *Children and Youth Services Review*, 32, 1086–1096.

Munro, E. & Manful, E. (2010). *Safeguarding children: A comparison of England's data with that of Australia, Norway and the United States* (No. DFE-RR198). United Kingdom: The Child Wellbeing Research Centre.

Nelson, E.C., Heath, A.C., Madden, P.A. et al. (2002). Association between self-reported childhood sexual abuse and adverse psychosocial outcomes: Results from a twin study. *Archives of General Psychiatry*, 59, 139–145.

Nelson, C.A., Zeanah, C.H., Fox, N.A. et al. (2007). Cognitive recovery in socially deprived young children: The Bucharest Early Intervention Project. *Science*, 318, 1937–1940.

Noll, J.G., Trickett, P.K., Susman, E.J. & Putnam, F.W. (2006). Sleep disturbances and childhood sexual abuse. *Journal of Pediatric Psychology*, 31, 469–480.

Norman, R.E., Byambaa, M., De, R. et al. (2012). The long-term health consequences of child physical abuse, emotional abuse, and neglect: A systematic review and meta-analysis. *PLoS Medicine*, 9, e1001349.

Osborne, C. & Berger, L.M. (2009). Parental substance abuse and child well-being: A consideration of parents' gender and coresidence. *Journal of Family Issues*, 30, 341–370.

Paras, M.L., Murad, M.H., Chen, L.P. et al. (2009). Sexual abuse and lifetime diagnosis of somatic disorders: A systematic review and meta-analysis. *JAMA*, 302, 550–561.

Pence, D.M. & Wilson, C.A. (1994). Reporting and investigating child sexual abuse. *Future of Children*, 4, 70–83.

Pretty, C., O'Leary, D., Cairney, J. & Wade, T.J. (2013). Adverse childhood experiences and the cardiovascular health of children: A cross-sectional study. *BMC Pediatrics*, 13, 208.

Scherrer, J.F., Xian, H., Kapp, J.M.K. et al. (2007). Association between exposure to childhood and lifetime traumatic events and lifetime pathological gambling in a twin cohort. *Journal of Nervous and Mental Disease*, 195, 72–78.

Sedlak, A. & Broadhurst, D. (1996). *The third national incidence study on child abuse and neglect (NIS-3)*. Washington, DC: US Department of Health and Human Services.

Sedlak, A.J., Mettenburg, J., Basena, M. et al. (2010). *Fourth National Incidence Study of Child Abuse and Neglect (NIS–4): Report to Congress*. Washington, DC: US Department of Health and Human Services, Administration for Children and Families.

Slack, K.S., Holl, J.L., McDaniel, M. et al. (2004). Understanding the risks of child neglect: An exploration of poverty and parenting characteristics. *Child Maltreatment*, 9, 395–408.

Spertus, I.L., Yehuda, R., Wong, C.M. et al. (2003). Childhood emotional abuse and neglect as predictors of psychological and physical symptoms in women presenting to a primary care practice. *Child Abuse & Neglect*, 27, 1247–1258.

Springer, K.W., Sheridan, J., Kuo, D. & Carnes, M. (2007). Long-term physical and mental health consequences of childhood physical abuse: Results from a large population-based sample of men and women. *Child Abuse & Neglect*, 31, 517–530.

Stith, S.M., Liu, T., Davies, L.C. et al. (2009). Risk factors in child maltreatment: A meta-analytic review of the literature. *Aggression and Violent Behavior*, 14, 13–29.

Stone, S. (2007). Child maltreatment, out-of-home placement and academic vulnerability: A fifteen-year review of evidence and future directions. *Children and Youth Services Review*, 29, 139–161.

Summit, R. (1983). Child Sexual Abuse Accommodation Syndrome. *Child Abuse & Neglect*, 11, 229–235.

Teicher, M., Samson, J., Polcari, A. & McGreenery, C. (2006). Sticks, stones, and hurtful words: Relative effects of various forms of childhood maltreatment. *American Journal of Psychiatry*, 163, 993–1000.

Trickett, P.K., Noll, J.G. & Putnam, F.W. (2011). The impact of sexual abuse on female development: Lessons from a multigenerational, longitudinal research study. *Development and Psychopathology*, 23, 453–476.

Ullman, S.E. & Filipas, H.H. (2005). Gender differences in social reactions to abuse disclosures, post-abuse coping, and PTSD of child sexual abuse survivors. *Child Abuse & Neglect*, 29, 767–782.

Vissing, Y.M., Straus, M.A., Gelles, R.J. & Harrop, J.W. (1991). Verbal aggression by parents and psychosocial problems of children. *Child Abuse & Neglect*, 15, 223–238.

Walsh, C., MacMillan, H.L. & Jamieson, E. (2003). The relationship between parental substance abuse and child maltreatment: Findings from the Ontario Health Supplement. *Child Abuse & Neglect*, 27, 1409–1425.

Widom, C.S., Czaja, S.J., Bentley, T. & Johnson, M.S. (2012). A prospective investigation of physical health outcomes in abused and neglected children: New findings from a 30-year follow-up. *American Journal of Public Health*, 102, 1135–1144.

Yen, C.-F., Yang, M.-S., Chen, C.-C. et al. (2008). Effects of childhood physical abuse on depression, problem drinking and perceived poor health status in adolescents living in rural Taiwan. *Psychiatry and Clinical Neurosciences*, 62, 575–583.

Young-Wolff, K.C., Kendler, K.S., Ericson, M.L. & Prescott, C.A. (2011). Accounting for the association between childhood maltreatment and alcohol-use disorders in males: A twin study. *Psychological Medicine*, 41, 59–70.

6

The Neurobiology and Genetics of Childhood Maltreatment

Eamon McCrory[1], Amy Palmer[2] and Vanessa Puetz[1]

[1] Developmental Risk and Resilience Unit, University College London, UK
[2] Veterans Affairs, Canada

The Impact of Maltreatment on Brain Development

Childhood maltreatment has been associated with a range of maladaptive outcomes such as poorer physical health (Widom, Czaja, Bentley & Johnson, 2012) and an increased risk of psychiatric disorder throughout an individual's life (Gilbert, Widom, Browne et al., 2009). The kind of psychiatric disorders that can follow the experience of maltreatment in childhood vary greatly, ranging from affective disorders, such as depression (Anda, Whitfield, Felitti et al., 2002) and anxiety (Scott, Smith & Ellis, 2010), to substance abuse disorders (Enoch, 2011) and schizophrenia (Read, Os, Morrison & Ross, 2005). From a clinical perspective it is noteworthy that individuals with a psychiatric disorder who have experienced childhood maltreatment are less likely to respond to standard treatment approaches (Nanni, Uher & Danese, 2012), and to develop symptoms earlier and at a greater level of severity (Hovens, Wiersma & Giltay, 2010). However, the biological mechanisms by which childhood maltreatment increases vulnerability to psychiatric disorders are not yet understood and research has only begun to elucidate the impact of childhood maltreatment on brain function. It is hoped that the study of neurobiological and genetic factors associated with maltreatment and psychiatric vulnerability may help shed light on the biological mechanisms underlying risk and resilience. Importantly, an increased awareness of biological influences may help clinicians to develop more targeted interventions.

This chapter is organised to present three main topics. The first part will review findings from neuroimaging studies of key brain structures involved in emotion processing, memory and regulation processes, with a particular emphasis on those findings that have employed magnetic resonance imaging (MRI). The second part will explore how genetic factors may be relevant in thinking about the interaction between maltreatment experience and maladaptive outcome. Finally, we will present a general discussion of some clinical implications of the research in this field to date.

The Wiley Handbook of What Works in Child Maltreatment: An Evidence-Based Approach to Assessment and Intervention in Child Protection, First Edition. Edited by Louise Dixon, Daniel F. Perkins, Catherine Hamilton-Giachritsis, and Leam A. Craig.
© 2017 John Wiley & Sons Ltd. Published 2017 by John Wiley & Sons Ltd.

Table 6.1 An overview of the characteristics, advantages and disadvantages of the main brain imaging modalities used to investigate the impact of childhood maltreatment.

Imaging modality	How it works	Advantages	Disadvantages
*ERP	Summarises electrical activity at the scalp following stimulus presentation	• Relatively inexpensive • High temporal resolution • Easy to use with very young children	• Poorer spatial resolution • Poorer spatial localisation • Limited to a pre-determined set of waveforms
*fMRI	Measures changes in blood oxygenation levels, which is taken as a proxy of brain activity	• High spatial resolution • Records from all regions of the brain simultaneously • Can examine activity networks of brain regions • Machine learning techniques can shed light on information processing within a functional region	• Expensive • Poorer temporal resolution • Susceptible to motion artefacts
*DTI	Measures the direction of water diffusion to detect the integrity of white matter tracts	• High spatial resolution • Technique that examines white matter tracts and measures connectivity	• Expensive • Indirect measure of white matter integrity

* ERP: Event Related Potential; fMRI: functional Magnetic Resonance Imaging; DTI: Diffusion Tensor Imaging.

For those less familiar with brain imaging research, we summarise the main imaging modalities in Table 6.1. In this chapter we focus on studies of children, first considering those that have investigated differences in brain structure followed by the smaller number of studies that have investigated the potential impact of childhood maltreatment on brain function.

Structural Differences

Much recent work has focused on differences in brain structure between those children who have experienced early adversity and those who have not (e.g., De Brito, Viding, Sebastian et al., 2013; De Bellis, Keshavan, Shifflett et al., 2002; see also Lim, Radua & Rubia, 2014 for a recent review). In this section we highlight research findings that relate to the impact of maltreatment on those brain structures thought to be critically involved in emotion processing and cognitive functioning.

Amygdala

The amygdala plays a central role in evaluating potentially threatening information, fear conditioning, emotional processing and memory (Pessoa & Adolphs, 2010) and as such has received particular attention in the field. Animal studies investigating chronic stress have reported increased dendritic arborisation (i.e., the expansion of a nerve cell's braches that transmits electrical signals in the brain) in the amygdala suggesting that maltreatment may be associated with increased amygdala volume in humans (Lupien, McEwen, Gunnar & Heim, 2009). However, generally findings in the field have not been consistent with this hypothesis. A meta-analysis of children with maltreatment-related PTSD found no difference in amygdala volume between those who had and had not experienced maltreatment (Woon & Hedges, 2008). A more recent meta-analysis which did not select studies based on co-morbid diagnoses, and therefore included a variety of psychiatric symptoms, found lower volume in children who had a history of maltreatment (Lim, Radua & Rubia, 2014). One possibility is that the length and onset of maltreatment influences structural differences in this region. In studies investigating the effects of early institutionalisation, an extreme form of early deprivation, amygdala volume was larger the longer the child had spent in institutional care (Tottenham & Hare, 2009).

Hippocampus

Animal research has shown that the hippocampus plays a central role in learning and memory and that these functions are impaired when animals are exposed to chronic stress (McEwen, 2004). Research in adults with a history of childhood maltreatment and maltreatment-related PTSD is fairly consistent in demonstrating a decreased volume of the hippocampus after exposure to early adversity (Lim, Radua & Rubia, 2014). A recent study in an adult sample showed reductions in hippocampal volume in patients with a diagnosis of major depression who had experienced childhood maltreatment compared to patients with depression without a history of childhood maltreatment, suggesting that childhood maltreatment is associated with structural brain changes in adulthood irrespective of a history of depression (Chaney, Carballedo, Amico et al., 2014).

By contrast, the majority of studies of children exposed to maltreatment have failed to detect the adult pattern of reduced hippocampal volume (McCrory, De Brito & Viding, 2010; Woon & Hedges, 2008). It is possible that the impact of this stress, while already showing effects at the behavioural level, does not manifest as structural brain differences until later in development. In other words, early stress has a protracted influence on hippocampal volume. Another possibility is that there are differences in sub-regions of the hippocampus, but that averaging across the whole region fails to capture developmental changes. As with the amygdala, the volume in this region has been shown to be influenced by the duration and severity of extreme childhood adversity, such that later-adopted children and children exposed to maltreatment for longer periods showed the smallest volumes relative to controls (Hodel, Hunt, Cowell et al., 2015; Teicher, Anderson & Polcari, 2012). There is also preliminary evidence that reductions in the hippocampus may mediate later psychiatric symptomatology. A recent investigation of structural differences after childhood maltreatment found that reductions in grey matter volume in the hippocampus and medial prefrontal cortex partly mediated the relationship between childhood maltreatment experience and anxiety later in life (Gorka, Hanson, Radtke & Hariri, 2014).

Prefrontal cortex

The prefrontal cortex (PFC) is a region of particular interest in the context of developmental research as it is the last part of the brain to fully mature, undergoing extensive re-organisation throughout childhood and especially adolescence (Gogtay, Giedd, Lusk et al., 2004). Through extensive connections to subcortical and other cortical regions, the PFC plays a regulatory role in cognitive and emotional processes (Ochsner & Gross, 2005). The findings in relation to the impact of childhood maltreatment on volumetric differences in this region are mixed and more complex to determine. Compared to the amygdala and hippocampus, both relatively small subcortical structures, the prefrontal cortex is a much larger and heterogeneous structure.

A recent meta-analysis found that inferior regions of the prefrontal cortex, such as the orbitofrontal cortex (OFC), which shares extensive connections with the amygdala, are especially vulnerable to maltreatment (Lim, Radua & Rubia, 2014). The orbitofrontal cortex plays a key role in the representation of the subjective value of rewards and is vital for emotional learning and decision-making (Rolls & Grabenhorst, 2008). We and others have found reductions in this region in children exposed to maltreatment at home who were not presenting with psychiatric disorders (De Brito, Viding, Sebastian et al., 2013; Hanson, Chung, Avants et al., 2010). More recently we have explored more fine-grained indices of cortical structure, looking for example at cortical thickness rather than overall volume. In the first study of its kind we found reduced cortical thickness in an extended frontal cluster that included the OFC and the anterior cingulate cortex (ACC) (Kelly, Viding, Wallace et al., 2013). Normally volumetric differences in the ACC are not observed in child samples; one interpretation is that the reduction in ACC cortical thickness in children represents a developmental precursor of the brain volume differences seen in adults. More recently, Hodel, Hunt, Cowell et al., 2015 investigated a group of previously institutionalised children in the same age range as those in Kelly, Viding, Wallace et al's. (2013) study. By contrast, they found that the differences in many sub-regions of the PFC showed reduced volumetric differences that were driven by reduced surface area and not cortical thickness. This suggests again that the timing, nature and duration of maltreatment experience may exert quite different effects on the structural indices of the brain.

White matter tracts (DTI-studies)

Recent advances in neuroimaging have enabled researchers to investigate white matter structure in maltreated children (i.e., brain tissue that contains insulated nerve fibres, which transmit signals between brain regions). These studies have employed a technique known as diffusion tensor imaging (DTI) and the DTI-derived measure of fractional anisotropy (FA), which measures variability of water diffusion in different directions and can be used as a marker of white matter tract integrity (Pierpaoli & Basser, 1996). To date, four studies have been conducted with children who were previously institutionalised, and these consistently point toward differences in frontal and temporal white matter regions. Two groups of researchers (Eluvathingal, Chugani, Behen et al., 2006; Govindan, Behen, Helder et al., 2010) found lower white matter directional organisation in the uncinate fasciculus, which is the main fibre bundle connecting the orbitofrontal cortex to the anterior temporal lobe, including the amygdala and hippocampus. The extent of the white matter differences observed by Govindan, Behen, Helder et al. (2010) was associated with longer periods within an orphanage and may underlie some of the socio-emotional and cognitive impairments exhibited by maltreated children. Additionally, when compared to non-institutionalised children, post-institutionalised children showed altered connectivity in fronto-striatal pathways that were associated with higher externalising behaviour (Behen, Muzik, Saporta et al., 2009).

A recent study by Hanson, Adluru, Chung et al. (2013) investigated white matter structure in 25 post-institutionalised children and also found lower FA values within the prefrontal cortex and white matter connecting the prefrontal cortex and temporal lobe, which were associated with poorer performance on a number of cognitive tasks. These findings are in line with behavioural evidence indicating that children who have experienced institutional care typically show poorer performance in domains that rely heavily on prefrontal cortex functioning (e.g., executive functioning, regulation of affect) and middle temporal lobe function (e.g., memory and emotion processing). These studies point consistently toward alterations in structural connectivity within fronto-limbic circuitries and suggest a more diffuse white matter organisation in maltreated youth.

Finally, differences have also been observed in the corpus callosum (CC), a large white matter structure connecting the right and left hemispheres, assumed to be central in interhemispheric communication. With the exception of one study, decreases in CC volume have consistently been reported in children and adolescents who have experienced maltreatment compared to non-maltreated peers (Jackowski, de Araújo, de Lacerda et al., 2009).

Structural differences: Conclusion

While this research has highlighted differences in a number of key brain regions implicated in emotion processing and cognitive functioning, these results nonetheless must be interpreted with caution. It is difficult to determine how these differences contribute to the function of a given region; a decrease in size of a particular brain region, for example, could index deficient functioning, or it could be that the region is operating more efficiently. The current state of the field, unfortunately, is such that we cannot often reliably make a claim in either direction.

Furthermore, because of the high rate of psychiatric disorders in children who have experienced childhood adversity, interpreting which effects are due to the co-morbid psychopathology and which are due to their childhood history is difficult. Nonetheless, as noted above, several regions are reliably found to be associated with childhood adversity across studies even in the absence of concurrent disorders, suggesting that maltreatment does indeed alter brain structure even in those children who do not present with mental health problems.

Functional Differences

In addition to the studies examining structural brain differences, a growing body of research has investigated possible functional correlates associated with maltreatment using brain imaging techniques such as functional MRI (fMRI) or electrophysiological techniques (e.g., ERP [Event Related Potential]; for a short description of these techniques see Table 6.1).

Event Related Potential (ERP) studies

Much of the existing ERP research has investigated institutionalised children's pattern of brain responses when processing facial expressions, an ability that is usually mastered by the preschool years. When compared with non-institutionalised peers, children who had been institutionalised and had experienced severe social deprivation showed a pattern of cortical hypoactivation when viewing emotional facial expressions, and familiar and unfamiliar faces (Parker & Nelson, 2005). A later study with institutionally reared children suggests, however, that the previously observed cortical hypoactivation was at least partially mediated by reductions in cortical white matter volume in institutionalised children who did not enter foster care, compared to those children who did enter foster care (Sheridan, Fox, Zeanah et al., 2012). These findings suggest that improved environmental conditions can potentially attenuate the impact of maltreatment on white matter, as has been shown for abnormal secretion of the stress hormone cortisol (Fisher, van Ryzin, & Gunnar, 2011).

In contrast, a second set of important studies has provided convincing evidence that school-aged children who had been exposed to physical abuse show increases in brain activity specific to angry faces and require more attentional resources to disengage from such stimuli (e.g., Pollak & Tolley-Schell, 2003). A recent study suggests that this hyper-responsivity to angry facial affect in children who have been maltreated is evident even in infants as young as 15 months and may extend in this younger sample to novel facial affect including happy faces (Curtis & Cicchetti, 2013). These differences in how facial affect is processed may represent one way in which an early adverse and emotionally unstable environment may contribute to an altered neurodevelopmental trajectory associated with difficulties in emotion processing and regulation.

fMRI studies

To date, only a limited number of fMRI studies have compared children who were maltreated to non-maltreated children. These studies however, have been relatively consistent in indicating alterations in fronto-limbic circuits, in line with findings from other neuroimaging modalities. Building on the experimental evidence that children who were maltreated show hypervigilance to threatening facial cues, several fMRI studies have examined the neural correlates of face processing in this population. These studies have reported that children who were maltreated are characterised by increased amygdala response to threatening cues in comparison to non-maltreated children (Maheu, Dozier, Guyer et al., 2010; McCrory, De Brito, Sebastian et al., 2011; Tottenham, Hare, Millner et al., 2011). One of the few studies to date investigating maltreated children who were not previously institutionalised (McCrory, De Brito, Sebastian et al., 2011) found greater activation in response to angry faces in the amygdala and the anterior insula – a neural signature previously associated with anxiety disorders (Etkin & Wager, 2007) and exposure to combat in adult soldiers (van Wingen, Geuze, Vermetten & Fernández, 2011). That these alterations in limbic system functioning occur in the earliest stages of affect processing is suggested by a study demonstrating heightened amygdala activity in maltreated children even when facial expressions were shown for periods of time that were outside conscious awareness (milliseconds range; see Figure 6.1) (McCrory, De Brito, Kelly et al., 2013).

The extent of amygdala activation to facial expressions has been associated with: (i) greater severity of the maltreatment experience; (ii) longer duration; (iii) younger age of onset of adversity; and (iv) the number of placements that a child has experienced (Maheu, Dozier, Guyer et al., 2010; McCrory, De Brito, Kelly et al., 2013), suggesting a dose-dependent relationship between the nature of the maltreatment experience and neural functioning (see Figure 6.1).

Overall, these fMRI findings are consistent with previous ERP evidence and suggest that some maltreated children spontaneously allocate more resources to threat-related cues, and remain hyper-vigilant to potential social threat in their environment. One consequence of this is that such children may have fewer attentional resources for more normative social and cognitive processes.

Other studies have observed altered activity in maltreated children and adolescents compared to controls in the anterior cingulate cortex (ACC), a brain structure with dense interconnections with the prefrontal cortex. One study assessed response inhibition in maltreated youth relative to controls and found impaired cognitive control and altered activation in the ACC associated with conflict monitoring (Mueller, Maheu, Dozier et al., 2010). Recent work on the neural correlates of peer rejection suggests that relative to non-maltreated peers, maltreated children report higher levels of exclusion and frustration during peer rejection and show altered activity and

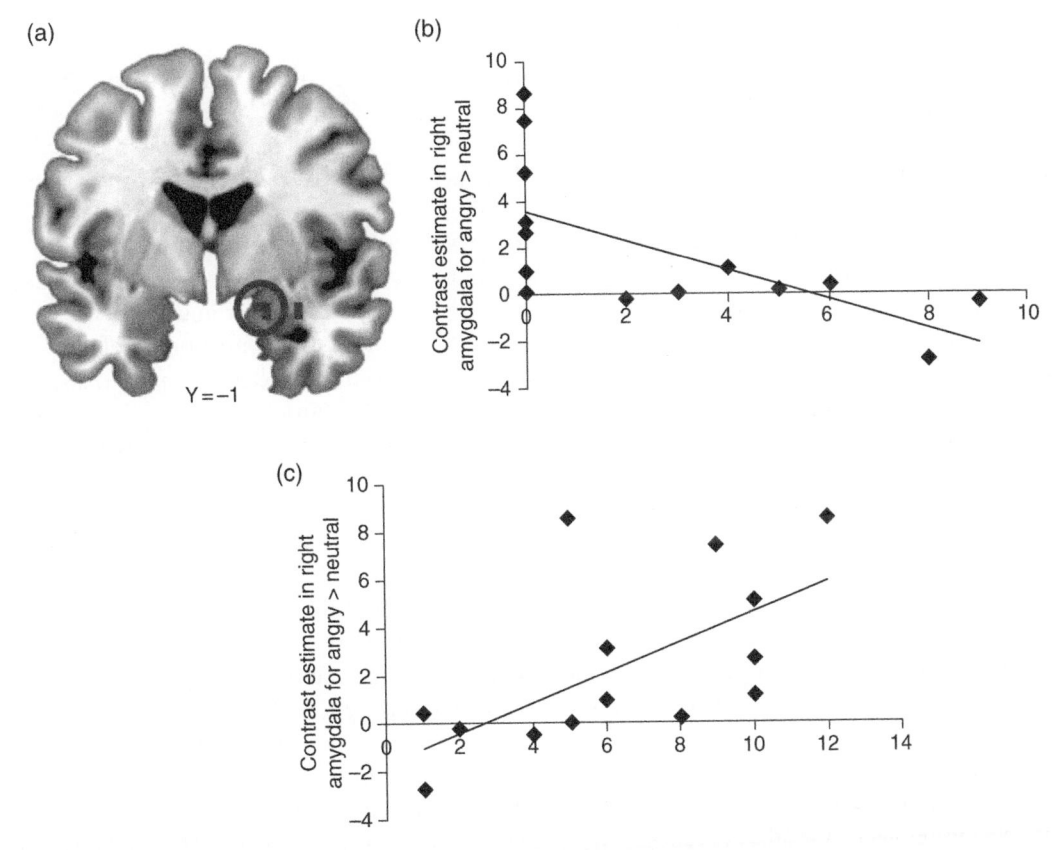

Figure 6.1 Brain activation and correlations in maltreated children during the processing of threat cues. a. Greater amygdala activation in children exposed to maltreatment during pre-attentive viewing of angry faces vs. neutral faces compared to control children; b. Scatterplot depicting the correlation between right amygdala activity during angry face processing and age of onset of emotional abuse in maltreated children; c. Scatterplot depicting the correlation between right amygdala activity during angry face processing and duration of emotional abuse in maltreated children. See McCrory, De Brito, Kelly et al., 2013 for full details.

connectivity within fronto-cingulate circuits previously implicated in negative affect regulation (Puetz, Kohn, Dahmen et al., 2014). These may represent a neural basis for impaired cognitive control in maltreated children, which, in turn, could confer risk for psychopathology, especially in the context of heightened subcortical responses such as that observed during affective processing.

Dillon, Holmes, Birk et al. (2009) investigated the neural response to reward cues in maltreated children and found a weakened response in the reward circuit (i.e., left globus pallidus), paralleling a reduction in the behavioural response to reward cues. This has important implications for reward learning and motivation in maltreated individuals, considering that reduced or altered motivational functioning for social rewards is a hallmark feature of major depression, PTSD and substance abuse (Hasler, Drevets, Manji & Charney, 2004), all of which are associated with maltreatment.

Taken together, these fMRI findings are in line with findings from other neuroimaging modalities and suggest alterations in fronto-limbic networks that likely affect emotion regulation abilities as well as the domains of reward learning and cognitive control, potentially increasing latent vulnerability for a range of psychiatric disorders.

The role of genetic influences

It is a common but often striking clinical experience to find that two children who have experienced very similar patterns of early adversity have very different outcomes. While this may be partly due to specific environmental or psychological factors characterising one child, but not the other, there is increasing evidence that such differential outcome may in part at least be due to genetic differences.

We now know that many of the psychiatric outcomes that are associated with maltreatment, such as PTSD, depression and antisocial behaviour, are partly heritable. However, it is incorrect to think that there are particular genes for these disorders. Rather, we are learning that there are a wide number of genetic variants that may subtly alter the structure and functioning of neural circuitry and hormonal systems that are crucial in calibrating our individual response to social affective cues, and in regulating our stress response (Viding, Williamson & Hariri, 2006). In recent years, researchers have focused in particular on the way in which such genetic variants and adverse environments may interact. Such GxE research has demonstrated that for a range of genetic variants (known as polymorphisms) childhood maltreatment can increase the risk of later psychopathology for some children more than others. For example, Caspi, McClay, Moffitt et al. (2002) were the first to report on an interaction of a measured genotype (MAOA) and environment (maltreatment) for a psychiatric outcome and demonstrated that individuals who are carriers for the low-activity allele (MAOA-l) were at increased risk for antisocial behaviour disorders following maltreatment. Imaging genetic studies have found that the risk genotype MAOA-l is related to hyper-responsivity of the brain's threat detection system and reduced activation in emotion regulation circuits. This work suggests a neural mechanism by which MAOA genotype engenders vulnerability to reactive aggression following maltreatment (Viding & Frith, 2006).

In other words, GxE research suggests that a child's genotype may partly determine their level of risk and resilience for adult psychiatric outcomes, including depression and PTSD following childhood maltreatment (e.g., Kaufman, Yang, Douglas-Palumberi et al., 2006). Note that positive environmental influences, such as social support, can promote resiliency, even in those children carrying 'risk' polymorphisms exposed to maltreatment (Kaufman, Yang, Douglas-Palumberi et al., 2006). This finding illustrates the important point that when considering a GxE interaction, positive environmental influences (e.g., contact with a supportive attachment figure) are as relevant to consider as negative environmental influences such as maltreatment. Future research will investigate the influence of clinical interventions as a positive environmental factor that may serve to moderate environmental and genetic risk.

Clinical implications

Over the last decade a small but growing body of neuroimaging research has documented a variety of changes to brain structure and function observed in children who have experienced maltreatment, and in adults reporting childhood experiences of maltreatment. But what do such differences mean? And do they have any clinical significance? Arguably, neurobiological correlates of maltreatment could be seen as a set of deleterious effects that are harmful for the child, and this kind of 'damage' narrative has been a relatively influential perspective in the field. However, a more evolutionary and developmentally informed view could contend that such changes are in fact adaptive responses to an early environment characterised by threat. If a child is to respond optimally to the challenges posed by their surroundings then early stress-induced changes in neurobiological systems could be seen as 'programming' or calibrating those systems to match the demands of a hostile environment.

This view has been recently articulated within the context of a theory of latent vulnerability (McCrory & Viding, 2015). Latent vulnerability can be understood as capturing the degree to which an ostensibly healthy individual previously exposed to maltreatment is at future risk of developing a psychiatric disorder. According to this theory, experiences of maltreatment and neglect in childhood may embed, causing enduring vulnerability to psychiatric disorder by altering the functioning of important neurocognitive systems during development. Such changes may reflect adaptations or patterns of atypical calibration that 'fit' with an early at-risk environment but which are, however, poorly suited to more normative environmental contexts (for example, a school setting or a safe foster care placement) and negotiating other kinds of future stressors.

Atypical development of neurocognitive systems that contribute to latent vulnerability can be thought of as hidden 'stress-weaknesses' in a building where the foundations have been shaped to accommodate one set of needs early in construction. However, as upper floors are added these internal configurations may confer a weakness to the building overall, when it is exposed to future environmental stressors.

There is good evidence to date that altered calibration of one candidate neurocognitive system – threat processing – may increase vulnerability to future psychopathology. Both psychological and neuroimaging findings suggest that maltreatment is associated with altered attentional allocation to threat and heightened neural responsiveness to threat cues. Such changes appear consistent with an early environment characterised by unpredictability and harm, but may become maladaptive in future more normative settings. Specifically, altered threat processing may gate attentional processes constraining other developmental inputs, and increase reactivity to internal and external threat cues in ways that may amplify stress and promote patterns of avoidance, increasing the likelihood of future psychiatric symptomatology. Other neurocognitive domains, however, including autobiographical memory and reward processing, represent equally promising candidates for indexing latent vulnerability, and warrant future enquiry.

From a practical perspective the operationalisation of latent vulnerability has the potential to fundamentally reconfigure our clinical approach to childhood maltreatment. Specifically, it may be possible to identify a subgroup of children exposed to maltreatment who are at most risk of future poor outcomes, and intervene in a way that can help offset their trajectory for future psychiatric risk. In other words, it may be possible to offer such children a preventative intervention that serves to reduce their risk of developing a future psychiatric disorder, rather than waiting for a disorder to present itself before offering treatment. What such a preventative intervention might look like remains an open question. The evidence from psychological, genetic and neurobiological research highlights the importance of a reliable adult caregiver, and the role they can play in helping to scaffold the child's ability to regulate stress (Dozier, Lindhiem, Lewis et al., 2009; Kaufman, Yang, Douglas-Palumberi et al., 2006), suggesting that enhancing social support and coping skills may be important components in any prevention package. In addition, clarifying which neurocognitive systems appear most associated with psychiatric risk may help inform how to best promote resilience and moderate the impact of early adversity, including at the neurobiological level.

References

Anda, R.F., Whitfield, C.L., Felitti, V.J. et al. (2002). Adverse childhood experiences, alcoholic parents, and later risk of alcoholism and depression. *Psychiatric Services*, 53, 1001–1009.

Behen, M.E., Muzik, O., Saporta, A.S. et al. (2009). Abnormal fronto-striatal connectivity in children with histories of early deprivation: A diffusion tensor imaging study. *Brain Imaging and Behavior*, 3, 292–297.

Caspi, A., McClay, J., Moffitt, T.E. et al. (2002). Role of genotype in the cycle of violence in maltreated children. *Science*, 297, 851–854.

Chaney, A., Carballedo, A., Amico, F. et al. (2014). Effect of childhood maltreatment on brain structure in adult patients with major depressive disorder and healthy participants. *Journal of Psychiatry & Neuroscience*, 39, 50–59.

Curtis, W.J. & Cicchetti, D. (2013). Affective facial expression processing in 15-month-old infants who have experienced maltreatment: An event-related potential study. *Child Maltreatment*, 18, 140–154.

De Bellis, M.D., Keshavan, M.S., Shifflett, H. et al. (2002). Brain structures in pediatric maltreatment-related posttraumatic stress disorder: A sociodemographically matched study. *Biological Psychiatry*, 52, 1066–1078.

De Brito, S.A., Viding, E., Sebastian, C.L. et al. (2013). Reduced orbitofrontal and temporal grey matter in a community sample of maltreated children. *Journal of Child Psychology and Psychiatry, and Allied Disciplines*, 54, 105–112.

Dillon, D., Holmes, A., Birk, J. et al. (2009). Childhood adversity is associated with left basal ganglia dysfunction during reward anticipation in adulthood. *Biological Psychiatry*, 66, 206–213.

Dozier, M., Lindhiem, O., Lewis, E. et al. (2009). Effects of a foster parent training program on young children's attachment behaviors: Preliminary evidence from a randomized clinical trial. *Child and Adolescent Social Work Journal*, 26, 321–332.

Eluvathingal, T.J., Chugani, H.T., Behen, M.E. et al. (2006). Abnormal brain connectivity in children after early severe socioemotional deprivation: A diffusion tensor imaging study. *Pediatrics*, 117, 2093–2100.

Enoch, M.A. (2011). The role of early life stress as a predictor for alcohol and drug dependence. *Psychopharmacology*, 214, 17–31.

Etkin, A. & Wager, T.D. (2007). Functional neuroimaging of anxiety: A meta-analysis of emotional processing in PTSD, social anxiety disorder, and specific phobia. *American Journal of Psychiatry*, 164, 1476–1488.

Fisher, P.A., van Ryzin, M.J. & Gunnar, M.R. (2011). Mitigating HPA axis dysregulation associated with placement changes in foster care. *Psychoneuroendocrinology*, 36, 531–539.

Gilbert, R., Widom, C.S., Browne, K. et al. (2009). Burden and consequences of child maltreatment in high-income countries. *The Lancet*, 373(9657), 68–81.

Gogtay, N., Giedd, J.N., Lusk, L. et al. (2004). Dynamic mapping of human cortical development during childhood through early adulthood. *Proceedings of the National Academy of Sciences of the United States of America*, 101, 8174–8179.

Gorka, A.X., Hanson, J.L., Radtke, S.R. & Hariri, A.R. (2014). Reduced hippocampal and medial prefrontal gray matter mediate the association between reported childhood maltreatment and trait anxiety in adulthood and predict sensitivity to future life stress. *Biology of Mood & Anxiety Disorders*, 4(12), 1–10.

Govindan, R.M., Behen, M.E., Helder, E. et al. (2010). Altered water diffusivity in cortical association tracts in children with early deprivation identified with Tract-Based Spatial Statistics (TBSS). *Cerebral Cortex*, 20, 561–569.

Hanson, J.L., Adluru, N., Chung, M.K. et al. (2013). Early neglect is associated with alterations in white matter integrity and cognitive functioning. *Child Development*, 84, 1566–1578.

Hanson, J.L., Chung, M.K., Avants, B.B. et al. (2010). Early stress is associated with alterations in the orbitofrontal cortex: A tensor-based morphometry investigation of brain structure and behavioral risk. *The Journal of Neuroscience*, 30, 7466–7472.

Hasler, G., Drevets, W.C., Manji, H.K. & Charney, D.S. (2004). Discovering endophenotypes for major depression. *Neuropsychopharmacology*, 29, 1765–1781.

Hodel, A.S., Hunt, R.H., Cowell, R.A. et al. (2015). Duration of early adversity and structural brain development in post-institutionalized adolescents. *NeuroImage*, 105, 112–119.

Hovens, J.G., Wiersma, J.E. & Giltay, E.J. (2010). Childhood life events and childhood trauma in adult patients with depressive, anxiety and comorbid disorders vs. controls. *Acta Psychiatrica Scandinavica*, 122, 66–74.

Jackowski, A.P., de Araújo, C.M., de Lacerda, A.L.T. et al. (2009). Neurostructural imaging findings in children with post-traumatic stress disorder: Brief review. *Psychiatry and Clinical Neurosciences*, 63, 1–8.

Kaufman, J. (2012). Child abuse and psychiatric illness. *Biological Psychiatry*, 71, 280–281.

Kaufman, J., Yang, B.-Z., Douglas-Palumberi, H. et al. (2006). Brain-derived neurotrophic factor-5-HTTLPR gene interactions and environmental modifiers of depression in children. *Biological Psychiatry*, 59, 673–680.

Kelly, P.A, Viding, E., Wallace, G.L. et al. (2013). Cortical thickness, surface area, and gyrification abnormalities in children exposed to maltreatment: Neural markers of vulnerability? *Biological Psychiatry*, 74, 845–852.

Lim, L., Radua, J. & Rubia, K. (2014). Gray matter abnormalities in childhood maltreatment: A voxel-wise meta-analysis. *The American Journal of Psychiatry*, 171, 854–863.

Lupien, S.J., McEwen, B.S., Gunnar, M.R. & Heim, C. (2009). Effects of stress throughout the lifespan on the brain, behaviour and cognition. *Nature Reviews Neuroscience*, 10, 434–445.

Maheu, F.S., Dozier, M., Guyer, A.E. et al. (2010). A preliminary study of medial temporal lobe function in youths with a history of caregiver deprivation and emotional neglect. *Cognitive, Affective & Behavioral Neuroscience*, 10, 34–49.

McCrory, E.J. & Viding, E. (2015). The theory of latent vulnerability: Reconceptualizing the link between childhood maltreatment and psychiatric disorder. *Development and Psychopathology*, 27, 493–505.

McCrory, E., De Brito, S.A. & Viding, E. (2010). Research review: The neurobiology and genetics of maltreatment and adversity. *Journal of Child Psychology and Psychiatry, and Allied Disciplines*, 51, 1079–1095.

McCrory, E.J., De Brito, S.A., Kelly, P.A. et al. (2013). Amygdala activation in maltreated children during pre-attentive emotional processing. *The British Journal of Psychiatry: The Journal of Mental Science*, 202, 269–276.

McCrory, E.J., De Brito, S.A., Sebastian, C.L. et al. (2011). Heightened neural reactivity to threat in child victims of family violence. *Current Biology*, 21, R947–8.

McEwen, B.S. (2004). Protection and damage from acute and chronic stress: Allostasis and allostatic overload and relevance to the pathophysiology of psychiatric disorders. *Annals of the New York Academy of Sciences*, 1032, 1–7.

Mueller, S.C., Maheu, F.S., Dozier, M. et al. (2010). Early-life stress is associated with impairment in cognitive control in adolescence: An fMRI study. *Neuropsychologia*, 48, 3037–3044.

Nanni, V., Uher, R. & Danese, A. (2012). Childhood maltreatment predicts unfavorable course of illness and treatment outcome in depression: A meta-analysis. *American Journal of Psychiatry*, 169, 141–151.

Ochsner, K.N. & Gross, J.J. (2005). The cognitive control of emotion. *Trends in Cognitive Sciences*, 9, 242–249.

Parker, S.W. & Nelson, C.A. (2005). An event-related potential study of the impact of institutional rearing on face recognition. *Development and Psychopathology*, 17, 621–639.

Pessoa, L. & Adolphs, R. (2010). Emotion processing and the amygdala: From a 'low road' to 'many roads' of evaluating biological significance. *Nature Reviews Neuroscience*, 11, 773–783.

Pierpaoli, C. & Basser, P.J. (1996). Toward a quantitative assessment of diffusion anisotropy. *Magnetic Resonance in Medicine*, 36, 893–906.

Pollak, S.D. & Tolley-Schell, S.A. (2003). Selective attention to facial emotion in physically abused children. *Journal of Abnormal Psychology*, 112, 323–338.

Puetz, V.B., Kohn, N., Dahmen, B. et al. (2014). Neural response to social rejection in children with early separation experiences. *Journal of the American Academy of Child & Adolescent Psychiatry*, 53, 1328–1337.

Read, J., Os, J.V., Morrison, A.P. & Ross, C.A. (2005). Childhood trauma, psychosis and schizophrenia: A literature review with theoretical and clinical implications. *Acta Psychiatrica Scandinavica*, 112, 330–350.

Rolls, E.T. & Grabenhorst, F. (2008). The orbitofrontal cortex and beyond: From affect to decision-making. *Progress in Neurobiology*, 86, 216–244.

Scott, K.M., Smith, D.R. & Ellis, P.M. (2010). Prospectively ascertained child maltreatment and its association with DSM-IV mental disorders in young adults. *Archives of General Psychiatry*, 67, 712–719.

Sheridan, M.A., Fox, N.A., Zeanah, C.H. et al. (2012). Variation in neural development as a result of exposure to institutionalization early in childhood. *Proceedings of the National Academy of Sciences*, 109, 12927–12932.

Teicher, M.H., Anderson, C.M. & Polcari, A. (2012). Childhood maltreatment is associated with reduced volume in the hippocampal subfields CA3, dentate gyrus, and subiculum. *Proceedings of the National Academy of Sciences of the United States of America*, 109, E563–72.

Tottenham, N. & Hare, T. (2009). Prolonged institutional rearing is associated with atypically large amygdala volume and difficulties in emotion regulation. *Developmental Science*, 13, 1–26.

Tottenham, N., Hare, T., Millner, A. et al. (2011). Elevated amygdala response to faces following early deprivation. *Developmental Science*, 14, 190–204.

van Wingen, G.A., Geuze, E., Vermetten, E. & Fernández, G. (2011). Perceived threat predicts the neural sequelae of combat stress. *Molecular Psychiatry*, 16, 664–671.

Viding, E. & Frith, U. (2006). Genes for susceptibility to violence lurk in the brain. *Proceedings of the National Academy of Sciences of the United States of America*, 103, 6085–6086.

Viding, E., Williamson, D.E. & Hariri, A.R. (2006). Developmental imaging genetics: Challenges and promises for translational research. *Development and Psychopathology*, 18, 877–892.

Widom, C.S., Czaja, S.J., Bentley, T. & Johnson, M.S. (2012). A prospective investigation of physical health outcomes in abused and neglected children: New findings from a 30-year follow-up. *American Journal of Public Health*, 102, 1135–1144.

Woon, F.L. & Hedges, D.W. (2008). Hippocampal and amygdala volumes in children and adults with childhood maltreatment-related posttraumatic stress disorder: A meta-analysis. *Hippocampus*, 18, 729–736.

7

Intimate Partner Violence and Child Maltreatment

Louise Dixon[1] and Amy M. Smith Slep[2]

[1] Victoria University of Wellington, NZ
[2] New York University, NY

Aggression and violence within the family has proven to be a common phenomenon (e.g., Dixon & Browne, 2003; Gelles & Cornell, 1990; Slep & O'Leary, 2005). There are five types of family violence and abuse, namely child, parent, sibling, elder and intimate partner abuse (IPV) (Browne & Herbert, 1997). Each type can encompass different forms of aggression, including physical, sexual, emotional and psychological abuse and neglect. Although this chapter recognises the different forms of abuse as important and necessary to understand it will limit its discussion to physical violence, as this is the form that the majority of empirical research in this area has investigated to date.

IPV and child maltreatment have arguably received the majority of empirical attention due to high international prevalence rates (e.g., Pinheiro, 2006; Krug, Dahlberg, Mercy et al., 2002). A review of child physical abuse (CPA) estimates in high-income countries found one-year prevalence rates of 4–16% (Gilbert, Widom, Browne et al., 2009). In some lower-resource countries (e.g., India, Republic of Korea), rates of CPA occur at high rates with one-third to one-half of all children experiencing CPA (World Health Organization, 2002). There is a high rate of co-occurrence among the different forms of child maltreatment (Gilbert, Widom, Browne et al., 2009; Higgins & McCabe, 2001). It is estimated that about 35–64% of victims of child maltreatment experience more than one form (Donga, Andaa, Felitti et al., 2004; Edwards, Holden, Felitti & Anda, 2003; Manly, Kim, Rogosch & Cicchetti, 2001). Of course, population surveys of CPA reveal higher rates than official records (e.g., Straus, Hamby, Finkelhor et al., 1998).

Physical IPV has a yearly prevalence of 15% in several nationally representative studies of US adults (e.g., Schafer, Caetano, & Clark, 1998). The lifetime and yearly prevalence rates from the 2010 Centers for Disease Control (CDC) National Intimate Partner and Sexual Violence Survey (Breiding, Chen & Black, 2014) are lower; however, CDC collected reports from individuals, whereas the Schafer et al. study interviewed couples (one of many methodological differences). Prevalence rates vary substantially across countries. The first European Union-wide

---

The Wiley Handbook of What Works in Child Maltreatment: An Evidence-Based Approach to Assessment and Intervention in Child Protection, First Edition. Edited by Louise Dixon, Daniel F. Perkins, Catherine Hamilton-Giachritsis, and Leam A. Craig.
© 2017 John Wiley & Sons Ltd. Published 2017 by John Wiley & Sons Ltd.

survey of IPV against women found lifetime rates of physical IPV ranging from 12% in many countries such as Spain and Poland to 31% in Latvia (European Union Agency for Fundamental Rights, 2012). In the World Health Organization (WHO) Multi-Country Study on Women's Health and Domestic Violence against Women (Garcia-Moreno, Jansen, Ellsberg et al., 2006) lifetime reports of physical IPV ranged from 13% in urban Japan to 27% in urban Brazil to between 40% and 50% in Samoa, rural Bangladesh, rural Tanzania, rural Ethiopia, rural Peru, and 61% in urban Peru. Surveys that have investigated rates of physical IPV for both sexes in different international samples vary in their results depending on the methodology used. For example, surveys that interview couples in the context of the family demonstrate approximately equal rates of victimisation between the sexes (e.g., yearly prevalence rates of 11.3% for men and 12.1% for women were reported in the US-based 1985 Family Violence Survey (Straus, 1990)). This is in comparison to surveys that interviewed one member of the couple in the context of an epidemiology and health survey (e.g., yearly rates of 5.8% for men and 12.7% for women were reported in a Ukraine-based survey (O'Leary, Tintle, Bromet & Gluzman, 2008)). Inconsistency in the survey methodology used makes it difficult to compare international rates of IPV (see Esquivel-Santovena & Dixon, 2012).

Traditionally, different types of family violence (e.g., CPA, physical IPV) have been studied and responded to in isolation. This is despite a wealth of evidence that has documented their co-occurrence. This overlap is particularly evident with IPV and child maltreatment (Bowen, 2000; Cox, Kotch & Everson, 2003; Hayzen, Connelly, Kelleher et al., 2004; Slep & O'Leary, 2005). Families who experience one type of violence and abuse have an increased likelihood of experiencing the other (Hughes, Humphrey & Weaver, 2005). This co-occurrence supports the need to study and respond to family violence in a holistic manner (Dixon & Browne, 2003; Slep & Heyman, 2008).

This chapter considers the child within the context of the family unit and explores the co-occurrence of physical IPV with CPA. It presents an overview of the co-occurrence rates, effects on the child, risk factors and theoretical explanations for this overlap and the implications this evidence has for research, policy and practice. It is argued that collectively the results highlight the need to adopt a systemic view and further explore and respond to patterns of family violence and abuse in research and practice. Although it is recognised that both types of family violence can manifest in a range of different forms of aggression, for the most part research has considered physical child and partner abuse in heterosexual relationships. As such, we mainly consider this evidence in our present discussion, however, we note the need to expand this knowledge base to understand a broad spectrum of family violence and abuse and its effects on parental care.

Co-occurrence

There is a great deal of empirical support for the co-occurrence of IPV and CPA within the family (e.g., Bowen, 2000; Cox, Kotch & Everson, 2003; Hayzen, Connelly, Kelleher et al., 2004; Slep & O'Leary, 2005). Research has highlighted co-occurrence rates of 30–60% (Edleson, 1999), 46–53% (Browne & Hamilton, 1999) and 40%, using a conservative definition of child abuse (Appel & Holden, 1998). However, the research methodology of studies should be carefully considered before interpreting and applying findings to the general population. For example, Appel and Holden's review of 31 studies showed differences in rates across studies depending on the type of sample accessed. Research focusing on samples of abused women or children found average co-occurrence rates of 40% (range 20–100%) in comparison to representative community samples, which provided an estimate base rate at 6% in the US. Slep and O'Leary (2005) found much higher rates of co-occurrence (reported below) in a representative sample of families with 3- to 7-year-old children using behaviourally specific assessments of physical aggression within the context of anonymous data collection. As always, rates gathered from clinical samples do not apply to community samples (Dutton, 2006). However, despite this discrepancy it is evident that where one type of family violence exists there is an increased likelihood that the other type will also exist.

Children living with IPV are not only at greater risk of being directly abused by one or both caregivers but can also be exposed to the parental violence directly or indirectly. Exposure to IPV can consist of the child hearing or seeing (witnessing) violence and/or its consequences, or simply being aware of IPV in the family home. Historically it has proven difficult to determine rates of exposure because of discrepancies in research methodology. However, international figures do highlight the sizeable problem of child exposure to IPV. Cawson's (2002) English national prevalence study of 2869 young men and women aged 18–24 reported that 26% of the sample witnessed violence between their parents at least once and 5% witnessed frequent and ongoing violence. Radford, Corral, Bradley and Fisher's (2013) more recent UK prevalence study provides an in-depth analysis of child maltreatment and other types of victimisation. Using computer-assisted self-interview techniques the authors determined the lifetime and yearly prevalence rates of a nationally representative sample of 2160 parents/caregivers of children aged 2 months to 10 years; 2275 children and young people aged 11–17 and their parents/caregivers; and 1761 young adults aged 18–24. In terms of exposure to parental domestic violence and abuse they determined lifetime prevalence rates of 12% for the under-11 age group; 17.5% for the 11–17 age group; and 23.7% for the 18–24 age group. The National Family Violence Surveys provide approximate figures for representative community samples in the US. Extrapolating from those samples to the general population, the 1975 survey reported that three million children witnessed minor to more severe acts of IPV each year (Straus, Gelles & Steinmetz, 1980) while adult retrospective reports in the 1985-survey approximated ten million (Straus, 1992).

Traditionally, the stereotypical family experiencing concurrent types of maltreatment is thought of as including an abusive male aggressing against his female partner, and either one or both of these parents responsible for maltreating the child, with the mother's ability to protect her child(ren) often coming into question. However, research has demonstrated that co-occurring physical abuse is common, and aggression by men and women in the same family is particularly common. In an attempt to go beyond the stereotype, Dixon and Browne (2003) proposed three hypothetical patterns of co-occurring abuse in the family, namely Paternal/Maternal, Hierarchical and Reciprocal family violence. In the Paternal/Maternal pattern the perpetrator aggresses against both their partner and child within the family unit. In some instances the child may also abuse the non-abusive adult, seeing them as powerless. In the Hierarchical pattern, family violence involves a hierarchy of violence where one adult is abusive to the other, and the victimised adult then in turn maltreats the child, but does not retaliate toward the adult. In some cases both adults may maltreat the child. Finally, the reciprocal pattern is characterised by bidirectional IPV, with both adults having the potential to abuse and/or neglect their child. Indeed, the potential to emotionally abuse the child through witnessing partner abuse is high. In all of the scenarios, it is suggested that children require support and intervention as victims of family violence.

In an initial study of these patterns of co-occurring family violence, Dixon, Browne, Hamilton-Giachritsis and Ostapuik (2010) examined concurrent abuse in a sample of 67 families referred to services for alleged child maltreatment that also evidenced concurrent physical

IPV. The three hypothesised patterns were found. The Paternal pattern characterised 14.9% of the sample; all aggressors were male in this instance. The Hierarchical pattern accounted for 43.3%; the man was the perpetrator of partner violence in all but three cases and both parents maltreated the child in the majority of instances. The reciprocal pattern constituted 41.8% of cases where both parents maltreated their child in the majority (21 out of 28 cases) of the families. This study considered more forms of child maltreatment than physical aggression. Further analysis demonstrated that Paternal fathers were always physically aggressive toward both their female partner and child. In Hierarchical families, fathers were significantly more likely to physically maltreat the child in comparison to the mother, who was significantly more likely to neglect him/her. In reciprocal families, both mother and father were significantly more likely to adopt the same child maltreatment strategy as each other, namely physical abuse or neglect.

Although this small clinical sample can only provide a first test of the predominance of these patterns in clinical populations, it supports the utility of understanding specific patterns of concurrent types of family aggression and the importance of including different forms of abuse in addition to physical maltreatment when considering those patterns. One critical implication of this line of research is that parents referred to treatment for either IPV or child abuse may have very different treatment needs depending on whether they engage in both types of maltreatment or only one, and depending on whether they are also a victim or solely a perpetrator. For example, the needs of a mother residing in a Hierarchical family who is a victim of partner violence and perpetrator of child maltreatment are those of both a victim and an offender. This is in comparison to a mother who is solely a victim in a Paternal pattern or a victim and a perpetrator in the reciprocal pattern. In reciprocal families the mother's partner violence needs to be addressed, in addition to the father's, rather than simply viewing her as a victim of his violence.

The reciprocal pattern may be even more predominant among families recruited from community samples. Slep and O'Leary (2005) assessed men's and women's physical aggression toward their partners and children in a US community sample of 453 families. In contrast to the often-expected Paternal pattern, the most common pattern of aggression (22% of all families) was characterised by both male and female partners aggressing against each other and their children. Instances of a sole perpetrator aggressing against both partner and child were rare with only 0.7% and 2.6% of fathers and mothers respectively perpetrating against family members in this manner. This was also true of severe physical violence with 11.3% of families reporting severe aggression abusing each other and the child and 2.1% of mothers and 0.7% of fathers aggressing against their partner and child only. Therefore, when considering the safety of a child, it is necessary to assess the family completely. This allows the clinician to understand all of the types of aggression that exist within the family. It is critical that these assessments be guided by evidence rather than based on stereotypical expectations.

Effects on the Child

Both exposure to IPV and experiencing child abuse can result in deleterious effects on a child's development – social (e.g., poor conflict resolution skills, vulnerability to further victimisation), emotional (e.g., shame, isolation, fear), behavioural (e.g., suicidal ideation, delinquency, substance abuse) and psychological (e.g., increased anxiety, depression, post-traumatic stress) development (e.g., Gewirtz & Edleson, 2007; Osofsky, 1999). Furthermore, in conjunction with the development of other risk factors, an increased likelihood of continuing the intergenerational cycle of family violence (e.g., Dixon, Browne & Hamilton-Giachritsis, 2005; Dixon, Hamilton-Giachritsis & Browne, 2005; Egeland, Bosquet & Chung, 2002) has been demonstrated. Experiencing both child abuse and exposure to IPV (in comparison to experiencing only one form) has been shown to result in greater negative effects for children (Chiodo, Leschied, Whitehead & Hurley, 2008; Herrenkohl & Herrenkohl, 2007; Herrenkohl, Sousa, Tajima et al., 2008). However, evidence on the unique effects of IPV exposure and child abuse is limited and mixed (Herrenkohl, Sousa, Tajima et al., 2008), primarily because these types of family violence have been researched independently. A common error in IPV research is to attribute any negative effects for the child to the exposure to IPV, rather than considering the possibility that those effects may be consequences of direct child abuse (Edleson, 1999; Herrenkohl, Sousa, Tajima et al., 2008). As the following section details, IPV and CPA share considerable overlap in risk factors and stressors and the existence of both types of aggression in the family unit is therefore plausible.

A further issue that is overlooked when considering the effects of IPV on the child is exposure to reciprocal aggression between parents. Evidence suggests children are more likely to be exposed to parental violence when it is reciprocal (Fusco & Fantuzzo, 2009) and are three times more likely to be physically abused by one or both parents in comparison to households where only one partner is violent (Slep & O'Leary, 2005). Considering that research has also found approximately 50% of relationships characterised by IPV can be categorised as bi-directional (Straus & Gelles, 1990), children's exposure to reciprocal partner violence is arguably an understudied issue. Exposure to partner violence increases children's risk for a host of emotional and behavioural problems, regardless of whether the perpetrator is their mother or father (English, Marshall & Stewart, 2003).

Finally, when considering the effects of living with IPV on the child it is important to understand the heterogeneity of different types of family violence and the varying effects for the child. Professionals need to understand that the experience of living with IPV is not the same for all children and although their safety is paramount their needs for support will vary (Jaffe, Johnston, Crooks & Bala, 2008). This is not always recognised, often due to a lack of joined-up thinking between services (Radford, Aitken, Miller et al., 2011). As D'Ambrosio (2008) states: 'Many jurisdictions handle domestic violence cases on a one-size-fits-all basis, with a presumption in favour of a finding of child neglect and removal when children are exposed to domestic violence. Such a standard fails to recognise that not all domestic violence is the same and not all families are equally affected' (p. 654). Arguably, further investigation into effective support for children and parents is required to inform policy and practice in this area. Indeed, Radford, Aitken, Miller et al. (2011) report that there is a clear need for 'better understanding among professionals and commissioners about what "work with children affected by domestic violence" means' (p. 19) and go on to state that for the most part 'work' has centred on therapeutic practice that has not been evaluated.

Risk Factors

Four published studies have addressed the question of distinctions between dually and singly aggressive individuals. Shipman, Rossman and West (1999) compared non-aggressive, partner-aggressive and partner-and-parent aggressive families and found that dual-form perpetrators reported higher levels of neighbourhood violence, family stress and more physical punishment in the father's family of origin. The authors concluded that these groups differed 'by the degree of severity of adversity and not in qualitative pattern of experience' (Shipman et al., 1999, p. 99).

Tajima (2004) examined differences among parent-and-partner-aggressive, parent-aggressive-only and partner-aggressive-only groups from the 1985 National Family Violence Survey (Straus & Gelles, 1990). Dually aggressive individuals reported higher levels of depressive symptoms and reported stomping out of the room more often during partner conflicts than individuals engaging in only one form of aggression. They also differed from parent-aggressive-only respondents in that they were younger and married for a shorter period and reported lower incomes and greater frequencies of all remaining non-violent conflict tactics (said things in spite, smashed things and insulted partner more) and of the husband being under the influence of drugs. Dually aggressive respondents differed from partner-aggressive-only respondents only in that the target child was older. These findings present an equivocal picture, suggesting that perhaps there are different risk profiles for dually aggressive individuals compared with parent-aggressive-only individuals, but perhaps this is not the case when distinguishing dually aggressive individuals from partner-aggressive-only individuals.

Using data from the National Study of Child and Adolescent Well-Being, Kohl, Edleson, English and Barth (2005) compared child welfare system families with and without domestic violence. They found that families with active domestic violence had an increased chance of child maltreatment being substantiated and were more likely to have prior reports of child maltreatment. Child welfare workers' assessments indicated that dually aggressive parents had higher rates of substance abuse, mental health problems, arrest and histories of child abuse and neglect in their own backgrounds. The nature of the variables available in this study makes it difficult to determine whether the differences between groups are in degree or in kind.

These three studies took an empirical approach to examining differences in risk factors for partner-aggressive-only, parent-aggressive-only and dually aggressive individuals. Slep and O'Leary (2009) proposed and tested an a priori framework to determine whether risk profiles differ among dually aggressive, singly aggressive and non-aggressive individuals. They began by examining the array of perpetrator risk factors that had been identified in the partner-and-parent aggression literatures at the time of the review (see Slep & O'Leary, 2001). A number of groups of risk factors were apparent: perpetrator personality characteristics, early life experiences, socio-demographics, cognitions, specific behaviours during interactions, emotional reactivity, adjustment and relationship qualities (see Black, Heyman & Slep, 2001; Schumacher, Feldbau-Kohn, Slep & Heyman, 2001). When examined in parallel, this literature suggested another organisation that seemed particularly relevant to understanding the conditions under which individuals perpetrate only one or both forms of family violence.

They proposed an organisation based on whether perpetrator risk factors are related or unrelated to an individual's specific role as a partner or a parent. Because role-independent factors (e.g., stress, depressive symptoms and trait anger) are typically associated with both partner and parent aggression (see Slep & O'Leary, 2001), Slep and O'Leary proposed they may not distinguish parent from partner aggressors, although dual perpetrators could have higher mean levels of such role-independent predictors. In contrast, many risk factors are specifically related to an individual's role as a parent or partner (e.g., jealousy in the partner aggression area or discipline style in the parent aggression area). They proposed that these role-specific risk factors would be uniquely related to one form of aggression. Thus, they conceptualised that dual, parent-only, and partner-only aggressors should each have distinct risk profiles in terms of level and type.

They tested this model in the sample of 453 parents of 3- to 7-year-olds described earlier. They found that dual aggressors were high on both parent and partner role-specific risk, which was consistent with the fact that they were aggressive in both roles. Dual aggressors were also high on role-independent risk and, especially for men, report elevations on risk factors of all types compared with both singly aggressive and non-aggressive individuals. Thus, targeting role-independent factors, such as depression or anger expression, might be particularly useful when intervening with dual aggressors. In fact, most of the role-independent factors for partner and parental physical aggression are risk factors for antisocial behaviour, crime and aggression in general (see Biglan, Brennan, Foster & Holder, 2004). Thus, it seems that role-independent risk factors for aggression toward a partner and aggression toward a child confer a general risk for family aggression and perhaps for all forms of aggression. Because these role-independent factors are not more tightly tied to one relationship than another, it seems reasonable that they may set the stage for aggression in the home against anyone who is perceived to provoke the perpetrator. In contrast, single aggressors generally have the most severe risk on the role-specific risk factors that match the type of aggression they perpetrate and have lower levels of risk on the role-specific risk factors pertaining to the other role. Furthermore, these findings regarding the specificity of relations of role-specific risk factors with aggression may also have important implications for theories of the processes and mechanisms responsible for the aetiology and maintenance of family aggression.

Slep and O'Leary (2001) found that partner and parent role-specific risk factors appear relevant to both singly and dually aggressive people. They propose that these factors are likely a function of both (a) qualities of the perpetrator and (b) specific contexts and particular interaction patterns. They further posited that among individuals for whom (a) role-specific factors are primarily a function of their qualities and not of contexts or partners or (b) there is a match between the level of dysfunction present across their qualities and both their parent and partner contexts, the level of elevation present in their parent and partner role-specific risk should match. That appeared to be the case among dual aggressors and non-aggressors in their study. When parent and partner role-specific risk levels do not match (which is the case for parent- and partner-only aggressors), a greater contribution of contextual influences and some inconsistency across their parent and partner contexts seems implied. This suggests that the ways in which role-specific risk factors relate to aggression differ depending on whether individuals aggress against both their partners and their children or against only their partners or their children.

Indeed, co-occurrence status might be a key source of heterogeneity and unexplained variability in findings reported in the family violence literature – an issue that has received a great deal of attention especially with respect to men's partner aggression (e.g., Capaldi & Kim, 2007; Dixon & Browne, 2003; Holtzworth-Munroe & Stuart, 1994; Johnson, 2004) and more recently women's partner aggression (e.g., Babcock, Miller & Siard, 2003). As dual-aggressor status is generally not considered in research, both dually and singly aggressive men are probably in many study samples adding some noise to what we think we know about these forms of aggression. That subgroups of aggressive parents or partners, as a function of co-occurrence of the other form of aggression, have substantially different risk profiles, both in severity and in kind, might have a particularly unpredictable influence on the findings of any given study and a varied impact on the literature as a whole. The importance of this possibility is underscored by the fact that the rate of dual aggression (detailed at the beginning of this chapter) appears to be approximately 40%. Of course, not all parents are partnered and not all partners have children. Therefore, any given study of either partner or parent aggression might have sampled predominantly dual aggressors or predominantly single aggressors, and the ratios of one to the other might affect results and interpretations without anyone's awareness. Slep and O'Leary (2001) found that the pertinent types of role-specific risk factors were, with one exception, higher than not only the other type of role-specific factor, but also the role-independent factors among single aggressors. Thus, research about co-occurrence status has clear implications for assessment and treatment.

Implications for Research, Practice and Policy

Although research has investigated the co-occurrence and effects of concurrent child maltreatment and IPV, the majority of studies examine the aetiology, maintenance and intervention of these forms of family aggression separately, with services and interventions often remaining distinct entities. This is despite an evidence base which suggests it would prove fruitful in prevention and intervention terms to consider family violence in a more holistic manner (Dixon & Browne, 2003; Slep & O'Leary, 2001). The message for professionals working in policy and practice is to incorporate the strong evidence of the connections between types of family violence in their practice and ensure 'joined-up thinking' occurs between professionals and agencies as much as possible. It is a disservice to clients when concurrent forms of abuse are not identified and responded to. Researchers can facilitate the responsiveness of practice and policy to the interconnections of types of family violence through the development of tools that aim to specifically identify co-occurring violence within a sample identified for one specific types of violence.

The need for joined-up thinking has been highlighted in recent research reports. In her review of the child protection system in England, Eileen Munro reported that children living with IPV have been overlooked, with priority often placed on the parent's needs. Conversely, if a focus is placed on child protection issues the needs of the abused parent can be overlooked (Munro, 2011). Therefore, the need for a joined-up approach between services and researchers examining effective support for the child and parent living in the abusive family is warranted (Radford, Aitken, Miller et al., 2011). Indeed, in their exploration of children living with domestic violence in London, Radford, Aitken, Miller et al. (2011) noted significant gaps in services addressing the needs of children and young people, that the most vulnerable children are the least likely to be able to access help, and that children are not often provided with a window to express their own views or be involved in decisions that affect them. Such issues will only be improved for children living with IPV through breaking down silos and thinking across issues and working collaboratively across agencies. As Peled, Jaffe and Edleson (1995) asserted, IPV and child maltreatment are a result of complex interactions among institutional, social and individual factors and as such a coordinated response across agencies is required for effective prevention and response.

One example of good practice that adheres to the evidence base is the introduction of Multi Agency Safeguarding Hubs (MASH) in England and Wales. MASH aims to 'improve the safeguarding response for children and vulnerable adults through better information sharing and high quality and timely safeguarding responses' (Home Office (HO), 2014, p. 4). Although no specific model of MASH is currently endorsed, the majority of local authorities adopting this model have located different agencies in the same building or local space to actively promote information sharing, joint decision-making and coordinated intervention (Home Office, 2014). While an outcome evaluation of MASH's effectiveness is yet to be completed, a recent review of 37 local authorities reports that those authorities who have established a MASH reported improved outcomes for children and families (Home Office, 2014). Furthermore, systemic approaches to the treatment of family violence, such as those described by Arlene Vetere in Chapter 24 of this edited book, provide promise for identifying and responding to the co-occurrence issue.

In addition to encouraging multi-agency work, the co-occurrence literature should encourage the development of practice that aims to comprehensively assess both types of family violence, which would lead to accurate identification of both when they co-occur. The co-occurrence of IPV and CPA and the presence of role-independent risk factors for both dual and single perpetrators (Slep & O'Leary, 2001) highlight the importance of assessing individuals who perpetrate violence toward their partner or child within the context of the family if patterns of aversive family interactions are to be clearly identified to inform effective intervention. Slep and O'Leary's work described above has implications for risk assessment. Considering that their findings showed dual perpetrators to have the highest levels of role-independent risk factors in comparison to singly and non-aggressive perpetrators, existing risk screeners, which typically include role-independent risk variables (e.g., Milner, 1986) along with role-specific risk variables, might be more effective at identifying dually aggressive individuals than singly aggressive individuals. Furthermore, as Slep and O'Leary showed role-specific factors to be prevalent among perpetrators carrying out each specific form of abuse, screeners specifically tailored to role-specific risk factors may be equally effective at identifying all perpetrators of parental aggression, for example, regardless of whether the respondents also perpetrate partner aggression. Joint screening tools would benefit from inclusion of both independent and role-specific risk factors weighted accordingly to best identify dual and singly aggressive individuals. However, further research is needed to develop such tools and inform the factors associated with the different categories of perpetrator. Arguably, as in the identification of other forms of violent behaviour, the need for theoretically driven risk factor and protective factor research to inform risk assessment is paramount (e.g., Bonta & Andrews, 2010). Indeed, professionals would be advised to adhere to the aforementioned evidence to inform their clinical judgement when assessing families.

Considering the role of assessment further, the development of structured risk assessment tools would enable professionals to carry out thorough, evidence-based and non-biased assessments to identify co-occurrence. This may be particularly useful when working in the domain of family violence where the majority of research to date has arguably focused on understanding IPV as male–female aggression in heterosexual relationships while most child maltreatment research has focused on mothers. Regardless of debates about the frequency of violence by either gender (e.g., see Dixon, Archer & Graham-Kevan, 2012), it is plausible that either parental figure (or both) may be perpetrating or experiencing IPV, and/or perpetrating child maltreatment. Professionals therefore need to be open to this view in their policy, assessments and further practice with families if prevention and intervention is to be accurate and effective (see Dixon & Graham-Kevan, 2011).

In addition, there is a need for research to adopt gender-inclusive methodology to inform practice and policy. Indeed, research has highlighted the reciprocal nature of IPV (Johnson, 2004; Slep & O'Leary, 2005) and overlap of this form of IPV with CPA (Dixon & Browne, 2003; Dixon, Browne, Hamilton-Giachritsis & Ostapuik, 2010; Slep & O'Leary, 2005). Furthermore, the importance of understanding male victimisation in heterosexual relationships (Celi, 2011; Douglas & Hines, 2011; Hines & Douglas, 2010a,b; 2013; Tilbrook, Allan & Dear, 2010) and the harm that this poses to children in their care has more recently been noted (Hines & Douglas, 2016). Further research to inform practice and policy in this area is much needed as understanding is in its infancy, as is research with same-sex couples with children.

Conclusion

In conclusion, research demonstrates the need for professionals to consider IPV in the context of the family and to understand the impact of impoverished family relations on the development and maintenance of all types of aggression in the home. The importance of using the evidence base to inform practice and policy is paramount, whereby joined-up thinking between services dealing with child protection and intimate partner violence is promoted, and tools to structure the formal assessment of both types of family violence are developed. Co-occurring family violence does not take only one form, and its implications for intervention (if carefully assessed and accurately identified) are likely quite strong. Conducting careful and accurate assessments of family violence is itself a challenge, as most parents are hesitant to be forthcoming in the context of an identifiable assessment. However, this is an area worthy of focused attention. Given the extraordinarily high rates of co-occurrence, coupled with the diversity of patterns of co-occurrence typical among both community and clinical samples, and in the context of the risk factor literature suggesting these different patterns may have different aetiologies and may require different interventions, we will do a disservice to children and families if these challenges are not faced head on. Definitional and assessment issues have begun to be more thoroughly addressed within the specific IPV and child maltreatment literatures (e.g., Heyman, Slep & Foran, 2015; Slep, Heyman & Foran, 2015). We must continue to take each step within those separate literatures and bring them within the family context and consider their implications for co-occurrence. Children live with their families experiencing their parents' treatment of them and each other simultaneously. Clearly our research must continue to do the same thing.

References

Appel, A.E. & Holden, G.W. (1998). The co-occurrence of spouse and physical child abuse: A review and appraisal. *Journal of Family Psychology*, 12, 578–599.

Babcock, J.C., Miller, S. A. & Siard, C. (2003). Toward a typology of abusive women: Differences between partner-only and generally violent women in the use of violence. *Psychology of Women Quarterly*, 27, 153–161.

Biglan, A., Brennan, P.A., Foster, S.L. & Holder, H.D. (2004). *Helping Adolescents at Risk: Prevention of Multiple Problem Behaviors*. New York: Guilford Press.

Black, D.A., Heyman, R.E. & Slep, A.M.S. (2001). Risk factors for child physical abuse. *Aggression and Violent Behavior*, 6, 121–188.

Bonta, J. & Andrews, D.A. (2010). *The Psychology of Criminal Conduct*, 5th edn. New York: Routledge.

Bowen, K. (2000). Child abuse and domestic violence in families of children seen for suspected sexual abuse. *Clinical Paediatrics*, 39, 35–40.

Breiding, M.J., Chen, J. & Black, M.C. (2014). *Intimate Partner Violence in the United States – 2010*. Atlanta: National Center for Injury Prevention and Control, Centers for Disease Control and Prevention.

Browne, K.D. & Hamilton, C.E. (1999). Police recognition of links between spouse abuse and child abuse. *Child Maltreatment*, 4, 136–147.

Browne, K.D. & Herbert, M. (1997). *Preventing Family Violence.* Chichester: John Wiley & Sons, Ltd.

Capaldi, D.M. & Kim, H.K. (2007). Typological approaches to violence in couples: A critique and alternative conceptual approach. *Clinical Psychology Review,* 27, 253–265.

Cawson, P. (2002). *Child maltreatment in the family: The experience of a national sample of young people.* London: NSPCC.

Celi, E. (2011). *Breaking the Silence: A Practical Guide for Male Victims of Domestic Abuse.* Victoria, AU: Global Publishing Group

Chiodo, D., Leschied, A.W., Whitehead, P.C. & Hurley, D. (2008). Child welfare practice and policy related to the impact of children experiencing physical victimization and domestic violence. *Children and Youth Services Review,* 30, 564–574.

Cox, C.E., Kotch, J.B. & Everson, M. (2003). A longitudinal study of modifying influences in the relationship between domestic violence and child maltreatment. *Journal of Family Violence,* 18, 5–17.

D'Ambrosio, Z. (2008). Advocating for comprehensive assessments in domestic violence cases. *Family Court Review,* 46, 654–669.

Dixon, L. & Browne, K.D. (2003). The heterogeneity of spouse abuse: A review. *Aggression and Violent Behavior,* 268, 1–24.

Dixon, L. & Graham-Kevan, N. (2011). Understanding the nature and etiology of intimate partner violence and implications for practice and policy. *Clinical Psychology Review,* 31, 1145–1155.

Dixon, L., Archer, J. & Graham-Kevan, N. (2012). Perpetrator programmes for partner violence: Are they based on ideology or evidence? *Legal and Criminological Psychology,* 17, 196–215.

Dixon, L., Browne, K.D. & Hamilton-Giachritsis, C. (2005). Risk factors of parents abused as children: A mediational analysis of the intergenerational continuity of child maltreatment (Part I). *Journal of Child Psychology and Psychiatry,* 46, 47–57.

Dixon, L., Hamilton-Giachritsis, C. & Browne, K.D. (2005). Attributions and behaviours of parents abused as children: A mediational analysis of the intergenerational continuity of child maltreatment (Part II). *Journal of Child Psychology and Psychiatry,* 46, 58–68.

Dixon, L., Browne, K.D., Hamilton-Giachritsis, C.E. & Ostapuik, E. (2010). Differentiating patterns of aggression in the family. *Journal of Aggression Conflict and Peace Research,* 2, 32–44.

Donga, M., Andaa, R.F., Felitti, V.J. et al. (2004). The interrelatedness of multiple forms of childhood abuse, neglect, and household dysfunction. *Child Abuse & Neglect,* 28, 771–784.

Douglas, E. & Hines. (2011). The helpseeking experiences of men who sustain intimate partner violence: An overlooked population and implications for practice. *Journal of Family Violence,* 26, 473–485.

Dutton, D.G. (2006). *Rethinking Domestic Violence.* Vancouver: University of British Columbia Press.

Edleson, J.L. (1999). The overlap between child maltreatment and woman battering. *Violence Against Women,* 5, 134–154.

Edwards, V.J., Holden, G.W., Felitti, V.J. & Anda, R.F. (2003). Relationship between multiple forms of childhood maltreatment and adult mental health in community respondents: Results from the adverse childhood experiences study. *American Journal of Psychiatry,* 160, 1453–1460.

Egeland, B., Bosquet, M. & Chung, A.L. (2002). Continuities and discontinuities in the intergenerational transmission of child maltreatment: Implications for breaking the cycle of abuse. In: K.D. Browne, H. Hanks, P. Stratton & C.E. Hamilton (eds), *Early Prediction and Prevention of Child Abuse: A Handbook.* Chichester: John Wiley & Sons, Ltd, 217–232.

English, D.J., Marshall, D.B. & Stewart, A.J. (2003). Effects of family violence on child behavior and health during early childhood. *Journal of Family Violence,* 18, 43–57.

Esquivel-Santovena, E.E. & Dixon, L. (2012). Investigating the true rate of physical intimate partner violence: A review of nationally representative surveys. *Aggression and Violent Behavior,* 17, 208–219.

European Union Agency for Fundamental Rights. (2012). FRA gender-based violence against women survey dataset, 2012, http://fra.europa.eu/DVS/DVT/vaw.php (accessed 3 July 2014).

Fusco, R.A. & Fantuzzo, J.W. (2009). Domestic violence crimes and children: A population-based investigation of direct sensory exposure and the nature of involvement. *Children and Youth Services Review*, 31, 249–256.

Garcia-Moreno, C., Jansen, H.A.F.M., Ellsberg, M., et al. (2006). Prevalence of IPV: Findings from the WHO multi-country study on women's health and domestic violence. *The Lancet*, 368, 1260–1269.

Gelles, R.J. & Cornell, C.P. (1990). *Intimate Violence in the Family*. Beverly Hills: Sage.

Gewirtz, A.H. & Edleson, J.L. (2007). Young children's exposure to intimate partner violence: Towards a developmental risk and resilience framework for research and intervention. *Journal of Family Violence*, 22, 151–163.

Gilbert, R., Widom, C.S., Browne, K. et al. (2009). Burden and consequences of child maltreatment in high-income countries. *The Lancet*, 373, 68–81.

Hayzen, A.L., Connelly, C.D., Kelleher, K. et al. (2004). Intimate partner violence among female caregivers of children reported for child maltreatment. *Child Abuse & Neglect*, 28, 301–319.

Herrenkohl, T.I. & Herrenkohl, R.C. (2007). Examining the overlap and prediction of multiple forms of child maltreatment, stressors, and socioeconomic status: A longitudinal analysis of youth outcomes. *Journal of Family Violence*, 22, 553–562.

Herrenkohl, T.I., Sousa, C., Tajima, E.A. et al. (2008). Intersection of child abuse and children's exposure to domestic violence. *Trauma, Violence and Abuse*, 9, 84–99.

Heyman, R.E., Slep, A.M.S. & Foran, H.M. (2015). Enhanced definitions of intimate partner violence for DSM-5 and ICD-11 may promote improved screening and treatment. *Family Process*, 54, 64–81.

Higgins, D.J. & McCabe, M.P. (2001). Multiple forms of child abuse and neglect: Adult retrospective reports. *Aggression and Violent Behavior*, 6, 547–578.

Hines, D.A. & Douglas, E.M. (2010a). A closer look at men who sustain intimate terrorism by women. *Partner Abuse*, 1, 286–313.

Hines, D.A. & Douglas, E.M. (2010b). Intimate terrorism by women towards men: Does it exist? *Journal of Aggression, Conflict, and Peace Research*, 2(3), 36–56.

Hines, D. & Douglas, E. (2013). Predicting potentially life-threatening partner violence by women toward men: A preliminary analysis. *Violence and Victims*, 28, 751–771.

Hines, D. & Douglas, E. (2016). Sexual aggression experiences among male victims of physical partner violence: Prevalence, severity, and health correlates for male victims and their children. *Archives of Sexual Behavior*, 45, 1133–1151.

Holtzworth-Munroe, A. & Stuart, G.L. (1994). Typologies of male batterers: Three subtypes and the differences among them. *Psychological Bulletin*, 116, 476–497.

Home Office (2014). *Multi agency working and information sharing project: Final report*. Home Office: London, https://www.gov.uk/government/uploads/system/uploads/attachment_data/file/338875/MASH.pdf (accessed date of January 2017).

Hughes, H.M., Humphrey, N.N. & Weaver, T.L. (2005). Advances in violence and trauma: Toward a comprehensive ecological model. *Journal of Interpersonal Violence*, 20, 31–38.

Jaffe, P., Johnston, J., Crooks, C. & Bala, N. (2008). Custody disputes involving allegations of domestic violence: Towards a differentiated approach to parenting plans, *Family Court Review*, 46, 500–522.

Johnson, M.P. (2004). Patriarchal terrorism and common couple violence: Two forms of violence against women. In: H.T. Reis & C.E. Rusbult (eds), *Close Relationships: Key Readings*. Philadelphia: Taylor & Francis, 471–482.

Kohl, P.L., Edleson, J.L., English, D.J. & Barth, R.P. (2005). Domestic violence and pathways into child welfare services: Findings from the National Survey of Child and Adolescent Well-Being. *Children and Youth Services Review*, 27, 1167–1182.

Krug, E.G., Dahlberg, L.L., Mercy, J.A. et al. (2002). *World report on violence and health*. Geneva: World Health Organization.

Manly, J.T., Kim, J.E., Rogosch, F.A. & Cicchetti, D. (2001). Dimensions of child maltreatment and children's adjustment: Contributions of developmental timing and subtype. *Development and Psychopathology*, 13, 759–782.

Milner, J.S. (1986). *The Child Abuse Potential Inventory: Manual*. Webster, NC: Psytec.

Munro, E. (2011). *The Munro Review of Child Protection. Final report: A child-centered system*, London: DfE, https://www.gov.uk/government/uploads/system/uploads/attachment_data/file/175391/Munro-Review.pdf (accessed January 2017).

O'Leary, K.D., Tintle, N., Bromet, E.J. & Gluzman, S.F. (2008). Descriptive epidemiology of intimate partner aggression in Ukraine. *Social Psychiatry and Psychiatric Epidemiology*, 43, 619–626.

Osofsky, J.D. (1999). The impact of violence on children. *The Future of Children*, 9, 33–49.

Peled, E., Jaffe, P.G. & Edleson, J.L. (1995). *Ending the Cycle of Violence: Community Responses to Children of Battered Women*. Thousand Oaks, CA: Sage.

Pinheiro, P. (2006). *World report on violence against children*. Geneva: United Nations.

Radford, L., Corral, S., Bradley, C. & Fisher, H. (2013). The prevalence and impact of child maltreatment and other types of victimization in the UK: Findings from a population survey of caregivers, children, young people and young adults. *Child Abuse & Neglect*, 37(10), 801–813.

Radford, L., Aitken, R., Miller, P. et al. (2011). *Meeting the needs of children living with domestic violence in London: Research Report*. London: Refuge/NSPCC, http://www.nspcc.org.uk/globalassets/documents/research-reports/meeting-needs-children-living-domestic-violence-london-report.pdf.

Schafer, J., Caetano, R. & Clark, C.L. (1998). Rates of intimate partner violence in the United States. *American Journal of Public Health*, 88, 1702–1704.

Schumacher, J.A., Feldbau-Kohn, S., Slep, A.M.S. & Heyman, R.E. (2001). Risk factors for male-to-female partner physical abuse. *Aggression and Violent Behavior*, 6, 281–352.

Shipman, K.L., Rossman, B.B.R. & West, J.C. (1999). Co-occurrence of spousal violence and child abuse: Conceptual implications. *Child Maltreatment*, 4, 93–102.

Slep, A.M.S & Heyman, R.E. (2008). Public health approaches to family maltreatment prevention: Re-setting family psychology's sights from the home to the community. *Journal of Family Psychology*, 22, 518–528.

Slep, A.M.S. & O'Leary, S.G. (2001). Examining partner and child abuse: Are we ready for a more integrated approach to family violence? *Clinical Child and Family Psychology Review*, 4, 87–107.

Slep, A.M.S. & O'Leary, S.G. (2005). Parent and partner violence in families with young children: Rates, patterns and connections. *Journal of Consulting and Clinical Psychology*, 3, 435–444.

Slep, A.M.S. & O'Leary, S.G. (2009). Distinguishing risk profiles among parent-only, partner-only, and dually-perpetrating physical aggressors. *Journal of Family Psychology*, 23, 705–716.

Slep, A.M.S., Heyman, R.E. & Foran, H.M. (2015). Child maltreatment in DSM-5 and ICD-11. *Family Process*, 54, 17–32.

Straus, M.A. (1990). The National Family Violence Surveys. In: M.A. Straus & R.J. Gelles (eds), *Physical Violence in American Families, Risk Factors and Adaptations to Violence in 8145 Families*. New Brunswick, NJ: Transaction Publishers, 3–15.

Straus, M.A. (1992). *Children as Witnesses to Marital Violence: A Risk Factor for Lifelong Problems among a Nationally Representative Sample of American Men and Women*. Columbus, OH: Ross Laboratories.

Straus, M.A. & R.J. Gelles (eds) (1990). *Physical Violence in American Families*. New Brunswick, NJ: Transaction Publishers.

Straus, M.A., Gelles, R.J. & Steinmetz, S.K. (1980). *Behind Closed Doors: Violence in the American Family*. New York: Anchor Books.

Straus, M.A., Hamby, S.L., Finkelhor, D. et al. (1998). Identification of child maltreatment with the Parent-Child Conflict Tactics Scales: Development and psychometric data for a national sample of American parents. *Child Abuse & Neglect*, 22, 249–270.

Tajima, E.A. (2004). Correlates of the co-occurrence of wife abuse and child abuse among a representative sample. *Journal of Family Violence*, 19, 399–410.

Tilbrook, E., Allan, A. & Dear, G. (2010). *Intimate Partner Abuse of Men*. Perth, Western Australia: Men's Advisory Network, http://static1.1.sqspcdn.com/static/f/455174/7045893/1406285128527/ECU_Final_Report.pdf?token=gxHH05PdLu%2F9friCnvk2sc5tG1M%3D.

World Health Organization. (2002). *World report on violence and health*. Geneva: World Health Organization.

Part II
Children's Services and Public Health Approaches to Prevention

9

Children's Services
Toward Effective Child Protection

Chris Goddard[1], Karen Broadley[2] and Susan Hunt[3]

[1] University of Hertfordshire and University of South Australia
[2] Monash University
[3] Central Queensland University

Introduction

Child protection is an essential service in safeguarding children. Statutory child protection work is one of the most complex and challenging areas of human service delivery (Goddard & Hunt, 2011; McPherson & Barnett, 2006; Sidebotham, 2015). The numerous reviews and inquiries into child protection systems are testament to these difficulties. In the Australian context, Wyles (2007) states that annual reviews into child protection are 'almost inevitable', and 'result in common recommendations about service improvements, increased resourcing, structural reorganisation and legislative reform' (p. 1). This chapter draws primarily on Australian examples, but the principles and issues presented are internationally relevant.

Empirical research is integral to improving legislation, policy, practice and ultimately children's safety. Not only is it important to translate research evidence into practice, we must obtain evidence and expertise from practice (Hanson, Finch, Allegrante & Sleet, 2012). Research to date into child protection practice reports a tendency of practitioners to think the best of parents, and to believe, despite evidence to the contrary, that parents will change (Stanley & Goddard, 2002). This reluctance to make negative judgements has been described as 'the rule of optimism' (Dingwall, Eelelaar & Murray, 1983; Munro, 2010). There are many reasons for practitioners' reluctance to make negative judgements. Many children who come to the attention of statutory child protection systems have parents who present with mental illness, disability, substance misuse and intimate partner violence (Bromfield, Lamont, Parker & Horsfall, 2010). These issues hinder successful participation in pro-social activities including education and employment. The families are often isolated and living in low-socio-economic areas. Their problems can both be the cause and consequence of their isolation and disadvantage. Practitioners are often 'keen to acknowledge the successes of the often disadvantaged, socially excluded parents' (Munro, p. 17).

Practitioners also hope to distance themselves from the mistakes of the past (Hansen & Ainsworth, 2006; Humphreys, 2012). Government policies of large-scale removal of children and the forcing

---

The Wiley Handbook of What Works in Child Maltreatment: An Evidence-Based Approach to Assessment and Intervention in Child Protection, First Edition. Edited by Louise Dixon, Daniel F. Perkins, Catherine Hamilton-Giachritsis, and Leam A. Craig.
© 2017 John Wiley & Sons Ltd. Published 2017 by John Wiley & Sons Ltd.

of unmarried mothers to place their children for adoption has had a major influence on child welfare policies and practices, particularly in Australia (Hansen & Ainsworth, 2006; Humphreys, 2012). This history, as well as the knowledge that many out-of-home care placements cause harm to children, reinforces family preservation ideology. These ideas and values influence how practitioners conduct assessments, and collect and analyse information. Information that challenges their preference for family preservation is often overlooked. As Brydon (2004, p. 370) explained:

> The tendency toward optimism has led to the minimisation of presenting risks and unrealistic expectations that parents will avail themselves of opportunity to gain parenting skills.

Similarly, Liddell, Donegan, Goddard and Tucci (2006) argue that the bias toward family preservation means that 'Child protection practitioners are then bound to implement plans that give parents almost limitless opportunities to change before decisive action is taken' (p. 8).

The ideas and values of practitioners inform their professional judgements and practice, which in turn influence the process of information gathering, analysis, assessment and decision-making (Rosnow & Rosenthal, 1997). Researchers may also be selective in their observations, by 'seeing' things that confirm their assumptions, expectations or hypotheses, and by overlooking information that does not (Rosnow & Rosenthal, 1997). This type of inferential error is known as 'confirmation bias' (Nickerson, 1998). Researchers can also make errors in interpretation and analysis, again reflecting their ideas and values (Rosnow & Rosenthal, 1997). Rosnow and Rosenthal suggest that:

> The history of science generally, and of psychology more specifically, suggests that more of us are wrong longer than we need to be because we hold our theories not quite lightly enough' (p. 18)

The main argument of this chapter is that many in the academic community have failed to acknowledge and address challenges inherent in family preservation ideology. These challenges are either ignored, or glossed over in research. We believe there is a type of 'groupthink' occurring within the research community, just as it has been noted in child protection (Beckett, 2007; Janis, 1972; Munro, 2008). Individuals and professional groups invest in a certain 'truth' about family preservation being the only way forward, and are reluctant to acknowledge evidence that may jeopardise this 'truth'. Consequently, statutory and non-statutory practitioners are left with the difficult task of actualising an ideology that has never been rigorously examined and tested. Ultimately, the safety of children is put at risk.

In this chapter we identify three challenges that prevent family preservation from living up to its name. We also consider solutions. We do not offer our comments out of disdain for the values of family preservation – we too would prefer children to remain with their families. It is essential, however, to be honest about the challenges:

1. For family preservation to be successful, an evidence base about the effectiveness of family support and related programmes must be built. Investing in interventions that work and empirically evaluating the effectiveness of programmes is critical to improving the lives of children and, when possible, their families. Saunders (2015, p. 21) stresses that this is an 'ethical duty'.
2. The most important aspect of family preservation is distinguishing between parents who are likely to benefit from intervention, and parents who are not. What criteria should practitioners use to decide which children should be removed from parental care?

3. An integral component of family preservation is the need to build partnerships with parents to achieve change. Many researchers and policy makers fail to consider that this can be impossible when parents are uncooperative, hostile, threatening or violent.

Family Preservation: Does It Work?

The history of child welfare in Australia, it has been claimed, has been based on a model of 'child rescue' (Lamont & Bromfield, 2015), taking children from 'unfit' parents to provide them with a better life. Many researchers argue that this did not work (Parton, Thomson & Harries, 2008), and in reaction have embraced family preservation. This ideology is based on the idea that, in order to achieve the best outcomes for the child, children need to live with their biological families. Family preservation is one of the apparent goals of a public health approach to child protection. Thus, government-funded family support services provide parents with resources, support, education, counselling and other services in order to prevent child abuse and neglect, while keeping children in parental care.

Child protection and family programmes: The evidence

The evidence for child protection is limited at best. Indeed, over a decade ago, Finkelhor (1999) wrote:

> First we need good epidemiological data to see the location and source of the child abuse problem, and also to be able to track and monitor its response to our efforts. This is something we currently do not have, at least at the level that would satisfy any even generous public health epidemiologist. Second, we need experimental studies to evaluate new and existing practices, so we can agree on what works...There is more experimental science in the toilet paper we use every day than in what we have to offer abused children or families at risk of abuse. (p. 969)

More recently, Munro (2009) agreed that 'There is only limited knowledge about good practice and the major need is to increase this, to find out more about what methods are effective' (p. 1015). McDonald, Higgins, Valentine and Lamont (2011) in their *Protecting Australia's Children Research Audit (1995–2010)* identified a number of gaps in the Australian research base. They noted that only a small proportion (19.6%) of the research projects in the audit were evaluations of child protection-related programmes, services or strategies, and that a number of these evaluations were not published or in the public domain. As a result, the effectiveness of family support programmes is questionable.

Family support programmes are family preservation interventions, and have been defined as 'secondary level initiatives with a strong parent education focus, and often employing a home visiting component' (Tomison & Poole, 2000, p. 72). Programmes include: home visitation, parent education, and early intervention and supported playgroups (Scerra, 2010). There are many professionals who focus on family preservation ideology (Brydon, 2004; Liddell, Donegan, Goddard & Tucci 2006; Lindsey, Martin & Doh, 2002) and appear reluctant to question its efficacy. This tendency 'to hold...theories not quite lightly enough' (Rosnow & Rosenthal, 1997, p. 18) is unhelpful to practitioners in the field. For instance, the Protecting Victoria's Vulnerable Children Inquiry found that:

> Submissions argued that there is a perception that both DHS (Department of Human Services) and the Court have failed to address issues of long-term child neglect and cumulative harm, leaving family services with inappropriate and unworkable responsibility for many such cases. (Cummins, Scott & Scales, 2012, p. 341)

This focus is dangerous to children. Lindsey, Martin & Doh (2002) reviewed 36 relevant studies and concluded that family preservation services made little difference in preventing placement in out-of-home care, or in improving children's safety. The authors conclude that the 'spectacular success reported in the number of early studies is reflective of poor research methodology and the hyperbole of program advocates' (p. 743). Examples of inadequate research design included lack of control group, non-randomised intervention allocation, and small sample sizes.

Scerra (2010) also reported conflicting results on the efficacy of a range of family support programmes. She identified a number of gaps in the literature, including but not limited to: a lack of longitudinal data on the long-term efficacy of initiatives; lack of knowledge about why the initiatives were effective; and insufficient research into case work and assessment. Moreover, O'Reilly, Wilkes, Luck and Jackson (2010) in their review of the family support, family preservation and home visiting literature, reported 'a paucity of qualitative research around the effectiveness of child abuse and neglect interventions' (p. 89). They further stated that much of the research that exists is outdated:

> the majority of research around the effectiveness of family-centred interventions for child abuse and neglect was published in the 1980s and 1990s. (p. 89)

In addition, the authors also found that much of the research was undertaken in the UK and US, and has not been confirmed within the Australian context (O'Reilly, Wilkes, Luck & Jackson, 2010). They suggested that focus tended to be on the experiences of the adults in the families, rather than the experiences and outcomes for children:

> the majority of research around child abuse and neglect has focused on outcome measurements for adults, with limited data on the effectiveness of interventions specific to children. (p. 89)

Accordingly, O'Reilly, Wilkes, Luck and Jackson (2010) recommended more research that is focused on children. This recommendation echoes Stanley and Goddard (2002) who stress that one clear measure of effectiveness must be that abuse and/or neglect ceases as a result of the intervention. Family preservation continues to be promoted despite a paucity of contemporary international or Australian evidence, and the lack of focus on the child. We must gain an improved understanding about what works, and whether there are ingredients for success. If there are such ingredients, we must be able to name, replicate, test and build on them.

Government secrecy

There are a number of reasons for the poor child protection knowledge base. In order to develop a knowledge base, it is essential for researchers to have access to data. However, governments need to present themselves in the most favourable light, and researchers are given little, if any, access to data. Australian researchers McDonald, Higgins, Valentine and Lamont (2011) have noted the lack of reliable data available to researchers. Goddard and Tucci (2008) agree that 'there has been a lack of independent research both allowed and supported into child protection' (p. 9) and that this restricts the capacity to build a knowledge base to inform public policy. Darlington and Scott (2002, p. 24) suggest that:

> government departments, may be concerned with the potential political ramifications of the research and at times research proposals may be thwarted, ostensibly on ethical grounds.

De Maria (2002) agrees that secrecy dominates the management of Australia's public affairs. Part of the reason for this culture of secrecy is the adversarial nature of politics:

> entrenched interparty conflicts and fierce electoral competition make secrecy an operational prerequisite. (p. 169)

De Maria (2002) suggests that secrecy flourishes with 'respect to a particular class of information – that which could expose government illegality, incompetence or breach of trust' (p. 172). Over the past decade there has been extensive criticism of child protection in every Australian jurisdiction. The tendency of governments to protect themselves from such criticism is understandable but not excusable. Improvements can only be achieved through systematic examination that by its nature will highlight both the effective and the ineffective strategies or programmes.

There are a range of policies in place to protect governments. Each of Australia's six states and two territories has a different child protection system. Many of the states and territories restrict child protection practitioners from speaking publicly about any aspect of their work; they are forbidden to talk to the media and are restricted from contributing their views and experiences to inquiries and reviews. We note that no serving child protection practitioner made a submission to the *Protecting Victoria's Vulnerable Children Inquiry*. Child protection practitioners are also restricted from submitting articles to academic journals if related to child protection practice, policy, legislation or initiative. This is an extraordinary situation, and amounts to the silencing of Australian practitioners. This restriction not only hinders professional development, but also prevents experienced practitioners from making an invaluable contribution to the knowledge base about the realities of the work. The *Code of Conduct for the Queensland Public Service* (The State of Queensland, 2010, p. 6) states that 'commenting on government policy is a matter for ministers not employees'. The New South Wales Department of Family and Community Services *Code of Ethical Conduct* (Family and Community Services, 2013, p. 24) places restrictions on child protection practitioners on making public comment and defines this as comment for:

> any media including social media, journals, books, other publications, the internet, chat rooms or at public speaking events.

The *Code of Conduct for Victorian Public Service Employees* (Victorian Government Public Sector Standards Commissioner, 2007) forbids public comment and defines it as providing information or comment to any media, the internet and speaking engagements.

The way forward

Government support and funding of independent research into child protection policies and programmes is needed to promote ongoing continuous quality improvement, thereby promoting child well-being. Researchers need to advocate change and promote a learning culture where the goal is to improve rather than lay blame.

According to Florini (2004):

> Even honest officials make mistakes that need correcting, and transparency is the most effective error-correction system humanity has yet devised. (p. 18)

Transparency enables the community to know whether 'a government's deeds match its words' (Australian Law Reform Commission, 2009, p. 46). Allowing, encouraging and funding research is the only way to establish a child protection knowledge base. At the very least, in-house research that is controlled by senior officials within government gives the appearance of built-in bias. Moreover, in-house research can be influenced by many factors such as previous policy decisions, financial constraints, and the need to protect the government of the day. Independent research is required because it can act as a check against vested interests of government. Allowing and encouraging child protection practitioners to publish articles that are honest and reflective will inform and develop the currently deficient child protection knowledge base.

In addition, in order to improve the knowledge base and develop a public health model of child protection, high-quality epidemiological surveillance data is essential (Jack, 2010; Webb & Bain, 2011; World Health Organization, 2006). There is no quality surveillance data in Australia, and consequently no effective public health model of child protection (Broadley & Goddard, 2015; Broadley, Goddard & Tucci, 2014). This lack of quality data appears to be an international problem. Governments must collect and disseminate high-quality, comparable and reliable data about child protection and child welfare activity in their jurisdictions. By doing so, effective strategies may be identified, including family preservation efforts.

Principles to Guide the Decision to Remove Children from Their Parents

Once it has been determined that a parent is abusing, neglecting or failing to protect his/her child, the parent should be given every assistance to change. In Victoria, this is enshrined in legislation. Section 10(3)(a) of the Children Youth and Families Act states:

> the need to give the widest possible protection and assistance to the parent and child as the fundamental group unit of society and to ensure that intervention into that relationship is limited to that necessary to secure the safety and wellbeing of the child. (Victorian Government, 2005, p. 21)

Most professionals feel empathy and compassion for parents. Many parents who come to the attention of child protection services, as noted above, present with problems such as mental illness, disability, substance misuse and intimate partner violence, and many have experienced abuse and trauma themselves (Banducci, Hoffman, Lejuez & Koenen, 2014; Dube, Felitti, Dong et al., 2003; Forrester & Harwin, 2011). In her research into parental drug addiction, Barnard (2007) found that:

> Many of these parents might be characterized as victims themselves, given their frequent accounts of childhoods marred by abuse and family dysfunction for which they carried the scars. (p. 61)

Deciding that parents cannot or will not change, and that their children should be removed from their care, is the most difficult and important decision a child protection practitioner must make. In a system that prefers family preservation, it is a decision that most practitioners would prefer not to make. Brydon (2004) states:

> within a context that favours family preservation, we may overlook a fundamental premise that not all parents can keep their children safe' (p. 365)

Brydon goes on to write:

> There appears a pervasive view that children are best looked after within their family of origin. It is difficult to make decisions to the contrary…at broad levels such consideration may arguably be at odds with the fundamental values of social work (p. 367)

The idea that some parents are 'untreatable' (Brydon, p. 365) and pose too great a risk to children seems to be ignored within the literature despite many examples of this occurring in practice. Some have argued that the criteria used to make these decisions should be made explicit (Dalgleish & Drew, 1989). Australian researchers Braithwaite, Harris and Ivec (2009) state that:

> Developing a clear understanding of the incidents or conditions that will trigger action by child protection agencies is critical for both those in the front line of the intervention attempting to protect children as well as parents and young people who are expected to comply with the agency's parenting standards (p. 15)

While it not possible to have absolute rules, because rules cannot capture the unique characteristics of each child, family and environment, there should at least be some principles for practitioners and courts to refer to when making these significant decisions. There is the 'need for reliable, consistent, and efficient decisions across cases' (Dalgleish & Drew, 1989, p. 491). In reviewing the literature, very few researchers have attempted to make these 'criteria', 'incidents' or 'conditions' explicit. Systematic criteria to make this decision should be explicitly presented in protocols that are evidence based and practitioner tested.

Predicting and testing parental change

Decisions about whether children remain in the care of their parents, or are placed in alternative care, should be made in one of two ways: (i) predicting whether parents are likely to change, or (ii) to test change. There is substantial benefit in assessing parental capacity to change early on, to prevent the re-abuse of children. However, there is no agreement about how to accomplish this. According to Turney, Platt, Selwyn & Farmer (2012), one limited way to do this is by assessing parental insight, intention to change, and engagement/cooperation with support and treatment. However, cooperation can be misleading. For instance, a parent may be cooperative, say all the correct things, and be believable – but still not be willing and/or able to change (Hunt, Goddard, Cooper et al., 2015; Turney, Platt, Selwyn & Farmer 2012): 'desire to change dangerous or neglectful behaviour does not equal the capacity to change' (Dwyer & Miller, 2014, p. 96). Some experts claim that assessments about capacity to change should also consider 'parental acceptance of responsibility for past acts and any damage done' (Turney, Platt, Selwyn & Farmer, 2012, p. 53).

Another limited way to predict whether a parent is willing and able to change may be through psychological assessment using a variety of tools and questionnaires (Broadley, 2012: Turney, Platt, Selwyn & Farmer, 2012). Some parents are able to 'fake good' on psychological tests (Broadley, p. 43) and there is a lack of agreed-upon tools for assessing parenting capacity (White, 2005), and for predicting the risk a particular parent poses to a particular child (Broadley, 2012; Goddard, Saunders, Stanley & Tucci, 1999):

> Traditional psychological tests, devised to measure intelligence and personality, were not designed to evaluate an adult's capacity to care for their children. They only bear an indirect relationship to

parenting capacity and research has not yet examined their ability to predict parenting effectiveness. Hence, opinions about parenting should not be over-reliant on such findings (White, p. 12)

Such risk assessments, of course, can be wrong. In practice this means that there is the danger of assessing a child as being at risk, removing the child, then the child losing emotional ties to a parent who does not pose a risk. There is also the danger of failing to identify a child who is at risk of harm, who is then harmed or murdered.

The second way to assess parental capacity to change is to test change over time. This involves testing whether a parent demonstrates a capacity to engage with support and treatment services, and change their parenting practices through '"managed" opportunities to change' (Turney, Platt, Selwyn & Farmer, 2102, p. 195). Turney, Platt, Selwyn and Farmer (2012) further state that:

> it is important to be clear what needs to change, how change will be measured or assessed, and over what timescale, how parents are to be supported, and the consequences if no, or insufficient changes are made (p. 195)

The obvious problem with this process is that giving parents the opportunity to demonstrate change while retaining primary care of their child can place children in real danger, particularly when the parental history involves significant levels of violence or sexual assault. When the concerns are related to emotional abuse and/or neglect, or where low-impact incidents of abuse and/or neglect are chronic, supporting and testing parental change over time may be appropriate.

The way forward

Providing practitioners with a set of criteria to use when making decisions about whether to remove a child from parental care is integral to protecting children (Meddin, 1985). A notable example of criteria informed by evidence from practice was offered by Meddin. The author assessed the views of 81 US child protection practitioners involved in decision-making and identified eight variables used to assess potential risk to a child. She then went on to recruit an additional 134 child protection investigators, supervisors and administrative personnel to evaluate the variables used to assess risk.

Drawing from her and our own work (Bessant & Broadley, 2014) we suggest the following 12 principles to guide child protection practitioners. Before detailing the principles, it should be noted that while it is often stressed that practitioners should learn as much information as possible about a child's situation, Goddard (1996) qualifies this requirement:

> it is never possible to know everything about anyone…workers will always be left with a sense that the job is incomplete. While assessment is a continuing process, there has to be clear acknowledgement that some information will always be missing. Secondly…collecting information…is only part of the task. Ordering it, and recognising its significance are also crucial tasks (p. 134)

In addition, this assessment takes place in a context where child abuse is often not treated as the crime that it is. Language may be used to minimise these adult crimes against children. Furthermore, the systems created to respond to this complex problem are themselves noted for their 'inherent' complexity (Munro, 2011, p. 22).

Decisions about whether to remove a child from parental care only need to be made in instances where either: (i) the abuse is not a criminal offence; or (ii) the abuse is a criminal offence but there is insufficient evidence to enable the criminal justice system to charge the perpetrator and remove the perpetrator from the home. Obviously it is preferable that perpetrators, not victims, be removed from their home. When perpetrators cannot be removed, these difficult decisions must be made.

1. The severity of the abusive incident The severity of the abusive incident is the key factor when determining future risk to the child (Meddin, 1985). There are no explicit criteria for determining severity and it would be beneficial for practitioners to be provided with relevant guidelines. In relation to physical abuse, a punch to a five-year-old child's head that results in a head injury is more serious than a squeeze to an arm that results in bruising. The former should be considered adequate reason to separate the child from the perpetrator. The latter may or may not be considered child abuse and the child may or may not be separated from the perpetrator. The incident must be considered in conjunction with a range of other situational criteria (e.g., the presence of chronic maltreatment, and the intent of the perpetrator).

2. The presence of chronic maltreatment Consideration must be given as to whether the primary concern for the child is in relation to a specific incident of abuse or neglect, or chronic maltreatment. Chronic maltreatment is the existence of compounded experiences of multiple episodes of abuse or 'layers' of neglect (Victorian Government Department of Human Services, 2007, p. 1). An isolated incident involving a parent angrily squeezing a child's arm causing bruising may not necessitate the removal of the child. However, an ongoing pattern of multiple 'low-impact' abusive incidents means that the effects are cumulative, and the harm experienced by the child is likely to be greater (Bessant & Broadley, 2014). A child who has suffered multiple 'low-impact' incidents of abuse or neglect may need to be removed from parental care, despite the most recent incident being less severe when considered in isolation.

3. The access of the perpetrator to the child The greater the access the perpetrator has to the child, the higher the risk (Meddin, 1985). A child who has been forced to live with intimate partner violence (Bedi & Goddard, 2007; Goddard & Bedi, 2010) may only be considered safe if the non-offending parent supports the removal of the perpetrator from the home, with a legal order in place. However, if the non-offending parent demonstrates an unwillingness to separate from the perpetrator by returning to the relationship, then removal of the child may be necessary.

4. The functioning and intentions of the parent Many child protection practitioners use the functioning and intentions of the parents to assess the risk to the child (Meddin, 1985). For example, parents who have drug or alcohol problems may have good intentions to care for their children. However, substance abuse has been found to increase the likelihood of violence (Ashrafioun, Dambra & Blondell, 2011; Dawe, Frye, David, et al., 2007; Holland, Forrester, Williams & Copello, 2014; Kroll & Taylor, 2003) and is a major obstacle in achieving change (Holland, Forrester, Williams & Copello, 2014) According to Laslett, Dietze and Room (2013), problematic drinking can 'interfere with care-givers' ability to successfully follow a [statutory child protection services] plan for remediation and thus make progression through the [child protection] system more likely' (p. 1398).

5. Whether the perpetrator has been responsible for previous incidents of child abuse, neglect and/or intimate partner violence It is sometimes known that a parent has a history of sexual assault or violence against another child or previous partner. In these cases, the following factors should be considered: (i) the severity of the previous incident, (ii) the time that has passed since the previous incident, (iii) the programmes and treatment undertaken by the perpetrator since the previous incident, (iv) the feedback from the treatment provider, and (v) the functioning and life situation of the parent currently and at the time of the previous incident.

Previous incidents of sexual assault or violence that are *known* to have occurred are often less than what has *actually* occurred. Intelligent offenders are more likely to 'get away' with additional incidents of violence and abuse than is officially reported (Broadley, 2012). Thus, research indicates a clear under-reporting in this area.

6. The cooperation of the parent The cooperation of the parent is important in assessing the future risk to the child, but must be viewed in conjunction with other factors:

> Cooperation must be viewed in terms of interacting with the functioning of the caretaker…A caretaker whose functioning is impaired either by physical or mental illness or incapacity, or, for example because of substance abuse, can be seen as creating a greater risk to the child…A tendency to violence on the part of the caretaker was seen as increasing the potential risk to the child (Meddin, 1985, p. 60)

Cooperation must also be viewed in conjunction with the severity of the incident. For instance, a man who has perpetrated an incident of very serious violence against a partner may agree to engage in a men's behaviour change programme. Completing the programme will not necessarily mean that change has occurred. Thus, ensuring an evidence-based programme is employed is critical.

Cooperation must also be considered in the context of whether the parent has been responsible for incidents of child abuse and neglect, but has not been able to achieve and sustain change despite receiving previous treatment and support. For instance, how useful is it to refer neglectful parents to a family support service if they have previously neglected their children and previously received similar assistance? Why might change occur this time? This is an example of an imprudent, perpetual 'rule of optimism' (Dingwall, Eelelaar, & Murray 1983).

7. The intent of the perpetrator A parent who grabs a child tightly on the arm causing bruising in order to stop the child from running onto a busy road should be viewed differently from a parent who squeezes the child's arm in anger. Other factors, such as parenting functioning, must also be considered. If the violence occurred while the parent was affected by alcohol then this would increase the future risk to the child.

8. The functioning of the child Considering the functioning of the child is critical when making a decision about risk:

> workers must assess the child's mental and physical capacity as well as the child's level of maturity in order to determine the child's ability to care and protect him/herself and thus reduce the potential risk of further abuse (Meddin, 1985, p. 59)

Whether a child has a disability, and if so, the nature and severity of the disability should influence the recommended action. Disability brings with it an increased vulnerability to abuse and neglect (Robinson, 2012). Vulnerability is magnified for children who have high support needs, are dependent on others for personal care, are physically and/or socially isolated, and do not have a trusted adult who they can communicate with and who can and will use influence on their behalf (Robinson). Children with disabilities are also less likely than their non-disabled peers to report abuse. The decrease in reporting may be because they have not been educated about sexuality and personal safety and are left without the language to describe abuse. Or it may be because they are without a trusted adult who they feel able to communicate with (Robinson). The importance of talking to children is emphasised below.

9. The voice and expressed wishes of the child   Historically, children who have suffered, or are at risk of, abuse and neglect, have been deliberately 'rendered inaudible' (Mudaly & Goddard, 2006, p. 18), in effect repeatedly silenced (Goddard, Hunt, Broadley, et al., 2014). Article 12 of the UN Convention on the Rights of the Child (UNCRC) (United Nations, 1989) states that the views of the child should be given 'due weight in accordance with the age and maturity of the child' (p. 4). Similarly, section 10, 3(d) of the Victorian Government Children Youth and Families Act 2005 requires that consideration be given to:

> the child's views and wishes if they can be reasonably ascertained, and they should be given such weight as is appropriate in the circumstances (Victorian Government, 2005, p. 22.)

It can be challenging to know what weight to put on what children want and say:

> What, for example, if a child aged ten says that he wants to return to a physically abusive parent?...What if a 15-year-old wants to stay overnight at a friend's house and the friend's parents are drug users? (Bessant & Broadley, 2014, p. 16)

There are no simple answers to these scenarios. Bessant and Broadley (2014) suggest that practitioners must, through experience, develop the ability to make good practical judgements. An effort should always be made to interview children on their own, although there are many obstacles in achieving this (Bessant & Broadley, 2014; National Society for the Prevention of Cruelty to Children, 2014). Knowing how to communicate with children and knowing what to think and feel in a particular situation is not easy. Practitioners need to maintain some distance but still connect, listen and respond appropriately to each unique child and situation (Bessant & Broadley, 2014). They also need to 'weigh up' what the child says against other criteria discussed here.

10. The age of the child   The age of the child should influence decision-making (Meddin, 1985). Infants are generally more vulnerable, and their need for protection is usually greater. Infants are entirely dependent on their primary carers to provide for basic needs and protection. Infants require stability and need to develop and maintain a secure attachment to their primary carer to live healthy lives (Sroufe, 2005). Some older children have a greater capacity to protect themselves, and to develop relationships with supportive adults, and may not require a highly interventionist statutory child protection response. In fact, such a response may be disempowering and detrimental to their personhood (Mudaly & Goddard, 2006; Broadley, 2014b).

11. Protective relationships available to the child   Information about the child's social network, including the existence of protective and supportive relationships, must be considered. Questions must be asked about the possibility of introducing and/or enhancing protective factors 'that may reduce or mitigate the negative impact of risk factors' (Hunter, 2012, p. 6). One significant factor for counteracting adverse circumstances is providing children with an enduring close relationship in which they are safe and valued (Gilligan, 2003). This could be with a supportive social worker or counsellor or, alternatively, a child protection practitioner may be instrumental in arranging contact with a buddy, mentor or youth worker. If the child of a drug-addicted mother can be made more safe as a result of extended family members regularly visiting the home, taking the child to school, or having the child for regular respite at their home, then this may build sufficient safety, and removal of the child may not be required. The willingness and appropriateness of others to assist must be weighed up in conjunction with the other criteria listed here.

12. The statutory requirement to 'cause no further harm' Out-of-home care placements can cause children and young people harm, thus, deciding to remove the child from the home requires due diligence in determining the safest path. Victorian and South Australian studies have found that many children and young people in out-of-home care experience poor-quality and multiple placements (Cummins, Scott & Scales, 2012; Mendes, Johnson & Moslehuddin, 2011; Office of the Guardian for Children and Young People, 2015) and frequent changes of school (Wise, Pollock, Mitchell et al., 2010). On leaving care, these young people lack the supports they need, particularly safe, secure and affordable housing (Broadley, 2014a; Mendes, Johnson & Moslehuddin, 2011). These system failures demand attention by increasing funding, transparency, and independent research into the experiences and outcomes of out-of-home care. The identification of evidence-based strategies within out-of-home care is critical to the promotion of child well-being and stemming the optimism bias. It is also essential that child protection assessments and decisions are informed by the statutory requirement to 'cause no further harm' (Bessant & Broadley, 2014, p. 279):

> A narrow focus on the abusive or neglectful parental actions or behaviours, or on the harm a child is suffering, can ignore even worse types of harms that child protection interventions and out-of-home-care may cause.

This is particularly relevant in Australia where long-term care can mean multiple placements as there are so few adoptions (Australian Institute of Health and Welfare, 2014).

Making the decision for the child to remain with the parent

If the final decision is for the child to remain in the care of parents who pose continued risk, then this risk must be acknowledged. Making the decision not to separate children from their parents does not mean denying risk. In fact, it is more important to acknowledge risk, and establish support systems to ensure there is a safety plan in place (e.g., for the child to have regular access to a counsellor or youth worker) to reduce risk. In some instances court orders should be sought to support these plans, and should remain in place until the child reaches adulthood. Moreover, establishing a monitoring system will enable researchers to understand the relapse rate and potentially provide more accurate guidance as to who the most likely offenders are.

Building Partnerships with Parents

An important aspect of family preservation ideology is the need to work with, support and build partnerships with parents, in order to achieve change. Many researchers and policy makers fail to consider that this is impossible when parents are uncooperative, hostile, aggressive and violent toward child protection practitioners (Stanley & Goddard, 2002).

The literature repeatedly encourages child protection practitioners to build partnerships with parents, and relationships are seen as the 'hallmark' of child protection practice (Lonne, Parton, Thomson & Harries, 2008, p. 181; Miller, 2009): 'Text after text places...a burden on those who are expected to create helping relationships' (Stanley & Goddard, 2002, p. 71). In the absence of a legal order, the key activities of a child protection intervention – gathering information, making an assessment, introducing interventions, and monitoring/testing change – require the cooperation of the parents.

Many parents do not want to provide information or allow their children to talk to child protection practitioners. Many parents are uncooperative, minimise or deny problems, and do not acknowledge the harm to their children (Stanley & Goddard, 2002). In addition, they are sometimes hostile, threatening and violent, significantly hampering the information-gathering and assessment process (Littlechild, 2005; Stanley & Goddard). Stanley and Goddard conducted a study of child protection practitioners in Victoria. They randomly selected 50 child protection practitioners and found that:

> Within a period of only six months, 9 of the 50 (child protection) workers interviewed had been subjected to physical assaults, and four workers to assault by a person wielding an object. There were a total of 68 episodes of threatened assault. Thus, 35 of the 50 workers were victims of at least one major trauma, in the form of assault, attempted or threatened assault, a death threat, or another form of major intimidation (p. 151)

Briggs, Broadhurst and Hawkins (2004) in their Australian research focused on a range of professionals from different sectors who all had child protection obligations:

> The majority of respondents (91%) had experienced intimidating behaviour in the course of their child protection duties. Many had experienced threats of violence (72%), and ongoing harassment (41%). A smaller group of respondents (24%) had experienced actual physical assault (p. 3)

In the UK, Littlechild's (2005) study into the experiences of English and Finnish child protection practitioners found that 'violence and aggression were constant features of the work' (p. 394). Another study conducted in the UK found that child protection practitioners frequently dealt with hostile or intimidating parents (Cooper, 2011; Wild, 2011). Further analysis of this data by Hunt, Goddard, Cooper et al. (2015) reported that the majority of participants had been threatened by parents (60.5%) in the previous six months. A third of participants (32.4%) were threatened three or more times. A third of participants (36.8%) reported being physically threatened, including 7.8% who had received death threats, 2.4% who had been threatened with firearms, 2.4% with knives, and 1% with bombs. Furthermore, 107 participants (18.1%) had been physically assaulted, including one participant who was permanently injured from a murder attempt. One practitioner wrote:

> Two incidents – difficult to say which was worst. 1) Pushed downstairs while parent was screaming and shouting, was taking 4 year old to contact. Suffered a miscarriage as a result. 2) Was removing an 11 year old girl from home where sexual abuse had been disclosed by siblings. Police were present. Mother assembled a lot of neighbours, all shouting abuse. Mother came at me and child with a garden fork – child was between me and her so moved child out of way and headed for the car. Focused on getting child out safely. Once in car realised that my leg was bleeding profusely and that the garden fork had gone into my leg. Needed stitches. Mother continued to make threats thereafter (full quote unpublished)

Overall there is strong evidence in Australia and internationally that child protection practitioners are likely to experience higher levels of violence than social workers addressing other challenges. Littlechild (2005) found acts of violence and aggression were often used by parents as a way of minimising statutory intervention, and often occurred during times when critical decisions were being made. In addition, Broadhurst, White, Fish et al. (2010) define one of the key pitfalls of assessing children:

> There is insufficient support/supervision to enable practitioners to work effectively with service users who are uncooperative, ambivalent, confrontational, avoidant or aggressive (p. 7)

The lack of supervision and organisational support for child protection practitioners facing hostile and intimidating parents is detailed in the UK research by Hunt, Goddard, Cooper et al. (2015).

Actual and potential violence impacts on practice

Both actual and potential violence cause major stress and anxiety, thereby causing practitioners to 'adopt unhelpful defence mechanisms as a way of coping' (Gibbs, 2009, p. 290) and can affect assessments and decision-making (Goddard & Carew, 1988; Littlechild, 2005; Stanley & Goddard, 2002). Stanley and Goddard suggest that child protection practitioners can demonstrate hostage-like behaviour. Threatening behaviour can be an effective parental strategy of limiting statutory involvement and even deterring court applications (Turney, Platt, Selwyn & Farmer, 2012), for when child protection practitioners don't know, they can't act (Goddard & Hunt, 2011). Hunt et al. (2015) found that as a result of threatened and actual violence, practitioners reported suffering from chronic stress, anxiety and disordered sleep. The violent and hostile behaviour experienced by practitioners was frequently reported as negatively impacting their practice and ability to protect children.

Moreover, parental non-cooperation, hostility and violence create difficulties for child protection practitioners as they seek to gain access to, and communicate with, children (Bessant & Broadley, 2014). For instance, parents with substance use problems may prevent their children from talking to social workers because they fear criminal proceedings, or feel ashamed (Barnard & Barlow, 2003; Moore, Noble-Carr & McArthur, 2010; Taylor & Kroll, 2004). Hill (2010) agrees that parents have a significant influence over the communication that occurs between child protection practitioners and children.

> For all children, arrangements to see them will be made usually with those carrying parental responsibility. In the case of younger children, these adults will also give their consent to the work...Yet, in statutory contexts, it may be the behaviour of some of these adults that is the cause for concern... for now, the point is that parental attitudes towards the involvement of social workers are likely to have a significant bearing on how the child understands the social worker's role and on what they are prepared to say to him or her. This is a problem with no easy solution; one has to be constantly aware of the possible influences on children (p. 89)

Given the amount of fear that *potential* as well as actual violence can produce in practitioners, we suggest that the problem of parental violence affects the approach and quality of the work that is done with *all* families.

Addressing the violence: Threat or realised

Researchers, educators, policy makers and employers must acknowledge the threatened and actual violence experienced by child protection practitioners. Practice guidelines that minimise the opportunity for violence and protect practitioners are needed (Koritsas, Coles & Boyle, 2010).

Such guidelines should be consistent across organisations and actually adhered to. For example, if a parent has a history of violence toward practitioners, no practitioner should be unaccompanied when in the child's home. Littlechild (2005) recommends that practitioners report all threatened and actual violence to management, and be educated about how an organisation should respond. Parents should also be informed that violence is unacceptable, will not be tolerated, and what to expect if it occurs. The police should be involved in potentially violent situations, as they have greater protective resources and training in working with hostile clients (Broadhurst, White, Fish et al., 2010). Violence against child protection practitioners is a criminal act and should be treated as such. Effective supervision and organisational support is integral in managing the negative impact of working with threatening or violent parents (DePanfilis & Zlotnik, 2008). Management support is seen as best practice in lowering the high attrition rates of child protection practitioners (Gibbs, 2001).

Other professions do not tolerate violence as just part of their role. Legislation was introduced in Victoria in 2014 stating that perpetrators of violence against emergency workers (police, firefighters, paramedics, nurses and doctors) will receive longer sentences. Similar legislation should be established for child protection practitioners and made clear to management, practitioners and parents.

Conclusion

As we stated at the beginning of this chapter, child protection work is one of the most complex and challenging areas of service delivery. The systems created to respond to this complexity are themselves 'inherently complex' and the number of agencies involved means that 'coordination and communication' are 'crucial to success' (Munro, 2011, p. 14).

This chapter has attempted to provide a way forward by providing a realistic assessment framework. The assessment occurs in a context where important elements are rarely fully acknowledged and are often overlooked completely, for example, the actual and threatened violence experienced by practitioners in child protection services. Theories should be held more lightly, less tightly (Rosnow & Rosenthal, 1997) and informed by the, at times, brutal reality and consequences of such violence. Research into and evaluation of the principles outlined above would offer hope of more effective child protection (Saunders, 2015).

Our focus has been on protective services, but the complexity and challenges of assessment are the same in all children's services. The lack of an adequate evidence base leads to unrealistic expectations of interventions and leaves child protection practitioners adrift. The lack of transparency and accountability leaves too many children who have been abused or neglected unaccounted for until the next scandal or review.

References

Ashrafioun, L., Dambra, C. & Blondell, R. (2011). Parental prescription opioid abuse and the impact on children. *The American Journal of Drug and Alcohol Abuse*, 37, 532–536.

Australian Institute of Health and Welfare (2014). *Adoptions Australia 2013–14 (Child welfare series no. 60. Cat. no. CWS 51)*. Canberra: AIHW.

Australian Law Reform Commission (2009). *Secrecy laws and open government in Australia (Report 112)*, http://www.alrc.gov.au/sites/default/files/pdfs/publications/ALRC112.pdf.

Banducci, A.N., Hoffman, E.M., Lejuez, C.W. & Koenen, K.C. (2014). The impact of childhood abuse on inpatient substance users: Specific links with risky sex, aggression, and emotion dysregulation. *Child Abuse & Neglect*, 38, 928–938.

Barnard, M. (2007). *Drug Addiction and Families*. Philadelphia, PA: Jessica Kingsley Publishers.

Barnard, M. & Barlow, J. (2003). Discovering parental drug dependence: Silence and disclosure. *Children & Society*, 17, 45–56.

Beckett, C. (2007). *Child Protection: An Introduction*. London: Sage.

Bedi, G. & Goddard, C. (2007). Intimate partner violence: What are the impacts on children? *Australian Psychologist*, 42, 66–77.

Bessant, J. & Broadley, K. (2014). Saying and doing: Child protective services and participation in decision making. *International Journal of Children's Rights*, 22, 710–729.

Braithwaite, V., Harris, N. & Ivec, M. (2009). Seeking to clarify child protection's regulatory principles. *Communities, Children and Families Australia*, 4, 7–23.

Briggs, F., Broadhurst, D. & Hawkins, R. (2004). Violence, threats and intimidation in the lives of professionals whose work involves children: Trends and issues in crime and criminal justice, *Australian Institute of Criminology*, 273, 1–6.

Broadhurst, K., White, S., Fish, S. et al. (2010). *Ten pitfalls and how to avoid them: What research tells us*. London: NSPCC.

Broadley, K. (2012). Sex offender risk assessments in the child protection context. Helpful or not? *Children Australia*, 37, 40–45.

Broadley, K. (2014a). Is there a role for adult protection services in the lives of young people with disabilities transitioning from out-of-home care? *Australian Social Work*, 61, 84–98.

Broadley, K. (2014b). Equipping child protection practitioners to intervene to protect children from cumulative harm: Legislation and policy in Victoria, Australia. *Australian Journal of Social Issues*, 49, 265–284.

Broadley, K. & Goddard, C. (2015). A public health approach to child protection: Why data matter. *Children Australia*, 40, 69–77.

Broadley, K., Goddard, C. & Tucci, J. (2014). *They count for nothing: Poor child protection statistics are a barrier to a child-centred national framework*. Melbourne: Australian Childhood Foundation and Child Abuse and Prevention Australia, Monash University.

Bromfield, L., Lamont, A., Parker, R. & Horsfall, B. (2010). Issues for the safety and wellbeing of children in families with multiple and complex problems. *National Child Protection Clearinghouse Issues Paper no. 33*. Melbourne: Australian Institute of Family Studies.

Brydon, K. (2004). Untreatable families: Suggestions from literature. *Australian Social Work*, 57, 365–373.

Cooper, J. (2011). Held hostage by hostile parents. *Community Care*, 1885, 18–20.

Cummins, P., Scott, D. & Scales, B. (2012). *Report of the Protecting Victoria's Vulnerable Children Inquiry*. Melbourne: Department of Premier and Cabinet.

Dalgleish, L.I. & Drew, E.C. (1989). The relationship of child abuse indicators to the assessment of perceived risk and to the court's decision to separate. *Child Abuse & Neglect*, 13, 491–506.

Darlington, Y. & Scott, D. (2002). *Qualitative research in practice: Stories from the field*. St Leonards, N.S.W.: Allen & Unwin.

Dawe, S., Frye, S., David, B. et al. (2007). *Drug use in the family, impacts and implications for children* (ANCD Research Paper 13). Canberra: Australian National Council on Drugs.

De Maria, B. (2002). Rescuing FoI: Rescuing democracy. *The Drawing Board: An Australian Review of Public Affairs*, 2, 167–185.

DePanfilis, D. & Zlotnik, J.L. (2008). Retention of front-line staff in child welfare: A systematic review of research. *Children and Youth Services Review*, 30, 995–1008.

Dingwall, R., Eelelaar, J. & T. Murray. (1983). *The Protection of Children: State Intervention and Family Life*. Oxford: Blackwell.

Dube, S.R., Felitti, V.J., Dong, M. et al. (2003). Childhood abuse, neglect, and household dysfunction and the risk of illicit drug use: The adverse childhood experiences study. *Pediatrics*, 111, 564.

Dwyer, J. & Miller, R. (2014). *Working with families where an adult is violent: Best interests case practice model: Specialist practice resource*. Melbourne: Victorian Government Department of Human Services.

Finkelhor, D. (1999). The science. *Child Abuse & Neglect*, 23, 969–974.

Florini, A. (2004). Behind closed doors: Governmental transparency gives way to secrecy. *Harvard International Review*, 26, 18–21.

Forrester, D. & Harwin, J. (2011). *Parents who misuse drugs and alcohol: Effective interventions in social work and child protection*. Chichester: Wiley-Blackwell.

Gibbs, J.A. (2001). Maintaining front-line workers in child protection: A case for refocusing supervision. *Child Abuse Review*, 10, 323–335.

Gibbs, J. (2009). Changing the cultural story in child protection: Learning from the insider's experience. *Child & Family Social Work*, 14, 289–299.

Gilligan, R. (2003). Promoting resilience in children and young people. *Developing Practice: The Child, Youth and Family Work Journal*, 5 (Summer), 29–36.

Goddard, C. (1996). *Child Abuse and Child Protection: A Guide for Health, Education and Welfare Workers*. Melbourne: Churchill Livingstone.

Goddard, C. & Bedi, G. (2010). Intimate partner violence and child abuse: A child-centred perspective. *Child Abuse Review*, 19, 5–20.

Goddard, C. & Carew, B. (1988). Protecting the child: Hostages to fortune? *Social Work Today*, 15, 12–14.

Goddard, C. & Hunt, S. (2011). The complexities of caring for child protection workers: The contexts of practice and supervision. *Journal of Social Work Practice*, 25, 413–432.

Goddard, C. & Tucci, J. (2008). *Policy analysis: Responding to child abuse and neglect in Australia*. Melbourne: Australian Childhood Foundation Protecting Children, Child Abuse Prevention Research Australia.

Goddard, C., Saunders, B.J., Stanley, J.R. & Tucci, J. (1999). Structured risk assessment procedures: Instruments of abuse? *Child Abuse Review*, 8, 251–263.

Goddard, C., Hunt, S., Broadley, K. et al. (2014). Silencing of children in Australia. In: J.R. Conte (ed) *Child Abuse and Neglect Worldwide*. Santa Barbara: Praeger Publishers, 257–283.

Hansen, P. & Ainsworth, F. (2006). Adoption in Australia. *Children Australia*, 31(4), 22–28.

Hanson, D.W., Finch, C.F., Allegrante, J.P. & Sleet, D. (2012). Closing the gap between injury prevention research and community safety promotion practice: Revisiting the public health model. *Public Health Reports*, 127, 147–155.

Hill, A. (2010). *Working in Statutory Contexts*. Cambridge: Polity Press.

Holland, S., Forrester, D., Williams, A. & Copello, A. (2014). Parenting and substance misuse: Understanding accounts and realities in child protection contexts. *British Journal of Social Work*, 44, 1491–1507.

Humphreys, C. (2012). 'Permanent' care: Is the story in the data? *Children Australia*, 37, 4–9.

Hunt, S., Goddard, C., Cooper, J. et al. (2015). 'If I feel like this, how does the child feel?' Child protection workers, supervision, management and organisational responses to parental violence. *Journal of Social Work Practice*, 30, 5–24.

Hunter, C. (2012). Is resilience still a useful concept when working with children and young people? *Child Family Community Australia*, 2, 1–11.

Jack, S.M. (2010). The role of public health in addressing child maltreatment in Canada. *Chronic Diseases in Canada*, 31, 39–44.

Janis, I.L. (1972). *Victims of Groupthink: A Psychological Study of Foreign-Policy Decisions and Fiascoes*. Oxford: Houghton Mifflin.

Koritsas, S., Coles, J. & Boyle, M. (2010). Workplace violence towards social workers: The Australian experience. *British Journal of Social Work*, 40, 257–271.

Kroll, B. & Taylor, A. (2003). *Parental Substance Misuse and Child Welfare*. London: Jessica Kingsley Publishers.

Lamont, A. & Bromfield, L. (2015). *History of Child Protection Services*. Canberra: Australian Institute of Family Studies.

Laslett, A., Dietze, P.M. & Room, R.G.W. (2013). Carer drinking and more serious child protection case outcomes. *British Journal of Social Work*, 43, 1384–1402.

Liddell, M., Donegan, T., Goddard, C. & Tucci, J. (2006). *The state of child protection: Australian child welfare and child protection developments*. Melbourne: Australian Childhood Foundation, Child Abuse Prevention Research Australia.

Lindsey, D, Martin, S., & Doh, J. (2002). The failure of intensive casework services to reduce foster care placements: An examination of family preservation studies. *Children & Youth Services Review*, 24, 743–775.

Littlechild, B. (2005). The stresses arising from violence: Threats and aggression against child protection social workers. *Journal of Social Work*, 2005, 5, 61–82.

Lonne, R., Parton, N., Thomson, J. & Harries, M. (2008). *Reforming Child Protection*. London: Routledge.

McDonald, M., Higgins, D., Valentine, K. & Lamont, A. (2011). *Protecting Australia's Children Research Audit (1995–2010)*. Canberra: Australian Institute of Family Studies.

McPherson, L. & M. Barnett. (2006). Beginning practice in child protection: A blended learning approach. *Social Work Education*, 25, 192–198.

Meddin, B.J. (1985). The assessment of risk in child abuse and neglect case investigations. *Child Abuse & Neglect*, 9, 57–62.

Mendes, P., Johnson, G. & Moslehuddin, B. (2011). *Young People Leaving State Out-Of-Home Care: A Research-Based Study of Australian Policy and Practice*. North Melbourne: Australian Scholarly Publishing.

Miller, R. (2009). Engagement with families involved in the statutory system. In: J. Maidment & R. Egan (eds), *Practice Skills in Social Work and Welfare Practice: More Than Just Common Sense*. Crows Nest: Allen & Unwin, 114–131.

Moore, T., Noble-Carr, D. & McArthur, M. (2010). Who cares? Young people with parents who use alcohol or other drugs talk about their experiences with services. *Family Matters*, 85, 18–27.

Mudaly, N. Goddard, C. (2006). *The Truth is Longer than a Lie: Children's Experiences of Abuse and Professional Interventions*. London and Philadelphia: Jessica Kingsley.

Munro, E. (2008). *Effective Child Protection*. London: Sage.

Munro, E. (2009). Managing societal and institutional risk in child protection. *Risk Analysis*, 29, 1015–1023.

Munro, E. (2010). *The Munro Review of Child Protection Part One: A systems analysis*. Department for Education: London.

Munro, E. (2011). *The Munro Review of Child Protection: Final report: A child-centred system* (vol. 8062). London: The Stationery Office.

National Society for the Prevention of Cruelty to Children (2014). *Assessing parenting capacity: An NSPCC factsheet*. London: NSPCC.

Nickerson, R.S. (1998). Confirmation bias: A ubiquitous phenomenon in many guises. *Review of General Psychology*, 2, 175.

Office of the Guardian for Children and Young People (2015). *Report on interim emergency care for children under guardianship*. Adelaide: Government of South Australia.

O'Reilly, R., Wilkes, L. Luck, L. & Jackson, D. (2010). The efficacy of family support and family preservation services on reducing child abuse and neglect: What the literature reveals. *Journal of Child Health Care*, 14, 82–94.

Robinson, S. (2012). *Enabling and protecting. Proactive approaches to addressing the abuse and neglect of children and young people with disability*. Melbourne: Children with Disability Australia.

Rosnow, R.L. & Rosenthal, R. (1997). *People Studying People: Artifacts and Ethics in Behavioral Research*. New York: W. H. Freeman and Company.

Saunders, B.E. (2015). Expanding evidence-based practice to service planning in child welfare. *Child Maltreatment*, 20, 20–22.

Scerra, N. (2010). Effective practice in family support services: A literature review. *Developing Practice: The Child, Youth and Family Work Journal*, 27, 19–27.

Sidebotham, P. (2015). The challenge and complexities of physical abuse. *Child Abuse Review*, 24, 1–5.

Sroufe, L.A. (2005). Attachment and development: A prospective, longitudinal study from birth to adulthood. *Attachment & Human Development*, 7, 349–367.

Stanley, J. & Goddard, C. (2002). *In the Firing Line: Violence and Power in Child Protection Work*. Chichester: John Wiley & Sons, Ltd.

State of Queensland (2010). *Code of Conduct for the Queensland Public Service*, www.emergency.qld.gov.au/ses/about/pdf/Code_of_Conduct_060313.pdf.

Taylor, A., & Kroll, B. (2004). Working with Parental Substance Misuse: Dilemmas for Practice. *British Journal of Social Work*, 34, 1115–1132.

Tomison, A.M. & Poole, L. (2000). *Preventing child abuse and neglect: Findings from an Australian audit of prevention programs*. Melbourne: National Child Protection Clearinghouse, Australian Institute of Family Studies.

Turney, D., Platt, D., Selwyn, J. & Farmer, E. (2012). *Improving Child and Family Assessments: Turning Research into Practice*. London: Jessica Kingsley Publishers.

United Nations General Assembly (1989). Convention on the Rights of the Child, www.ohchr.org/en/professionalinterest/pages/crc.aspx.

Victorian Government (2005). *Children, Youth and Families Act*. Melbourne: Department of Human Services.

Victorian Government (2007). *Cumulative harm: A conceptual overview (Best Interest Series)*. Melbourne: Department of Human Services.

Victorian Government Public Sector Standards Commissioner (2013). *Code of Conduct for Victorian Public Sector Employees*, http://ssa.vic.gov.au/images/stories/product_files/810_CodeofConduct2007.pdf.

Webb, P. & Bain, C. (2011). *Essential Epidemiology: An Introduction for Students and Health Professionals*, 2nd edn. Cambridge: Cambridge University Press.

White, A. (2005). *Assessment of parenting capacity: Literature review*. Ashfield, New South Wales: New South Wales Department of Community Services.

Wild, J. (2011). Hostile witnesses. *Community Care*, 1879, 16–17.

Wise, S., Pollock, S., Mitchell, G. et al. (2010). *Care-system impacts on academic outcomes*, www.anglicarevic.org.au/index.php?pageID=11144&action=filemanager&folder_id=806&form_action=list&sectionID=11103.

World Health Organization (2006). *Preventing child maltreatment: A guide to taking action and generating evidence*. Geneva: WHO Press.

Wyles, P. (2007). When the bough breaks the cradle will fall: Child protection and supervision: Lessons from three recent reviews into the state of child protection in Australia. *Communities, Children & Families Australia*, 2, 49–58.

11

The Prevention of Child Maltreatment
The Case for a Public Health Approach to Behavioural Parenting Intervention

Matthew R. Sanders and John A. Pickering
The University of Queensland, Brisbane, Australia

The family provides the first and most important context for human development. Findings from behaviour genetics research, as well as epidemiological, correlational and experimental studies, all support the notion that parenting practices have a major influence on children's development and life course. Of concern, however, is that parents account for over 70% of all persons believed to be responsible for perpetrating the majority of substantiated cases of child maltreatment (Australian Institute of Health and Welfare [AIHW], 2005). Therefore, parenting programmes that address multiple aspects of family functioning are potentially the most effective and cost-effective interventions available to promote the mental health and wellbeing of children and keep them safe. This chapter makes the case that not only is improved parenting the cornerstone of child maltreatment prevention and treatment, but a population approach to parenting support is the most likely means of reducing the unacceptably high rate of child maltreatment. We make the case for 'proportionate universalism' in the design of population-based parenting programmes and document the steps required to achieve population-level reductions in rates of child maltreatment. A parenting intervention known as Pathways Triple P is used to illustrate the case. Implications for policy makers, researchers, parents and their children are discussed.

Why Parenting is so Important

The quality of parenting that children receive has a major influence on their development, wellbeing and life opportunities (Griffin, Botvin, Scheier et al., 2000; Repetti, Taylor & Seeman, 2002). Parenting programmes that seek to improve parenting practices while simultaneously enhancing child development are vital to establishing a nurturing environment that acts to offset

---

The Wiley Handbook of What Works in Child Maltreatment: An Evidence-Based Approach to Assessment and Intervention in Child Protection, First Edition. Edited by Louise Dixon, Daniel F. Perkins, Catherine Hamilton-Giachritsis, and Leam A. Craig.
© 2017 John Wiley & Sons Ltd. Published 2017 by John Wiley & Sons Ltd.

the development of behavioural and psychological problems and lays the foundation for children to contribute to a healthy and functional society (Biglan, Flay, Embry & Sandler, 2012). There is now broad scientific and interdisciplinary consensus that behaviourally oriented active skills training programmes that teach parents positive parenting and contingency management skills are effective. Such programmes have transformed child and family-focused mental health support services and prevention services (Comer, Chow, Chan et al., 2013; McCart, Priester, Davies & Azen, 2006; Menting, de Castro & Matthys, 2013).

Parenting programmes are potentially powerful tools in the prevention and treatment of a range of child social, emotional and behavioural problems including challenging behaviour in children with developmental disabilities (Tellegen & Sanders, 2014; Whittingham, Sanders, McKinlay & Boyd, 2014), persistent feeding problems (Adamson, Morawska & Sanders, 2013), anxiety disorders (Rapee, Kennedy, Ingram et al., 2010), recurrent pain syndromes (Sanders, Cleghorn, Shepherd & Patrick, 1996), and childhood obesity (West, Sanders, Cleghorn & Davies, 2010). Positive intervention effects on child and parent outcome measures have been reported across diverse cultures (Mejia, Calam & Sanders, 2014; Turner, Richards & Sanders, 2007), family types (Stallman & Sanders, 2007), stages of child development (Salari, Ralph & Sanders, 2014), and delivery settings (Morawska, Sanders, Goadby et al., 2011). Positive intervention effects have typically been found to be maintained over time (Heinrichs, Kliem & Hahlweg, 2014) without the need for further booster sessions.

Recent research has also demonstrated how different parenting styles and strategies influence various aspects of brain development. One study showed how harsh parenting reduces telomere length in the brain (Mitchell, Hobcraftb, McLanahanc et al., 2014), while another demonstrated how even in environments of poverty, altering the ways children are raised can help alleviate some of the adverse effects of disadvantage and promote healthy brain development in children (Luby, Belden, Botteron et al., 2013).

Although studies on parenting programmes for parents of teenagers are far less extensive compared to studies with younger children (Kazdin, 2005), such programmes have been demonstrated to improve parent–adolescent communication and reduce family conflict (Barkley, Edwards, Laneri et al., 2001; Chu, Farruggia, Sanders & Ralph, 2012; Dishion & Andrews, 1995), reduce the risk of adolescents developing and maintaining substance abuse, delinquent behaviour and other externalising problems, and leave parents feeling more confident and using more effective parenting strategies (Mason, Kosterman, Hawkins et al., 2003; Spoth, Redmond & Shin, 1998). Connell, Dishion, Yasui and Kavanagh (2007) found that a family-centred, school-based intervention improved academic achievement and attendance in school. The study showed that compared with matched controls, adolescents whose parents received the intervention maintained satisfactory results into high school. Interestingly, intervention engagement was associated with improved attendance, with high-risk families the most likely to engage in the intervention.

Parenting and Child Maltreatment

Evidence clearly indicates that maltreating parents tend to differ from non-maltreating parents in their inability to cope with anger-provoking situations (Rodriguez & Green, 1997). Of greater concern, maltreated children are more likely to suffer antisocial outcomes including externalising behaviours (Kotch, Lewis, Hussey et al., 2008; Lansford, Berlin, Bates & Pettit, 2007; Maas, Herrenkohl & Sousa, 2008), and internalising problems (McHolm, MacMillan & Jamieson, 2003; Widom, Dumont & Czaja, 2007). Fortunately, significant inroads have been made in the last decade toward understanding how parents' cognitive factors influence their affect and behaviour toward their children (Azar & Weinzierl, 2005; Dix, Reinhold & Zambarano, 1990; Kolko & Swenson, 2002; Sanders, Pidgeon, Gravestock et al., 2004). Much of the research has centred on various forms of maladaptive schemas, unrealistic expectations, and negative attributional bias in interpreting child behaviour and negative parenting behaviour (Miller & Azar, 1996; Pidgeon & Sanders, 2009; Sanders, Pidgeon, Gravestock et al., 2004).

A growing body of evidence has highlighted a clear link between parents who are at risk of maltreating their children and the extent to which they possess faulty causal attributional processes toward their explanations of their children's problem behaviours (Milner, 2003; Pidgeon & Sanders, 2009). It is reasoned that faulty attributions indirectly contribute to child maltreatment by increasing parental anger, over-reactivity and use of severe discipline strategies such as threats, yelling, hitting, grabbing and pushing (Dix, Ruble & Zambarano, 1989; Nix, Pinderhughes, Dodge et al., 1999). Parental anger is also a common factor underlying the act of parents physically abusing children (Kolko 1996; Mammen, Kolko & Pilkonis, 2002). It stands to reason, therefore, that if efforts can be made to address parental anger and negative attributional processes then improvements in rates of child maltreatment may occur. Parenting programmes that address anger and attributional style, as well as other parenting skills more broadly, hold particular promise in reducing the rates of child maltreatment.

Evidence available with maltreating parents suggests that parent training leads to improvements in parenting competence and parent behaviour (James, 1994; Wekerle & Wolfe, 1998). These changes in parenting practice reduce the risk of further abusive behaviour toward children, reports to protective agencies, and visits to hospital. However, as the number of official reports of child maltreatment in most Western countries continues to rise each year (AIHW, 2008; US Department of Health and Human Services, 2008; World Health Organization, 2009) questions remain pertaining to the most effective methods for reducing the unacceptably high rates of child maltreatment. There is a general lack of consensus among researchers, policy makers and support workers about the best approach to take in combating the issue.

One potential solution to this issue is to reconsider the approach undertaken in applying a parenting programme within the community. Traditional approaches to parent training to resolve child maltreatment involve working with individual families or small groups of parents; although effective, such programmes reach relatively few parents and consequently are unlikely to reduce rates of serious child-development problems related to inadequate parenting (Prinz & Sanders, 2007). Thus, the benefits derived from participating in parenting programmes are seldom fully realised across communities (Prinz & Sanders, 2007).

However, a paradigm shift in the way evidence-based parenting interventions are developed, trialled and disseminated is currently underway. Fundamentally, the shift is away from a focus on the individual parent or family unit, toward a community-wide, population-level focus. Biglan, Flay, Embry and Sandler (2012) described the shift as being toward a public health paradigm that valued the prevalence of nurturing environments and has, at its core, multiple efforts that act to prevent most mental, emotional and behavioural disorders. The Triple P – Positive Parenting Program is an example of a system of parenting intervention that operates through a population-level lens.

The Triple P System of Population-Level Parenting Intervention

The Triple P – Positive Parenting Program (see Sanders, 2012) is a system of parenting support and intervention that seeks to increase parents' confidence and skill in raising their children, thereby enhancing children's developmental outcomes. The standout feature of

Triple P is that it is built on the principle of *proportionate universalism* (Marmot, 2010) whereby it works as both an early intervention and prevention model to help create a society of healthy, happy, well-adjusted individuals with the skills and confidence they need to do well in life. Triple P adopts a public health approach to parenting support which aims to make highly reliable, evidence-based parenting support available and accessible to all parents. To achieve this, Triple P targets the multiple factors that lay the foundation for lifelong prosperity for both the individual and broader community.

Triple P employs an iterative, consumer engagement model of programme development to develop a range of evidence-based tailored variants and flexible delivery options (see Pickering & Sanders, 2013). The programme targets children at five different developmental stages: infants, toddlers, preschoolers, primary schoolers and teenagers. Within each developmental period the reach of the intervention can vary from being very broad (targeting an entire population) to quite narrow (targeting only vulnerable high-risk children or parents). The five levels of Triple P incorporate universal media messages for all parents (Level 1), low-intensity large group sessions (Level 2), topic-specific parent discussion groups (Level 3), group and individual programmes (Level 4), and more intense offerings for high-risk or vulnerable parents (Level 5). Figure 11.1 describes Triple P's multilevel system of parenting support geared toward normalising and destigmatising parental participation in parenting education programmes.

The rationale for Triple P's multilevel strategy is that there are differing levels of dysfunction and behavioural disturbance in children and adolescents, and parents have different needs and preferences regarding the type, intensity and mode of assistance they may require. The multilevel approach of Triple P follows the principle of selecting the 'minimally sufficient' intervention as a guiding principle for serving the needs of parents in order to maximise efficiency,

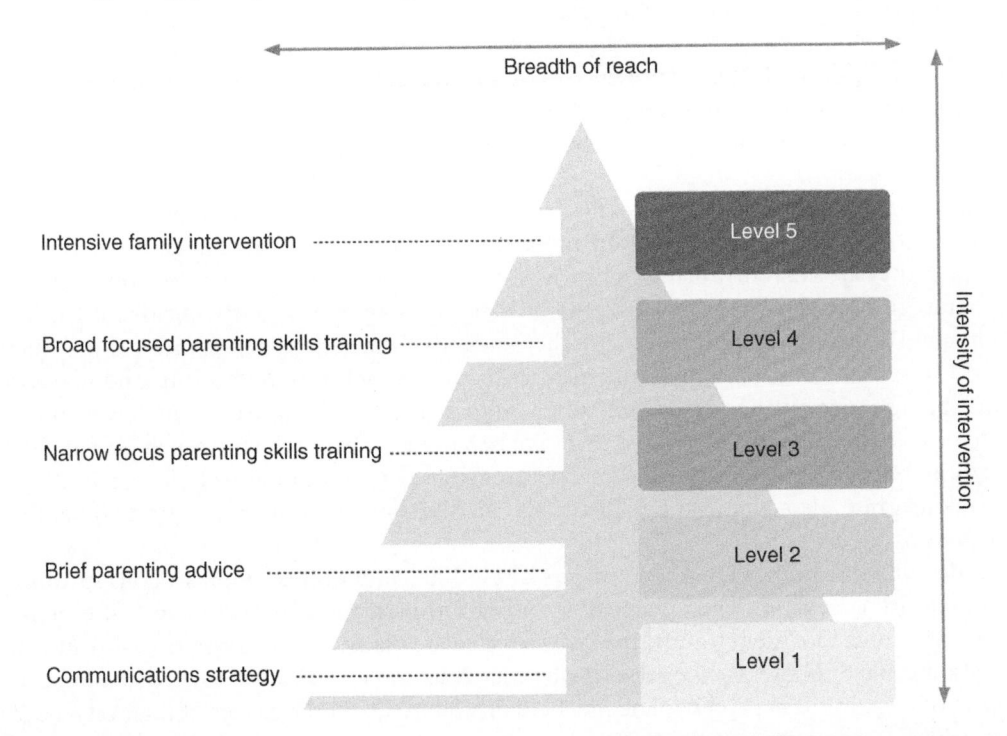

Figure 11.1 The population multilevel, multiformat Triple P system of parenting support and intervention.

contain costs, avoid over-servicing, and ensure that the programme becomes widely available to parents in the community. The model avoids a one-size-fits-all approach by using evidence-based tailored variants and flexible delivery options (e.g., web, group, individual, over the phone, self-directed) targeting diverse groups of parents. The need for a flexible system of intervention was demonstrated by Sanders, Markie-Dadds, Rinaldis et al. (2007), who found that 75% of respondents to a national household survey who had a child with an emotional or behavioural problem had not participated in a parenting programme (Sanders, Markie-Dadds, Rinaldis et al., 2007). The multidisciplinary nature of Triple P, combined with its flexibility, makes it well placed to address the critically important issue of child maltreatment.

The Pathways Triple P – Positive Parenting Program

Pathways Triple P (PTP) is a specific variant within the larger Triple P system of intervention designed specifically for families with indicated risk factors for child abuse or neglect. When compared to other Triple P variants, the main variation of PTP is that it hones in on parental attributional and anger processes that place parents at risk of child maltreatment. Although the content of Pathways Triple P is relevant for all parents, this variant of the Triple P system has been developed as an intensive intervention programme for parents who have difficulty regulating their emotions and as a result are considered at risk of physically or emotionally abusing their children. Consequently, it is viewed as an intervention for clients who are involved in the child protection system. Parents are generally referred to Pathways Triple P if the initial intake assessment and clinical interview reveal the following: (i) presence of coercive or harsh parenting or other elevated scores on standardised measures such as the Parenting Scale (Arnold, O'Leary, Wolff & Acher, 1993) or the Parent's Attributions for Child's Behaviour Measure (Pidgeon & Sanders, 2004); (ii) presence of dysfunctional attributions; (iii) parent reports difficulty implementing positive parenting skills after exposure to less intense variants of Triple P; (iv) suspected or substantiated child abuse and neglect; (v) parent is literate and willing to participate.

Parents are taught a variety of skills aimed at challenging and countering their maladaptive attributions for parent–child interactions and changing any negative parenting practices they are currently using in line with these attributions. The attributional retraining strategies focus on teaching parents how to counter their misattributions regarding their child's negative behaviour, and their negative parenting behaviour toward their child. This involves teaching parents how to challenge their misattributions and generate more benign attributions regarding their child's negative behaviour and fewer anger-justifying attributions for their own negative behaviour. These sessions teach parents how to counter and alter not only their anger-intensifying attributional style for their child's behaviour, but also their anger-justifying attributions for their negative parenting behaviour.

As described in Table 11.1, the Pathways Triple P intervention component consists of five two-hour group sessions where parents are invited to participate in discussion and exercises designed to orientate them toward the factors which are placing them at risk of maltreatment. Parents are asked to identify the reasons why they react in negative ways toward children, the impact of negative or harsh discipline practices on children, and the causes of their own negative behaviour toward their child. The exercises are also designed to teach parents how to prevent anger escalation and negative parenting practices, a process which involves teaching

Table 11.1 The Pathways Triple P system of intervention.

Pathways Triple P	Group Triple P sessions					Pathways Triple P sessions				Group Triple P session
Intake session	Session 1	Session 2	Session 3	Session 4		Module 1 Session 1	Module 1 Session 2	Module 2 Session 1	Module 2 Session 2	Closure session Session 8
Provide overview of programme. Explain what's involved. Obtain commitment. Conduct intake interview. Complete Assessment Booklet 1.	Principles of positive parenting. Identifying causes of child behaviour. Monitoring children's behaviour. Monitoring own behaviour. Setting developmentally appropriate goals. Setting practice tasks. Self-evaluation of strengths and weaknesses. Setting personal goals for change.	**Parent–child relationship enhancement skills** Spending quality time. Talking with children. Physical affection. **Encouraging desirable behaviour** Giving descriptive praise. Giving non-verbal attention. Providing engaging activities. **Teaching new skills and behaviours** Setting a good example. Using Ask, Say, Do. Using behaviour charts.	**Manage misbehaviour** Establishing ground rules. Using directed discussion. Using planned ignoring. Giving clear, calm instructions. Using logical consequences. Using quiet time. Using time-out.	**Preventing problems in high-risk situations** Planning and advance preparation. Discussing ground rules for specific situations. Selecting engaging activities. Providing incentives. Providing consequences. Holding follow-up discussions.		**Parent traps** Identifying parent traps. Understanding impact of own behaviour on children. Identifying dysfunctional attributions.	**How to get out of a parent trap** Understanding the reasons parents get caught in parent traps. Thought switching. Breaking out of a Parent Trap.	**Understanding anger** Recognising and understanding anger. Stopping anger from escalating. Abdominal breathing and relaxation techniques. Planning pleasurable activities.	**Coping with anger** Catching unhelpful thoughts. Developing personal anger coping statements. Challenging unhelpful thoughts. Developing coping plans for high-risk situations.	Family survival tips. Phasing out the programme. Strategies for maintaining change. Problem-solving for the future. Future goals. Complete Assessment Booklet 2.

parents to challenge and control their anger-intensifying attributions and mistaken explanations for their child's misbehaviour. Parents are also introduced to the emotion of anger and its physical effects, and are provided with a variety of techniques and strategies for becoming physically and mentally relaxed. Parents are also introduced to cognitive therapy concepts as they apply to anger management, which includes catching unhelpful thoughts, developing alternative coping statements in arousing situations, and challenging thoughts that lead to aggressive responses. Identifying high-risk anger situations and developing coping plans to manage anger in these situations are also covered.

After the group intervention phase, parents participate in four individual telephone consultations (15–30 minutes duration each). Parents receive a copy of two workbooks, *Avoiding Parent Traps* and *Coping with Anger*, which outline the principles taught in the two modules (focusing on the risk factors and on countering parents' misattributions for parent–child interactions and anger management). These parent workbooks have been published together with the existing practitioner's workbook (see Pidgeon & Sanders, 2005; Sanders & Pidgeon, 2005a, 2005b, 2005c).

Evidence for Triple P

Triple P is built on more than 35 years of programme development and evaluation. A recent meta-analysis of Triple P (Sanders, Kirby, Tellegen & Day, 2014) looked at 101 studies (including 62 randomised controlled trials) involving more than 16,000 families. Studies were included in the analyses if they reported a Triple P evaluation, reported child or parent outcomes, and provided sufficient original data. In these analyses, significant moderate effect sizes were identified for children's social, emotional and behavioural outcomes ($d=0.473$), parenting practices ($d=0.578$), and parenting satisfaction and efficacy ($d=0.519$). Significant small-to-moderate effects were also found for the distal outcomes of parental adjustment ($d=0.340$) and parental relationship ($d=0.225$). Significant positive effect sizes were found for each level of the Triple P system for children's social, emotional and behavioural outcomes, although greater effect sizes were found for the more intense interventions (Levels 4 and 5).

Several studies have demonstrated the effectiveness of Pathways Triple P in improving parenting practices and reducing the risk of child maltreatment. Sanders, Pidgeon, Gravestock et al. (2004) randomly assigned 98 parents experiencing significant difficulties in managing their own anger in their interactions with their preschool-aged children to either Pathways Triple P, which included attributional retraining, or a standard version of Triple P that provided training in parenting skills alone. At post-intervention, both conditions were associated with lower levels of observed and parent-reported disruptive child behaviour, lower levels of parent-reported dysfunctional parenting, greater parental self-efficacy, less parental distress and relationship conflict, and similarly high levels of consumer satisfaction. Whereas the Pathways intervention showed a significantly greater short-term improvement on measures of negative parental attributions for children's misbehaviour, potential for child abuse and unrealistic parental expectation, at six-month follow-up both conditions showed similarly positive outcomes on all measures of child abuse potential, parent practices, parental adjustment, and child behaviour and adjustment. Importantly, the Pathways intervention resulted in sustained and greater change in negative parental attributions.

In further support of the efficacy of the Pathways intervention, Wiggins, Sofronoff and Sanders (2009) examined the effects of Pathways Triple P on parents who met the inclusion criteria of borderline to clinically significant relationship disturbance and child emotional and behavioural problems. Participants were randomly allocated into either an intervention or a wait-list control group. The intervention was delivered in a group format for nine weeks and consisted of parent skills training and cognitive behaviour therapy targeting negative attributions for child behaviour. Participants in the Pathways condition reported significantly greater improvement in parent–child relationship quality from pre- to post-intervention compared to participants in the control group with benefits maintained at three-month follow-up. Participants in the intervention condition also reported a significant reduction in the use of dysfunctional parenting practices (laxness, verbosity and over-reactivity), blameworthy and intentional attributions for child behaviour, and child externalising behaviour problems from pre- to post-intervention, with reductions maintained at three-month follow-up.

Adopting a Public Health Approach to Child Maltreatment

Drawing on the principle of proportionate universalism (Marmot, 2010), the public health approach emphasises the needs of individual families while remaining sensitive to the universal relevance of parenting assistance so that the larger community of parents embraces and supports parents being involved in parenting programmes. From a population-level perspective, intervention developers must consider how their programme fits with local needs and policy, and be mindful of the cost-effectiveness of their proposed solution. Improved parenting is a potentially powerful cornerstone of any prevention and early intervention strategy designed to promote positive outcomes for children and the community.

In a groundbreaking study, Prinz, Sanders, Shapiro et al. (2009) examined the value of a public health approach to the prevention of child maltreatment in what was known as the US Triple P system population trial. Eighteen counties in South Carolina were randomly assigned either to the Triple P system or to services-as-usual. Professional training for an existing workforce (over 600 service providers) in the Triple P countries was provided, and universal media and communication strategies pertaining to positive parenting were deployed via local newspapers, radio, school newsletters, mass mailings to family households, publicity at community events and website information. These strategies implementing the system's universal facet are intended to destigmatise parenting and family support, make effective parenting strategies readily accessible to all parents, and facilitate help-seeking by parents who need higher intensity intervention.

Large improvements were found in three measured outcomes: substantiated child maltreatment, child out-of-home placements, and child maltreatment injuries. The findings came from three separate sources: the child protective services, the foster care system, and the hospital system respectively. This study is the first to randomise geographical areas and show the preventative impact of evidence-based parenting interventions on child maltreatment at a population level. This population trial demonstrated that offering parenting and family support via a broad system like Triple P, without singling out parents because of risk characteristics, could actually help prevent maltreatment and related problems. Further, the infrastructure costs associated with implementing the Triple P system (i.e., Levels 1–5) in the United States (Prinz, Sanders, Shapiro et al., 2009) was $12 per participant, a cost that could be recovered in a year by as little as a 10% reduction in the rate of abuse and neglect (Foster, Prinz, Sanders & Shapiro, 2008). Although these savings are striking, it is unclear who absorbs the cost of delivering parenting programmes such as Triple P to the community.

Implications and Challenges

An effective parenting support strategy needs to address a number of significant challenges within a robust implementation framework in order to succeed (Damschroder & Hagedorn, 2011). Of primary consideration, parenting interventions need to be delivered in a non-stigmatising way. Currently, parenting interventions are perceived by many vulnerable and at-risk parents as only being for inadequate, ignorant, failed or wayward parents. To be effective and non-stigmatising, a whole-of-population approach to parenting support has to emphasise the universal relevance of parenting assistance so that the larger community of parents embraces and supports parents being involved in parenting programmes. A non-stigmatised example is found in prenatal (birth) classes, which parents across a broad array of economic and cultural groups (and family configurations) find useful and do not perceive as stigmatising. Parenting programmes must be considered equally as 'routine' as undertaking prenatal classes and preparing for life as a parent.

Parenting support also needs to be flexible with respect to delivery formats (e.g., group, individual, online) to meet the needs of parents in the child welfare system. Having every family receive an intensive intervention at a single location is not only cost ineffective but also unnecessary and undesirable from a family's perspective. A careful consideration of the cost-effectiveness of interventions is essential when developing and disseminating programmes at a population level. Morawska, Tometzki and Sanders (2014) provided an excellent example of flexible delivery formats in action. They evaluated whether administering parenting strategies over the radio could significantly improve parenting practice and child behaviour problems. The study revealed parents who were randomised to listen to the radio podcasts showed significant improvements in key parent and child outcome measures. Such examples of flexible delivery formats are cost-effective and potentially highly effective at reducing problematic parenting practices across communities.

Governments can choose to directly invest in these programmes as part of their social welfare and mental health policies. However, in an environment of intense competition for public funds and resources, sustained investment in parenting programmes is ultimately a matter of priority, which points to the importance of continued advocacy by researchers, agencies and consumers for government investment in prevention programmes. Flexibility of programme offering will also make the intervention useful for mandated services – parenting support for foster and adoptive parents and support for families within the child welfare system who are not involved with child protective services.

Investment in a population approach to parenting support would enable every family in the community to have access to evidence-based parenting information and support when needed, regardless of where they live. Under a population approach, the vast majority of families would be able to access all the help they need through the multilevel suite of programmes contained within systems of intervention such as Triple P. Programmes could be promoted through non-stigmatising, universal access points such as long daycare services, kindergartens, playgroups, schools, churches and other community groups. Families would be free to choose whether they take advantage of the Triple P services.

Conclusion

Preventing the maltreatment of children should be given priority as a major public health challenge. There is considerable scope for parenting interventions to improve children's developmental outcomes for any mental health, physical health or social problem where potentially modifiable parenting and family variables have been causally implicated in the onset, maintenance, exacerbation or relapse of a problem. However, the limited reach of most parenting programmes ensures that these programmes make little impact on prevalence rates of social and emotional problems of children and child maltreatment at a population level. The limited impact of available parenting interventions on children's problems at a population level underpins the need for implementation of Triple P as a public health system of parenting support and intervention. Triple P adopts a public health approach to the delivery of universal parenting support with the goal of increasing parental self-efficacy, knowledge and competence in the use of skills that promote positive development in children and adolescents. This change in focus has enabled millions more children around the world to experience the benefits of positive parenting and family environments that promote healthy development and, as a consequence, fewer children are likely to have developed behavioural and emotional problems or experienced episodes of maltreatment.

The Parenting and Family Support Centre is partly funded by royalties stemming from published resources of the Triple P – Positive Parenting Program, which is developed and owned by The University of Queensland. Royalties from the program are also distributed to the Faculty of Health and Behavioural Sciences at UQ and contributory authors of Triple P programs. Triple P International (TPI) Pty Ltd is a private company licensed by Uniquest, Pty Ltd, a commercialization company of UQ, to publish and disseminate Triple P worldwide. Dr Sanders and Dr Pickering have no share or ownership of TPI but Dr Sanders receives royalties and consultancy fees from TPI. TPI had no involvement in the study design, collection, analysis or interpretation of data, or writing of this report. Drs Sanders and Pickering were employees of The University of Queensland.

References

Adamson, M., Morawska, A. & Sanders, M.R. (2013). Childhood feeding difficulties: A randomized controlled trial of a group-based parenting intervention. *Journal of Developmental and Behavioural Pediatrics*, 34, 293–302.

Arnold, D.S., O'Leary, S.G., Wolff, L.S. & Acher, M.M. (1993). The Parenting Scale: A measure of dysfunctional parenting in discipline situations. *Psychological Assessment*, 5, 137–144.

Australian Institute of Health and Welfare (2005). *Child Protection Australia 2003–2004* (Child Welfare Series No. 36). Canberra: Australian Institute of Health and Welfare.

Australian Institute of Health and Welfare (2008). *Child Protection Australia 2006–2007* (Child Welfare Series No. 43). Canberra: Australian Institute of Health and Welfare.

Azar, S.T. & Weinzierl, B.S. (2005). Child maltreatment and childhood injury research: A cognitive behavioural approach. *Journal of Pediatric Psychology*, 30, 598–614.

Barkley, R.A., Edwards, G., Laneri, M. et al. (2001). The efficacy of problem-solving communication training alone, behavior management training alone, and their combination for parent–adolescent conflict in teenagers with ADHD and ODD. *Journal of Consulting and Clinical Psychology*, 69, 926–941.

Biglan, A., Flay, B.R., Embry, D.D. & Sandler, I.N. (2012). The critical role of nurturing environments for promoting human well-being. *American Psychologist*, 67, 257–271.

Chu, J.T.W., Farruggia, S.P., Sanders, M.R. & Ralph, A. (2012). Towards a public health approach to parenting programmes for parents of adolescents. *Journal of Public Health*, 34(S1), i41–i47.

Comer, J.S., Chow, C., Chan, P. et al. (2013). Psychosocial treatment efficacy for disruptive behavior problems in young children: A meta-analytic examination. *Journal of the American Academy of Child and Adolescent Psychiatry*, 52, 26–36.

Connell, A.M., Dishion, T.J., Yasui, M. & Kavanagh, K. (2007). An adaptive approach to family intervention: Linking engagement in family-centered intervention to reductions in adolescent problem behavior. *Journal of Consulting and Clinical Psychology*, 75, 568–579.

Damschroder, L.J. & Hagedorn, H.J. (2011). A guiding framework and approach for implantation research in substance use disorders treatment. *Psychology of Addictive Behaviors*, 25, 194–205.

Dishion, T.J. & Andrews, D.W. (1995). Preventing escalation in problem behaviors with high-risk young adolescents: Immediate and 1-year outcomes. *Journal of Consulting and Clinical Psychology*, 63, 538–548.

Dix, T., Reinhold, D.P. & Zambarano, R.J. (1990). Mothers' judgments in moments of anger. *Merrill-Palmer Quarterly*, 36, 465–486.

Dix, T., Ruble, D.N. & Zambarano, R.J. (1989). Mothers' implicit theories of discipline: Child effects, parent effects, and the attribution process. *Child Development*, 60, 1373–1390.

Foster, E.M., Prinz, R.J., Sanders, M.R. & Shapiro, C.J. (2008). The costs of a public health infrastructure for delivering parenting and family support. *Children and Youth Services Review*, 30, 493–501.

Griffin, K.W., Botvin, G.J., Scheier, L.M. et al. (2000). Parenting practices as predictors of substance use, delinquency and aggression among urban minority youth: Moderating effects of family structure and gender. *Psychology of Addictive Behaviors*, 14, 174–184.

Heinrichs, N., Kliem, S. & Hahlweg, K. (2014). Four-year follow-up of a randomized controlled trial of Triple P group for parent and child outcomes. *Prevention Science*, 15, 233–245.

James, J.E. (1994). Foundation education as a means of disseminating behavioural innovation to non-psychologists. *Behavior Change*, 11, 19–26.

Kazdin, A.E. (2005). *Parent Management Training: Treatment for Oppositional, Aggressive, and Antisocial Behavior in Children and Adolescents*. New York: Oxford University Press.

Kolko, D.J. (1996). Clinical monitoring of treatment course in child physical abuse: Psychometric characteristics and treatment comparisons. *Child Abuse & Neglect*, 20, 23–43.

Kolko, D.J. & Swenson, C.C. (2002). *Assessing and Treating Physically Abused Children and Their Families: A Cognitive-Behavioural Approach*. Thousand Oaks, CA: Sage Publications.

Kotch, J.B., Lewis, T., Hussey, J.M. et al. (2008). Importance of early neglect for childhood aggression. *Pediatrics*, 121, 725–731.

Lansford, M.J., Berlin, D., Bates, J. & Pettit, G.S. (2007). Early physical abuse and later violent delinquency: A prospective longitudinal study. *Child Maltreatment*, 12, 233–245.

Luby, J., Belden, A., Botteron, K. et al. (2013). The effects of poverty on childhood brain development: The mediating effect of caregiving and stressful life events. *JAMA Pediatrics*, 167, 1135–1142.

Maas, C., Herrenkohl, T.I. & Sousa, C. (2008). Review of research on child maltreatment and violence in youth. *Trauma, Violence, & Abuse*, 9, 56–67.

Mammen, O.K., Kolko, D.J. & Pilkonis, P.A. (2002). Negative affect and parental aggression in child physical abuse. *Child Abuse & Neglect*, 26, 407–424.

Marmot, M. (2010). *Fair Society Health Lives*. London: The Marmot Review.

Mason, W.A., Kosterman, R., Hawkins, J.D. et al. (2003). Reducing adolescents' growth in substance use and delinquency: Randomized trial effects of a parent-training prevention intervention. *Prevention Science*, 4, 203–212.

McCart, M.R., Priester, P.E., Davies, W.H. & Azen, R. (2006). Differential effectiveness of behavioural parent training and cognitive-behavioral therapy for antisocial youth: A meta-analysis. *Journal of Abnormal Child Psychology*, 34, 527–543.

McHolm, A.E, MacMillan, H.L. & Jamieson, E. (2003). The relationship between childhood physical abuse and suicidality among depressed women: Results from a community sample. *American Journal of Psychiatry*, 160, 933–938.

Mejia, A., Calam, R. & Sanders, M.R. (2014). Examining delivery preferences and cultural relevance of an evidence-based parenting program in a low-resource setting of Central America: Approaching parents as consumers. *Journal of Child and Family Studies*.

Menting, A.T.A, de Castro, B.A. & Matthys, W. (2013). Effectiveness of the Incredible Years parent training to modify disruptive and prosocial child behavior: A meta-analytic review. *Clinical Psychology Review*, 33, 901–913.

Miller, L.R. & Azar, S.T. (1996). The pervasiveness of maladaptive attributions in mothers at-risk of child abuse. *Family Violence and Sexual Assault Bulletin*, 12, 31–37.

Milner, J.S. (2003). Social information processing in high-risk and physically abusive parents. *Child Abuse & Neglect*, 27, 7–20.

Mitchell, C., Hobcraftb, J., McLanahanc, S.S. et al. (2014). Social disadvantage, genetic sensitivity, and children's telomere length. *Proceedings of the National Academy of Sciences*, 111, 5944–5949.

Morawska, A., Sanders, M.R., Goadby, E. et al. (2011). Is the Triple P-Positive Parenting Program acceptable to parents from culturally diverse backgrounds? *Journal of Child and Family Studies*, 20, 614–622.

Morawska, A., Tometzki, H. & Sanders, M.R. (2014). An evaluation of the efficacy of a Triple P-Positive Parenting Program Podcast series. *Journal of Developmental and Behavioral Pediatrics*, 35, 128–147.

National Institute Clinical Excellence Social Care (NICE). 2006. Parent-training/education programmes in the management of children with conduct disorders. London: NICE.

National Research Council and Institute of Medicine (2009). *Preventing mental, emotional, and behavioural disorders among young people: Progress and possibilities.* Committee on the Prevention of Mental Disorders and Substance Abuse Among Children, Youth, and Young Adults: Research Advances and Promising Interventions. M.E. O'Connell, T. Boat and K.E. Warner (eds), Board on Children, Youth, and Families, Division of Behavioural and Social Sciences and Education. Washington, DC: The National Academies Press.

Nix, R.L., Pinderhughes, E.E., Dodge, K.A. et al. (1999). The relation between mothers' hostile attribution tendencies and children's externalizing behaviour problems: The mediating role of mothers' harsh discipline strategies. *Child Development*, 70, 896–909.

Pickering, J.A. & Sanders, M.R. (2013). Enhancing communities through the design and development of positive parenting interventions. *Journal of Applied Research on Children: Informing Policy for Children at Risk*, 4(2), Article 18, digitalcommons.library.tmc.edu/childrenatrisk/vol4/iss2/18.

Pidgeon, A.M. & Sanders, M.R. (2004). The parent's attributions for child behaviour measure. Brisbane, Australia: The University of Queensland.

Pidgeon, A.M. & Sanders, M.R. (2005). *Pathways to positive parenting. Module 1: Avoiding parent traps.* Brisbane, Australia: Triple P International.

Pidgeon, A.M. & Sanders, M.R. (2009). Attributions, parental anger and risk of maltreatment. *International Journal of Child Health and Human Development*, 2, 57–69.

Prinz, R.J. & Sanders, M.R. (2007). Adopting a population-level approach to parenting and family support interventions. *Clinical Psychology Review*, 27, 739–749.

Prinz, R.J., Sanders, M.R., Shapiro, C.J. et al. (2009). Population-based prevention of child maltreatment: The US Triple P system population trial. *Prevention Science*, 10, 1–12.

Rapee, R.M., Kennedy, S.J., Ingram, M. et al. (2010). Altering the trajectory of anxiety in at-risk young children. *American Journal of Psychiatry*, 167, 1518–1525.

Repetti, R.L., Taylor, S.E. & Seeman, T.E. (2002). Risky families: Family social environments and the mental and physical health of offspring. *Psychological Bulletin*, 128, 330–366.

Rodriguez, C.M. & Green, A.J. (1997). Parenting stress and anger expression as predictors of child abuse potential. *Child Abuse & Neglect*, 21, 366–377.

Salari, R., Ralph, A. & Sanders, M.R. (2014). An efficacy trial: Positive parenting program for parents of teenagers. *Behaviour Change*, 31, 34–52.

Sanders, M.R. (2012). Development, evaluation, and multinational dissemination of the Triple P-Positive Parenting Program. *Annual Review of Clinical Psychology*, 8, 345–379.

Sanders, M.R. & Pidgeon, A.M. (2005a). *Pathways to positive parenting. Module 2: Coping with anger.* Brisbane, Australia: Triple P International.

Sanders, M.R. & Pidgeon, A.M. (2005b). *Pathways to positive parenting. Module 3: Maintenance and closure.* Brisbane: Triple P International.

Sanders, M.R. & Pidgeon, A.M. (2005c). *Practitioner's manual for Pathways Triple P.* Brisbane, Australia: Triple P International.

Sanders, M.R., Cleghorn, G.J., Shepherd, R.W. & Patrick, M. (1996). Predictors of clinical improvement in children with recurrent abdominal pain. *Behavioural and Cognitive Psychotherapy*, 24, 27–38.

Sanders, M.R., Kirby, J.N., Tellegen, C.L. & Day, J.J. (2014). Towards a public health approach to parenting: A systemic review and meta-analysis of the Triple P-Positive Parenting Program. *Clinical Psychology Review*, 32, 337–357.

Sanders, M.R., Markie-Dadds, C., Rinaldis, M. et al. (2007). Using household survey data to inform policy decisions regarding the delivery of evidence-based parenting interventions. *Child: Care, Health and Development*, 33, 768–783.

Sanders, M.R., Pidgeon, A.M., Gravestock, F. et al. (2004). Does parental attributional retraining and anger management enhance the effects of the Triple P-Positive Parenting Program with parents at risk of child maltreatment? *Behavior Therapy*, 35, 513–535.

Spoth, R.L., Redmond, C. & Shin, C. (1998). Direct and indirect latent-variable parenting outcomes of two universal family-focused preventive interventions: Extending a public health-oriented research base. *Journal of Consulting and Clinical Psychology*, 66, 385–399.

Stallman, H.M. & Sanders, M.R. (2007). 'Family Transitions Triple P': The theoretical basis and development of a program for parents going through divorce. *Journal of Divorce & Remarriage*, 47(3–4), 133–153.

Tellegen, C.L. & Sanders, M.R. (2014). A randomized controlled trial evaluating a brief parenting program with children with autism spectrum disorders. *Journal of Consulting and Clinical Psychology*, 82, 1193–2000.

Turner, K.M.T., Richards, M. & Sanders, M.R. (2007). Randomised clinical trial of a group parent education programme for Australian indigenous families. *Journal of Paediatrics and Child Health*, 43, 429–437.

US Department of Health and Human Services (2008). *Administration on children youth and families. Child Maltreatment* 2006. Washington, DC: US Government Printing Office.

Washington State Institute for Public Policy (July, 2015). *Benefit-Cost Technical Documentation*, www.wsipp.wa.gov/BenefitCost?programSearch=Triple+P+ (accessed 14 July 2015).

Wekerle, C. & Wolfe, D.A. (1998). The role of child maltreatment and attachment style in adolescent relationship violence. *Development and Psychopathology*, 10, 571–586.

West, F., Sanders, M.R., Cleghorn, G.J. & Davies, P.S.W. (2010). Randomised clinical trial of a family-based lifestyle intervention for childhood obesity involving parents as the exclusive agents of change. *Behaviour Research and Therapy*, 48, 1170–1179.

Whittingham, K., Sanders, M.R., McKinlay, L. & Boyd, R.N. (2014). Interventions to reduce behavioural problems in children with cerebral palsy: An RCT. *Pediatrics*.

Widom, C.S., Dumont, K.A. & Czaja, S.J. (2007). A prospective investigation of major depressive disorder and comorbidity in abused and neglected children grown up. *Archives of General Psychiatry*, 64, 49–56.

Wiggins, T.L., Sofronoff, K. & Sanders, M.R. (2009). Pathways Triple P-Positive Parenting Program: Effects on parent–child relationships and child behavior problems. *Family Process*, 48, 517–530.

World Health Organization (2009). *Preventing violence through the development of safe, stable and nurturing relationships between children and their parents and caregivers. Series of briefings on violence prevention: the evidence*. Geneva, Switzerland: World Health Organization.

12

What Works to Prevent the Sexual Exploitation of Children and Youth

Sandy K. Wurtele[1] and Cindy Miller-Perrin[2]

[1] University of Colorado, Colorado Springs, US
[2] Pepperdine University, CA, US

> *No violence against children is justifiable; all violence against children is preventable.*
> Source: UNICEF, 2006, p. 5

Violence against children, including sexual abuse and exploitation, is a serious public health problem of global magnitude. Childhood sexual abuse (CSA) refers to the involvement of a child in sexual activity to provide sexual gratification or financial gain to the offender. Children are at risk of being sexually exploited and abused by adults in residential care, youth-serving organisations (YSOs), and while using information and communication technologies (ICTs), including the internet and smartphones. The internet is used by adults to create, collect, and exchange sexually abusive images of children, to engage in inappropriate sexual communication with minors, and to solicit sex from minors (Durkin & DeLong, 2012). The internet is also integral to the commercial sexual exploitation of children (CSEC), which involves any exchange of sexual activity with a minor for money, shelter, food, drugs or any other goods or services. CSEC takes many forms, including prostitution, abusive imagery, sex trafficking, and child sex tourism, and CSEC can occur online as well as offline (APSAC, 2013; IOM & NRC, 2013; Miller-Perrin & Wurtele, 2017). Although 'child sexual abuse' (CSA) is the most commonly used term, we refer to all forms of sexual exploitation and abuse – commercial and non-commercial – as the sexual exploitation of children and youth. Exploitation is the common element in adult–child sexual abuse, whether for commercial or personal gain.

Although prevalence estimates of CSA vary because of differing definitions (e.g., contact abuse and non-contact abuse) and different methods of data collection (e.g., interviews and surveys), it is clear that children of all nationalities and ethnicities are sexually exploited. For example, two recent meta-analyses demonstrated that the global prevalence of CSA is alarmingly high, with about 20% of women and 8% of men reporting sexual abuse during childhood (Pereda, Guilera, Forns & Gomez-Benito, 2009; Stoltenborgh, van IJzendoorn, Euser & Bakermans-Kranenburg, 2011). Furthermore, CSA has been associated with an array of emotional, behavioural, physical and social difficulties across the lifespan (e.g., Maniglio, 2009;

The Wiley Handbook of What Works in Child Maltreatment: An Evidence-Based Approach to Assessment and Intervention in Child Protection, First Edition. Edited by Louise Dixon, Daniel F. Perkins, Catherine Hamilton-Giachritsis, and Leam A. Craig.
© 2017 John Wiley & Sons Ltd. Published 2017 by John Wiley & Sons Ltd.

Pérez-Fuentes, Olfson, Villegas et al., 2013). Based on the global prevalence and short- and long-term negative physical and mental health outcomes, CSA has been identified as a significant public health challenge by the US Centers for Disease Control and Prevention (CDC) (Whitaker, Lutzker & Shelley, 2005) and as one of the leading global risks to health by the World Health Organization (Butchart, Phinney Harvey, Mian & Fürniss, 2006).

Given the ubiquity and negative consequences, primary prevention efforts are clearly warranted, which are broadly conceptualised as interventions that reduce risk and promote variables that protect against problems (Romano, 2015). With respect to the sexual exploitation of children and youth, primary prevention aims to reduce the number of new cases (incidence) by providing services to everyone, regardless of risk status (i.e., universal prevention efforts). Public health experts recognise that this problem arises from multiple ecological levels (i.e., from individual to societal levels) and recommend that prevention not only target factors at an individual level but also address conditions in the macro-system that promote or support the sexual exploitation of children. Given the rise in cyber sexual exploitation, an additional level – the online world – must be added to this framework to keep youth safe in cyberspace. This chapter will review current prevention efforts and provide direction for future initiatives to prevent the sexual exploitation of children and youth. We briefly describe international primary prevention strategies using an ecological framework targeting many segments of society, including children, parents/caretakers, youth-serving organisations, society and cyberspace.

Child-Focused Approaches: Educating Youth to Avoid Sexual Victimisation

School-based empowerment programmes to help children avoid sexual victimisation were created and widely disseminated in both the United States and Canada starting in the early 1980s. The focus of these educational programmes has primarily been to teach young children personal safety knowledge and skills through group-based instruction, usually conducted in schools. School systems evolved as the obvious choice for teaching children about personal safety, given that their primary function is to inform and educate, and also because of their ability to reach large numbers of diverse children in a relatively cost-efficient fashion. A universal primary prevention approach of this nature also eliminates the stigma of identifying specific children or families as at risk for sexual abuse, and thus avoids costly and intrusive interventions into family privacy. Most educational initiatives for young children share common goals, including the 5Rs of: (a) helping children *recognise* potentially abusive situations or potential abusers, (b) encouraging children to *refuse* sexual requests by saying 'No', (c) teaching children to *resist* by getting away from the perpetrator, (d) encouraging children to *report* previous or ongoing abuse to a trusted authority figure and (e) explaining that secret or inappropriate touching is never the child's *responsibility* (Wurtele, 2008). Of these goals, the first three address primary prevention – the focus of this review.

A sizeable number of reviews and meta-analyses have been published that examine empirical studies that were conducted mostly in the US, with additional studies from Canada, UK, Ireland, Australia and China. Reviews consistently conclude that children benefit from participating in these programmes. Specifically, programme participants have demonstrated increased knowledge of sexual abuse and protective behaviours (Kenny & Wurtele, 2010a; MacMillan Wathen, Barlow et al., 2009; Mikton & Butchart, 2009; Topping & Barron, 2009; Wurtele, 2002; Wurtele & Kenny, 2010b, 2012; Zwi, Woolfenden, Wheeler et al., 2007). Studies also find that programmes increase participants' willingness to disclose, enhance positive feelings and correct terminology about their bodies and genitals, and help children learn that it is not their fault if abuse occurs (Kenny & Wurtele, 2009; Wurtele & Owens, 1997).

Reviews also conclude that child-focused educational programmes can build children's knowledge and self-protective skills without producing negative side effects (e.g., elevated anxiety, making false allegations, over-generalising to appropriate touches) and may actually produce positive effects (e.g., increased parent–child communication) (Wurtele, 2009). However, studies are inconclusive about whether these programmes actually *prevent* CSA. Only one study has attempted to determine whether participation in personal safety programmes might prevent sexual victimisation. In 2000, Gibson and Leitenberg asked 825 undergraduate women in the US to report their past histories of CSA as well as their participation in school-based prevention programmes. Women who had not participated in a prevention programme in childhood were about twice as likely to have experienced CSA as those who had participated in a programme. Even though this study used a relatively weak, non-experimental design, it provides tentative support for the assertion that, at least for women, school-based CSA prevention programmes are associated with a decreased occurrence of sexual abuse. In his review of child-focused educational programmes, childhood victimisation expert Finkelhor (2007) concluded that 'the weight of currently available evidence shows that it is worth providing children with high-quality prevention education programs' (p. 644).

Several characteristics of 'high-quality' programmes have been determined. Young children can learn personal safety skills if they are taught concrete concepts in a clear, developmentally appropriate way, and are given adequate time for learning, across multiple sessions and involving skill-building exercises. Reviews have consistently concluded that programmes which incorporate modelling (i.e., demonstrating the skill to be learnt) and rehearsal (e.g., role plays) are more effective than programmes that primarily rely on individual study or passive exposure (Davis & Gidycz, 2000; Topping & Barron, 2009; US General Accounting Office, 1996; Wurtele, 2008, 2009; Wurtele & Kenny, 2010b, 2012; Wurtele & Owens, 1997; Zhang, Chen, Feng et al., 2013, 2014). In addition, programmes for young children are more effective if they are longer in duration (four sessions or more), if they repeat important concepts across spaced sessions rather than massed presentation, and if they are based on concrete rules rather than abstract concepts (e.g., rights, feelings, good/bad touch) (Collin-Vézina, Daigneault & Hébert, 2013; Kenny & Wurtele, 2010a; Topping & Barron, 2009; Wurtele & Owens, 1997). Programmes should avoid using the 'good touch and bad touch' approach for teaching children how to recognise inappropriate touches. Not only has this approach been shown to be confusing, especially for young children (Charlesworth & Rodwell, 1997; Kenny & Wurtele, 2010b; Wurtele, Kast, Miller-Perrin & Kondrick, 1989), but it also potentially communicates to children that all sexual touches are 'bad'.

For all their benefits, child-focused educational programmes have their limitations. They have been criticised for expecting children to be solely responsible for their own protection, when 'the responsibility for the protection of minors lies with adults' (Zollner, Fuchs & Fegert, 2014, p. 5). Another limitation is that the majority of programmes target the early childhood years and neglect the adolescent years. As educational programmes move from preschool to high school, educational approaches should prepare youth as they begin to experience sexual thoughts, feelings and attractions to others; help them adjust to the biological and physical changes of puberty; and assist adolescents with the transition to establishing sexual identities and intimate relationships (Wurtele & Kenny, 2011).

Adolescence is an excellent opportunity to provide young people with universal sex education that promotes healthy sexual behaviour free of coercion and respectful of both partners' desire and consent (Lavoie, Thibodeau, Gagné & Hébert, 2010; Wurtele, 2009). Young people need help recognising, for example, that adult–teen sexual relationships are punishable crimes, regardless of whether the teen is 'in love' with the offender and 'consents' to what they may believe is a 'reciprocal' sexual relationship (Oudekerk, Farr & Reppucci, 2013; Tener, Walsh, Jones & Kinnish, 2014). Child-focused approaches have also been criticised for over-emphasising secondary or tertiary prevention, such as disclosing present or past abuse, while underemphasising primary prevention – that is, stopping the development of perpetrating behaviours. As adolescence is a key developmental risk period for the onset of sexual arousal to children (Smallbone, Marshall & Wortley, 2008), there needs to be more of a focus on stopping the development of sexual offending behaviours among youth. Educational approaches should prepare youth as they begin to experience sexual thoughts, feelings and attractions to others, and emphasise that it is morally and legally wrong to sexually experiment with or exploit children (Wurtele, 2009). In addition to targeting this age group, innovative ways to educate teens about sexuality and prevention of exploitation are sorely needed (e.g., using the internet or online interactive games). Evaluations of web-based training to prevent CSA are appearing and showing promise (e.g., Müller, Röder & Fingerle, 2014).

Another criticism of child-focused prevention programmes has been the lack of attention and sensitivity to diverse populations and cultural differences of participants. Some programmes shown to be effective for building knowledge and skills among children in an average socio-economic environment (Hébert, Lavoie, Piché & Poitras, 2001) have been less effective in a multi-ethnic and underprivileged urban environment (Daigneault, Hébert, McDuff & Frappier, 2012). In the US, cultural-specific prevention programmes are being developed and evaluated (e.g., Baker, Gleasono, Naai et al., 2012; Kenny, Wurtele & Alonso, 2012). Plummer's (2001) review of 87 child-focused CSA prevention programmes found that only 17% of programmes addressed diversity, while only about one-third addressed special-needs populations (e.g., deaf, developmentally or physically disabled). Children who are deaf or hard of hearing (DHH) are at increased risk of sexual abuse, particularly DHH youth who attend residential schools (Schenkel, Rothman-Marshall, Schlehofer et al., 2014). Encouragingly, much-needed guidance for adapting prevention information for children with disabilities is appearing (e.g., McEachern, 2012). Although initial findings demonstrate promising results, more efforts to meet the unique needs of diverse populations and to tailor interventions to groups of youth shown to be at high risk for commercial and non-commercial forms of sexual exploitation (e.g., sexual minority youth; homeless youth; previously victimised youth) is needed (Miller-Perrin & Wurtele, 2017; Whittle, Hamilton-Giachritsis, Beech & Collings, 2013).

Child-focused programmes in high-income countries also primarily focus on preventing CSA rather than CSEC (i.e., child sex trafficking) (Wurtele & Miller-Perrin, 2012). In a few countries with higher rates of CSEC, information about trafficking has been introduced into the school curriculum. There have also been initiatives to promote educational success and teach schoolchildren life skills to reduce the likelihood that they will be trafficked for sexual purposes. In the UK, Barnardo's produces a pamphlet for young people and family members entitled *Sexual Exploitation: Sex, Secrets and Lies* to help users understand what sexual exploitation can be and providing tips for staying safe, both offline and online (available at: www.barnardos.org.uk). In addition, Barnardo's has produced *Real Love Rocks*, designed to provide extensive guidance and materials to enable professionals to feel confident in talking to adolescents about sexual exploitation (available at: www.barnardosrealloverocks.org.uk). Education about CSEC is particularly important because youth may not recognise either their risk for, or actual, victimisation (IOM & NRC, 2014; Walker, 2013). Unfortunately, child-focused interventions to prevent CSEC are limited and have not been evaluated rigorously enough to determine their effectiveness (IOM & NRC, 2014; President's Interagency Taskforce, 2014; van der Laan, Smit, Busschers & Aarten, 2011).

To prevent technology-related sexual solicitation and victimisation of adolescents, teen-focused safety education programmes are sorely needed. Although almost half of US youth in one survey reported receiving prevention messages at school about online sexual solicitation (Mitchell, Jones, Finkelhor & Wolak, 2013), a recent review of internet safety education materials revealed that these programmes are of dubious quality and many of their safety recommendations have questionable protective logic (Jones, Mitchell & Walsh, 2012). Awareness-building strategies are needed to help youth recognise that emotionally manipulative adults exist, whether online or in-person, who will exploit their sexual curiosity and take advantage of their normal needs for affection, intimacy and romantic connections. The warning signs that they are being groomed online need to be described, covering such inappropriate sexual advances as being asked personal questions, talking about sex, being asked to send or receive sexually explicit images, or being told to keep the relationship a secret (Wurtele, 2012b). Perhaps youth hearing from victims of online abusers would be helpful, especially about how easy it was to become enmeshed in the relationship, and the variety of manipulation techniques used throughout the grooming process, like being offered payment for sexual services or the promise of modelling work (Shannon, 2008). It is also important to counter the belief that only girls are targeted online (Davidson & Martellozzo, 2008).

In addition to recognising inappropriate sexual advances, young people need instruction on how to respond to solicitations and how to report such incidents to prevent offline contact (Wolak & Finkelhor, 2013). Although teenagers rarely inform their parents when they receive sexual solicitations online (Mitchell, Jones, Finkelhor & Wolak, 2013), they often tell their friends (Katz, 2013; Whittle, Hamilton-Giachritsis, Beech & Collings, 2013) who, if informed about how to respond to disclosures of online relationships, could intervene. Chat-room or social-networking users could also be recruited to become 'cyber-bystanders' (Palasinski, 2012) and encouraged to warn the adolescent about the possibility that they are being sexually exploited. Educators can assist students in preventing cyber sexual solicitation by integrating online safety into lessons about cyber-bullying, health, and sex education, with specific strategies and tailored interventions for students who may be at higher risk for online victimisation (Burrow-Sanchez, Call, Zheng & Drew, 2011; van Ouytsel, Walrave & van Gool, 2014).

Children and youth should be informed about their right to be protected from all forms of sexual exploitation and how to exercise that right; consistent with the spirit and intent of the United Nation's Convention on the Rights of the Child (see www.ohchr.org). Indeed, Finkelhor (2009) argues that it is 'morally reprehensible' *not* to equip children with knowledge and skills that could help keep them safe from sexual exploitation. Although child-focused personal safety programmes play an important part in the effort to keep children safe from sexual exploitation, they cannot single-handedly prevent the sexual victimisation of youth.

Parent-Focused Prevention Strategies

An additional prevention strategy to combat the sexual exploitation of youth includes the involvement of supportive adults present in a child's environment, most importantly, their parents or caregivers. A major reason for targeting parents is that the home is the most proximal level of the child's ecology. Forming a 'prevention partnership' (Wurtele & Miller-Perrin, 1992) with parents has long been recommended and has several advantages (Babatsikos, 2010; Elrod & Rubin, 1993; Reppucci, Jones & Cook, 1994; Wurtele & Kenny, 2010a). Parents can play an important role in empowering their own children to protect themselves either by supporting their child's participation in a school-based programme or by providing personal safety education in the home. Parents can practice and review the content of school-based programmes, and can also teach and reinforce personal safety rules at home. In addition, many of the factors that heighten a child's risk for sexual exploitation relate to the home environment (e.g., lack of supervision or privacy, presence of unrelated males, restricted parent–child communication about sexuality, lack of screening of substitute caregivers, children taught blind obedience to authority figures, etc.). Educating parents about these risk factors can enable them to improve the safety of the home environment by increasing monitoring and supervision, enhancing their communication with their children about sexuality, and screening substitute caregivers (Mendelson & Letourneau, 2015; Wurtele & Berkower, 2010; Wurtele & Kenny, 2010a). Parents can also be provided with suggestions about how to limit access of potential perpetrators to their children, informed about sexual grooming, and provided with descriptions of the ploys and manipulations used by sex offenders (Babatsikos & Miles, 2015; Kaufman, Mosher, Carter & Estes, 2006; Wurtele, 2010, 2012b; Wurtele & Berkower, 2010).

Studies in several countries indicate that parents want to be involved in preventing CSA, either by supporting school-based education or by being their children's first educators on this topic (Hunt & Walsh, 2011; Walsh & Brandon, 2012). Research also supports the need to educate parents about the realities of child sexual exploitation. Despite the fact that most sexual abuse is carried out by someone known to the child and their family, the majority of parents (80–95%) focus their CSA prevention discussions on 'stranger-danger' warnings (Chen & Chen, 2005; Chen, Dunne & Han, 2007; Deblinger, Thakkar-Kolar, Berry & Schroeder, 2010; Ige & Fawole, 2011; Wurtele, Kvaternick & Franklin, 1992). Parents in China feared that discussing CSA prevention concepts would lead to their children knowing too much about sex, and were more likely to provide prevention messages to their daughters than to their sons, as they viewed boys at low risk of abuse (Chen & Chen, 2005; Chen, Dunne & Han, 2007). A study of parents in Africa revealed that many blamed children for sexual abuse (e.g., because they dressed provocatively) (Mathoma, Maripe-Perera, Khumalo et al., 2006). Involving the family in the educational process may also help reduce the secrecy surrounding the topic and can stimulate parent–child discussions about sexual abuse in the context of healthy sexuality, providing an important protective factor within the child's home. Indeed, certain parent–child interactions, such as regularly asking questions of and listening to children, have been associated with a lower risk of sexual abuse in Columbian children (Ramíreza, Pinzón-Rondónb & Botero, 2011).

There have been a limited number of studies evaluating CSA parent educational training. The few studies conducted to date have primarily focused on either increasing parent knowledge or enhancing parent–child communication about CSA. Studies in the US, Canada and Ireland have reported increases in parents' knowledge about children's disclosure and help-seeking resources (MacIntyre & Carr, 1999), the characteristics of perpetrators (Wurtele, Moreno & Kenny, 2008), that CSA rarely involves physical evidence or penetration, that children from all socio-economic backgrounds are sexually abused, and that a child who is sexually abused often loves the offender in spite of the abuse. Parent education not only increased parents' reported intentions to talk to their children about CSA, but also the amount of parent–child discussions (Burgess & Wurtele, 1998; Wurtele, Moreno, & Kenny, 2008).

Although parents are of critical importance to the success of child-focused educational programmes, the full potential of 'parent partnerships' has yet to be realised (Hunt & Walsh, 2011; Mendelson & Letourneau, 2015; Walsh & Brandon, 2012; Wurtele, 2009; Wurtele & Kenny, 2010a). For example, recruiting and retaining parents for educational programmes have proven significant challenges for researchers and educators. Attendance rates at informational meetings have been quite low (e.g., 21% of parents in Tutty, 1997; 20% in Hébert, Lavoie, Piché, & Poitras, 2001), and fathers rarely attend (Elrod & Rubin, 1993; Tang & Yan, 2004). In an exploration of Chinese adults' intentions to participate in CSA prevention programmes, only 24% definitely intended to participate (Tang & Yan, 2004). Parents often cite scheduling conflicts or lack of time as barriers to attending programmes (Babatsikos, 2010; Wurtele & Kenny, 2010a). Parent educators have offered numerous suggestions to enhance parental participation, especially for fathers, and encouraged the development of web-based training and educational modules (Wurtele & Kenny, 2012). Compared to attending workshops, the internet offers a confidential and more convenient way to get information about CSA. Internet-based interventions (IBIs) may be especially useful for parents, yet few existing IBIs are aimed at parent–child dyads (Amstadter, Broman-Fulks, Zinzow et al., 2009). Web-based intervention can reach a large population at relatively low cost, and can be accessed privately and conveniently from home – a plus for parents who may be reluctant or unable to attend school-based meetings.

Additional challenges include the fact that the majority of programmes and materials are targeted at parents of young children, with less attention paid to parents of adolescents. Similar to child-focused programmes, parent-focused strategies rarely include information about other forms of CSEC, such as victimisation through prostitution, online solicitation and sex trafficking. Given the potential for adolescents to be abused through online sexual solicitation, parents needed to be informed about safe internet use and how to talk to their children about cyber safety (e.g., Wurtele, 2012b; Wurtele, in press; Wurtele & Miller-Perrin, 2014). Parents need to discuss the dangers of meeting a new internet friend offline, how to handle receiving sexually explicit images or messages, especially when sent to them by adults, and how to recognise and respond to e-grooming (Wurtele, 2009), including what 'exit strategies' (Tynes, 2007) to adopt if they are sexually solicited online by an adult. Parents are also encouraged to talk about online behaviours shown to increase risk of sexual solicitation (e.g., flirting and having sexual conversations with strangers, posting provocative pictures, sexting and visiting pornography sites). In the US, the National Center for Missing and Exploited Children has developed an awareness campaign directed at children and their parents that emphasises the need for parental knowledge about computers and the internet, as well as the importance of parents' involvement in the lives of their children (www.netsmartz.org/InternetSafety). The UK Safer Internet Centre provides resources for parents and carers of children in two age groups: 3–11 and 11–19 (www.saferinternet.org.uk). Programme evaluation is needed to determine how successful such campaigns are at increasing parental knowledge and preventing online sexual victimisation of adolescents.

Certain family characteristics have been found to increase the risk for adolescent sexual exploitation, both online and offline, along with commercial and non-commercial forms of abuse. Family variables found to increase the likelihood of sexual exploitation include family violence, parental substance use, witnessing or experiencing family abuse (emotional, sexual or physical), along with having only one biological parent and absence of family support or parental monitoring (Clarke, Clarke, Roe-Sepowitz & Fey, 2012; Martin, Najman, Williams, et al., 2011; Noll, Shenk, Barnes & Haralson, 2013; Pérez-Fuentes, Olfson, Villegas, et al.,

2013; Roe-Sepowitz, 2012; Whittle, Hamilton-Giachritsis, Beech & Collings, 2013; Wildsmith, Barry, Manlove & Vaughn, 2013). In these cases, sexual exploitation may be secondary to neglect and the failure to protect the child from potential perpetrators or dangerous situations (Wekerle, Bennett & Francis, 2013). Thus, there may be a limit to what parent-focused programmes can do for some children and youth. Recognising the limitation of relying exclusively on parents to prevent the sexual exploitation of youth, we now turn to the vital role youth-serving organisations play in protecting children and young people in their care.

Preventing Sexual Exploitation in Youth-Serving Organisations

Along with their parents, children interact with and depend on many adults as they grow up – teachers, coaches, faith leaders, and other mentors in youth-serving organisations. Youth-serving organisations (YSOs) are establishments, institutions and clubs that provide various services to children. They include schools, youth groups, foster care, correctional facilities, faith-based institutions and recreational or sporting clubs. As noted by Trocmé and Schumaker (1999), 'participation in these activities provide children with important protective factors against sexual abuse including increased self-esteem and skills development, relationships with adults outside the home who may act as role models and confidants, and relationships with peers' (p. 631). Many of these organisations foster close and caring relationships between youths and adults outside the family, but this same closeness can provide opportunities for sexual exploitation.

Every YSO requires prevention, protection, and monitoring policies and procedures to minimise the risk of sexual abuse of youth in their care. Like others (e.g., Kaufman, Tews, Schuett & Kaufman, 2012), we approach abuse in organisations through the lens of situational prevention theory (Tonry & Farrington, 1995), which shifts attention from an exclusively individual level to the context in which the potential offender and victim interact. Situational prevention of CSA calls for broad approaches to protecting children from abuse in institutions, including screening, establishing safety and protection policies and procedures, training, along with monitoring and supervision (Wurtele, 2012a; Wurtele & Kenny, 2012).

In the US, guidelines for screening staff are provided in a document produced by the Centers for Disease Control and Prevention entitled *Preventing Child Sexual Abuse Within Youth-Serving Organizations* (Saul & Audage, 2007). A standard recommendation is to conduct criminal background checks on potential candidates, and US agencies typically conduct checks of criminal offences and determine if the potential employee or volunteer is listed on a Sex Offender Registry. In the UK, the Safeguarding Vulnerable Groups Act of 2006 and the Safeguarding Vulnerable Groups Order (Northern Ireland) of 2007 set up a Vetting and Barring Scheme that lists those disqualified from working with children (Erooga, 2009). Although checking for criminal records is essential, the majority of those who have abused children while in positions of trust do not have criminal records. According to Erooga, Allnock and Telford (2012), convicted offenders reported that screening and interview procedures for their organisational positions were often not rigorous (e.g., interviews were not particularly challenging and screening of references was insufficient), suggesting the need for a range of screening and hiring measures.

Organisations need to establish specific policies, procedures, guidelines and ethical standards to ensure the safety and protection of children in their care. Organisations can establish policies limiting physical access to children (Cranley, 2015; Noble & Vermillion, 2014; Read, 2013; Saul & Audage, 2007; Wurtele, 2012a; Wurtele & Kenny, 2012). One strategy is to minimise opportunities for staff to be alone with children. For example, in the US, the Boy

Scouts of America (BSA) has a 'two-deep leadership' policy, which requires at least two adults to present on all trips and outings and which prohibits youth workers from transporting children alone in a vehicle (Boy Scouts Association (BSA), n.d.). Others recommend that contacts between staff and youth are limited to organisation-sanctioned activities and restrict out-of-programme contact (Lanning & Dietz, 2014; Wurtele, 2012a; Wurtele & Kenny, 2012). Codes of conduct, providing clear guidance to staff on standards of behaviour, are also important. Convicted sex offenders have reported that organisations are often not clear about regulations and expectations about relationships between staff and children (Erooga, Allnock & Telford, 2012). Ethical and behavioural standards for the clergy and other church personnel are available from faith-based institutions (e.g., National Board for Safeguarding Children, 2008; Unitarian Universalist Association, 2004). Several standards of practice for preventing the sexual abuse of children in sport are also available (Child Protection in Sport Unit, 2003; Irish Sports Council, 2000; Play By The Rules, 2011; Queen's Printer for Ontario, 2002; USA Gymnastics, 2009; USOC's Safe Sport programme at www.safesport.org).

Recognising that youth are vulnerable to technology-facilitated sexual grooming, YSOs must develop and implement responsible-use-of-technology policies, outlining the acceptable and unacceptable uses of digital devices and electronic communications, including guidelines for communication between staff and youth on social-networking sites (SNSs) and via cell phones. For example, in the US, the New York City Department of Education (DOE) publishes Social Media Guidelines for both employees and students, recommending that DOE employees maintain separate professional and personal SNSs and e-mail accounts, and that they only communicate with students through these school-based professional social media sites and e-mail accounts. However, the guidelines do not address one-to-one communication via cell phones and text messaging between teachers and students, which have been more widespread and problematic (Chen & McGeehan, 2012). In contrast, the Board of Education in Paramus, New Jersey, prohibits teachers from giving out cell phone numbers to students or calling students under the age of 18 on their cell phones without parent authorisation. Stricter e-communication guidelines are meeting resistance from some teachers because of the increasing importance of technology as a teaching tool and of the benefits of social media for engaging with students (Preston, 2011). In addition to schools, other YSOs are developing and implementing policies to limit digital contact between staff and youth in their care (e.g., Boy Scouts of America; USA Swimming, n.d.).

Once selected for positions, it is critical that in-service training be offered to all employees and volunteers to raise their awareness of sexual exploitation in YSOs (Lanning & Dietz, 2014; Saul & Audage, 2007; Wurtele, 2012a). In-service training informs all employees and volunteers about the organisation's commitment to child protection, along with its prevention policies and procedures. Trainees need opportunities to discuss ethical principles and values underlying their care of youth, particularly the need to maintain professional boundaries, knowing what constitutes sexual misconduct, and acknowledging the potential for exploiting their greater status and power. Training should also be provided on how to recognise and respond to questionable behaviours or boundary violations exhibited by fellow staff members, like when a co-worker has a special relationship with a particular child, is seen touching the child in question in inappropriate ways, or communicates with a child (via cell phone, text messages or letters) about personal or intimate issues. In the US, one adult-focused CSA prevention programme is offered by the non-profit organisation Darkness to Light (see www.d2l.org), whose mission is to empower adults to prevent CSA. Darkness to Light's (2004; 2013) *Stewards of Children* program teaches adults in YSOs (i.e., staff, volunteers and parents) how to prevent, recognise and react responsibly to CSA. The programme is available both in-person and online. Rheingold and colleagues (Rheingold, Zajac & Chapman, 2014; Rheingold, Zajac & Patton, 2012) have conducted studies showing the programme's promise for efficacy and have also compared different formats, both in-person and web-based. Additional research on the online version likewise found support for the programme's convenience and cost-effectiveness (Paranal, Thomas & Derrick, 2012).

YSOs also need to develop monitoring and supervision protocols (Gula, 2010; Noble & Vermillion, 2014; Saul & Audage, 2007; Wurtele, 2012a). All employees and volunteers should be informed about the monitoring protocol and be clear about their roles and responsibilities in response to observed, disclosed or suspected sexual abuse. Organisations must have policies for dealing appropriately with allegations of staff–child sexual abuse. There needs to be easily accessible ways for children to disclose abuse. Saul, Patterson and Audage (2010) recommended empowering youth by encouraging them to intervene or tell someone when they see inappropriate interactions between adults and youth.

There are challenges to implementing prevention efforts in institutions. Lack of personnel and resources to provide educational programmes for staff is frequently mentioned (Parent & Demers, 2011; Read, 2013; Wiersma & Sherman, 2005; Wurtele, 2012a). Another potential problem is reticence on the part of employees to address the subject. Agency administrators are sometimes concerned that promoting prevention may arouse fear within the organisation, possibly leading members to worry that measures are being implemented because sexual abuse exists in their organisation (Parent & Demers, 2011). Staff members might also become fearful of false allegations due to heightened sensitivity and monitoring by parents, co-workers and supervisors about engaging in various forms of non-sexual physical contact, e-communication, and social media with students (Andrzejewski & Davis, 2008; Preston, 2011; Vamos, 2001). There may be denial among employees and administrators that CSA abuse exists within their organisation (Malkin, Johnston & Brackenridge, 2000; Wurtele, 2012a), with staff refusing to believe that their colleagues are capable of such behaviour (Hendrie, 1998; Lanning & Dietz, 2014; Noble & Vermillion, 2014). Administrative difficulties have also been cited as potential challenges to implementing CSA prevention policies. For example, administrators of sports programmes have been observed to encounter problems in carrying out policies due to delays in criminal background checks or reluctance to share information about offending coaches (Noble & Vermillion, 2014), along with a lack of support from senior management (Hartill & Lang, 2014).

Although the various strategies described above are potentially promising ways to prevent CSA from occurring in YSOs, there is a dearth of research available to confirm their effectiveness. In this final section, we turn to societal-level prevention efforts.

Societal-Level Prevention Strategies

Societal-level factors that might contribute to the sexual exploitation of youth include social norms, societal values, and shared beliefs and attitudes (Miller-Perrin & Wurtele, 2017; UNICEF, 2014). This final section describes prevention efforts targeting societal risk factors that support and possibly condone the sexual exploitation of youth, including strategies such as public awareness campaigns, statewide planning and programming, and media campaigns. Unfortunately, very little research has addressed societal-level risk factors, despite the calls for prevention efforts targeting adults and systems within the broader macro-system (e.g., UNICEF, 2014).

Cross-cultural studies on attitudes and beliefs about adult–child sex provide evidence of a lack of understanding about the social problem of sexual exploitation of youth (e.g., Jones & Jemmott, 2009; Stop It Now!, 2010). There is also a widespread lack of understanding about commercial sexual exploitation of children (Miller-Perrin & Wurtele, 2017). Studies have found a low level of knowledge and awareness among law enforcement, prosecutors, judges, and jurors about the crime of human trafficking, as well as negative attitudes from law enforcement toward human trafficking victims, who are often seen as responsible for their own victimisation (Farrell, McDevitt, Pfeffer, et al., 2012; Mikton, Power, Raleva, et al., 2013).

One key societal factor in shaping attitudes and norms related to the sexual exploitation of youth, and in shaping public policy, is the media. Reviews of news coverage of CSA cases suggest that the news tends to report on criminal justice responses rather than contextual information about causes of and solutions to CSA, making sexual crimes against minors appear as though they occur in a vacuum, instead of being the product of broader social conditions (Dorfman, Mejia, Cheyne & Gonzalez, 2011). In addition, prevention-oriented solutions rarely appear. Only 18% of articles described a preventative measure, and half of these suggested education for children and their parents. By contrast, only 4% of articles suggested policy changes or broad-scale prevention activities focused on either potential victims or potential perpetrators (Dorfman, Mejia, Gonzalez & Cheyne, 2012; Mejia, Cheyne & Dorfman, 2012). Clearly there is a need to move attitudes about CSA from a criminalisation perspective to a public health threat warranting primary prevention efforts. Education for media professionals about the empirical realities of CSA is greatly needed (Letourneau, Eaton, Bass et al., 2014; Mejia, Cheyne & Dorfman, 2012). The development of comprehensive toolkits to help the media disseminate information would be helpful (Collin-Vézina, Daigneault & Hebert, 2013).

Few media campaigns targeting CSA have been mounted in the US. One exception is the Stop It Now! programme which includes affiliates in the US and UK and uses social marketing campaigns to advance two ideas: (i) Many people who sexually exploit children want treatment to control their impulses; and (ii) All adults are responsible for noticing warning signs and engaging with people at risk of sexually abusing a child before a child is harmed (see www.stopitnow.org). Prevention messages are delivered through newspaper advertisements, television and radio ads, talk shows, articles, billboards, transit posters and news features. A confidential toll-free Helpline (1–888-PREVENT) is available for information and referrals.

In the US, the Enough Abuse Campaign is a statewide education and community mobilisation effort whose mission is 'to prevent people from sexually abusing children now and to prevent children from developing sexually abusive behaviours in the future' (Massachusetts Citizens for Children, 2010). The campaign provides information about conditions and social norms associated with the occurrence of CSA and offers training for parents and child care professionals to identify and respond to sexual behaviours of children. Along with media coverage and community presentations and workshops, a variety of CSA prevention materials and resources are available on their website (www.enoughabuse.org). The campaign also supports efforts to affect public policies related to CSA (e.g., reforming the State's statute of limitations) (Schober, Fawcett & Bernier, 2012a). Evaluations are promising. Following the campaign, more Massachusetts residents believed that adults, rather than children, should take responsibility for preventing CSA (an increase from 69% in 2003 to 93% in 2007; Schober, Fawcett & Bernier, 2012a). As another potential indicator of programme impact, substantiated reports of CSA in Massachusetts declined 69% from 1990 to 2007. Similar effects were observed in Georgia, as substantiated reports decreased in four of the five years of the implementation period (Schober, Fawcett, Thigpen et al., 2012b). These findings suggest that a statewide effort can impact abuse rates and promote community responsibility for prevention.

Evaluations of CSA-targeted media campaigns in the US have shown promise (e.g., Self-Brown, Rheingold, Campbell & de Arellano, 2008). An evaluation of Stop It Now! was shown to effectively change public awareness and knowledge about CSA over a two-year period (Chasen-Taber & Tabachnick, 1999). Other evaluations of media campaigns in other US cities, as well as other countries (see Lalor & McElvaney, 2010), show similar positive outcomes (e.g., increased knowledge, awareness and disclosure). Despite methodological limitations of these evaluations, public awareness initiatives hold great promise for focusing on the most appropriate targets: potential offenders and bystanders. In Berlin, the Prevention Project Dunkelfeld aims to prevent the sexual abuse of children by providing clinical and support services to individuals who are sexually interested in children and want help controlling their interests. An initial evaluation of the project demonstrated its effectiveness in reaching potential offenders via a media campaign, and persuading them to enrol in a treatment programme (Beier, Ahlers, Goecker et al., 2009; Beier, Neutze, Mundt et al., 2009).

In the US, few media campaigns specifically target the prevention of commercial sexual exploitation (CSEC) of children. Internationally, however, there has been significant media coverage about CSEC in sex tourist destination countries (e.g., the Philippines, Thailand, Taiwan, Brazil, Nicaragua and Costa Rica) largely as a result of grassroots efforts. For example, in Costa Rica an information campaign was launched entitled, 'Behind a job promise could be a destination of pain!' aimed at adolescent girls to increase their awareness of risks and enable them to resist what might seem like tempting offers of work or travel that could lead to exploitation in the sex industry (US Department of State, 2010, p. 121). Evaluations of media campaigns focusing on CSEC are not yet available.

Other examples of societal-level prevention efforts include criminal justice system responses targeting offenders. All US states have criminal laws prohibiting sexual relationships between adults and youth (Myers, 2011). In addition to criminal charges and incarceration, criminal justice responses also include community protection policies such as lifetime offender registries, lifetime online community notification, indefinite post-incarceration civil commitment, and expansive sex offender residency restrictions (Finkelhor, 2009; Letourneau & Levenson, 2011). These approaches are most often considered to be tertiary rather than primary prevention strategies (since they apply after abuse has occurred). However, because of the potential deterrent effect on future acts of abuse, they could be considered primary prevention. Unfortunately, most legislative initiatives have not been adequately evaluated and what research is available suggests that sex offender policies including notification, registration and residency restrictions do not prevent sex offenders from repeating their crimes (Letourneau & Levenson, 2011; Letourneau, Eaton & Bass, 2014; Zandbergen, Levenson & Hart, 2010). Thus, the impact of these legislative initiatives on primary prevention of CSA perpetration is unknown.

With regard to the commercial sexual exploitation of children (CSEC), the US enacted the Trafficking Victims Protection Act in 2000 (TVPA; P.L. 106–386). TVPA is considered to be the seminal piece of US legislation to combat human trafficking and help victims as it criminalises human trafficking on a federal level (Adams, Owens & Small, 2010). TVPA's three main components, referred to as the '3P' paradigm, include Protection, Prosecution and Prevention. The Act extended existing anti-trafficking criminal statutes and also strengthened efforts to prosecute traffickers, along with increasing prevention efforts (US Department of Justice, 2010a, 2010b). TVPA was reauthorised in 2003, 2005, and in 2008 with the William Wilberforce Trafficking Victims Protection Reauthorization Act (P.L. 110–457).

The reauthorisation of TVPA in 2013 enhanced law enforcement capacity to combat sex tourism by prosecuting US citizens who travel or live abroad and purchase children for sex (Alliance to End Slavery and Trafficking [ATEST], 2014). Over the past ten years since TVPA was enacted, the number of cases of human trafficking (including cases of child sex trafficking) investigated, charged and prosecuted in the US has increased (US Department of Justice, 2010b). However, some experts believe that progress is too slow. For example, Farrell, McDevitt, Pfeffer, et al. (2012) found that as of 2012, only 700 cases of trafficking suspects had been federally prosecuted while only 18 states had attempted prosecutions under state human trafficking statutes.

Several international treaty and human rights instruments are essential tools to effectively protect the rights of children. The First World Congress against Commercial Sexual Exploitation of Children held in Stockholm, Sweden in 1996 is often identified as the first international effort to both acknowledge the problem of commercial exploitation of children and to offer guidelines for combating child sex trafficking. Since the First World Congress, many additional international legal frameworks to combat child sex trafficking have been established. One of the most influential human rights organisations is the United Nations (UN), which has been instrumental in combating CSEC. In 1989, for example, the United Nations General Assembly adopted the Convention on the Rights of the Child (CRC). Article 34 of the CRC states that national governments are obliged to protect children from all forms of sexual exploitation and sexual abuse and that they should take all appropriate measures to prevent children from being sexually exploited. Other international human rights instruments include: the Optional Protocol to the CRC on the Sale of Children, Child Prostitution and Child Pornography, which entered into force in 2002; the Protocol to Prevent, Suppress, and Punish Trafficking in Persons, Especially Women and Children, which entered into force in 2003; the African Charter on the Rights and Welfare of the Child, which entered into force in 1999; and the Council of Europe Convention on the Protection of Children against Sexual Exploitation and Sexual Abuse, also known as the Lanzarote Convention, which entered into force in 2010 (Council of Europe, 2012; UNICEF, 2014; United Nations General Assembly, 2000). The Lanzarote Convention is perhaps the most comprehensive legal instrument on the protection of children against sexual exploitation and sexual abuse, as it covers all possible kinds of sexual offences against minors (including sexual abuse, child prostitution, child pornography, and solicitation of children for sexual purposes, including internet grooming) and includes commercial and non-commercial forms of sexual exploitation. It also promotes national and international cooperation, and facilitates the exchange of stakeholders' views and experiences on good practices in preventing and combating sexual exploitation and sexual abuse of children (see www.coe.int/lanzarote).

National action plans for preventing child maltreatment are beginning to appear which incorporate many of the societal-level approaches described in this section. For example, the World Health Organization's Regional Committee for Europe recently released a national action plan for Europe entitled *Investing in children: The European child maltreatment prevention action plan 2015–2020* (WHO, 2014). The plan calls for both population-level actions and selective approaches for high-risk groups and outlines the following objectives:

- Make health risks more visible by setting up information systems
- Strengthen governance through partnerships and multi-sectoral action by developing national plans
- Reduce risks by strengthening health systems.

Australia has developed a similar national action plan entitled *Protecting Children Is Everyone's Business*, the goal of which is to ensure the safety and well-being of Australia's children (Commonwealth of Australia, 2010). Many action plans target general child health and well-being, rather than specifically preventing child maltreatment in general or sexual exploitation in particular. Risk factors for sexual exploitation are different from other forms of child maltreatment, and thus CSA prevention strategies must be unique (Dubowitz, 2014; Olafson, 2011). To that end, Sri Lanka's establishment in 1998 of the National Child Protection Authority (NCPA; see www.childprotection.gov.lk) is notable. Authority board members, representing many disciplines (law, psychology, non-governmental organisations, education, social services, tourism, media), report directly to the President of Sri Lanka (de Zoysa, 2002). Functions of the NCPA include advising the government in the formulation of a national policy on the prevention of child abuse and creating an awareness of children's rights to be protected from abuse. In the US, a group of individuals formed the National Coalition to Prevent Child Sexual Abuse and Exploitation (www.preventtogether.org) and in 2012 produced the *National Plan to Prevent the Sexual Abuse and Exploitation of Children*. The plan calls for six action areas to accomplish the goals of prevention including promoting research, increasing public awareness, targeting factors to end demand, encouraging policies and organisational practices, promoting collaborative practices, and increasing funding. Another action plan developed in the US focuses specifically on human trafficking, including child sex trafficking. In 2012, President Obama created an inter-agency task force to monitor and combat trafficking in persons, which developed an action plan for 2013–2017 seeking to create a victim-centered approach to treatment, public awareness, and outreach efforts for those affected by human trafficking (President's Interagency Taskforce, 2014).

Given that social, cultural and economic factors all contribute to commercial sexual exploitation of children, national child protection plans are sorely needed. Child sex traffickers exploit conditions in impoverished countries in Asia, Eastern Europe, Africa and Latin America, for example, that offer few employment opportunities, have limited educational opportunities, and are characterised by high rates of organised crime and violence against women and children, discrimination against women, government corruption, political instability, and armed conflict, all of which render women and children vulnerable to sexual exploitation (Miller-Perrin & Wurtele, 2017; United Nations Office on Drugs and Crime, 2009). Confronting CSEC should be a priority matter under the public agenda and must involve national child protection agencies, departments of health and education, and mass media to generate a culture of zero tolerance of sexual exploitation of children and adolescents.

Conclusion

Although the research and approaches reviewed in this paper hold much promise, what works to prevent the sexual exploitation and abuse of youth has yet to be definitively determined through programme evaluation. Several challenges to prevention efforts exist, including the fact that sexual exploitation of youth is a complex, sensitive and alarmingly widespread problem; one that elicits strong emotional reactions from adults (Letourneau, Eaton & Bass, 2014; Zollner, Fuchs & Fegert, 2014), which can make disseminating knowledge and improving understanding about the topic difficult. In addition, prevention programmes are costly and, unfortunately, child sexual exploitation does not receive the same funding as other public health problems. The US Centers for Disease Control and Prevention conducted a review of public health agencies and found that 71% offered programmes targeting intimate partner violence, whereas only 20% offered CSA prevention programmes (CDC, 2010). Increased federal, state and foundational funding for CSA-related research and prevention implementation is arguably needed. When weighed against the psychological, medical and economic costs of the sexual exploitation of youth, investing in its prevention is clearly a worthwhile endeavour.

As described throughout this chapter, risk factors for the sexual exploitation of youth exist at various levels of the child's ecology (including cyberspace), and thus solutions will require complex multilevel frameworks along with the involvement of multiple stakeholders. The joint efforts of parents, educators, health care professionals, law enforcement, researchers, policy makers, the media, private sector entities and youth themselves are needed to ensure that young people are never sexually exploited. Prevention interventions that modify both the individual and the environment hold the most promise for eradicating the sexual exploitation of youth. Concerted and coordinated efforts in these new directions are essential to uphold children's fundamental rights to live free of all forms of violence, including sexual exploitation and abuse.

References

Adams, W., Owens, C. & Small, K. (2010). Effects of federal legislation on the commercial sexual exploitation of children. US Department of Justice, Office of Juvenile Justice and Delinquency Prevention.

Alliance to End Slavery and Trafficking [ATEST] (2014). *Recommendations for a trafficking in persons focus country approach*, www.endslaveryandtrafficking.org/coming-into-focus-how-the-us-government-can-tip-the-fight-against-human-trafficking/.

American Professional Society on the Abuse of Children [APSAC] (2013). *The commercial sexual exploitation of children: The medical provider's role in identification, assessment and treatment*, www.apsac.org.

Amstadter, A.B., Broman-Fulks, J., Zinzow, H. et al. (2009). Internet-based interventions for traumatic stress-related mental health problems: A review and suggestions for future research. *Clinical Psychology Review*, 29, 410–420.

Andrzejewski, C.E. & Davis, H.A. (2008). Human contact in the classroom: Exploring how teachers talk about and negotiate touching students. *Teaching and Teacher Education*, 24, 779–794.

Babatsikos, G. (2010). Parents' knowledge, attitudes and practices about preventing child sexual abuse: A literature review. *Child Abuse Review*, 19, 107–129.

Babatsikos, G. & Miles, D. (2015). How parents manage the risk of child sexual abuse: A grounded theory. *Journal of Child Sexual Abuse*, 24, 55–76.

Baker, C.K., Gleasono, K., Naai, R. et al. (2012). Increasing knowledge of sexual abuse: A study with elementary school children in Hawai'i. *Research on Social Work Practice*, 23, 167–178.

Beier, K.M., Ahlers, C.J., Goecker, D. et al. (2009). Can pedophiles be reached for primary prevention of child sexual abuse? First results of the Berlin Prevention Project Dunkelfeld (PPD). *The Journal of Forensic Psychiatry & Psychology*, 20, 851–867.

Beier, K.M., Neutze, J., Mundt, I.A. et al. (2009). Encouraging self-identified pedophiles and hebephiles to seek professional help: First results of the Prevention Project Dunkelfeld. *Child Abuse & Neglect*, 33, 545–549.

Boy Scouts of America [BSA] (n.d.). *Youth protection*, www.scouting.org/Training/YouthProtection.htm.

Burgess, E.S. & Wurtele, S.K. (1998). Enhancing parent–child communication about sexual abuse: A pilot study. *Child Abuse & Neglect*, 22, 1167–1175.

Burrow-Sanchez, J.J., Call, M.E., Zheng, R. & Drew, C.J. (2011). How school counselors can help prevent online victimization. *Journal of Counseling & Development*, 89, 3–10.

Butchart, A., Phinney Harvey, A., Mian, M. & Fürniss, T. (2006). *Preventing child maltreatment: A guide to taking action and generating evidence*. Geneva: WHO.

Centers for Disease Control and Prevention [CDC] (2010). *Findings from the 2009 child maltreatment prevention environmental scan of state public health agencies*. Atlanta, GA: CDC.

Charlesworth, L.W. & Rodwell, M.K. (1997). Focus groups with children: A resource for sexual abuse prevention program evaluation. *Child Abuse & Neglect*, 21, 1205–1216.

Chasen-Taber, L. & Tabachnick, J. (1999). Evaluation of a child sexual abuse prevention program. *Sexual Abuse: A Journal of Research and Treatment*, 11, 279–292.

Chen, D.W. & McGeehan, P. (2012, May 1). *Social media rules limit New York student-teacher contact*, www.nytimes.com/2012/05/01/nyregion/social-media-rules-for-nyc-school-staff-limits-contact-with-students.html.

Chen, J.Q. & Chen, D.G. (2005). Awareness of child sexual abuse prevention education among parents of Grade 3 elementary school pupils in Fuxin City, China. *Health Education Research*, 20, 540–547.

Chen, J.Q., Dunne, M.P. & Han, P. (2007). Prevention of child sexual abuse in China: Knowledge, attitudes and communication practices of parents of elementary school children. *Child Abuse & Neglect*, 31, 747–755.

Child Protection in Sport Unit. (2003). *Standards for safeguarding and protecting children in sport*. Leicester, UK: Child Protection in Sport Unit, www.therfl.co.uk/~therflc/clientdocs/CPSU%20Standards.pdf.

Clarke, R.J., Clarke, E.A., Roe-Sepowitz, D. & Fey, R. (2012). Age at entry into prostitution: Relationship to drug use, race, suicide, education level, childhood abuse, and family experiences. *Journal of Human Behavior in the Social Environment*, 22, 270–289.

Collin-Vézina, D., Daigneault, I. & Hébert, M. (2013). Lessons learned from child sexual abuse research, prevalence, outcomes, and preventive strategies. *Child and Adolescent Psychiatry and Mental Health*, 7(22), 1–9.

Commonwealth of Australia. (2010). *Protecting children is everyone's business: National framework for protecting Australia's children* 2009–2020, https://www.dss.gov.au/sites/default/files/documents/pac_annual_rpt_0.pdf.

Council of Europe (2012). *Council of Europe Convention on the Protection of Children against Sexual Exploitation and Sexual Abuse*. Strasbourg Cedex: Council of Europe Publishing, www.coe.int/t/dghl/standardsetting/children/default_en.asp.

Cranley, D. (2015). *8 Ways to Create Their Fate: Protecting the Sexual Innocence of Children in Youth Serving Organizations*. Mustang, OK: Tate Publishing.

Daigneault, I., Hébert, M., McDuff, P. & Frappier, J. (2012). Evaluation of a sexual abuse prevention workshop in a multicultural, impoverished urban area. *Journal of Child Sexual Abuse*, 21, 521–542.

Darkness to Light (2004; 2013). *Stewards of children*. Charleston, SC: Darkness to Light, www.d2l.org.

Davidson, J.C. & Martellozzo, E. (2008). Protecting vulnerable young people in cyberspace from sexual abuse: Raising awareness and responding globally. *Police Practice and Research*, 9, 277–289.

Davis, M.K. & Gidycz, C.A.(2000). Child sexual abuse prevention programs: A meta-analysis. *Journal of Clinical Child Psychology*, 29, 257–265.

De Zoysa, P. (2002). Child sexual abuse in Sri Lanka: The current state of affairs and recommendations for the future. *Journal of Child Sexual Abuse*, 11, 97–113.

Deblinger, E., Thakkar-Kolar, R.R., Berry, E.J. & Schroeder, C.M. (2010). Caregivers' efforts to educate their children about child sexual abuse: A replication study. *Child Maltreatment*, 15, 91–100.

Dorfman, L., Mejia, P., Cheyne, A. & Gonzalez, P. (2011). *Case by case: News coverage of child sexual abuse*. Berkeley, CA: Berkeley Media Studies Group.

Dorfman, L., Mejia, P., Gonzalez, P. & Cheyne, A. (2012). *Breaking news on child sexual abuse: Early coverage of Penn State*. Berkeley, CA: Berkeley Media Studies Group.

Dubowitz, H. (2014). The Safe Environment for Every Kid (SEEK) Model: Helping promote children's health, development, and safety. *Child Abuse & Neglect*, 38, 1725–1733.

Durkin, K.F. & DeLong, R.L. (2012). Internet crimes against children. In: Z. Yan (ed), *Encyclopedia of Cyber Behavior*. Hersey, PA: IGI Global, 799–807.

Elrod, J.M. & Rubin, R.H. (1993). Parental involvement in sexual abuse prevention education. *Child Abuse & Neglect*, 17, 527–538.

Erooga, M. (2009). *Towards safer organisations: Adults who pose a risk to children in the workplace and implications for recruitment and selection*. London: NSPCC, www.nspcc.org.uk/inform.

Erooga, M., Allnock, D. & Telford, P. (2012). *Towards safer organisations II: Using the perspectives of convicted sex offenders to inform organisational safeguarding of children*. London: NSPCC, www.nspcc.org.uk.

Farrell, A., McDevitt, J., Pfeffer, R. et al. (2012). *Identifying challenges to improve the investigation and prosecution of state and local human trafficking cases*. Washington, DC: US Department of Justice, Office of Justice Programs, National Institute of Justice, www.ncjrs.gov/pdffiles1/nij/grants/238795.pdf.

Finkelhor, D. (2007). Prevention of sexual abuse through educational programs directed toward children. Pediatrics, 120, 640–645.

Finkelhor, D. (2009). The prevention of childhood sexual abuse. The Future of Children, 19(2), 53–78.

Gibson, L.E. & Leitenberg, H. (2000). Child sexual abuse prevention programs: Do they decrease the occurrence of child sexual abuse? *Child Abuse & Neglect*, 24, 1115–1125.

Gula, R.M. (2010). *Just ministry: Professional ethics for pastoral ministers*. Mahwah, NJ: Paulist Press.

Hartill, M. & Lang, M. (2014). 'I know people think I'm a complete pain in the neck': An examination of the introduction of child protection and 'safeguarding' in English sport from the perspective of National Governing Body Safeguarding Lead Officers. *Social Sciences*, 3, 606–627.

Hébert, M., Lavoie, F., Piché, C. & Poitras, M. (2001). Proximate effects of child sexual abuse prevention program in elementary school children. *Child Abuse & Neglect*, 25, 505–522.

Hendrie, C. (1998). Sex with students: When employees cross the line. *Education Week*, 18(14), 1–5.

Hunt, R. & Walsh, K. (2011). Parents' views about child sexual abuse education: A systematic review. *Australian Journal of Early Childhood*, 36, 63–76.

Ige, O.K. & Fawole, O.I. (2011). Preventing child sexual abuse: Parents' perceptions and practices in urban Nigeria. *Journal of Child Sexual Abuse*, 20, 695–707.

IOM (Institute of Medicine) and NRC (National Research Council) (2013). *Confronting Commercial Sexual Exploitation and Sex Trafficking of Minors in the United States*. Washington, D.C.: The National Academies Press.

IOM (Institute of Medicine) and NRC (National Research Council) (2014). *Commercial Sexual Exploitation and Sex Trafficking of Minors in the United States: A Guide for the Health Care Sector*. Washington, D.C.: The National Academies Press.

Irish Sports Council (2000). *Code of ethics and good practice for children's sport*, www.irishsportscouncil.ie/Participation/Code_of_Ethics/.

Jones, A.D. & Jemmott, E.T. (2009). *Child Sexual Abuse in the Eastern Caribbean*. United Nations Children's Fund Action for Children and University of Huddersfield, Huddersfield.

Jones, L.M., Mitchell, K.J. & Walsh, W.A. (2012). *Evaluation of Internet child safety materials used by ICAC task forces in school and community settings*, www.ncjrs.gov/pdffiles1/nij/grants/242016.pdf.

Katz, C. (2013). Internet-related child sexual abuse: What children tell us in their testimonies. *Children and Youth Services Review*, 35, 1536–1542.

Kaufman, K.L., Mosher, H., Carter, M. & Estes, L. (2006). An empirically based situational prevention model for child sexual abuse. In: S. Smallbone & R. Wortley (eds), *Situational prevention of child sexual abuse, Crime prevention studies (Vol. 19)*.Monsey, NY: Criminal Justice Press.

Kaufman, K.L., Tews, H., Schuett, J.M. & Kaufman, B.R. (2012). Prevention is better than cure: The value of situational prevention in organisations. In: M. Erooga (ed), *Creating Safer Organisations: Practical Steps to Prevent the Abuse of Children by Those Working with Them*. Chichester: Wiley-Blackwell, 140–169.

Kenny, M.C. & Wurtele, S.K. (2009). A counselor's guide to preventing childhood sexual abuse. *Counseling and Human Development*, 42, 1–14.

Kenny, M.C. & Wurtele, S.K. (2010a). Child sexual abuse prevention: Choosing, implementing, and evaluating a personal safety program for young children. In: K.L. Kaufman (ed), *The Prevention of Sexual Violence: A Practitioner's Sourcebook*. Holyoke, MA: NEARI Press, 303–317.

Kenny, M.C. & Wurtele, S.K. (2010b). Children's abilities to recognize a 'good' person as a potential perpetrator of childhood sexual abuse. *Child Abuse & Neglect*, 34, 490–495.

Kenny, M.C., Wurtele, S.K. & Alonso, L. (2012). Evaluation of a personal safety program with Latino preschoolers. *Journal of Child Sexual Abuse*, 21, 368–385.

Lalor, K. & McElvaney, R. (2010). Child sexual abuse, links to later sexual exploitation/high-risk sexual behavior, and prevention/treatment programs. *Trauma, Violence & Abuse*, 11, 159–177.

Lanning, K.V. & Dietz, P. (2014). Acquaintance molestation and youth-serving organizations. *Journal of Interpersonal Violence*, 29, 2815–2838.

Lavoie, F., Thibodeau, C., Gagné, M.H. & Hébert, M. (2010). Buying and selling sex in Quebec adolescents: A study of risk and protective factors. *Archives of Sexual Behavior*, 39, 1147–1160.

Letourneau, E.J. & Levenson, J.S. (2011). Preventing sexual abuse: Community protection policies and practice. In: J.E.B. Myers (ed), *The APSAC Handbook on Child Maltreatment*, 3rd edn. Thousand Oaks, CA: Sage, 307–321.

Letourneau, E.J., Eaton, W.W., Bass, J. et al. (2014). The need for a comprehensive public health approach to preventing child sexual abuse. *Public Health Reports*, 129, 222–228.

MacIntyre, D. & Carr, A. (1999). Evaluation of the effectiveness of the Stay Safe primary prevention program for child sexual abuse. *Child Abuse & Neglect*, 23, 1307–1325.

MacMillan, H.L., Wathen, C.N., Barlow, J. et al. (2009). Interventions to prevent child maltreatment and associated impairment. *The Lancet*, 373, 250–266.

Malkin, K., Johnston, L. & Brackenridge, C. (2000). A critical evaluation of training needs for child protection in UK sport. *Managing Leisure*, 5, 151–160.

Maniglio, R. (2009). The impact of child sexual abuse on health: A systematic review of reviews. *Clinical Psychology Review*, 29, 647–657.

Martin, A., Najman, J.M., Williams, G.M. et al. (2011). Longitudinal analysis of maternal risk factors for childhood sexual abuse: Early attitudes and behaviours, socioeconomic status, and mental health. *The Australian and New Zealand Journal of Psychiatry*, 45, 629–637.

Massachusetts Citizens for Children (2010). *Enough Abuse Campaign*, www.enoughabuse.org.

Mathoma, A.M., Maripe-Perera, D.B., Khumalo, L.P. et al. (2006). Knowledge and perceptions of parents regarding child sexual abuse in Botswana and Swaziland. *Journal of Pediatric Nursing*, 21, 67–72.

McEachern, A.G. (2012). Sexual abuse of individuals with disabilities: Prevention strategies for clinical practice. *Journal of Child Sexual Abuse*, 21, 386–398.

Mejia, P., Cheyne, A. & Dorfman, L. (2012). News coverage of child sexual abuse and prevention, 2007–2009. *Journal of Child Sexual Abuse*, 21, 470–487.

Mendelson, T. & Letourneau, E.J. (2015). Parent-focused prevention of child sexual abuse. *Prevention Science*, 16, 844–852.

Mikton, C. & Butchart, A. (2009). Child maltreatment prevention: A systematic review of reviews. *Bulletin of the World Health Organization*, 87, 353–361.

Mikton, C., Power, M., Raleva, M. et al. (2013). The assessment of the readiness of five countries to implement child maltreatment prevention programs on a large scale. *Child Abuse & Neglect*, 37, 1237–1251.

Miller-Perrin, C. & Wurtele, S.K. (2017). Sex trafficking and the commercial sexual exploitation of children. *Women and Therapy*, 40, 123–151.

Mitchell, K.J., Jones, L.M., Finkelhor, D. & Wolak, J. (2013). Understanding the decline in unwanted online sexual solicitations for US youth 2000–2010: Findings from three Youth Internet Safety Surveys. *Child Abuse & Neglect*, 37, 1225–1236.

Müller, A.R., Röder, M. & Fingerle, M. (2014). Child sexual abuse prevention goes online: Introducing 'Cool and Safe' and its effects. *Computers & Education*, 78, 60–65.

Myers, J.E.B. (2011). Criminal prosecution of child maltreatment. In: J.E.B. Myers (ed), *The APSAC Handbook on Child Maltreatment*, 3rd edn. Thousand Oaks, CA: Sage Publications 87–99.

National Board for Safeguarding Children (2008). *Safeguarding children: Standards and guidance document for the Catholic Church in Ireland*, www.achonrydiocese.org/safeguarding.pdf.

Noble, J. & Vermillion, M. (2014). Youth sport administrators' perceptions and knowledge of organizational policies on child maltreatment. *Children and Youth Services Review*, 38, 52–57.

Noll, J.G., Shenk, C.E., Barnes, J.E. & Haralson, K.J. (2013). Association of maltreatment with high-risk Internet behaviours and offline encounters. *Pediatrics*, 123, e510–e517.

Olafson, E. (2011) Child sexual abuse: Demography, impact, and interventions. *Journal of Child & Adolescent Trauma*, 4, 8–21.

Oudekerk, B.A., Farr, R.H. & Reppucci, N.D. (2013). Is it love or sexual abuse? Young adults' perceptions of statutory rape. *Journal of Child Sexual Abuse*, 22, 858–877.

Palasinski, M. (2012). The roles of monitoring and cyberbystanders in reducing sexual abuse. *Computers in Human Behavior*, 28, 2014–2022.

Paranal, R., Thomas, K.W. & Derrick, C. (2012). Utilizing online training for child sexual abuse prevention: Benefits and limitations. *Journal of Child Sexual Abuse*, 21, 507–520.

Parent, S. & Demers, G. (2011). Sexual abuse in sport: A model to prevent and protect athletes. *Child Abuse Review*, 20, 120–133.

Pereda, N., Guilera, G., Forns, M. & Gomez-Benito, J. (2009). The prevalence of child sexual abuse in community and student samples: A meta-analysis. *Clinical Psychology Review*, 29, 328–338.

Pérez-Fuentes, G., Olfson, M., Villegas, L. et al. (2013). Prevalence and correlates of child sexual abuse: A national study. *Comprehensive Psychiatry*, 54, 16–27.

Play By The Rules (2011). *Making sport inclusive, safe and fair*, www.playbytherules.net.au.

Plummer, C.A. (2001). Prevention of child sexual abuse: A survey of 87 programs. *Violence and Victims*, 16, 575–588.

President's Interagency Taskforce to Monitor and Combat Trafficking in Persons (2014). *Federal Strategic Action Plan on Services for Victims of Human Trafficking in the United States 2013–2017*. Washington, D.C.: US Department of Justice, US, www.ovc.gov/pubs/FederalHumanTraffickingStrategicPlan.pdf.

Preston, J. (2011). *Rules to stop pupils and teachers from getting too social online*, www.nytimes.com/2011/12/18/business/media/rules-to-limit-how-teachers-and-students-interact-online.html.

Queen's Printer for Ontario (2002). *Making it safeR: Preventing sexual abuse of children in sport*. Toronto, ON: Queen's Printer for Ontario, www.tourism.gov.on.ca.

Ramíreza, C., Pinzón-Rondónb, A.M. & Botero, J.C. (2011). Contextual predictive factors of child sexual abuse: The role of parent–child interaction. *Child Abuse & Neglect*, 35, 1022–1031.

Read, D. (2013). It takes a team. *Athletic Management*, 25(2), 31–35.

Reppucci, N.D., Jones, L.M. & Cook, S.L. (1994). Involving parents in child sexual abuse prevention programs. *Journal of Child and Family Studies*, 3, 137–142.

Rheingold, A.A., Zajac, K. & Patton, M. (2012). Feasibility and acceptability of a child sexual abuse prevention program for childcare professionals: Comparison of a web-based and in-person training. *Journal of Child Sexual Abuse*, 21, 422–436.

Rheingold, A.A., Zajac, K., Chapman, J.E. et al. (2014). Child sexual abuse prevention training for childcare professionals: An independent multi-site randomized controlled trial of Stewards of Children. *Prevention Science*, 1–12.

Roe-Sepowitz, D.E. (2012). Juvenile entry into prostitution: The role of emotional abuse. *Violence Against Women*, 18, 562–579.

Romano, J.L. (2015). *Prevention Psychology: Enhancing Personal and Social Well-Being*. Washington, DC: American Psychological Association.

Saul, J. & Audage, N. (2007). *Preventing child sexual abuse within youth-serving organizations: Getting started on policies and procedures.* Atlanta, GA: Centers for Disease Control and Prevention, www.cdc.gov/ncipc/dvp/PreventingChildSexualAbuse.pdf.

Saul, J., Patterson, J. & Audage, N. (2010). Preventing sexual maltreatment in youth-serving community organizations. In: K.L. Kaufman (ed), *The Prevention of Sexual Violence: A Practitioner's Sourcebook.* Holyoke, MA: NEARI Press, 449–463.

Schenkel, L.S., Rothman-Marshall, G., Schlehofer, D.A. et al. (2014). Child maltreatment and trauma exposure among deaf and hard of hearing young adults. *Child Abuse & Neglect*, 38, 1581–1589.

Schober, D.J., Fawcett, S.B. & Bernier, J. (2012a). The Enough Abuse Campaign: Building the movement to prevent child sexual abuse in Massachusetts. *Journal of Child Sexual Abuse*, 21, 456–469.

Schober, D.J., Fawcett, S.B., Thigpen, S. et al. (2012b). An empirical case study of a child sexual abuse prevention initiative in Georgia. *Health Education Journal*, 71, 291–298.

Self-Brown, S., Rheingold, A.A., Campbell, C. & de Arellano, M.A. (2008). A media campaign prevention program for child sexual abuse: Community members' perspectives. *Journal of Interpersonal Violence*, 23, 728–743.

Shannon, D. (2008). Online sexual grooming in Sweden—Online and offline sex offences against children as described in Swedish police data. *Journal of Scandinavian Studies in Criminology and Crime Prevention*, 9, 160–180.

Smallbone, S., Marshall, W.L. & Wortley, R. (2008). *Preventing Child Sexual Abuse: Evidence, Policy and Practice.* Portland, OR: Willan.

Stoltenborgh, M., van IJzendoorn, M.H., Euser, E.M. & Bakermans-Kranenburg, M.J. (2011). A global perspective on child sexual abuse: Meta-analysis of prevalence around the world. *Child Maltreatment*, 16, 79–101.

Stop It Now! (2010). *What do US adults think about child sexual abuse? Measures of knowledge and attitudes among six states,* www.StopItNow.org/rdd_survey_reportfrt.

Tang, C.S. & Yan, E.C. (2004). Intention to participate in child sexual abuse prevention programs: A study of Chinese adults in Hong Kong. *Child Abuse & Neglect*, 28, 1187–1197.

Tener, D., Walsh, W.A., Jones, L.M. & Kinnish, K. (2014). 'It all depends on the guy and the girl': A qualitative study of youth experiences with statutory victimization relationships. *Journal of Child Sexual Abuse*, 23, 935–956.

Tonry, M. & Farrington, D. (1995). *Building a Safer Society; Strategic Approaches to Crime Prevention.* Chicago, IL: Chicago University Press.

Topping, K.J. & Barron, I.G. (2009). School-based child sexual abuse prevention programs: A review of effectiveness. *Review of Educational Research*, 79, 431–463.

Trocmé, N. & Schumaker, K. (1999). Reported child sexual abuse in Canadian schools and recreational facilities: Implications for developing effective prevention strategies. *Children and Youth Services Review*, 21, 621–642.

Tutty, L.M. (1997). Child sexual abuse prevention programs: Evaluating 'Who Do You Tell?' *Child Abuse & Neglect*, 21, 869–881.

Tynes, B.M. (2007). Internet safety gone wild? Sacrificing the educational and psychosocial benefits of online social environments. *Journal of Adolescent Research*, 22, 575–584.

Unitarian Universalist Association (2004). *Balancing acts: Keeping children safe in congregations,* www.uua.org.

United Nations Children's Fund [UNICEF] (2006). *United Nations secretary-general's study on violence against children,* www.nicef.org/violencestudy/reports/SG_violencestudy_en.pdf.

United Nations Children's Fund [UNICEF] (2014). *Hidden in plain sight: A statistical analysis of violence against children.* New York: UNICEF.

United Nations General Assembly (2000). *Optional Protocol to the Convention on the Rights of the Child on the Sale of Children, Child Prostitution and Child Pornography.* New York: United Nations, www.ohchr.org/EN/ProfessionalInterest/Pages/OPSCCRC.aspx.

United Nations Office on Drugs and Crime (2009). *Annual report* 2009, www.unodc.org/documents/about-unodc/AR09_LORES.pdf.

US Department of Justice (2010a). *Attorney General's annual report to congress and assessment of US Government activities to combat trafficking in persons: Fiscal year 2009*, www.state.gov/documents/organization/125840.pdf.

US Department of Justice (2010b). *Report on the tenth anniversary of the Trafficking Victims Protection Act*, www.justice.gov/crt/about/crm/trafficking_newsletter/tvpaanniversaryreport.pdf.

US Department of State (2010). *Trafficking in persons report*, www.state.gov/j/tip/rls/tiprpt/2010/index.htm.

US General Accounting Office (1996). *Preventing child sexual abuse: Research inconclusive about effectiveness of child education programs*. Washington, DC: US Government Printing Office.

USA Gymnastics (2009). *Participant welfare policy*, www.californiatnt.com/USA%20Welfare.pdf.

USA Swimming (n.d.). *Model policy: Electronic communication*, www.usaswimming.org/protect.

Vamos, M. (2001). The concept of appropriate professional boundaries in psychiatric practice: A pilot training course. *The Australian and New Zealand Journal of Psychiatry*, 35, 613–618.

Van der Laan, P.H., Smit, M., Busschers, I. & Aarten, P. (2011). Cross-border trafficking in human beings: Prevention and intervention strategies for reducing sexual exploitation. *Campbell Systematic Reviews*, 9.

Van Ouytsel, J., Walrave, M. & van Gool, E. (2014). Sexting: Between thrill and fear—How schools can respond. *The Clearing House*, 87, 204–212.

Walker, K. (2013). *Ending the commercial sexual exploitation of children: A call for multisystem collaboration in California*. Sacramento, CA: California Health and Human Services Agency.

Walsh, K. & Brandon, L. (2012). Their children's first educators: Parents' views about child sexual abuse prevention education. *Journal of Child and Family Studies*, 21, 734–746.

Wekerle, C., Bennett, T. & Francis, K. (2013). Child sexual abuse and adolescent sexuality. In: D.S. Bromberg & W.T. O'Donohue (eds), *Handbook of Child and Adolescent Sexuality: Developmental and Forensic Psychology*. New York: Academic Press, 325–345.

Whitaker, D.J., Lutzker, J.R. & Shelley, G.A. (2005). Child maltreatment prevention priorities at the Centers for Disease Control and Prevention. *Child Maltreatment*, 10, 245–259.

Whittle, H., Hamilton-Giachritsis, C., Beech, A. & Collings, G. (2013). A review of young people's vulnerabilities to online grooming. *Aggression and Violent Behavior*, 18, 135–146.

Wiersma, L.D. & Sherman, C.P. (2005). Volunteer youth sport coaches' perspectives of coaching education/certification and parental codes of conduct. *Research Quarterly for Exercise and Sport*, 76, 324–338.

Wildsmith, E., Barry, M., Manlove, J. & Vaughn, B. (2013, October). *Dating and sexual relationships*, www.childtrends.org/wp-content/uploads/2013/10/2013-04DatingSexualRelationships.pdf.

Wolak, J. & Finkelhor, D. (2013). Are crimes by online predators different from crimes by sex offenders who know youth in-person? *Journal of Adolescent Health*, 53, 736–741.

World Health Organization [WHO] (2014). *Investing in children: The European child maltreatment prevention action plan 2015–2020*, www.uro.who.int/en/about-us/governance/regional-committee-for-europe/64th-session/documentation/working-documents/eurrc6413-investing-in-children-the-european-child-maltreatment-prevention-action-plan-20152020.

Wurtele, S.K. (2002). School-based child sexual abuse prevention. In: P.A. Schewe (ed), *Preventing Violence in Relationships*. Washington, DC: American Psychological Association, 9–25.

Wurtele, S.K. (2008). Behavioral approaches to educating young children and their parents about child sexual abuse prevention. *The Journal of Behavior Analysis of Offender and Victim Treatment and Prevention*, 1, 52–64.

Wurtele, S.K. (2009). Preventing sexual abuse of children in the twenty-first century: Preparing for challenges and opportunities. *Journal of Child Sexual Abuse*, 18, 1–18.

Wurtele, S.K. (2010) *Out of Harm's Way: A Parent's Guide to Protecting Young Children from Sexual Abuse*. Seattle, WA: Parenting Press.

Wurtele, S.K. (2012a). Preventing the sexual exploitation of minors in youth-serving organizations. *Children and Youth Services Review*, 34, 2442–2453.

Wurtele, S.K. (2012b). *Safe Connections: A Parent's Guide to Protecting Young Teens from Sexual Exploitation*. Seattle, WA: Parenting Press.

Wurtele, S.K. (in press). Preventing cyber sexual solicitation of adolescents. In: R. Alexander & N. Guterman (eds), *Prevention of Child Maltreatment*. St. Louis, MO: STM Learning, Inc.

Wurtele, S.K. & Berkower, F. (2010). *Off Limits: A Parent's Guide to Keeping Kids Safe from Sexual Abuse*. Brandon, VT: Safer Society Press.

Wurtele, S.K. & Kenny, M.C. (2010a). Partnering with parents to prevent childhood sexual abuse. *Child Abuse Review*, 19, 130–152.

Wurtele, S.K. & Kenny, M.C. (2010b). Primary prevention of child sexual abuse: Child- and parent-focused approaches. In: K.L. Kaufman (ed), *The Prevention of Sexual Violence: A Practitioner's Sourcebook*. Holyoke, MA: NEARI Press, 107–119.

Wurtele, S.K. & Kenny, M.C. (2011). Normative sexuality development in childhood: Implications for developmental guidance and prevention of childhood sexual abuse. *Counseling and Human Development*, 43(9), 1–24.

Wurtele, S.K. & Kenny, M.C. (2012). Preventing childhood sexual abuse: An ecological approach. In: P. Goodyear-Brown (ed), *Handbook of Child Sexual Abuse: Identification, Assessment and Treatment*. Hoboken, NJ: Wiley Press, 531–565.

Wurtele, S.K. & Miller-Perrin, C.L. (1992). *Preventing Child Sexual Abuse: Sharing the Responsibility*. Lincoln, NE: University of Nebraska Press.

Wurtele, S.K. & Miller-Perrin, C.L. (2012). Global efforts to prevent sexual exploitation of minors. In: H. Dubowitz (ed), *World Perspectives on Child Abuse*, 10th edn. Denver, CO: International Society for Prevention of Child Abuse and Neglect, 82–88.

Wurtele, S.K. & Miller-Perrin, C.L. (2014). Preventing technology-initiated sexual victimization of youth: A developmental perspective. In: M.C. Kenny (ed), *Sex Education: Attitude of Adolescents, Cultural Differences and Schools' Challenges*. New York: Nova, 147–175.

Wurtele, S.K. & Owens, J. (1997). Teaching personal safety skills to young children: An investigation of age and gender across five studies. *Child Abuse & Neglect*, 21, 805–814.

Wurtele, S.K., Kvaternick, M. & Franklin, C.F. (1992). Sexual abuse prevention for preschoolers: A survey of parents' behaviors, attitudes, and beliefs. *Journal of Child Sexual Abuse*, 1, 113–128.

Wurtele, S.K., Moreno, T. & Kenny, M. (2008). Evaluation of a sexual abuse prevention workshop for parents of young children. *Journal of Child and Adolescent Trauma*, 1, 1–10.

Wurtele, S.K., Kast, L.C., Miller-Perrin, C.L. & Kondrick, P.A. (1989). A comparison of programs for teaching personal safety skills to preschoolers. *Journal of Consulting and Clinical Psychology*, 57, 505–511.

Zandbergen, P.A., Levenson, J.S. & Hart, T.C. (2010). Residential proximity to schools and daycares: An empirical analysis of sex offense recidivism. *Criminal Justice and Behavior*, 37, 482–502.

Zhang, W., Chen, J., Feng, Y. et al. (2013). Young children's knowledge and skills related to sexual abuse prevention: A pilot study in Beijing, China. *Child Abuse & Neglect*, 37, 623–630.

Zhang, W., Chen, J., Feng, Y. et al. (2014). Evaluation of a sexual abuse prevention education for Chinese preschoolers. *Research on Social Work Practice*, 24, 428–436.

Zollner, H., Fuchs, K.A. & Fegert, J.M. (2014). Prevention of sexual abuse: Improved information is crucial. *Child & Adolescent Psychiatry & Mental Health*, 8(5), 1–9.

Zwi, K.J., Woolfenden, S.R., Wheeler, D.M. et al. (2007). School-based education programmes for the prevention of child sexual abuse (Review). *Cochrane Database of Systematic Reviews*, 3, Art. No.: CD004380.

Part II

Assessment

Part III
Assessment

13

Evidence-Based Assessments of Children and Families
Safeguarding Children Assessment and Analysis Framework

Stephen Pizzey[1], Arnon Bentovim[1], Liza Bingley Miller[1] and Antony Cox[2]

[1] Child and Family Training Ltd
[2] Guy's King's and St Thomas' School of Medicine

Safeguarding children is the action we take to promote the welfare of children and protect them from harm. Child protection refers to the activity that is undertaken to protect specific children where there is reasonable cause to believe they are suffering maltreatment. The purpose of this chapter is to introduce the Safeguarding Children Assessment and Analysis Framework (SAAF; Bentovim, Cox, Bingley Miller & Pizzey, 2009; Pizzey, Bentovim, Cox et al., 2015), to describe the seven-stage model in assessment, analysis, and planning and implementing intervention and provide practical guidance on each step of the process. The chapter also includes details of evaluation of the SAAF.

Purpose and Principles of SAAF

SAAF is a structured decision-making tool that has been designed to enhance and facilitate the quality of decision-making by professionals in cases where the statutory agency/child protection services have reasonable cause to suspect that a child is being maltreated.[1] Child and family strengths are identified and considered in developing a multi-agency plan to protect the child from harm and monitor progress. The SAAF is designed to be used:

- In a complex case where government agencies or non-governmental agencies are providing help/services but, despite this, the child's needs are not being met and there are concerns about whether there should be a child protection investigation;

---

[1] The SAAF was initially developed for the English and Welsh jurisdictions to be consistent with the Children Act 1989. It has subsequently been adapted for use in other national jurisdictions and it is this latter version that is described in this chapter.

- Where there has been a child protection investigation and decisions must be made about what action to take, i.e., a statutory agency/child protection service has reasonable cause to suspect that a child who lives, or is found, in their area is suffering, or is likely to suffer, maltreatment, and makes such enquiries as they consider necessary to enable them to decide whether they should take any action to safeguard or promote the child's welfare as required by legislation for the investigation of allegations of abuse or neglect;
- When considering whether a child should be made the subject of, or remain the subject of, a multi-agency plan to protect the child from harm;
- In applications by a statutory child protection service for a court child welfare order to either remove the child from their parents or to require the child and family to have services provided by the state child protection services. In these situations, a civil/family court must be satisfied that the legislative requirements for the compulsory removal of the child from their parents' care are met;
- In private family law (i.e., civil/family court cases that do not involve the State), where there are concerns the child might be suffering maltreatment; and,
- When considering the rehabilitation of an accommodated child to their parent/carer.

The SAAF provides a structure for making professional judgements. It is designed to help practitioners make sense of the complexity involved in child protection work. It helps social workers and other professionals[2] describe the extent of harm suffered by the child, predict the likely outlook for the child if nothing changes, assess the prospects for successful intervention, formulate interventions and identify outcomes and how they can be measured. It is designed to assist social workers to remain open-minded throughout the assessment process and to base their conclusions and consequent decisions on the available evidence.

The use of the SAAF helps social workers and their managers analyse information gathered during the assessment and communicate clearly to other agencies and the courts about each child and their family's needs and the rationale for future plans. It is designed to enhance social workers' expertise and their ability to make sound professional judgements and enable them to give sound, evidence-based opinions in multidisciplinary contexts, including the courts, about actions required in order to prevent children suffering future harm.

The key principles underpinning the SAAF are in line with the Framework for Assessment (Department of Health, Department for Education and Employment, and Home Office, 2000, p.10) that assessments and interventions should be:

- child centred
- rooted in child development
- ecological in their approach which means the child should be understood within the context of their family, culture and environment
- focused on identifying strengths as well as difficulties
- open-minded and analytical
- grounded in evidence-based knowledge
- aimed at improving outcomes for children.

---

[2] The term social worker and practitioner are interchangeably used in this chapter but the SAAF can be used by any professional required to make assessments in child protection cases and carry out statutory child protection functions.

SAAF applies these principles to analysis and to assessing the prospects of bringing about change in complex child protection and children-in-need cases.

The SAAF Seven-Stage Model

The SAAF sets out the following seven-stage model in assessment, analysis and planning and implementing intervention:

- Consider the referral and aims of the assessment
- Gather assessment information on the child's developmental needs, the parenting capacity, and family and environmental factors
- Establish the nature and level of impairment of the child's health and development
- Analyse the patterns of harm and protection
- Child protection decision-making and care planning: The safeguarding analysis
- Develop and implement a plan of intervention
- Identify outcomes and measures for assessing change.

Each stage will be considered in turn.

Stage 1: Consider the referral and aims of the assessment

This involves:

- consideration of whether the child is at immediate risk of suffering harm
- establishing the focus and the aims of the assessment.

In safeguarding, the first consideration on receiving a new referral is to decide whether, and if so what, steps need to be taken to ensure the child's safety, i.e., removal from family or carers, removal of abusive adult from the household, or removal to different family members. Ongoing consideration of the safety of the child is important throughout the assessment process. If this is not an immediate concern, then the next step is to review the referral and establish the focus and the aims of the assessment. These should set out how extensive and deep the exploration should be, judged on the basis of the nature of the referral and any available information.

The aims of the assessment need to be directed to the concerns about the child and their health and development, and any relevant parenting and family and environmental factors. For example, is it essential to have a thorough assessment of the child's developmental status? Is it vital to have a full appraisal of the family? Are there environmental factors, which need to be better understood? This stage can involve the re-assessment of a case in the light of new information (Bentovim, Cox, Bingley Miller & Pizzey, 2009; Pizzey, Bentovim, Cox et al., 2015).

Stage 2: Gather assessment information on the child's developmental needs, the parenting capacity, and family and environmental factors

This involves:

- collecting information from available sources using an appropriate range of methods and approaches
- creating a chronology of salient information.

Information gathering should be guided by the aims of the assessment. The approach should be systematic to ensure that the data obtained are adequate in their scope and well-evidenced, and that time is used effectively. Sources of information should be considered. These include family members and professionals/agencies who have been involved with the child and their family. Thought should be given to the combination of family members that might be seen and in what contexts – this is important because what will be learnt will be influenced by the combination and the context. For example, different information is likely to be obtained from seeing a child alone than from interviewing them with a parent and according to whether they are in their own home or at school.

Which approaches to use to gather information should be considered. They range from reviewing existing files and requesting reports from agencies previously involved or already engaged, to interviewing, observation, and use of standardised assessment tools. These tools include the *HOME (Home Observation for the Measurement of the Environment) Inventory* (Caldwell & Bradley, 2003; Cox, Pizzey & Walker, 2009), the *Family Pack of Questionnaires and Scales* (Cox & Bentovim, 2000), the *Family Assessment* (Bentovim & Bingley Miller, 2001), *In My Shoes* (Calam, Cox, Glasgow et al., 2000) and the *Attachment Style Interview* (Bifulco, Moran, Ball & Lillie, 2002), and referral for specialist assessment. When gathering information, it is essential to collect information about past history relating to factors being considered in each dimension and domain. This will assist in the task of preparing a chronology of salient information (Pizzey, Bentovim, Cox et al., 2015).

Stage 3: Establish the nature and level of impairment of the child's health and development

This involves:

- organising the information using the Assessment Framework
- identifying strengths and difficulties in all dimensions.

Once information has been gathered, the next step is to organise that information to ascertain what is known, to identify crucial information that is *not yet known and needs to be known*, and to prepare for analysis. The Assessment Framework triangle provides a map for collecting together and then analysing the available information on a child's developmental needs and the factors affecting them (Department of Health [DoH], 2000). The information obtained is organised according to the domains and dimensions of the Assessment Framework triangle (Figure 13.1, DoH, 2000). Assessments should include relevant history in every dimension of the three domains. This enables the practitioner to understand current issues and concerns better when analysing the information collected.

Child's developmental needs. The child's developmental needs domain assesses what is happening to a child, and each aspect of a child's developmental progress is examined in the context of their age and stage of development and the history of their health and development. Account must be taken of any particular vulnerability, such as a learning disability or a physically impairing condition, and the impact that these may be having on progress in any of the developmental dimensions.

Children who have been maltreated may suffer impairments to their health and development as a result of injuries sustained and/or the impact of the trauma caused by their abuse. A clear understanding of what a particular child is capable of achieving successfully at each

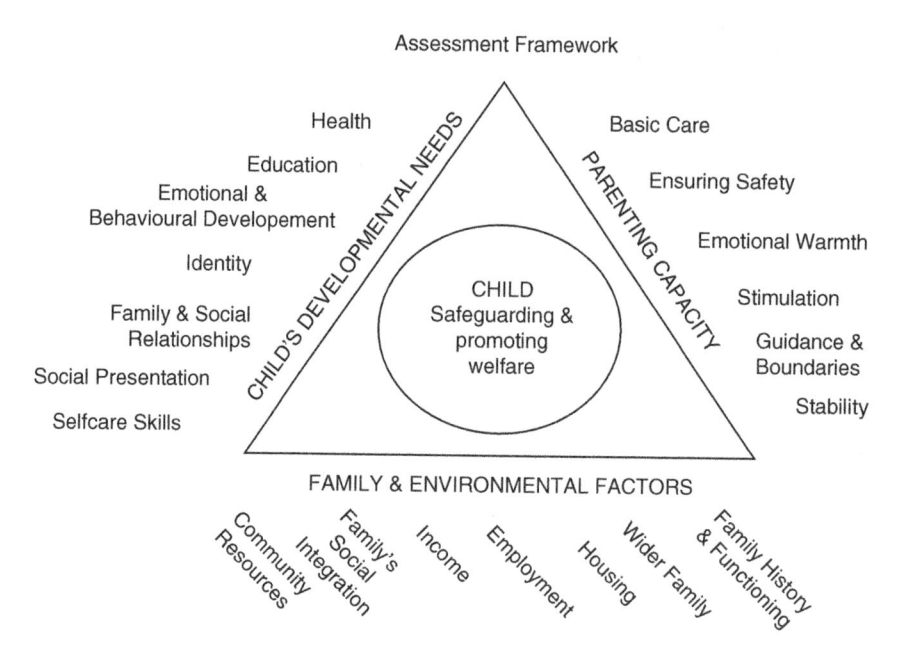

Figure 13.1 Framework for the Assessment of Children in Need and their Families (Department of Health, Department for Education and Employment, and Home Office, 2000).

stage of development is required, in order to ensure that they have the opportunity to achieve their full potential (DoH, 2000, p. 18).

Parenting capacity. The parenting capacity domain assesses the ability of parents and caregivers to ensure that the child's developmental needs are being appropriately and adequately responded to, and to adapt to the child's changing needs over time (Department of Health, 2000, p. 20).

Family and environmental factors domain. This domain takes account of the influence of the cultural norms of the family on the care and upbringing of children. All family members are influenced both positively and negatively by the wider family, the neighbourhood and social networks in which they live. The history of the child's family and of the individual family members may have a significant impact on the child and parents. A range of environmental factors can either help or hinder a family's functioning (DoH, 2000, p. 22). Consideration should be given to the social and environmental disabling factors that have an impact on the child's development, such as limited access to resources for those who have a disability and other forms of discrimination.

At this stage there should be no attempt to explore how the different factors/items are affecting each other, i.e., how different pieces of information are linked. The practitioner will be beginning to form ideas, often referred to as 'hypotheses', about what is going on with the child, their parents and in the family, and other factors which may be relevant, but these hypotheses need to be noted and put on hold until all the information has been organised.

If links are made too early, false assumptions can be made about a child's developmental needs, the nature of and reasons for any difficulties and strengths in parents'/carers' capacity to care, and the family and environmental factors affecting the child and/or their carers. In a safeguarding context, this can lead in turn to misplaced planning for the changes thought appropriate to ensure the child's health and development and safety. Interventions are then less likely to be targeted in an appropriate and effective way.

In organising the information there should be a clear distinction as to which domain is appropriate, otherwise hypotheses about processes involving the child and their family may be mistaken. Strengths as well as difficulties should be noted. The key questions at this stage are 'what is the current situation?' and 'how does it relate to the past?'

Throughout the information/data gathering stage, it is vital to monitor what dimensions mapped on the Assessment Framework triangle have been covered in detail and those where knowledge is lacking. There will always be aspects that are not fully understood. Once the available relevant information has been mapped into the Assessment Framework triangle, it may become obvious that crucial information is missing, e.g., how a child is doing at school; whether a parent protects their child from witnessing domestic violence; whether there are members of the wider family who might be able to offer support. In some areas significant historical data may be missing.

Being clear about *what is not yet known that needs to be known* is important and helps to guide what should be explored further. It may be clear that without this information it will be hard to assess and understand whether the child's needs are being met and whether there is any risk to their safety, health and development. Ideally, such information will be gathered and mapped before moving on to detailed analysis (Bentovim, Cox, Bingley Miller & Pizzey, 2009, pp. 76–77). In addition, when assessing the severity of child and family difficulties, frequency and duration should be considered. For example, impairments or stressors can be short-lived, recurrent, persistent or lifelong. History is therefore explored and the timing of changes in impairments and factors potentially affecting them should be noted.

The use of the Assessment Framework in assessments of unborn children will differ from assessments of children post-birth. As the child has not been born yet, fewer dimensions in the child developmental needs and parenting capacity domains can be completed. The family and environmental factors domain can be fully completed. This includes parenting of other children in both the past and present. The evidence gathered will be relevant to forming hypotheses about the likely parenting that would be provided to the unborn child following the birth and its likely impact on the child's health and development (Pizzey, Bentovim, Cox et al., 2015).

Stage 4: Analyse the patterns of harm and protection

This involves:

- considering the chronology of salient information
- generating hypotheses or theories about which processes (i.e., the pattern of influences of one item of information over others) may be affecting the child's health and development.

The fourth stage is to hypothesise which processes may be affecting the child's health and development (Bentovim, Cox, Bingley Miller & Pizzey, 2009; Pizzey, Bentovim, Cox et al., 2015). The aim is first to raise hypotheses/theories about how the dimensions in the three domains are impacting on each other both within and across the domains of the Assessment Framework triangle. For example:

- How the child's strengths and difficulties are impacting on each other
- How the child impacts on the parents and their parenting, e.g., the parents' mental health
- How parenting strengths and difficulties are affecting each other
- How family and environmental factors are affecting each other

- How the parenting being provided for the child is affecting the child's health and development both in terms of resilience and protective factors, and vulnerability and risk
- How family and environmental factors are impacting on parenting and/or on the child directly.

Careful checks need to be made as to whether there is evidence to confirm or refute the hypotheses, which should be reviewed as new information emerges.

To understand further the child's developmental needs and the factors affecting their health and development, it is necessary to analyse the processes which are in operation (i.e., the pattern of influences of one factor over others) and their impact (i.e., the weight/effect of the factors or processes involved). When examining processes, time relationships between impairments and life events and stressors should be considered as they point to connections that may be significant (e.g., arrival of stepfather, onset of bedwetting) and thus lead to hypotheses. The chronology of impairments/ improvements in the child's health and development, and the timing of events and/or changes in influences, can raise hypotheses about processes influencing the child's health and development, and the parenting, as well as the family and environmental factors potentially influencing these.

The most useful starting place for analysis is to look at the child's developmental needs and seek to understand any areas of difficulty or strength. This involves looking at the processes which may have brought about these difficulties or strengths and/or may be maintaining them. In trying to understand how factors are affecting a child's developmental needs, it is useful to distinguish conceptually between linear and circular processes to learn more about:

- the processes which may have brought something about
- the factors and processes which may be keeping something going.

Both of these can help to predict what might happen in the future (Figure 13.2).

A linear process is when two factors are thought to be directly linked so that alterations in one lead to changes in the other. For example, Shane, aged 11, has stopped attending school because he broke his leg. The broken leg causes his non-school attendance.

Circular processes can serve to sustain a strength or a difficulty. The identification of circular processes affects choice of intervention. Circular processes are recurrent. For example, Louise, aged 14, is missing school. Her mother is lonely and depressed and encourages Louise to stay

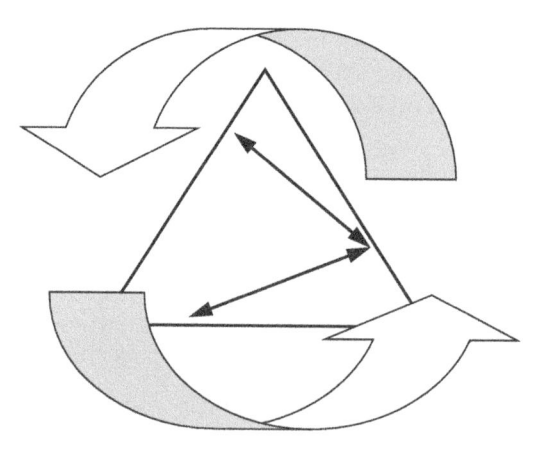

Figure 13.2 Linear and circular processes underlying analysis.

at home to keep her company. Louise sees less of her peers and becomes depressed and anxious, and reluctant to leave home or return to school.

In analysing information gathered during an assessment, what is paramount is whether there is impairment or likelihood of impairment of the child's development. This means holding in mind that difficulties and impairments in parenting capacity or broader family and environmental factors may or may not be producing impairments in the child's health and development. It is easy to assume factors are linked, but it is always essential to have evidence as this will affect hypotheses about processes and intervention and expected outcomes. False assumptions about the links will be likely to result in incorrectly targeted interventions and therefore in children and families being unlikely to achieve the hoped-for outcome.

Once the processes (i.e., pattern of influences and factors) have been analysed, it is useful to look at impact – the severity of any negative processes and/or the weight of any positive processes (Angold, Prendergast, Cox et al., 1995). In other words:

- what processes seem to be having the biggest effect on the child's health and development or on processes that affect them
- which are the greatest protective processes that might help to mitigate against any difficulties.

Analysing the impact of positive or negative factors and processes provides a fuller assessment of risk and protective factors. This helps to prioritise where interventions may be needed most urgently and where strengths can be most readily enhanced. Ultimately, the greater the effect/impact a factor has on a child's development, the more severe or beneficial it is. For example, if a child's anxiety is persistent and present in all situations in the day, keeps them awake at night and adversely affects their relationships, it is severe. The analysis of the weight or severity of positive and negative factors or processes affecting the child's health and development helps to provide an accurate assessment of the risk of harm, i.e., future impairment of the child's health and development if no action is taken.

Analysis of the negative factors and processes in the parenting capacity and family and environmental factors domains affecting the child and their needs helps identify the nature of the steps or interventions which may be required to safeguard that child. Analysis of the positive factors operating in and across all three domains points to protective factors and sources of resilience that should be supported in planning interventions.

Severe negative factors in the parenting or family and environmental domains may signify the likelihood of impairment in the child's health and development even where none is detectable at the time of assessment. In exploring the degree of severity of negative factors, it is usually the case that:

- the more dimensions of the domains that show difficulty
- the more frequently those difficulties are manifest
- the longer they have existed
- the less modifiable they are, and
- the more they intrude upon/adversely affect the child's health and development

then the greater the severity of the problem to be addressed.

Consideration of the balance between positive and negative factors and processes influencing the child's health and development can point to the need for safeguarding. When a wide range of negative factors or processes in the parenting capacity and/or family and environmental domains have been acting over a considerable period, they point in that direction.

Regarding unborn children, the evidence gathered and organised about foetal health, the parenting being provided to the unborn child, and the family and environmental factors (including any history of parenting of other children) will be relevant to forming hypotheses about the likely parenting that would be provided to the unborn child and its likely impact on their health and development. The principles set out above can be applied to form hypotheses about the likely processes that will occur after the birth of the baby and their likely impact on the baby's health and development. For example, will a father with personality disorder be able to tolerate his baby's incessant crying without lashing out or will a mother with severe learning difficulties be capable of changing the baby's nappy (Hart, 2010, p. 237)?

Stage 5: Child protection decision-making and care planning: The safeguarding analysis

This involves:

- creating a profile of the harm to and impairment of the child's health and development
- predicting the likely outlook for the child: the risks of re-abuse or likelihood of future harm (the systemic analysis)
- determining the prospects of successful intervention
- summarising the safeguarding analysis.

This stage is concerned with predicting the likely future health and development of the child if either they continue to live at home or a return to their parents/carers is being contemplated.

To analyse the profile of harm to and impairment of the child's health and development and the associated levels of concern, it is helpful to draw together the information (which has been organised using the domains and dimensions of the Assessment Framework) about the situation at the point when the child has been subjected to harmful behaviour or is at risk of being harmed. These can be considered as static factors as they largely relate to the past and present rather than the future.

Strengths and difficulties in all domains of the Assessment Framework must be considered on a continuum of lower to higher levels of concern, or rating scales, in order to establish the extent of severity or difficulty. Strengths should be noted as they may become particularly relevant when forming plans and when considering interventions. The analysis of the profile of harm to and impairment of the child's health and development thus involves consideration of the following:

- child's developmental needs
  - severity of impairment of the child's health and development and impact on child
- parenting capacity
  - severity of parenting difficulties
- family and environmental factors
  - severity of individual and family difficulties
  - severity of environmental difficulties
- parenting, protection and therapeutic help the child requires.

Rating scales for each of these areas are set out in the form of tables. Descriptors are provided for strengths and difficulties related to factors which are important to consider in safeguarding/child protection cases. These are analysed in terms of a lower or higher level of concern. The evidence upon which the judgement about level of concern is based is included in each table. To establish the level of severity of difficulty, factors are considered in terms of pervasiveness, intrusiveness, modifiability, frequency, duration and unusualness. In the higher level of concern column, assessment of severity is necessary for all the listed prompts: sometimes presence alone is enough to meet a higher level of concern (e.g., sexualised behaviour); at other times only severity of difficulty would raise concern (e.g., eating or sleeping difficulty). An example of 'severity of impairment of the child's health and development and impact on the child' is provided in Figure 13.3.

The rating scales are summarised in summary grids which provide a quantitative 'picture' of the level of concern identified by the practitioner. This enables supervisors to explore with the

Severity of impairment of the child's health and development and impact on child		
Level of functioning	Areas to be considered	Level of functioning
LOWER LEVEL OF CONCERN	• History of severe impairments of child's health and/or development and/or previous harm • Child's health, growth and care • Educational/psychological development • Emotional development–attachments, mood and behaviour • Identity • Family and social relationships • Social presentation and self-care skills	HIGHER LEVEL OF CONCERN
Satisfactory history of early development in all dimensions and no evidence of previous harm.		History of impairments in any of the dimensions and/or history of previous harm.
Fewer, less severe and less sustained injuries. Satisfactory growth, care patterns and health.		Repeated or severe injuries, lengthy or repeated hospitalisation, growth failure, repeated infections/ infestations, lack of immunisation, persistent feeding/ sleeping problems, fabricated illness.
Satisfactory unfolding of cognition and language, educational progress and learning skills		Significant delays or deviance in development of cognition, language or educational skills.
Satisfactory emotional development, secure attachments. Limited traumatic effects, reasonably well-modulated (regulated) arousal, mood variable, reasonably compliant, empathic and responsive.		Impaired emotional or behavioural development, disorganised, indiscriminate attachments, evidence of the impact of trauma (e.g., sleep disturbance, flashbacks, intense emotions triggered by specific experiences), poorly modulated arousal states, pervasive and/or persistent mood disturbance, aggressive and/or oppositional behaviour, lack of empathy.
Satisfactory self-esteem, confidence, sense of belonging, self-worth, positive self-regard.		Persistent low self-esteem, low confidence, sense of alienation, self-hatred.
Satisfactory relationships, no sustained patterns of withdrawal and hostility, more collaborative, friendly, caring, discriminating. Demonstrates trust in relationships including with professionals.		Unsatisfactory relationships, sustained withdrawal, over-dependency, hostility, unresponsive, exploitative, fighting, controlling, rivalrous, abusive, antisocial, indiscriminate, precocious sexuality. Untrusting in relationships including with professionals.
Child's social presentation and self-care skills appropriate.		Major issues with child's social presentation or self-care skills.

Figure 13.3 Severity of impairment of the child's health and development and impact on the child.

Severity of impairment of child's health and development and impact on child					
The overall levels of harm, past and present, and the impact on the child's health, safety, educational issues, emotional life, behaviour and identity, and the child's previous health and development and harm.					
(please tick a box)	LOWER LEVEL OF CONCERN				HIGHER LEVEL OF CONCERN
History of severe impairments of development and/or previous harm					
Child's health, growth and care					
Educational/psychological development					
Emotional development–attachments, mood and behaviour					
Identity					
Family and social relationships					
Social presentation and self-care					

Figure 13.4 Severity of impairment of the child's health and development and impact on the child, summary grid.

practitioner the evidence base for their rating of the level of concern. An example of 'severity of impairment of the child's health and development and impact on the child' summary grid is provided in Figure 13.4.

The systemic analysis (see Figure 13.5) draws together the identified factors and processes leading to patterns of harm to the child. In order to predict the likely outlook for the child if nothing changes, consideration needs to be given to the processes and the severity of impact identified in Stage 4.

Although there is a distinction between factors that may initiate positive or negative processes and those that may maintain them, it is vital to retain a historical perspective and an open mind. For example, there may be antecedent factors that predispose to later difficulty, but do not necessarily lead to it; for example, one childhood disability may predispose to other disabilities, but this may not happen if there is appropriate support. Similarly, difficulties in the relationship between mother and child may be more likely where a mother has suffered severe postnatal depression, but this does not necessarily follow.

Safeguarding comes into focus where the child's developmental needs are of such magnitude and/or the negative factors that impinge on those needs are of such severity that a change in home circumstances must be considered.

The systemic analysis (Figure 13.5) brings together the elements of the assessment described thus far, in diagrammatic form, leading to a prediction of the outlook for the child if nothing changes in their circumstances. It comprises the following:

- The child's current health and development including the harm and impairment of development. This involves the current impact on the child of the harm they have experienced and are experiencing. It relates to where the child is at in terms of their health and development currently. For an unborn child this would involve knowledge about foetal health.

```
┌─────────────────────────────────────────────────────────────────────┐
│ Pre-disposing Factors                                               │
│ and Processes:                                                      │
└──────┬───────────────────────┬──────────────────┬──────────┬────────┘
       ▼                       ▼                  ▲          ▼
┌─────────────────┐  ┌──────────────────────────────┐  ┌─────────────────┐
│ Harmful         │  │ Precipitating Trigger        │  │ Protective      │
│ Maintaining     │  │ Factors and Processes:       │  │ Maintaining     │
│ Factors and     │  │                              │  │ Factors and     │
│ Processes       │←→│                          ←→  │  │ Processes:      │
│ Present:        │  │   ┌──────────────────────┐   │  │                 │
│                 │  │   │ The Child's Current  │   │  │                 │
│                 │  │   │ Health and Development│  │  │                 │
│                 │  │   │ Including Harm to    │   │  │                 │
│                 │←→│   │ the Child:           │   │←→│                 │
│                 │  │   └──────────────────────┘   │  │                 │
│                 │  │   ┌──────────────────────┐   │  │                 │
│                 │  │   │ Predicting Likely    │   │  │                 │
│                 │  │   │ Future of Child's    │   │  │                 │
│                 │  │   │ Health and           │   │  │                 │
│                 │←→│   │ Development:         │   │←→│                 │
│                 │  │   └──────────────────────┘   │  │                 │
└─────────────────┘  └──────────────────────────────┘  └─────────────────┘
```

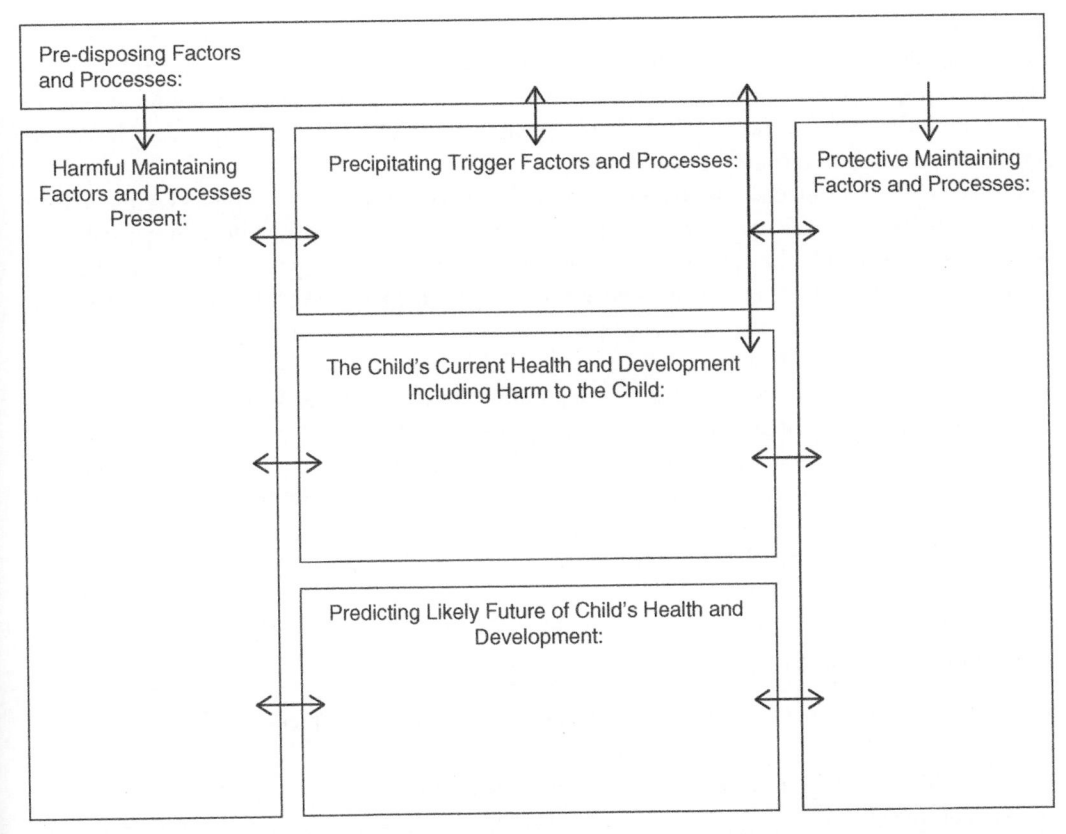

Figure 13.5 Systemic analysis of the identified factors and processes leading to patterns of harm to the child.

- Predisposing factors and influences. These relate to past or longer-term factors and processes, which may influence harm or increase the likelihood of harm, for example, difficulties in the parent's childhood upbringing. They are associated with what has brought things about. They may have contributed to past impairments of child development and may contribute to future impairments.
- Precipitating trigger factors and processes in the past which may have resulted in harm to the child. Again, these relate to how things came about. These factors may activate latent processes or precipitate new ones as, for example, when a parent gains a new partner.
- Harmful maintaining factors and processes. These are patterns of actions/behaviours which keep the harm to the child going in the present.
- Protective maintaining factors and processes. These are the resilience factors and processes operating in the present which protect the child from the adverse effects of potentially harmful factors and processes.
- Predicting the likely future of the child's health and development. This involves considering the outlook for the child in the future if things carry on as they are doing. It is helpful to look at this in the short term and then the long term.

Determining the prospects for successful intervention requires an understanding of the factors and processes associated with parental child-centredness (i.e., the capacity of the parents to recognise, understand, acknowledge and take responsibility for difficulties), the parents' level of modifiability (i.e., their level of motivation and capacity for change), and their readiness and ability to cooperate with professionals and agencies. These can be seen as 'dynamic' factors in that they represent the potential for change and the SAAF includes suggested interview approaches to help ascertain this information.

Of particular relevance is future modifiability; in other words, can the child's circumstances be improved safely within a reasonable time period taking account of the developmental stage and needs of the child (the child's developmental timeframe) if they stay in their current home setting? For there to be the possibility that matters can be changed for the better, partnership with the parents/carers has to be developed. Indicators that parental cooperation will not be forthcoming point to the need to safeguard the child.

Factors associated with substantial recurrent abuse in children and families are the number of previous episodes of abuse, neglect, severe and longstanding family conflict and/or parental personality or mental health problems, particularly where there is an inability on the part of the parents/carers to appreciate adequately the child's needs and respond to them. This will also be the case where the child is unwanted or used to gratify a parent's/carer's needs in a manner that impairs the child's development (Bentovim, Cox, Bingley Miller & Pizzey, 2009; Hindley, Ramchandani & Jones, 2006).

The prospects for successful intervention are analysed using rating scales in a series of tables and summary grids covering:

- nature of harm suffered and child or young person's wishes and feelings
- parental child-centredness regarding
  - child's health and development and any harm suffered and its impact
  - parenting
  - individual, family and environmental factors and processes
- modifiability, i.e., parents' level of motivation and capacity for change regarding difficulties in
  - impairment of child's development and any harm suffered
  - parenting
  - individual, family and environmental factors and processes
- parents' ability to cooperate with professionals and agencies.

Figure 13.6 provides an example of one of the tables of rating scales for the above areas together with its associated summary grid. A summary of the safeguarding analysis brings together the results of the three instruments and comprises an overall summary of each element:

- quantitatively on a three-point scale; and
- qualitatively by setting out the evidence that led to the rating.

The care plan for the child will be affected by the risk of the child suffering re-abuse or the likelihood of the child suffering future harm and the prospects for intervention. Child protection decision-making involves weighing up the combination of outcomes of the summary of the safeguarding analysis taking account of the developmental stage and needs of the child (the child's developmental timeframe) in order to formulate a plan for the child (Brown & Ward, 2013). The younger the child the shorter their timeframe will be, given their need to establish permanent attachments in their early years. The more the child's health and development has been impaired through harm, the shorter their timeframe, given the urgency of ensuring their development is maximised.

Level of functioning	Areas to be considered	Level of functioning
BETTER PROSPECTS FOR INTERVENTION	• Potential for change in individual and family factors to impact on parenting to meet child's needs • Extensiveness of personality, mental health, drugs/alcohol or relationship problems • History of family's and family members' response to previous intervention • Extensiveness of environmental difficulties • Availability of therapeutic resources/support services • Ability of family and family members to benefit from intervention	**POORER PROSPECTS FOR INTERVENTION**
Individual relationship and family factors and processes impacting on parenting and the child's safety and welfare are modifiable within child's timeframe.		Extensive severe individual family and relationship factors and processes impacting on parenting and the child's safety and welfare are highly unlikely to be changeable within child's timeframe.
Few personality, mental health, drugs/alcohol or relationship problems.		Extensive personality, mental health, drugs/alcohol or relationship problems.
History of family and family members responding positively to interventions.		History of family and family members responding poorly to interventions.
Few environmental difficulties.		Extensive environmental difficulties.
Therapeutic resources/support services available.		Requisite therapeutic resources/support services unavailable.
Family and family members able to benefit from intervention in individual and family factors and processes impacting on parenting and consequent meeting of child's needs.		Family and family members unable to benefit from intervention in individual and family factors and processes impacting on parenting and consequent meeting of child's needs.

Figure 13.6 Example rating scale table with associated summary grid.

The overall outlook is reasonably hopeful where the risks of re-abuse are low or moderate and there are good prospects for intervention, i.e., there are sufficient factors to feel that a positive outcome can be achieved within the child's developmental timeframe. Frequently there is a degree of doubt about the outlook because, for example, although the risk of

Assess the potential for change in individual and family factors and to respond to intervention and improve parenting to meet the child's needs.					
(please tick a box)	BETTER PROSPECTS				POORER PROSPECTS
Potential for change in individual and family factors to impact on parenting to meet child's needs					
Extensiveness of personality, mental health, drugs/alcohol or relationship problems					
History of family's and family members' response to previous intervention					
Extensiveness of environmental difficulties					
Availability of therapeutic resources/support services					
Ability of family and family members to benefit from intervention					

Figure 13.6 (Continued)

re-abuse is not high, there may be considerable doubts about the parents' response to intervention or rehabilitation. Alternatively, there may be considerable risks of re-abuse but a high level of parental motivation and better prospects for intervention.

Some areas (e.g., past history of abuse, acceptance of responsibility for the child's state, current psychiatric history) may indicate grave concerns. In such situations, further assessment or intervention may be required to determine whether the situation is hopeful and a plan of intervention can be initiated or, conversely, whether the prospect of safe care is unlikely to be achieved. The overall outlook is poor if the risk of re-abuse is so high and the prospects for intervention are so limited that it is highly unlikely that a safe context can be achieved for the child and a plan for long-term permanent alternative arrangements for the child's care needs to be made.

Stage 6: Develop and implement a plan of intervention

This involves:

- developing a plan of intervention that considers the likelihood of achieving sufficient change within the child's developmental timeframe
- deciding what the sequence/order of interventions should be in order to best meet the child's and family's needs
- identifying how it will be known if the child's health and development has improved and whether this improvement is related to the intervention(s)
- undertaking interventions with the child and family in accordance with the plan.

At the end of the previous stage, a judgement should have been made as to what is the most appropriate plan for the child and other children in the family on the basis of the level of harm which has occurred, the risks of re-abuse and the prospects for rehabilitation, taking all these factors into account.

In developing a plan for intervention, it is helpful to consider plans for each area of parenting in terms of providing basic care, ensuring safety, providing emotional warmth, stimulation, guidance and boundaries and stability, as well as the specific needs of the children and parents as individuals. It is useful to consider the following questions:

- What interventions are required to ensure the safety of the child?
- What are the options for interventions that might:
  (a) help support strengths in the child's health and development and/or
  (b) help reduce impairments in the child's health and development?
- Toward which strength/impairment in health and development is each intervention targeted?
- What resources are available?
- Which of those available is the family most likely to cooperate with?
- Which intervention is likely to produce the most immediate benefit and which might take time?
- What should be the sequence of interventions and why?
- What is the likelihood of achieving sufficient change within the child's developmental timeframe?

These questions are useful in building targeted, child-focused and realistic plans for intervention. It is useful to consider options for interventions which might help support strengths as well as those which might help reduce impairments in the child's health and development. It is essential to be clear as to which strength or impairment of the child's health and development is targeted, so that interventions can be effectively monitored. Bentovim and Elliott (2014) carried out an analysis of the most effective approaches to modifying harmful parenting, promoting good quality care, and responding to impairments of children's health and development. A set of modules has been developed from which practitioners can choose which interventions will best respond to the child's and family's assessed needs and thereby construct a collaborative intervention plan.

Plans need to be based on the resources actually available in the area and grounded in practical reality. The focus is therefore on what is available and not on what the practitioner thinks should be available in the area in which they work. Existing strengths (for example, good relationships or positive activities) should be used and developed. The next question is which of those available resources and approaches are the family most likely to cooperate with or engage with? There is little point in suggesting interventions which the family might struggle to understand or would have little motivation to engage with.

Some interventions are likely to produce immediate benefits whereas others might take time. For example, practical assistance might have an immediate benefit. Family therapy is likely to take time. It is also important to consider what sequence of interventions will meet the child's and family's needs best. All too often families are given a raft of interventions to engage with, and they struggle with them. It is a better use of resources and more manageable for the family to limit the number of interventions and deliver them in a sequence which makes sense to the child, family and practitioner. It may be that some interventions need to be prioritised over others. Experience shows that a success in one intervention is likely to have benefits in other areas.

In planning interventions, given the severity of impairments of the child's development and the capacity of the family to cooperate, it is important to consider the likelihood of achieving sufficient change within the child's developmental timeframe and adjust plans accordingly. This involves identifying how we will know:

- whether there has been an improvement in the child's health and development, i.e., whether the child's impairments in health and development have been improved or resolved
- whether that improvement is related to what has been done, e.g., the intervention(s). For example, was the intended intervention implemented and was it implemented at the frequency intended and with the appropriate skill? Has the process or factor at which the intervention is targeted been changed in the desired direction (Bentovim, Cox, Bingley Miller & Pizzey, 2009; Pizzey, Bentovim, Cox et al., 2015)?

Stage 7: Identify outcomes and measures for assessing change

This involves:

- establishing outcomes related to your hypotheses about how the interventions are expected
  - to improve the child's health and development
  - to have an impact on the factors and processes considered to be influencing the child's developmental needs
- identifying measures for assessing whether change has been achieved for each outcome.

Outcomes should be established related to hypotheses about how the interventions are expected (a) to improve the health and development of the child and (b) those factors and processes considered to be influencing the child's developmental needs. Measures for assessing whether change has been achieved also need to be identified for each outcome in order to indicate whether interventions have been successful. These measures then need to be applied before and after interventions.

The overall aim is to understand the child's progress or lack of it and the reasons for this, so that interventions can be modified appropriately. The assessment of outcomes of intervention necessitates the capacity to measure change over time in:

- the child's health and development
- the factors and processes thought to influence the child's health and development.

To assess change there must have been a baseline assessment and follow-up measures so that any changes over the time of the intervention can be identified. The aims in identifying outcomes for a child are to enable practitioners to assess or measure change following intervention. The outcomes must relate to the analysis of the child's developmental needs and the contribution of the parenting they are receiving to meeting their needs (or not) and the impact of family and environmental factors on both the parenting and the child's needs directly. The aims in measuring outcomes therefore are to assess:

- the child's developmental progress with respect to a specific starting point
- changes in factors/dimensions of parenting or in the family and environmental factors with respect to the starting point
- the effectiveness of any interventions.

At the starting point or commencement of a focused intervention, an assessment will have identified dimensions of the child's health and development that need to be enhanced. Intervention may have addressed some of these directly rather than by attempting to influence factors affecting parenting. For example, a remedial reading scheme may have been instituted for a child with reading difficulties. Outcome assessment aims to check whether the child has progressed on the relevant dimension. If there has been no progress, the process will need to be examined.

During an assessment, hypotheses will have been formed about processes that are thought to be affecting the child's health and development in either a positive or negative way. Interventions may have been aimed to work on these processes. Assessment of processes seeks to determine whether changes in those processes relate to child development outcomes or a factor thought to be crucial to the child's progress. It is not just a matter of assessing factors; processes need to be explored also. This must be done systemically in the light of original hypotheses. For example, it was hypothesised that a mother's unresponsive parenting was due to her depression. The mother's mental state could be monitored and matched with her responsivity toward her child.

Baseline and follow-up measures need to be valid, i.e., they must measure what they are intended to measure. This means the practitioner knows that the factor(s) they wish to be assessed are addressed by the measure being used. The measures also need to be reliable (replicable over time and give the same results when used by different practitioners). This means that the 'measure' returns similar results over at least short time periods and that trained practitioners under comparable circumstances obtain similar scores when used with the same individual or family. An example might be when a scale is used by different practitioners or the school register is used by different teachers.

Standardised measures often provide population norms and scores that can help understand the significance of any change. The term 'population norms' means the range of scores obtained in research with a large, general population. Norms are the spread of scores found for a defined population of respondents. Thus, it is possible to state what percentage of the population score at different points on the possible range of scores. For example, with the Strengths and Difficulties Questionnaire (Goodman, 1997) it is possible to predict what percentage of the population (within the relevant age range) would be expected to get the score that a particular child has got. This gives an indication about the likely level of strengths and difficulties being presented by that child in terms of their emotional and behavioural development and well-being.

For baseline measures to be replicated at a follow-up, they need to be standardised or operationally defined. It is then possible to assess whether change has taken place between the time of original (baseline) assessment and once the interventions have been implemented. Standardised measures are those assessment tools which have operationally defined items which are then scored. Examples outlined above include the *Family Pack of Questionnaires and Scales*, the *HOME Inventory*, the *Family Assessment* and the *Attachment Style Interview*. Other measures include the *Edinburgh Postnatal Depression Scale* (Cox, Holden & Sagovsky, 1987) and the *UK-WHO Growth Charts* (World Health Organization, 1978).

Case-specific measures can also be used provided they are operationally defined so that they can be replicated over time or used in a comparable fashion by different practitioners. To be operationally defined they need to have agreed criteria which can be counted or rated.

Ratings must be guided by markers for each point on a scale, otherwise there can be no certainty that baseline and follow-up assessments are comparable. Ratings of behaviour over a period of time, such as a school day, may be unreliable. It may be easier to achieve reliable results by methods that count defined behaviours such as a bedwetting chart, counting the number of days a child is excluded from school, counting the number of days a child has taken medication for hyperactivity or scoring the number of times a child is 'on task' at fixed times during the day.

Examination of the various factors involved in these processes leads to a better understanding and assessment of whether interventions are working. Measures can employ a variety of modes such as questionnaire, interview and observation, and may be conducted with any relevant person, child, teacher or parent, and in several different settings. The issue for outcome is that the measure, person and setting must be the same at follow-up as at baseline. Children's behaviour may vary according to situation so that outcomes need to be assessed in all appropriate contexts (Bentovim, Cox, Bingley Miller & Pizzey, 2009; Pizzey, Bentovim, Cox et al., 2015).

Evaluation of SAAF

Barlow, Fisher and Jones (2012) reviewed a range of analytical tools, including the *Graded Care Profile* (Srivastava & Polnay, 1997) and *Signs of Safety* (Turnell & Edwards, 1999) and found that the SAAF was the 'only one of the family assessment tools that we identified [that] included an assessment of the possibilities of future change and how success or otherwise might be gauged' and that it was 'consistent with the *Assessment Framework*; assessed a much wider range of domains compared with other available tools' and as such is 'more comprehensive', and 'compared with current practice [it provides] practitioners with clear guidance about what to assess, and how to analyse and "make sense of" the data collected' (pp. 73–74).

The SAAF is currently the subject of a cluster-randomised controlled trial commissioned (RCT) by the Department for Education in England (Macdonald, Lewis, Macdonald et al., 2014). This is a multi-site RCT in which teams of child protection social workers, stratified by site, are randomly allocated to one of two arms:

(i) SAAF training followed by implementation of SAAF in child protection cases and complex children-in-need cases;
(ii) Management as usual in child protection cases and complex children-in-need cases.

An implementation evaluation will run concurrently with the trial to explore the experience of using the SAAF, how it is integrated into working processes, and the barriers and facilitators to successful intervention. The study will also explore participant social workers' experience of taking part in the trial. The findings of the study are due to be published in 2017.

Conclusion

The Safeguarding Assessment and Analysis Framework is one of a set of evidence-based approaches to assist practitioners to adopt an evidence-based approach to their practice. It is designed to help practitioners make sense of, and manage, the complexity involved in child protection work. By describing the process of an assessment of safeguarding concerns from initial consideration, through the assessment and analysis phases, to planning an intervention, the practitioner has a set of evidence-based frameworks which can act as a 'third party' to their work.

The practitioner has to position themselves using a variety of lenses to view the task, their professional role and the expectations of their organisation, the courts and the society they work and live in. They bring their experiences into the picture and must remain open-minded in order to understand the child's and family's viewpoints, and process the information which they derive directly and indirectly through interviews and observation, reviewing records, and from other agencies. Pressures to influence the processes of forming a judgement about the best interests of the child abound: to believe or be sceptical; to maintain a balance between the child's and the parents' wishes; to be mindful of the potential impact of protection and intervention; and to be aware of the realities of the long-term impact of harmful parenting, and the potential for change, and recovery.

The assessment and analysis frameworks described in this chapter are meant to be a guide to judgement. A clear, balanced, realistic, evidence-based picture should emerge of the prospects for the child if the situation remains unchanged, the prospects for intervention, the plan needed to promote the child's health and development, the interventions that would be best suited to bring about positive change in the child's situation, and how the success or otherwise of those interventions can be measured.

References

Angold, A., Prendergast, M., Cox, A. et al. (1995). The Child and Adolescent Psychiatric Assessment (CAPA). *Psychological Medicine*, 25, 739–753.

Barlow J., Fisher J.D. & Jones D. (2012). *Systematic Review of Models of Significant Harm*. London: Department for Education.

Bentovim, A. & Bingley Miller, L. (2001). *The Family Assessment: Assessment of Family Competence, Strengths and Difficulties*. York: Child and Family Training.

Bentovim, A. & Elliott, I. (2014). Hope for children and families: Targeting abusive parenting and the associated impairment of children. *Journal of Clinical Child & Adolescent Psychology*, 43, 270–285.

Bentovim A., Cox A., Bingley Miller L. & Pizzey, S. (2009). *Safeguarding Children Living with Trauma and Family Violence: A Guide to Evidence-Based Assessment, Analysis and Planning Interventions*. London: Jessica Kingsley.

Bifulco, A., Moran, P., Ball, C. & Lillie, A. (2002). Adult Attachment Style II. Its relationship to psycho-social depressive-vulnerability. *Social Psychiatry and Psychiatric Epidemiology*, 37, 60–67.

Brown, R. & Ward, H. (2013). *Decision-making within a child's timeframe: An overview of current research evidence for family justice professionals concerning child development and the impact of maltreatment*, 2nd edn. London: Childhood Wellbeing Research Centre, https://www.gov.uk/government/uploads/system/uploads/attachment_data/file/200471/Decision-making_within_a_child_s_timeframe.pdf.

Calam, R.M., Cox, A.D., Glasgow, D.V. et al. (2000). Assessment and therapy with children: Can computers help? *Child Clinical Psychology and Psychiatry*, 5, 329–343.

Caldwell, B.M. & Bradley, R.H. (2003). *HOME Inventory: Administration Manual Comprehensive Edition*. Little Rock, AR: University of Arkansas for Medical Sciences.

Children Act 1989. London: Her Majesty's Stationery Office.

Cox, A. & Bentovim, A. (2000). *The Family Pack of Questionnaires and Scales*. London: The Stationery Office.

Cox, A., Pizzey, S. & Walker, S. (2009). *The HOME Inventory: A Guide for Practitioners – The UK Approach*. York: Child and Family Training.

Cox, J.L., Holden, J.M. & Sagovsky, R. (1987). Detection of postnatal depression: Development of the 10-item Edinburgh Postnatal Depression Scale. *British Journal of Psychiatry*, 150, 782–786.

Department for Education (2015). *Working Together to Safeguard Children: A Guide to Inter-Agency Working to Safeguard and Promote the Welfare of Children.* London: Department for Education.

Department of Health, Department for Education and Employment and Home Office (2000). *Framework for the assessment of children in need and their families.* London: The Stationery Office.

Goodman, R. (1997). The Strengths and Difficulties Questionnaire: A research note. *Journal of Child Psychology and Psychiatry*, 35, 581–586.

Hart, D. (2010). Assessment before birth. In: J. Horwath (ed), *The Child's World: The Comprehensive Guide to Assessing Children in Need*, 2nd edn. London: Jessica Kingsley, 229–240.

Hindley, N., Ramchandani, P. & Jones, D.P.H. (2006). Risk factors for recurrence of maltreatment: A systematic review. *Archives of Disease in Childhood*, 91, 744–752.

Macdonald, G., Lewis, J., Macdonald, K. et al. (2014). The SAAF Study: Evaluation of the Safeguarding Children Assessment and Analysis Framework (SAAF), compared with management as usual, for improving outcomes for children and young people who have experienced, or are at risk of, maltreatment: Study protocol for a randomised controlled trial. *Trials*, 15, 453.

Pizzey S., Bentovim A., Cox A. et al. (2015). *The Safeguarding Children Assessment and Analysis Framework.* York: Child and Family Training.

Srivastava, O.P. & Polnay, L. (1997). Field trial of graded care profile (GCP) scale: A new measure of care. *Archives of Disease in Childhood*, 76, 337–340.

Turnell, A. & Edwards, S. (1999). *Signs of Safety: A Solution and Safety Oriented Approach to Child Protection Casework.* New York: W.W. Norton & Co.

World Health Organization (1978). *A growth chart for international use in maternal and child health care.* Guidelines for primary health care personnel. Geneva: World Health Organization.

14
Utilising an Attachment Perspective in Parenting Assessment

Carol George

Mills College, Oakland, CA, USA

Professionals and parents alike have an intuitive sense of what attachment is and it is often assumed that children who are receiving services, rehabilitation, or in intervention programmes have parents who cannot provide for their children's basic attachment needs. Discussion of how to support a child's attachment security is often drawn into treatment and legal decisions, many of which change the life course of a child's living arrangements and access to parents. Yet practitioners do not agree on what constitutes attachment, and there are many inconsistencies and contradictory interpretations of parents' contributions to children's attachments (George, Isaacs & Marvin, 2011; McIntosh, 2011).

The chapter delineates an attachment theory approach to parenting so as to provide professionals with intentional knowledge that can contribute to intervention and advise family outcomes. The chapter begins with an overview of attachment theory, describing the fundamental elements of the core features for the development of attachment in children. The discussion then moves to an attachment theory perspective of parenting. The association between patterns of caregiving and individual differences in patterns of children's attachment are described. Finally, the chapter addresses the tools available for evidence-based assessment of parenting from an attachment perspective.

What is Attachment?

Attachment is an evolutionary-based concept that identifies a specific intimate human social relationship and influences development across the life span (Bowlby, 1969/1982). The term 'attachment' is shorthand for a complex set of interrelated behaviour and thought patterns directed toward a parent figure. Attachment behaviour is guided by a biologically based behavioural system that evolved to ensure protection and safety (Bowlby, 1969/1982). Attachment organises motivational, emotional, cognitive and memory processes. It begins in infancy and affects development, behaviour in other relationships (including parenting the next generation of children), risk-taking, and mental health throughout the life span (Bowlby, 1969/1982, 1973, 1980; Cassidy & Shaver, 2008). The attachment is distinguished from other social relationships by the following constellation of behaviours and processes: (i) proximity seeking; (ii) distress when separation is not understandable; (iii) happiness at reunion; (iv) grief/sadness at loss; (v) secure-base behaviour – capacity to explore when attachment figure is present (Ainsworth 1989); (vi) confidence that the attachment figure has an enduring commitment to the relationship; and (vii) capacity for mutual enjoyment or vicarious joy (Bowlby, 1969/1982; George & Solomon, 2008; Kobak, Cassidy & Ziv, 2004).

Attachment behaviour is adaptive. Selected by human evolution as a protection strategy, it increases children's chances for survival. Attachment is guided by a neurologically based system; it has specific biological substrates that influence physiological homeostasis (Bowlby, 1973; Cassidy & Shaver, 2008). This system, formally termed the attachment behavioural system, is activated by stress or threat, which creates the desire for physical or psychological contact or proximity with attachment figures (Bowlby, 1969/1982, 1973). Internal cues (illness, fatigue, hunger, pain) and external cues (frightening and stressful events) activate attachment behaviour (Bowlby, 1973). Some activating events are universal to humans and shared by non-human primates (e.g., fear of the dark or of situations or features associated with pain); others are learnt or taught by parents (Bowlby, 1973).

Understanding the evolutionary and neurobiological foundations of attachment are critical components to thinking about attachment and parenting. Attachment behaviours signal distress and the need for care and comfort in many situations that are programmed by human biology (e.g., being left alone and separation). This programming is so fundamental that young children, and even sometimes adults, have little control over how distressed or frightened they feel. Attachment behaviour, especially in early childhood, is a form of communication (Bowlby, 1969/1982, 1973). Attachment needs are based on genuine feelings elicited by real experiences. These experiences are associated with affects that regulate children's responses to parental proximity, soothing and protection, as well as parents' attunement to children's goals for protection (Bowlby, 1969/1982; Cassidy & Shaver, 2008; George & Solomon, 2008). These affects foster the intimacy and shared enjoyment, which are essential in deepening attachment relationships (Bowlby, 1969/1982). Relationships that lack mutual enjoyment and in which the parent does not share the child's attachment goals and respond to the child's real attachment needs foster chronic intense negative affect. As a result, negative feelings – anger, sadness, depression, anxiety and fear (often the product of relationship trauma) – compromise emotion regulation, exploration, cognitive competence, relationships, and ultimately, mental health (Bowlby, 1973, 1980; Cassidy & Shaver, 2008; Lyons-Ruth & Jacobvitz, 2008). In short, a perspective that views attachment behaviour as irrational, infantile, or manipulative is not useful (Bowlby, 1973). The origins of 'dependency' or 'manipulative' communications ultimately serve children's needs for proximity to parents when these goals are frustrated or truncated, often because parents misconstrue the mean of attachment behaviour in their children's early years.

The concept of representation is core to understanding these regulatory functions, originally described by Bowlby (1969/1982) as the 'internal working model' of attachment. Children's representational models of attachment act as a synthesising and internal guidance system that regulates how and when to signal needs (Bowlby, 1969/1982; Bretherton & Munholland, 2008). By ages three and four years, representational models are automatic mechanisms that evaluate, emotionally appraise, and organise real life experience. Representational models are not static; they are updated and reworked to achieve internal consistency and are available for use in novel situations or as the basis of future plans (Bowlby, 1969/1982; Bretherton & Munholland, 2008). This process continues through childhood and adolescence and representational models about one's own childhood attachment figures lay the foundation for parenting (George & Solomon, 2008; Hesse, 2008).

Children develop preferred attachment relationships with parents and a finite number of other caring adults (e.g., foster parents or daycare providers); relationships that are balanced by parental sensitivity and the child's desire to cooperate with parental care contribute to age-appropriate development across all domains, an integrated and confident sense of self, and developmental resilience (George & Solomon, 2008; Lyons-Ruth & Jacobvitz, 2008; Sroufe, Egeland, Carlson & Collins, 2005). By contrast, dysregulated relationships in which balance is compromised is associated with maladaptive developmental risk, including difficulty maintaining relationships, and increased likelihood of being diagnosed with mental health problems in childhood, adolescence and adulthood (Lyons-Ruth & Jacobvitz, 2008; Solomon & George, 2011a). Dysregulated child attachment patterns are prevalent in high-risk parent–child relationships such as maltreatment, intense parent conflict, and parent psychiatric disorder or chemical dependency.

Children's attachment patterns become increasingly stable and resistant to change during early childhood (infancy through age five) as relationships become internalised through the development of representational skills. Continuity and discontinuity, however, are connected to experiences with parents. Changes in attachment patterns occur when there are significant changes in parental sensitivity and responsiveness due to life events that can stabilise (infant mental health intervention) or threaten (loss of a parent) attachment security (McConnell & Moss, 2011).

Parenting: An Attachment Theory Perspective

Attachment theory posits that parents' responses to their children are guided by a biologically based caregiving behavioural system, and the goal of proximity in the service of protection is the same for parents and their children (Bowlby, 1969/1982). The difference between attachment and caregiving is that parents must make a fundamental shift away from being the one who seeks protection and care from an attachment figure to becoming the person who provides protection and care for their child (George & Solomon, 2008). As such, the behavioural goal of the caregiving system is delineated as providing protection for the child by keeping the child close, and paying attention to the child's attachment cues and contextual demands for safety and care. Parents continue to have their own attachment needs, but for the parent–child relationship to progress normally, parents must direct these needs to their own attachment figures and not to their children (George & Solomon, 2008). Parents who cannot do this are role-reversed and children's development is compromised by such adultification (Bowlby, 1969/1982; George & Solomon, 2008).

Parenting then involves a biologically based caregiving behavioural repertoire that serves the system's protective function (Bowlby, 1969/1982; George & Solomon, 2008). When the caregiving system is 'working' as human evolution intended, parents automatically step in to protect and comfort children when they are frightened, endangered or distressed. These situations include (but are not limited to) separation, child endangerment, and the child's signals (direct or oblique) of discomfort and distress. In these moments, parents swoop in and get children to keep them close, or call or signal children to follow or come toward parents for safety. George and Solomon (2008) proposed that the tension created by needing to care for children in any particular situation cannot be assuaged until parents successfully achieve physical (and as the child grows older) psychological proximity and see visible signs that children are comforted, contented or satisfied. As with attachment, the successes or failures of caregiving are associated with strong feelings, and these feelings not only regulate behaviour, but are also associated with regulatory behavioural and biochemical responses. When the caregiving system is balanced and attuned to children's attachment needs, parents should experience feelings of intense pleasure and satisfaction. They understandably become angry, sad, anxious, or desperate when separated from the child or when their ability to protect and comfort their children is threatened. And when the risk of these feelings becoming overpowering is heightened, they are managed by defensive processing that helps as well as possible to maintain balanced and thoughtful responsiveness (George & Solomon, 2008). For distressed, angry or distracted parents, these defensive processes misalign or even block caregiving responses to children's attachment needs.

Following the attachment theory model, the caregiving system, and thus parenting behaviour, is regulated by representational models. As noted earlier, caregiving representations are influenced by parents' own attachment representations. The association between past and present, however, is not linear and not so simple. Caregiving representations are heavily influenced by current experiences with children and parenting contexts, including those that are often seen in high-risk families such as parent death or mental illness, family violence, or high-conflict custody disputes. In short, caregiving representations as regulatory mechanisms reflect reciprocal and transactional evaluations of being the parent of a particular child in the context of current situations.

Patterns of Caregiving and Attachment

All young children who receive some form of regular care select attachment figures, suggesting that simple proximity and social interactions with a caregiver are sufficient for an attachment to develop (Bowlby, 1969/1982). Not all caregiving-attachment relationships are the same, even in the same family (van IJzendoorn, Moran, Belsky et al., 2000). The field of attachment uses the term 'patterns' to describe attachment. These patterns provide a qualitative lens for understanding how parents are able, or not able, to provide protection of care for their children. Patterns range from providing security to normative compromises to security to dysregulated relationships that are associated with vulnerability and the highest developmental risk. Our knowledge of the parenting behaviours and representations associated with these different patterns has been established over more than four decades of empirical study.

Flexible caregiving and secure attachment. Sensitive and flexible caregiving are the hallmark features of a parenting pattern associated with children's attachment security. Maternal sensitivity has been established as a central contributor to security and the link between sensitivity and security is an attachment postulate that is supported in a wide range of child rearing contexts and cultures (Ainsworth, Blehar, Waters & Wall, 1978; Bakermans-Kranenburg, van IJzendoorn & Juffer, 2003; Behrens, Parker & Haltigan, 2011; Bigelow, MacLean, Proctor et al., 2010; De Schipper, Oosterman & Schuengel, 2012; De Wolff & van IJzendoorn, 1997; Huang, Lewin, Mitchell & Zhang, 2012; Jin, Jacobvitz, Hazen & Jung, 2012; Koren-Karie, Oppenheim, Dolev & Yirmiya, 2009; Leerkes, 2011; Lucassen, Tharner, van IJzendoorn et al., 2011; McElwain

& Booth-LaForce, 2006; Mills-Koonce, Gariepy, Sutton & Cox, 2008; NICHD, 2001; True, Pisani & Oumar, 2001; von der Lippe, Eilertsen, Hartmann & Killen, 2010). Flexible care appears to be characteristic of all humans, despite vast differences in caregiving behaviour (e.g., Posada, Gao, Wu & Posada, 1995). Flexibility represents parents' capacities to notice and think about their children's attachment needs and respond in ways that integrate these needs within relational and interpersonal systems, including family, context, cultural and developmental agendas in such a way that children are confident in parents' protective capacity and availability for comfort (George & Solomon, 2008).

Mothers of securely attached children are relaxed and enjoy being with their children (Stevenson-Hinde & Shouldice, 1995). Mothers of securely attached children have been shown to monitor children's play and are comfortable when children return to them, and to engage in more harmonious positive interaction and collaboration, less instruction, and less discipline in structured tasks than mothers of insecurely attached children (Britner, Marvin & Pianta, 2005; Bus & van IJzendoorn, 1988; Moss, St-Laurent & Parent, 1999; Stevenson-Hinde & Shouldice, 1995). Secure dyads as compared with insecure dyads have been found to engage in higher levels of attunement, respect, willingness to negotiate, reciprocity, and balanced emotional expression during unstructured interaction (Britner, Marvin & Pianta, 2005; Dubois-Comtois & Moss, 2008; Humber & Moss, 2005; Moss, Rousseau, Parent et al., 1998; Moss & St-Laurent, 2001; Solomon, George & Silverman, 1990).

Mothers' representations of caregiving emphasise flexibility and sensitivity. They describe their commitment to being parents, and trust, cooperation, knowledge of self and child as individuals, the ability and desire to communicate clearly about caregiving and attachment goals, especially when in conflict, and the joy associated with being a parent (Bernier & Dozier, 2003; George, 1996; George & Solomon, 1999; Grienenberger, Kelly & Slade, 2005; Slade, Grienenberger, Bernbach et al., 2005; Steinberg & Pianta, 2006). Mothers' representations are also relatively undefended (George & Solomon, 2008). Parenting experiences and evaluations of their children and caregiving contexts are described openly without shifting to other topics or overemphasising negative or positive qualities in self or child (George & Solomon, 2008). These parents admit to making mistakes or having to take drastic measures (e.g., hide children from the landlord who does not know children are living in the apartment), but are thoughtful about these situations, the cost to the child or themselves, and how to remedy the risk of repetition as compared with rationalisation or defensiveness (George & Solomon, 2008).

This quality of parenting supports children's attachment security. *Secure* children signal needs promptly and clearly, and clearly show preferences for parental care above all others (e.g., Ainsworth, Blehar, Waters & Wall, 1978; Thompson, 2008; Weinfield, Sroufe, Egeland & Carlson, 2008). Secure children are confident that the parent is accessible, sensitive, responsive, and will follow through as promptly and completely as possible (Ainsworth, Blehar, Waters & Wall, 1978). Security fosters competence, cooperation, and the child's desire to explore and achieve mastery (e.g., Ainsworth, Blehar, Waters & Wall, 1978; Thompson, 2008; Weinfield, Sroufe, Egeland & Carlson, 2008). The parents of the secure child views him/her as deserving care and work hard to meet their child's attachment needs as well as their own needs in a developmentally and contextually appropriate manner (George & Solomon, 2008). In sum, the secure caregiving-attachment relationship is balanced, mutually satisfying, comfortable, and characterised by emotional sharing and the co-construction of plans and activities – a balanced working partnership (Bowlby, 1969/1982; George & Solomon, 2008; Marvin & Britner, 2008).

Inflexible caregiving and insecure attachment. Parents who are inflexible, because their caregiving is out of balance because of their own or their children's needs, contribute to attachment insecurity that compromises relationship and biological homeostasis. These compromises demand behavioural adjustment and representational defensive processes to manage distress, exclusion or transformation of attachment experience and affect, and maintain physical and psychological proximity, the reciprocal goals of caregiving and attachment. In spite of chronic anxiety, parents and children develop a relationship rule system of how to be together that provides children with a sense of what George and Solomon (2008) conceived of, in relation to this quality of care, as 'good enough', as long as parenting conditions remain stable. These relationships are termed in the field of attachment as 'insecure', sometimes also called 'ordered insecure' (Marvin & Britner, 2008), which acknowledges the quality of functioning from predictable and ordered rules. These forms of insecure parenting are associated with some level of developmental compromise in their children, but at least these parents communicate a basic protective capacity that keeps their relationship organised.

Parenting in this group is characterised by two different overarching patterns. One pattern is to *discourage closeness*. These parents emphasise the importance of children's secure-base behaviour (i.e., exploration) at the expense of providing a safe haven (i.e., do not encourage closeness and provide limited comfort) (Britner, Marvin & Pianta, 2005; Marvin, Cooper, Hoffman & Powell, 2002). Parents focus on their own needs, including the need for personal space or adhering to a parenting role emphasising the guidelines that define parenting adults as children's main agents for socialisation and proper behaviour (George & Solomon, 2008). They use distancing strategies and rejection to manage parenting, which helps diffuse anger by maintaining an emotional façade of calm neutrality (George & Solomon, 2008). This position is not always fully effective, however; distress can leak through, for example, as maternal separation anxiety from children or negativity toward self and feelings of parental inadequacy (George & Solomon, 2008; Lutz & Hock, 1995). Parenting behaviour and caregiving representations emphasise didactic teaching and independence, discouraging children from showing their distress, and discipline and transgression management (Britner, Marvin & Pianta, 2005; George & Solomon, 2008; Main, 1990). Parent–child interaction centres on taking care of children's physical needs (e.g., injuries) without intimacy or comfort (Britner, Marvin & Pianta, 2005; George & Solomon, 2008). Although these parents can be pleasant and their attention to injury and exploration is often misinterpreted as providing security, their behaviour and thinking about being a parent shows little emotion, with the exception of irritation at what they evaluate as children's signals for attachment or other needs as manipulative or testing parent limits (Britner, Marvin & Pianta, 2005; George & Solomon, 2008). In middle childhood, these parents add children's peer relationships to their list of major concerns, which represents yet another attention shift away from children's attachment needs to focus on achievement in both the intellectual (i.e., exploration) and peer domains (George & Solomon, 2008).

Their children's attachment patterns are *avoidant*. Avoidant children ignore and even push parents away, creating an outward sense to those who see them as being independent and not needing care (Ainsworth, Blehar, Waters & Wall, 1978). They turn away from parents when they need care in order to cope with distress and anger in attachment situations because their need to express their distress and need for comfort directly to the parent cannot be met (Ainsworth, Blehar, Waters & Wall, 1978). Like their parents, however, their distress can leak through, especially when they are separated from their parents (Ainsworth, Blehar, Waters & Wall, 1978; Solomon, George & De Jong, 1995). Avoidant children show less coordination and close communication with their parents than secure children, keeping conversation focused on play or the environment and away from topics related to the parent–child relationship (Dubois-Comtois, Cyr & Moss, 2011). They mirror their parents' emotional neutrality and distance keeping (Dubois-Comtois, Cyr & Moss, 2011). In spite of their parents' emphasis on exploration and achievement, play quality, mastery motivation, and school achievement is compromised as compared with secure children (Moss & St-Laurent, 2001; Pederson & Moran, 1996).

The other caregiving pattern is *heightened caregiving and sentimentality*. These parents emphasise the importance of their role as providing their children with a haven of safety; their caregiving goals emphasise intimacy and togetherness at the expense of encouraging exploration (Britner, Marvin & Pianta, 2005; Marvin, Cooper, Hoffman & Powell, 2002). They focus on children's vulnerability and need for care, fortified by sentimentality, at the expense of taking care of their own needs as parents and adults (George & Solomon, 2008). This defensive position can be so exhausting that parents vacillate between wanting to be close and seeking respite from parenting, vacillations that are unpredictable and confusing even to the parents (George & Solomon, 2008). Parenting behaviour and caregiving representations emphasise the importance of intimacy and feelings, but parents are unable to sustain these topics or intimate behaviour, noticeably shifting conversation and activities to their needs rather than their children's (e.g., what they did that day rather than asking children about their day) (Britner, Marvin & Pianta, 2005; George & Solomon, 2008). Interaction and discussion are drawn out way beyond what is required in situations (e.g., over-analysis, overly long good-byes), punctuated with anxiety and confusion, and guilt about how to understand and respond to their children's attachment needs (Britner, Marvin & Pianta, 2005; George & Solomon, 2008). Ultimately, these parents want to be comfortable, happy, and to have fun with their children, but confusion, frustration, anger, and intolerance of children's negative affect undermine their attempts to maintain this idyllic façade.

Their children's attachment patterns are *ambivalent-resistant*. These children are preoccupied with and confused by their parents' potential for sensitivity but incapability for consistency. Ambivalent-resistant children understandably seek but are not satisfied with their parents' caregiving. Their signals are often confusing and contradictory; moods and affective states are intense because of compromised capacity for affect regulation, especially anger (Ainsworth, Blehar, Waters & Wall, 1978). They can be difficult to soothe, immature, feisty, and angry (Dubois-Comtois, Cyr & Moss, 2011; Marvin & Britner, 2008). They are not comfortable with exploration because parents have communicated that being away from the parent is not safe; play, mastery motivation, and school achievement, therefore, are compromised as compared with secure children (Moss & St-Laurent, 2001; Pederson & Moran, 1996).

Dysregulated caregiving and attachment. Dysregulated caregiving and attachment are most prevalent in families with high risk; the proportion of dysregulated forms of attachment ranges from 13– 90%, depending on risk factors (e.g., maltreatment, chemical dependency, poverty, war/neighbourhood terror) (Lyons-Ruth & Jacobvitz, 2008). The patterns of caregiving associated with this form of parenting are quite different from those associated with distance and heightened-sentimental patterns. Dysregulated caregiving is defined by the breakdown of the organising behaviour and defensive processes that maintain ordered caregiving and attachments (i.e., secure, avoidant, ambivalent-resistant). Parents are either incompetent or passive, clearly unable to take on the parenting role as needed (Britner, Marvin & Pianta, 2005). Parenting behaviour and representation are characterised by *abdication and failed protection* (George & Solomon, 2008, 2011; Solomon & George, 1996, 2011a).

Caregiving and attachment relationships are completely out of balance in these parent–child dyads. Caregiving and attachment are dysregulated at the behavioural, representational and biological levels (Solomon & George, 2011a). Children's natural desire to seek and maintain proximity to the parent is blocked by parental abdication and failure to provide care and comfort at the very moment the child needs them (George & Solomon, 2008). The aetiology of the disorganised/controlling relationship appears to be a complex interaction of the parent's current experience with past attachment trauma, which contributes to (i) extreme parental psychological or physical withdrawal and 'invisibility' (dissociative behaviour); (ii) unresolved, contradictory or unpredictable frightening experiences (rage, hostile-intrusive interaction) sometimes associated with certain forms of psychopathology (anxiety disorder, borderline personality disorder, depression), abuse, alcoholism, or parental conflict; (iii) helplessness; (iv) child empowerment/deference (glorification – the child viewed as more capable of caring for others than the parent); and (v) dissolution of parent–child boundaries (parent merged with child and/or acts like a child, and/or treats child like a spouse) (Lyons-Ruth & Jacobvitz, 2008; Solomon & George, 2011b). The single underlying thread in this list is the fear generated by feelings of abdicated parental care.

In infancy, their children appear disorganised and disoriented in response to their parents. The disorganised terminology stemmed from observations of infants' reunions with parents following separation (Main & Solomon, 1990). These infants appear disoriented (in a trance-like state), frightened (freezing, apprehensive), conflicted about proximity (head uncomfortably averted), and hostile (aggression without apparent cause) (Main & Solomon, 1990). Children under the age of three act frightened and helpless to get their needs met. Typically by ages three to five years, disorganised children have developed *controlling* strategies and get their needs met by directing their parents' behaviour (Marvin & Britner, 2008; Solomon & George, 2008).

There are two predominant forms of dysregulated parenting. One is *helpless/out of control*. Caregiving associated with this form is punctuated by overwhelming feelings of being afraid and vulnerable, for themselves and their children (George & Solomon, 2008). Children and parenting situations that should normally elicit protective feelings and actions rather threaten to unleash disproportionate anger, cruelty and hostility, or helpless hesitation that truncates connectedness and involvement (George & Solomon, 2008; Lyons-Ruth & Spielman, 2004; Solomon & George, 2011b). Parents risk drowning in their worst fears about themselves and their children (George & Solomon, 2008). These parents describe their children as often going wildly out of control (e.g., acting like 'maniacs', hysterical, and threatening), conveying messages of defiance and sometimes evil spirit that parents are helpless to combat (George & Solomon, 2008). As a result, parents' caregiving and children's attachment systems are markedly out of balance and, parents desperately struggle and fight with their children to remain in control (George & Solomon, 2008).

How this form of parenting correlates with infant attachment disorganisation is not yet clear. By ages three to five years, children's attachment patterns are described as *controlling-punitive*. Furious at parents' failure to protect them, these children dominate and punish their parents in ways that mirror their parents' anger and hostility (George & Solomon, 2008; Main & Cassidy, 1988). Unlike avoidant children, they are unable to turn away from their parents to modulate their emotions, especially their anger. Their commands and punitive rudeness are likely efforts they have developed to push parents back into role of authority; even if angry, authoritarian parents take charge and children can perhaps hope to experience some kind of parental protection (George & Solomon, 2008). From an attachment theory perspective, however, these strategies are maladaptive because children must first assume the role of the adult in charge in order to try to get their parents to reverse roles (Dubois-Comtois, Cyr & Moss, 2011; George & Solomon, 2008). Representational assessments of these children's attachment relationships with their parents suggest, however, that their hopes are dashed and they remain feeling unprotected, vulnerable, out of control, and helpless to protect themselves (Solomon, George & De Jong, 1995).

The other form is *constricted*. Constricted caregiving is conceived of as a brittle defensive guard or heightening of segregating exclusion processes that prevents dysregulated representational and behavioural states from emerging (George & Solomon, 2008; Solomon, George & De Jong, 1995). Constriction appears to prevent parents from thinking about how they and their children both contribute to their relationship. Constricted thinking is associated with constricted parenting behaviour, such as totally removing themselves from parenting situations (e.g., locking themselves in the bathroom), often leaving the child in distress, in order to prevent breaking down and losing self-control (George & Solomon, 2008). These parents can also expect their children to take over parenting responsibilities, evaluating children as perfect and possessing precocious and amazing, sometimes supernatural, abilities to manage and control people and situations in which the mother would have been incompetent (i.e., adultification, role reversal; (Ackerman & Dozier, 2005; George & Solomon, 2008). It follows then that parents describe feeling good about their relationships with their children over time and describe their children as very adaptable (Dubois-Comtois, Cyr & Moss, 2011). They may also psychologically merge with their children (e.g., 'we have a special understanding of each other', 'the child and I are one'). Whether precociously competent or merged, constricted parents can only think of their children in terms of themselves, rendering their children and the caregiving-attachment relationship as invisible (George & Solomon, 2008).

As with helpless and out-of-control parenting, there is no information in the field of attachment to date that has established correlates of constricted parenting in infancy. By ages three to five years, the children's attachment patterns are described as *controlling-caregiving*. Frightened by their parents' incapacity to provide protection, but also threatened by parental disappearance and psychological invisibility as compared with hostile combat for the punitive children, it is understandable that these children develop gentle caregiving strategies to nurture and care for their parents. These strategies are thought to build parents' confidence and desire to step into the parent role, thus as with the other pattern providing children with hopes for protection (George & Solomon, 2008). Representational assessments of these children's attachment suggest that they may hang on to these hopes at all costs by constricting or refusing to think about how frightened and unprotected they feel (Solomon, George & De Jong, 1995). They will refuse to complete attachment story stems, often sitting on their hands, protesting that they do not know what to do, or stating that there are too many ways to tell attachment stories for them to decide (Solomon, George & De Jong, 1995).

Children with dysregulated attachments are at the highest developmental risk of any of the attachment patterns (Lyons-Ruth & Jacobvitz, 2008). For dysregulated dyads, reintegration blocked by the breakdown of the caregiving-attachment partnership, that is, behavioural systems collapse (Solomon & George, 1996, 1999), is evidenced by role reversal or disorientation in toddlerhood and continuing into middle childhood and beyond (Bureau, Ann Easlerbrooks & Lyons-Ruth, 2009; Henninghausen, Bureau, David et al., 2011; Macfie, Fitzpatrick, Rivas & Cox, 2008; Macfie, McElwain, Houts & Cox, 2005; Solomon & George, 2008). Disorganised attachment in infancy predicts dissociative symptoms and high psychopathology ratings in adolescence (Lyons-Ruth & Jacobvitz, 2008).

Research that differentiates between the two forms of dysregulation shows that controlling-punitive children typically are at the greatest levels of developmental risk. The punitive parent–child dyads show the poorest levels of communication of all the caregiving-attachment groups (Dubois-Comtois, Cyr & Moss, 2011; George & Solomon, 2016). Coordination, affective quality, praise and affirmation were reported to be especially lacking in dyads in controlling-punitive subgroup, with maternal communications and interactions described as the most inconsistent, role-reversed, role inappropriate, and incongruent (Moss, Rousseau, Parent et al., 1998; Moss & St-Laurent, 2001; Solomon, George & Silverman, 1990). Punitive children's social–emotional problems include fussiness and disruptive behaviour, internalising and externalising problems; peer aggression; defiance; coercion, poor self-esteem, poor social competence, and fantasies of helplessness, destruction and death (Dubois-Comtois, Cyr & Moss, 2011; Lyons-Ruth & Jacobvitz, 2008; Solomon, George & De Jong, 1995). Children in this attachment group were the only children to be at academic risk when they reached school age, suggesting that in the absence of IQ differences these children are not able to consolidate and integrate cognitive skills, which later are associated with metacognitive thinking and abstract thought (Dubois-Comtois, Moss, Cyr & Pascuzzo, 2013; Moss, Bureau, Béliveau et al., 2009).

The constricted strategies of controlling-caregiving children appear, at least on the surface, to serve them well in terms of developmental risk. Parent–child dyadic communication and synchrony are as poor as in punitive dyads, however, they are not evaluated by parents or teachers as showing elevated levels of externalising social–emotional risk (Dubois-Comtois, Cyr & Moss, 2011; George & Solomon, 2016). Externalising problems, including overt signs of anger and disruption, are likely low because this behaviour could be threatening to parents and make them even more physically and psychological invisible (Dubois-Comtois, Cyr & Moss, 2011; George & Solomon, 2011). Whether or not the controlling-caregiving pattern is associated with internalising risk is unclear, and their empathy and caregiving demeanour can be refreshing and pleasing to other children and adults alike (Dubois-Comtois, Cyr & Moss, 2011; George & Solomon, 2011). These children have not been found to be at academic risk; however they do seem to express lower levels of mastery motivation than secure children (Dubois-Comtois, Cyr & Moss, 2011).

The Attachment Component in Evaluating Parenting

Observing the quality and characteristics of parenting through the attachment theory lens can provide a fundamental perspective in understanding the roles of both distress and mutual enjoyment in child–parent relationships. Behaviour that might otherwise be interpreted as dependent or manipulative is viewed as fundamental to achieving the physical and psychological proximity required to feel safe and foster development.

Therapeutic practice that integrates an attachment perspective necessitates the use of validated assessments the can be used systemically to make informed recommendations for treatment based on the established empirical evidence of children's developmental outcomes as associated with different attachment patterns. The need is the greatest when family systems are high risk for maltreatment and/or when evaluations and recommendations have legal implications for interrupting or blocking access to parents (McIntosh, 2011).

This final chapter section provides a brief synopsis of the attachment assessments most frequently used to evaluate parenting from an attachment perspective. Attachment is a relationship model; it represents the intersection and synchrony established between parents and their children. These assessments are relationship-specific; they provide information about the parent's relationship with a particular child. There are behavioural and representational measures of parent–child interaction or parent-caregiving representations that elucidate the patterns described earlier in this chapter. A summary of these measures is shown in Table 14.1.

Table 14.1 Parenting interaction and representational assessments.

Age of Child	Method	Patterns identified	Kind of information provided	Length of assessment	Use requirements	Training
Parenting Behaviour – Naturalistic Observation						
Infant/toddler through age 7 yrs	Structured parent–child separation & reunion; toy clean-up[1]	Secure; Organised-insecure (avoidant, ambivalent-resistant); Disorganised/dysregulated	▲Attachment 'in action' when the dyad is under stress ▲Interactive rating scales: e.g., proximity seeking, contact maintaining, disorganisation	▲~30 minutes ▲Analysed from video	▲Observation or unfamiliar consulting room ▲Stranger & toys ▲Video	▲Training to administer ▲Interpretation training required *or* reliable evaluators are available for scoring
Parent Caregiving – Representational Assessments						
Adolescent and adult parents of children aged infant to adolescent	Caregiving Interview[2]	Caregiving groups associated with children's attachment: Secure; Organised-insecure (distanced; heightened); Helpless	▲Descriptions and parents' evaluations of parenting and interaction with child	▲60 minutes ▲Evaluated from transcript	▲Interview protocol ▲Private space, individualised administration ▲Audio tape transcription	▲Training to administer ▲Interpretation training required *or* reliable evaluators are available for scoring
Adult parents of children ages infant–12	Caregiving Helplessness Questionnaire (CHQ)[3]	3 dysregulation scales: Helpless; Parent–child frightened; Child caregiving	▲3 scales indicating risk of disorganised caregiving	▲10 minutes, 26 items	▲CHQ questionnaire	▲Administration: paper and pencil, or administrator reads and fills out for parent
Adult parents of children infant–preschool	Parent Development Interview[4]	▲Parent interactive scales (e.g., sensitivity) + states of mind scales	▲Transcript record of perceptions and evaluations of parenting	▲60 minutes ▲Evaluated from transcript	▲Interview protocol ▲Private space ▲Audio tape ▲Transcription	▲Interpretation training required *or* reliable evaluators are available for scoring

| Adult parents of young children with disabilities | Reaction to Diagnosis Interview[5] | ▶ Parent's ability to 'resolve' a child's disability diagnosis (i.e., re-organise parenting) | ▶ Transcript record of parent's response to diagnosis | ▶ 60 minutes
▶ Evaluated from transcript | ▶ Interview protocol
▶ Private space
▶ Audio tape
▶ Transcription | ▶ Scoring instructions available from author |

[1] Ainsworth, Blehar, Waters & Wall, 1978; Britner, Marvin & Pianta, 2005; Main & Cassidy, 1990.
[2] George & Solomon, 1989, 2008.
[3] George & Solomon, 2011.
[4] Slade, Belsky, Aber & Phelps, 1999; Pianta, Marvin, Britner & Borowitz, 1996.
[5] Pianta, Marvin, Britner & Borowitz, 1996.

Parent and Parent–Child Interaction Measures

Behavioural Parenting Assessments. Several good frameworks exist for guiding and evaluating observations of parent response to the child in play and response to 'reunion' after parent–child separation. These observations support evaluations of the parent's reciprocal interactive behaviour that complements our understanding of the child's attachment pattern (Britner, Marvin & Pianta, 2005; Main & Cassidy, 1988).

Representational Parenting Assessments. Parenting representations encompass parents' current thoughts, feelings and evaluations of being the parent of a particular child. Like interactive behaviour, caregiving representations are relationship-specific. Parenting representations are most often assessed through clinical-style interview. Interviews provide information about caregiving events that may be ambiguous or not observable during home visits or other settings (e.g., separation and reunion, stressful parenting situations such as parents getting ready for work or mealtimes) (George & Solomon, 1989, 1996, 2008; Grienenberger, Kelly & Slade, 2005; Pianta, Marvin, Britner & Borowitz, 1996; Pianta, Marvin & Mong, 1999; Slade, Belsky, Aber & Phelps, 1999). Interviews provide information not only about events but also importantly the meanings that parents' associate with these events. Interviews also provide practitioners' access to parents' affects about being a parent, which can be obscured or even manipulated during observations of parent–child interactions.

The *Caregiving Interview* (George & Solomon, 1996, 2008) identifies caregiving patterns associated with the attachment groups described at the beginning of this chapter. It can be used to provide an overall group placement of parents' caregiving (i.e., flexible, inflexible, dysregulated). One of the most elegant features of this approach is the interview's capacity to evaluate the complete range of caregiving patterns that underscore parenting strengths and difficulties rather than just assigning parents to a single prototypic group.

Conclusions

This chapter provides a comprehensive view of how to utilise an attachment theory perspective in assessing parenting. The attachment approach is grounded in human evolution and attachment patterns are conceived as manifestations of emotion and neurobiological regulation patterns, a model that has been substantiated by over 40 years of empirical scrutiny. Valid attachment assessments used systemically with parents can be especially important for making recommendations, especially when children's mental and developmental health, trauma, and access to parents are concerned. Identification of these patterns can help practitioners develop recommendations to support parenting flexibility and strategies for organising dysregulated relationships and risk factors for insecurity in the family system. This approach can help pinpoint how to support parents by capitalising on their strengths and interrupt the risk of perpetuating traumatic parenting cycles.

References

Ackerman, J.P. & Dozier, M. (2005). The influence of foster parent investment on children's representations of self and attachment figures. *Journal of Applied Developmental Psychology*, 26, 507–520.

Ainsworth, M.D.S. (1989). Attachment beyond infancy. *American Psychologist*, 44, 709–716.

Ainsworth, M.D.S., Blehar, M., Waters, E. & Wall, S. (1978). *Patterns of Attachment: A Psychological Study of the Strange Situation.* Hillsdale, NJ: Erlbaum.

Bakermans-Kranenburg, M.J., van IJzendoorn, M.H. & Juffer, F. (2003). Less is more: Meta-analyses of sensitivity and attachment interventions in early childhood. *Psychological Bulletin*, 129, 195–215.

Behrens, K.Y., Parker, A.C. & Haltigan, J.D. (2011). Maternal sensitivity assessed during the Strange Situation Procedure predicts child's attachment quality and reunion behaviors. *Infant Behavior and Development*, 34, 378–381.

Bernier, A. & Dozier, M. (2003). Bridging the attachment transmission gap: The role of maternal mind-mindedness. *International Journal of Behavioral Development*, 27, 355–365.

Bigelow, A.E., MacLean, K., Proctor, J. et al. (2010). Maternal sensitivity throughout infancy: Continuity and relation to attachment security. *Infant Behavior and Development*, 33, 50–60.

Bowlby, J. (1969/1982). *Attachment and Loss: Vol. 1. Attachment.* New York: Basic Books.

Bowlby, J. (1973). *Attachment and Loss: Vol. 2. Separation: Anxiety and Anger.* New York: Basic Books.

Bowlby, J. (1980). *Attachment and Loss: Vol. 3. Loss: Sadness and Depression.* New York: Basic Books.

Bretherton, I. & Munholland, K.A. (2008). Internal working models in attachment relationships. In: J. Cassidy & P.R. Shaver (eds), *Handbook of Attachment: Theory, Research, and Clinical Applications*, 2nd edn. New York: Guilford Press, 102–127.

Britner, P.A., Marvin, R.S. & Pianta, R.C. (2005). Development and preliminary validation of the caregiving behavior system: Association with child attachment classification in the preschool Strange Situation. *Attachment and Human Development*, 7, 83–102.

Bureau, J.F., Ann Easlerbrooks, M. & Lyons-Ruth, K. (2009). Attachment disorganization and controlling behavior in middle childhood: Maternal and child precursors and correlates. *Attachment and Human Development*, 11, 265–284.

Bus, A.G. & van IJzendoorn, M.H. (1988). Mother-child interactions, attachment, and emergent literacy: A cross-sectional study. *Child Development*, 59, 1262–1272.

Cassidy, J. & Shaver, P.R. (eds) (2008). *Handbook of Attachment: Theory, Research and Clinical Applications.* New York: Guilford Press.

De Schipper, J.C., Oosterman, M. & Schuengel, C. (2012). Temperament, disordered attachment, and parental sensitivity in foster care: Differential findings on attachment security for shy children. *Attachment and Human Development*, 14, 349–365.

De Wolff, M.S. & van IJzendoorn, M.H. (1997). Sensitivity and attachment: A meta-analysis on parental antecedents of infant attachment. *Child Development*, 68, 571–591.

Dubois-Comtois, K. & Moss, E. (2008). Beyond the dyad: Do family interactions influence children's attachment representations in middle childhood? *Attachment and Human Development*, 10, 415–431.

Dubois-Comtois, K., Cyr, C. & Moss, E. (2011). Attachment behavior and mother-child conversations as predictors of attachment representations in middle childhood: A longitudinal study. *Attachment and Human Development*, 13, 335–357.

Dubois-Comtois, K., Moss, E., Cyr, C. & Pascuzzo, K. (2013). Behavior problems in middle childhood: The predictive role of maternal distress, child attachment, and mother-child interactions. *Journal of Abnormal Child Psychology*, 41, 1311–1324.

George, C. (1996). A representational perspective of child abuse and prevention: Internal working models of attachment and caregiving. *Child Abuse & Neglect*, 20, 411–424.

George, C. & Solomon, J. (1989). Internal working models of caregiving and security of attachment at age six. *Infant Mental Health Journal*, 10, 222–237.

George, C. & Solomon, J. (1996). Representational models of relationships: Links between caregiving and attachment. *Infant Mental Health Journal*, 17, 198–216.

George, C. & Solomon, J. (1999). Attachment and caregiving: The caregiving behavioral system. In: J. Cassidy & P.R. Shaver (eds), *Handbook of Attachment: Theory, Research, and Clinical Applications*, 1st edn. New York: Guilford Press, 649–670.

George, C. & Solomon, J. (2008). The caregiving system: A behavioral systems approach to parenting. In: J. Cassidy & P.R. Shaver (eds), *Handbook of Attachment: Theory, Research, and Clinical Applications*, 2nd edn. New York: Guilford Press, 833–856.

George, C. & Solomon, J. (2011). Caregiving helplessness: The development of a screening measure for disorganized maternal caregiving. In: J. Solomon & C. George (eds), *Disorganized Attachment and Caregiving*. New York: Guilford Press, 133–163.

George, C. & Solomon, J. (2015). The relationship between mothers' caregiving representations of sensitivity and helplessness, mother-child interaction, and attachment in 5-year olds. Manuscript in preparation.

George, C. & Solomon, J. (2016). The Attachment Doll Play Assessment (ADPA): Predictive validity for concurrent mother-child interaction and maternal caregiving representations. *Frontiers in Psychology*, 7.

George, C., Isaacs, M. & Marvin, R.S. (2011). Incorporating attachment assessment into custody evaluations: The case of a 2-year old and her parents. *Family Court Review*, 49, 483–500.

Grienenberger, J., Kelly, K. & Slade, A. (2005). Maternal reflective functioning, mother-infant affective communication, and infant attachment: Exploring the link between mental states and observed caregiving behavior in the intergenerational transmission of attachment. *Attachment and Human Development*, 7, 299–311.

Henninghausen, K.H., Bureau, J.F., David, D.H. et al. (2011). Disorganized attachment behavior observed in adolescence. In J.S.C. George (ed), *Disorganized Attachment and Caregiving*. New York: Guilford Press, 207–244.

Hesse, E. (2008). The Adult Attachment Interview: Protocol, methods of analysis, and empirical studies. In: J. Cassidy & P.R. Shaver (eds), *Handbook of Attachment: Theory, Research, and Clinical Applications*, 2nd edn. New York: Guilford Press, 552–598.

Huang, Z.J., Lewin, A., Mitchell, S.J. & Zhang, J. (2012). Variations in the relationship between maternal depression, maternal sensitivity, and child attachment by race/ethnicity and nativity: Findings from a nationally representative cohort study. *Maternal and Child Health Journal*, 16, 40–50.

Humber, N. & Moss, E. (2005). The relationship of preschool and early school age attachment to mother-child interaction. *American Journal of Orthopsychiatry*, 75, 128–141.

Jin, M.K., Jacobvitz, D., Hazen, N. & Jung, S.H. (2012). Maternal sensitivity and infant attachment security in Korea: Cross-cultural validation of the Strange Situation. *Attachment and Human Development*, 14, 33–44.

Kobak, R., Cassidy, J. & Ziv, Y. (2004). Attachment-related trauma and posttraumatic stress disorder: Implications for adult adaptation. In: W.S. Rholes & J.A. Simpson (eds), *Adult Attachment: Theory, Research, and Clinical Implications*. New York: Guilford Press, 388–407.

Koren-Karie, N., Oppenheim, D., Dolev, S. & Yirmiya, N. (2009). Mothers of securely attached children with autism spectrum disorder are more sensitive than mothers of insecurely attached children. *Journal of Child Psychology and Psychiatry*, 50, 643–650.

Leerkes, E.M. (2011). Maternal sensitivity during distressing tasks: A unique predictor of attachment security. *Infant Behavior and Development*, 34, 443–446.

Lucassen, N., Tharner, A., van IJzendoorn, M.H. et al. (2011). The association between paternal sensitivity and infant–father attachment security: A meta-analysis of three decades of research. *Journal of Family Psychology*, 25, 986–992.

Lutz, W.J. & Hock, E. (1995). Maternal separation anxiety: Relations to adult attachment representations in mothers of infants. *Journal of Genetic Psychology*, 156, 57–73.

Lyons-Ruth, K. & Jacobvitz, D. (2008). Attachment disorganization: Unresolved loss, relational violence, and lapses in behavioral and attentional strategies. In: J. Cassidy & P.R. Shaver (eds), *Handbook of Attachment: Theory, Research, and Clinical Applications*, 2nd edn. New York: Guilford Press, 666–697.

Lyons-Ruth, K. & Spielman, E. (2004). Disorganized infant attachment strategies and helpless-fearful profiles of parenting: Integrating attachment research with clinical intervention. *Infant Mental Health Journal*, 25, 318–335.

Macfie, J., Fitzpatrick, K.L., Rivas, E.M. & Cox, M.J. (2008). Independent influences upon mother-toddler role reversal: Infant-mother attachment disorganization and role reversal in mother's childhood. *Attachment and Human Development*, 10, 29–39.

Macfie, J., McElwain, N.L., Houts, R.M. & Cox, M.J. (2005). Intergenerational transmission of role reversal between parent and child: Dyadic and family systems internal working models. *Attachment and Human Development*, 7, 51–65.

Main, M. (1990). Cross-cultural studies of attachment organization: Recent studies, changing methodologies and the concept of conditional strategies. *Human Development*, 33, 48–61.

Main, M. & Cassidy, J. (1988). Categories of response to reunion with the parent at age 6: Predictable from infant attachment classifications and stable over a 1-month period. *Developmental Psychology*, 24, 1–12.

Main, M. & Solomon, J. (1990). Procedures for identifying infants as disorganized/disoriented during the Ainsworth Strange Situation. In: M.T. Greenberg, D. Cicchetti & E.M. Cummings (eds), *Attachment in the Preschool Years*. Chicago, IL: University of Chicago Press, 121–160.

Marvin, R.S. & Britner, P. (2008). Normative development: The ontogeny of attachment. In: J. Cassidy & P.R. Shaver (eds), *Handbook of Attachment: Theory, Research, and Clinical Applications*, 2nd edn. New York: Guilford Press, 269–294.

Marvin, R.S., Cooper, G., Hoffman, K. & Powell, B. (2002). The Circle of Security project: Attachment-based intervention with caregiver–pre-school child dyads. *Attachment and Human Development*, 4, 107–124.

McConnell, M. & Moss, E. (2011). Attachment across the life span: Factors that contribute to stability and change. *Australian Journal of Educational and Developmental Psychology*, 11, 60–77.

McElwain, N.L. & Booth-LaForce, C. (2006). Maternal sensitivity to infant distress and nondistress as predictors of infant-mother attachment security. *Journal of Family Psychology*, 20, 247–255.

McIntosh, J.E. (2011). Guest editor's introduction to special issue on attachment theory, separation, and divorce: Forging coherent understandings for family law. *Family Court Review*, 49, 418–425.

Mills-Koonce, W.R., Gariepy, J.-L., Sutton, K. & Cox, M.J. (2008). Changes in maternal sensitivity across the first three years: Are mothers from different attachment dyads differentially influenced by depressive symptomatology? *Attachment and Human Development*, 10, 299–317.

Moss, E. & St-Laurent, D. (2001). Attachment at school age and academic performance. *Developmental Psychology*, 37, 863–874.

Moss, E., St-Laurent, D. & Parent, S. (1999). Disorganized attachment and risk at school age. In: J.S.C. George (ed), *Disorganized Attachment*. New York: Guilford Press, 160–186.

Moss, E., Bureau, J.-F., Béliveau, M.-J. et al. (2009). Links between children's attachment behavior at early school-age, their attachment-related representations, and behavior problems in middle childhood. *International Journal of Behavioral Development*, 33, 155–166.

Moss, E., Rousseau, D., Parent, S. et al. (1998). Correlates of attachment at school age: Maternal reported stress, mother-child interaction, and behavior problems. *Child Development*, 69, 1390–1405.

NICHD (2001). Child-care and family predictors of preschool attachment and stability from infancy. *Developmental Psychology*, 31, 847–862.

Pederson, D.R. & Moran, G. (1996). Expressions of the attachment relationship outside of the Strange Situation. *Child Development*, 67, 915–927.

Pianta, R.C., Marvin, R.S. & Mong, M.C.(1999). Resolving the past and present: Relations with attachment organization. In: J. Solomon & C. George (eds), *Attachment Disorganization*. New York: Guilford Press, 379–398.

Pianta, R.C., Marvin, R.S., Britner, P. & Borowitz, K. (1996). Parents' reactions to their child's diagnosis: Relations with security of attachment. *Infant Mental Health Journal*, 17, 239–256.

Posada, G., Gao, Y., Wu, F. & Posada, R. (1995). The secure-base phenomenon across cultures: Children's behavior, mother's preferences, and experts' concepts. *Monographs of the Society for Research in Child Development*, 60, Serial No. 244, 27–48.

Slade, A., Belsky, J., Aber, J.L. & Phelps, J.L. (1999). Mothers' representations of their relationships with their toddlers: Links to adult attachment and observed mothering. *Developmental Psychology*, 35, 611–619.

Slade, A., Grienenberger, J., Bernbach, E. et al. (2005). Maternal reflective functioning, attachment, and the transmission gap: A preliminary study. *Attachment and Human Development*, 7, 283–298.

Solomon, J. & George, C. (1996). Defining the caregiving system: Toward a theory of caregiving. *Infant Mental Health Journal*, 17, 183–197.

Solomon, J. & George, C. (1999). The place of disorganization in attachment theory: Linking classic observations with contemporary findings. In: J. Solomon & C. George (eds) *Attachment Disorganization*. New York: Guilford Press, 3–32.

Solomon, J. & George, C. (2008). The measurement of attachment security in infancy and childhood. In: J. Cassidy & P.R. Shaver (eds), *Handbook of Attachment: Theory, Research, and Clinical Applications*, 2nd edn. New York: Guilford Press, 383–416.

Solomon, J. & George, C. (2011a). The disorganized attachment-caregiving system: Dysregulation of adaptive processes at multiple levels. In: J. Solomon & C. George (eds), *Disorganized Attachment and Caregiving*. New York: Guilford Press, 3–24.

Solomon, J. & George, C. (2011b). Dysregulation of maternal caregiving across two generations. In: J. Solomon & C. George (eds), *Disorganization of Attachment and Caregiving*. New York: Guilford Press, 25–51.

Solomon, J., George, C. & De Jong, A. (1995). Children classified as controlling at age six: Evidence of disorganized representational strategies and aggression at home and at school. *Development and Psychopathology*, 7, 447–463.

Solomon, J., George, C. & Silverman, N. (1990). *Maternal caretaking Q-sort: Describing age-related changes in mother-child interaction*. Unpublished manuscript.

Sroufe, L.A., Egeland, B., Carlson, E.A. & Collins, A.W. (2005). *The Development of the Person*. New York: Guilford Press.

Steinberg, D.R. & Pianta, R.C. (2006). Maternal representations of relationships: Assessing multiple parenting dimensions. In: O. Mayseless (ed), *Parenting Representations: Theory, Research, and Clinical Implications*. New York Cambridge University Press, 41–78.

Stevenson-Hinde, J. & Shouldice, A. (1995). Maternal interactions and self-reports related to attachment classifications at 4.5 years. *Child Development*, 66, 583–596.

Thompson, R.A. (2008). Early attachment and later development: Familiar questions, new answers. In: J. Cassidy & P.R. Shaver (eds), *Handbook of Attachment: Theory, Research and Clinical Applications*, 2nd edn. New York: Guilford Press, 348–365.

True, M.M., Pisani, L. & Oumar, F. (2001). Infant-mother attachment among the Dogon of Mali. *Child Development*, 72, 1451–1466.

Van IJzendoorn, M.H., Moran, G., Belsky, J. et al. (2000). The similarity of siblings' attachments to their mother. *Child Development*, 71, 1086–1098.

Von der Lippe, A., Eilertsen, D.E., Hartmann, E. & Killen, K. (2010). The role of maternal attachment in children's attachment and cognitive executive functioning: A preliminary study. *Attachment and Human Development*, 12, 429–444.

Weinfield, N.S., Sroufe, L.A., Egeland, B. & Carlson, E. (2008). Individual differences in infant-caregiver attachment. In: J. Cassidy & P.R. Shaver (eds), *Handbook of Attachment: Theory, Research, and Clinical Applications*, 2nd edn. New York: Guilford Press, 78–101.

15

Evidence-Based and Developmentally Appropriate Forensic Interviewing of Children

Annabelle Nicol[1], David La Rooy[2] and Michael E. Lamb[3]

[1] Abertay University
[2] Royal Holloway University of London
[3] University of Cambridge

The Need to Conduct Developmentally Appropriate Interviews

Forensic interviews are conducted with children when there is suspicion that they may have been abused or maltreated. The purpose of the forensic interview is to help determine whether or not something has happened to the child, to elicit an account(s) of the incident(s) if something has happened, and to ascertain whether the child is at any further risk and needs to be protected (Ministry of Justice, 2011; Scottish Executive, 2003, 2011). Who is considered an appropriate person to interview the child and the way that they are expected to conduct the interview varies across jurisdictions worldwide. Professionals such as police officers (Sternberg, Lamb, Davies & Westcott, 2001), social workers (Aldridge & Cameron, 1999), forensic psychologists, specialist child justice centre interviewers and specialist youth investigators from child crime units (Lamb, Hershkowitz, Sternberg et al., 1996b) conduct interviews with children in various countries around the world, and each interviewer will be expected to follow agreed practice guidelines of their country or organisation.

Interest in children's testimony has become a topic of public interest in recent years. An increased rate of reporting of child abuse and high estimates of abuse (11.3% of 18- to 24-year-olds in the UK reported experiencing sexual abuse before they turned 18; Aldridge & Cameron, 1999; NSPCC, 2015) has highlighted the need for children's testimony to be obtained appropriately. Additionally, high-profile cases in which risky interviewing practices led to false accusations of child sexual abuse were highly publicised in the media, sparking debate about whether or not children can be relied upon as eyewitnesses (see Schreiber, Bellah, Martinez et al., 2006, for a discussion of the McMartin Preschool and Kelly Michaels cases and also Kitzinger, 2000, for a discussion of the Cleveland and Orkney cases). This fuelled a wealth of laboratory and field studies, focusing on the competencies of children and the optimal conditions under which they can be afforded the best opportunity to provide accurate and reliable accounts of their experiences.

Children's Cognitive Competencies and Limitations

The forensic interview is primarily a test of memory because it involves asking children to recall events they have experienced. In order to understand how to best question children about suspected abuse, the development and dynamics of all aspects of how children remember their experiences must be understood, as well as the other factors that can impact children's ability to recount their experiences. The following section will focus on the strengths and limitations of these abilities during childhood.

Memory

There is evidence that different kinds of information are processed by different parts of the brain. Localised brain damage has been shown to affect performance on some memory tasks, while performance on other types of memory tasks remains unaffected (Scoville & Milner, 1957). This has led to a categorisation of memory systems, with a main dichotomy proposed between procedural memory and declarative memory. *Procedural memory* relates to skills and habits that require no conscious awareness to transfer to memory and no conscious effort to recall or utilise the knowledge in the present. *Declarative memory* relates to data-based materials, facts and knowledge, and memories of experienced events that require thought or directed conscious attention to bring back into conscious awareness and to utilise the information stored.

In 1972, Endel Tulving proposed that declarative memory can be further categorised into subsystems: working memory, semantic memory and episodic memory. *Working memory* is a short-term store that actively holds multiple pieces of transitory information in the mind, where they can be manipulated. *Semantic memory* processes facts and knowledge while *episodic memory* represents memory for our experiences and specific autobiographical events. Age differences in declarative memory have long been noted; generally, older children and adults perform better on memory such tests than younger children. Brainerd, Kingma and Howe (1985) noted that, while both storage and retrieval processes improve through early childhood to adolescence, the largest improvement in storage processes happens in the preschool years while improvements in retrieval processes occur during middle childhood and adolescence. Therefore, older children's superior memory abilities may reflect 'retrieval forgetting' rather than 'storage forgetting' and, while the memory trace may still be available to the younger children, their poorer performance may reflect the lack of an 'algorithm' or 'retrieval cue' required to access the memory.

These studies tested children's retention and recognition performance on word lists. When interviewing a child in forensic contexts, interviewers aim to elicit an eyewitness account of a personally experienced event or series of events, stored in episodic memory. Episodic memory is a late-developing memory system that emerges gradually over the preschool years (Nelson & Fivush, 2004; Tulving, 2002b). It is difficult to establish exactly when children begin to use episodic memory, as some of Tulving's criteria specify the need for autonoetic consciousness (an awareness that this event happened to 'me' in the past that does not accompany retrieval of other kinds of memories; Tulving, 2002a, 2002b) and chronesthesia (a consciousness that allows the rememberer to mentally time travel not only backwards but also forwards). Without verbal reporting, it is difficult to determine whether young children are engaged in episodic or some other form of memory. Tulving (2002b) and other commentators (Nelson 1993; Nelson & Fivush, 2004; Perner & Ruffman, 1995) believe that until roughly four years of age, children are not capable of forming and retaining episodic memories. Others have argued that children as young as three years of age do possess at least a rudimentary form of episodic memory (Russell & Hanna, 2012; Scarf, Gross, Colombo & Hayne, 2013).

Preschool children must undergo substantial brain and neurological maturation before they have the facilities to support episodic memory. Neurological developments in structures that are not fully developed at birth contribute to this emerging faculty. These include the hippocampus, which is thought to be of particular importance to encoding new episodic memories (Usher & Neisser, 1993), and the prefrontal cortex, which plays a specific role in retrieval and in memory for temporal order (Carver & Bauer, 2001). However, biological factors alone do not account for the appearance of episodic memory; social and cultural factors, the development of language and the developing sense of self also contribute to its emergence.

When asked about their past experiences, young children may rely on 'scripts', reporting what usually occurs instead of reporting details of specific experiences, using the general 'you' and present tense ('You do x'; Hudson, Fivush & Kuebli, 1992). Even very young children have general, well-organised scripts that are organised in a qualitatively similar manner to those of older children and adults, although usually less complete (Hudson, Fivush & Kuebli, 1992). When children recall details that occurred in a specific occurrence of a repeated experience, fixed items (details that are the same every time) are well remembered while variable items (details of repeated items that change in different occurrences, e.g., ordering a cheeseburger on one trip to McDonald's and Chicken McNuggets on another) are commonly misattributed to the incorrect time (Connolly & Lindsay, 2001). According to the schema confirmation-deployment model (Farrar & Goodman, 1990), children should be able to recall new items (unique to a specific occurrence) because they are inconsistent with an already formed script of a repeated experience and so are episodically encoded, leading to enhanced memory for these details. Brubacher, Glisic, Roberts and Powell (2011) found children were better at attributing new details (details that only occurred in one instance of a repeated play event) to the correct time they had experienced them than they were for details that were variable across events. These findings are consistent with the idea that basic episodic memory, as evidenced in young children, is thought to be part of a general episodic-like memory that becomes more script-like if similar experiences occur (Nelson & Hudson, 1988).

Many researchers, however, have found that preschoolers can retain memories for specific unique episodes and recall their experiences in great detail. Hamond and Fivush (1991) interviewed three- to five-year-olds who had visited Disneyland either 6 or 18 months earlier, when they were between 33 and 54 months of age. Children recalled a mean of 40 propositions and inaccuracies were 'virtually non-existent' (p. 437). There was no effect of age or retention interval; even the youngest children gave highly accurate and detailed accounts of personally experienced events even after an 18-month delay, performing as well as older peers who experienced only a six-month delay. Similarly, Fivush, Gray and Fromhoff (1987) asked 29- to 35-month-olds about events that they had experienced only once or twice. Approximately half of the events were recent (up to three months previously) and half distant (occurring more than three months beforehand). The children recalled as much about distant events as they did about recent events; all children recalled at least one event that occurred more than six months earlier, demonstrating that young children are capable of remembering personally experienced events, even when they have only been experienced once. This has led researchers to theorise that the nature of experiences plays a role in how long they are remembered. For example, going to Disneyland may well be remembered because it is likely to arouse positive emotions in the children (Hamond & Fivush, 1991), while Fivush, Gray & Fromhoff (1987) similarly asked the children in their study about events such as trips to the zoo or their birthday parties. These events were all of a meaningful and personally salient nature, and these features likely played a role in their high memorability (nature of events to be recalled will be covered later in this chapter).

Indeed, age-related differences have been found in preschoolers' memories for laboratory play events, which may be less personally meaningful. Hayne and Imuta (2011) asked When–What–Where questions about children's experiences of hiding some toys and also provided them the opportunity to non-verbally demonstrate their memory by finding the toys they had watched the interviewer hide. Four-year-olds were superior to the three-year-olds in verbal recall; however, non-verbally they only outperformed the 3-year-olds on the test of 'when' (the order in which the toys were hidden). Reliance on verbal recall underestimates younger children's memory abilities; while they were not as able to verbally recall the event, their ability to behaviourally demonstrate their memory of it shows they are capable of remembering single episodes that have happened to them at an earlier point in time. These findings also raise an important question relating to language and memory; can the experiences of pre-verbal infants be recalled verbally once sufficient language skills have developed?

Language

As children grow older, their ability to recall personally experienced events improves – and this improvement coincides with the development of language. Children begin to reminisce with adults about their past experiences, and this rehearsal and repetition is known to consolidate memory. The development of language skills must thus play a crucial role in forming memories of experiences (Nelson, 1993).

Language also allows us to organise our experiences into a coherent form aiding retention of entire experiences rather than fragments. As causal understanding of the narrative structure of an event improves, memory for the event has been shown to also improve (Fivush & Hamond, 1990). The superior performance of older children at recalling episodic memories can be thus attributed in part to increased understanding of the relationships between the individual components of events. Pillemer, Picariello and Pruett (1994) interviewed 3½- and 4½-year-olds about their experience of an emergency evacuation at preschool, both two weeks later and after seven years. Only the older children, whose first interview narratives showed evidence of temporal and causal understanding of the evacuation at the time, were able to produce an intact narrative account of the event after a seven-year delay. This suggests that comprehension of an experience aids its retention; the children who did not show comprehension of the event when they experienced it were not able to recall it at a later date (also see Murachver, Pipe, Gordon et al., 1996). These findings have important implications for forensic interviewing; investigative interviewers must be sensitive to the fact that children's age at the time of the interview may not necessarily predict their ability to provide a logical account of what has happened to them. Children are more likely to report things that they understand and actions that are connected logically; if there has been a delay between the abuse and interview, despite having since gained the skills necessary to report what they have experienced, they may not have understood the abusive events that happened to them at the time of their occurrence, making them less likely to be recalled at a later date.

Furthermore, it has been hypothesised that the development of language actually supports the development of verbally accessible memory. Simcock and Hayne (2002) tested 2- to 3-year-old children's verbal and non-verbal memory of participating in a novel event (playing the game 'magic shrinking machine') after either a 6- or 12-month delay, during which time the children's language skills had improved to the point that they could easily produce the target words necessary to describe the event. The children demonstrated that they remembered the event by behaviourally re-enacting the game, but did not perform so well when asked to verbally recall the event. Despite having developed the language skills necessary to describe the event, none of the children ever used any word in their verbal recall that had not been part of their vocabulary at the time of encoding the event – they instead relied on non-verbal representations. Children appear unable to turn their pre-verbal memories into language, which may be what prevents these experiences from becoming part of autobiographical memory.

Peterson and Rideout (1998) similarly found that 18- to 24-month-olds who had language skills at the time they experienced an injury and hospital treatment could recall the incident a year later, while children who were pre-verbal at the initial experience could not. Conversely, studies in which children engaged in conversations with adults while participating in events (e.g., trips to a museum) have shown that aspects of the events not discussed during their occurrence were not recalled later (Haden, Ornstein, Eckerman & Didow, 2001; Tessler & Nelson, 1994).

Language allows us to share our experiences with others. Complex questions, as indexed by the way they are worded or the content they contain, can undermine children's recollections. When children are asked questions that are too complicated for them to understand, they do not have the opportunity to express the information they may possess. For example, Saywitz and Camparo (1998) describe a court case in which a preschooler denied seeing a *weapon* at a crime scene, but answered 'yes' when asked if he saw a *gun*.

In addition to failing to obtain knowledge held by children, asking developmentally inappropriate questions can further undermine their competency because they tend to answer questions even if they do not understand what they are being asked (Hughes & Grieve, 1980; Pratt, 1990). This may be in part due to the difficulty children have when it comes to comprehension monitoring; that is, they may not yet have the skills necessary to identify when they do not understand the question they are being asked, particularly when they are being asked complex questions (Perry, McAuliffe, Tam et al., 1995). Researchers have attempted to teach children to engage in comprehension monitoring (CMT) by showing them how to identify confusing questions. Peters and Nunez (1999) found that when CMT was coupled with TDT (task demand training), which emphasises that adults make mistakes and children should tell the interviewer when they do not know, children requested question rephrasing more often than children trained in TDT alone.

Self-relevance, personal salience and delay

Once children have developed the relevant language skills to be able to describe their experiences, one should not assume that they will be able to recall everything that they have experienced, as some aspects of our experiences are more likely to be remembered than others. Memory is facilitated by a self-referencing bias; events are better remembered when they were actively participated in than when observed. Tobey and Goodman (1992) questioned four-year-olds either about their own personal experience of interacting with a 'babysitter' or about another four-year-old's experience of interacting with a 'babysitter' who they had watched on videotape. When questioned, those who had directly participated in an encounter with the babysitter recalled the actions that happened during the encounter more accurately and were less suggestible than those who had only watched the encounter.

The organisation of episodic memories is temporal and loose so they are more vulnerable to decay and modification than other types of memory. Memory decay or forgetting occurs rapidly after experiencing an event so delay in being asked to recall can have a serious impact on the amount and accuracy of the information recalled, unless the event undergoes rehearsal in memory, thus strengthening the memory trace. It is thus not surprising that recall delay has attracted considerable attention from researchers (Fivush, McDermott Sales, Goldberg et al., 2004; Goodman, Batterman-Faunce, Schaaf & Kenney, 2002; Jack, Simcock & Hayne, 2012; Quas, Goodman, Bidrose et al., 1999; Van Abbema & Bauer, 2005).

Flin, Boon, Knox and Bull (1992) examined memory for events after both short and long delays. They interviewed six-year-olds, nine-year-olds and adults about a staged event. No group differences in accuracy were found between age groups when participants were interviewed the following day. Interviews occurring five months later revealed that children had forgotten more and were less accurate than adults. The accuracy of the six-year-old participants reduced to a greater extent when compared to the nine-year-olds. Interestingly, following the delay, all participants in all age groups acquiesced to suggestive questions more than they had in the initial interview.

Peterson and colleagues studied children's memory for a naturally occurring stressful event after delays of up to five years. These memories were self-relevant, personally salient and upsetting, making them comparable to children's testimony in forensic contexts. Peterson (1996) interviewed two- to nine-year-olds about their memories of sustaining injuries and the subsequent treatment they received in the hospital, both after a short delay (two to five days) and a long delay (six months). The initial interviews were more accurate than after the six-month delay, but the later inaccuracies were related to the hospital treatment and all children were 100% accurate when reporting information about the events surrounding the sustaining of the injury after both the short and long delay. Therefore, salient features of personally relevant events may be well remembered, even by very young children (two to three years old). Interestingly, none of the errors was made in the children's free recall; they all came when the children were directly questioned. Two years later, all the children were re-interviewed and some received an extra interview one year after the target event (Peterson, 1999). All children recalled just as much information two years later as they did initially, but were less accurate. Accuracy rates for children that had participated in just three interviews fell from 98% to 80%, while the children who received the extra interview had slightly less of a drop in accuracy from 95% to 83%.

Even though the children's accuracy in these studies decreased after delays (at least for the peripheral components of their experiences), this was also true for the adults in Flin, Boon, Knox and Bull's (1992) study. The accuracy rates for the injuries themselves remained at 100% when discussing the injury event even after six months. Therefore, the type of event being recalled seems to be one of the most important factors affecting the quality of recall. When participants were asked to freely recall their experiences, they were highly accurate, but the way questions were posed affected the accuracy of the children's answers. Direct or focused questions were more likely to elicit inaccuracies than prompts for free recall, whether asked of children or adults. In addition, risky question types (i.e., those that may increase suggestibility) were more problematic when compounded with delay.

Suggestibility

Memory is a reconstructive process (Roediger & McDermott, 1995). This is one of the reasons why the type of question asked can exert such a powerful influence on our memories. Memories can be shaped and changed simply by mental rehearsal or by recalling and discussing them with others, even when no suggestive questions have been posed. This means that influences from others, whether direct or indirect, can affect the accuracy of our memories. Suggestibility can be manifest in different forms: memories for experiences can be altered through the presentation of misleading information or by hearing post-event information, which can be incorporated into memory traces. In other situations, people may come to believe that they have actually experienced entire non-experienced events; these memories are known as 'false memories'. Suggestive techniques such as imagining partaking in events, or being questioned repeatedly about the events by someone who communicates their belief that they really happened, can also play a role in the development of false memories.

Factors thought to be involved in vulnerability or resistance to suggestion are complex, and they may also interact with other factors to enhance the likelihood that suggestions will be acquiesced to or resisted. Suggestibility is negatively correlated with greater cognitive capacity such as source monitoring ability (the ability to distinguish the origin or source of information; Giles, Gopnik & Heyman, 2002), pre-existing knowledge about experienced events (Goodman, Quas, Batterman-Faunce et al., 1997), cognitive inhibitory control (Melinder, Endestad & Magnussen, 2006) and intelligence (Chae, Goodman, Eisen & Qin, 2011). Cognitive factors that are still under-developed in children and improve with age may, in part, explain age differences in suggestibility, with preschoolers seeming to be the most vulnerable to misleading information (Bjorklund, Cassel, Bjorklund, et al., 2000; Ceci & Bruck, 1993). However, is it important to note that under certain conditions no such age differences have been found; indeed, research has sometimes shown 'reverse developmental effects' where conversely older children and adults have been more susceptible to certain types of suggestions than younger children (Brainerd, Reyna & Ceci, 2008; Otgaar, Howe, Peters et al., 2013).

Other explanations of suggestibility are psychosocial ones; acquiescence to interviewers' suggestions may not reflect changes to existing memories, but merely changes to the responses given (see McCloskey & Zaragoza, 1985, for their discussion on misleading post-event information influencing response choice as opposed to memory traces). Personality factors, such as compliance or low self-esteem, may also be influential. Children may feel that interviewers are authority figures or want to please them, for example, by changing their answers when asked repeated questions (Bjorklund, Bjorklund, Brown & Cassel, 1998).

In addition to the cognitive and social factors that can have an effect on children's vulnerability to suggestibility, researchers have considered whether abuse status (the type of abuse children have experienced) has any effect on children's suggestibility. The few studies comparing abused and non-abused children's recall of episodic memories have revealed consistent results: abuse status does not predict memory or suggestibility in children. This is true for recall of both neutral interactive events (Chae, Goodman, Eisen & Qin, 2011; Goodman, Bottoms, Rudy et al., 2001) and stressful events (Eisen, Goodman, Qin et al., 2007; Eisen, Qin, Goodman & Davis, 2002). There were thus no significant differences between abused and non-abused children's correct recall in response to free-recall questions, the number of errors made in response to specific questions, or the number of incorrect responses to misleading questions. Chae, Goodman, Eisen and Qin (2011) reported instead that children's level of general cognitive functioning (based on a composite score generated from the results of tests of short-term memory, intelligence and receptive verbal comprehension) was associated with suggestibility; children with lower cognitive functioning made more errors in response to misleading questions. Maltreated children appear no better or worse than their non-maltreated peers when asked to recall both neutral and traumatic events.

It should be noted that sexually and physically abused children provided more correct information in response to open-ended questions, made fewer omission errors, and were less suggestible than neglected children (Eisen, Goodman, Qin et al., 2007). It has been theorised that neglected children may perform worse on a variety of tasks including those assessing memory because neglected children have suffered from a lack of parental attention to their basic needs, which may have jeopardised their cognitive functioning (Gaudin, 1999). However, the paucity of research on the short- and long-term effects of child neglect means that more research is needed in this area before any firm conclusions can be drawn.

While undoubtedly many factors such as age, linguistic proficiency, number of times an event has been experienced, comprehension of the event at the time it took place and the length of the delay between the event and time of questioning will impact children's ability to remember and describe their experiences, there are ways interviewers can capitalise on children's strengths to maximise the quality of the information they elicit in the forensic interview. The most appropriate way to question children and to structure interviews will be the focus of the remainder of this chapter.

Interviewing Strategies

Research has shown that the way children are questioned may be as important as their underlying cognitive skills. In comparison with older children, less information may be gleaned from younger children who may also be more suggestible; however, when questioned appropriately, all children are capable of providing detailed and accurate reports about their experiences. Many guidelines have been established in order to guide interviewers through the task of conducting developmentally appropriate interviews, and most converge on a similar basic structure (see for example: Achieving Best Evidence (ABE), Office for Criminal Justice Reform, 2011; The Memorandum of Good Practice (MOGP), Home Office, 1992; National Institute of Child Health and Human Development (NICHD) Protocol, Lamb, Orbach, Hershkowitz et al., 2007a; Scottish Executive Guidelines: Guidance on Interviewing Child Witnesses in Scotland, 2003; Guidance on Joint Investigative Interviewing of Child Witnesses in Scotland, 2011). All advocate a rapport-building phase to engage children and put them at ease, the eliciting of a narrative account of what happened in the children's own words, focused questions delayed until the end, and a closure phase where neutral topics are discussed before the interview ends.

Introductions

The rapport phase serves a variety of important functions: putting the children at ease, allowing interviewers to gauge the children's capabilities (e.g., their language skills) and to adapt their questioning to meet the children's needs if necessary. Interviewers can gauge children's willingness to talk and may wish to spend longer in this phase with reluctant children. This phase also provides the opportunity to set out the purpose, 'ground rules', and roles and expectations regarding the interview.

The forensic interview is an unusual situation for children for many reasons. Children are not used to correcting adults and need to be told it is acceptable for them to do so. Also, children are used to being questioned by adults about topics that they already know the answers to and children are encouraged to guess if they do not know the correct answer. In forensic situations, this is problematic, which is why interviewers are advised to establish ground rules such as 'correct me if I make a mistake' and 'don't guess', before questioning children, in order to prepare them for their role as informants.

Brubacher, Poole and Dickinson (2015) conducted a review of the research on ground rules, concluding that more research is needed with different populations in order to learn how to deliver them most effectively. The relevant skills that children must possess in order to understand and to utilise these instructions, such as theory of mind and metacognition, may not yet be developed in some age groups, therefore, not all children will benefit from the standardised delivery. Once ground rules have been established, a practice interview (otherwise known as narrative elaboration training) is recommended. The topic for the practice interview should be a neutral, personally experienced event, such as a birthday party or a holiday celebration. If possible, interviewers should pick events that took place near in time to the event(s) under investigation; allowing interviewers to gauge whether the children are able to remember events from the relevant timeframe. The interviewers should ask children to describe the events from beginning to end using open questions, thereby providing opportunities to practice the narrative style that will be used in the substantive phase of the interviews as this is not the usual style of responding to adults' questions.

Price, Roberts and Collins (2013) found that children provided more details in response to substantive open-ended prompts when practice narratives preceded them, compared to when no practice narrative was conducted. The relationship was enhanced when the practice narratives were conducted as recommended (i.e., 60% or more of the prompts were open-ended). Overall, the mean number of details elicited was almost five times greater when practice interviews were conducted. Similarly, Sternberg, Lamb, Hershkowitz et al. (1997) found that when interviewers built rapport using open prompts, children provided 2½ times as many details and words in response to the first substantive utterance. In addition, they continued to respond more informatively to open-ended utterances during the remainder of the interview, than did children whose rapport-building session involved direct questions, even though the rapport phases were of the same duration and covered the same topics.

Free-recall narrative account

After the introduction, accounts of each of the alleged incident(s) should be obtained, in the children's own words using open prompts. Open prompts are questions, statements or imperatives that are free from interviewer input or constraints, and so do not introduce information that has not already been mentioned by the children and do not dictate or limit what information children may disclose. Open questions probe recall memory, which requires respondents to conduct memory searches so as to provide as much relevant information as they 'remember', whereas focused questions involve recognition processes which do not require this search (Sternberg, Lamb, Hershkowitz et al., 1997).

Field studies conducted by Lamb and colleagues have shown that when interviewers use open questions with children, they elicit longer and more detailed responses from children than do directive, option-posing and suggestive questions (Lamb, Hershkowitz, Sternberg et al., 1996b; Sternberg, Lamb, Hershkowitz et al., 1996; Lamb, Orbach, Hershkowitz et al., 2007a, b). Importantly, when researchers can assess the accuracy of details provided in field interviews, it is clear that a high level of accuracy is also obtained (Orbach & Lamb, 1999), while more focused prompts are, in turn, more likely to elicit erroneous information (Lamb, Orbach, Hershkowitz et al., 2007b; Lamb & Fauchier, 2001; Orbach & Lamb, 1999, 2001).

Lamb, Orbach, Hershkowitz et al. (2007b) compared accounts provided by victims of child sexual abuse with the confessional accounts given by the perpetrators of the abuse in order to assess the convergence between the details provided. Each detail reported by the alleged victim was classified as confirmed, contradicted, ambiguous or ignored by the suspect. About 30% of the details elicited using open prompts (e.g., 'Tell me what happened') were confirmed by the suspects, making this type of prompt significantly superior to focused prompts with respect to the proportion of reported details that were confirmed. Additionally, although the superiority of open-ended utterances was even greater when older children were involved (Lamb, Hershkowitz, Sternberg et al., 1996b; Sternberg, Lamb, Hershkowitz et al., 1996), even preschoolers (who pose the greatest problems for investigators; Ceci & Bruck, 1995) respond to open prompts with longer and more detailed narratives than to focused questions (Orbach & Lamb, 2000).

The NICHD protocol (Lamb, Orbach, Hershkowitz et al., 2007a) provides examples of additional ways to enhance children's testimony using varied prompts and cues. Riskier focused questions are often unavoidable and may, in fact, be necessary in some cases, such as when children fail to mention details that interviewers intended to enquire about. It is recommended that these types of prompt are asked as late as possible in order to avoid contaminating the children's accounts. Open-prompts, however, are equally effective at any stage of the interview (Orbach & Lamb, 2000). This allows 'pairing' techniques to be used, with leading questions 'paired with' (i.e., followed by) open-ended prompts that return the child to free-recall responding. For example, when interviewers are investigating genital touching but children have only reported general touching, they may ask 'Were you touched anywhere else on your body?' and if the child responds affirmatively they can then 'pair' the previous question with an open prompt such as 'Tell me everything about that touching' (Lamb, Sternberg & Esplin, 1994).

Memories for repeated experiences often form 'scripts' (what usually happens). Thus, in the case of repeated abuse, interviewers need to use techniques that elicit individual accounts of separate incidents rather than 'gist' accounts. Separation of incidents should be achieved by using episodic prompts (Schneider, Price, Roberts & Hedrick, 2011) and unique labels associated with each different incident (e.g., 'the first time', 'the last time', or 'the time you said x happened' (Powell & McMeeken, 1998)). Further, these labels should be generated by the children themselves to prevent interviewers' cues biasing their memory searches (Brubacher, Malloy, Lamb & Roberts, 2013). Overall, children who have been abused repeatedly must be interviewed in a style designed to tap episodic rather than generic script memory.

Questioning

Focused questions or recognition prompts (such as option-posing 'yes/no' and 'forced-choice' questions), which require the child to affirm, negate or select an investigator-given option, are problematic. They rely on recognition memory processes, which do not require interviewees to search memory, but instead allow them to acquiesce and to guess the answers to questions (Waterman, Blades & Spencer, 2000). By their very definition, they allow the introduction of information (which in turn reflects the investigators' hypotheses). More problematically, they elicit erroneous information and allow interviewees to go along with misleading information (Brady, Poole, Warren & Jones, 1999; Waterman, Blades & Spencer, 2004). Studies in laboratory contexts have repeatedly shown that errors of commission are much more likely to occur when recognition memory is probed using focused questions (Dent, 1986; Dent & Stephenson, 1979; Oates & Shrimpton, 1991).

Lamb and Fauchier (2001) compared the details elicited in interviews of young children with details the same children provided later, in order to assess what types of questions elicited information most likely to be contradicted later. Significantly fewer details that were contradicted later were elicited using open prompts whereas suggestive questions elicited significantly more details that were later contradicted. Similarly, Orbach and Lamb (2001) looked at within-interview contradictions made by a five-year-old who had been asked an excessive number of repeated, leading and suggestive questions. Forty-one per cent of the option-posing and suggestive questions were involved in self-contradictions and 94% of the contradictory details were elicited using option-posing or suggestive utterances. Both studies found that details elicited using open-ended questions never contradicted earlier reported details.

Once an account of all alleged incidences has been elicited, the protocol recommends eliciting information about any disclosures that have been made prior to the interview. Eliciting information regarding prior disclosures is important for many reasons, such as (but not limited to) identifying additional witnesses who may be able to verify the account to build the case against the alleged perpetrator or in cases of delayed disclosure to enhance the child's credibility if the case goes to court, as a jury may be interested as to why a child may have delayed disclosing (Schaeffer, Leventhal & Asnes, 2011).

Closure

The closure phase of the interview should always be conducted, even if no disclosure is made or the children do not appear distressed. Neutral topics should be discussed. The children should be thanked for their participation and made aware of what will happen next, provided with contact details and offered the opportunity to ask any questions they may have.

Additional techniques

While interviewer aids such as anatomical dolls and body diagrams are still used in many interviews, their use is extremely controversial but it is beyond the scope of this chapter to cover all of the research on this topic. Much of the research regarding the appropriateness of such aids has been conducted in laboratory studies, because it is generally impossible to gain a measure of accuracy in field interviews, unless there is evidence in addition to the victim's testimony. Lamb, Hershkowitz, Sternberg et al. (1996a) compared field reports of abuse elicited from two groups of children (aged 4–12 years) interviewed either with or without an anatomical doll in an effort to determine the effect of anatomic doll use on the length (number of words) and richness (number of details) of the children's reports. They found that the group interviewed without the dolls gave longer and more detailed responses. This could suggest that the use of anatomical dolls, instead of facilitating children's accounts as they are designed to do, in fact may inhibit them. The authors' noted that they failed to find any clear benefits from using the dolls, and so suggested that caution should be exercised if any of these aids were used in forensic interviews.

Training

In order to qualify as forensic interviewers of children, child protection workers must undergo additional training to provide them with the knowledge and skills needed when conducting best-practice interviews with children. Typically, investigative interviewer courses are short intensive courses, completed in one stint, lasting for a few days or a week (Powell, Wright & Clark, 2010). While the content of individual courses varies, there are national standards and curricula that courses are expected to meet. All courses aim to impart background knowledge about issues pertinent to interviewing children such as the dynamics of child abuse, child development, children's memory and suggestibility, and the role of interviews in the wider context of the legal process. Participants may also be instructed in how to conduct a best-practice interview, perhaps with a focus on the ideal structure and the types of questions that are suitable for eliciting information from children. Finally, interviewers may have the opportunity to put what they have learnt into practice and conduct mock interviews, on which they will receive feedback from trainers (Aldridge & Cameron, 1999; Warren, Woodall, Thomas et al., 1999).

Despite the emphasis on educating trainees about the desirability of asking open questions and explaining the effect of the different types of question on children's testimony, most training does not have the desired effect on performance in actual forensic interviews. Field research has consistently shown that the quality of interviews with children is typically poor, with some studies reporting as little as 2.2% of all incident-related questions being open (Lamb, Hershkowitz, Sternberg et al., 1996b). Instead, interviewers typically rely on option-posing and suggestive questions, and structure their interviews poorly. This has been shown in Britain (Aldridge & Cameron, 1999; Sternberg, Lamb, Davies & Westcott, 2001), Sweden (Cederborg, Orbach, Sternberg & Lamb, 2000), Israel (Lamb, Hershkowitz, Sternberg et al., 1996b) and the US (Warren, Woodall, Thomas et al., 1999). Mastering the use of open prompts has proved a difficult task for interviewers, with myriad factors working against interviewers, including the natural tendency to ask focused questions (Powell, 2000a). Interviewers continue to maintain their use of focused prompts even when receiving little information from witnesses (Powell, 2008). Interestingly, even when interviewers have been instructed to employ open prompts in the pre-substantive phase of their interviews and thus elicited longer and more detailed responses from children, they still reverted back to using the more risky focused questions in the substantive phase of their interviews (Sternberg, Lamb, Hershkowitz et al., 1997).

Currently, training programmes are subject to time and financial constraints, with training, feedback, and ongoing practice and support often unavailable or inappropriate (Powell & Wright, 2008). One of the most important components of investigative interviewers' training is practising interviewing skills in a controlled environment where feedback can be provided, yet the mock interview formats used on training courses provide inconsistent opportunities to practice the necessary skills. Trainees may be given the opportunity to practice their interviewing skills on fellow trainees, on children recalling a neutral event only, or on adult actors playing the role of abused children.

While interviewers have reported that interviewing real children provides invaluable practice establishing rapport and familiarising them with talking to children, eliciting recall of a staged event does not present the same challenges as attempting to elicit disclosures of negative abusive events because, for example, the children did not require as much prompting (Powell & Wright, 2008). Concerns have also been raised about the use of adult respondents in mock interviews because their responses in simulated interviews often reflect superior memory and language skills than that typically portrayed by child witnesses in investigative interviews (Powell, 2002).

Powell, Cavezza, Hughes-Scholes and Stoové (2010) compared interviewers' performance in two mock interview contexts (a mock interview with an adult actor playing the role of an abused child and a mock interview with a real child recalling an innocuous event) with each other and against one of their field interviews. They found that performance was relatively stable; if problem behaviours were exhibited in one interview situation, interviewers were likely to exhibit the same problematic behaviours in other interview contexts. When it came to questioning behaviour, the adult-actor interviews produced performance that was more similar to the field interviews than did interviews in which schoolchildren recalled innocuous events. As mock interview exercises and field interviews prompt similar behaviours and questioning strategies, problematic behaviours and inappropriate questioning strategies should be apparent in training and can therefore be addressed and improved during training.

Not only are mock interviews with adult actors more similar to field interviews than other mock interviews contexts, they are also more effective contexts in which to reinforce best-practice questioning, provided that the adult respondents are trained to respond appropriately. Powell, Fisher and Hughes-Scholes (2008) paired interviewers with either fellow participants (untrained actors) or research assistants (trained actors) who followed a set of rules about how to respond like children in mock interviews. Trainees who had practised by interviewing the trained actors used proportionally more open-ended questions in both immediate post-training assessments and 12 weeks later than colleagues who had practised with untrained fellow participants. The fact that trained actors 'rewarded' interviewers with information when they used open-ended questions may have reinforced the interviewers' perceptions of the value of open-ended questions.

In addition to multiple practice opportunities, research recommends training programmes should include using a structured interview protocol, and provide expert feedback and spaced learning opportunities (Poole & Lamb, 1998). One recent training programme in Sweden that increased the use of open prompts and reduced the use of option-posing questions combined the NICHD protocol and the PEACE interviewing model, which involved training spaced over six months, extensive supervision and feedback in a variety of forms (verbal and written), and instruction on how to evaluate one's own interviews (Cederborg, Alm, Lima da Silva Nises & Lamb, 2013).

Due to difficulties in changing interviewing behaviour, researchers have examined additional ways to improve performance. Coding interviews may promote a deeper understanding of question type because, in order to categorise questions, coders must focus their attention on the structure of different prompt types. Notably, tasks that give interviewers practice distinguishing and categorising questions using an objective coding scheme increase the use of open prompts in mock interviews (Yii, Powell & Guadagno, 2014) and field interviews (Cederborg, Alm, Lima da Silva Nises & Lamb, 2013). Learning to code interviews also allows investigators to evaluate their own work, which was one of the most useful elements of training highlighted by trainee interviewers (Powell & Wright, 2008). Positive correlations have been found between performance in a mock interview and on tasks requiring both generating and choosing open prompts from a variety of options (Yii, Powell & Guadagno, 2014). Improving interviewers' use of open prompts can also be done using online activities centred on eliciting best-practice accounts of abuse (Powell, Guadagno & Benson, 2014). However, knowledge alone of best practice does not necessarily affect performance in the field (Warren, Woodall, Thomas et al., 1999); for example performance on a knowledge quiz was not associated with performance in the mock interview (Yii, Powell & Guadagno, 2014). Instead, training interviewers to identify and use open prompts is more effective than knowledge-based training.

In sum, training programmes that focus mainly on knowing about open prompts and best-practice questioning may not effectively equip interviewers to conduct best-practice interviews with children. Training programmes that provide multiple opportunities to conduct practice interviews and receive feedback over spaced learning intervals may be the key to improving interviewers' proficiency using open prompts. Further, the type of training exercises employed should be carefully considered. Conducting mock interviews with trained adult actors can be very effective. Finally, exercises that involve generating and categorising prompts may promote deeper learning and understanding of question type.

Conclusions

While age undoubtedly influences children's memory, recall ability and vulnerability to suggestion, even very young children are capable of remembering their experiences accurately. How well events are remembered may be affected by how well they were understood at the time of encoding, how much time has passed since the events, and the nature of the events themselves. Forgetting occurs during the time between experiencing an event and being questioned about it, though personally meaningful events, events with high self-reference and experiences that are understood are remembered better, even after very long delays. Children's verbal abilities at the time of the event powerfully affect how well children report their experiences; pre-verbal experiences are unlikely to be verbally recalled though may be elicited using behavioural measures. Additionally, the types of questions asked and language used also affects children's accuracy; when they are asked open questions and allowed to give free narrative accounts they are capable of providing highly accurate information, whereas when asked focused, misleading or suggestive questions, the numbers of errors and inaccuracies rises they make.

Interviewers must play to children's strengths by letting them recount what has happened in their own words, asking open questions that do not dictate responses, and using cues drawn from the children's accounts when probing for further recall. Children should be interviewed as soon as possible after allegations of maltreatment are made, because delay has a negative impact on memory, particularly on the peripheral details which may not have been well remembered initially. Investigative interviewers' training should aim to teach interviewers not only to recognise open prompts, but also to understand their structure and how to generate them, with multiple practice and feedback opportunities. Training exercises that produce experiences similar to real forensic interviews, such as practising interviews with adult actors, are desirable because they allow problem behaviours to be observed early in training, and can be tailored to individual interviewer needs. Following a structured protocol, such as the NICHD Protocol, which has been shown to elicit longer, most detailed and more accurate responses from alleged victims, is recommended because field research has shown that interviewers have trouble adhering to guidelines after training. Therefore, the implementation of a structured protocol that guides interviewers through the interview process and provides examples of appropriate questions, is another way of supporting interviewers striving to conduct best-practice interviews with children.

References

Aldridge, J. & Cameron, S. (1999). Interviewing child witnesses: Questioning techniques and the role of training. *Applied Developmental Science*, 3, 136–147.

Bjorklund, D.F., Bjorklund, B.R., Brown, R.D. & Cassel, W.S. (1998). Children's susceptibility to repeated questions: How misinformation changes children's answers and their minds. *Applied Developmental Science*, 2, 99–111.

Bjorklund, D.F., Cassel, W.S., Bjorklund, B.R. et al. (2000). Social demand characteristics in children's and adults' eyewitness memory and suggestibility: The effect of different interviewers on free recall and recognition. *Applied Cognitive Psychology*, 14, 421–433.

Brady, M.S., Poole, D.A., Warren, A.R. & Jones, H.R. (1999). Young children's responses to yes-no questions: Patterns and problems. *Applied Developmental Science*, 3, 47–57.

Brainerd, C.J, Kingma, J. & Howe, M.L. (1985). On the development of forgetting. *Child Development*, 56, 1103–1119.

Brainerd, C.J., Reyna, V.F. & Ceci, S.J. (2008). Developmental reversals in false memory: A review of data and theory. *Psychological Bulletin*, 134, 343.

Brubacher, S.P., Glisic, U., Roberts, K.P. & Powell, M. (2011). Children's ability to recall unique aspects of one occurrence of a repeated event. *Applied Cognitive Psychology*, 25, 351–358.

Brubacher, S.P., Malloy, L.C., Lamb, M.E. & Roberts, K.P. (2013). How do interviewers and children discuss individual occurrences of alleged repeated abuse in forensic interviews? *Applied Cognitive Psychology*, 27, 443–450.

Brubacher, S.P., Poole, D.A. & Dickinson, J.J. (2015). The use of ground rules in investigative interviews with children: A synthesis and call for research. *Developmental Review*.

Carver, L.J. & Bauer, P.J. (2001). The dawning of a past: The emergence of long-term explicit memory in infancy. *Journal of Experimental Psychology: General*, 130, 726–754.

Ceci, S.J. & Bruck, M. (1993). Suggestibility of the child witness: A historical review and synthesis. *Psychological Bulletin*, 113, 403–439.

Ceci, S.J. & Bruck, M. (1995). *Jeopardy in the Courtroom: A Scientific Analysis of Children's Testimony*. Washington, DC: American Psychological Association.

Cederborg, A.C., Alm, C., Lima da Silva Nises, D. & Lamb, M.E. (2013). Investigative interviewing of alleged child abuse victims: An evaluation of a new training programme for investigative interviewers. *Police Practice and Research: An International Journal*, 14, 242–254.

Cederborg, A.C., Orbach, Y., Sternberg, K.J. & Lamb, M.E. (2000). Investigative interviews of child witnesses in Sweden. *Child Abuse & Neglect*, 24, 1355–1361.

Chae, Y., Goodman, G.S., Eisen, M.L. & Qin, J. (2011). Event memory and suggestibility in abused and neglected children: Trauma-related psychopathology and cognitive functioning. *Journal of Experimental Child Psychology*, 110, 520–538.

Connolly, D.A. & Lindsay, D.S. (2001). The influence of suggestions on children's reports of a unique experience versus an instance of a repeated experience. *Applied Cognitive Psychology*, 15, 205–223.

Dent, H.R. (1986). An experimental study of the effectiveness of different techniques of questioning mentally handicapped child witnesses. *British Journal of Clinical Psychology*, 25, 13–17.

Dent, H.R. & Stephenson, G.M. (1979). An experimental study of the effectiveness of different techniques of questioning child witnesses. *British Journal of Social and Clinical Psychology*, 18, 41–51.

Eisen, M.L., Qin, J., Goodman, G.S. & Davis, S.L. (2002). Memory and suggestibility in maltreated children: Age, stress arousal, dissociation, and psychopathology. *Journal of Experimental Child Psychology*, 83, 167–212.

Eisen, M.L., Goodman, G.S., Qin, J. et al. (2007). Maltreated children's memory: Accuracy, suggestibility, and psychopathology. *Developmental Psychology*, 43, 1275–1294.

Farrar, M.J. & Goodman, G.S. (1990). Developmental differences in the relation between script and episodic memory: Do they exist? In: R. Fivush & J. Hudson (eds), *Knowing and Remembering in Young Children*. New York: Cambridge University Press, 30–64.

Fivush, R. & Hamond, N. R. (1990). Autobiographical memory across the preschool years: Toward reconceptualizing childhood amnesia. In: R. Fivush & J.A. Hudson (eds), *Knowing and Remembering in Young Children*. New York: Cambridge University Press, 223–248.

Fivush, R., Gray, J.T. & Fromhoff, F.A. (1987). Two-year-olds talk about the past. *Cognitive Development*, 2, 393–409.

Fivush, R., McDermott Sales, J., Goldberg, A. et al. (2004). Weathering the storm: Children's long-term recall of Hurricane Andrew. *Memory*, 12, 104–118.

Flin, R., Boon, J., Knox, A. & Bull, R. (1992). The effect of a five-month delay on children's and adults' eyewitness memory. *British Journal of Psychology*, 83, 323–336.

Gaudin, J.M. (1999). Child neglect: Short-term and long-term outcomes. In: H. Dubowitz (ed), *Neglected Children*. Thousand Oaks, CA: Sage, 89–108.

Giles, J.W., Gopnik, A. & Heyman, G.D. (2002). Source monitoring reduces the suggestibility of preschool children. *Psychological Science*, 13, 288–291.

Goodman, G.S., Batterman-Faunce, J.M., Schaaf, J.M. & Kenney, R. (2002). Nearly 4 years after an event: Children's eyewitness memory and adults' perceptions of children's accuracy. *Child Abuse & Neglect*, 26, 849–884.

Goodman, G.S., Bottoms, B.L., Rudy, L. et al. (2001). Effects of past abuse experiences on children's eyewitness memory. *Law and Human Behavior*, 25, 269.

Goodman, G.S., Quas, J.A., Batterman-Faunce, J.M. et al. (1997). Children's reactions to and memory for a stressful event: Influences of age, anatomical dolls, knowledge, and parental attachment. *Applied Developmental Science*, 1, 54–75.

Haden, C.A., Ornstein, P.A., Eckerman, C.O. & Didow, S.M. (2001). Mother–child conversational interactions as events unfold: Linkages to subsequent remembering. *Child Development*, 72, 1016–1031.

Hamond, N.R. & Fivush, R. (1991). Memories of Mickey Mouse: Young children recount their trip to Disneyworld. *Cognitive Development*, 6, 433–448.

Hayne, H. & Imuta, K. (2011). Episodic memory in 3- and 4-year-old children. *Developmental Psychobiology*, 53, 317–322.

Hudson, J.A., Fivush, R. & Kuebli, J. (1992). Scripts and episodes: The development of event memory. *Applied Cognitive Psychology*, 6, 483–505.

Hughes, M. & Grieve, R. (1980). On asking children bizarre questions. *First Language*, 1, 149–160.

Jack, F., Simcock, G. & Hayne, H. (2012). Magic Memories: Young children's verbal recall after a 6-year delay. *Child Development*, 83, 159–172.

Kitzinger, J. (2000). Media templates: Patterns of association and the (re)construction of meaning over time. *Media, Culture and Society*, 22, 61–84.

Lamb, M.E. & Fauchier, A. (2001). The effects of question type on self-contradictions by children in the course of forensic interviews. *Applied Cognitive Psychology*, 15, 483–491.

Lamb, M.E., Sternberg, K.J. & Esplin, P.W. (1994). Factors influencing the reliability and validity of statements made by young victims of sexual maltreatment. *Journal of Applied Developmental Psychology*, 15, 255–280.

Lamb, M.E., Hershkowitz, I., Sternberg, K.J. et al. (1996a). Investigative interviews of alleged sexual abuse victims with and without anatomical dolls. *Child Abuse & Neglect*, 20, 1251–1259.

Lamb, M.E., Hershkowitz, I., Sternberg, K.J. et al. (1996b) Effects of investigative utterance types on Israeli children's responses. *International Journal of Behavioral Development*, 19, 627–637.

Lamb, M.E., Orbach, Y., Hershkowitz, I. et al. (2007). A structured forensic interview protocol improves the quality and informativeness of investigative interviews with children: A review of research using the NICHD Investigative Interview Protocol. *Child Abuse & Neglect*, 31, 1201–1231.

Lamb, M.E., Orbach, Y., Hershkowitz, I. et al. (2007). Does the type of prompt affect the accuracy of information provided by alleged victims of abuse in forensic interviews? *Applied Cognitive Psychology*, 21, 1117–1130.

McCloskey, M. & Zaragoza, M. (1985). Misleading post-event information and memory for events: Arguments and evidence against memory impairment hypotheses. *Journal of Experimental Psychology: General*, 114, 1–16.

Melinder, A., Endestad, T.O.R. & Magnussen, S. (2006). Relations between episodic memory, suggestibility, theory of mind, and cognitive inhibition in the preschool child. *Scandinavian Journal of Psychology*, 47, 485–495.

Memorandum of Good Practice (1992). London: Her Majesty's Stationery Office.

Murachver, T., Pipe, M.E., Gordon, R. et al. (1996). Do, show, and tell: Children's event memories acquired through direct experience, observation, and stories. *Child Development*, 67, 3029–3044.

Nelson, K. (1993). The psychological and social origins of autobiographical memory. *Psychological Science*, 4, 7–14.

Nelson, K. & Hudson, J. (1988). Scripts and memory: Functional relationships in development. In: F.E. Weinert & M. Perlmutter (eds), *Memory Development: Universal Changes and Individual Differences*. New Jersey: Lawrence Erlbaum Associates, 87–105.

Nelson, K. & Fivush, R. (2004). The emergence of autobiographical memory: A social cultural developmental theory. *Psychological Review*, 111, 486.

Oates, K. & Shrimpton, S. (1991). Children's memories for stressful and non-stressful events. *Medicine, Science and the Law*, 31, 4–10.

Office for Criminal Justice Reform (2011). Achieving best evidence in criminal proceedings: Guidance for vulnerable or intimidated witnesses, including children. London: Office for Criminal Justice Reform.

Orbach, Y. & Lamb, M.E. (1999). Assessing the accuracy of a child's account of sexual abuse: A case study. *Child Abuse & Neglect*, 23, 91–98.

Orbach, Y. & Lamb, M.E. (2000). Enhancing children's narratives in investigative interviews. *Child Abuse & Neglect*, 24, 1631–1648.

Orbach, Y. & Lamb, M.E. (2001). The relationship between within-interview contradictions and eliciting interviewer utterances. *Child Abuse & Neglect*, 25, 323–333.

Otgaar, H., Howe, M.L., Peters, M. et al. (2013). Developmental trends in different types of spontaneous false memories: Implications for the legal field. *Behavioral Sciences & the Law*, 31, 666–682.

Perner, J. & Ruffman, T. (1995). Episodic memory and autonoetic consciousness: Developmental evidence and a theory of childhood amnesia. *Journal of Experimental Child Psychology*, 59, 516–548.

Perry, N., McAuliffe, B.D., Tam, P. et al. (1995). When lawyers question children. Is justice served? *Law and Human Behavior*, 19, 609–629.

Peters, W.W. & Nunez, N. (1999). Complex language and comprehension monitoring: Teaching child witnesses to recognize linguistic confusion. *Journal of Applied Psychology*, 84, 661–669.

Peterson, C. (1996). The preschool child witness: Errors in accounts of traumatic injury. *Canadian Journal of Behavioural Science*, 28, 36–42.

Peterson, C. (1999). Children's memory for medical emergencies: 2 years later. *Developmental Psychology*, 35, 1493–1506.

Peterson, C. & Rideout, R. (1998). Memory for medical emergencies experienced by 1- and 2-year-olds. *Developmental Psychology*, 34, 1059–1072.

Pillemer, D.B., Picariello, M.L. & Pruett, J.C. (1994). Very long-term memories of a salient preschool event. *Applied Cognitive Psychology*, 8, 95–106.

Poole, D.A. & Lamb, M.E. (1998). *Investigative interviews of children: A guide for helping professionals*. Washington, DC: American Psychological Association.

Powell, M.B. (2000a). Interviewing of Aboriginal people. *Australian Police Journal*, 54, 209–212.

Powell, M.B. (2002). Specialist training in investigative and evidential interviewing: Is it having any effect on the behaviour of professionals in the field? *Psychiatry, Psychology and Law*, 9, 44–55.

Powell, M.B. (2008). Designing effective training programs for investigative interviewers of children. *Current Issues in Criminal Justice*, 20, 189–208.

Powell, M.B. & McMeeken, L. (1998). 'Tell me about the time when …': 9 Golden rules for interviewing a child about a multiple offence. *Australian Police Journal*, 52, 104–108.

Powell, M.B. & Wright, R. (2008). Investigative interviewers' perceptions of the value of different training tasks on their adherence to open-ended questions with children. *Psychiatry, Psychology and Law*, 15, 272–283.

Powell, M.B., Fisher, R.P. & Hughes-Scholes, C.H. (2008). The effect of using trained versus untrained adult respondents in simulated practice interviews about child abuse. *Child Abuse & Neglect*, 32, 1007–1016.

Powell, M.B., Guadagno, B. & Benson, M. (2014). Improving child investigative interviewer performance through computer-based learning activities. *Policing and Society: An International Journal of Research and Policy*, ahead of print, 1–10.

Powell, M.B., Wright, R. & Clark, S. (2010). Improving the competency of police officers in conducting investigative interviews with children. *Police Practice and Research: An International Journal*, 11, 211–226.

Powell, M.B., Cavezza, C., Hughes-Scholes, C. & Stoové, M. (2010). Examination of the consistency of interviewer performance across three distinct interview contexts. *Psychology, Crime & Law*, 16, 585–600.

Pratt, C. (1990). On asking children — and adults — bizarre questions. *First Language*, 10, 167–175.

Price, H.L., Roberts, K.P. & Collins, A. (2013). The quality of children's allegations of abuse in investigative interviews containing practice narratives. *Journal of Applied Research in Memory and Cognition*, 2, 1–6.

Quas, J.A., Goodman, G.S., Bidrose, S. et al. (1999). Emotion and memory: Children's long-term remembering, forgetting, and suggestibility. *Journal of Experimental Child Psychology*, 72, 235–270.

Roediger, H.L. & McDermott, K.B. (1995). Creating false memories: Remembering words not presented in lists. *Journal of Experimental Psychology: Learning, Memory, and Cognition*, 21, 803.

Russell, J. & Hanna, R. (2012). A minimalist approach to the development of episodic memory. *Mind & Language*, 27, 29–54.

Saywitz, K. & Camparo, L. (1998). Interviewing child witnesses: A developmental perspective. *Child Abuse & Neglect*, 22, 825–843.

Scarf, D., Gross, J., Colombo, M. & Hayne, H. (2013). To have and to hold: Episodic memory in 3- and 4-year-old children. *Developmental Psychobiology*, 55, 125–132.

Schaeffer, P., Leventhal, J.M. & Asnes, A.G. (2011). Children's disclosures of sexual abuse: Learning from direct inquiry. *Child Abuse & Neglect*, 35, 343–352.

Schneider, L., Price, H.L., Roberts, K.P. & Hedrick, A. (2011). Children's episodic and generic reports of alleged abuse. *Applied Cognitive Psychology*, 25, 862–870.

Schreiber, N., Bellah, L.D., Martinez, Y. et al. (2006). Suggestive interviewing in the McMartin Preschool and Kelly Michaels daycare abuse cases: A case study. *Social Influence*, 1, 16–47.

Scottish Executive (2003). Guidance interviewing child witnesses and victims in Scotland. Edinburgh: Scottish Executive.

Scottish Executive (2011). Guidance on joint investigative interviewing of child witnesses in Scotland. Edinburgh: Scottish Executive.

Scoville, W.B. & Milner, B. (1957). Loss of recent memory after bilateral hippocampal lesions. *Journal of Neurology, Neurosurgery, and Psychiatry*, 20, 11–21.

Simcock, G. & Hayne, H. (2002). Breaking the barrier? Children fail to translate their pre-verbal memories into language. *Psychological Science*, 13, 225–231.

Sternberg, K.J., Lamb, M.E., Davies, G.M. & Westcott, H.L. (2001). The memorandum of good practice: Theory versus application. *Child Abuse & Neglect*, 25, 669–681.

Sternberg, K.J., Lamb, M.E., Hershkowitz, I. et al. (1996). The relation between investigative utterance types and the informativeness of child witnesses. *Journal of Applied Developmental Psychology*, 17, 439–451.

Sternberg, K.J., Lamb, M.E., Hershkowitz, I. et al. (1997). Effects of introductory style on children's abilities to describe experiences of sexual abuse. *Child Abuse & Neglect*, 21, 1133–1146.

Tessler, M. & Nelson, K. (1994). Making memories: The influence of joint encoding on later recall by young children. *Consciousness and Cognition*, 3, 307–326.

Tobey, A.E. & Goodman, G.S. (1992). Children's eyewitness memory: Effects of participation and forensic context. *Child Abuse & Neglect*, 16, 779–796.

Tulving, E. (1972). Episodic and semantic memory 1. In: E. Tulving & W. Donaldson (eds), *Organization of Memory*. London: Academic Press, 381–402.

Tulving, E. (2002a). Chronesthesia: Conscious awareness of subjective time. In: D. Stuss & R. Knight (eds), *Principles of Frontal Lobe Function*. New York: Oxford University Press, 311–325.

Tulving, E. (2002b). Episodic memory: From mind to brain. *Annual Review of Psychology*, 53, 1–25.

Usher, J.A. & Neisser, U. (1993). Childhood amnesia and the beginnings of memory for four early life events. *Journal of Experimental Psychology: General*, 122, 155–165.

Van Abbema, D. & Bauer, P. (2005). Autobiographical memory in middle childhood: Recollections of the recent and distant past. *Memory*, 13, 829–845.

Warren, A.R., Woodall, C.E., Thomas, M. et al. (1999). Assessing the effectiveness of a training program for interviewing child witnesses. *Applied Developmental Science*, 3, 128–135.

Waterman, A.H., Blades, M. & Spencer, C. (2000). Do children try to answer nonsensical questions? *British Journal of Developmental Psychology*, 18, 211–225.

Waterman, A.H., Blades, M. & Spencer, C. (2004). Indicating when you do not know the answer: The effect of question format and interviewer knowledge on children's 'don't know' responses. *British Journal of Developmental Psychology*, 22, 335–348.

Yii, S.L.B., Powell, M.B. & Guadagno, B. (2014). The association between investigative interviewers' knowledge of question type and adherence to best-practice interviewing. *Legal and Criminological Psychology*, 19, 270–281.

16

Considering Parental Risk in Parenting (Child Custody) Evaluation Cases Involving Child Sexual Exploitation Material

Hannah L. Merdian[1], David M. Gresswell[1] and Leam A. Craig[2]

[1] University of Lincoln, UK
[2] Forensic Psychology Practice Ltd, UK and University of Birmingham, Birmingham City University, UK

Introduction

In 2010, Witt, Merdian, Connell and Boer published a set of best-practice recommendations on the assessment of parental risk in child custody evaluation cases involving online sexual behaviours, including explicit sexual chats or compulsive viewing of pornography. The authors also tentatively approached the issue of engagement with illegal online material, such as child sexual exploitation material (CSEM), reflecting on the limited research base available at the time. Since the publication of the original article, research and theoretical development concerning individuals involved in online sex offending against minors has significantly advanced, but remains in many ways contradictory and equivocal. The current chapter is aimed at exploring and specifying the assessment of parental risk in child custody evaluation cases where one or both parents, usually the father, is reported to have possessed and/or engaged in the distribution, trading and/or production of CSEM. We hope to provide professionals with some guidance for formulating custody cases by providing systemic and reflective insight into the current legal and psychological context of CSEM, by reviewing the evidence concerning the link between CSEM and contact sexual offences (CSO) against minors, and by reflecting on the function and contextualised assessment of this offending behaviour, by considering cases from our own experience as CSEM researchers and assessors for court.

Investigative, Legal and Empirical Context of the Offending Behaviour

In the UK, the Protection of Children Act 1978 c. 37 section 1 regulates the taking, permission to take, making, distributing, possessing, publishing and distributing of *indecent photographs* or *pseudo-photographs*[1] of children, defined as 'an indecent film, copy of a photograph or film, or computer data capable of conversion into a photo or copy, of a person who is under 18 years of age'. A conviction is dependent on three aspects: (i) the defendant is deliberately and/or knowingly engaged in the behaviour; (ii) the person depicted is classified as a *child* (currently defined as under 18 years); and (iii) the (pseudo)-photograph is classified as *indecent*. Until recently, the only tool that had been developed to systemically rate the content of images was the COPINE scale (Taylor, Holland & Quayle, 2001), which consisted of a ten-level typology based on analysis of images ranging from Level 1 non-erotic and non-sexualised pictures (e.g., children in underwear and swimwear) to Level 10 sadistic/bestiality, pictures showing children being bound, beaten, whipped or otherwise subject to something that implies pain, or, pictures where an animal is involved in some form of sexual behaviour with a child.

Following a Court of Appeal (*R v Oliver* [2003]) hearing, the UK Sentencing Advisory Panel adapted the COPINE scale to provide a five-level scale giving an objective estimation of the level of victimisation in the images collected. The age of the child was classified as an additional factor for sentencing with the age categories: (i) under 13 years, (ii) 13–15 years and (iii) 16–17 years old. From the 1 April 2014, these five levels were replaced and have since been revised to a three-level distinction of sexual explicitness: Category A – images involving penetrative sexual activity, images involving sexual activity with an animal or sadism; Category B – images involving non-penetrative sexual activity; and Category C – other indecent images not falling within Categories A or B (Sentencing Council, 2014).

In 2010, the Coroners and Justice Act 2009 came into force regarding the possession of a *prohibited* image of a child, a pornographic or obscene image depicting (in)direct sexualisation of a child, such as sexual activities performed in the presence of a child. While this Act is limited to image material, sexual depictions of children without an identifiable victim, including drawings, sound- and text-based stories, are prosecuted under the Obscene Publication Act 1959. The *production* of indecent material of children is classified under the Sexual Offences Act 2003 c.42, Abuse of children though prostitution and pornography. Thus, in this chapter, the terminology *Child Sexual Exploitation Material* (CSEM) is used to linguistically incorporate all material types and levels of sexual explicitness in their contents, referring to offending behaviour covered in all three pieces of legislation.

A specific challenge in the policing and investigation of CSEM offending is that a prosecution is dependent on the analysis of the individual's computer-based technology, such as hard-drives, mobile phones, cloud contents or chat logs. This process can take considerable amounts of time and can have a significant impact on the individual and his family environment (e.g., loss of job and financial resources; need to leave family home; strained/broken relations with spouse, family and friends; enhanced anxiety/ stress response). Thus, professional opinion for child custody evaluations may be sought prior to a person being charged or convicted for CSEM-related offending behaviour and the evaluation may be influenced by bail conditions that restrict parental contact with the child.

---

[1] A pseudo-photographs is defined as 'an image, whether made by computer graphics or otherwise, which appears to be a photograph' (section 160, Criminal Justice Act 1988).

Due to the increase of internet availability, offender management services in recent years have had to deal with a rise of CSEM-related offending. For 2013–2014, the Crown Prosecution Service (2014) reported a total of 20,373 child abuse image offences (where a prosecution was commenced), which constitutes a rise of 1,476 prosecutions from 2008–2009. One of the most significant questions relates to the risk of crossover, or escalation (Quayle, 2009), from viewing CSEM to contact sex offending (CSO), and thus the risk an individual may present in terms of contact with children, including their own. However, while escalation implies a unidirectional process to contact offending, Seto and Eke (2005) found that crossover could also have occurred prior to accessing CSEM.

The empirical data show very little crossover between CSEM and CSO. A large-scale meta-analysis (Seto, Hanson & Babchishin, 2011) identified 12.2% of CSEM users with historical contact sex offences (17.3% if additional self-report data was included) but did not differentiate by victim type (e.g., adult vs. child victims). Predictably, the empirical research on this topic reflects the discrepancy between official and self-reported data that has also become apparent in studies on undetected CSEM users (see Neutze, Seto, Schaefer et al., 2011) or studies involving CSEM users' polygraph assessment as a form of information validation (e.g., Buschman, Bogaerts, Foulger et al., 2010). In terms of re-conviction rates, progression from viewing CSEM to CSO appears to be rare. In their meta-analysis, Seto, Hanson & Babchishin (2011) found that less than 5% of online offenders (N = 2630) re-offended with any sex offence within the follow-up period of six years, including 2% CSO offences. Faust, Bickart, Renaud and Camp (2015) provided re-offending rates of US online sex offenders (N = 638) over a nine-year follow-up, reporting a 3% recidivism rate for CSO and 1.6% CSEM offending. Such low base rates of (detected) CSO within the CSEM population limit the utility of probabilistic risk predictions. Thus, existing risk-assessment tools for contact sex offenders (e.g., Risk Matrix 2000; Thornton, Mann & Webster, 2003) require validation regarding the offending base rates of CSEM users and are unlikely to make reliable and accurate estimations of future risk when applied to this group (Middleton, Mandelville-Norden & Hayes, 2009; Osborn, Elliott, Middleton & Beech, 2010; Wakeling, Howard & Barnett, 2011).

Consequently, recent research has aimed to identify potential predictors of crossover to CSO. Based on a meta-analysis comparing CSEM users (N = 2284) and offenders with convictions for both CSEM and CSO (N = 1086), Babchishin, Hanson and VanZuylen (2015) pointed to four potential predictors of crossover to CSO: (i) sexual interest in children (measured through self-report or implicit assessment), (ii) access to children, (iii) high levels of anti-sociality, and (iv) few psychological barriers to acting on the sexual interest. Babchishin, Hanson and VanZuylen referred to a range of variables as indicators of *anti-sociality*, including high scores on psychometric assessments such as the Minnesota Multiphasic Personality Inventory (Psychopathic Deviate sub-scale; Butcher, Dahlstrom, Graham et al., 1989) as well as behavioural indicators, such as prior offending, supervision failures, employment problems/unemployment and substance use. These suggested predictors map well onto Seto's (2013) *Motivation-Facilitation Model (M-F Model)*, an explanatory model that conceptualises a sexual interest in children as an internal motivator that, in combination with offence-facilitative factors of the individual (i.e., anti-sociality) and situational facilitators (i.e., access to children), may lead to an exacerbation of CSEM viewing to CSO.

Although consideration of these predictors of crossover is a helpful starting point in a risk assessment, they are also evidence of the heterogeneity of CSEM users, both in terms of their behavioural characteristics as well as their psychological (psychometric) profiles. This suggests that a connection between CSEM consumption and CSO may exist but if so, it is probably limited to a subgroup of CSEM users. Group-based typologies of CSEM offending propose that different types of CSEM users can be identified, who present unique risks and needs with differential impact on investigative prioritisation, re-offending risk, assessment, and treatment planning (Beech, Elliott, Birgden & Findlater, 2008; Long, Alison & McManus, 2013; Merdian, Curtis, Thakker et al., 2013). However, none of these typologies are empirically validated at present, and thus cannot be relied upon in individualised assessments of parental risk and capability. Nevertheless, these group-based approaches communicate an attempt to differentiate CSEM-offending behaviour based on its *function* for the individual. Previous research has identified a range of functions associated with CSEM, extending from its use as a masturbatory template to a grooming tool for potential victims (Caple, 2008; Holt, Blevins & Burkert, 2010; Sheldon & Howitt, 2007; Surjadi, Bullens, van Horn & Bogaerts, 2010; Taylor & Quayle, 2003, 2005); it is further known that CSEM offending can hold multiple functions for an individual, and that these functions may change over time and are influenced by contextual variables (Merdian, Wilson, Thakker et al., 2013; Seto, Reeves & Jung, 2010). Such functions include sexual explanations (sexual attraction to minors and replacement for an adequate sexual object) and emotional explanations (a relief aspect combating feelings of depression, anxiety and loneliness or feeling in control).

In line with the focus on functional analysis, Merdian, Perkins, Dustagheer, and Glorney (under review) developed a CSEM-specific case formulation model, based on interviews and psychometric testing of CSEM users at both post-arrest and post-conviction stages (Figure 16.1). The resulting model identified key stages in an individual's pathway to CSEM

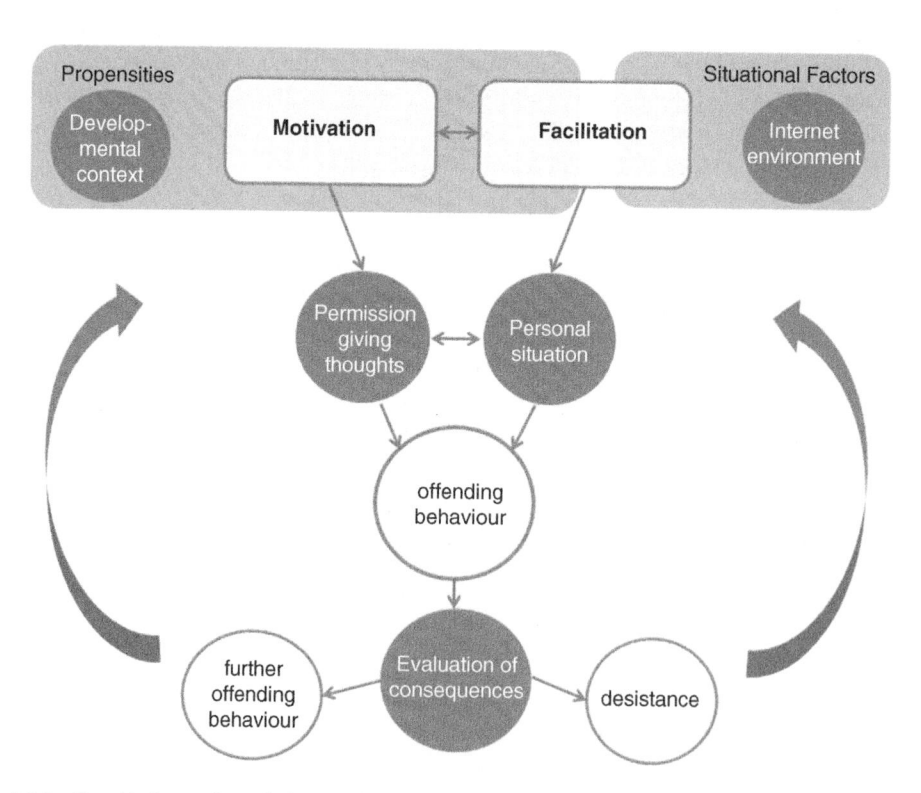

Figure 16.1 Empirical case formulation model for CSEM users (Merdian, Perkins, Dustagheer & Glorney, in review). Reprinted with permission of the authors.

offending, integrating offence-related vulnerabilities (including developmental factors, e.g., paraphilias or socio-emotional dysfunctionality) and their interaction with the broader offending context (i.e., the accessibility, affordability and anonymity of the internet – the so-called Triple A driver, Cooper, 1998) and the immediate circumstances surrounding the offending. Finally, the model points to the positive and negative consequences of the behaviour, such as the sexual gratification linked to CSEM or stress-relief, which either support or deter future offending behaviour.

This empirical model reflects the motivational and facilitational distinction of Seto's (2013) M-F Model, but broadens it toward integrating Finkelhor's (1984) *Four Pre-Conditions of Abuse*, a model used to explain the decision process of an individual committing a CSO. Finkelhor postulated that four components are necessary to commit a CSO, namely (i) the thinking (motivational) stage, (ii) overcoming internal inhibitions (permission-giving), (iii) overcoming external inhibitions (creating the opportunity), and (iv) overcoming the victim's resistance. The first two preconditions refer to characteristics of the offender, while the two remaining preconditions are arguably characteristics of the environment. When applying Finkelhor's model to CSEM users, Merdian, Perkins, Dustagheer & Glorney (under review) proposed that the initial stage is influenced by both motivational factors (such as a sexual interest in children) and enabling internal states, thus separating the facilitative factors proposed by Seto (2013) into internal propensities (e.g., oppositional thinking) as well as situational factors (e.g., the offence-enabling internet environment, considered in Precondition Three). The third stage, overcoming external inhibitions, is facilitated through the contextual factors of the internet (e.g., ease of access to CSEM material) but may also relate to the identification of idiosyncratic offence opportunities, such as use of the computer out of sight of family members. In the case of CSEM-offending behaviour, Finkelhor's fourth precondition ('overcoming victim resistance') has been carried out by proxy by the creators of the material, and thus is not directly assessed here.

Considering Parental Risk

In applying the literature above to clinical assessments for the courts, we will consider two anonymised cases, which are typical of the referrals received by clinical forensic psychologists in CSEM family cases. The task of the assessor is to provide responses to the questions of the courts; such questions are generally pragmatic and primarily consider two domains:

1. What is the risk of the CSEM user committing a contact offence against a child in the family and/or one of their friends or relatives?
2. Can the perceived risk be managed, and if so, how? A common sub-theme to this question is the non-offending parent's ability to protect the child.

In approaching a court assessment of a CSEM user, a psychologist, acting within the Scientist–Practitioner Model (Shakow, 1942; cited in Baker & Benjamin, 2000), has access to a range of resources such as data collection and evaluation tools, including: interviews with the client, interviews with family members or relevant others, psychometric assessments of the CSEM user, witness statements, research data, established risk-assessment protocols and psychological theory. Based on the review of the literature set out above, we will comment on each resource in turn before applying best-practice principles to the assessments of our cases.

Interviews with the client and related parties

Conducting interviews with CSEM users for family court assessments is a complex process given the potentially severe consequences for the client depending on the outcome of the assessment. Levels of shame associated with admitting a sexual interest in children are often overwhelming and denial (as a function of the interaction between client, interviewer and context) is very common (see Seto, Reeves & Jung, 2010). In addition, an interviewee's cooperation may be mitigated through external forces, such as a lawyer's advice not to disclose certain information. Denial or part-admissions have not been empirically linked to an increased risk of re-offending (Yates, 2009), and should therefore only be considered as a responsivity factor of the individual. A comprehensive interview should aim to include an account of the client's developmental history (including sexual and relationship history), identify the predisposing and precipitating factors of the offending behaviour, detail the exact nature of the offending behaviour, including CSEM content, involvement and trajectory of the offending behaviour, and specify the context and function of the behaviour. In addition, the interview will allow exploration of potential crossover to contact offending, such as a history of online chats with minors or indications of grooming behaviour. Semi-structured interview guidelines are available (e.g., Parsons, Honyara, Delmonico & Griffin, 2013; Quayle, 2009), alongside self-report assessment tools for CSEM content (e.g., Glasgow, 2010). Psychosexual history interviews commonly focus on the nature and range of materials including any paraphilic materials which may indicate sexual preoccupation (see Ireland & Craig, 2011).

While the current empirical knowledge on CSEM users' risks is limited, recent research has pointed to enhanced risk of re-offending in those CSEM users with previous contact sex offence histories (Seto & Eke, 2015); it may thus be useful to explore the presence of established predictors for contact sex offending in the assessment. A semi-structured interview schedule, known as the Structured Assessment of Risk and Need: Treatment Needs Analysis (SARN:TNA; Craig & Rettenberger, 2016; Wakeling, Beech & Freemantle, 2013), is widely used by the National Offender Management Service within prison and probation services in England and Wales, to assess for the presence of sexual preoccupation, sexual preference for children, interests in sexual violence, and other sexual offence-related behaviours (see Craig & Rettenberger, 2016). The SARN:TNA comprises of 15 dynamic risk factors organised into four domains: (i) Sexual Interests Domain; (ii) Offence-Supportive Attitudes Domain; (iii) Relationships Domain; and (iv) Self-Management Domain. Assessed either psychometrically or clinically, the Sexual Interests Domain has moderate to good predictive accuracy in identifying those contact sex offenders who are re-convicted for further sex offences (Craig, Thornton, Beech & Browne, 2007; Tully, Browne & Craig, 2015).

Interviews with other related parties can be used to add to the knowledge about the client and their situation, and to cross-validate the information provided.

Psychometric assessments

Psychological assessors may find it informative to include psychometric measures of relevant variables, such as the client's mental health, intellectual functioning, depression levels or sexual history and fantasy. In terms of assessment tools specific to CSEM users, recent developments have focused on the endorsement of offence-supportive cognitions (Children and Sexual Activities, Howitt & Sheldon, 2007; Internet Behaviors and Attitudes Questionnaire, O'Brien & Webster, 2007); however, none of these measures is sufficiently validated to date to allow them to be relied upon in court.

Witness statements and related reports

The assessor may have access to reports prepared by the police, providing a detailed breakdown of the hard drive and related content analysis. Digital evidence of interest may include the type, content and explicitness ratings of CSEM found, the ratio of CSEM to other pornographic material, access ways, search terms used, level of categorisation and labels used, chat histories, online postings or related emails received. Other information of potential interest to the assessor includes the client's criminal and mental health history, or previous engagement with social services.

Research data

A useful resource for the psychological assessor is the empirical literature: based on the review presented at the start of the chapter, the existing literature on CSEM and CSO can be summarised as follows:

(a) The vast majority of CSEM users do not appear to progress to committing a CSO against a child.
(b) The best current predictors for CSEM users who crossover to a contact offence are signs of significant anti-sociality (though most CSEM user do not share this characteristic), deviant sexual interest and access to children.
(c) CSEM can have different functions for different users, and different functions for the same user in different contexts.

In applying this research data to the assessment of CSEM users, the risk prediction most accurate in the majority of cases is to state that a CSEM user who does not display a history of anti-sociality is unlikely to progress to a CSO. When trying to predict low-base-rate events (such as crossover offending), the error rate increases as the base rate reduces, leading to a high number of false positives (Craig, Browne & Beech, 2008).

Considering parental risk of CSEM users: A scientist–practitioner approach

A number of standardised risk-assessment tools have been developed for contact sex offenders, such as the Static-99 (Hanson & Thornton, 1999) or the Stable 2007 (Hanson, Harris, Scott & Helmus, 2007). While most existing risk-assessment tools can be used with CSEM users with a historical CSO, the psychological assessor still faces the difficulty of translating the group-derived outcome probability of an actuarial tool to the unique circumstances of a specific individual. In addition, the accuracy of actuarial risk-assessment instruments becomes compromised as the individual shares less characteristics with the cohort developmental sample (Craig, Browne & Beech, 2008).

As the above review outlines, reliable, well-validated measures of crossover from CSEM to CSO have yet to be developed, and there is currently no risk-assessment tool available that can successfully predict re-offending with another CSEM offence. Overall, there is professional consensus that best practice in sex offender risk assessment combines different risk measures, referred to as a 'convergent approach' to risk assessment (Singer, Boer & Rettenberger, 2013; Craig, Browne, Hogue & Stringer, 2004); ideally, expert opinion is based on variables with a reliable, statistically significant relationship to criminal offending, or, in their absence, is anchored in the existing psychological theory and empirical data, making the assessment both transparent and defensible to the court and client. Thus, in the absence of established risk-assessment tools for CSEM users, the assessing psychologist, acting as a scientist–practitioner, will set up a series of hypotheses based on the scientific derived body of theory and knowledge, and test the hypotheses against the evidence/case material available. The assessor also needs to communicate transparency with regard to their own bias within this process; the choice of data that is abstracted as relevant; and that the theories that are applied are not immune to the assessor's a priori assumptions.

Clinical Analysis of CSEM Offending and Risk in Family Settings: Two Case Studies

The following will describe a clinical analysis of parental risk applied to two separate case studies (Mr A and Mr B). In both scenarios, there was evidence that the father had been viewing CSEM but only Mr B had been convicted. Neither of the mothers was thought to be aware of their husband's use of CSEM and there was no evidence that either father had sexually abused their children. There were indications that both Mr A and Mr B had experience of stable adult relationships and there was evidence that both men had an interest in, and experience of, adult heterosexual sexual activity. Both Mr A and Mr B were referred for psychological evaluation and risk assessment by the courts. Table 16.1 summarises the core case information.

It has been outlined above that CSEM users are a heterogeneous population, generally perceived to be at low risk of re-offending and crossover to CSO. Psychological theories and models are still developing to account for the development of the behaviour, and for crossover (or lack of crossover) to CSO. However, the similarity of emerging models (Babchishin, Hanson & VanZuylen, 2015; Seto, 2013) to Finkelhor's (1984) four preconditions model shows a convergence of thinking within the field with respect to explanatory models of contact offending, and provides a strong theoretical guidance for the clinical assessor. Thus, in using a scientist–practitioner model to approach these psychological assessments, a series of hypotheses were derived from Finkelhor's model, informed by the research evidence on CSEM offenders who crossover, and tested against the clinical evidence available.

Precondition One: Motivation

Finkelhor's model proposes motivation as the first precondition to sexual abuse, which is supported by Seto (2013) and Babchishin, Hanson & VanZuylen (2015). Thus, the following hypothesis was deducted from the above reviewed literature: *A CSEM offender is more likely to commit a CSO when the primary function of their CSEM use is to facilitate a sexual interest in children (e.g., use of CSEM for sexual arousal and private masturbation, or grooming purposes).*

Finkelhor (1984) identified three types of offence motivations: Emotional Congruence, Sexual Arousal and Blockage. Emotional congruence refers to the idea that some offenders use sexual contact with a child to meet their emotional as well as sexual needs. The literature on the role of emotional congruence in the use of CSEM is sparse; in their meta-analysis, Babchishin, Hanson & VanZuylen (2015) found that CSEM users were less likely to show emotional congruence with children than contact sex offenders and were more likely to develop secure adult relationships.

Sexual arousal to children is the biggest single predictor of recidivism among contact sex offenders (Hanson & Morton-Bourgon, 2004); however, as might be expected for such a

Table 16.1 Introduction to the cases.

Case of Mr A	Case of Mr B
Index Behaviour and Reason for the Assessment In 2013, Mr A (41 yrs, married[1]) was arrested on suspicion of viewing indecent images of children (on 'pay to view' internet sites) and was subsequently bailed on condition not to have contact with children. Subsequently all contact between Mr A and his son (2 yrs[1]) was arranged and supervised by social services. As a result of a police investigation a large quantity of adult pornography was found on computer drives owned by Mr A. However, many computer files were encrypted (Mr A claimed he had forgotten the passwords) and the encoded material could not be viewed by police officers. Nevertheless, a record of Mr A's internet use revealed 'a list of video clips and images with names, ages and descriptions' (e.g., 'pre-teen hard-core') which were strongly indicative of him having viewed illicit sexual images of children over a period of time. Mr A was unwilling to provide an explanation of his behaviour and when interviewed by the police did not comment, on the advice of his solicitor. Mr A said that his solicitor had also advised against cooperating with the psychological assessment in case he incriminated himself. In July 2014, the police decided not to prosecute Mr A; however, at that point social services became more actively involved and the couple (who had lived apart since Mr A's arrest) formally separated in August 2014, with Mrs A indicating that she would instigate divorce proceedings.	**Index Behaviour and Reason for the Assessment** Mr B (35 yrs, married[1]). Social services first became involved with the B family in 2010 when over 300 indecent images of children were found on Mr B's computer: these images were rated at Levels[2] 1 to 5. The images had been seen by a babysitter who reported Mr B to the police. In July 2010, Mr B pleaded guilty to 24 specimen charges of 'Having or Making Indecent Photographs' and was sentenced to six months' imprisonment. Mr and Mrs B were said to have separated at that time but following Mr B's release from prison he was found to be having unsupervised contact with his two children (son, then aged 3 yrs; daughter, then aged 9 yrs). In March 2011, a psychological assessment of both parents was commissioned from Dr X, a Consultant Clinical Psychologist. Following that, Mrs B was allowed to supervise contact between Mr B and the children until November 2013 when she and the children moved seemingly so that Mrs B could be close to her aunt (a relative who she claimed was a major source of social support). However, after Mrs B and her children had moved, Mr B was found to be living with the family. Mr B had also moved to the same area to be close to the children and said he was staying in the family home temporarily while he looked for suitable single accommodation. Social services asked Mr B to leave the family home and although he complied the couple indicated that they wanted to be assessed so that they could live together openly.
Psychological Interview Mr A presented as a partial admitter; he admitted to having 'accidentally seen' CSEM but denied actively looking for it or being sexually aroused by it. There was no evidence of a CSO, with Mr A denying being sexually aroused by his son, and affirming his commitment to his wife. Given his circumstances, the assessor was aware of the risk that Mr A was not entirely honest about his behaviour and, by implication, sexual preferences, which was commented on in the assessment reports produced for court.	**Psychological Interview** Mr B presented as a partial admitter, claiming to have 'accidentally' come across CSEM despite overwhelming evidence in the form of records of search terms and organised folders. He denied any sexual arousal to CSEM and to his children, and stated his commitment to his wife. A note was included in the assessment report about the limits of his self-report statement.

Table 16.1 (Cont'd)

Case of Mr A	Case of Mr B
Psychometric Assessments None were conducted for this case.	**Psychometric Assessments** None were conducted for this case.
Witness Statements and Other Reports Information about Mr A was derived from secondary sources. Because Mr A's investigation focused on CSEM, available statements were mainly restricted to the specific police investigations. Detailed breakdowns of the number and types of images viewed (incl. CSEM) were missing for Mr A.	**Witness Statements and Other Reports** As Mr B's investigation focused on CSEM, available statements were mainly restricted to the specific police investigations. Breakdowns of the number and types of images (incl. CSEM) were available but lacked detail. A previous assessment indicated that Mrs B had a mild learning disability.

[1] At the time of assessment.
[2] These levels refer to the original guidelines by the UK Sentencing Advisory Panel (2012). Mr B's material ranged from *Erotic posing* (Level 1) to *Sadism/penetration by an animal* (Level 5).

complex behaviour, correlation is low ($d = .34$, measured by effect size). Babchishin, Hanson, and Hermann (2010) and Babchishin, Hanson & VanZuylen (2015) found that online offenders appeared more sexually deviant than offline offenders (using phallometric and psychometric assessments). However, it should be acknowledged that the modus of phallometric assessments is similar to the CSEM offence experience (e.g., viewing of images of children) and hence may lead to higher arousal profiles. Indeed, Schmidt, Mokros and Banse (2013) identified equal rates of sexual preference for children among extra-familial contact sex offenders and CSEM users when implicit methods of assessment were used.

Blockage refers to the lack of other sources of sexual gratification. When considering CSEM offenders, it is perhaps tempting to dismiss this aspect given the range of sexual material available online. However, in considering crossover to CSO, this may relate specifically to limited access to physical sources of sexual gratification. In addition, Babchishin, Hanson & VanZuylen, (2015) reported higher rates of sexual preoccupation and higher sexual self-regulation problems among CSEM users, and Jahnke, Imhoff and Hoyer (2015) pointed toward the crucial role of emotional loneliness and stigmatisation experience of people who identify as paedophilic. Table 16.2 outlines the case material available to test against the hypothesis.

In the absence of a full disclosure from either Mr A or Mr B, it was impossible in either case to refute the hypothesis that the CSEM used reflects a specific sexual interest and was used as an aid to masturbation. In case of Mr B, there was also some role play involving sexualisation of minors, given his disclosure of having an interest in school uniforms and given that his partner had shaved off her pubic hair on previous occasions. Finally, for Mr B, the 'discovery' of CSEM by his babysitter could be conceptualised as the outcome of a potential grooming process (see next section). There is no information available to comment on the emotional identification with children, or about risk specificity (e.g., preferred victim type). Both cases indicate a preference for prepubescent females; however, this is in line with CSEM availability online (Wolak, Finkelhor & Mitchell, 2005). Other indications of risk include claims of blocked alternatives for both men: Mr A complained of physical illness which affected his libido and sexual performance while Mr B claimed that his wife had lost interest in sex following the birth of their second child. In summary, our recommendation is that the first precondition (motivation to offend) is potentially met for both men, but with a stronger evidence base for Mr B.

Table 16.2 Indications of motivation to offend.

Mr A	Mr B
No history of sexual abuse. Denied having any sexual interest in children. Denied any homosexual interest or experience. Achieved puberty at 13 yrs. No history of sexual dysfunction or of STDs.	No history of sexual abuse. Denied having any sexual interest in children. Denied any homosexual interest or experience. Achieved puberty at 16 yrs. No history of sexual dysfunction or of STDs.
In school, began using pornographic magazines (obtained from friends) for private masturbation; prefers 'readers' wives' ('real women') to glamour models. Began viewing internet pornography from mid-90s when internet became more widely available. Reports a preference for adult 'classic erotica'. Denied searching for images of children but said he had seen 'pop-ups' advertising images of children when visiting adult pornography sites. Could not explain why the police found references entitled '12-year-old XX performs [various sexual] acts', nor why there was a list of video clips and images with names, ages and descriptions (e.g., 'pre-teen hard-core') which were strongly indicative of him having viewed illicit sexual images of children over a period of time, on his computer drive.	Had used adult magazine pornography from the age of 18 yrs; started using pornography again in 2008 to aid masturbation after 'Mrs B lost interest in sex' following the birth of their second child. Police analysis of Mr B's computer indicated the presence of adult pornography (details not available) and over 400 illicit images of female children (6–13 yrs; 350 were at Level 1 to 3, 45 were at Level 4, and four were at Level 5). Mr B claimed the images had been viewed accidentally while searching for adult material and could not explain why he had saved them to his hard drive. Mr B admitted that he had used search terms such as: 'Lolita', 'teen-porn', 'young/hard-core', 'shy-teen', 'Asian schoolgirls' and 'incest' but stressed that he thought that he would only see legal images of people aged over 18 yrs. The CSEM had been discovered by the 15-year-old babysitter who had been given permission to use Mr B's computer; she indicated that the images were visible as soon as the computer was turned on. No other information was available.
Mr A described himself as 'not confident with women'. He had no sexual experiences before early 20s; thereafter, he had had one long-term consenting adult heterosexual relationship before his current marriage. Disclosed having a genital piercing and, prior to his marriage, to exposing his genitals to show this off while drunk. Mr and Mrs A had made video recordings of themselves performing a range of sexual acts (also encrypted). Mr A indicated a significant reduction in his sex drive as a result of complications following an operation for haemorrhoids which led to him having repeated infections.	Mr B had had two longer-term sexual partners (and one affair) before meeting and marrying Mrs B. Mr B disclosed that his wife would dress up in a schoolgirl outfit and shave off her pubic hair but he claimed he felt neutral about this behaviour.

Precondition Two: Overcoming internal inhibitions

According to Finkelhor (1984), the offender must also have the ability to overcome any internal (cognitive) inhibitors against offending. This precondition overlaps with both Babchishin, Hanson and VanZuylen's (2015) and Seto's (2013) argument for the role of anti-sociality in crossover, and the finding that crossover offenders have fewer psychological barriers to acting on their sexual interests than the typical CSEM user. Thus, the following hypothesis is proposed: *A CSEM offender is more likely to commit a CSO if he has low internal inhibitions against committing a contact sex offence against a child.*

When considering the characteristics of the environment that could contribute to overcoming internal inhibitions, Cooper's (1998) concept of the 'Triple A driver' suggests that accessing CSEM may be perceived as a lower-risk behaviour relative to the risks associated with committing CSO. Thus, an assessment of how a client overcame inhibitions against accessing CSEM materials online is not necessarily transferable to the contact offending process. As outlined above, internal inhibitions can be overcome through a variety of cognitive processes such as estimates of the probability of getting caught and/or of harming the victim, or, for example, by redefining the offence as an expression of love or education or as a mutual consenting sexual act. CSEM users often adopt the stance that viewing CSEM does not directly harm the child (Howitt & Sheldon, 2007). For Finkelhor (1984), affective states such as high levels of sexual arousal, which can focus the offender on the short-term benefits of the offence over the long-term potential negative consequences/risks for them, can also be disinhibiting. Further, misuse of substances (alcohol/drugs; Babchishin, Hanson & Hermann, 2010), mental health issues (Laulik, Allam & Sheridan, 2007), or a negative change in one's personal circumstances at the time of offending (Merdian, Perkins, Dustagheer & Glorney, under review) may have a disinhibitory effect. Table 16.3 lists the case information regarding Precondition Two.

Table 16.3 Indications of ability to overcome internal inhibitions.

Mr A	*Mr B*
No significant mental health history preceding his arrest. Does not meet criteria for diagnosis of personality disorder.	No significant mental health history preceding his arrest. Does not meet criteria for diagnosis of personality disorder.
No history of drug or alcohol abuse.	No history of drug or alcohol abuse.
No history of general criminality.	No history of general criminality.
Was 'shocked' when saw first CSEM image and reported it to his internet service provider.	Blames use of pornography on 'being in a dark depressed place at the time'; claims he was downloading on 'autopilot'.
Had seen images of 17-year-olds and reported to find the illicit activity arousing in itself.	Tendency to make external attributions for a range of social, employment and relationship problems, including motivation to access CSEM. Presents self as a victim of circumstances.
Claimed he had become anxious and had 'wiped' all pornography (including CSEM seen 'accidentally' but not images of wife and 'classic erotica') from computer hard drive; re-formatted his hard drive several months before arrest.	Ignored supervision sanctions and justified move back into the family home 'while looking for a new place to live'.
Admitted to masturbating to adult pornographic images in the family living room after Mrs A had gone to bed.	Reportedly used pornography to stay awake at night while caring for infant son.
Some history of exposing genital piercings, when drunk, in public place.	When asked why he had used the search term 'incest', Mr B insisted that this was not as result of a direct sexual interest in incestuous behavior but because he was trying to understand a television programme about an incestuous relationships.
	The circumstances of babysitter discovering CSEM materials on Mr B's computer are suggestive of him beginning a 'grooming process' with a teenage female non-relative.

According to the empirical evidence outlined above, most CSEM users appear to have strong internal inhibitions against committing a CSO against a child. There is little evidence to refute this with respect to Mr A. He has a history of exposing himself and of masturbating while viewing pornography in the shared family rooms (while his wife and child were asleep) but there is no evidence of direct boundary violations or disinhibition with children. With Mr B, the situation appears more complex; the circumstance in which CSEM was discovered is suggestive of a grooming process of the teenage babysitter. In addition, the evidence that he had used the search term 'incest' when looking for CSEM could be indicative of an interest in such a boundary violation. Thus, the above hypothesis cannot be confidently refuted for Mr B, but is not upheld for Mr A.

Precondition Three: Overcoming external inhibitions

Both Seto (2013) and Babchishin, Hanson & VanZuylen (2015) stressed the role of the environment (e.g., access to victim) in the crossover from accessing CSEM to CSO. However, given that neither Mr A nor Mr B has committed a contact offence, consideration of contextual variables identified as Preconditions Three and Four are necessarily speculative. The difference between observation and speculation/extrapolation must be made clear in any advice to the courts and protective agencies.

In terms of environmental influences, Precondition Three postulates for the potential offender to be able to physically and/or socially separate the potential victim from protectors; poor supervision of children can be an important factor in facilitating sexual abuse. Potential protective agents include family members, relatives and friends as well as agencies in the wider community. Thus, we suggest the following hypothesis: *A CSEM user is more likely to commit a CSO if external inhibitions can be overcome*. The relevant case information is presented in Table 16.4.

Table 16.4 Indications of ability to overcome external inhibitions.

Mr A	Mr B
Was able to view pornography (as well as CSEM) without Mrs A knowing.	Was able to view pornography (as well as CSEM) without Mrs B knowing.
Was able to masturbate while watching pornography in the living room while Mrs A was in bed without her knowing.	Was able to masturbate while watching pornography upstairs in the house while Mrs B was in bed without her knowing.
Mrs A was initially very protective of Mr A pointing out that he had looked at female-oriented CSEM and that their child was male.	Mrs B has mild learning difficulty.
	Mrs B has colluded with Mr B to allow him back into the house and has moved areas.
Mrs A participates in creation of erotic/sexually explicit video recordings.[1]	Mrs B has acted out Mr B's sexual fantasies indicative of an interest in prepubescent female children by shaving pubic hair and dressing in school girl uniform.[1]

[1] This sexual behaviour could be considered within the normal range of adult sexual activity and is not evidence of deviant sexual interest in and of itself; however, the issue here is one of consent/coercion and function of the behaviour, which needs to be established by the assessor.

At the point of assessment, neither Mr A nor Mr B had committed a CSO, and Mr A did not have a criminal record; thus, all information provided here is speculative. Both men had demonstrated an ability to view CSEM within the family environment but neither man had come to the attention of the authorities as a result of family members being aware of their activities. Both Mr A and Mr B's partners had been involved in activities related to their internet pornography use: Mrs A had acted out sexual scenes congruent with Mr A's disclosed adult sexual preferences while being videoed. Mrs B had dressed up as a schoolgirl and shaved her pubic hair which would appear consistent with Mr B's CSEM preferences. Mrs B was also assessed (by a different agency) as less able to protect her children than the average mother given her mild learning disability.

Both Mrs A and Mrs B were supportive of their partners. Mrs A was initially very defensive of Mr A and did not perceive him to present a risk to their son. (Following the court report, Mrs A changed her view of both Mr A's presented risk to the son and of their relationship and instigated divorce proceedings.) Mrs B had seemingly colluded with Mr B to allow him to live back in the family home and had moved to a new area in a way which made social services concerned that she was trying to evade their supervision.

At the point of assessment, it was felt that for both men there was insufficient evidence to refute the default hypothesis and therefore it was concluded that Precondition Three was likely to be partially met for both Mr A and Mr B. However, given the change in Mrs A's behaviour following the court report, it appears that Precondition Three is no longer met for Mr A. Alongside the speculative element in the analysis, the assessor should also acknowledge that the relevance of normal behaviours may become overemphasised through a post-hoc bias. For example, the creation of sexually explicit videos by Mr and Mrs A may in the presented context appear indicative of Mr A's (potentially deviant) sexual interest in recorded materials; however, this behaviour is also within the range of normal adult sexual engagement.

Precondition Four: Overcoming victim resistance

In order to fulfil Finkelhor's (1984) Precondition Four, the offender must have access to a vulnerable victim and be able to overcome their resistance. Having access to children has been identified as a key factor in crossover by both Babchishin, Hanson & VanZuylen (2015) and Seto (2013), however, the research evidence (based on re-conviction rates) indicates that crossover is an unusual behaviour for this group of men, leading to the following hypothesis: *A CSEM offender is more likely to commit a CSO if he is able to find a vulnerable victim and overcome their resistance.* The related evidence in the case material is set out in Table 16.5 but is inevitably the most speculative part of the analysis.

In effect there is no clear evidence that is strongly consistent with the hypothesis or strong enough to refute it. With regards to Precondition Three, we provided some evidence that both Mr A and Mr B can be persuasive; however, influencing one's partner is not comparable to coercing a child into sexual activity. It could be argued that Mr B has transgressed into

Table 16.5 Indications of ability to overcome victim resistance.

Mr A	Mr B
Own child is infant male.	Has female and male child.
	Set-up of computer so 15-year-old babysitter sees CSEM; suggestive of grooming of child outside the family.

potential grooming behaviour by allowing his babysitter use of his computer with ready access to his CSEM. Nevertheless, on balance, and given the lack of clear evidence either way, we cannot refute the hypothesis, with both Mr A and Mr B having some potential to fulfil Precondition Four, but typically being unlikely to do so based on the research evidence.

Recommendations

With respect to Mr A, our view was that he initially fulfilled Precondition One (CSEM use to facilitate a sexual interest in children) and Precondition Four (Overcoming Victim Resistance); however, he appeared to endorse internal inhibitors toward CSO (Precondition Two) and, due to the recent change in Mrs A's behaviour, there were difficulties in overcoming external inhibitors (Precondition Three), as Mrs A claimed she would deny Mr A contact with their son until he was successfully treated. There appears to be no guidance with respect to the potential weighting of preconditions in Finkelhor's (1984) model. While it is known that strong situational drivers are linked to CSEM offending (Merdian, Perkins, Dustagheer & Glorney, under review; Taylor & Quayle, 2006, 2008; Wortley, 2009), these appear to be mediated by internal processes, such as permission-giving thoughts, and we thus assume that Preconditions One and Two, referring to the assessee's internal states, will outweigh Preconditions Three and Four as necessary precursors to the offending behaviour. Thus, Mr A's presentation would lead us to recommend that he should only have supervised contact with children until Precondition One had been dealt with more thoroughly, for example, through participation in a treatment programme.

For Mr B, the listed material appears to provide some evidence for all preconditions, with the strongest support for Precondition One (CSEM use to facilitate a sexual interest in children), and Preconditions Two and Three (overcoming internal and external inhibitors) being at least partially met. Thus, on balance, we could not recommend Mr B's rehabilitation to the family without indications of significant participation in therapy aimed at addressing issues covered in Preconditions One and Two, and significant input for Mrs B with respect to Precondition Three.

Conclusion

In this chapter, we have considered the research evidence and theoretical models regarding CSEM usage and crossover to CSO, and have shown how the existing knowledge can be applied to parental risk evaluation cases. Our review pointed to the need for more specialised empirical and theoretical research in this area. Thus, our first recommendation for the assessor was to clearly communicate the limitations of the existing research body, alongside the uncertainty with respect to interpretation of the research data, the paucity of convincing theory, and the unreliability of evidence gained from both the clients and official sources. Our second recommendation for the assessor was, in response to the lack of empirical evidence, to default to existing explanatory models of CSO in adopting a scientist–practitioner approach. Although in previous work (Dawson & Gresswell, 2010), we have argued for the adoption of functional analysis as a method for making sense of complex case material and for establishing working hypotheses about the function and consistency of behaviour, the level of uncertainty arising from a lack of confidence in the evidence derived and an absence of independent observations in these CSEM cases does not lend itself to this type of analysis. Still, as could be seen in the presented cases, the psychologist's role as a scientist–practitioner has been stretched when it comes to assessing, analysing, predicting and managing the risk presented by real CSEM users in real family settings.

Although the environment has changed, viewing sexual imagery of children or grooming children for sexual purposes existed long before the advent of the internet (Seto, 2009), and while the topography and methods may have adjusted, the underlying function of the behaviour remains the same. However, the internet has now become the principal medium for CSEM purposes (Laulik, Allam & Sheridan, 2007). Hence, a related finding from CSEM investigations and research was the acknowledgement that it was previously underestimated how many adults are interested in accessing such material (Taylor & Quayle, 2005). The democratisation of CSEM availability will lead to many more people accessing it than will go on to offend; indeed the evidence to date appears to be that CSEM is being used by significant numbers of men who will not go on to commit a contact offence. As stated above, follow-up studies of CSEM users generally report very low re-offending rates, with the majority of sexual re-offences being internet-related as opposed to a contact sex offence (Faust, Bickart, Renaud & Camp, 2015; Seto, Hanson & Babchishin, 2011). Overall, the recidivism data suggests that CSEM offenders with no known contact offence history are at relatively low risk of contact offending (Eke, Seto & Williams, 2011; Seto, Hanson & Babchishin, 2011; Seto & Eke, 2015).

The endorsement of a sexual interest in children in a community population has been neglected as a research topic, and may be more widespread than previously assumed. In 1989, Briere and Runtz reported comparably high rates of paedophilic fantasies among male undergraduate students (21% indicated some sexual attraction to children, 7% reportedly would engage in sexual contact if immunity was guaranteed) and Gannon and O'Connor (2011) found that 57% of their sample of community males did not reject an interest in child sexual abuse.

Thus, relying too heavily on sexual interest, expressed through using CSEM, as a major risk indicator for CSO is likely to lead to high false positive rates. Instead, it is recommended that practitioners seek to explore the motivation underlying the individual's CSEM use, history of anti-sociality and the maintaining factors of the offending behaviour. In addition, to further our commitment to the scientist–practitioner approach, we aim to continuously enhance the empirical basis of our work, and for our practice to inform the kind of questions that drive psychological research. In this chapter, we have argued that in adopting a scientist–practitioner role, we need to be transparent about the limits of knowledge base, the transferability of our theoretical stance, our reasoning and our methods, to allow the courts to balance the evidence available and make informed decisions in the interests of the children and parents.

References

Babchishin, K.M., Hanson, R.K. & Hermann, C.A. (2010). The characteristics of online sex offenders: A meta-analysis. *Sexual Abuse: A Journal of Research and Treatment*, 23, 92–123.

Babchishin, K.M., Hanson, R.K. & VanZuylen, H. (2015). Online child pornography offenders are different: A meta-analysis of the characteristics of online and offline sex offenders against children. *Archives of Sexual Behavior*, 44, 45–66.

Baker, D.B. & Benjamin, L.T. (2000). The affirmation of the scientists-practitioner: A look back at Boulder. *American Psychologist*, 55, 241–247.

Beech, A.R., Elliott, I.A., Birgden, A. & Findlater, D. (2008). The internet and child sexual offending: A criminological review. *Aggression and Violent Behavior*, 13, 216–228.

Briere, J. & Runtz, M. (1989). University males' sexual interest in children: Predicting potential indices of 'pedophilia' in a nonforensic sample. *Child Abuse & Neglect,* 13, 65–75.

Buschman, J., Bogaerts, S., Foulger, S. et al. (2010). Sexual history disclosure polygraph examinations with cybercrime offenses: A first Dutch explorative study. *International Journal of Offender Therapy and Comparative Criminology,* 54, 395–411.

Butcher, J.N., Dahlstrom, W.G., Graham, J.R. et al. (1989). *The Minnesota Multiphasic Personality Inventory-2 (MMPI-2): Manual for Administration and Scoring.* Minneapolis, MN: University of Minnesota Press.

Caple, T. (2008). *A comparison of the characteristics and motivations of abusing and non-abusing child pornography offenders* (Unpublished doctoral dissertation). James Cook University, Townsville, AUS.

Cooper, A. (1998). Sexuality and the internet: Surfing into the new millennium. *CyberPsychology and Behavior,* 1, 187–193.

Craig, L.A. & Rettenberger, M. (2016). A brief history of sexual offender risk assessment. In: D.R. Laws and W. O'Donohue (eds), *Treatment of Sexual Offenders: Strengths and Weaknesses in Assessment and Intervention.* New York, Springer, 19–44.

Craig, L.A., Browne, K.D. & Beech, A.R. (2008). *Assessing Risk in Sex Offenders: A Practitioner's Guide.* Chichester: John Wiley & Sons, Ltd.

Craig, L.A., Browne, K.D., Hogue, T.E. &. Stringer, I. (2004). New directions in assessing risk for sex offenders. In: G. Macpherson & L. Jones (eds), *Risk Assessment and Management: Issues in Forensic Psychology.* Leicester, UK: The British Psychological Society.

Craig, L.A., Thornton, D., Beech, A. & Browne, K.D. (2007). The relationship of statistical and psychological risk markers to sexual reconviction in child molesters. *Criminal Justice & Behavior,* 34, 314–329.

Crown Prosecution Service (2014). *Violence against women and girls: Crime report 2013–14,* http://www.cps.gov.uk/data/violence_against_women/vawg_2013_14_report.html.

Dawson, D.L. & Gresswell, D.M. (2010). Offense paralleling behavior and multiple sequential functional analysis. In: M. Daffern, L. Jones and J. Shine (eds), *Offense Paralleling Behavior: A Case Formulation Approach to Offender Assessment and Intervention.* Chichester: John Wiley & Sons, Ltd.

Eke, A.W., Seto, M.C. & Williams, J. (2011). Examining the criminal history and future offending of child pornography offenders: An extended prospective follow-up study. *Law and Human Behavior,* 35, 466–478.

Faust, E., Bickart, W., Renaud, C. & Camp, S. (2015). Child pornography possessors and child contact sex offenders: A multilevel comparison of demographic characteristics and rates of recidivism. *Sexual Abuse: A Journal of Research and Treatment,* 27, 460–478.

Finkelhor, D. (1984). *Child Sexual Abuse: New Theory and Research.* New York: Free Press.

Gannon, T.A. & O'Connor, A. (2011). The development of the interest in child molestation scale. *Sexual Abuse: A Journal of Research and Treatment,* 23, 474–494.

Glasgow, D. (2010). The potential of digital evidence to contribute to risk assessment of internet offenders. *Journal of Sexual Aggression,* 16, 87–106.

Hanson, R.K. & Morton-Bourgon, K.E. (2004, February). *Predictors of sexual recidivism: An updated meta-analysis (PS3-1/2004-2E-PDF).* Ottawa, ON: Public Safety and Emergency Preparedness Canada, www.publicsafety.gc.ca/cnt/rsrcs/pblctns/2004-02-prdctrs-sxl-rcdvsm-pdtd/2004-02-prdctrs-sxl-rcdvsm-pdtd-eng.pdf.

Hanson, R.K. & Thornton, D. (1999). *Static-99. Improving actuarial risk assessment for sex offenders.* Ottawa, ON: Department of the Solicitor General of Canada, www.courtdiagnostic.com/Static%2099-02.pdf.

Hanson, R.K., Harris, A.J.R., Scott, T.L. & Helmus, L. (2007). *Assessing the risk of sex offenders on community supervision: The Dynamic Supervision Project (User Report 2007–05).* Ottawa, ON: Public Safety Canada.

Holt, T.J., Blevins, K.R. & Burkert, N. (2010). Considering the paedophile subculture online. *Sexual Abuse: A Journal of Research and Treatment,* 22, 3–24.

Howitt, D. & Sheldon, K. (2007). The role of cognitive distortions in paedophilic offending: Internet and contact offenders compared. *Psychology, Crime and Law,* 13, 469–486.

Ireland, C. & Craig. L.A. (2011). Adult sex offender assessment. In: D.P. Boer., R. Eher., L.A. Craig, M.H. Miner. & F. Pfaefflin (eds), *International Perspectives on the Assessment and Treatment of Sexual Offenders: Theory, Practice and Research*. Chichester, UK: Wiley-Blackwell, 13–33.

Jahnke, S., Imhoff, R. & Hoyer, J. (2015). Stigmatization of people with pedophilia: Two comparative surveys. *Archives of Sexual Behaviour*, 44, 21–34.

Laulik, S., Allam, J. & Sheridan, L. (2007). An investigation into maladaptive personality functioning in internet sex offenders. *Psychology, Crime and Law*, 13, 523–535.

Long, M.L., Alison, L.A. & McManus, M.A. (2013). Child pornography and likelihood of contact abuse: A comparison between contact child sexual offenders and non-contact offenders. *Sexual Abuse: A Journal of Research and Treatment*, 25, 370–395.

Merdian, H.L., Perkins, D.E., Dustagheer, E. & Glorney, E. (under review). Development of a case formulation model for users of child sexual exploitation material. *International Journal of Offender Therapy and Comparative Criminology*.

Merdian, H.L., Curtis, C., Thakker, J. et al. (2013). The three dimensions of online child pornography offending. *Journal of Sexual Aggression*, 19, 121–132.

Merdian, H.L., Wilson, N., Thakker, J. et al. (2013) 'So why did you do it?': Explanations provided by child pornography offenders. *Sexual Offender Treatment*, 1–19, http://researchcommons.waikato.ac.nz/bitstream/handle/10289/7976/So%20why%20did%20you%20do%20it.pdf?sequence=1&isAllowed=y.

Middleton, D., Mandelville-Norden, R. & Hayes, E. (2009). Does treatment work with internet sex offenders? Emerging findings from the Internet Sex Offender Treatment Programme (i-SOTP). *Journal of Sexual Aggression*, 15, 5–19.

Neutze, J., Seto, M.C., Schaefer, G.A. et al. (2011). Predictors of child pornography offenses and child sexual abuse in a community sample of pedophiles and hebephiles. *Sexual Abuse: A Journal of Research and Treatment*, 23, 212–242.

O'Brien, M.D. & Webster, S.D. (2007). The construction and preliminary validation of the Internet Behaviors and Attitudes Questionnaire (IBAQ). *Sexual Abuse: A Journal of Research and Treatment*, 19, 237–256.

Osborn, J., Elliott, I.A., Middleton, D. & Beech, A.R. (2010). The use of actuarial risk assessment measures with UK internet child pornography offenders. *Journal of Sexual Aggression, Conflict and Peace Research*, 2, 16–24.

Parsons, R., Honyara, N., Delmonico, D.L. & Griffin, E.J. (2013). *The child abuse material instrument (CAMI): Collecting and utilizing forensic data in child pornography cases*, http://ranconsulting.net/uploads/Perspectives_V38_N1_P94CAMI.pdf.

Quayle, E. (2009). Assessment of internet sexual abuse. In: M.C. Calder (ed), *Sexual Abuse: Using and Developing Frameworks for Practice*. Dorset, UK: Russell House Publishing, 250–263.

R v Oliver and others [2003] 2 Cr.App.R. (S) 15.

Schmidt, A.F., Mokros, A. & Banse, R. (2013). Is pedophilic sexual preference continuous? A taxometric analysis based on direct and indirect measures. *Psychological Assessment*, 25, 1146–1153.

Sentencing Council (2014). *Sexual offenses: Definitive Guideline*, www.sentencingcouncil.org.uk/wp-content/uploads/Final_Sexual_Offences_Definitive_Guideline_content_web1.pdf.

Seto, M. (2013). *Internet Sex Offenders*. Washington, DC: American Psychological Association.

Seto, M.C. (2009, March). *Assessing the risk posed by child pornography offenders*. Position Paper prepared for the G8 Global Symposium 'Global symposium for examining the relationship between online and offline offenses and preventing the sexual exploitation of children', University of North Carolina, Chapel Hill, www.iprc.unc.edu/G8/Seto_Position_Paper.pdf.

Seto, M.C. & Eke, A.W. (2005). The criminal histories and later offending of child pornography offenders. *Sexual Abuse: A Journal of Research and Treatment*, 17, 201–210.

Seto, M.C. & Eke, A.W. (2015). Predicting recidivism among adult male child pornography offenders: Development of the Child Pornography Offender Risk Tool (CPORT). *Law and Human Behaviour*, 39, 416–429.

Seto, M.C., Hanson, R.K. & Babchishin, K.M. (2011). Contact sexual offending by men with online sexual offenses. *Sexual Abuse: A Journal of Research and Treatment*, 23, 124–145.

Seto, M.C., Reeves, L. & Jung, S. (2010). Explanations given by child pornography offenders for their crimes. *Journal of Sexual Aggression*, 16, 169–180.

Shakow, D. (1942). The training of the clinical psychologist. *Journal of Consulting Psychology*, 6, 277–288.

Shakow, D. (n.d.). The training of the clinical psychologist. AAAP Professional Training in Clinical Psychology, 1939–1941, Box 691, American Psychological Association Papers, Library of Congress, Washington, DC.

Sheldon, K. & Howitt, D. (2007). *Sex Offenders and the Internet*. Chichester: John Wiley & Sons, Ltd.

Singer, J.C., Boer, D.P. & Rettenberger, M. (2013). A convergent approach to sex offender risk assessment. In: K. Harrison & B. Rainey (eds), *The Wiley-Blackwell Handbook of Legal and Ethical Aspects of Sex Offender Treatment and Management*. Hoboken, NY: John Wiley & Sons Inc., 341–355.

Surjadi, B., Bullens, R., van Horn, J. & Bogaerts, S. (2010). Internet offending: Sexual and non-sexual functions within a Dutch sample. *Journal of Sexual Aggression*, 16, 47–58.

Taylor, M. & Quayle, E. (2003). *Child Pornography: An Internet Crime*. Hove, UK: Brunner-Routledge.

Taylor, M. & Quayle, E. (2005). Abusive images of children and the internet: Research from the COPINE project. In: S.W. Cooper, R.J. Estes, A.P. Giardino, N.D. Kellogg & V.I. Vieth (eds), *Medical, Legal and Social Science Aspects of Child Sexual Exploitation: A Comprehensive Review of Pornography, Prostitution, and Internet Crimes*. St Louis, MO: GW Medical Publishing, 257–275.

Taylor, M. & Quayle, E. (2006). The internet and abuse images of children: Search, pre-criminal situations and opportunity. In: R. Wortley & S. Smallbone (eds), *Crime Prevention Studies Vol. 19: Situational Prevention of Child Sexual Abuse*. Devon, UK: Willan Publishing and Criminal Justice Press, 169–195.

Taylor, M. & Quayle, E. (2008). Criminogenic qualities of the internet in the collection and distribution of abuse images of children. *The Irish Journal of Psychology*, 29, 119–130.

Taylor, M., Holland, G. & Quayle, E. (2001). Typology of paedophile picture collections. *The Police Journal*, 74, 97–107.

Thornton, D., Mann, R., Webster, S. et al. (2003). Distinguishing and combining risks for sexual and violent recidivism. In: R. Prentky, E. Janus, M. Seto & A.W. Burgess (eds), *Annals of the New York Academy of Sciences (Vol. 989): Sexually Coercive Behavior: Understanding and Management*. New York: New York Academy of Sciences, 225–235.

Tully, R., Browne, K.D. & Craig, L.A. (2015). An examination of the predictive validity of the Structured Assessment of Risk and Need Treatment Needs Analysis (SARN TNA) in England and Wales. *Criminal Justice and Behaviour*, 42, 509–528.

UK Coroners and Justice Act 2009, www.legislation.gov.uk/ukpga/2009/25/section/62.

UK Obscene Publication Act 1959, www.legislation.gov.uk/ukpga/Eliz2/7-8/66/contents.

UK Protection of Children Act 1978 c. 37 section 1, www.legislation.gov.uk/ukpga/1978/37.

UK Sexual Offences Act 2003 c. 42, www.legislation.gov.uk/ukpga/2003/42/contents.

Wakeling, H., Beech, A.R. & Freemantle, N. (2013). Investigating treatment change and its relationship to recidivism in a sample of 3773 sex offenders in the UK. *Psychology, Crime and Law*, 19, 233–252.

Wakeling, H.C., Howard, P. & Barnett, G. (2011). Comparing the validity of the RM2000 Scales and OGRS3 for predicting recidivism by internet sex offenders. *Sexual Abuse: A Journal of Research and Treatment*, 23, 146–168.

Witt, P.H., Merdian, H.L., Connell, M. & Boer, D.P. (2010). Assessing parental risk in parenting plan (child custody) evaluation cases involving internet sexual behavior. *Open Access Journal of Forensic Psychology*, 2, 216–236, http://media.wix.com/ugd/166e3f_032e2a11611c4a88acd6acde2b8fe816.pdf.

Wolak, J., Finkelhor, D. & Mitchell, K.J. (2005). *Child-pornography possessors arrested in internet-related crimes: Findings from the National Juvenile Online Victimization Study.* Alexandra, VA: National Center for Missing and Exploited Children, www.unh.edu/ccrc/pdf/jvq/CV81.pdf.

Wortley, R. (2009, April). *Situational prevention of child sexual abuse in the new technologies.* Position Paper prepared for the G8 Global Symposium 'Global symposium for examining the relationship between online and offline offenses and preventing the sexual exploitation of children', University of North Carolina, Chapel Hill, www.iprc.unc.edu/symposium.shtml.

Yates, P.M. (2009). Is sexual offender denial related to sex offense risk and recidivism? A review and treatment implications. *Psychology, Crime and Law*, 15, 183–199.

17

Assessments in Child Care Proceedings
Observations in Practice

Martin C. Calder
Calder Training & Consultancy Limited, UK

Introduction

Evidence-based practice raises challenges for frontline practitioners who are facing high caseloads, most containing a multitude of problems, and variable access to research and detailed training. The government definition for social care practice is that it must comprise the best of theory, research and practice wisdom. Practitioners are, however, lacking the access to, and the time to read and digest, much of the best materials available. They are also dealing with new kinds of case work where research and theory has yet to emerge and practitioners are developing approaches by drawing on the closest proximate materials from their experience. This chapter attempts to offer a view from practitioners operating frequently in the gaps between theory and research and provides a summary of professional observations of current practice in child care proceedings and emerging themes. It examines the changing court context in England and Wales for child care proceedings and the challenges and consequences of a move designed to streamline the process, but which, in doing so, is arguably in danger of losing sight of the child. The context that allows such a move will be examined followed by practice-based suggestions that aim to keep the children the priority within child care proceedings.

The Context

The child protection system in England and Wales in recent times has been shaped by four key driving forces: the importance of the safety and welfare of children and young people; a belief held by many that uncertainty in child protection work can be eradicated; a tendency in inquiries

---

The Wiley Handbook of What Works in Child Maltreatment: An Evidence-Based Approach to Assessment and Intervention in Child Protection, First Edition. Edited by Louise Dixon, Daniel F. Perkins, Catherine Hamilton-Giachritsis, and Leam A. Craig.
© 2017 John Wiley & Sons Ltd. Published 2017 by John Wiley & Sons Ltd.

to focus on professional error without examining the causes of any error; and the undue weight given to performance information and targets (Morrison, 2009).

Assessment is a key task for all social work professionals and a good assessment should:

- Recognise that some users may be the best assessors of their own needs and solutions.
- Consider the needs and strengths of individuals in the context of their everyday lives.
- Be separate from a decision about allocation of services.
- Strike a balance between invading privacy and obtaining sufficient information.
- Be ethnically and culturally sensitive.

Child and parental assessments are the heartbeat of all social work practice and provide the pathway to sensitive decision-making that strives to achieve optimum outcomes for vulnerable children and their families. Historically, in the UK child care policy has created a standardised set of templates that were mandatory for social workers to use in their assessment practice (Department of Health [DoH], 2000). Allied to this was a rigid requirement to complete different parts of the process in prescribed timescales that formed the principal measure of practice competence by government. For example, a referral had to be dealt with in 24 hours, an initial assessment in seven days and a more detailed core assessment in 35 days (DoH, 1999). It could be argued that the drive to comply with the timescales diverted worker focus from the needs of the case toward compliance with the procedure and performance measure. The tight timeframes for conducting the required assessments led workers to become output rather than outcome compliant, and the perceptions of practice were that the child was forced to work within the timescales rather than the professionals working at the child's pace.

Complex cases involving children frequently require consideration within a legal framework and there have been significant changes to this framework in England and Wales in recent years. Historically, the perception has been one of concern that the timetabling and conclusion of cases has been too protracted to accommodate professional capacity and anxieties at the expense of timely decisions affecting the children concerned. The *Public law outline: Guide to case management in public law proceedings* (PLO: Ministry of Justice, 2008) came into force with effect from 6 April 2010. The PLO sets out streamlined case management procedures for dealing with public law children's cases. The aim is to identify and focus on the key issues for the child, with the aim of making the best decisions for the child within the timetable set by the court, and avoiding the need for unnecessary evidence or hearings. Under the revised section 32(1)(a) of the Children Act 1989 (introduced by section 14 of the Children and Families Act 2014), care and supervision proceedings must be completed without delay, and, in any event, within 26 weeks beginning with the day on which the application was issued.

Concerns of excessive control, bureaucracy and box-ticking led the UK government to commission a review of child protection procedures known as the Munro Report of Child Protection (Munro, 2011). The introduction of this report, in part, relieved some of the perception of excessive control but unfortunately this has been replaced by rigid inflexible timescales adopted by the courts and also by local council elected members who oversee local practice. Lawyer Edward Lloyd-Jones has argued that the PLO should be scrapped due to concerns of bureaucratic restrictions on human complexity (cited in Gillen, 2009). Lloyd-Jones has also noted that where assessments are carried out under the eye of the court, during proceedings all parties can contribute to the identification and instruction of the expert and thereby fully participate. The danger of in-house assessments is that they may not have the confidence of all parties nor subsequently of the court, which could lead to further delay (cited in Gillen, 2009).

As a result of the new working arrangements, social workers are being socialised into accepting that there are serious resource constraints and there is a danger that they may make recommendations on attainable rather than desirable outcomes. There is some evidence of stress-related illness, linked to both physical and mental health, within the health and social care workforce as a result of increasing demands and decreasing resources (Calder, 2016). Social workers are also at greater risk of becoming desensitised to the emotional impact of their roles, and thus, less able to give the best therapeutic care to those on the receiving end of services. The consequences for organisations include: absenteeism and long-term sick leave, high staff turnover and use of agency staff and management consultancies, expensive and ongoing recruitment and retention processes, and errors and impaired quality and safety of social and health care (Calder, 2008a, 2008b; Morrison, 1990).

Since the review of child protection procedures by Munro (2011), there has been no escape from the review or public scrutiny of social and children's services. There has been no decline in the number of referrals to children's services or early years' intervention or in the number of children that come into care. Wider austerity cuts have led to reductions in funding to services, and changes in the terms and conditions of employment, and training and support of social workers. Online fora for social workers reveal anxieties and stress in practitioners in attempting to balance the needs and demands of courts with the needs and wishes and feelings of vulnerable children and families (Social Work Matrix, 2015).

Children and Family Court Advisory and Support Service (CAFCASS)

CAFCASS represents children in family court cases, with the role of making sure that children's voices are heard and decisions are taken in their best interests. They are independent of the courts, social services, education and health authorities and all similar agencies. CAFCASS as an organisation has endured significant challenges in the course of its evolution and this has impacted on the quality and confidence of the employees who conduct the court orchestra in many cases.

An ideal response to challenges over practice is to evolve better, more detailed and more coherent procedures. In CAFCASS the perception has conceivably been one of a bureaucratic drive toward a compliance culture with performance targets at its heart, although many other examples of prescriptive practice exist. The unfortunate issuing of the Domestic Violence Toolkit (CAFCASS, 2007), which set out the prescribed approach practitioners should adopt in their work, was a response to concerns about practice in this area of work. However, arguably, it was premature and misaligned as the system of response was premised on the Multi Agency Risk Assessment Conference (MARAC) system, which is principally adult victim focused rather than child-focused. MARAC is a monthly multi-agency meeting, chaired by police, focusing on the safety of victims of domestic abuse identified as being at high risk. The identification of high-risk victims of domestic abuse has been made possible by the use of a risk-identification tool. In a single meeting, the MARAC combines up-to-date risk information with a timely assessment of a victim's needs and links those directly to the provision of appropriate services for all those involved in a domestic abuse case: victim, children and perpetrator. Information is shared and joint decisions made on the most appropriate way to reduce or manage the identified risks.

CAFCASS Cymru, based in Wales, commissioned a set of materials that re-focused on the child in conjunction with the child welfare checklist (Harold & Shelton, 2008). The Child and

Adolescent Welfare Assessment Checklist (CC-CAWAC; Harold & Shelton, 2008) examines the impact upon a child of seeing or hearing inter-parental conflict – allowing workers to better assess through evidence-based means the psychological and social risk of individual children being subject to inter-parental conflict. Importantly, this is also of significance in private law cases where significant problems for children emerge but the pressure of time allocated to these pieces of work often precludes detailed examination of such issues as the focus is on the resolution of adult disputes (Harold & Shelton, 2008).

The Office for Standards in Education, Children's Services and Skill (Ofsted) is a non-ministerial department of the UK government, which has been accused of approaching their task with a 'high criticism, low warmth' mentality that is perceived as demotivating, persecutory and unhelpful. For example, Burns (2015) reported council concerns that their approach to inspecting child protection services is 'blinkered', not least because they fail to assess the work of 'crucial agencies', such as health services and police. Before making practice-based suggestions on improvements to current assessment frameworks, it is important to also consider the impact that various non-child care-specific legislation has on child care proceedings.

Lack of Protection for Practitioners

The latest concern for social workers is that practitioners in care cases can now be identified online. The Right Honourable Lord Justice James Munby, President of the Family Court Division in the UK, ruled in 2013 that family courts should not prevent parents, the media and websites from identifying social workers once care proceedings have ended (*Re J (a child)* [2013]). The decision related to Staffordshire Council's bid to stop the publication of names, images and video footage of social workers involved in the case of Child J, who was subject to an emergency protection order after birth in April 2014. On the day Child J was removed from his family, the father posted a comment on Facebook comparing social workers involved in the case with the Nazi SS paramilitaries. Child J's father then posted secret video footage on the internet which showed social services taking the baby away. The footage was later uploaded to YouTube by the website UK Column Live, which followed this by publishing a video interview with the parents in which the child was named. In his judgement Lord Justice Munby ruled that injunctions that prevented the identification of the children's guardian, the council and the social workers should only be granted if there were compelling reasons. The need for open justice means that courts should not gag those with objections, founded or otherwise, to the family justice system. Instead courts should balance the child's right to privacy with people's right to freedom of expression (Donovan, 2013).

Nicolas (2014) reported a further name and shame case where three social workers from North East Lincolnshire have been named and criticised by Judge Simon Jack for their role in care proceedings. This was in line with the High Court ruling from Lord Justice Munby who had made his position clear on the need for open justice and transparency in the family court. However, the perception is that such a move may drive people away from the profession entrusted with protecting children, as well as ruining the lives of the professionals involved. The real issue however is the concern expressed by some that the social workers were 'hung out to dry' by their organisation playing the blame game – thus creating a toxic scenario (Calder, 2015) where staff are faced with an environment for practice pervaded by fear, blame and a lack of trust (Ayre & Calder, 2010).

Evidence-Based Practice: Challenges and Consequences

The UK government introduced an expectation that practitioners' assessments and decisions should be grounded in evidence-based practice, to reduce the possibility of appeals, as well as in recognition of the fact that the demise of expert appointees to conduct assessments required enhanced credibility of the assessments being provided by frontline (generic) staff. 'Expressions of opinion must be supported by detailed evidence and articulated reasoning' (*Re M* [2003]).

Evidence-based practice comprises the best of theory, research and practice wisdom. Unfortunately, social workers undertaking assessments are often discouraged from using the theory unless it is departmentally sanctioned (such as systems approaches), and have to adhere to carefully selected 'commonly accepted' (government-related) research. Their practice wisdom is often considered, scrutinised and rejected by the court system.

The skills needed for evidence-based practice include an ability to formulate an answerable question from a clinical or service issue, search using bibliographical databases (such as Medline) and find shortcuts to good quality evidence, be confident in critically appraising research findings, interpret and apply results for use in a particular clinical situation, or in developing service provision, and evaluate one's own clinical practice.

There would be little disagreement with the view that good practice ought to derive from research evidence about either the nature, causes or typical pathways of social problems or about the success of particular methods to deal with those problems (Hill, 1991). The evidence-based practice movement therefore urges practitioners to seek out and critically assess relevant research literature and findings. Evidence-based practitioners should themselves collect data systemically, specify outcomes in measurable terms and systemically monitor and evaluate their interventions (Hill, 1991, p. 20).

There are, however, some potential pitfalls of evidence-based practice and these include the question whether research should be the sole basis for developing or sustaining services, whether things as complex as human interactions can be measured, and whether paying attention to the efficacy of interventions diverts attention away from the root of problems.

While the directions adopted within the Assessment Framework (the standardised and mandated framework in England and Wales for professionals involved in child care work) allows for the use of practice wisdom to offset any research and conceptual limitations, this is problematic since it is commonly cited as the lowest form of evidence on the evidence-base continuum (Ramchandani, Joughin & Zwi, 2001) and practitioners lack the opportunity for reflective practice or time to read and digest the emerging materials.

Some of the questions that evidence-based practice can help to answer include effectiveness, risk/prognosis, description, assessment and prevention. However, court judgements need to be based on sound research, defined by its methods, sampling and analysis, and the suggestion is that practitioners are not supported in searching out, or being critical of the case-specific relevance of research, or being encouraged to ask questions of the research. Some of the other issues raised about evidence-based practice include research lagging behind practice, the research having limited applicability to presenting practice situations, searching for material being time-consuming and expensive, and the fact that research is often discouraged by legal advocates (Calder, 2014). Calder (2014) identified a number of obstacles to evidence-based practice that include:

- Inadequate access to research information – access being costly, time-consuming and frequently undertaken in personal time.
- Lack of knowledge about how to find or appraise research – given the shift from reflective to regulatory supervision.

- Insufficient time or resources and competing priorities.
- Lack of support from colleagues.
- A culture of acting before reflecting – with overwhelmed staff on a conveyor belt of unrelenting work and expectation (Calder, 2008a, 2008b).
- Poor communication of research within organisations – often individuals rather than wider systems.
- Perceived threats to professional autonomy – especially since staff feel that they represent the department's interests as opposed to the child's.
- Lack of relevant and timely evidence – as new problems do not wait for research and theory.
- Perceptions of research – need to be understood as well as the motivation and aim of the authors.

Elevated Expectations

There has been a shift toward expecting that most assessments will have been completed by the start of the care proceedings, as directed within the PLO timeframe (Ministry of Justice, 2008). This is often in a climate of diminishing resources and thus access to experts; therefore, staff are elevated to the role of expert. This is more challenging if practitioners lack experience or detailed training in the absence of departmentally mandated assessment tools and specialist/reflective supervision. The Legal Guidance (prepared by the Crown Prosecution Service for England and Wales) defines an expert as: 'a person whose evidence is intended to be tendered before a court and who has relevant skill or knowledge achieved through research, experience or professional application within a specific field sufficient to entitle them to give evidence of their opinion and upon which the court may require independent, impartial assistance' (para 36.2, Crown Prosecution Service, 2010). The role of an expert witness is to break complex problems down into manageable components, to rationalise them so that they are controllable and so that interventions can be applied which will lead to predictable and positive outcomes. Interestingly, however, Power (2004, p. 14) has argued that:

> Experts who are being made increasingly accountable for what they do are now becoming more preoccupied with managing their own risks. Specifically, secondary risks to their reputation are becoming as significant as the primary risks for which experts have knowledge and training. This trend is resulting in a dangerous flight from judgement and a culture of defensiveness that create their own risks for organisations in preparing for and responding to a future they cannot know.

A challenge for some social workers is the notion of having their assessment tempered by the organisation – especially if the two clash or even are polar opposites. The assessment clearly needs to focus on the child's journey and what can be achieved by formal intervention, but the danger is that such an approach will identify resources that are not available. Therefore, the perception is that they are diluted to achieve a match between plans and available resources. Effective assessments remain child-focused and bravely assert what is needed to effect change.

Transforming Social Workers

Practice wisdom has been defined as 'a particular type of professional expertise involving the capacity for wise judgements in uncertain situations' (O'Sullivan, 2005, p. 222). O'Sullivan (2005) argued that practice wisdom needs to be critical, accountable and knowledge-based and requires distinctive knowledge-production processes, an ability to make reasoning explicit, as well as credible and valuable knowledge. There are two types of reasoning: intuitive and analytical. Social workers are often encouraged to prioritise analysis over intuition as it is considered by many to be more formal and defensible. Indeed, Munro (2008) argued that child protection work makes heavy demands on reasoning skills.

Intuition is the use of tacit knowledge and emotions to make judgements and decisions without deliberation. Analytical reasoning involves the capacity to analyse and synthesise information into hypotheses about particular situations. Analytical reasoning requires flexible conceptual frameworks and the social work difficulty in explaining reasoning maybe a symptom of the lack of such frameworks. Perceptions of frontline practice suggest that it may be more appropriate to cultivate wise rather than evidence-based practice. Wise practice involves balancing, weighing, integrating what is known and making judgements. It is clear however that the increase in regulatory practice undermines any worker's capacity to act wisely with the overwhelming prioritisation of process and task over need and reflection.

Courts are reasonably expecting social workers to predict the future in order that they make the appropriate assessment of risk in the case. Unfortunately, the expectation that one can predict parenting in the future – especially if this is a relatively new case – on the basis of a tight court timetable is unrealistic. Snapshot assessments create multiple errors and this is evidenced with over-optimistic projections that people who change can stay changed – especially drug- and alcohol-using adults (Calder, unpublished). Courts expect social workers to assess parenting holistically, but given that this is complicated and protracted, the best that can be assessed is compliance within the judicial timeframe (parenting ability) rather than their parenting capacity, which requires observations over a sustained period of time (Calder, 2013). Effective assessments require the necessary time to sequence the assessment needed rather than holding to a timeframe which precludes informed prediction potential due to a lack of time to observe and cross-check with other professionals as well with as historical data.

Ideas for a Framework for Assessment

Good assessment is fundamental to good practice for all potential service users, regardless of age. It is an analytical process that requires intelligence, logic, flexibility, open-mindedness and creativity, and it should be experienced by the consumer as a positive contribution to their life (Middleton, 1997). The often-reported and -observed challenges in delivering good assessments (e.g., Calder, 2010; 2015) include:

- Generic is too general – although it does ensure that all presenting risks are identified rather than having to act on the originating concerns.
- Multiple specialist tools are required – to capture the increasing co-existence of problems – although the cause and consequence debate persists (Calder, 2010) and the multiplicity of harms grows.
- Analysis follows particular assessments – and it is more difficult to balance the risks and strengths across multiple different frameworks.
- Information sharing – an alarmingly pervasive and persistent problem meaning that effective assessment is too often retrospective as opposed to prospective.
- Challenges to multidisciplinary working – all struggling with increased complexity and caseloads.

- Perverse consequences of early help successes – where the assembly of information accelerates the move to child protection as opposed to heading it off.
- Actuarial or clinical assessment – often means that even when professionals are communicating with each other, there is no guarantee that they are talking about the same thing, or that they even acknowledge a difference of interpretation exists.
- Tri-partite risk assessments – need to be meaningfully holistic and embrace resistance and resilience, as well as risk.
- Emotions, resilience and resources – professionals become contaminated by the emotive nature of the work, the lack of care for the staff and the accommodation of personal responsibility when things go wrong (Calder, 2015).

Good assessments should recognise that some users may be the assessors of their own needs and solutions; consider the needs and strengths of individuals in the context of their everyday lives; be separate from a decision about allocation of services; strike a balance between invading privacy and obtaining sufficient information; and be ethically and culturally sensitive. Table 17.1 sets out the essential ingredients for good assessments described by Middleton (1997).

Considering the aforementioned points, good assessments should arguably:

- Be based on defined theoretical models and research.
- Recognise the individuality of each client, the context, family, assets and difficulties.
- View the client and their needs holistically.
- Have access to information from a range of sources.
- Expect denial from involuntary clients and employ techniques to motivate and engage the client and their families.
- Promote confidence in the help that can be offered and the achievability and potential benefits of change.
- Provide a hypothesis on problem formation, future risk, risk management and clear interventions plans.
- Ensure liaison with child protection and other relevant agencies.
- Feedback to the client, their family and other professionals.

Table 17.1 Good assessment (adapted from Middleton, 1997).

GOOD ASSESSMENT	
Starts with an open mind	Thinks about a range of options
Starts where the individual is involved and empowers the user as a partner	Does not put pressure on the user to choose the option the assessor wants or resources prescribe
Relates to their perceived problem and explores the reasons for it	Negotiations with the individual, and with existing and potential service providers, to find an acceptable and feasible solution
Puts the information in the context of its collection	Makes recommendations which relate to the information collected
Analyses the problem using the data	Makes arrangements for review
Explores the pros and cons of a range of solutions	Attends to how the user views the range of options and sees the match between options and the strengths of the user/circumstances

The social work assessment is a key document in child care proceedings. It should contain the history and current circumstances of a child's situation, an analysis of the meaning of that situation and the implications for risk and at least some alternatives for the court to consider in making decisions aimed at alleviating that risk (Precey, 2001).

Courts are required to assess and balance the risks involved in each case. Some element of risk may be involved in the initial stage of deciding whether the threshold criteria for making an order have been established, if there is an issue as to whether a child is likely to suffer significant harm; but at this stage no balancing exercise is needed. Assessing and balancing risks really come to the fore when the court reaches the next stage of considering whether it is in the child's welfare for an order to be made.

The process may start with the court identifying the risks likely to arise in a particular case. Each of these risks then has to be assessed. Assessing a risk involves evaluating both (a) the chances of that risk materialising and (b) the likely harm if it does materialise. The weight attached to a particular risk is likely to depend on a combination of these two factors. The balancing of the risks then takes place, accompanied by weighing of the risks against any other relevant items in the checklist (e.g., the child's wishes). It is a result of this balancing exercise that the decision on what to do will be determined. The balance of risk will not necessarily be decisive. There may be cases (e.g., where the identified risks are negligible or finely balanced) where other factors – such as the child's wishes – may be decisive.

The court may well use the following factors to identify and assess risks:

- Past events (e.g., significant harm already suffered by a relevant child).
- The characters and conduct of the relevant adults (e.g., their ability and willingness to protect their child from harm).
- The particular attributes and needs of the child concerned (e.g., any special needs).
- Any significant changes in the situation which give rise to the institution of care proceedings.
- The availability of professional guidance and support to help the relevant adults to avoid or minimise risks to the child.
- The views, experience and judgement of relevant professionals, such as social workers, health visitors and teachers.
- Examinations and/or research by experts such as paediatricians, psychiatrists and psychologists.
- The investigation and views of the children's guardian.

When assessing risks, it is obviously necessary to be as objective and precise as possible. However, since one is dealing with unpredictable factors of human behaviour and future events, it is unrealistic to expect that such an exercise can be conducted with the mathematical accuracy applied to the solution of a problem in mechanics (Craig, Browne, Stringer & Beech, 2004). This is particularly true when looking at the chances of a particular risk materialising. In many cases it is usually difficult to do more than place these chances within a fairly broad band, such as 'negligible', 'very high' or 'about 50/50' – and even then it would be hard to avoid an appreciable element of speculation. However, it is usually easier to predict the likelihood of a risk materialising in the future if that risk has actually materialised in the past, than if it is, as yet, a purely hypothetical risk. In risk assessment this is sometimes referred to as anamnestic risk assessment, meaning that history will repeat itself (Melton, Petrila, Poythress & Slobogin, 1997). Anamnestic risk assessment assumes there is a series of events and circumstances (behavioural chain) which resulted in the outcome behaviour. However, the seriousness of the harm already done is not a predictor that future harm will be more or less serious, only that the likelihood of it is increased, unless relevant interventions can be made that will lessen that risk.

Forensic Approach to Assessment

Munro (2011) argued for the recapturing of a forensic approach to the conduct of assessments as there is ample evidence of too much information being collected that bears no reference to the risks being assessed and makes any analysis more difficult as we try to separate the wood from the trees. Akin to this approach is the well-established stepwise model suggested by Samra-Tibbets and Raynes (1999), which organises information into five keys areas: plan, hypothesise, gather information, test information and evaluate.

Plan

In the first block, **planning** is essential. This is often left out by the practitioners as they feel pressured to get on with the task, particularly when working to tight timeframes. This may be safe where practitioners work together on a regular basis, but is more concerning where they have never worked together beforehand. There needs to be a careful look at the information held already, and what still needs to be gathered. There needs to be some agreement on channels of communication, as it is unrealistic for the social worker to expect to know everything at every stage of the process.

Hypothesise

The second block attends to issues of **hypotheses**. This is considered to be the starting point for an investigation. There is some suggestion that social workers sometimes begin the assessment with one particular hypothesis and gather evidence to support this. This can be dangerous as it actually involves the formation of a conclusion before the assessment has begun. The social worker should consider all possible hypotheses, be open-minded in gathering evidence, and prioritise hypotheses only where there is clear evidence to do so. They need to take a step back from the early intervention in order to generate the maximum number of possibilities, so as not to shut down any avenue prematurely. Gawlinski, Carr, McDonnell and Irving (1988) offered the following characteristics of a hypothesis: it is stated in specific rather than vague terms; the statements within the hypothesis are logically connected; it is comprehensive and so takes account of most available significant information; it contains statements about predisposing and precipitating factors; it identifies factors which continue to place the family at risk for further child abuse; and it points to a clear action plan and also suggests courses of action that should be avoided. The initial hypothesis is necessarily speculative and is used as the basis for gathering more information that will either confirm or refute it.

Gather information

In the third block, there is a need to **gather information**. Nothing is more sterile than information collecting for the purpose of information collecting. The kind and amount of information collected will be dictated by the defined problem for work and the preliminary goals that are established. It is difficult to deal with areas of data collection concretely because the specific areas to be explored depend on the situation. There are, however, some principles that should be considered. It is a joint process and the client should be involved in helping to determine the areas to be explored. The client should be aware of the sources being used for data collection (e.g., they may not always be asked for their permission).

There should be a connection between the problems identified and the data collected, and the client should be aware of any connection and helped to understand the areas the worker seeks to explore. Data collection goes on all the time, but it is critical to the problem identification, goal-setting and assessment stages of work. It is crucial that the social worker understands the client's view of all areas of data collection – their thinking, feelings and actions (Compton & Galaway, 1999).

There is a tendency to gather too much information, and we need to guard against too much information as well as irrelevant information. We may modify our original hypothesis many times as the new information is gathered from the family. It is not necessary to wait for a definitive hypothesis before intervening, as many times only the interventions themselves produce crucial information. Since the major purpose of a hypothesis is to make connections, how information is gathered is extremely important. The social worker must take a neutral position and try not to imply any moral judgements or to align themselves with any one faction of the family. Change often comes about through the social worker's ability to stand outside the family and gain a holistic view. The intervention is then geared at the most relevant of the presenting problems. In gathering information, it is helpful to keep the following questions in mind: What function does the symptom serve in stabilising the family? How does the family function in stabilising the symptom? What is the central theme around which the problem is organised? What will be the consequences of change?

Test information

The fourth step requires that the information collected is **tested**. Different professionals will come together with information around levels of risk, potential and targets for change, and there needs to be some analysis about what evidence there is to either support or refute their views. Strategies for achieving change or the management of risk in the interim do need to be agreed, as do areas where gaps exist and further information may need to be gathered. The following risk assessment checklist is helpful in identifying areas for testing out the information, which leads us into the next block around deciding on the probability of future harm:

- What is the nature of the concern?
- What is the category of abuse?
- Check out how your own attitudes and values will affect your responses.
- Are there racial, cultural, linguistic or other issues that need consideration?
- Are the injuries/incidents acute/cumulative/episodic?
- When and how is the child at risk?
- Did the injuries/incidents result from spontaneous actions, neglect or intent?
- What are the parents'/carers' attitudes and response to your concerns?
- Is their explanation consistent with the injury/incident?
- What does the child mean to the family?
- What are the child's views/needs/wishes?
- What is the potential for change in the family?

- Are incidents/injuries likely to re-occur? and
- How safe is the child? What are the possibilities? What is the probability? How imminent is the likely risk? How grave are the likely consequences?

Make evaluation and decision

In the **evaluation and decision** block, the professional group is being asked to make recommendations for the longer-term child protection plan, through the child protection review. The professionals may have to make recommendations for the future protection of children in contact with the perpetrator. These may be to the civil or criminal courts or the child protection conference. In the final step, there is a need to review the way forward. This may include the potential for change within both the perpetrator and his family; the viability and focus of the necessary work; any mandate needed; any relaxation of contact restrictions; and any family re-constitution. The assessment needs to move beyond the changes required to identify whether change is possible and what motivation exists for change. In some ways, the client may well experience some element of discomfort with their current situation for them to be motivated to change. Accompanying this must be some hope of reaching the goal, an ability to consider what has gone wrong and some opportunity for change in the situation (Compton & Galaway, 1999).

Samra-Tibbets and Raynes' (1999) stepwise model provides a roadmap for workers throughout the life of an assessment and it is consistent with other helpful frameworks. Table 17.2 aims to summarise the essential considerations at each step to enhance the relevance, depth and quality of the information collected.

Risk Assessment

When assessing potential risk of future harm, the perception is that the prescribed templates and supporting literature in the government's recommended portfolio do not address wide-ranging risk factors and scenarios. Preferring to over-focus on strengths, there has been a need to introduce a series of generic questions that provide workers – particularly inexperienced ones – with some structure to risk assessment practice (Calder, 2008c).

Based on practitioner observations in practice, Calder (2002) offered the following framework for conducting risk assessments:

- Assess all areas of identified risk – write each down and ensure each is considered separately, e.g., child, parent, family, surrounding environment, type and nature of maltreatment, intervention issues.
- Define the behaviour to be predicted – rather than focusing on the 'risky' individual. Assess each worrying behaviour individually as each is likely to involve different risk factors.
- Grade the risks, and be alert for especially serious risk factors – e.g., previous corroborated or uncorroborated concerns; unwillingness or inability to protect. While numerical weighting is hard to give, some weighting has to be given to significance. A less-likely event with a serious outcome if it occurred would need to be weighted, e.g., injury, death, traumatic emotional impact. A more-likely event with a high frequency, even though with a not-too-serious outcome, would need to be weighted. Who is affected could add to the gravity, e.g., harm to a child is often greater than harm to an adult.

Table 17.2 Ideas for a framework for assessment.

Data gathering	Familiar to all workers
	Relevant information is gathered from different areas
	Positive and negative factors identified
	Direct observation of individuals and families
	Historical information and records
Weighing relative significance	How much weight do positive factors have for the child?
	How much force do negative factors have on the child?
	What are the potential interactions between the different factors?
Assessment of the current situation	Sets out current status of the child from welfare perspective
	Draws together the factors discussed
	Formulates a coherent evaluation of the child's situation
	Worker should state exactly what they think about the child's situation
Circumstances that might alter the child's welfare	Need to identify factors and circumstances which might affect the child's future welfare
	Include proposed intervention strategies
	Consider all the domains and dimensions within the single assessment framework that are likely to impact on child outcomes
Prospects for change	Consider the likelihood for change in the situation facing the child
	Alternative outcomes should be described
	What is the prognosis?
Criteria for gauging effectiveness	Set out the criteria to be used to evaluate the outcome of the intervention
	Involve parents and children as appropriate
	Desired outcomes should be made explicit
Timescale proposed	How long is a reasonable period of time within which to expect changes to be made?
	Consideration should be given to review timescales
The action plan	Each risk has to be explicit in the plan
	Each child should have a unique plan
	Multiple plans have to be consistent rather than contradictory or confusing

- Be aware of risk factors that may interact in a dangerous manner – e.g., a case of physical injury where the abuser is drinking heavily at present. Take into account both internal and external factors – almost all behaviour is the result of interaction between characteristics of the individual (e.g., attitudes, skills, controls) and those of the environment (e.g., demands, constraints, stressors, etc.).
- Examine the nature of the risk factors – how long have they been operating for? How severe are they? Risk factors that are long-term and relatively uncontrollable generally signal a higher level of risk.

- Avoid focusing exclusively on the severity of the abuse – we need to consider other factors that point to future risk, not just committed harm. Distinguish between the probability and the cost of the behaviour – we need to distinguish the likelihood of the behaviour occurring from the seriousness of it if it does occur. Failure to do so makes any decision-making more problematic.
- Assess family strengths and resources – while risk assessment is essentially a negative process, workers should be examining family strengths and resources that may be used to counteract the risk factors present. For example, good bonding; supportive networks. It is argued that the assessment process is incomplete in the absence of this dimension. Protective factors can be understood as circumstances that moderate the effects of risk in a positive direction.
- Use specific and descriptive terms to document the risk factors – do not rely on terms such as 'multi-problem family'. These are too subjective and are used in many different scenarios that can result in multiple interpretations and cultivate variation in understanding in professionals, families and between the two groups.
- Gather real and direct evidence whenever possible – do not relay on hunches, hearsay or circumstantial information. Intuition should not be ignored, and should lead to further enquiry to try to understand the reason behind the concern, but it cannot be accepted as an end in itself. For example, the worker may have some unresolved issues themselves that they are projecting on to a case and as such may offer a biased, unhealthy building block from which to work.
- Check whether all necessary information has been gathered – in some cases, few sources of data may be needed to develop a strong understanding of the behaviour, whereas in others we may need to qualify any predictions made due to entirely inadequate or irrelevant material. Too frequently we follow templates to guide our assessment and since these cover all children and all circumstances, they are very broad and may not be relevant to the particular case you are working with. This means that too much irrelevant information is being collected and thus it is often much more difficult to make sense of it and to develop a coherent plan.
- Identify if/when specialists or other outsiders need to be involved – predictive accuracy is often improved when we utilise the combined skills across agencies and sometimes beyond, such as extended family, neighbours etc. (Broadhurst et al., 2010). Where this is lacking, workers should explicitly state how their recommendations have been affected by such omissions.
- Be aware of probable sources of error – which may come from the person being assessed (e.g., their poor reliability as an informant), the assessor (e.g., a difficulty in suspending personal values) or the context (such as an agency bias in favour of one or other party involved). What workers have to be alert to is what outcome the client desires and what information they may wish to provide to enhance the likelihood of this happening; the personal views of the assessor related to their own values, experiences and outlook; as well as the presence of an agency preference for the outcome, such as choosing between a foster or an adoptive placement. This is particularly necessary when the English government is providing a combination of enticements to pursue adoption above all else, coupled with consequences for failure to meet the prescribed targets.
- Plan key interventions – because a sound assessment of risk will be based on the formulation of the mechanisms underlying the behaviour, it will automatically identify those processes which appear to be key elements in increasing or reducing such risk, e.g., within the individual or the couple.

Calder (2003) extended this to include:

- Previous incidents of abuse or neglect. Detail any previous incident of abuse or neglect (type and frequency) in this family OR any record of the current caretakers having abused or neglected other children. Is there a pattern of abuse (such as physical abuse being repeated) or is it changing (such as the concerns spanning a range of categories of child abuse)? There is widespread research evidence that children are more at risk in the care of those who have previously abused or neglected children (Hamilton & Browne, 2002). Do the caretakers accept any of the previous concerns? Do they have any insight into their previous behaviour? If so, why the lapse? Do they accept or reject themselves as a continuing risk?

Conclusions

This chapter has attempted to offer a view from practitioners operating in the gaps between theory and research. It has utilised professional observations of current practice in child care proceedings and emerging themes to outline the challenging context in which social work practitioners are working in order to keep within governmental and judicial policy in England and Wales. In attempting to overcome some of these difficulties, this chapter has suggested a number of strategies and frameworks for use when assessing risk of harm and potential for change in parents involved in child care proceedings.

Practitioners are encouraged to be clear about what a good assessment involves and to retain this as a non-negotiable platform to guide their work. They should be aware of the system and process challenges that have the potential to adjust their focus from the client and their potential outcomes to the system and the desired outputs. It is suggested that bureaucracy and regulation inhibit rather than promote sound assessments. The most contentious and complex cases are often processed at some point through the court process and this now raises additional challenges that require management. Workers need to ensure they adopt an evidence-based approach to their work, recognising that this will inevitably and frequently require considerable time and resources. The need is to retain the child as the focus of everything that is done and to ensure practitioners work at their pace where it is safe to do so. The challenge is to source the best of the available evidence to guide the work while also freeing workers up to engage with the child and their family.

References

Ayre, P. & Calder, M.C. (2010). The de-professionalisation of child protection: reversing the vicious spiral. In: P. Ayre and M. Preston-Shoot (eds) *Children's Services: Future Directions*. London: MacMillan.

Broadhurst, K., White, S., Fish, S. et al. (2010). *Ten Pitfalls and How to Avoid Them*. London: NSPCC.

Burns, J. (2015). Ofsted 'blinkered' on child protection. BBC News website, 20 January 2015, www.bbc.co.uk/news/education-30888641?print=true.

CAFCASS (2007). *Domestic Violence Toolkit*. London: CAFCASS.

Calder, M.C. (2002). A framework for conducting risk assessment. *Child Care in Practice*, 8, 1–18.

Calder, M.C. (2003). *RASSAMM*. Leigh: Calder Consultancy. Available to license from author by local authorities.

Calder, M.C. (2008a). Organisational dangerousness: Causes, consequences and correctives. In: M.C. Calder (ed), *Contemporary Risk Assessment in Safeguarding Children*. Dorset, UK: Russell House Publishing, 119–165.

Calder, M.C. (2008b). Professional dangerousness: Causes, correctives and contemporary features. In: M.C. Calder (ed), *Contemporary Risk Assessment in Safeguarding Children*. Lyme Regis, UK: Russell House Publishing, 61–86.

Calder, M.C. (2008c). Risk and child protection. In: M.C. Calder (ed), *Contemporary Risk Assessment in Safeguarding Children*. Lyme Regis, UK: Russell House Publishing, 206–223.

Calder, M.C. (2010). Risk assessment with parents who have mental illness or a dual diagnosis. Keynote presentation to Hillingdon SCB conference, Civic Centre Uxbridge, 4 November 2010.

Calder, M.C. (2013). *Parenting Assessment Framework*. Leigh: Calder Training & Consultancy Limited. Available to license from author by local authorities.

Calder, M.C. (2014). Evidence-based assessment: Challenges for frontline practice. Workshop at Belfast Trust Family Centres.

Calder, M.C. (2015). Complex assessments: A masterclass for Leeds Social Care. Thackray Medical Museum, 23 February 2015.

Calder, M.C. (2016). *Risk in Child Protection: Assessment Challenges and Frameworks for Practice*. London: Jessica Kingsley.

Calder, M.C. (unpublished). Analysis of re-referrals and re-registrations in a local authority cohort. Salford City Council.

Children and Families Act 2014. Published by The Stationery Office, http://www.legislation.gov.uk/ukpga/2014/6/pdfs/ukpga_20140006_en.pdf.

Compton, B.R. & Galaway, B. (1999). *Social Work Processes*, 6th edn. Pacific Grove, CA: Brooks/Cole Publishing Company.

Craig, L.A., Browne, K.D., Stringer, I. & Beech, A. (2004). Limitations in actuarial risk assessment of sexual offenders: A methodological note. *The British Journal of Forensic Practice*, 6, 16–32.

Crown Prosecution Service (2010). Prosecution Policy and Guidance, Legal Guidance. Disclosure Manual Chapter 36: Expert Witnesses – Prosecution Disclosure Obligations, www.cps.gov.uk/legal/d_to_g/disclosure_manual/disclosure_manual_chapter_36/#a25.

Department of Health (1999). *Working together to safeguard children: A guide to inter-agency working to safeguard and promote the welfare of children*. London: The Stationery Office.

Department of Health (2000). *Framework for the assessment of children in need and their families*. London: The Stationery Office.

Donovan, T. (2013). Social workers in care cases can be identified online, rules High Court. *Community Care*, 6 September 2013.

Gawlinski, G., Carr, A., McDonnell, D. & Irving, N. (1988). Thurlow House Association Programme for families with physically abused children. *Practice*, 2, 208–220.

Gillen, S. (2009). How the public law outline is affecting care cases in the wake of Baby P. Community Care, 13 January 2009.

Hamilton, C. & Browne, K. (2002). Predicting physical maltreatment. In: K.D. Browne, H. Hanks, P. Stratton and C. Hamilton (eds), *Early Prediction and Prevention of Child Abuse: A Handbook*. Chichester: John Wiley & Sons, Ltd, 41–56.

Harold, G. & Shelton, K. (2008). *Research review – Highlighting the voice of the child – Assessing the psychological impacts of witnessing inter-parental conflict and domestic violence on children: Introducing the Child and Adolescent Welfare Assessment Checklist*. Community Care Inform.

Hill, M. (1991). *Social Work and the European Community*. London: Jessica Kingsley.

Melton, G.B., Petrila, J., Poythress, N. & Slobogin, C. (1997). *Psychological Evaluations for the Courts: A Handbook for Mental Health Professionals and Lawyers*. New York: Guilford.

Middleton, L. (1997). *The Art of Assessment*. Birmingham: Venture Press.

Ministry of Justice (2008). *The public law outline: Guide to case management in public law proceedings*, http://www.familylaw.co.uk/system/uploads/attachments/0000/2168/public_law_outline.pdf.

Morrison, T. (1990). The emotional effects of child protection work on the worker. *Practice: Social Work in Action*, 4, 253–271.

Morrison, T. (2009). The strategic leadership of complex practice: Opportunities and challenges. Founder's lecture to BASPCAN conference, 14 September 2009, Swansea.

Munro, E. (2008). *Effective Child Protection*. London: Sage Publications Limited.

Munro, E. (2011). *The Munro Review of Child Protection, Final report*. Cm 8207. London: The Stationery Office, https://www.gov.uk/government/uploads/system/uploads/attachment_data/file/175391/Munro-Review.pdf.

Nicolas, J. (2014). Naming and shaming social workers helps no one. *Guardian*, 9 December 2014.

O'Sullivan, T. (2005). Some theoretical propositions on the nature of practice wisdom. *Journal of Social Work*, 5, 221–242.

Power, M.L. (2004). *The Risk Management of Everything: Rethinking the Politics of Uncertainty*. London: Demos.

Precey, G. (2001). *The role of the social work assessment in child care proceedings*. Dissertation submitted for MA in Child Studies, King's College, University of London.

Ramchandani, P., Joughin, C. & Zwi, M. (2001). Evidence-based child and adolescent mental health services: Oxymoron or brave new dawn? *Child Psychology and Psychiatry Review*, 6, 59–64.

Re J (A Child) [2013] EWHC 2694 (Fam).

Re M [2003] 2 FLR 171. Care Proceedings Judicial Review.

Samra-Tibbets, C. & Raynes, B. (1999). Assessment and planning. In: M.C. Calder and J. Horwath (eds), *Working for Children on the Child Protection Register: An Inter-Agency Practice Guide*. Aldershot, UK: Arena, 81–117.

Social Work Matrix, The (2015). https://hownottodosocialwork.wordpress.com/2014/05/24/the-social-work-matrix/ (accessed 9 March 2015).

Part IV

Interventions with Children and Families

18

Evidence-Based Approaches to Empower Children and Families at Risk for Child Physical Abuse to Overcome Abuse and Violence

Melissa K. Runyon, Stephanie Cruthirds and Esther Deblinger
Rowan University, School of Osteopathic Medicine, NJ, US

Child physical abuse (CPA) is a global public health problem associated with an estimated 57,000 deaths attributed to homicide among children in the year 2000, with infants and very young children being at the greatest risk (Krug, Dahlberg, Mercy et al., 2002). Of the countries surveyed in the WorldSafe study (Krug, Dahlberg, Mercy et al., 2002), incidence rates of children being hit with an object (defined as severe physical punishment) ranged from 4% to 36%, with the United States and Chile having the lowest rates and India reporting the highest rates. The United Nations (UN) Secretary General's study on violence against children, released in 2006, documents that 80% to 98% of children experience physical punishment in their homes with at least 30% experiencing severe physical punishment with implements (UN, 2006).

Definitions and responses to CPA by the State/government vary across the world with 52 countries defining physical abuse as any type of physical/corporal punishment or discipline, so that it is illegal to use any physical discipline with youth in the home, school or other settings, with others defining CPA as physical discipline that leaves marks or causes injuries. To date, all member countries of the United Nations, with the exception of the United States and one other, have ratified the Convention on the Rights of the Child, which protects the rights of children across a number of domains (e.g., freedom of speech and privacy). Although it does not specifically outline what form of discipline parents should use, there is a clear statement that discipline should not involve any form of violence.

CPA has been associated with an array of psychological and physical sequelae in children that may persist into adulthood, including Post-Traumatic Stress Disorder (PTSD; Giardino, Harris & Giardino, 2009; Leeb, Lewis & Zolotor, 2011), other psychiatric disorders (Copeland, Keeler, Angold & Costello, 2007), significant stress and impairment (Margolin &

The Wiley Handbook of What Works in Child Maltreatment: An Evidence-Based Approach to Assessment and Intervention in Child Protection, First Edition. Edited by Louise Dixon, Daniel F. Perkins, Catherine Hamilton-Giachritsis, and Leam A. Craig.
© 2017 John Wiley & Sons Ltd. Published 2017 by John Wiley & Sons Ltd.

Vickerman, 2007), as well as lasting anatomical changes to the brain, such as reduction in brain volume, changes to the corpus callosum, hippocampus, and amygdala, and changes to the stress-response system (Leeb, Lewis & Zolotor, 2011). These children are at greater risk of having interpersonal difficulties, perhaps due to their sensitivity to the environment and a tendency to interpret benign interactions as hostile (Dodge, Pettit & Bates, 1994), to experience anxiety, depression, and poor self-esteem, and to exhibit a variety of difficulties related to anger, aggression, and non-compliance (see Kolko and Kolko [2010] for a review of the impact of CPA on children). These symptoms can persist throughout adulthood (Sugaya, Hasin, Olfson et al., 2012; Thompson, Kingree & Desai, 2004).

In general, parents who engage in physically abusive behaviour present with more difficulties (e.g., anxiety, depression, anger and substance use) relative to their non-violent counterparts (Milner & Chilamkurti, 1991); display skills deficits, including a lack of knowledge about child development parenting skills (Wolfe, 1985); have poor emotional regulation; and are more likely to have a history of CPA (see Runyon & Deblinger, 2014). They tend to have fewer interactions overall and more aversive parent–child interactions compared to non-maltreating parents (Wilson, Rack, Shi & Norris, 2008). Parents who engage in coercive parenting often lack empathy for the impact of their behaviour on the child (de Paul, Pérez-Albéniz, Guibert et al., 2008), tend to overreact to their children's behaviour, and misinterpret their child's behaviours as intentional and negative (Milner, 2000, 2003) which, in turn, contributes to ongoing coercive interactions.

Given the prevalence of CPA, the deleterious impact of CPA on children across the lifespan, and the complex needs of families who are at risk for CPA, there is a need for comprehensive evidence-based therapies (EBTs) that address the needs of the parent, child and family. In this chapter we will introduce the reader to five EBTs that have been applied to the CPA population, are included on the California Evidence-based Clearinghouse for Child Welfare website, and have at least one supporting controlled trial. These EBTs are primarily based on CBT and in some capacity after children thus have overlapping tenets, similar components, and include both parents and children. Described below are: SafeCare (Lutzker & Rice, 1984); Parent–Child Interaction Therapy (PCIT; Eyberg & Robinson, 1983); Multisystemic Therapy for Child Abuse and Neglect (MST-CAN; Swenson, Schaeffer, Henggeler et al., 2010); Alternatives for Families: A Cognitive Behavioural Therapy (AF-CBT; Kolko, 1996a); and Combined Parent–Child Cognitive Behavioural Therapy (CPC-CBT; Runyon, Deblinger & Schroeder, 2009). CPC-CBT is one of the few interventions for this population that emphasises treating the child's PTSD in the context of the parent's treatment with data demonstrating the model's utility in helping youth overcome PTSD. Given this unique aspect of CPC-CBT, a case is presented to illustrate the powerful therapeutic value of including the child in the 'at-risk' or 'offending' parent's treatment, particularly given the hesitation that some therapists might have about treating the parent and child together.

Review of Evidence-Based Therapies (EBTs) to Address CPA

SafeCare

SafeCare is an evidence-based, in-home service model developed by John Lutzker to address the needs of families involved in the child welfare system, primarily involving those where neglect and CPA has been present. SafeCare includes modules that address parenting, home safety and child health issues, but does not directly address the child's emotional reactions. Research demonstrates that SafeCare is associated with lower rates of recurring child maltreatment compared to treatment as usual (TAU; e.g., family preservation) in one quasi-experimental (Gershater-Molko, Lutzker & Welsh, 2002) and two controlled trials (Chaffin, Bard, Bigfoot & Maher, 2012; Chaffin, Hecht, Bard et al., 2012). Participation in SafeCare is also associated with improvements on a number of child, parent and family factors in the child maltreatment population (Silovsky, Bard, Chaffin et al., 2011). Self-Brown, McFry, Montesanti et al. (2014) note that, to date, there is no data examining the impact of SafeCare on children's emotional functioning.

Parent–Child Interaction Therapy

PCIT (Eyberg & Robinson, 1983) is an EBT that has efficacy for reducing children's behaviour problems with these changes generalising to multiple settings (e.g., office to home, home to school) and being maintained long term (Campbell, Chaffin & Funderburk, 2014). PCIT is based on social learning principles, has an intensive positive-interaction training component, incorporates both parent and child in each treatment session, provides a mechanism to change the pattern of the dysfunctional parent–child relationship, and involves the use of live coaching. Traditional PCIT consists of 14 weekly one-hour sessions that are delivered across two phases, child-directed interaction (CDI) and parent-directed interaction (PDI), with seven sessions devoted to each phase. PCIT is implemented in a very structured, systematic manner that involves closely adhering to session outlines to enhance treatment integrity.

While PCIT has a wealth of data collected over the past 30 plus years demonstrating positive outcomes for enhancing positive parenting behaviours and decreasing behaviour problems in young children with disruptive behaviour disorders, PCIT has been successfully implemented with CPA for more than a before decade (Chaffin, Silovsky, Funderburk et al., 2004; Timmer, Urquiza, Zebell & McGrath, 2005). In a well-designed controlled comparison examining the efficacy of PCIT with parents who engage in abusive behaviour, Chaffin, Silovsky, Funderburk et al. (2004) randomly assigned 110 parent–child dyads to PCIT, PCIT plus individualised enhanced services, or a community parenting group. For those assigned to the PCIT conditions, there were significantly fewer new CPA incidents (19% vs. 49%) and a relative improvement in parent–child interactions compared to those in the standard community parenting group. However, PCIT plus individualised services did not result in better outcomes than PCIT alone (Chaffin, Silovsky, Funderburk et al., 2004). This finding suggests that more services are not necessarily better and may not be the best use of scarce therapeutic resources.

While this initial study (Chaffin, Silovsky, Funderburk et al., 2004) included a pre-treatment motivational component, Chaffin, Valle, Funderburk et al. (2009) conducted a dismantling study to determine the added value of the motivational component above and beyond the PCIT intervention. Prior to treatment, 193 parent–child dyads were randomly assigned to either a motivational or informational intervention. After the initial intervention, the remaining 153 dyads were randomly assigned to PCIT vs. community parenting. Findings indicated that combining PCIT with the motivational intervention yielded a better retention rate of 85% when compared to the 61% cumulative retention rate for the study. Thus, the motivational intervention increased retention for PCIT but not for the community parenting group. In a second publication associated with this clinical trial, Chaffin, Funderburk, Bard et al. (2011) report that the motivational intervention plus PCIT was also associated with lower recidivism rates, particularly when children returned to their homes more quickly.

While PCIT was developed primarily as a parenting model, there is a growing body of research that identifies PCIT as an effective evidence-based parenting programme for high-risk and abusive families. However, professionals have posited that it is necessary to directly address the child's internalising symptoms (e.g., PTSD, depression, anxiety), which the parent may misinterpret as oppositional or defiant behaviour, which, in turn, may escalate interactions between the parent and the child (Runyon, Deblinger & Schroeder, 2009; Runyon & Deblinger, 2014). Indeed, recent adaptations of PCIT have included modules to address internalising difficulties and have yielded promising results (Lenze, Pautsch & Luby, 2011; Puliafico, Comer & Pincus, 2012). To date, there do not appear to be any published randomised controlled trials evaluating these adaptations of PCIT.

Multisystemic Therapy

Multisystemic Therapy (MST; Henggeler, Schoenwald, Borduin et al., 2009), another EBT, has a wealth of research to support its effectiveness for treating adolescents with serious emotional difficulties, chronic health care conditions, and those who commit juvenile offences (Swenson, Schaeffer, Henggeler et al., 2010). Swenson, Schaeffer, Henggeler et al. (2010) describe MST as involving a number of critical features: 'addressing the multidetermined nature of serious clinical problems, viewing the family as key to effective behaviour change, using a home-based model of service delivery to overcome barriers to service access, integrated evidence-based interventions, and using a quality assurance system to support therapist fidelity', p. 498. Based on a thorough assessment of the families' needs, standard MST typically involves systemically identifying, developing and prioritising an individually tailored menu of evidence-based services provided in the home, the family's ecological setting, over a period of four to six months to address the needs identified.

More recently, MST was adapted as MST-CAN (Swenson, Schaeffer, Henggeler et al., 2010) for the child abuse and neglect population. MST-CAN includes all of the standard features of MST, but the treatment length was extended beyond four to six months in order to address safety concerns and parenting difficulties that may be unique to the CPA population. Other features in the MST-CAN adaptation are the development of a safety plan, working closely with child protective services (CPS), incorporating specific cognitive behavioural strategies to address specific skills deficits, and an abuse clarification process (Kolko & Swenson, 2002; Lipovsky, Swenson, Ralston & Saunders, 1998; Runyon & Deblinger, 2014; Runyon, Deblinger & Schroeder, 2009).

In a controlled trial examining MST-CAN (Swenson, Schaeffer, Henggeler et al., 2010), 86 families, with children ranging from 10 to 17 years of age, who were involved in CPS due to CPA were randomly assigned to either MST-CAN or Enhanced Outpatient Treatment (EOT). Families completed assessment measures at baseline, 2, 4, 10 and 16 months. While each treatment group received an equal dose (hours) of treatment, those youth who received MST-CAN reported relative improvements in PTSD and depression compared to those receiving the enhanced treatment. Parents in the MST-CAN group reported significant decreases for youth on measures of PTSD symptoms as well as internalising behaviours. Parents receiving MST-CAN reported relative improvements in psychiatric distress. MST-CAN was associated with less coercive and violent parenting tactics as reported by the parent and/or youth (depending on type and severity of parenting tactic) as well as parent reports of increased social support. MST-CAN was also associated with fewer out-of-home placements for youth after treatment.

Alternatives for families – Cognitive Behavioural Therapy

CBT models developed for this population that directly address children's emotional distress, parent–child interactions, and parenting style have been empirically examined and have been associated with positive outcomes for both children and parents (Kjellgren, Svedin & Nilsson, 2013;

Kolko, 1996b; Runyon, Deblinger & Schroeder, 2009; Runyon, Deblinger & Steer, 2010). For example, AF-CBT includes child-directed, parent-directed and family-directed components that are delivered over the course of 12 to 24 hourly sessions, across three phases: (i) psychoeducation and engagement, (ii) individual and family skills training, and (iii) family applications. Child-directed components include effective coping skills training, as well as cognitive processing related to coercive and/or abusive experiences. Essential components for the parent involve engagement, rapport building, and an examination of the reason for referral and causes of the coercive behaviour among family members. Cognitive strategies address parental beliefs about coercion and violence and unrealistic developmental child expectations that may contribute to aggressive parent–child interactions. Parents are also offered affect regulation and parenting skills training to promote more positive parenting strategies. Family components include physical abuse psychoeducation, abuse clarification including the development of a safety plan, communication skills training and non-violent problem-solving skills training.

In Kolko's (1996b) seminal study, children and parents were randomly assigned to one of three conditions: individual CBT, family therapy, or TAU. Individual CBT and family therapy were associated with greater improvements on measures of child externalising behaviour problems, parental distress, abuse risk, coercive parenting and family conflict and cohesion relative to those who received TAU. However, CBT was superior to family therapy and TAU for reducing parent-reported anger and use of physical punishment (Kolko, 1996a). Given the positive outcomes associated with both individual CBT and family therapy, these protocols were integrated into AF-CBT.

Another study examined outcomes for 52 families who received AF-CBT delivered by community practitioners who were trained in the model two and five years prior to the study (Kolko, Iselin & Gully, 2011). The abuse-specific content of AF-CBT was related to improvements on parents' reports of children's externalising behaviours, anger, anxiety and social competence, and ratings by both parent and therapist of the child's functioning at discharge (i.e., child more safe, less scared/sad, more appropriate with peers) even after accounting for the amount of training therapists received in other EBTs.

Combined Parent–Child Cognitive Behavioural Therapy (CPC-CBT)

CPC-CBT, similar to the models mentioned above, was developed by the authors of this chapter (Runyon & Deblinger, 2014) to meet the complex needs of families struggling with issues related to CPA and violence. The developers of CPC-CBT believed it would be beneficial to families if one comprehensive model helped the child heal from the trauma of the physical abuse, empowered and motivated parents to modulate their emotions and use effective non-coercive parenting strategies, enhanced parent–child interactions and strengthened parent–child relationships while helping families stop the cycle of violence. This approach involves both the at-risk parent and the child(ren) as opposed to referring the parent and child to separate therapists. Rather, in the context of CPC-CBT, typically one therapist utilises a combination of individual parent sessions, individual child sessions and joint parent–child sessions to address the individual therapeutic needs and skills deficits of each member, while simultaneously engaging in joint work to engage parents and children in activities that support more effective communication and empathy as well as enhanced parent–child relationships. This approach may be preferable given the level and frequency of communication that would be required between multiple therapists and agencies to coordinate effective treatment and monitor safety risks that may arise when treating a child who remains in the home with a parent who engages in physically abusive behaviour toward that child. As noted earlier, recent research suggests that multiple service providers are not necessarily more effective than a singular EBT in helping families overcome difficulties related to CPA (Chaffin, Silovsky, Funderburk et al., 2004).

It should also be noted that CPC-CBT is one of few models in which therapists provide direct intervention and processing of children's PTSD symptoms, similar to the process in Trauma-Focused Cognitive Behavioural Therapy (TF-CBT; Deblinger, Mannarino, Cohen et al., 2015) in the context of the child's and the parent's treatment with families at risk for CPA. Outcome data (including a controlled trial) for CPC-CBT demonstrates the model's utility for reducing children's PTSD symptoms along with other internalising and behavioural difficulties for this population (Kjellgren, Svedin & Nilsson, 2013; Runyon, Deblinger & Schroeder, 2009; Runyon, Deblinger & Schroeder, 2010; Runyon, Deblinger & Steer, 2010). In the first study examining the comprehensive model, Runyon, Deblinger & Schroeder (2009) conducted a pilot study examining the feasibility of group CPC-CBT that incorporated the child into the 'at-risk' or 'offending' parent's therapy. After their participation in treatment, both parents ($N=12$) and children ($N=21$) reported reductions in PTSD symptoms and parental use of physical punishment. CPC-CBT was also associated with significant improvements in parental anger toward their children and consistent parenting as reported by the parents. Parents also reported significant improvements in children's behavioural problems (Runyon, Deblinger & Schroeder, 2009). These pilot data suggested the potential value and feasibility of offering services in a group format and having the child participate with the parent in sessions. However, there was no control group or follow-up to assess the long-term benefits of their participation.

To address the limitations of the initial study and to determine the added benefit of including the child in the parent's treatment, a controlled trial funded by the National Institute of Mental Health (NIMH) compared CPC-CBT (24 parents, 34 children) to parent-only CBT (20 parents, 26 children; Runyon, Deblinger & Steer, 2010). Children and parents completed assessment measures across three time periods (i.e., prior to treatment, after 15 sessions and at three-month follow-up). Those participants randomly assigned to CPC-CBT showed significantly greater improvements with respect to children's PTSD symptoms and parents' positive parenting skills as compared to the condition where only the parent received treatment. These gains were maintained at a three-month follow-up for those who were assessed.

Results from these studies suggested that CPC-CBT is promising in helping children and parents overcome a number of issues relevant to the CPA population. The most unique findings are the usefulness of implementing CPC-CBT in a group format as well the ability to help children overcome PTSD symptoms related to CPA in the context of their parent's treatment. When CPC-CBT was disseminated to community therapists through training efforts, supervisors and therapists wanted to implement CPC-CBT in an individual format given the delay in services waiting for a group to form (e.g., children within specified age range, similar referral situations). To determine whether individual CPC-CBT would be associated with similar outcomes for families, pre- to post-treatment pilot data was examined for 40 children and their 35 caregivers. After completing individual CPC-CBT, children reported significant improvements in emotional symptoms while parents reported improvements in their emotional functioning and school-age children's externalising behaviour problems. Both parents and children reported significant reductions in coercive parenting tactics (Runyon, Deblinger & Steer, 2010).

CPC-CBT has also been evaluated in mental health settings outside the setting where the model was developed. As part of a Swedish dissemination project, referred to as KIBB, researchers collected pilot data from children and families who were served by professionals from four agencies who were trained by a treatment developer (Kjellgren, Svedin & Nilsson, 2013). After their participation in CPC-CBT, parents ($N=26$) reported significant gains in relation to depression, violent parenting tactics, inconsistent parenting and children's trauma symptoms. It is worth noting that 94% of the caregivers took responsibility for their abusive behavior towards their children. The children also reported significant post-treatment improvements on measures of trauma and depressive symptoms, coercive parenting tactics and positive parenting for their parents. These findings replicated a majority of the outcomes in the initial CPC-CBT pilot study in the United States (Runyon, Deblinger & Schroeder, 2009). While the definition of CPA involves a much lower threshold of coercion compared to CPA by definition in the United States, CPC-CBT appears promising for treating CPA in Sweden. To further evaluate CPC-CBT in Sweden, researchers are currently conducting a clinical trial comparing CPC-CBT to TAU.

In another pilot dissemination project involving the National Child Traumatic Stress Network's Learning Collaborative (LC) framework, 12 clinicians from three community mental health centres in the Gulf Coast region of the United States were trained and delivered CPC-CBT to families. After their participation in the 12-month training experience, therapists and supervisors reported significant changes in organisational practices and clinicians' therapeutic practices. Therapists also reported significant increases in the use of a number of CPC-CBT components and skills during parent, child and conjoint sessions after the training. Preliminary analyses indicated that families who were provided CPC-CBT by participating therapists reported significant improvements in parenting, reductions in the use of corporal punishment, and improvements in children's emotional symptoms from pre- to post-treatment.

Summary of CPC-CBT Components: A Case Illustration

CPC-CBT is a short-term (16 to 20 sessions), components-based therapy programme for children ages 3 to 17 years, and their caregivers who engage in a range of coercive parenting strategies. These families include those who have been substantiated for CPA, those who have had multiple unsubstantiated referrals, and those who fear they may lose control with their child. CPC-CBT targets an array of difficulties in children, including PTSD symptoms, depression and externalising behaviours. CPC-CBT is grounded in cognitive behavioural theory and incorporates elements (e.g., trauma narrative and processing, positive reinforcement, time out, behavioural contracting) from CBT models for families who have experienced sexual abuse, physical abuse, and/or domestic violence (Deblinger, Mannarino, Cohen et al., 2015; Kolko & Swenson, 2002; Runyon, Basilio, van Hasselt & Hersen, 1998), as well as elements from motivational, family systems, trauma and developmental theories. CPC-CBT helps the child heal from the trauma of the physical abuse, empowers and motivates parents to modulate their emotions and use effective non-coercive parenting strategies, and strengthens parent–child relationships while helping families stop the cycle of violence. The treatment is delivered across four phases which are described below in conjunction with a case example to illustrate key components.

Mr Green was widowed when his wife died suddenly in a car accident when their son Joel was only one-year-old. Since then, Mr Green has devoted himself to raising his son, while working full time as a contractor. He was referred for CPC-CBT after he hit 10-year-old Joel with a belt because Joel lied about completing his homework. Mr Green hit his son on his buttocks, lower back and legs, leaving welts on Joel's legs and a buckle mark on his lower back. The next day at school, Joel's teacher noticed him grimacing when attempting to sit in his chair. The teacher sent Joel to the school nurse who saw the welts on his legs. When the nurse asked him what happened, Joel disclosed that his father 'beat' him. The nurse immediately called CPS to report the incident.

After Joel was interviewed by the CPS investigative worker, he was seen for a medical examination by a child abuse paediatrician who documented his physical injuries as well as his statements about the abusive interaction between him and his father. Subsequently, Joel and his father were referred for a course of CPC-CBT to address issues secondary to substantiated CPA by Mr Green.

During the initial therapy assessment, Joel reported that his father frequently hits him. He met criteria for PTSD, presented with significant depression symptoms, and stated that he was fearful of his father and did not feel as though his father loved him. Mr Green reported frequent use of physical discipline and stated that it was not his intent to physically harm his son, but was adamant that Joel's repetitive lying had to stop. He also reported significant behaviour problems for Joel that he reported were stressful to manage.

CPC-CBT is designed to meet the needs of children and families who are at risk for CPA. Only a small percentage of children (13% to 18%) in the child welfare population receive individual therapy after an abuse disclosure (Kolko, Selelyo & Brown, 1999). Furthermore, parents who are involved with CPS due to harsh or abusive parenting are often distrustful and consequently hesitant to seek services for fear of being judged negatively and criticised and, consequently, drop out of parenting classes. Thus, it is critical to emphasise the use of engagement strategies with parents. Researchers have developed evidence-based engagement strategies to promote attendance at initial therapy sessions and completion of therapy (McKay, Stoewe, McCadam & Gonzales, 1998). Simple strategies, such as addressing barriers to treatment and past therapeutic experiences, have been associated with increased attendance to trauma-focused therapy by foster parents (Dorsey, Pullmann, Berliner et al., 2014). Motivational procedures have also been important in retaining clients in therapy, specifically those receiving PCIT due to CPA (Chaffin, Valle, Funderburk et al., 2009). CPC-CBT incorporates engagement strategies and a motivational procedure as described below. In a controlled trial, Runyon, Deblinger & Steer (2010) found that only 12% of parents dropped out of a 16-session course of CPC-CBT after completing the first two sessions which focus on engagement and motivation.

The first phase of CPC-CBT (engagement and psychoeducation) focuses primarily on engagement and motivation of parents and psychoeducation about abuse, violence and coercion and their emotional and behavioural impact on children. The initial two sessions of CPC-CBT involve empathy building, motivational interviewing skills, and review of consequences to build rapport with parents and to enhance their buy-in and motivation to change behavior. The therapist makes a concerted effort to empathise with the parent's stress related to parenting while not condoning the parent's abusive behaviour and to offer the parent support in a non-judgemental therapeutic environment. For many parents, this may be the first time they have felt supported and understood with respect to their personal struggles with their children. It is important to use the parent's words (e.g., spanking in Mr Green's case) to describe the referral incident in these early engagement sessions.

To engage Mr Green, the therapist initiated the session by discussing Mr Green's previous experiences with therapy, any barriers to attending sessions, as well as Mr Green's goals for treatment. By exploring the aforementioned with Mr Green, the therapist was able to provide education about how CPC-CBT differs from his previous treatment experiences and can help Mr Green achieve his current goals.

THERAPIST: Mr Green, I would like to talk a little about your past experiences with therapy. Have you ever been in therapy before?
MR GREEN: Yes, when I was a teenager.
THERAPIST: What was it like? What was helpful or not helpful?

MR GREEN:	I don't know. We just talked a lot about what was happening on that particular day or week. It really felt like it was a waste of time because I don't feel like it helped. I had to go for almost two years. And that's a lot of time to waste.
THERAPIST:	How would you like this experience to be different?
MR GREEN:	Well I want to feel like we are working towards something and not just talking about my day or week.
THERAPIST:	That is totally understandable that you want to be working towards something. This treatment approach is structured but also flexible, meaning that there will be certain skills or discussion topics to cover every week. With that being said, we will discuss topics that will help you and your son reach your goals. This treatment is also time limited. It could range from 16 to 20 sessions, maybe less, maybe more, depending on the needs of your family.

The therapist then engaged Mr Green in an activity to process the sequence of events surrounding the reason he and his son were referred for treatment as well as his related thoughts and feelings before, during and after the incident occurred. This activity not only allows the therapist to understand the details of the referral incident and to assess how much responsibility the parent takes for the abusive behaviour, but most importantly at this critical stage allows the therapist to empathise and align with Mr Green and his experiences as a parent.

THERAPIST:	Mr Green, tell me about what happened between you and Joel that led to you being referred for treatment?
MR GREEN:	He lied about doing his homework so I spanked him.
THERAPIST:	Mr Green, I want to hear more about what that experience was like for you as a parent. Parenting can be the most challenging job at times. You have already mentioned that parenting Joel can be very stressful and that you are struggling with helping Joel manage his behaviour. I really want to understand what it is like for you on that after on a daily basis to parent Joel. Tell me more about what led up to you spanking Joel.

Mr Green then provided a detailed account of the events that precipitated him 'spanking' Joel. According to Mr Green, he was 'at wits end', because Joel repeatedly lied 'about everything', which Mr Green perceived as very disrespectful. One of his primary goals for Joel was for Joel to do well in school and obtain a college degree so Joel didn't have to work so hard performing manual labour like Mr Green. Yet, Joel repeatedly failed to complete his homework, lied about having assignments when asked, and his grades were significantly declining. The teacher contacted Mr Green every day during the week to tell him that Joel had failed to complete his homework and that his behaviour was disruptive in class. Mr Green said when Joel came home 'I met him at the door with the belt.' After the teacher called, 'I kept thinking about how he lied again, how disrespectful he was, and how he was throwing his future away.' When asked how he was feeling when he had those thoughts, Mr Green stated that he felt angry, frustrated and betrayed. He indicated that his level of anger was a 6 on a scale from 1 to 10 while he was talking to the teacher, but progressively escalated to a 9 by the time Joel arrived home. The therapist pointed out to Mr Green that he had experienced this tension and stress for nearly 90 minutes while waiting for Joel. The therapist empathised with Mr Green's intense emotions.

Next, Mr Green identified the consequences he experienced that resulted from him spanking Joel, such as CPS being involved with the family, he and Joel having to attend therapy, and Joel acting afraid of him. The therapist was able to use Mr Green's disclosure of the referral incident as well as the subsequent review of consequences to empathise with, engage and motivate him to change his behaviour to avoid these negative experiences in the future.

THERAPIST: Mr Green, you mentioned that you have experienced a few consequences since spanking Joel. You indicated that your relationship with Joel is different, you now have to attend counselling and you have CPS involved with your family. I can't imagine how difficult this has been for you.

[Therapist continues to explore the meaning of these consequences and empathise with Mr Green.]

THERAPIST: If we could work together to improve your relationship with Joel and complete counselling while reducing the chance of CPS being involved in your life in the future, would that be helpful for you?

MR GREEN: Yeah that'd be great if we could do that.

After spending the initial two sessions processing the referral incident, conducting a motivational procedure, establishing goals and gaining Mr Green's commitment to therapy, the therapist introduced education about abuse and violence to Mr Green. Psychoeducation focuses on educating parents and children about a range of coercive and violent behaviours across all types of violence (e.g., emotional, physical and sexual) as opposed to focusing only on what is defined as CPA by law. To diffuse defensiveness about the discussion of violence and its potential impact on children, the conversation is initiated by discussing any violence that the parent and/or child might have been exposed to in the home or community. Frequently, parents begin by disclosing their own experiences of violence, which provides the opportunity to elicit the emotional, behavioural and physical impact of these experiences on the parents during childhood and throughout their lives, and draw parallels between their own experiences and those of their children. By approaching the impact of violence from a broader perspective and inquiring about the parent's personal history, the therapist works to convey empathy, while gaining the parent's commitment to working toward creating a peaceful, non-coercive home environment.

THERAPIST: Mr Green, I want to spend some time discussing different types of abuse/violence that you and Joel may have experienced in your community or home.

The therapist and Mr Green discussed examples of different types of violence. Mr Green then provided a personal history of being bullied in school as well as his father 'beating' him a few times. The therapist then explored with Mr Green the impact of violence on him as well as the impact of the 'beatings' on his relationship with his father.

THERAPIST: Mr Green, you indicated that your father beat you a few times when you were growing up. Tell me about your relationship with your father when you were a child.

MR GREEN: Well, he wasn't around much. He was always working. But when he was around, I listened to him and respected him.

THERAPIST: What was it about him that made you listen to and respect him?

MR GREEN: Well, he was my father, that's what I was supposed to do. He also worked really hard to make sure we had food, clothes and shelter. He would also try and spend time with me sometimes.

THERAPIST: So when he would beat you for a certain behaviour, you never did that behaviour again?

MR GREEN: Well I might have, but I just tried not to get caught. (laughs)

THERAPIST: So, if your behaviour didn't change, what did the beatings accomplish?

MR GREEN: Well, I don't know.

THERAPIST: How did you feel about your father after he beat you?

Mr Green:	I was mad at him. I was scared of him.
Therapist:	Is it possible that that is how Joel felt after you spanked him? Mad at you and scared of you? You mentioned that he doesn't talk to you about his day or ask you to practice soccer as much.
Mr Green:	I guess it's possible. I didn't think that he might be coming to me less because he was mad or scared. But I want him to respect me.
Therapist:	But you noted that it was your father's hard work and his attempt at spending time with you that made you respect him while the beatings made you feel scared of him. Can you think of other ways that don't involve spanking that you can gain Joel's respect?

After the engagement period, the therapist gained a commitment to no violence from Mr Green, repeatedly emphasised the consequences associated with his behaviour to encourage him to change, and conducted weekly assessments with Mr Green and Joel independently to assess the presence of ongoing coercive parenting and positive parenting practices.

During the engagement phase, the therapist worked on building rapport with Joel who was sceptical that his father would alter his behaviour, but was willing to participate with some encouragement and review of the pros and cons associated with his participation. Psychoeducation about violence and the impact of loss of a parent was also offered to Joel.

Positive parenting skills are a critical part of CPC-CBT and are integrated across all phases of treatment with the goal of assisting parents to learn effective, non-coercive parenting strategies that shape children's behaviour and enhance the parent–child relationship. The therapist serves as a coach to empower the parent to effectively implement positive parenting skills and active listening and communication skills during parent–child interaction sessions. Parents are encouraged to role play and practice skills independently with the therapist, during joint sessions with their children, and then to implement skills at home. Parents are offered an array of parenting skills beginning with praise and positive reinforcement as the foundation for all parenting skills.

The therapist introduced praise to Mr Green early on in treatment. Mr Green was encouraged to be specific and purely positive when praising Joel. Mr Green was also provided with the rationale behind praising a child. Initially Mr Green was resistant to praising Joel.

Mr Green:	I honestly don't think that I should have to tell him he did a good job doing something that he is supposed to do. He knows one of his chores is washing the dishes; therefore he is responsible for doing them. If I tell him I like how he did the dishes he may feel entitled and always expect to hear it.
Therapist:	Mr Green, I understand that you are somewhat hesitant to use praise with Joel. Sometimes we can feel uncomfortable when giving praise to others or even when receiving praise from someone. The world we live in can be a negative place at times. Do you ever watch the news or read the newspaper?
Mr Green:	Yes.
Therapist:	What kind of stories lead the news?
Mr Green:	Well they aren't good stories.
Therapist:	That's right, many times news stories are negative. Negativity seems to lead a lot of times. For example, you may not hear from Joel's teachers unless there is a problem with his school work or behaviour. We can't control a lot of the negativity that may go on around us but you do have an opportunity to bring some positivity into your son's life in a way that will build a foundation for him…a foundation in which he has a positive self-esteem and sense of self. That way when he gets older, he won't look toward others to tell him when he is doing well at something. He will have that confidence within himself.

The second phase of CPC-CBT, effective coping skills, involves helping both the child and parent develop an array of effective coping skills (e.g., emotional expression and regulation skills, assertiveness and anger management, cognitive coping skills, self-care, stress management and problem-solving skills) that will promote a safe, non-coercive home environment and enhance their abilities to cope with significant stressors in their lives. These skills also prepare the child to discuss, process and make meaning of interactions with the parent, particularly those that the child perceived as scary, uncomfortable or traumatic.

During the coping skills phase of treatment, Mr Green was taught cognitive coping and anger management while Joel learnt about assertiveness and anger management. Prior to a conjoint session where Joel was to practice assertiveness, the therapist met with Mr Green to prepare him for the joint session. Mr Green was initially resistant to having Joel make requests in an assertive way, but he was reminded that Joel was learning to not be aggressive in his interactions with others. It was further explained that this work was critical to addressing Joel's externalising behaviour problems. Mr Green would be encouraged to not only model assertive behaviour for his son, but by acknowledging and praising Joel for appropriate assertiveness even when it is directed toward him, Mr Green would help Joel to be more effective in his interactions with peers as well as authority figures.

Mr Green: I don't think he needs to be assertive with me. I feel like he needs to know that I am in charge and he can't just tell me what he wants and expect me to give it to him.

Therapist: I completely understand you wanting Joel to know that you are still the parent. And just because he communicates to you in an assertive way does not mean that he is going to get everything he wants. Let me ask you this. Would you rather Joel use other ways to communicate with you, like yelling, screaming, or slamming things, or would you rather that he use his words in a way that is direct and respectful?

Mr Green: I would definitely rather he use words.

Therapist: That is basically what we mean when we teach kids assertiveness. We teach them to communicate in a way that lets others know what they want in a way that is not aggressive or passive, but is assertive and respectful at the same time.

The third phase of CPC-CBT involves family safety planning. Family safety planning focuses on utilisation of skills learnt thus far in treatment to help manage situations and behaviours in order to enhance safety. Once the therapist has assessed a family's readiness for safety planning, the therapist works with the parent and child independent of one another in developing a plan in which the family utilises a code word to signal that the conflictual situation is escalating. When the code word is used, family members go to separate rooms for a designated amount of time to deescalate. After the specified amount of time, the family then comes back together to continue their interaction. The clinician has the family practice and role play the safety plan in session and then the family is asked to practice the plan at home.

The therapist worked with Mr Green and Joel on developing a family safety plan. Mr Green and Joel agreed on the code word 'potato' that would be used to signal that a cooling-down period was needed. Mr Green presented to the session with concerns that the plan did not work.

Mr Green: So this past weekend, Joel came home an hour after he was supposed to be home. By the time he got home I was furious. He came in acting like he had done nothing wrong and then he saw me. I started yelling at him for being so late and he started yelling back at me. I ended up saying some really mean things to him before he stormed off to his room.

After the therapist processed the aforementioned incident with Mr Green and Joel independent of one another, the therapist had Mr Green and Joel role play using the safety plan with the therapist individually as well as together. Mr Green and Joel were also advised to practice the plan at home. By practising in session and at home, Mr Green and Joel became more comfortable in their understanding and practice of the plan resulting in more successful implementation during escalating interactions in the future.

The abuse clarification phase is an opportunity for the child and parent to openly discuss the abusive interaction in order to help reduce the child's trauma symptoms and enhance the parent's empathy for the child while simultaneously strengthening the parent–child relationship. During the abuse clarification phase, the child develops a trauma narrative in which he processes his thoughts and feelings related to the abuse. At the same time, the parent develops a clarification letter in which the parent takes responsibility for the abuse and addresses any cognitive distortions or concerns the child may have. Following the development of the narrative and clarification letter, when determined to be clinically appropriate, the parent and child meet jointly with the therapist and share their work. It is, however, very important to carefully assess the parent's emotional stability prior to sharing the child's narrative with the parent and/or sharing such in a conjoint session. Most parents and children benefit a great deal from reviewing the child's narrative and the parent's clarification letter together in conjoint sessions after preparation. However, it is important to prepare all parties very well for these sessions. It is worth noting that, on occasion, the therapist may determine that the sharing of the trauma narrative with a particular parent(s) may be counterproductive for the child (e.g., when parent is unstable, child adamantly refuses to write or share the narrative).

In his trauma narrative, Joel expressed his thoughts and feelings related to his father hitting him with the belt. Joel stated, 'I felt very scared and so angry at him when he was hitting me. I just wanted him to stop. I was thinking, why is he hitting me? I thought I deserve to be hit. If I hadn't lied to him then none of this would have happened. Maybe I am not a good enough son. Maybe that is why I don't have a mother.' Joel further noted, 'After he left the room, I felt hurt and alone. I thought he doesn't love me because if he did then he wouldn't have hurt me. He probably hates having a son like me who gets bad grades.' Joel also included a chapter in his narrative about his feelings related to the loss of his mother and growing up without her in his life. In his clarification letter, Mr Green responded to Joel's thoughts and feelings. Mr Green stated, 'Joel, I am very sorry that I hit you that day. You did not deserve to be hit. I could have chosen a different way to discipline you. Also, I want you to know that I think you are very capable of getting good grades and I want to help you and support you in doing that. But no matter what grades you get I will always love you.' Mr Green also told Joel that in the future when he is angry he will use skills that he has learnt in counselling to calm down before disciplining Joel and encouraged Joel to continue using their code word. With support from the therapist, Mr Green talked to Joel about his mother and for the first time told Joel how much his mother loved him. Joel had many questions for his father about his mother and they agreed to create an album about Joel's mother that would include pictures of Joel in his first year of life. The session concluded with Mr Green assuring Joel of his love for him and he and Joel hugging.

Shortly before the final session, Mr Green completed standardised measures that documented his progress both in terms of the development of more effective parenting and coping skills as well as significant reductions in Joel's noncompliant behaviours. During their last session, the therapist helped Joel and Mr Green review all they had learnt in therapy. They both exchanged specific praise, highlighting the positive changes that each had made since the start of therapy. In addition, Mr Green agreed to continue the rituals and practices he had begun since the start of the therapy and reminded Joel how proud he was to be his father. Finally, the therapist presented both Joel and his father with graduation certificates.

Conclusion

In sum, CPA is a highly prevalent childhood trauma that can significantly disrupt children's social, emotional, cognitive, behavioural and brain development. Parents at risk for physically abusive behaviour often struggle with emotional difficulties, may be under considerable stress, and may have significant deficits in parenting knowledge and skills. In recent years, EBTs have been developed to address the varied psychosocial factors associated with CPA. Though there is still much to be learnt and a great need for ongoing research, there is considerable evidence that early evidence-based interventions appear to be highly effective in addressing the therapeutic needs of families at risk for CPA, thereby reducing the likelihood of ongoing abuse.

References

Campbell, C., Chaffin, M. & Funderburk, B. (2014). Parent–child interaction therapy in child welfare settings. In: R.M. Reece, R.F. Hanson & J. Sargent (eds), *Treatment of Child Abuse: Common Ground for Mental Health, Medical, and Legal Practitioners*, 2nd edn. Baltimore, MD: John Hopkins University Press, 39–49.

Chaffin, M., Bard, D., Bigfoot, D.S. & Maher, E.J. (2012). Is a structured, manualized, evidence-based treatment protocol culturally competent and equivalently effective among American Indian parents in child welfare? *Child Maltreatment*, 17, 242–252.

Chaffin, M., Funderburk, B., Bard, D. et al. (2011). A combined motivation and parent–child interaction therapy package reduces child welfare recidivism in a randomized dismantling field trial. *Journal of Consulting and Clinical Psychology*, 79, 84–95.

Chaffin, M., Hecht, D., Bard, D. et al. (2012). A statewide trial of the SafeCare home-based services model with parents in child protective services. *Pediatrics*, 129, 509–515.

Chaffin, M., Silovsky, J.F., Funderburk, B. et al. (2004). Parent–child interaction therapy with physically abusive parents: Efficacy for reducing future abuse reports. *Journal of Consulting and Clinical Psychology*, 72, 500–510.

Chaffin, M., Valle, L.A., Funderburk, B. et al. (2009). A motivational intervention can improve retention in PCIT for low-motivation child welfare clients. *Child Maltreatment*, 14, 356–368.

Copeland, W.E., Keeler, G., Angold, A. & Costello, J. (2007). Traumatic events and posttraumatic stress disorder in childhood. *Archives of General Psychiatry*, 64, 577–584.

Deblinger, E., Mannarino, A.P., Cohen, J.A. et al. (2015). *Child Sexual Abuse: A Primer for Treating Children, Adolescents, and Their Nonoffending Parents*, 2nd edn. New York: Oxford University Press.

De Paul, J., Pérez-Albéniz, A., Guibert, M. et al. (2008). Dispositional empathy in neglectful mothers and mothers at high risk for child physical abuse. *Journal of Interpersonal Violence*, 23, 670–684.

Dodge, K.A., Pettit, G.S. & Bates, J.E. (1994). Effects of physical maltreatment on the development of peer relations. *Developmental Psychopathology*, 6, 43–55.

Dorsey, S., Pullmann, M.D., Berliner, L. et al. (2014). Engaging foster parents in treatment: A randomized trial of supplementing Trauma-focused Cognitive Behavioral Therapy with evidence-based engagement strategies. *Child Abuse & Neglect*, 38, 1508–1520.

Eyberg, S.M. & Robinson, E.A. (1983). Conduct problem behavior: Standardization of a behavioral rating. *Journal of Clinical Child Psychology*, 12, 347–354.

Gershater-Molko, R.M., Lutzker, J.R. & Welsh, D. (2002). Using recidivism to evaluate project SafeCare: Teaching bonding, safety, and health care skills to parents. *Child Maltreatment*, 7, 277–285.

Giardino, A., Harris, T.B. & Giardino, E. (2009). Child abuse and neglect, posttraumatic stress disorder. *Pediatrics: Developmental and Behavioral*, http://emedicine.medscape.com/article/916007-print.

Henggeler, S.W., Schoenwald, S.K., Borduin, C.M. et al. (2009). *Multisystemic Therapy for Antisocial Behavior in Children and Adolescents*, 2nd edn. New York: Guilford Press.

Kjellgren, C., Svedin, C.G. & Nilsson, D. (2013). Child physical abuse – experiences of combined treatment for children and their parents. A pilot study. *Child Care in Practice*, 19, 275–290.

Kolko, D.J. (1996a). Clinical monitoring of treatment course in child physical abuse: Psychometric characteristics and treatment comparisons. *Child Abuse & Neglect*, 20, 23–43.

Kolko, D.J. (1996b). Individual cognitive-behavioral treatment and family therapy for physically abused children and their offending parents: A comparison of clinical outcomes. *Child Maltreatment*, 1, 322–342.

Kolko, D.J. & Kolko, R.P. (2010). Psychological impact and treatment of child physical abuse. In: C. Jenny (ed), *Child Abuse and Neglect: Diagnosis, Treatment, and Evidence*. New York: Elsevier, 476–489.

Kolko, D.J. & Swenson, C.C. (2002). *Assessing and Treating Physically Abused Children and Their Families: A Cognitive-Behavioral Approach*. Thousand Oaks, CA: Sage.

Kolko, D.J., Iselin, A.M. & Gully, K.J. (2011). Evaluation of the sustainability and clinical outcome of Alternatives for Families: Cognitive-Behavioral Therapy (AF-CBT) in a child protection center. *Child Abuse & Neglect*, 35, 105–116.

Kolko, D.J., Selelyo, J. & Brown, E.J. (1999). The treatment histories and service involvement of physically and sexually abusive families: Description, correspondence, and clinical correlates. *Child Abuse & Neglect*, 23, 459–476.

Krug, E.G., Dahlberg, L.L., Mercy, J.A. et al. (2002). *World report on violence and health*. Geneva: World Health Organization.

Leeb, R.T., Lewis, T. & Zolotor, A.J. (2011). A review of physical and mental health consequences of child abuse and neglect and implications for practice. *American Journal of Lifestyle Medicine*, 5, 454–468.

Lenze, S.N., Pautsch, J. & Luby, J. (2011). Parent–child interaction therapy emotion development: A novel treatment for depression in preschool children. *Depression and Anxiety*, 28, 153–159.

Lipovsky, J., Swenson, C., Ralston, M. & Saunders, B. (1998). The abuse clarification process in the treatment of intrafamilial child abuse. *Child Abuse & Neglect*, 22, 729–741.

Lutzker, J.R. & Rice, J.M. (1984). Project 12-Ways: Measuring outcome of a large in-home service for treatment and prevention of child abuse and neglect. *Child Abuse & Neglect*, 8, 519–524.

Margolin, G. & Vickerman, K.A. (2007). Post-traumatic stress in children and adolescents exposed to family violence: I. Overview and issues. *Professional Psychology Research Practice*, 38, 613–619.

McKay, M., Stoewe, J., McCadam, K. & Gonzales, J. (1998). Increasing access to child mental health services for urban children and their caregivers. *Health and Social Work*, 23, 9–15.

Milner, J.S. (2000). Social information processing and child physical abuse: Theory and research. In: D.J. Hansen (ed), *Motivation and Child Maltreatment: Volume 46 of the Nebraska Symposium on Motivation*. Lincoln, NE: University of Nebraska Press, 39–84.

Milner, J.S. (2003). Social information processing in high risk and physically abusive parents. *Child Abuse & Neglect*, 27, 7–20.

Milner, J.S. & Chilamkurti, C. (1991). Physical child abuse perpetrator characteristics: A review of the literature. *Journal of Interpersonal Violence*, 6, 345–366.

Puliafico, A.C., Comer, J.S. & Pincus, D.B. (2012). Adapting parent–child interaction therapy to treat anxiety disorders in young children. *Child and Adolescent Psychiatry Clinics in North America*, 21, 607–619.

Runyon, M.K. & Deblinger, E. (2014). *Combined Parent–Child Cognitive Behavioral Therapy: An Approach to Empower Families At-Risk for Child Physical Abuse.* New York: Oxford University Press.

Runyon, M.K., Deblinger, E. & Schroeder, C.M. (2009). Pilot evaluation of outcomes of Combined Parent–Child Cognitive-Behavioral group therapy for families at-risk for child physical abuse. *Cognitive and Behavioral Practice*, 16, 101–118.

Runyon, M.K., Deblinger, E. & Schroeder, C.M. (2010). *Preliminary analyses of pre to posttreatment changes in families after their participation in Combined Parent–Child Cognitive Behavioral Therapy.* Unpublished manuscript.

Runyon, M.K., Deblinger, E. & Steer, R. (2010). Group cognitive behavioral treatments for parents and children at-risk for physical abuse: An initial study. *Child & Family Behavior Therapy*, 32, 196–218.

Runyon, M.K., Basilio, I., Van Hasselt, V.B. & Hersen, M. (1998). Child witnesses of interparental violence: Child and family treatment. In: V.B. Hasselt & M. Hersen (eds), *Handbook of Psychological Treatment Protocols for Children and Adolescents* Mahwah, NJ: Lawrence Erlbaum Associates, 224–300.

Self-Brown, S., McFry, E., Montesanti, A. et al. (2014). SafeCare: A prevention and intervention program for child neglect and physical abuse. In: R.M. Reece, R.F. Hanson & J. Sargent (eds), *Treatment of Child Abuse: Common Ground for Mental Health, Medical, and Legal Practitioners*, 2nd edn. Baltimore, MD: John Hopkins University Press, 50–58.

Silovsky, J.F., Bard, D., Chaffin, M. et al. (2011). Prevention of child maltreatment in high-risk rural families: A randomized clinical trial with child welfare outcomes. *Children and Youth Services Review*, 33, 1435–1444.

Sugaya, L., Hasin, D.S., Olfson, M. et al. (2012). Child physical abuse and adult mental health: A national study. *Journal of Traumatic Stress*, 25, 384–392.

Swenson, C.C., Schaeffer, C.M., Henggeler, S.W. et al. (2010). Multisystemic therapy for child abuse and neglect: A randomized effectiveness trial. *Journal of Family Psychology*, 24, 497–507.

Thompson, M., Kingree, C.J. & Desai, S. (2004). Gender differences in long-term health consequences of physical abuse of children: Data from a nationally representative survey. *American Journal of Public Health*, 94, 599–604.

Timmer, S., Urquiza, A.J., Zebell, N. & McGrath, J. (2005). Parent–child interaction therapy: Application to maltreating parent–child dyads. *Child Abuse & Neglect*, 29, 825–842.

United Nations, General Assembly. (2006). *Report of the independent expert for the United Nations study on violence against children, A/61/299*, www.unviolencestudy.org.

Wilson, S.R., Rack, J.J., Shi, X. & Norris, A.M. (2008). Comparing physically abusive, neglectful, and non-maltreating parents during interactions with their children: A meta-analysis of observational studies. *Child Abuse & Neglect*, 32, 897–911.

Wolfe, D. (1985). Child abusive parents: An empirical review and analysis. *Psychological Bulletin*, 97, 462–482.

19

Effective Therapies for Children and Non-offending Caregivers in the Aftermath of Child Sexual Abuse or Other Traumas

Esther Deblinger, Elisabeth Pollio and Melissa K. Runyon

Rowan University, NJ

Childhood trauma can have a significant and long-lasting impact. Research has repeatedly documented emotional, behavioural, social and neurobiological effects exhibited by children in the aftermath of trauma (e.g., Goenjian, Walling, Steinberg et al., 2005; Putnam, 2003; Trickett & McBride-Chang, 1995). The Adverse Childhood Experiences studies (e.g., Chapman, Anda, Felitti et al., 2004; Dube, Felitti, Dong et al., 2003; Felitti, Anda, Nordenberg et al., 1998) suggest the impact of trauma in childhood can lead to a host of psychological and physical difficulties in adulthood including substance abuse, depression, heart disease, lung disease and cancer, as well as an increased risk of premature death. Although children are resilient and some recover without treatment, many children require intervention to ameliorate trauma's significant negative effects. It is therefore critical that children negatively impacted by trauma receive effective therapy. This chapter provides a review of the research on those treatments for childhood trauma deemed 'Well-Supported by Research Evidence' or 'Supported by Research Evidence' by the California Evidence-Based Clearinghouse for Child Welfare (CEBC; www.cebc4cw.org). Trauma-Focused Cognitive Behavioural Therapy (TF-CBT; Cohen, Mannarino & Deblinger, 2017; Deblinger, Mannarino, Cohen et al., 2015), a well-supported treatment originally designed for families impacted by child sexual abuse, will be explored in greater detail as this model has the strongest evidence base among treatments for childhood trauma with effectiveness documented in over 50 scientific studies, including 20 randomised trials.

Brief Review of Research for Treatments in the Supported by and Well-Supported by Research Evidence Categories

While many diverse treatments have been developed to help children overcome childhood trauma(s), the efficacy of relatively few treatments has been rigorously evaluated. One treatment that meets the requirements for the Supported by Research Evidence category of the CEBC in the area of childhood trauma is Child–Parent Psychotherapy (CPP; Lieberman, Van Horn & Ghosh Ippen, 2005). Three treatment models have met the more rigorous requirements for the Well-Supported by Research Evidence category of the CEBC in the area of childhood trauma: Eye Movement Desensitisation and Reprocessing for Children and Adolescents (EMDR) (Shapiro, 2001), Prolonged Exposure for Adolescents (PE-A; Foa, Chrestman & Gilboa-Schechtman, 2008), and Trauma-Focused Cognitive Behavioural Therapy (TF-CBT; Cohen, Mannarino & Deblinger, 2017). Each of these models and relevant research support will be presented. Given the depth of research supporting TF-CBT, this model, developed by the first author of this chapter in collaboration with Judith Cohen, M.D. and Anthony Mannarino, Ph.D., will be described in greater detail, along with a case study that illustrates its practical implementation.

CPP (Lieberman, Van Horn & Ghosh Ippen, 2005) is an intervention model for children zero through five years of age who have experienced trauma. The treatment is rooted in attachment theory and an emphasis is placed on the child–primary caregiver relationship. This dyad participates together in therapy. One randomised controlled trial involved 75 preschoolers (ages 3–5 years) who had been exposed to marital violence, and their mothers (Lieberman, Van Horn & Ghosh Ippen, 2005). Participants were randomly assigned to CPP or case management plus treatment as usual in the community. Children in the CPP group experienced significantly greater improvements in traumatic stress disorder symptoms, diagnostic status and behavioural difficulties. Mothers in both groups demonstrated significant reductions in total Post-traumatic Stress Disorder (PTSD) symptoms and global severity of symptoms but only mothers in the CPP group evidenced significant reductions in PTSD avoidance symptoms. At the six-month follow-up, children in the CPP group continued to show significant reductions in behavioural difficulties and mothers in the CPP group showed significant reductions in the global severity of symptoms as compared to the control group (Lieberman, Ghosh Ippen & Van Horn, 2006).

A re-analysis of the data from the Lieberman, Van Horn and Ghosh Ippen (2005) randomised trial was utilised to assess the efficacy of CPP with preschoolers exposed to multiple traumatic and stressful events (Ghosh Ippen, Harris, Van Horn & Lieberman, 2011). Results indicated that preschoolers in the CPP group with four or more traumatic and stressful events showed significantly greater improvements in PTSD symptoms and diagnosis, depressive symptoms and behavioural difficulties than the comparison group. Mothers in this group showed significant decreases in symptoms of PTSD and depression. Treatment gains were maintained at the six-month follow-up for the CPP group with four or more traumatic and stressful events.

A randomised controlled trial of 137 younger children (age one year) from maltreating families and their mothers compared the effects of Infant-Child Psychotherapy (IPP; an adaptation of CPP for infants), a psychoeducational parenting intervention (PPI), and a community standard control group (Cicchetti, Rogosch & Toth, 2006). A low-income normative comparison group of non-maltreating families (N=52) was also utilised. Results indicated that only children in the IPP and PPI groups demonstrated significant increases in secure attachment.

As noted earlier, only three evidence-based interventions, including EMDR, PE-A and TF-CBT, met the criteria set forth by the CEBC to be regarded as well-supported interventions for this population. EMDR (Shapiro, 2001) uses an eight-phase approach to treating trauma and its sequelae. An important element of EMDR is the use of dual stimulation through focus on bilateral eye movements, audio tones or hand taps while concentrating on the traumatic memory. Chemtob, Nakashima, and Carlson (2002) utilised a randomised lagged-groups design involving 32 children (ages 6–12 years) with disaster-related PTSD. Results indicated that EMDR significantly reduced symptoms of PTSD, depression and anxiety. These gains were maintained at a six-month follow-up assessment.

EMDR was compared to a wait-list control (WLC) group in a randomised controlled trial of 33 children (ages 6–16 years) with a diagnosis of PTSD due to varying types of trauma (Ahmad, Larsson & Sundelin-Wahlsten, 2007). Children in the EMDR group had significantly greater improvements on scales related to total post-traumatic stress symptoms and PTSD-related symptoms, as well as subscales of re-experiencing and avoidance. The WLC group evidenced significantly greater reductions in symptoms on the PTSD-non-related scale, which may have been due to a natural healing process of those symptoms. Another comparison of EMDR and a WLC group involved 27 children (ages 6–12 years) with PTSD symptoms secondary to a motor vehicle accident (Kemp, Drummond & McDermott, 2009). Significantly greater improvements in child-reported and clinician-rated PTSD symptoms were found for the EMDR group as compared to the WLC group. Parent-reported PTSD and symptoms on non-trauma measures did not yield significant improvement. Treatment gains were maintained at three-month and 12-month follow-up assessments.

EMDR also has been compared to cognitive behavioural therapy (CBT) in randomised controlled trials. A study of 14 girls (ages 12–13 years) who had experienced sexual abuse indicated that both treatments resulted in significant improvements in PTSD symptoms (Jaberghaderi, Greenwald, Rubin et al., 2004). The mean number of sessions was significantly lower in the EMDR group; however, the CBT group had a required minimum number of sessions that was not required of the EMDR group. Another comparison of EMDR and CBT involved 52 children (ages 4–18 years) with trauma-related symptoms secondary to a fireworks factory explosion (de Roos, Greenwald, den Hollander-Gijsman et al., 2011). Significant reductions in PTSD, anxiety, depression, and behavioural difficulties were found for both groups. The EMDR group completed treatment in fewer sessions. Treatment gains were maintained at a three-month follow-up for both groups.

There has been one randomised controlled trial to date comparing EMDR and TF-CBT (Diehle, Opmeer, Boer et al., 2015). This study involved 48 children (ages 8–18 years) who met partial or full criteria for PTSD due to varying traumatic experiences. Participants were randomly assigned to a maximum of eight sessions of EMDR or eight sessions of TF-CBT. Both treatment groups demonstrated significant reductions in PTSD with no significant differences between groups on PTSD symptoms or length of treatment. Significant improvements in child-reported symptoms of depression and anxiety were found within both groups. However, parent-reported improvement of depressive symptoms and hyperactivity was significant for the TF-CBT group but not the EMDR group. Moreover, the investigators reported increases in conduct problems in the EMDR group only.

PE-A (Foa, Chrestman & Gilboa-Schechtman, 2008) is another well-supported cognitive behavioural therapy to address trauma symptoms with a foundation in emotional processing theory. Components of the treatment include psychoeducation about trauma and treatment planning, in vivo exposure, imaginal exposure and relapse prevention. One study involved the random assignment of 38 adolescents (ages 12–18 years) with a PTSD diagnosis secondary to a single-event trauma to PE-A or time-limited psychodynamic psychotherapy (TLDP-A), a non-directive, non-trauma-focused intervention that served as the active control condition (Gilboa-Schechtman, Foa, Shafran et al., 2010). Results indicated that both treatments decreased distress and improved functioning but PE-A was superior to TLDP-A in the reduction of PTSD and depressive symptoms and in the improvement of overall functioning. Significant differences between groups were observed at post-treatment and at six-month follow-up but not at the 17-month follow-up, although treatment gains within groups were maintained. Another randomised controlled trial compared PE-A to supportive counselling among 61 adolescent females (ages 13–18 years) with a PTSD diagnosis secondary to sexual abuse (Foa, McLean, Capaldi & Rosenfield, 2013). Both treatments demonstrated significant improvements in PTSD symptoms, rates of PTSD diagnosis, depressive symptoms and overall functioning but the improvement of participants in the PE-A group was significantly greater as compared to those in the supportive counselling group. These significant differences remained at the 12-month follow-up.

Review of TF-CBT Research

The efficacy of TF-CBT (Cohen, Mannarino & Deblinger, 2017) has been evaluated in more than 20 randomised controlled trials to date. The model integrates cognitive behavioural principles and trauma-sensitive interventions with aspects of attachment, developmental neurobiology, family, empowerment and humanistic theories. Typically, children, adolescents and non-offending caregivers are engaged in individual sessions as well as conjoint caregiver–child sessions that are designed to provide psychoeducation, skills training and opportunities for the therapeutic processing of traumatic memories.

Based on early research documenting the prevalence of post-traumatic stress symptoms as well as other emotional and behavioural difficulties among children who had experienced sexual abuse (e.g., Cohen & Mannarino, 1988; Deblinger, McLeer, Atkins et al., 1989), research began at separate clinical sites to develop and evaluate the efficacy of treatment models designed to address children's trauma-related difficulties. The initial treatment protocols were developed and tested through several independent randomised trials examining trauma-focused individual therapy formats (Cohen & Mannarino, 1996, 1998; Deblinger, Lippmann & Steer, 1996) as well as a trauma-focused group format (Deblinger, Stauffer & Steer, 2001). Recognising that these demonstrably effective treatment models were highly similar, the developers, Drs Cohen, Mannarino and Deblinger, integrated their approaches as described in their treatment manual (Cohen, Mannarino & Deblinger, 2017) and conducted several large-scale randomised controlled trials that have been replicated by other investigators over the last decade.

While space limitations of this chapter preclude the review of all of the TF-CBT quasi-experimental and experimental investigations completed, it is worth noting that over 50 TF-CBT related studies have been published to date. Below are summaries of several of the randomised trials with other treatment outcome findings highlighted that have been consistent across studies and/or critical to the optimal understanding and implementation of TF-CBT.

The first multi-site site investigation of this model examined the efficacy of TF-CBT with children, adolescents and their caregivers in the aftermath of child sexual abuse (CSA) at clinical sites in Pittsburgh, PA and Stratford, NJ (Cohen, Deblinger, Mannarino & Steer, 2004). In the context of this study, youngsters and their caregivers were randomly assigned to receive approximately 12 sessions of TF-CBT or a child-centred treatment approach. While children and caregivers across the alternative treatment conditions all showed significant improvements, children assigned to TF-CBT showed significantly greater improvements with respect to PTSD, depression, behaviour problems, feelings of shame and dysfunctional abuse-related attributions. Similarly, caregivers assigned to TF-CBT, as compared to the client-centred condition, reported significantly greater improvements with respect to personal depressive symptomatology, abuse-specific distress, parenting skills and parental support of the child. The follow-up assessments revealed that these findings generally were sustained over a one-year period (Deblinger, Mannarino, Cohen & Steer, 2006).

A more recent multi-site study examined the impact of length of treatment and the use of a written narrative with young children (ages 4–11 years) impacted by CSA (Deblinger, Mannarino, Cohen, Mannarino & Iyengar, 2011). While the findings of this dismantling randomised trial documented the efficacy of TF-CBT in 8-session as well as 16-session formats with and without the written narrative, the 8-session condition with the written narrative appeared to be the most efficient and effective condition in terms of alleviating abuse-related fear and generalised anxiety in young children. However, the skill-building 16-session condition without the written narrative produced significantly greater improvements with respect to externalising behaviour problems and parenting practices, thereby replicating earlier findings highlighting the importance of parenting skill-building in terms of addressing children's behaviour problems (Deblinger, Lippmann & Steer, 1996; Deblinger, Mannarino, Cohen et al., 2011).

The efficacy of TF-CBT has also been evaluated in studies involving children and teens impacted by other diverse traumas. Caregivers and children impacted by intimate partner violence, for example, were randomly assigned to TF-CBT or treatment as usual in a community setting (Cohen, Mannarino & Iyengar, 2011). The findings of this investigation documented the superior efficacy of TF-CBT in terms of children's PTSD symptom improvement as well as anxiety as compared to treatment as usual.

Several TF-CBT investigations have been implemented with children in foster care with histories of diverse and multiple traumas. A quasi-experimental study of TF-CBT with this population not only replicated previous findings in terms of significant reductions in traumatic stress symptoms, but also demonstrated the superior effects of TF-CBT in leading to significantly greater reductions in placement disruptions and runaway incidents from foster care as compared to treatment as usual (Lyons, Weiner & Scheider, 2006). Another recent randomised controlled trial compared TF-CBT plus an evidence-based engagement procedure with standard TF-CBT for children in foster care (Dorsey, Pullmann, Berliner et al., 2014). While no differences were found in the post-treatment outcomes across these conditions, there were significantly fewer dropouts and greater completion rates among those foster families assigned to the TF-CBT plus engagement condition.

The above findings documenting the efficacy of TF-CBT in addressing the therapeutic needs of children and caregivers in the United States have been replicated in studies conducted around the world. Two randomised trials examining TF-CBT delivered to boys and girls highly traumatised as a result of war zone experiences in the Democratic Republic of the Congo replicated earlier findings in terms of the efficacy of TF-CBT delivered in group formats (McMullen, O'Callaghan, Shannon et al., 2013; O'Callaghan, McMullen, Shannon et al., 2013). In addition, a randomised controlled trial conducted in Norway comparing TF-CBT to treatment as usual with youth (ages 10–18 years) impacted by diverse traumas also replicated earlier findings (Jensen, Holt, Ormhaug et al., 2014). Norwegian children assigned to TF-CBT demonstrated significantly greater improvements with respect to PTS symptoms, depression, general mental health problems, and functional impairments as compared to those assigned to treatment as usual.

Finally, while the above reviews only provide a sample of TF-CBT outcome research conducted to date, a preliminary examination of the cost effectiveness of TF-CBT as compared to treatment as usual in community settings is important to highlight. Greer, Grasso, Cohen, and Webb (2014) examined mental health service costs over a one-year period. Their findings suggested that low-end outpatient mental health services cost twice as much for children who received TF-CBT as compared to those who received treatment as usual. However, five times more was spent on children who received treatment as usual for high-end mental health services during follow up as compared to those who received TF-CBT.

Description of TF-CBT

TF-CBT is a components-based, hybrid approach to treating children who have experienced trauma and their non-offending caregivers. The treatment integrates cognitive behavioural principles and trauma-sensitive interventions with aspects of attachment, developmental neurobiology, family, empowerment and humanistic theories. TF-CBT includes individual work with the child, individual work with the non-offending caregiver, and conjoint work with the child and caregiver together. The individual work with child and caregiver generally proceeds in parallel through the TF-CBT components, which can be summarised by the acronym PRACTICE (Psychoeducation and Parenting, Relaxation, Affective Expression and Modulation, Cognitive Coping, Trauma Narration and Processing, In Vivo Mastery, Conjoint Sessions, and Enhancing Safety and Future Development). Therapeutic activities encouraged between sessions, referred to as PRACTICE assignments, are often utilised to enhance the skills through practice in everyday situations. The TF-CBT components will be briefly described below; further information on TF-CBT is provided in the treatment manuals (Cohen, Mannarino & Deblinger, 2017; Cohen, Mannarino & Deblinger, 2012; Deblinger, Mannarino, Cohen et al., 2015) and the online training site 'TF-CBT *Web*' (http://tfcbt.musc.edu).

The initial phase of TF-CBT focuses on stabilisation and skill-building and is comprised of the 'PRAC' components. **P**sychoeducation begins the gradual exposure process by acknowledging the trauma experienced at the start of therapy and maintaining the trauma focus throughout the course of treatment. This component involves providing information about the trauma(s) experienced and the impact to help normalise the reactions of the child and caregiver, as well as to provide and reinforce accurate information about the trauma. Psychoeducation about TF-CBT also helps caregivers and children have a general understanding of what treatment will entail and how it will address the trauma symptoms experienced. This educational information often instils hope, given the strong research support for the efficacy of the TF-CBT treatment model. The **P**arenting component provides caregivers with parenting skills designed to encourage positive, adaptive child behaviours, while enhancing caregiver–child communication and reducing the occurrence of more challenging child behaviours. Maintaining structure and consistency for children is particularly important in the aftermath of a traumatic experience. Skills such as praise, reflective listening, selective attention, time out and contingency reinforcements are valuable tools for caregivers to utilise, even with children who do not exhibit significant behavioural difficulties.

The **R**elaxation component involves teaching children, as well as their caregivers, various techniques to reduce the physiological manifestations of stress, anxiety and PTSD. Such techniques typically include focused breathing, progressive muscle relaxation, positive imagery and mindfulness.

Affective expression and modulation involves helping children to identify and label feelings, thereby enhancing their feelings vocabulary. There is also an emphasis on sharing feelings in an appropriate manner, particularly with caregivers, as well as identifying various strategies to cope with distressing feelings. Additionally, this component involves enhancing problem-solving and social skills. Affective expression and modulation skills are taught in relation to feelings in general as well as related to the trauma more specifically. It is often helpful for children to create a coping skills toolkit that lists affect regulation strategies, such as their favourite positive activities, listening to music and discussing feelings with others. Of note, exercise can be a beneficial affect modulation strategy, as exercise has been found to be as effective as antidepressant medication in the treatment of depression (Blumenthal, Babyak & Moore, 1999).

Cognitive coping involves identifying thoughts, understanding the interrelationship of thoughts, feelings, and behaviours (cognitive triangle), and ultimately challenging unhelpful and inaccurate thoughts and replacing them with more helpful and accurate thoughts. It may be beneficial to incorporate body sensations into the cognitive triangle, particularly among children with physical manifestations of anxiety and PTSD. Cognitive coping focuses only on non-trauma-related thoughts with children at this point in treatment, whereas eliciting both non-trauma-related and trauma-related thoughts from caregivers is encouraged. Trauma-related thoughts will be elicited and processed with children during the trauma narrative component, which will be discussed next.

The second phase of TF-CBT focuses on the development of a Trauma narrative and processing. During this phase, children are encouraged to share the details of their traumatic experience(s), including their thoughts, feelings and body sensations, in a gradual manner. The trauma narrative is the next step in the gradual exposure process, as children have been exposed to trauma-related material in a graduated manner throughout treatment through psychoeducation about the trauma, use of relaxation skills when upset by trauma reminders, discussing feelings related to the trauma, etc. Children often create a written trauma narrative but other means of expression can be utilised (e.g., song, artwork, talk show, and re-enactment with dolls/puppets). Typical chapters of a trauma narrative include the traumatic event itself (the first time, last time, and most distressing time if multiple incidents), the disclosure and/or investigation, and other events preceding and/or following the trauma. During the processing portion of this component, any inaccurate and unhelpful thoughts are challenged and ultimately replaced by more accurate and helpful thoughts through the use of Socratic questioning. Children also create a final chapter that briefly summarises the traumatic experience(s), describes what was learnt in therapy about themselves, others, and the world, includes any messages to other children who have had a similar experience, acknowledges positive interactions with caregivers or others who helped, and describes expectations for the future. Work with the caregiver in this phase also involves gradual exposure to trauma-related details. The clinician is assessing the caregiver's reaction to this exposure to determine the clinical appropriateness of sharing some or all of the child's trauma narrative. During this phase, caregivers also continue to practise their parenting and coping skills.

The final phase of TF-CBT focuses on consolidation and closure, and is comprised of the 'ICE' components. Invivo mastery involves decreasing trauma-related avoidant behaviour through a process of gradual exposure. Trauma-related avoidant behaviour often decreases during the trauma narrative and processing component but if avoidant behaviours that interfere with functioning remain after completion of the narrative, an in vivo plan can be created to desensitise the child to these innocuous stimuli. This component may be initiated earlier in treatment if the avoidant behaviours interfere significantly with day-to-day functioning (e.g., school refusal or sleep refusal). Conjoint sessions involve working with the child and caregiver together. Earlier in treatment conjoint work often involves brief skill-building sessions in which caregivers practice parenting skills (such as praise, reflective listening and active ignoring) and children demonstrate and practice coping skills (such as teaching caregivers focused breathing, expressing their feelings to caregivers, and sharing their coping skills toolkit with caregivers). In the final phase of treatment, conjoint sessions become increasingly trauma-focused. Some typical activities include playing the 'What Do You Know' psychoeducation card game (Deblinger, Neubauer, Runyon & Baker, 2006), sharing trauma-related artwork, sharing the trauma narrative (when clinically appropriate), discussing sex education and role-playing personal safety skills. Children and caregivers are always carefully prepared in individual sessions for the conjoint session activities.

The Enhancing safety and future development component can include age-appropriate sex education for children who have been sexually abused or at-risk teens, enhancing confident communication, improving problem-solving skills, and role-playing personal safety skills (e.g., how to handle bullying, exposure to violence, sexual abuse, etc.). It is important to praise children for the skills they did use when they were faced with the trauma in an effort to minimise any self-blame. An emphasis is placed on involving the caregiver and/or other trusted adult in handling potentially dangerous situations (e.g., disclosing to the caregiver about bullying, sexual abuse, an unsafe situation, etc.). TF-CBT concludes with a review of progress and skills learnt, and plans to address trauma reminders that might surface in the future are discussed. Finally, it is important to acknowledge and celebrate the children's and caregivers' progress and hard work in therapy. Thus, an end of therapy celebration, including music, balloons, special snacks and a graduation ceremony is often planned collaboratively by the child, caregiver and therapist to reinforce well-deserved feelings of pride and strength in overcoming the trauma(s) endured.

TF-CBT Case Study

James, a 12-year-old male, was referred for TF-CBT, after being sexually abused on multiple occasions by his male soccer coach, Mr Smith. James was a very gifted athlete who found a safe environment at the local centre in a community that was plagued by gangs and community violence. Mr Smith was well respected in the community and was known for helping young men cultivate their athletic talents, showcasing them to important officials, and for helping many of the young men in this neighbourhood get into college.

Over the course of a little more than a year, Mr Smith engaged in a grooming process in which he increasingly violated appropriate boundaries and engaged in increasingly abusive sexual behaviours toward James. Mr Smith frequently told James that he was special and had athletic talents that surpassed those of any other young man he had coached. As a result, James felt very proud of himself and increasingly relied on Mr Smith for his guidance as a trusted mentor. James' single mother was grateful that her son seemed to have a positive male role model in Mr Smith. Mr Smith also consistently gave James the sports equipment and items (e.g., cleats) that James' family was unable to afford. James, who grew up in a home with four older sisters and a strong, supportive, yet firm single mother, viewed Mr Smith as 'the father he never had'. Over time, Mr Smith began scheduling private coaching sessions with James, while encouraging him to help with odd jobs around the centre that were rewarded with weekend camping and fishing trips. Mr Smith's sexually inappropriate behaviour toward James was uncovered when another adult witnessed Mr Smith sexually abusing James in a public bathroom at a campground. The adult intervened to stop Mr Smith and then immediately contacted the police.

Following the investigation of the sexual assault allegations, James was referred for a medical examination to diagnose and treat the impact of the sexual assault. The child abuse paediatrician who conducted the examination assessed for any physical injury and sexually transmitted infections, and took a complete medical history during which James disclosed that the sexually abusive experiences occurred over the course of approximately one year. Mr Smith was charged and arrested for multiple counts of sexual assault of a minor and endangering the welfare of a minor. Subsequently, James was referred for a course of TF-CBT to assist him in overcoming the impact of CSA as well as exposure to community violence.

During his initial therapy assessment, James disclosed that the sexual abuse began with Mr Smith hugging him a lot, which made James feel loved yet uncomfortable at times. He shared little additional detail, but acknowledged the relief and embarrassment he felt when the hiker discovered Mr Smith sexually abusing him. James was quite avoidant of any further discussion about the sexual abuse, but was able to share more about frightening exposures to community violence that led him to seek refuge at the community recreation centre in the first place. In response to a trauma history inventory, James disclosed that he had frequently witnessed property and gun violence and fighting among youth and adults in his community. According to James, there had been times he was fearful of being harmed while walking to and from school. He added that he felt safe at the community centre with Mr Smith until Mr Smith 'hurt me'.

In assessment of Ms Johnson, James' mother, she revealed that James had historically been a bright, athletic, and talented child who was very kind and helpful to others. She indicated that she recently noticed he was somewhat irritable and withdrawn at home and there had been a few incidents where he had minor physical altercations with peers at school and at the community centre. At the time, she reportedly dismissed his behaviour as 'boys being boys'. Ms Johnson became tearful and said that she should have known that her son was being abused because of these changes in his behaviour. She also blamed herself for encouraging her son to interact with Mr Smith because she thought he needed a positive male role model.

Based on his responses to standardised assessment measures, James met criteria for PTSD, had mild depressive symptoms, and reported feelings of shame associated with the abuse he experienced. His mother reported a significant level of depression as well as significant behaviour problems for James.

During the initial phase of TF-CBT, the stabilisation and skill-building phase, the 'PRAC' components (i.e., psychoeducation, parenting, relaxation, affective expression and modulation, and cognitive coping skills) were presented to James and Ms Johnson in individual sessions. Separate sessions were important to help mother and son have a place to let down their guard and share any feelings and thoughts that were troubling them. During these individual sessions, the therapist offered psychoeducation about trauma responses to normalise both James' and his mother's symptoms and responses, provided basic information about the prevalence, impact and dynamics of sexual abuse and community violence, and reviewed what they could expect from treatment, while also highlighting the documented efficacy of TF-CBT. The therapist instilled hope by emphasising that James had two things that were associated with the best possible outcome for a youth exposed to sexual assault and violence: a supportive parent who responded appropriately to support him and his participation in effective treatment.

Coping skills were then introduced to help James and his mother cope with general life stressors as well as trauma reminders and the associated thoughts, feelings and behaviours that those reminders elicited. Noting that James was somewhat avoidant of discussing the sexual abuse, the therapist initially encouraged him to share a positive narrative about spending time with a school friend the past weekend. Next, he was gently encouraged to provide a similar narrative (i.e., baseline trauma narrative) about the last sexual assault incident or about talking to the police about the sexual abuse. James responded by disclosing that Mr Smith had 'done some bad stuff' to him. When asked to define 'bad stuff', James hesitantly replied, 'You know, he touched me and did sexual stuff.' The therapist reflected back James' statements about the sexual abuse, thereby acknowledging the abuse and validating his feelings. Going forward, the therapist's goal would be to gently encourage James to talk about abuse and violence in general, with gradual exposure to brief questions related to his experiences. While the development of a trauma narrative was not mentioned in the initial phase, the therapist hoped that the psychoeducation and skill-building activities would gradually prepare James for the trauma narrative and processing component that would come later in treatment.

Given that parenting is a critical part of TF-CBT, Ms Johnson was reminded of the importance of providing a great deal of structure, clear limits, and positive feedback to children after they have experienced traumatic events in order to enhance their sense of safety, security and confidence. The therapist emphasised the benefits of specific praise and positive reinforcement as a powerful tool for increasing James' positive, pro-social behaviours. Ms Johnson was instructed to praise James every time he was kind, expressed his anger in a calm, appropriate manner, or interacted in a positive way with peers or adults. After a few sessions, a behavioural contract was also negotiated between James and his mother where the expectation that James would not be aggressive toward others as well as consequences for this behaviour and rewards for pro-social behaviour were clearly communicated, recorded and agreed upon by both James and his mother.

Next, James and his mother were engaged in coping skills practice activities with respect to relaxation, affective expression and modulation, and cognitive coping. With James, there was an emphasis on emotional regulation and expression skills given that James' expressed emotions tended to be limited to anger. The therapist helped him identify a range of emotions by examining the feelings that were underneath his surface reaction of anger, including feeling betrayed, sad, scared, shameful and embarrassed. He also practised removing himself from anger-provoking situations and using exercise and running in conjunction with calming self-talk so he could handle these situations in a calm manner. As James began implementing these skills, there was a noticeable change in his aggressive behaviour. The therapist utilised praise and positive feedback to shape and encourage the use of these skills. She also encouraged Ms Johnson to praise James' efforts at expressing his emotions verbally in order to further shape and strengthen these adaptive behaviours.

Ms Johnson reported feelings of guilt and self-blame. The therapist helped her utilise cognitive coping skills to identify possible dysfunctional thoughts underlying those distressing feelings. For example, Ms Johnson was repeatedly blaming herself for encouraging her son to spend time with the coach and thinking she should have known something was wrong when James' behaviour changed and he became more irritable and aggressive toward his peers. The therapist provided education and used Socratic questioning to challenge Ms Johnson's distressing thoughts by asking 'How could you or anyone else have known the coach was capable of sexually abusing children without witnessing this behaviour? How did the person who reported him to the police know? Are there other things that could account for the change in James' behaviour or should we automatically think that any time a child's behaviour changes that he/she is being sexually abused?' Ms Johnson was asked to list all of the positive things that Mr Smith had done for local children and the community – a very long list including fundraising, mentoring children, building the community centre, serving as soccer coach and setting up meetings with talented children, their parents and scouts. After reviewing the list, Ms Johnson was asked why she or anyone would have been suspicious of the coach or suspected him of hurting their children. Psychoeducation was also provided about the strategies perpetrators use to ensure that their abusive behaviour is kept a secret. Ms Johnson reported feeling less depressed as she worked between sessions at catching and challenging her dysfunctional thoughts related to the assault of her son. Ms Johnson began to realise that the coach had fooled everyone, but now she and her son were working with law enforcement to stop him from abusing others in the future.

To continue psychoeducation and gradual exposure, the therapist introduced a card game to James with questions about information related to sexual abuse and other forms of violence (Deblinger, Neubauer, Runyon & Baker, 2006). The therapist also shared a book with James about boys who were sexually abused and exposed to violence. The therapist also reviewed a list of celebrities, including a famous athlete, who had disclosed his own exposure to sexual abuse and violence. These strategies provided additional psychoeducation about youths' reactions to sexual assault and violence and also prepared James for the second phase of therapy. After some individual sessions, the therapist prepared James and his mother to meet for brief skills-focused conjoint sessions. During these sessions, James often proudly taught his mother the coping skills he was mastering and James and his mother would exchange specific praise they had prepared for one another, thereby ending sessions on a positive note.

During the second phase of TF-CBT, youth are encouraged to discuss and/or write about the details of their traumatic experiences including their related thoughts and feelings. James was reluctant to discuss the sexual abuse, but seemed a bit more receptive to discussing the community violence. The therapist reviewed the coping skills with James and reminded him that deep breathing and other strategies would enhance his sense of control and comfort throughout the process. James also learnt how to use the subjective units of distress scale (SUDS) to keep the therapist aware of how he was feeling. These SUDS scores would help the therapist to pace the sessions ensuring that James would have an opportunity to utilise his skills to bring down his distress levels before ending sessions each week. James seemed to favour the use of focused breathing to help him manage his distress. The therapist then provided James with a choice to write about a time he witnessed violence in his community or to write about the most recent sexual abuse episode. James continued to hesitate to write about anything so the therapist offered James the opportunity to create a poster for other kids that outlined all the different types of community violence and sexual abuse that children should know about. After creating this poster James was asked to circle those types of violence and abuse he had experienced. His circled answers revealed exposure to gun violence as well as increasingly invasive sexual abuse incidents with Mr Smith fondling James, James being encouraged to fondle Mr Smith, oral sex performed by and on both parties, and the final incident being the sexual assault that involved all of these acts and anal penetration. The therapist encouraged James to create a trauma narrative that would not only help him but might also help the therapist understand how these types of experiences affect boys so the therapist could potentially help others more effectively. In response to this treatment rationale, James agreed to write a brief introductory chapter in which he indicated his age and grade, and described his family as well as his favourite hobbies, and then he chose to write a chapter about an exposure to community violence that occurred before the sexual abuse began. He began by writing about and sharing his thoughts and feelings about an incident in which he and a friend witnessed gang-related gun violence. As therapy continued, the therapist gave James a choice each session between two incidents of sexual abuse that he reported experiencing to describe in a chapter of his trauma narrative. James started by writing about his first introduction to the coach and his early positive interactions with him and then he progressed to writing about the confusing touches with the coach, the fondling and oral sex with the coach, and the most recent sexual assault that was reported. The therapist carefully recorded and read each chapter back and offered encouragement as James worked to share the details as well as his thoughts and feelings about several distinct abusive episodes. Each time, he reported feeling relief and his SUDS scores over time reflected less anxiety after he completed a chapter. After he added a chapter for each of the incidents, he was asked to put his chapters in chronological order.

Through the narrative, James expressed many unhelpful cognitive distortions related to the abuse, including 'Why did he pick me?', 'Why did he betray me?', 'Why did my body feel good when he touched me?', 'It's my fault. I liked the gifts and didn't tell anyone', 'I should have told someone the first time I felt uncomfortable.' Thus, after completing the narrative, the therapist used psychoeducation, Socratic questioning and best-friend role plays to help James process his experiences, while also identifying, challenging and replacing dysfunctional thoughts with healthy, productive thoughts that were incorporated into his narrative. James also worked on adding a positive ending to his book by writing a chapter about what he learnt in therapy and what he felt proud of in general and in relation to coping with the violence and abuse he experienced. He ended his narrative by sharing positive feelings about his family and friends and things he looked forward to in the future. Over the course of treatment, the therapist determined that the sharing of the narrative in a conjoint session would be therapeutic for both James and his mother. Thus, as James completed the chapters, the therapist shared the chapters with his mother to gradually assist her in coping with these experiences, and to assess whether she could respond to her son in a supportive manner during conjoint sessions in the next and final phase of TF-CBT.

The final phase of TF-CBT focuses on the consolidation of skills and closure with an emphasis on in vivo mastery (when indicated), trauma-focused conjoint sessions and final therapeutic activities that enhance safety and future development. James had not been on the soccer field since the sexual abuse by his coach was discovered, thus a focus on in vivo mastery was discussed as a way of encouraging him to face his fear of returning to participating in the sport he previously enjoyed. Initially the team was angry and supported the coach, but as other victims of the coach stepped forward, parents were increasingly grateful that James had bravely disclosed the abuse when it was reported to the police. The in vivo mastery process began with the assignment of watching soccer games on YouTube with his mother in order to reduce his abuse-related anxiety that had generalised to the soccer field. These assignments gradually progressed, beginning with James watching soccer on the computer, to watching with his mother others playing soccer, going to the field with a friend, putting on his uniform and practising shooting goals with a friend, and finally meeting with the new coach and participating in an actual practice with the team. Both the therapist and Ms Johnson provided James with enthusiastic praise and encouragement for each effort he made toward playing soccer. After he worked his way through each assignment, James reported no anxiety related to soccer or the field; in fact, he stated with a smile on his face, 'Thank you for helping me enjoy the sport I love again.'

As noted earlier, the therapist helped Ms Johnson prepare for conjoint sessions in which James read his trauma narrative. During the conjoint session, the therapist encouraged James to pause after each chapter thereby allowing time for his mother to reflect back some of his words, acknowledge his feelings, and praise his ability to write and describe his experiences in detail. After James read his final chapter in which he thanked his mother for coming to therapy with him, Ms Johnson praised James for his hard work in therapy and his ability to continue to excel in school despite the abuse and its aftermath. The therapist also provided James with education about healthy sexuality, healthy relationships, dating and dating violence. In both individual and conjoint sessions, James practised safety skills and problem-solving when faced with violent or uncomfortable situations in the context of role plays. James and Ms Johnson also completed standardised measures that demonstrated objective improvements in James' PTSD and depressive symptoms and aggressive behaviour as well as improvements in Ms Johnson's overall mood and functioning. Given the significant reduction in symptoms reported by James and his mother, a graduation celebration was planned that involved a review of therapy progress and the display of posters James created to help other kids, as well as the sharing of some favourite snacks that Ms Johnson provided, graduation certificates, and music.

Conclusion

Research findings have repeatedly documented that abuse or violence experienced in childhood increases children's risk of developing significant emotional, behavioural, cognitive and/or medical difficulties that can impair functioning and well-being throughout the lifespan. Though more research is needed, the evidence-based trauma-focused interventions described in this chapter have been found to not only effectively address the immediate impact of trauma, but the results of follow-up studies suggest these interventions show promise in reducing children's long-term risk of experiencing ongoing difficulties. Future research is needed to reduce the overall incidence and prevalence of abuse in childhood and to enhance our understanding of factors that can increase children's resilience as well as their responsiveness to treatment when trauma is experienced.

References

Ahmad, A., Larsson, B. & Sundelin-Wahlsten, V. (2007). EMDR treatment for children with PTSD: Results of a randomized controlled trial. *Nordic Journal of Psychiatry*, 61, 349–354.

Blumenthal, J.A., Babyak, M.A., Moore, K.A. et al. (1999). Effects of exercise training on older patients with major depression. *Archives of Internal Medicine*, 159, 2349–2356.

Chapman, D.P., Anda, R.F., Felitti, V.J. et al. (2004). Adverse childhood experiences and the risk of depressive disorders in adulthood. *Journal of Affective Disorders*, 82, 217–225.

Chemtob, C.M., Nakashima, J. & Carlson, J.G. (2002). Brief treatment for elementary school children with disaster-related posttraumatic stress disorder: A field study. *Journal of Clinical Psychology*, 58, 99–112.

Cicchetti, D., Rogosch, F.A. & Toth, S.L. (2006). Fostering secure attachment in infants in maltreating families through preventive interventions. *Development and Psychopathology*, 18, 623–649.

Cohen, J.A. & Mannarino, A.P. (1988). Psychological symptoms in sexually abused girls. *Child Abuse & Neglect*, 12, 571–577.

Cohen, J.A. & Mannarino, A.P. (1996). A treatment outcome study for sexually abused preschool children: Initial findings. *Journal of the American Academy of Child & Adolescent Psychiatry*, 35, 42–50.

Cohen, J.A. & Mannarino, A.P. (1998). Interventions for sexually abused children: Initial treatment outcome findings. *Child Maltreatment*, 3, 17–26.

Cohen, J.A., Mannarino, A.P. & Deblinger, E. (2017). *Treating Trauma and Traumatic Grief in Children and Adolescents*, 2nd edn. New York: Guilford Press.

Cohen, J.A., Mannarino, A.P. & Deblinger, E. (2012). *Trauma-Focused CBT for Children and Adolescents: Treatment Applications*. New York: The Guilford Press.

Cohen, J.A., Mannarino, A.P. & Iyengar, S. (2011). Community treatment of posttraumatic stress disorder for children exposed to intimate partner violence: A randomized controlled trial. *Archives of Pediatrics & Adolescent Medicine*, 165, 16–21.

Cohen, J.A., Deblinger, E., Mannarino, A.P. & Steer, R. (2004). A multisite randomized controlled trial for sexually abused children with PTSD symptoms *Journal of the American Academy of Child & Adolescent Psychiatry*, 43, 393–402.

Deblinger, E., Lippmann, J. & Steer, R. (1996). Sexually abused children suffering posttraumatic stress symptoms: Initial treatment outcome findings. *Child Maltreatment*, 1, 310–321.

Deblinger, E., Stauffer, L.B. & Steer, R.A. (2001). Comparative efficacies of supportive and cognitive behavioral group therapies for young children who have been sexually abused and their nonoffending mothers. *Child Maltreatment*, 6, 332–343.

Deblinger, E., Mannarino, A.P., Cohen, J.A. & Steer, R.A. (2006). A follow-up study of a multisite, randomized, controlled trial for children with sexual abuse-related PTSD symptoms *Journal of the American Academy of Child & Adolescent Psychiatry*, 45, 1474–1484.

Deblinger, E., Neubauer, F., Runyon, M.K. & Baker, D. (2006). *What Do You Know? A Therapeutic Card Game about Child Sexual and Physical Abuse and Domestic Violence*. Stratford, NJ: CARES Institute.

Deblinger, E., Mannarino, A.P., Cohen, J.A. et al. (2011). Trauma-focused cognitive behavioral therapy for children: Impact of the trauma narrative and treatment length. *Depression and Anxiety*, 28, 67–75.

Deblinger, E., Mannarino, A.P., Cohen, J.A. et al. (2015). *Child Sexual Abuse: A Primer for Treating Children, Adolescents, and Their Nonoffending Caregivers*, 2nd edn. New York: Oxford University Press.

Deblinger, E., McLeer, S., Atkins, M. et al. (1989). Post-traumatic stress in sexually abused, physically abused, and nonabused children. *Child Abuse & Neglect*, 13, 403–408.

De Roos, C., Greenwald, R., den Hollander-Gijsman, M. et al. (2011). A randomized comparison of cognitive behavioural therapy (CBT) and eye movement desensitisation and reprocessing (EMDR) in disaster-exposed children. *European Journal of Psychotraumatology*, 2, 5694.

Diehle, J., Opmeer, B.C., Boer, F. et al. (2015). Trauma-focused cognitive behavioral therapy or eye movement desensitization and reprocessing: What works in children with posttraumatic stress symptoms? A randomized controlled trial. *European Child & Adolescent Psychiatry*, 24, 227–236.

Dorsey, S., Pullmann, M., Berliner, L. et al. (2014). Engaging foster parents in treatment: A randomized trial of supplementing trauma-focused cognitive behavioral therapy with evidence-based engagement strategies. *Child Abuse & Neglect*, 38, 1508–1520.

Dube, S.R., Felitti, V.J., Dong, M. et al. (2003). Childhood abuse, neglect and household dysfunction and the risk of illicit drug use: The Adverse Childhood Experience Study. *Pediatrics*, 111, 564–572.

Felitti, V.J., Anda, R.F., Nordenberg, D. et al. (1998). Relationship of childhood abuse and household dysfunction to many of the leading causes of death in adults: The Adverse Childhood Experiences (ACE) Study. *American Journal of Preventive Medicine*, 14, 245–258.

Foa, E.B., Chrestman, K. & Gilboa-Schechtman, E. (2008). *Prolonged Exposure Manual for Children and Adolescents Suffering from PTSD*. New York: Oxford University Press.

Foa, E.B., McLean, C.P., Capaldi, S. & Rosenfield, D. (2013). Prolonged exposure vs supportive counseling for sexual abuse-related PTSD in adolescent girls: A randomized clinical trial. *Journal of the American Medical Association*, 310, 2650–2657.

Ghosh Ippen, C., Harris, W.W., Van Horn, P. & Lieberman, A.F. (2011). Traumatic and stressful events in early childhood: Can treatment help those at highest risk? *Child Abuse & Neglect*, 35, 504–513.

Gilboa-Schechtman, E., Foa, E.B., Shafran, N. et al. (2010). Prolonged exposure versus dynamic therapy for adolescent PTSD: A pilot randomized controlled trial. *Journal of the American Academy of Child & Adolescent Psychiatry*, 49, 1034–1042.

Goenjian, A.K., Walling, D., Steinberg, A.M. et al. (2005). A prospective study of posttraumatic stress and depressive reactions among treated and untreated adolescents 5 years after a catastrophic disaster. *American Journal of Psychiatry*, 162, 2302–2308.

Greer, D., Grasso, D.J., Cohen, A. & Webb, C. (2014). Trauma-focused treatment in a state system of care: Is it worth the cost? *Administration and Policy in Mental Health and Mental Health Services Research*, 41, 317–323.

Jaberghaderi, N., Greenwald, R., Rubin, A. et al. (2004). A comparison of CBT and EMDR for sexually-abused Iranian girls. *Clinical Psychology and Psychotherapy*, 11, 358–368.

Jensen, T.K., Holt, T., Ormhaug, S.M. et al. (2014). A randomized effectiveness study comparing trauma-focused cognitive behavioral therapy with therapy as usual for youth. *Journal of Clinical Child & Adolescent Psychology*, 43, 356–369.

Kemp, M., Drummond, P. & McDermott, B. (2009). A wait-list controlled pilot study of eye movement desensitization and reprocessing (EMDR) for children with post-traumatic stress disorder (PTSD) symptoms from motor vehicle accidents. *Clinical Child Psychology and Psychiatry*, 15, 5–25.

Lieberman, A.F., Ghosh Ippen, C. & Van Horn, P. (2006). Child-parent psychotherapy: 6-month follow-up of a randomized controlled trial. *Journal of the American Academy of Child and Adolescent Psychiatry*, 45, 913–918.

Lieberman, A.F., Van Horn, P. & Ghosh Ippen, C. (2005). Toward evidence-based treatment: Child-Parent psychotherapy with preschoolers exposed to marital violence. *Journal of the American Academy of Child and Adolescent Psychiatry*, 44, 1241–1248.

Lyons, J.S., Weiner, D.A. & Scheider, A. (2006). *A field trial of three evidence-based practices for trauma with children in state custody*. Report to the Illinois Department of Children and Family Services. Evanston, IL: Mental Health Resources Services and Policy Program, Northwestern University.

McMullen, J., O'Callaghan, P., Shannon, C. et al. (2013). Group trauma-focused cognitive behavioural therapy with former child soldiers and other war-affected boys in the DR Congo: A randomised controlled trial. *Journal of Child Psychology and Psychiatry*, 54, 1231–1241.

O'Callaghan, P., McMullen, J., Shannon, C. et al. (2013). A randomized controlled trial of trauma-focused cognitive behavioral therapy for sexually exploited, war-affected Congolese girls. *Journal of the American Academy of Child & Adolescent Psychiatry*, 52, 359–369.

Putnam, F.W. (2003). Ten-year research update review: Child sexual abuse. *Journal of the American Academy of Child & Adolescent Psychiatry*, 42, 269–278.

Shapiro, F. (2001). *Eye Movement Desensitization and Reprocessing: Basic Principles, Protocols, and Procedures*, 2nd edn. New York: Guilford Press.

Trickett, P.K. & McBride-Chang, C. (1995). The developmental impact of different forms of child abuse and neglect. *Developmental Review*, 15, 311–337.

20

Effectiveness of Cognitive and Behavioural Group-Based Parenting Programmes to Enhance Child Protective Factors and Reduce Risk Factors for Maltreatment

Tracey Bywater

Department of Health Sciences, University of York, UK

Effectiveness of Cognitive and Behavioural Group-Based Parenting Programmes

A parent[1] is an extremely powerful influence in a child's life, and how a child is parented can influence long-term life outcomes. The important, yet sometimes challenging, role of *parenting* can be defined as '...the process of **promoting** and **supporting** the physical, emotional, social, and intellectual development of a child from infancy to adulthood' (Davies, 2000, p. 245). However, promoting *morality* – and possibly *faith* or *religion* – could also be included in this quote.

Neglect and emotional abuse of children occurs when the role of parenting, as described above, is not undertaken adequately. Neglect and emotional abuse are the two most common reasons for children in the UK needing protection from abuse (NSPCC, 2014, Child Protection Register statistics). Indeed, neglect is the most common reason for a child to be the subject of a Child Protection Plan or on a Child Protection Register in the UK, with one in ten children having experienced it (Radford, Corral & Bradley et al., 2011).

Neglect is defined as the ongoing failure to meet a child's basic needs by lack of provision of food, clean clothes, shelter, supervision, medical or health care, with children perhaps not getting the love, care and attention they need from their parents. In addition, children may

---

[1] *Parent* in this chapter refers to anyone in a significant parenting role, that is, the activity of raising a child, regardless of whether or not there is a biological relationship (e.g., foster parents).

The Wiley Handbook of What Works in Child Maltreatment: An Evidence-Based Approach to Assessment and Intervention in Child Protection, First Edition. Edited by Louise Dixon, Daniel F. Perkins, Catherine Hamilton-Giachritsis, and Leam A. Craig.
© 2017 John Wiley & Sons Ltd. Published 2017 by John Wiley & Sons Ltd.

not be protected from physical or emotional harm. Neglect can cause serious, long-term damage, and may even result in death (NSPCC, 2014). Neglect occurs where parents are either unwilling or unable to fulfil their child's needs. Parents may be unable to parent adequately through lack of knowledge, skills or support, or through issues such as mental health, drug and alcohol problems, or poverty.

Emotional abuse is the ongoing emotional maltreatment or emotional neglect of a child, sometimes referred to as psychological abuse; it can impact seriously on a child's emotional health and development. Emotional abuse can involve deliberately humiliating, scaring, threatening, scapegoating, isolating or ignoring a child. Other types of emotional abuse include being too controlling, not allowing a child to have friends, never expressing positive feelings or congratulating a child on successes, never showing kindness or caring in interactions, not recognising a child's limitations by pushing them too hard, or exposing a child to distressing events or interactions such as domestic abuse or drug taking. Notably, children who are emotionally abused usually also suffer another type of abuse or neglect, such as neglect or physical abuse.[2] A recent report by the NSPCC (Radford, Corral & Bradley et al., 2011) surveyed individuals from 11 to 24 years of age. Adults aged 18–24 years reported that, over their lifetime, 23% (N=435) had suffered physical violence, physical neglect and emotional abuse by their parent or guardian. For smacking alone, 45.9% (N=616) of 11- to 17-year-olds reported being smacked within the previous year. Although there is a relationship between low-family-income levels and higher rates of child maltreatment, there is limited research exploring types of neglect specifically encountered by children living in middle- and high-income households.[3] However, recent US research shows that depression and anxiety is almost twice the normal rate in children whose parents earn more than £100,000 a year due to parents pushing their children too hard to succeed or achieve (Luthar, Barkin & Crossman, 2013). Other research suggests child maltreatment and neglect has a prevalence rate of less than 10% in US households with incomes above the median income (Melton & Barry, 1994).

Parents may engage in emotional abuse during times of high stress and tension, such as living in poverty or being unemployed. These worrying issues may leave parents unable to provide the emotional love and support that a child needs. Alternatively parents may not have the tools to parent adequately if they themselves have been raised in an abusive or neglectful household.

Most parents are able to raise their children to be pro-social, well-balanced, hard-working individuals. However, parenting is a tough and demanding job, and can be made more difficult when stressors are present such as disadvantage, unemployment, lack of social support, housing difficulties, mental health issues, residing in an abusive or overcrowded household, or suffering from alcohol- or drug-related issues. These stressors can be referred to as *risk factors* and may form a barrier for children being able to achieve their best potential. In addition, a child raised with multiple risk factors, including ineffective parenting practices, may repeat the cycle when parenting their own child/ren. *Improved parenting* is the most important goal of child abuse prevention (Barth, 2009; Sanders & Pickering, Chapter 11 of this book).

Protective factors are interactive factors that attenuate children's exposure to risk and facilitate positive outcomes in difficult circumstances. They include: applying developmentally appropriate parenting skills; supporting child social, emotional and academic development; growing a strong support network consisting of family, friends and local services; utilising effective

---

[2] For further information please see www.nspcc.org.uk/preventing-abuse/child-abuse-and-neglect/neglect/.
[3] The report by Radford, Corral & Bradley et al. (2011) states that this will be explored in the near future using their UK survey data.

communication skills; anger management; problem-solving; making sound health choices; and not living in poverty or overcrowded conditions.[4] Parenting programmes increase many of these protective factors through focusing on positive parent–child interaction, and building of support networks (Hutchings, Gardner & Lane, 2004). Importantly, research has demonstrated that the absence of protective factors is more predictive of abuse than are risk factors (Dixon, Browne & Hamilton-Giachritsis, 2009), thus highlighting the potential utility of programmes that are delivered to parents early in their parenting role, or early in a child's life.

It is well documented that the consequences of child maltreatment extends beyond childhood to affect educational and employment outcomes, mental and physical health, relationship quality, and antisocial and criminal behaviour (e.g., Mersky & Topitzes, 2010). This is at a cost to the individual, society and local services. In the US, direct public expenditures in response to child abuse and neglect are over $25 billion annually (Scarcella, Bess, Zielewski & Green, 2006).

As outlined by Hamilton-Giachritsis & Pellai in Chapter 3 of this text, risk and protective factors for child neglect, physical or emotional maltreatment exist at the individual, familial and the larger social system/community levels (known as the ecological model). Ideally interventions should, therefore, be directed at these multiple levels depending on the specific needs of the family. The need for multilevel or multi-modal interventions is further highlighted by the findings from the recent NSPCC UK survey, which found that children and young people who experience maltreatment, or severe maltreatment from a parent or guardian, are at greater risk than those who are not maltreated of also experiencing abuse from others (Radford, Corral & Bradley et al., 2011). These findings reflect the wider literature showing that specific forms of abuse are good predictors of there being other types (Finkelhor, Turner, Ormrod & Hamby, 2009).

Whole-system approaches

Communities That Care and *Evidence2Success* are examples of whole-system approaches. *Communities That Care* (CTC) is a US model that employs a proven community-change process for promoting healthy child and youth development through tested and effective programmes and policies. CTC uses prevention science and guides local coalitions through a tested five-phase process. A rigorous scientific trial of CTC demonstrated reductions in rates of youth violence, crime, alcohol and tobacco use. The Community Youth Development Study reports youths from 12 CTC communities were 25% to 33% less likely to have health and behaviour problems than youths from 12 matched control communities (Monahan, Oesterle, Rhew & Hawkins, 2014). Additionally, at the end of Grade 8 (UK Year 9, 13- to 14-year-olds), youths from CTC communities reported higher levels than controls of protective factors that support positive development. Social skills, interaction with pro-social peers, school recognition for pro-social involvement, and community opportunities for pro-social involvement were significantly improved among CTC youth (Van Horn, Fagan, Hawkins & Oesterle, 2014).

CTC takes a local level view to ascertain in the first instance the level of need in certain areas (e.g., education, well-being, child behaviour, etc.), and then identifies effective or evidence-based programmes to reduce or enhance the identified and agreed required outcome.

Evidence2Success (E2S) is a similar UK model based on CTC collaboratively developed with the Social Research Unit at Dartington, the Social Development Research Group at the

---

[4] See Chapters 3, 4 and 6 of this book for further discussion on risk and protective factors and their interaction with both genetics and environmental factors.

University of Washington and the Annie E. Casey Foundation in Baltimore (for more information see http://dartington.org.uk/projects/evidence2success/). E2S is a community-based strategy development and implementation process that involves leaders of public services and community leaders working together to improve children's outcomes by commissioning, designing and implementing evidence-based children's services.

The process requires robust data on children's needs to inform evidence-based commissioning strategies, evidence on what works to improve children's outcomes, and cost–benefit analysis of proven programmes to inform commissioning strategies. In addition, an understanding of expenditure on children at the local level is needed in order to identify shifts in spending on evidence-based prevention and early intervention.

E2S is currently being delivered in Perth and Kinross, Scotland and will be applied to support the Big Lottery Fund's five UK Better Start areas (Bradford, Blackpool, Southend, Lambeth, Nottingham). The Better Start £215m initiative is a place-based initiative to transform *early years* services using evidence of what works and intends to implement system change in order to support child outcomes in three main areas: social and emotional well-being, language and communication, and nutrition and health. The five Better Start locations have been awarded up to £50m each for up to ten years to concentrate on improving long-term outcomes for children under three years of age. The initiative aims to produce a step change at the system level for 60,000 children across the sites, by delivering projects and programmes aimed at the family and individual level, such as child literacy programmes to enhance parent involvement in reading with their child, and antenatal or peri-natal parent programmes, such as the Family Links antenatal programme, and the Incredible Years Infant and Toddler Parent Programmes in Bradford Better Start.

Bradford Trident will lead the partnership in Bradford to support 20,000 babies and children over ten years. Bradford has significant deprivation and within the three target wards there are high rates of infant mortality, child poverty, poor oral health and child obesity, low numbers of school readiness, and high rates of domestic violence and child protection orders. Local data shows one in five children in the three wards have poor communications skills at the school-readiness stage, and one in three children have poor social and emotional development when starting school.

It is imperative that in initiatives such as CTC, E2S and Better Start that the operating 'systems' in which the family- and individual-level programmes are to be embedded are flexible, or adaptable, enough to accommodate and successfully implement specific programmes as they were designed to be delivered to ensure replicable outcomes. If the systems are not able to support delivery of a programme with fidelity then effectiveness may be compromised. Programmes need to be carefully chosen with a strong theory of change matching the desired outcomes, with previous evidence of effectiveness in similar contexts if possible. So, what do we actually mean by a 'programme'?

Programmes are defined here as manualised, structured interventions, with clear guidelines for implementation and fidelity. Manualised facilitator expertise is required to deliver the programme responsively to the population and context. Programmes can be delivered in a group format, or in an intensive one-to-one format with a practitioner working with one family at a time.

The family, child and parent strategies outlined below have demonstrated some success in enhancing protective factors or reducing risk factors for children of different ages in a preventative or treatment approach. However, the parent level is arguably the most effective of levels, and can be implemented as a preventative approach in the early years, or antenatally, before a baby is even born.

Family-centred strategies

These involve parents, children of varying ages, and possibly other members of the family. Coordination of multiple service providers may be required to support a family's needs, focusing on enhancing skills and potentially recovery from neglect. This may include training in behavioural and social skills, setting short-term goals with clearly defined action steps, providing in-home teaching and skills training to parents to improve parent–child interactions, and teaching home-management skills.

These strategies can also be applied in a preventative model to encourage attachment, appropriate feeding and childcare practices, infant/toddler stimulation, child development, successful money management, and nutrition, and should be provided during subsequent pregnancies for high-risk families and during the postpartum period (Thomlison, 2004).

Treatment and intervention approaches Examples of *treatment* programmes for families returning from neglect are outlined below.

Multidimensional Treatment Foster Care. MTFC (www.mtfc.com) is an intensive, targeted US programme that aims to apply parent management training methods to support foster carers providing short-term care for children and young people with serious behaviour problems, which may have developed through inadequate or ineffective parenting practices, such as neglect or emotional abuse, in the home. Foster carers receive specialist training and support, but the programme also works therapeutically with the children and their own families to prepare for a return home. The programme requires close monitoring of the child, minimal association with antisocial peers, and enforcement of rules, with consistent consequences for unacceptable behaviour.

MTFC has been trialled successfully in the US (Chamberlain, Price, Leve et al., 2008) and Sweden (Westermark, Hansson & Olsson, 2010). In 2002, the British government introduced a national implementation of MTFC, a wrap-around multi-modal foster care intervention for children with challenging behaviour, originally developed by the Oregon Social Learning Centre in the USA. A quasi-experimental pilot evaluation in England examined the use of MTFC with 47 young offenders. While in foster care the MTFC group were less likely to be reconvicted (39% of the MTFC group were reconvicted compared to 75% of the comparison group), committed fewer and less serious known offences, and took three times longer to re-offend than the comparison group (Biehal, Ellison & Sinclair, 2011). However, a follow-up one year after they left their placements found no significant differences in re-conviction patterns.

In the UK, MTFC has been trialled through the Care Placement Evaluation (CaPE) working with looked-after children aged 12–16 years. A randomised controlled trial of the MTFC, the low sample in the trial was due to only eight of the participating local authorities agreeing to randomisation of children to receive either MTFC or carry on receiving usual services. For the primary outcomes of mental health and social and physical functioning there were no significant differences between the intervention or control arms of the trial (Green, Biehal, Roberts et al., 2014).

It is clear that further research is required in the UK to explore any long-term benefits. A UK project called 'Step Change' has just begun, implemented by Action for Children, to evaluate the MTFC programme and two other targeted US family interventions, Functional Family Therapy (FFT) (www.fftllc.com/) and Multisystemic Therapy (MST) (http://mstuk.org/). Step Change aims to improve long-term outcomes for 450 young people. The structured interventions FFT and MST average two-hour weekly sessions over 10–12 weeks, and are delivered in health or community settings with a group, or with individual parents.

Functional Family Therapy. FFT is useful to families of at-risk children and young people aged 11–18 years. It aims to improve behaviour by helping family members to reduce defensive communication patterns, increase supportive interactions and promote positive parenting skills, such as supervision and effective non-violent discipline. FFT (Sexton & Alexander, 2004) is a clinic-based intervention that aims to improve behaviour by helping family members understand how their behaviour affects others, and also addresses supervision and effective discipline. FFT phases include an engagement and motivation phase to reduce maladaptive perceptions, beliefs and emotions within the family. Phase two involves behavioural change techniques such as communication skills, basic parenting skills and conflict management. The final 'generalisation' phase involves families applying learnt skills. The programme comprises 8–12 sessions over three to four months, but it can be extended to up to 30 sessions for more needy cases.

US trial outcomes of FFT show reductions in crime, violence, antisocial behaviour, drug and alcohol problems, and the likelihood of going into care (Alexander & Sexton, 2002). An RCT of FFT in the US (with juvenile offenders who had been sentenced by a court to probation randomly assigned to either the FFT programme or control) found FFT was associated with a significant reduction in felony (35%) and violent crimes (30%; Sexton & Turner, 2010). Cost–benefit analysis of FFT estimates savings of $7.69 for every $1 invested (Aos, Lieb, Mayfield & Miller, 2004).

In England, FFT has been evaluated by the National Academy for Parenting Research through the Study of Adolescents' Family Experiences (SAFE project[5]), which focused on young offenders aged 12–17 and their families, and in the Step Change project (Blower, Dixon, Ellison et al., 2016).

Multisystemic Therapy. MST is an intensive programme that aims to reduce severe behaviour problems in children typically aged 12–18 years. It combines family and individual cognitive therapy with support services tailored to specific family needs by addressing the key predictors of antisocial behaviour, family conflict and the adolescent's functioning at school. It could include child skills training, parenting training, distancing from deviant peers, and methods for improving attachment to school. Delivery is through a team of purpose-trained therapists who are on-call 24 hours a day.

MST evaluations have found improved youth functioning, decreased substance use problems, improved school functioning and decreased re-arrests at 18-month follow-up (Timmons-Mitchell, Bender, Kishna & Mitchell, 2006). Not all trials have, however, produced positive results, particularly those that have not included the developer (Littell, 2005). Two recent meta-analyses found very different results. Curtis, Ronan and Borduin (2004) found youths and their families who had received MST were functioning better than controls; yet Littell, Campbell, Green and Toews (2005) suggested there was no evidence that MST was more effective than regular services. The programme developers have conducted the majority of evaluations of MST, which may have increased fidelity levels; indeed Curtis, Ronan and Borduin (2004) suggested the involvement of the developer can increase the effectiveness threefold.

In an independent RCT of MST in Norway (Ogden & Hagen, 2006), adolescents referred from child welfare services for serious behaviour problems received MST treatment while control adolescents received regular services. MST adolescents were less likely than the control group to be placed out of home after the intervention (72% vs. 55%), and more likely to score in the normal range on the Child Behaviour Check List (38% vs. 21%). A two-year follow-up achieved similar results. Greater effectiveness was related to greater programme fidelity (see Chapter 21 of this text for detailed discussions on fidelity).

---

[5] Results forthcoming.

Systemic Therapy for At Risk Teens (START) is a national RCT to evaluate MST in the UK context (Fonagy, Butler, Goodyer et al., 2013). It is a pragmatic trial that will inform policy-makers, commissioners of services and professionals about the potential of MST in the UK context. The trial is being conducted at ten clinical sites across the UK staffed by a team of therapists. Previous results from a randomised UK pilot showed reductions in reoffending 18 months after completing the programme (Butler, Baruch, Hickey & Fonagy, 2011).

Although there is evidence that the programme is effective it is also very costly due to its intensity and length. Nevertheless a cost–benefit analysis of the programme by Aos and colleagues (Aos, Lieb, Mayfield & Miller, 2004) suggests $2.64 is saved for every $1 invested.

Prevention Preventative family-centred strategies aimed at intervening *prior* to maltreatment occurring and/or reducing the risk, include *Families and Schools Together* (FAST) (www.savethechildren.org.uk/about-us/where-we-work/united-kingdom/fast). FAST is a multi-modal preventative programme that aims to bring together families, schools, the community and local services within disadvantaged areas. Five versions of FAST from 'baby' to 'teen' have been developed. It uses a combination of different approaches, such as kids clubs, parent sessions and structured peer time to enhance family functioning and reduce school failure, violence, delinquency, substance abuse and family stress. US trials of FAST demonstrated improvements in academic performance and classroom behaviours, including aggression and social skills, and family adaptability for children aged four to nine years, up to two years following intervention (Crozier, Rokutani, Russett et al., 2010; Kratochwill, McDonald, Levin et al., 2009).

There is no UK RCT evidence of FAST as yet.

Child-centred strategies

Child-centred strategies provide children 'at risk of', or already experiencing, neglect or physical abuse with the skills and support to overcome maltreatment successfully. Preschool interventions focus on parent–child interactions, attachment, educational play and school readiness to enhance self-control, communication and problem-solving skills, and also, for older children, how to resist negative social influences (Thomlison, 2004). Potential interventions include paediatric care, mentoring, or behavioural and mental health treatment. Schools are increasingly important in enhancing children's social and emotional skills, in addition to their academic learning. Evidence-based approaches to preventing antisocial behaviour include programmes for improving children's problem-solving and social–emotional skills, as well as 'whole school' approaches to alter the institutional ethos and ensure consistency in behaviour management. Many school-based programmes are universal, but some are targeted toward children who need additional social and emotional coaching.[6]

Parent-centred strategies

Rather than working on the whole system or family, parent-centred strategies enable parents to promote the safety and well-being of the child by focusing on promoting protective factors while reducing risk factors. Programmes to enhance parenting skills and the parent–child relationship are relevant, as are those that address parent depression, substance abuse and domestic

---

[6] Child-centred strategies to enhance social–emotional well-being or increase resiliency are outside of the scope of this chapter. For a summary of programme evidence in the UK on this topic please see Bywater and Sharples, 2012.

violence. It is important that *all* parents receive parent support in proportion to their level of need, which could be offered through a public health service model, to increase the chances for parents and children in achieving positive life outcomes (Marmot, Allen, Goldblatt et al., 2010). Preventative and treatment programmes also exist for parent-centred strategies as they do for family- and child-centred strategies. When risk factors are identified services can support families to reduce risk factors and strengthen protective factors, thereby preventing child neglect. Effective programmes focus on developing basic problem-solving skills and behaviour management strategies, and on addressing environmental factors where possible. Programmes that change, or modify, thoughts (cognitions) and behaviour are described as cognitive behavioural programmes. In the UK parent programmes are delivered by a variety of facilitators such as health visitors, midwives, social workers, parents and teachers; by Children's Centres; Child and Adolescent Mental Health; and by a range of voluntary organisations. They aim to help parents understand their children and their development, to strengthen their relationships with their children, and to find non-physical ways of managing difficult behaviour.

Cognitive behavioural group-based parent programmes Behavioural and cognitive behavioural parenting interventions can be delivered in a group format and are increasingly implemented to address ineffective parenting practices. For instance, a Cochrane review of such interventions for parents of children aged 3–12 years (Furlong, McGilloway, Bywater et al., 2012) found a statistically significant reduction in negative or harsh parenting practices according to both parent reports (SMD -0.77; 95% CI -0.96 to -0.59) and independent assessments (SMD -0.42; 95% CI -0.67 to -0.16), and improvements in parent mental health (SMD -0.36; 95% CI -0.52 to -0.20), and positive parenting skills, based on both parent reports (SMD -0.53; 95% CI -0.90 to -0.16) and independent reports (SMD -0.47; 95% CI -0.65 to -0.29).

These kinds of group-based parenting programmes typically involve an interactive and collaborative learning format in which programme facilitators discuss and model key behavioural principles and parenting skills (for example, play, praise, rewards, discipline) to parents and caregivers, who then practise the skills. Key elements of effective programmes include how and when to use positive parenting skills; observation; modelling; behaviour rehearsal (for example, role play); discussion; homework assignments; using peer support; reframing unhelpful cognitive perceptions about their child or about child management in general; and tackling barriers to attendance (Hutchings, Gardner & Lane, 2004). However, behavioural and cognitive behavioural parenting programmes vary in the extent to which they include these components; for example, it has been shown that differences in the duration of the programme, which may range from 4 to 24 weekly group sessions, affects the amount of time dedicated to practice and may impact upon the mechanism of group support. In addition, some programmes incorporate additional material on parent-related stress factors and social support.

Behavioural and cognitive behavioural interventions may incorporate social learning principles and techniques from cognitive therapy alongside principles of operant and classical learning. Operant learning theory emphasises the environmental antecedents and consequences of behaviour. Thus, programmes based on operant learning theory involve teaching techniques of positive and negative reinforcement to parents, helping them to focus on the child's positive behaviour (by praising and rewarding the desired behaviour) and to ignore or introduce limit-setting and 'time-out' consequences for the child's negative behaviour. Parents also learn how to pinpoint proximal and distal antecedents for identified positive and negative target behaviours for their child. Social learning theory posits that children learn how to behave by imitating the behaviour modelled by others in their environment and, therefore, if this behaviour is reinforced it is likely to be repeated. Programmes based on this principle help parents to model appropriate behaviour. In addition, group facilitators and leaders have the opportunity, within certain group-based behavioural programmes, to model key parenting skills in each session, while parents imitate and practise the new skills through role plays and homework assignments (Hutchings, Gardner & Lane, 2004). Parents may also be encouraged to act as empathic and supportive role models for each other.

However, it is important to note that the frequency and quality of positive role-modelling, and the level of support provided by facilitators and other parents, varies between programmes. The cognitive component of parenting interventions focuses on problematic thinking patterns in parents that have been associated with conduct problems in their children. For instance, typical cognitive distortions include globalised 'all or nothing' thinking, such that one minor setback may trigger a negative automatic thought (for example, 'I am a bad parent') thereby leading to feelings of stress, hopelessness, low self-esteem, a perceived inability to cope with the situation and learnt helplessness. Thus, behavioural and cognitive behavioural parenting interventions are aimed at helping parents to learn how to reframe distorted cognitions or misattributions and to coach them in the use of problem-solving and anger management techniques.

There are now a variety of group-based cognitive behavioural parent programmes delivered preventatively or as a treatment model during the antenatal period up to when the child is in his/her teenage years. The table below presents a selection of cognitive behavioural group-based parent programmes (available in the UK), highlighting the population, the outcomes it hopes to achieve and the evidence base for each programme. In recent years, a variety of 'standards of evidence' have emerged, such as those applied by the UK Early Intervention Foundation, NESTA, Blueprints and others.

The UK Parenting Programme Evaluation Tool (PPET) (now archived on the Department for Education website: http://webarchive.nationalarchives.gov.uk/20140311170415/http://education.gov.uk/commissioning-toolkit/Programme/InfoCommissioners) is, as the name suggests, specifically applicable to parent programmes and assesses programmes on four domains:

1. The specificity of the programme's target population (Who is it for?)
2. The programme's theories and activities (What does it do?)
3. The programme's training and implementation support systems (Who delivers the programmes and how?)
4. The strength of the programme's evaluation evidence (How we know the programme works?)

Programmes receive a rating from 0 to 4 stars (****) within each category, resulting in five ratings. A rating of four means that the programme meets all of the criteria in the category and is strongly developed in this domain, while a rating of zero means it does not meet any of the criteria.

Table 20.1 highlights that although a variety of group-based cognitive behavioural parent programmes are available in the UK, the evidence and/or readiness to scale-up (become embedded in many areas) is variable or sometimes limited. One of the programmes with the most solid evidence base, with rigorous processes in place for scale-up, is the Incredible Years parent programme. Furthermore there is UK evidence for IY, while, to date, FAST has not completed a UK RCT, and a UK RCT of Triple P found non-significant treatment effects (Little, Berry, Morpeth et al., 2012). The subsequent section therefore focuses on IY as a good example of a parent (and multi-modal) programme that is effective in the UK.

Table 20.1 Parent programmes available in the UK, rated against standards of evidence.

Name of programme Ascending order prenatal, infant to toddler	PPET rating and evidence	Type and delivery setting	Who is it for?	What are the outcomes?	Cost information
New Beginnings For more information see http://www.annafreud.org/pages/new-beginnings-programme-for-mothers-and-babies-in-prison.html	*** UK RCT Note: According to the website training is currently only offered by the developer so scale-up may be an issue.	**Level of need:** Moderate, high, complex **Format:** Group 12 months and younger. **Classification:** Targeted, specialist **Setting:** Mother–baby unit in their prison **Length:** 12 sessions, 2 hrs, twice per wk, over 6 wks delivered by a practitioner and co-practitioner	Mothers and infants (under 12 mos) in prison experiencing difficulties in the parent–child relationship. Mothers may have mental health issues.	Child: Improved child general well-being, mental health. Parent: Improved parenting practices/competency.	No information as yet.
Triple P (TP) A multilevel parent programme for a variety of family set-ups and level of need. For more information see http://www.triplep.net/glo-en/the-triple-p-system-at-work/the-system-explained/level-4/	**** (for standard TP) Multiple RCTs in UK, US, Australia. Results mixed – for meta-analyses see: http://www.ncbi.nlm.nih.gov/pubmed/23121760 http://www.biomedcentral.com/1741-7015/10/145 http://link.springer.com/article/10.1023%2FA%3A1021843613840.	**Level of need:** Universal to moderate-high **Format:** Group (and 1:1) **Classification:** Universal to targeted **Setting:** Clinics, community settings, media (home) **Length:** 8 sessions for standard group level 4 Triple P: 4 × 2 hr group sessions followed by 4 × 30-minute individual telephone consultations.	Baby programme for pre-birth up to age 1, toddler programme for age 1–2 years with same format, and older (e.g., Stepping Stones TP for children with physical or learning difficulties, Family Transitions TP for families undergoing separation). Other TP programmes are for parents of children up to teenage.	Child: Child well-being and behaviour. Parent: Parenting competencies, individual coping skills, couple relationship skills.	The developer has explored the cost-effectiveness and cost benefits of the programmes. See http://www.ncbi.nlm.nih.gov/pubmed/17464705

(Continued)

Table 20.1 (Cont'd)

Name of programme Ascending order prenatal, infant to toddler	PPET rating and evidence	Type and delivery setting	Who is it for?	What are the outcomes?	Cost information
Anna Freud Centre Parent Infant Project (PIP)	** Note: According to website training is currently only offered by the developer so scale-up may be an issue. The Anna Freud Centre has conducted UK RCT (end 2012), see: http://www.annafreud.org/pages/parent-infant-psychotherapy-randomised-controlled-trial-pip-rct.html.	**Level of need:** Moderate, complex, high **Format:** Individual or group **Classification:** Targeted, specialist, highly specialist **Setting:** Family home, children's centre, school, community centre/faith-based centre, clinic/health centre **Length:** 10 wks	Parents and infants under 1 year of age experiencing difficulties in the parent-baby relationship.	Child: Improved child general well-being and mental health. Parent: Parent practices and mental health.	No information as yet.
Mellow Parenting For more information see www.mellowparenting.org/	** No definitive RCT as yet, pre-post only. Pilot RCT underway, see http://www.abdn.ac.uk/iahs/research/crh/projects/mellow-babies.php.	**Level of need:** Complex, high **Format:** Group **Classification:** Targeted, specialist **Setting:** Family home, children's centre, school, community centre/faith-based centre, clinic/health centre **Length:** 6–14 weekly sessions	Mothers and fathers (plus separate fathers programme) with high levels of social and health needs, as well as child protection concerns. Mellow Bumps: antenatal, Mellow Babies: < 18 mos, Going Mellow: 2–5 yrs. Plus fathers' programmes: Dad Matters: antenatal, Mellow Dads: 0–18 mos, 2–5 yrs.	Child: Reduced child maltreatment (actual or risk). Parent: Improved parenting practices/competency.	No information as yet.

Programme	Evidence	Level/Format/Setting/Length	Target & Outcomes	Cost-effectiveness
The Incredible Years Parent Programmes For more information see shttp://incredibleyears.com/programs/parent/	**** Toddler programme: 2 RCTs (US & UK); additional RCT underway in Ireland and England (combined with IY Infant programme). BASIC IY for parents with children aged 3+ has rigorous evidence of effectiveness, independent of the developer, in several countries. See IY website.	**Level of need:** Low-moderate, complex **Format:** Group **Classification:** Targeted prevention, targeted specialist **Setting:** Children's centre, school, community centre/faith-based centre, clinic/health centre **Length:** Toddler IY is 12 weeks, BASIC is now 14 weeks (adjuncts can be added to extend length due to parent need)	Parents with a child aged 0–12 years at risk of developing conduct disorder, social-emotional difficulties, or a substance misuse problem when older. Suitable for parents with mental health issues, at risk of maltreatment, social/economic disadvantage. Child: Improved child behaviour, improved child general well-being/mental health, reduced risk of child substance misuse. Parent: Improved parenting practices/competency, mental health.	IY for ages 3–7 has cost-effectiveness analyses demonstrating good value (see Furlong, Bywater McGilloway, et al., 2012). Micro-costing conducted for IY Infant & Toddler, see IY website.
Parents Plus Early Years (PPEY) For more information see http://parentsplus.ie/node/6	*** Promising evidence from three evaluations including a good quasi-experimental trial.	**Level of need:** Low-moderate, complex **Format:** Individual, group **Classification:** Universal, selected prevention, targeted, specialist **Setting:** Family home, children's centre, school, community centre/faith-based centre, clinic/health centre **Length:** 8–10 weekly sessions.	Any parent concerned about their child's behaviours (including ADHD), emotional problems, and/or development and learning. Toddlerhood (1–2 yrs), Preschool (3–5 yrs), Primary (5–11 yrs). Child: Improved child behaviour. Parent: Improved parent well-being, reduced parent stress/depression/mental health problems.	No information as yet.
Fostering Changes For more information see http://www.fosteringchanges.com/	** Preliminary evidence from small RCT in UK.	**Level of need:** High **Format:** Group **Classification:** Targeted prevention, targeted specialist **Setting:** Family home, children's centre, school, community centre/faith-based centre, clinic/health centre **Length:** 12 weekly sessions	Foster carers with children aged: Toddlerhood (1–2 yrs), Preschool (3–5 yrs), Primary (5–11 yrs). Child: Improved child behaviour, improved child general well-being/mental health. Parent: Reduced parent stress/depression/mental health problems, other.	No information as yet.

(*Continued*)

Table 20.1 (Cont'd)

Name of programme Ascending order prenatal, infant to toddler	PPET rating and evidence	Type and delivery setting	Who is it for?	What are the outcomes?	Cost information
Families and Schools Together (FAST) For more information see http://education.gov.uk/commissioning-toolkit/Programme/Detail/37	**** Evidence from US RCTs: Kratochwill, McDonald, Levin et al. (2009).	**Level of need:** Low-moderate **Format:** Group **Classification:** Universal, targeted **Setting:** School, community centre/faith-based centre **Length:** Eight weekly 2.5-hour group sessions	Social/economic disadvantage. Any parent interested in supporting their child's development and being involved in their community. Preschool (3–5 yrs), Primary (5–11 yrs).	Child: Improved child behaviour, achievement, social skills, reduced risk of child substance misuse, reduced risk of child offending. Parent: Improved parenting practices/ competency, improved parent well-being.	No information as yet.
Family Links Nurturing Programme (FLNP) For more information see http://familylinks.org.uk/	** UK RCT (children aged 2–4 yrs) showed no effect possibly due to implementation issues. Family Links addressing this weakness. Pre-post studies found positive effects.	**Level of need:** Low-moderate **Format:** Group **Classification:** Universal, targeted **Setting:** Family home, children's centre, school, community centre/faith-based centre, clinic/health centre **Length:** 10 weekly 2-hr sessions for groups of 6–10 parents	Any parent interested in improving their relationship with their child of 0–18 yrs, but best suited for 4–11 yrs, Preschool (3–5 yrs), Primary (5–11 yrs).	Child: Improved child behaviour, mental health. Parent: Improved parent well-being, parent skills/practices.	UK RCT could not demonstrate cost-effectiveness due to non-significant results.

Solihull Approach Parenting Group (SAPG)	** Preliminary pre-post evidence of effectiveness Note: Developers working to tackle implementation and dissemination issues.	**Level of need:** Low-moderate **Format:** Group **Classification:** Universal, targeted prevention **Setting:** Family home, children's centre, school, community centre/faith-based centre, clinic/health centre **Length:** 10 weekly sessions	Any parent interested in improving their relationship with their child, Preschool (3–5 yrs), Primary (5–11 yrs).	Child: Improved child behaviour. Parent: Reduced parent stress/depression/mental health problems.	No information as yet.
Strengthening Families Strengthening Communities (SFSC) For more information see www.education.gov.uk/commissioning-toolkit/Programme/Detail/28 and www.raceequalityfoundation.org.uk/sfsc	** No RCT, but some evidence from pre-post as was one of the PEIP (less effective than IY or TP) programmes, and small quasi-experiment.	**Level of need:** Low-moderate **Format:** Group or online **Classification:** Universal, selective prevention, targeted **Setting:** Family home, children's centre, school, community centre/faith-based centre, clinic/health centre **Length:** 13 weekly 3-hr sessions, 8–12 parents Online is 6 weeks (under 5s)	Any parents (particularly BME) interested in improving their relationship with their child, and those who want to reduce the risks associated with family and community violence. Suggested age 3–18, but more appropriate for Primary (5–11 yrs), Secondary (11–14 yrs).	Child: Improved child behaviour, improved child general well-being/mental health. Parent: Improved parent well-being, practices/skills.	Race Equality are working to produce this information

Note: Information correct at time of writing.

In Focus: Incredible Years (IY)

IY (see: www.incredibleyears.com) is a parent programme frequently accessed, oftentimes by parents identified with children at risk, with parents attending either voluntarily or by being mandated. It was developed in the US by Professor Carolyn Webster-Stratton in the 1970s and has been successfully transported across to the UK. IY has an extensive reach and a worldwide evidence base. It is a suite of multi-modal programmes including those for parents, children and teachers. IY parent programmes are becoming more multilevel, but mostly they remain targeted by developmental or chronological age, rather than intensity of delivery, and are delivered individually or in a group format. The aim of IY is to prevent, or treat, child (0–12 years) conduct problems/disorder and antisocial behaviour by enhancing the protective factors, such as strengthening relationships and social–emotional well-being. For more detail on IY and its evidence base please see Webster-Stratton and Bywater (in press).

The Core Parent Programmes

The IY BASIC (core) parent training consists of four curricula designed to fit the developmental stage of the child: Baby Programme (1–9 months), Toddler Programme (1–3 years), Preschool Programme (3–5 years) and School-Age Programme (6–12 years). The programmes run from 8–22 weeks, for two hours per week, depending on the specific programme selected and the risk level of the population. The recommended programme delivery length is longer for higher risk and child welfare-referred families, and parents whose children have conduct issues, Attention Deficit Disorder or developmental delays.

Two trained IY group facilitators deliver the programme, which includes showing short DVD vignettes of modelled parenting skills to groups of 10–12 parents. The vignettes demonstrate child development and parenting principles, and encourage focused discussions. Self-reflection, problem-solving, practice exercises and collaborative learning are key programme elements. The programmes support parents' understanding of typical child developmental milestones, child safety-proofing and adequate monitoring, as well as age-appropriate child-management skills.

All the programmes focus on ways to strengthen parent–child relationships and attachment and encourage children's language, social and emotional development. Programme goals include: (a) promoting parent competencies by increasing positive parenting, parent–child attachment, and self-confidence about parenting; (b) increasing parents' child-directed play interactions to coach children's social–emotional, academic, verbal and persistence skills; (c) reducing critical and physically violent discipline and increasing positive discipline strategies; (d) increasing family support networks; and (e) strengthening home–teacher bonding and parents' involvement in school-related activities, and positive connections with teachers.

Incredible Years Adjuncts to Parent Programmes

Supplemental or adjunct parenting programmes can be combined with the core IY BASIC programme (see below for references).

ADVANCE. The ADVANCE parenting programme, offered after completion of the BASIC preschool or school-age programmes, was designed for selective high-risk and indicated populations and focuses on parents' interpersonal risk factors such as anger and depression management, effective communication, ways to give and get support, problem-solving between adults, and ways to teach children problem-solving skills.

School Readiness Programme. This preschool programme for children ages 3–4 years is designed to help parents support their children's preliteracy and interactive reading readiness skills.

Attentive Parenting Programme. A third optional adjunct for the Toddler, Preschool and early School-Age programmes is the *Attentive Parenting Programme* for children ages two to six years. This universal group prevention programme is designed to teach all parents social, emotional and persistence coaching, reading skills and how to promote their children's self-regulation and problem-solving skills.

IY programme to support foster/kinship carer. 'Parent' has been defined in this chapter to describe those with a significant caring role of a child; this includes foster carers who may look after a child on a long-term basis or with a view to returning the child to their family. In 2008, there were 80,000 looked-after children in local authority care in the UK (UK National Statistics, 2008). Looked-after children often have a difficult start in life and approximately 16% experience three placements in the course of a year. 'Care' does not always address emotional and behavioural difficulties, and can therefore lead to a vicious cycle of failed placements, poor school achievement and exclusion, poor social relationships and escalating challenging and antisocial behaviour resulting in high use of health, social care and local authority special educational services.

There is a 37% prevalence of conduct disorder in looked-after children (Tapsfield & Collier 2005), which is almost three times that found in the general population. Given the high levels of conduct problems among looked-after children and the added cost to families, society and services, there is a pressing need to support foster carers in the care and management of this behaviour. Foster carers' parenting capacity can be markedly reduced when experiencing stress during placement and they are less likely to meet their foster children's needs, such as integration or fostering independence, with significantly higher disruption rates being experienced by strained carers (Farmer, Lipscombe & Moyers, 2005). It is therefore important to support carers in their difficult task of nurturing looked-after children.

The UK government has recognised a need to improve training for foster carers in order to support the health, well-being and educational attainment of looked-after children (Tapsfield & Collier 2005). The IY parenting programme has proved effective with foster carers in the UK (Bywater, Hutchings, Linck et al., 2010) and their looked-after children (aged 2–17 years), with reduced stress levels for carers and reduced problematic child behaviour at a six-month follow-up, compared to those who did not receive IY. A similar study in the US also found IY to be effective for foster carers and the looked-after child's biological parents (Linares, Montalto, Li & Oza, 2006).

Evidence base for IY

A recent IY parent programme meta-analysis included 50 studies with 4745 participants (2472 for intervention groups and 2273 for comparison groups; Menting, Orobio de Castro & Matthys, 2013). Results showed IY to be statistically effective, with a mean effect size of $d = .27$ for disruptive child behaviour across informants (e.g., teacher and parents) and $d = .23$ for prosocial behaviour. Mean effect sizes based on observations ($d = .37$) were larger than mean effect sizes based on parents' ($d = .30$) or teachers' judgements ($d = .13$). Pre-treatment intensity of children's problem behaviour proved to be the strongest predictor of the IY's intervention effects on parental report, with larger effects for studies that included more severe cases.

The School-Age BASIC programme for parents of 3- to 6-year-olds (12–16 sessions) has demonstrated effectiveness in targeted RCTs in the UK in Wales and England (e.g., Hutchings, Bywater, Daley et al., 2007; Bywater, Hutchings, Daley et al., 2009; Little, Berry, Morpeth et al., 2012), and in Ireland (McGilloway, Ni Mhaille, Bywater et al., 2012). Families were recruited to these trials if they lived in disadvantaged areas and had a child scoring over the cut-off on a behavioural screener. Results were similar, with child behaviour effect sizes ranging from

.5 to .89 across the three trials. The Welsh and Irish trial (Hutchings, Bywater, Daley et al., 2007; McGilloway, Ni Mhaille, Bywater et al., 2012) independently observed critical parenting (by observers who did not know whether parents had attended IY or not) and significant differences were found, indicating that intervention group parents used significantly fewer aversive parenting strategies at follow-up when compared to control group parents. In addition parent mental health for intervention parents improved in the studies that measured it (Hutchings, Bywater, Daley et al., 2007; McGilloway, Ni Mhaille, Bywater et al., 2012).

The BASIC programme can be combined with the ADVANCE parent programme (nine sessions) to make 18–22 sessions of 2–2½ hours. This combined programme was delivered to families with 'high-risk' children aged 8 to 13 years as part of the Pathfinders Early Intervention Programme, demonstrating (pre-post) improvements in parenting skills and reductions in child behaviour problems (Hutchings, Bywater, Williams et al., 2011), thus reflecting the results obtained via the RCTs of this programme on a younger age group.

Webster-Stratton (2011) highlights why IY is suitable for parents at risk of maltreating their child(ren), or with substantiated cases of maltreatment, and highlights a variety of evidence and published articles, with a discussion on adaptations for this specific population. The families may experience domestic violence, substance abuse, maternal depression, mental illness and/or family instability, yet IY has several aspects making it suitable for this population, such as cognitive restructuring, emotional regulation strategies and behavioural practice methods, in order to bring about cognitive and behavioural change. Although other parenting programmes have evidence of effectiveness, for example Triple P, IY is currently the only programme that has robust UK evidence in addition to a broad international evidence base.

Parenting Programme Moderators and Limitations

Research suggests that the impact of behavioural and cognitive behavioural parenting programmes may be moderated by socio-economic factors, such as socio-economic disadvantage arising from low levels of income or low levels of educational attainment and employment (e.g., Reyno & McGrath, 2006). Some research has found that lower socio-economic status *reduces* the effectiveness of parenting programmes, although other research (e.g., Gardner, Hutchings, Bywater & Whitaker, 2010) indicates that specific parenting programmes may achieve positive outcomes for *all* parents, irrespective of socio-economic status. Menting, Orobio de Castro and Matthys (2013) found child behaviour to be the biggest predictor of outcomes, that is, if the initial severity of problem behaviour were high there would be more of an effect following attendance on the programme. Other moderators included number of sessions attended (although this finding may be biased if relying purely on parent report – if a parent attends many sessions they may perceive that they have made more changes than those who attended less).

Another important moderator of impact may include implementation fidelity (see Chapter 21); that is, the extent to which programmes delivered in more naturalistic service settings adhere to the original design of the programme. Thus, if monitoring (that is training and supervision of programme deliverers) is critical to programme success, a programme might be efficacious within experimental research settings but not effective when rolled out within more naturalistic settings.

It is recommended, therefore, that effectiveness trials should also include a full process and cost evaluation. This will ensure that UK implementation issues and barriers can be addressed, and implementation costs are transparent, in order to inform decision makers more fully. A process evaluation will establish the programme's acceptability to the deliverers as well as to the end recipients, feasibility, attendance and retention levels. Local and national commissioners of parent programmes also need to be aware not only of process and outcome evaluation findings, but also, crucially, what the financial costs are to initiate, implement and scale-up a programme. A programme needs to be cost-effective and also to demonstrate potential cost benefits in the future.

The Washington State Institute of Public Policy is currently playing a leading role in developing cost–benefit methods in the UK and their implications for policy. The reduction in public spending has stimulated interest in cost-effective services offered at the earliest opportunity in life; the question is – if the pounds are saved in relation to other services later in the child's life, then who should financially invest in the early interventions? (Allen, 2011a).

Conclusions

Emotional abuse and neglect are important, yet common, public health problems. Some family- or community-level risk factors for emotional and physical abuse and neglect cannot be modified; however, intervening to change parenting practices can prove effective at reducing or preventing the abuse. Parenting programmes are focused, short-term interventions aimed at improving parenting practices and other risk factors such as parental mental well-being, attitudes and practices.

Evidence of the growing range of successful interventions demonstrates that while it is never too early to intervene preventatively, it is also never too late. Interventions for high-risk groups may, however, need to be multi-modal or multilevel in order to tackle the multiple risks in children's lives and acknowledge the increasingly varied influences on their life trajectories (Bywater & Utting, 2012). Given the strength of available evidence in relation to reducing the risk factors linked to ineffective parenting, we can be optimistic that interventions for parents at risk of neglecting their child can make a valuable and constructive contribution to preventing child neglect and emotional abuse.

The shift toward funding effective, evidence-based approaches should ultimately result in long-term savings to families and society (Allen, 2011b). Access to UK evidence to inform local and national strategies is easier with the existence of databases or toolkits; for instance, the Commissioning Toolkit of parent programmes. However, current availability of interventions can be localised and patchy, even when – as with MTFC – they are listed in the menu of community sentences theoretically available to the Youth Court. Therefore, further work is needed to ensure adequate availability of programmes, delivered with fidelity.

Summary of policy and practice implications

- Programmes may be applied at the child, parent, family, school or community level, or at multiple levels, depending on factors such as the identification pathway, the developmental stage and age of the child, and the mental health and ability of the parent.
- A continuum of support is needed from pregnancy onward to extend and reinforce earlier learning.
- Given the patterns of multiple risks that neglected and/or physically abused children may live with, it is likely that multi-modal interventions will be especially effective in providing a holistic approach that reinforces resilience and protection.
- Practitioners and policy-makers can choose from an expanding suite of effective programmes for parents and their children across the age range, although there are still limited

programmes for parents of the younger age groups and limited 'UK home-grown' programmes.
- The UK evidence base is expanding but requires development, including a commitment to rigorous evaluation of outcomes, process and costs, and greater availability of proven programmes.
- There is a lack of offerings for foster or kinship carers to work in parallel with or alongside parents in building effective, consistent, parenting practices.

References

Alexander, J.F. & Sexton, T.L. (2002). Functional Family Therapy: A model for treating high-risk, acting-out youth. In: J. Lebow (ed), Wiley Series in Couples and Family Dynamics and Treatment. *Comprehensive Handbook of Psychotherapy, volume IV: Integrative/Eclectic.* Hoboken: John Wiley & Sons, Inc.

Allen, G. (2011a). *Early Intervention: Smart Investment, Massive Savings.* London: Cabinet Office.

Allen, G. (2011b). *Early Intervention: The Next Steps.* London: Cabinet Office.

Aos, S., Lieb, R., Mayfield, J. & Miller, M. (2004). *Benefits and costs of prevention and early intervention programs for youth.* Olympia: Washington State Institute for Public Policy.

Barth, R. (2009). Preventing child abuse and neglect with parent training: Evidence and opportunity. *The Future of Children*, 19(2).

Biehal, N., Ellison, S., & Sinclair, I. (2011). Intensive fostering: An independent evaluation of MTFC in an English setting. *Children and Youth Services Review*, 33, 2043–2049.

Blower, S., Dixon, J, Ellison, S., et al. (2016). Step Change: an evaluation (Research Report DFE-RR568). London, DfE.

Butler, S., Baruch, G., Hickey, N. & Fonagy, P. (2011). A randomized controlled trial of multisystemic therapy and a statutory therapeutic intervention for young offenders. *Journal of the American Academy of Child and Adolescent Psychiatry*, 50, 1220–1235.

Bywater, T. & Sharples, J. (2012). Effective, evidence-based interventions for emotional well-being: Lessons from policy and practice. Special Issue 'Emotional and Social Justice in Education: Interdisciplinary Perspectives', *Research Papers in Education*, 27, 389–408.

Bywater, T. & Utting, D. (2012). Support from the start: Effective programmes for nine to 13 year-olds. *Journal of Children's Services*, 7, 41–52.

Bywater, T., Hutchings, J., Daley, D. et al. (2009). A pragmatic randomised control trial of a parenting intervention in sure start services for children at risk of developing conduct disorder; Long term follow-up. *British Journal of Psychiatry*, 195, 318–324.

Bywater, T., Hutchings, J., Linck, P. et al. (2010). Incredible Years parent training support for foster carers in Wales: A multi-centre feasibility study. *Child Care Health and Development*.

Chamberlain, P., Price, J., Leve, L.D. et al. (2008). Prevention of behavior problems for children in foster care: Outcomes and mediation effects. *Prevention Science*, 9, 17–27.

Crozier, M., Rokutani, L., Russett, J.L. et al. (2010). A multi-site programme evaluation of families and schools together (FAST): Continued evidence of a successful multi-family community-based prevention programme. *The School Community Journal*, 20, 187–207.

Curtis, N.M., Ronan, K.R. & Borduin, C.M. (2004). Multisystemic treatment: A meta- analysis of outcome studies. *Journal of Family Psychology*, 18, 411.

Davies, M. (2000). *The Blackwell Encyclopaedia of Social Work.* Oxford: John Wiley & Sons, Ltd. 245.

Dixon, L., Browne, K.D. & Hamilton-Giachritsis (2009). Patterns of risk and protective factors in the intergenerational cycle of maltreatment. *Journal of Family Violence*, 24, 111–122.

Farmer, E., Lipscombe, J. & Moyers, S. (2005). Foster carer strain and its impact on parenting and placement outcomes for adolescents. *British Journal of Social Work*, 35, 237–253.

Finkelhor, D., Turner, H., Ormrod, R. & Hamby, S.L. (2009). Violence, abuse, and crime exposure in a national sample of children and youth. *Pediatrics*, 124, 1411–1423.

Fonagy, P., Butler, S., Goodyer, I. et al. (2013). Evaluation of multisystemic therapy pilot services in the Systemic Therapy for At Risk Teens (START) trial: Study protocol for a randomised controlled trial. *Trials*, 14, 265.

Furlong, M., McGilloway, S., Bywater, T. et al. (2012). Behavioral and cognitive-behavioural group-based parenting interventions for early-onset conduct problems in children age 3–12 years. *Cochrane Database of Systematic Reviews* (2).

Gardner, F., Hutchings, J., Bywater, T. & Whitaker, C. (2010). Who benefits and how does it work? Moderators and mediators of outcome in an effectiveness trial of a parenting intervention. *Journal of Clinical Child & Adolescent Psychology*, 39(4), 1–13.

Green, J., Biehal, N., Roberts, C. et al. (2014). Multidimensional treatment foster care for adolescents in English care: Randomised trial and observational cohort evaluation. *British Journal of Psychiatry*, 204, 214–221.

Hutchings, J., Bywater, T., Daley, D. et al. (2007). A pragmatic randomised control trial of a parenting intervention in sure start services for children at risk of developing conduct disorder. *British Medical Journal*, 334, 678–682.

Hutchings, J., Bywater, T., Williams, M.E. et al. (2011). The extended School Age Incredible Years parent programme. *Child and Adolescent Mental Health*, 16, 136–143.

Hutchings, J., Gardner, F. & Lane, E. (2004). Making evidence based interventions work in clinical settings: Common and specific therapy factors and implementation fidelity. In: C. Sutton, D. Utting & D. Farrington (eds), *Support from the start: Working with Young Children and Their Families to Reduce the Risks of Crime and Antisocial Behaviour*. Research Report 524. London: Department for Education and Skills.

Kratochwill, T.R., McDonald, L., Levin, J.R. et al. (2009). Families and schools together: An experimental study of multi-family support groups for children at risk. *Journal of School Psychology*, 47, 245–265.

Linares, L.O., Montalto, D., Li, M. & Oza, V.S. (2006). A promising parenting intervention in foster care. *Journal of Consulting and Clinical Psychology*, 74, 32–41.

Littell, J.H. (2005). Lessons from a systematic review of effects of multisystemic therapy. *Children and Youth Services Review* 27, 445–463.

Littell J.H., Campbell, M., Green, S. & Toews, B. (2005). Multisystemic therapy for social, emotional, and behavioral problems in youth aged 10–17. Cochrane Database of Systematic Reviews 2005, 4, Art. No.: CD004797.

Little, M., Berry, V., Morpeth, L. et al. (2012). The impact of three evidence-based programmes delivered in public systems in Birmingham, UK. *International Journal of Conflict and Violence*, 6, 260–272.

Luthar, S.S., Barkin, S.H. & Crossman, E.J. (2013). 'I can, therefore I must': Fragility in the upper-middle classes. *Development and Psychopathology, 25th Anniversary Special Issue*, 25, 1529–1549.

Marmot, M., Allen, J., Goldblatt, P. et al. (2010) *Fair Society, Healthy Lives*. VSSP Policy Briefing.

McGilloway, S., Ni Mhaille, G., Bywater, T. et al. (2012). A parenting intervention for childhood behavioral problems: A randomised controlled trial in disadvantaged community-based settings. *Journal of Consulting and Clinical Psychology*, 80, 116–127.

Melton, G.B. & Barry, F.D. (1994). *Protecting Children from Abuse and Neglect: Foundations for a New National Strategy*. New York, NY: Guilford Press.

Menting, A., Orobio de Castro, B. & Matthys, W. (2013). Effectiveness of the Incredible Years parent training to modify disruptive and prosocial child behavior: A meta-analytic review. *Clinical Psychology Review* 33 (2013), 901–913.

Mersky, J.P. & Topitzes, J. (2010). Comparing early adult outcomes of maltreated and non-maltreated children: A prospective longitudinal investigation. *Children and Youth Services Review*, 32, 1086–1096.

Monahan, K.C., Oesterle, S., Rhew, I. & Hawkins, J.D. (2014). The relation between risk and protective factors for problem behaviors and depressive symptoms, antisocial behavior, and alcohol use in adolescence. *Journal of Community Psychology*, 42, 621–638. (2014), www.nspcc.org.uk/preventing-abuse/child-abuse-and-neglect/neglect/.

Ogden, T. & Hagen, K.A. (2006). Multisystemic therapy of serious behaviour problems in youth: Sustainability of therapy effectiveness two years after intake. *Child and Adolescent Mental Health*, 11, 142–149.

Radford, L., Corral, S., Bradley, C. et al. (2011). *Child Abuse and Neglect in the UK Today*. London: NSPCC.

Reyno, S.M. & McGrath, P.J. (2006). Predictors of parent training efficacy for child externalizing behavior problems — A meta-analytic review. *Journal of Child Psychology and Psychiatry*, 47, 99–111.

Scarcella, C.A., Bess, R., Zielewski, E.H. & Green, R. (2006). *The cost of protecting vulnerable children V: Understanding state variation in child welfare financing*. Washington, DC: Urban Institute.

Sexton T.L. & Alexander J.F. (2004). *Functional Family Therapy Clinical Training Manual*. Annie E. Casey Foundation.

Sexton, T.L. & Turner, C.W. (2010). The effectiveness of functional family therapy for youth with behaviour problems in a community practice setting. *Journal of Family Psychology*, 24, 339–348.

Tapsfield, R. & Collier, F. (2005). *The cost of foster care: Investing in our children's future*. London: British Association for Adoption and Fostering (BAAF) and The Fostering Network.

Thomlison, B. (2004). A risk and protective factor perspective in child maltreatment. In: M. W. Fraser (ed), *Risk and Resilience in Childhood: An Ecological Perspective*, 2nd edn. Washington, DC: National Association of Social Workers Press, 89–131.

Timmons-Mitchell, J., Bender, M.B., Kishna, M.A. & Mitchell, C.C. (2006). An independent effectiveness trial of multisystemic therapy with juvenile justice youth. *Journal of Clinical Child and Adolescent Psychology*, 35, 227–236.

UK National Statistics (2008). Children looked after statistics Scotland; England; and Wales, http://www.statistics.gov.uk/hub.

Van Horn, M.L., Fagan, A.A., Hawkins, J.D. & Oesterle, S. (2014). Effects of the Communities That Care System on cross-sectional profiles of adolescent substance use and delinquency. *American Journal of Preventive Medicine*, 47, 188–197.

Webster-Stratton, C., & Bywater, T. (in press). The Incredible Years® Series: An Internationally Evidenced Multi-modal Approach to Enhancing Child Outcomes. In M Whisman, M Celano, K Deater-Deckard, and E Jouriles (eds) *The APA Handbook of Contemporary Family Psychology*.

Webster-Stratton, C. (2011). *The Incredible Years: Parents, Teachers and Children Training Series*. Seattle, US: Incredible Years.

Westermark, P.K., Hansson, K. & Olsson, M. (2010). Multidimensional treatment foster care (MTFC): Results from an independent replication. *Journal of Family Therapy*, 33, 1–23.

21

Critical Factors in the Successful Implementation of Evidence-Based Parenting Programmes
Fidelity, Adaptation and Promoting Quality

Nick Axford[1], Tracey Bywater[2], Sarah Blower[2], Vashti Berry[3], Victoria Baker[1] and Louise Morpeth[1]

[1] Dartington Social Research Unit, UK
[2] University of York, UK
[3] University of Exeter Medical School, UK

Introduction

Implementation fidelity refers to the extent to which an intervention is delivered as it was originally intended by the programme developers; in other words, that it follows the model (Dusenbury, Brannigan, Falco & Hansen, 2003; Carroll, Patterson, Wood et al., 2007; Harn, Parisi & Stoolmiller, 2014; Hasson, 2015). The word fidelity conveys the sense of being *true* or *faithful* to the design. Sometimes the term intervention *integrity* has the same meaning. Scholars in prevention and implementation science propose that programmes for children and families that follow closely to their original proven model (high fidelity) are more likely to result in positive outcomes for participants than those programmes that deviate significantly from the original model (low fidelity).

This chapter focuses on programme fidelity in relation to parenting interventions. It discusses the importance of fidelity, outlines strategies for promoting fidelity, and emphasises fidelity and evidence-based parenting programmes. Fidelity levels can become a barrier to testing the evidence base of a programme effectively, an issue that will also be discussed.

Parenting Interventions

What are they?

A *parent* is an individual who may or may not have a biological relationship to the child and is in a significant childrearing and child care role (see Bywater, Chapter 20 of this text). *Parenting programmes*, for the purpose of this chapter, are defined as manualised, structured interventions for parents that include clear guidelines for implementation and fidelity and are designed to modify parenting behaviour in order to improve child behaviour and/or prevent or reduce child maltreatment and neglect (see Bywater, Chapter 20 of this text). They can be delivered in a group format or in an intensive one-to-one format in which a practitioner works with one family at a time.

Parenting programmes may aim to change parent cognitions, beliefs and behaviours and are increasingly implemented to address ineffective parenting practices to mediate child behavioural and social–emotional problems and attachment issues (Furlong, McGilloway, Bywater et al., 2012). Behavioural and cognitive behavioural group-based parenting programmes typically draw on social learning theory (Bandura, 1977) and involve an interactive and collaborative learning format in which programme facilitators discuss and model key behavioural principles and parenting skills (e.g., play, praise, rewards and discipline) to parents and caregivers, who then practise the skills. Key elements of effective programmes include the following: learning how and when to use positive parenting skills, employing observation, modelling, practising behaviour rehearsal (e.g., role play), applying discussion, completing homework assignments, using peer support, reframing unhelpful cognitive perceptions about the child or about child-management in general, and tackling barriers to attendance (Hutchings, Gardner & Lane, 2004).

Structured, group-based parenting programmes are usually delivered weekly or fortnightly for at least three sessions, or the sessions may range from four (Martin & Sanders, 2003) to 24 weekly group sessions (Webster-Stratton & Hammond, 1997), with each session lasting between one and two hours (Furlong, McGilloway, Bywater et al., 2012). The delivery setting includes community venues, children's centres, schools or clinics. Important considerations in choosing delivery venues include that the locations must be non-stigmatising, comfortable, non-threatening, easily accessible, and have the potential for holding a crèche. To encourage fathers' engagement, a non-feminised venue is favoured (Tracey, Bywater, Blower et al., 2014). Children's centres are sometimes considered too feminised and are, therefore, threatening for fathers (e.g., there may be posters on domestic violence). These factors need to be taken into account to ensure that both mothers and fathers are able to easily locate and access the venue, do not feel threatened in entering the venue, and are comfortable remaining in the venue. These are pragmatic considerations which can become barriers to attendance, responsiveness and retention in relation to parent programmes.

Parenting programmes have become increasingly popular as a means of improving parent–child attachment and interaction, addressing conduct problems in childhood (Webster-Stratton & Hammond, 1997; Sanders & McFarland, 2000; Hutchings, Bywater, Daley et al., 2007; Kling, Forster, Sundell & Melin, 2010), and reducing child maltreatment or neglect (see Bywater Chapter 20 of this text). They are suitable for parents at all stages of childrearing, from pregnancy, in which the programme can be delivered as part of a targeted preventative approach such as Family Nurse Partnership (e.g., Olds, Henderson, Chamberlin & Tatelbaum, 1986), and as a treatment approach in programmes such as Multi-Treatment Foster Care (MTFC) (e.g., Westermark, Hansson & Olsson, 2011).

What is known about the effectiveness of parenting programmes?

There are a variety of systematic reviews and meta-analyses demonstrating the effectiveness (or lack of effectiveness) of parenting programmes. The systematic review by Furlong, McGilloway, Bywater et al. (2012) explored the effectiveness of different cognitive behavioural parenting programmes for parents of children aged 3–12 who were deemed at risk of developing conduct disorder. The findings supported parenting programmes in general as they were found to be effective in improving parent (mother) mental health, parenting skills and child pro-social behaviour. Several Cochrane reviews have highlighted the effectiveness of group-based parenting programmes in promoting child and parent well-being (for children aged three years and older) (e.g., Barlow, Smailagic, Huband et al., 2012), and a review of programmes for 0- to 3-year-olds calls for more research with younger age groups (Barlow, Smailagic, Ferriter et al., 2010). A meta-analysis of Triple P (Sanders, Kirby, Tellegen & Day, 2014) included 101 Triple P studies that spanned 33 years of research and found significant effect sizes on child and parent outcomes in the short term and long term.

In the United Kingdom, the most robust evidence comes from studies of imported programmes, such as Incredible Years from the United States (Scott, Spender, Doolan et al., 2001; Gardner, Burton & Klimes, 2006; Hutchings, Bywater, Daley et al., 2007; Little, Berryl, Morpeth et al., 2012). These are 'transportable' programmes, which indicates that they have demonstrated effectiveness in various countries, with diverse populations, and possibly in different contexts or settings (Gardner, Montgomery & Knerr, 2015).

A variety of parenting programmes are available in the UK that are routinely delivered, for example, Triple P from Australia. Triple P has been shown to be effective in other countries (e.g., Bodenmann et al., 2008) and is widely available in the UK, although the single UK trial found no impact (Little, Berryl, Morpeth et al., 2012). Other parent programmes available in the UK are home-produced, such as Family Links, Solihull and Mellow Parenting (Simkiss, Snooks, Stallard et al., 2013; Puckering, Cox, Mills et al., 2013; Johnson & Wilson, 2012). Yet the evidence for these programmes is weak, and, for some routinely delivered programmes, the evidence of impact is non-existent (Axford, Barlow, Coad et al., 2015). An increasing number of online databases outline the level of evidence available for parenting programmes (and other interventions for children and families).[1]

Often the evidence behind programmes is mixed, which may reflect the fact that programmes can be classed as 'complex interventions' because they have multiple components and tackle issues in several domains (MRC, 2008). A parenting programme may, therefore, impact one domain, such as enhancing parent support, but not other domains, such as child behaviour. Specific expected outcomes should be clearly defined in a programme's theory of change to ensure that an informed choice of programme can be made by policy-makers or commissioners. Parenting programmes may also vary in effectiveness with different types of families, such as those who are most at risk or children with the most severe problems (Gardner, Hutchings, Bywater & Whitaker, 2010).

Fidelity

What is fidelity?

Different ways of subdividing the concept of fidelity exist. Some authors refer to content, frequency, duration, coverage and timeliness (Carroll, Patterson, Wood et al., 2007; von Thiele Schwartz, Hasson & Lindfors, 2015). These subcategories capture whether the intervention's

---

[1] For example, see www.blueprintsprograms.com and http://guidebook.eif.org.uk/.

active ingredients have been received by intended participants at the right times and as often and for as long as was planned (Hasson, 2015). Another widely used categorisation refers to adherence, exposure (or dose), quality of delivery, participant responsiveness and programme differentiation (Dusenbury, Brannigan, Falco & Hansen, 2003; Mihalic, 2004). Some of these dimensions are often used interchangeably with fidelity; however, it may be more helpful to view these elements as *aspects* of fidelity rather than the concept in its entirety.

The first dimension, *adherence*, refers to whether all the core components – known or hypothesised – of the intervention are delivered as designed with staff trained to the appropriate standard using the right protocols, techniques and materials and in the proper sequence and in prescribed locations and contexts. Adherence, therefore, is good if practitioners cover relevant material, conduct set exercises, show the right DVDs, convey specified messages, and so on. This said, the concept of 'core components' is not simple. Core components may be distinguished in terms of *principles* – for example, delivering material and exercises that focus on sensitivity, reinforcement, positive interactions, clarity, consistency and child-development education/knowledge – and *procedures* – for instance, how material and exercises are delivered (e.g., homework, modelling, role play, practising skills, information dissemination). 'Core' may also be defined in terms of the critical or active ingredients for effectiveness, if known (which is rare), or in terms of what is central to the logic model or theory of change, if active ingredients are hypothesised (which is more common).

Second, *exposure* refers to whether an intervention is delivered in the specified dose or amount (e.g., the number of parenting sessions in a course and their frequency and length). Just as courses of medical treatment usually stipulate how many pills must be taken over what period in order to make the patient better, interventions in children's services increasingly specify the number of sessions, the length and frequency of sessions, the period (duration), and the timing (timeliness). As with core components, however, the recommended dose is rarely based on strong empirical evidence as few studies test the dose–response relationship prospectively.

Third, *quality* refers to the manner in which the intervention is delivered. This includes the practitioner's preparation, attitude, enthusiasm and ability to respond to and engage with participants (e.g., having a collaborative style, starting with the participants' needs/goals, empathy, group facilitation skills). For example, is the practitioner sensitive, warm and empathetic? Does he/she encourage all parents in a session to engage in group discussions, or does the practitioner allow some parents to remain uninvolved? Clearly this will affect how much each participant is able to contribute to the group and how much he/she gains from the intervention.

The fourth dimension is user engagement or *responsiveness*. This refers to the extent to which the children, parents or families are engaged and involved in the activities and content of the programme and is seen as a judgement about how relevant the programme is to the participants' needs. How consistently do participants stick with the programme? Do they attend? Do they like it? Do they get involved (e.g., do they take part in discussion, and do they try to use new techniques or behaviours)?

The fifth dimension, programme *differentiation*, refers to identifying unique features or components of interventions and determining which elements are essential for the programme's success. Programme differentiation is important; however, it involves something distinct from fidelity (Carroll, Patterson, Wood et al., 2007). Therefore, including *reach* (or coverage) instead, namely the extent to which the intervention reaches the intended target group, may be more accurate and helpful. Do participants fit the target group criteria? What proportion of the target group is taking part? Are other children and families also involved?

Fidelity refers in part to what the practitioner does but also to the participant; in other words, fidelity is a product of the interaction between the actions of these two agents in the relationship. Adherence, for example, is predominantly a *practitioner* aspect of fidelity (i.e., adherence to core components), but it can also define *parent* adherence to programme requirements (i.e., whether he/she complies with expectations). Exposure is affected by what a practitioner does – how much was delivered (e.g., 12 two-hour sessions) – and also by how much a parent actually attends/receives (e.g., 10 weeks). Quality of delivery is clearly a provider aspect of fidelity, whereas user engagement is primarily a participant aspect, albeit a function of the quality of delivery.

When and why is fidelity important?

Implementation fidelity acts as a potential moderator of the relationship between interventions and the intended outcomes (Carroll, Patterson, Wood et al., 2007). Put another way, the fidelity with which an intervention is implemented affects how well it succeeds in achieving its goals.

There is substantial empirical evidence that programme effects are related to fidelity. Higher fidelity has been linked to improved programme outcomes for participants, and results tend to be weaker where implementation fidelity is poor (e.g., Blakely, Mayer, Gottschalk et al., 1987; Botvin, Baker, Dusenbury et al., 1990; Botvin, Baker, Filazzola & Botvin, 1990; Pentz, Trebow, Hansen et al., 1990; Hansen, Graham, Wolkenstein & Rohrbach, 1991; Rohrbach, Graham & Hansen, 1993; Kam, Greenberg & Walls, 2003; Durlak & DuPre, 2008; Eames, Daley, Hutchings et al., 2009; Lee, August, Realmuto et al., 2008). Failure to achieve fidelity may also have a wider adverse effect if it results in low or no impact for participants. Specifically, the community may become disillusioned with ineffective prevention efforts and withdraw their support from such initiatives (Lee, August, Realmuto et al., 2008).

This association between fidelity and outcomes should not be surprising. Programmes are essentially vehicles for delivering a theory of change (a hypothesis for how intervention activities will achieve the desired outcomes). Tampering with the core components, known or hypothesised, of the programme can, therefore, reduce the likelihood of the theory of change being delivered. Yet this is common:

> As efficacious interventions are disseminated to natural practice settings and implemented under broader, less controlled, and more complicated real-world conditions, the chances increase for key program components to be modified or deleted and for inconsistencies in program delivery to develop (Dane & Schneider 1998). This is particularly true for new interventions and interventions with complex delivery systems. For example, programs with multiple intervention components (e.g., child-, parent-, and school foci), tailored approaches, and extended time lines place substantial demands on local implementers who may have little or no previous experience delivering mental health interventions and limited infrastructure to support program implementation efforts. Over time, complex interventions are often simplified at the expense of key program objectives and strategies (Lee, August, Realmuto et al., 2008, p. 215)

Although fidelity is clearly important, there is debate around how much fidelity is sufficient (Kretlow & Bartholomew, 2010). In a review of over 500 studies that link implementation fidelity to outcomes, Durlak and DuPre (2008) argue that expecting perfect implementation is unrealistic (few studies achieve more than 80%), and that positive results have often been achieved with levels around 60%. The issue is less about 'how much' but rather 'which things' must be done and which things are flexible. There has been a tendency for measuring fidelity to become a counting exercise, but there is a strong case for moving it away from quantity and toward quality.

Fidelity is important, first, in *efficacy trials* when one is testing a hypothesised theory of change because one needs to test the intervention to determine if it is feasible, acceptable and efficacious. Second, fidelity is important in effectiveness trials (and scale-up) when one is seeking the same proven efficacy impacts in a real-world setting (i.e., the same intervention in a less-controlled or uncontrolled environment). However, variation in practice (i.e., non-adherence) can be useful when one wants to test whether different components are more or less critical or in intervention development where there may be different procedures for delivering the same principles. The ability to identify the areas that can be adjusted for the sake of local adaptation is important for its acceptance and wider use.

Fidelity and Adaptation

Programme adaptation can involve an addition/enhancement to or deletion from the original model, a modification of existing components, or changes in the manner or intensity of programme delivery. Adaptations can broadly be categorised in terms of changes to intervention *content* and changes to the form of intervention *delivery* (Castro, Barrera & Martinez, 2004). A spectrum of adaptation also exists from subtle accommodations, such as, for cultural reasons, replacing a 'piggy bank' (as pigs may be offensive to Muslims) with a 'Moses basket' to 'store' thoughts in a parenting session, to a larger adaptation, such as removing or adding a new session. Increasingly, parenting programmes are being adapted for specific groups or populations, for example, children presenting with Attention Deficit Hyperactivity Disorder (ADHD) or autism and families at risk of child maltreatment. While there is insufficient evidence currently to support the use of parenting programmes to treat abuse and neglect, there is support for targeting this group in improving some outcomes associated with abusive parenting, such as poor attachment and child behaviour and emotional disorders (Barlow, Johnston, Kendrick et al., 2006; Berry, Axford, Blower et al., 2014). In addition, where parenting programmes have been adapted by adding components related to abuse, such as dealing with anger and stress, the evidence suggests the programmes are more effective (Barlow, Johnston, Kendrick et al., 2006).

Dusenbury, Brannigan, Falco and Hansen (2003) identified two opposing perspectives regarding fidelity and adaptation. Advocates of strict adherence to the original model, the 'profidelity' perspective, argue that deviations or 'drift' are likely to reduce programme effectiveness (e.g., Elliott & Mihalic, 2004; Bumbarger & Perkins, 2008). Even in clinical settings, attempts to replicate positive results often fail because a programme has been adapted in ways that prevent it from achieving the same outcomes as those found in efficacy trials (Mihalic, Fagan, Irwin et al., 2002). Profidelity strives to maintain all programme components because it is rarely understood which components are actually core, and which ones are not. It must be proven empirically that a programme component is optional or modifiable (Mihalic, Fagan, & Argamaso, 2008). Supporters of a 'pro-adaptation' or 'reinvention' perspective, by contrast, argue that allowing freedom to modify a programme to fit the local needs (e.g., practitioner motivations, organisational climate, management capacity and support) increases the likelihood of programme effectiveness and sustainability (e.g., Berman & McLaughlin, 1978). Most scholars in the field of prevention and implementation science believe that some adaptation to accommodate local needs is acceptable and desirable with the condition that the causal mechanism of the programme is preserved. As such, a 'balance between adaptation and implementation with high fidelity' is needed (Webster-Stratton, Newcomer, Herman & Reinke, 2011, p. 524).

The case for fidelity to the model was discussed above: fidelity increases impact. So why adapt in practice? At least three reasons are explored in the literature.

First, modifying practices can assist with implementation, programme sustainability, and practitioner motivation (Dearing, 2008). Ensuring there is a match between the intervention and the context in which it is to be delivered is essential if a programme is to be successfully implemented and sustained long term (Durlak, 2010; von Hippel, 2005).

Second, adaptation can help to improve outcomes. Adhering too strictly to the programme model may compromise programme effectiveness if local needs are not met. Factors that may affect the need to adapt include time constraints, community norms, culture mores, resources and local regulations. For example, exposure or dose might be adjusted if the intervention is too long to fit the allotted time or resources (e.g., delivering fewer sessions to fit within a school term). Or the procedures for ensuring engagement may be adapted to address particular cultural practices (e.g., forming a women-only group). Similarly, vignettes or videos produced in one country could be unsuitable for another country and need to be redone. In parent programmes, a typical adaptation is the adjustment of content delivery to the pace of the group. So, a group of parents who are struggling with concepts introduced in the first two weeks would not move on to the third week until they understood the early concepts. Practitioners would repeat and reinforce the concepts and make a decision to progress when the group was ready. Flexibility should be built into programmes to account for such factors (Dearing, 2008; Webster-Stratton, Newcomer, Herman & Reinke, 2011).

Third, adaptation will happen naturally: consumers or local adopters often reinvent or change innovations to meet their own needs and to derive a sense of ownership (Dusenbury, Brannigan, Falco & Hansen, 2003). Given this, adaptations should arguably be planned rather than improvised (Bumbarger & Perkins, 2008). This involves considering and fully understanding the underpinning theory and critical components of an intervention and appreciating how altering them could impact programme outcomes (Harn, Parisi & Stoolmiller, 2014). Modifying dose, content and other delivery factors and measuring the impact on participant outcomes can help with identifying which components are critical to success (Gersten, Fuchs, Compton et al., 2005).

There are several common strategies for resolving the tension between adaptation and adherence. One is to involve the programme developer. The developer usually has a unique understanding of the theoretical underpinnings of an intervention and knows what modifications have been tried and with what success. Ideally, the developer would work with practitioners who are aware of the local conditions. In addition to adapting the programme to fit the local context, another strategy is to adapt the organisation to fit the programme – this is 'mutual adaptation'. Indeed, involving different hierarchical levels in an organisation is needed because changes to programme content and delivery may have wider implications for an organisation, and the power to make decisions and the reasons for them vary at different levels (Hasson, 2015). Adaptation strategies should also be guided by a clear and culturally informed theory, model or cultural framework as this will make the strongest contribution to outcomes (Castro, Barrera & Martinez, 2004). Any changes made to the programme need to be systemically examined for their impact on children and families (Fixsen, Louis de la Parte Florida Mental Health Institute & University of South Florida, 2005).

Parenting Interventions and Fidelity

Several studies exist that are designed specifically to test whether a *causal* relationship occurs between fidelity in the implementation of parenting programmes and their impact on children and families. Research on this topic is largely correlational and reveals mixed findings in relation to the link between fidelity and the outcomes of parenting programmes. A number of studies report a positive and significant relationship between fidelity and outcomes (e.g., Eames, Daley, Hutchings et al., 2009; Forgatch, Patterson, & DeGarmo, 2006). Two independent fidelity observation measures have been developed specifically to assess fidelity in the delivery of Incredible Years (Scott, Carby & Rendu, 2008; Eames, Daley, Hutchings et al., 2009). Analyses showed that the higher the levels of fidelity with regard to facilitator skill in delivering programme content and principles, the greater the positive outcomes on parents and, ultimately, on children. These measures are valuable because with self-report measures subjective bias can influence the results (Green, Goldman & Salovey, 1993).

However, the evidence about the relationship between fidelity and outcomes is not unequivocal. A number of studies have reported finding mixed or no significant relationships between fidelity and parent or child outcomes (Breitenstein, Fogg, Garvey et al., 2010). For example, Hogue, Henderson, Dauber et al. (2008) observed no effects of therapist competence in multidimensional family therapy on adolescent behavioural outcomes (though this study did report a significant relationship between adherence and reduced behaviour difficulties). In a large study of Triple P, Malti, Ribeaud and Eisner (2011) examined the link between fidelity and outcomes using propensity score matching techniques. A comparison of a subsample of highly adherent parents from the intervention group, those who completed the full course of Triple P, with a matched subsample of control parents found no consistent effects on any of the outcome measures.

There are a number of potential explanations for these conflicting results, such as variation in the ways that fidelity has been defined, operationalised and measured across different studies. The programmes under study also have discernible differences in their core components and intended outcomes, despite fitting loosely under the broad heading of parenting programme. Another potential source of contradictory findings relates to evaluation readiness. The pre-installation phase in the implementation of evidence-based programmes and innovations is often overlooked in both research and practice. Parenting programmes are generally described as complex interventions and, therefore, require sufficient lead-in time to ensure successful set-up and to become embedded within real-world service contexts (Forgatch, Patterson & Gewirtz, 2013). A complex set of factors and processes influence this stage of implementation, such as organisational readiness and programme fit.

The UK evaluation of MTFC demonstrates issues with organisational readiness and willingness for delivery to be evaluated by a randomised controlled trial (RCT) (Green, Biehal, Roberts et al., 2014; Dixon, Biehal, Green et al., 2014). These issues and barriers are common in many pragmatic trials and reduce the opportunity to evaluate the true fidelity. Research that assesses programme fidelity and outcomes during the first year of implementation, when staff are newly trained and programmes are delivered for the first time, is unlikely to observe optimal levels of fidelity (Forgatch & DeGarmo, 2011). As such, facilitators who lead parent groups as part of impact evaluations should conduct practice sessions before the study begins.

A study of the effectiveness and cost-effectiveness of the Family Links Nurturing Programme (FLNP) (Simkiss, Snooks, Stallard et al., 2013) illustrates the challenges of evaluation readiness and the importance of implementation factors in interpreting evidence of impact. The study was a multi-centre RCT of FLNP that involved 286 families and found no significant differences in outcomes for children and families between the intervention and control groups. The authors report low levels of exposure (just over a third of the families allocated to receive FLNP attended no sessions and less than half completed the whole course). One of the FLNP groups received delivery below the expected standards for the programme (Simkiss, Snooks, Stallard et al., 2013). Further research is needed to establish whether FLNP can be implemented with fidelity and to determine the programme's impact on outcomes. In a constructive response to the findings of this study, Family Links have embarked on a process of reviewing the fidelity of practitioners and their processes for quality control monitoring, and Family Links have appointed an in-house researcher to contribute to programme evaluation and state that 'it is now standard practice for everyone trained in the Nurturing Programme to take part in a Refresher day 12 months after the initial training; this is included in the initial training cost' (Mountford & Darton, 2013).

Outcomes from evidence-based parenting programmes are reliant on facilitator skills. Facilitators, therefore, need appropriate training, support, resources and materials in order to deliver with fidelity. But to what extent are parenting programmes implemented with strategies to support implementation? Many evidence-based parenting programmes have an infrastructure to support the monitoring and promotion of fidelity – some more extensive than others. Garbacz, Brown, Spee et al. (2014) reviewed the use of strategies to promote fidelity as reported in 65 research trials of evidence-based parent training programmes designed to reduce child and adolescent behavioural difficulties. The review utilised the Intervention Fidelity Assessment Checklist (IFAC), a tool developed to aid consistency in the assessment of the use of fidelity-promoting and -monitoring strategies in evaluation studies of behaviour change interventions (Bellg, Borrelli, Resnick et al., 2004). The IFAC examines 25 different strategies under the five headings of treatment design, training provider, delivery of treatment, receipt of treatment and enactment of treatment skills. Garbacz, Brown, Spee et al. (2014) report that 75% of the 65 studies describe the use of fidelity strategies; however, only 8% reported high adherence to strategies in all five categories. The review did not explore the link between fidelity and outcomes.

In relation to the five dimensions of fidelity outlined earlier in this chapter, parenting programmes generally incorporate adherence, quality and user engagement in order to be effective (see Hutchings, Gardner & Lane, 2004). In terms of *adherence*, parenting programmes typically include the following intervention components and procedures:

- Relationship-enhancing and discipline or limit-setting strategies;
- Emphasis on parents learning principles, such as the need for sensitivity and reinforcement, rather than prescriptions for parent–child interaction;
- Child development knowledge and awareness of children's capabilities;
- Videotaped vignettes prompt discussion and problem-solving;
- Role play rehearsal of new skills;
- Homework with practice assignments;
- Parents are encouraged to keep records of their practice at home and to set their own weekly goals; and
- Parents receive weekly feedback from group facilitators.

In terms of *quality* and *participant/parent engagement*, Hutchings, Gardner and Lane (2004) include the following:

- A collaborative, reciprocal relationship, which assumes that the facilitators and the parents both have expertise. Facilitators solicit parents' ideas, and parents participate in goal-setting and are encouraged to adapt the intervention to meet their own individual needs.
- Parents are empowered to find their own solutions. Research shows that this reduces attrition and increases motivation and commitment.
- Parents are encouraged to help each other, which reduces isolation and builds support networks, by, for example, making calls to one another during the course.
- Group facilitators phone parents during the course and contact parents who miss any sessions.

In relation to the tension identified earlier between fidelity and adaptation, parenting programme developers increasingly pre-empt this in two ways. The first is by developing tailored versions of programmes for specific populations. For example, the Incredible Years parenting programme has been adapted for families in the child welfare system (Webster-Stratton & Reid, 2010), and the Triple P programme has been adapted for perpetrators of domestic violence.[2] It is also common for parenting programmes to be adapted to reflect differences in the developmental stages and ages of children. Second, developers 'design-in' flexibility and specify programme elements that can be adapted (sometimes with ideas for how to do this). For instance, in Incredible Years, trainers teach practitioners about core programme principles and when variation can and should occur to match the programme context. This includes factors such as class size, personnel and student demographics. A good example of this is the provision of additional social–emotional materials to be used by a practitioner where children are displaying challenging behaviour. Teachers are trained to identify when and how to use these available adaptations (Webster-Stratton, Newcomer, Herman & Reinke, 2011).

Promoting Quality Implementation

Two major barriers to high fidelity are intervention complexity and a lack of fidelity-facilitation strategies, such as the provision of manuals, guidelines, training, monitoring and feedback, capacity building and incentives (Carroll, Patterson, Wood et al., 2007). With these obstacles in mind, six ways to promote programme fidelity will be described.

First, a manual should explain what the programme is and how it should be implemented. Interventions that have detailed and specific descriptions tend to obtain higher levels of implementation adherence (Carroll, Patterson, Wood et al., 2007). Manuals should specify components and activities in detail and explicitly state whether components are core or flexible. Instructions should be clear and simple rather than ambiguous. Since the realities of real-world practice can differ from manualised situations, examples of challenges or instructions on how to adapt in the face of unexpected situations should be included. For example, vignettes could be used (Dusenbury, Brannigan, Falco & Hansen, 2003). Parenting programmes such as Incredible Years and Triple P have very detailed manuals.

Second, it is necessary to identify and deliver the programme to the 'right' families. This is about ensuring the correct *reach*. When evidence-based parenting programmes are implemented in real-world settings, they often fail to produce the results shown in efficacy trials. One reason is it is difficult to engage parents. For example, only about a third of invited families enrol in prevention projects – they attend at least one programme session; of these, 40–60% drop out even when financial incentives, childcare, refreshments and transportation are provided (Baker, Arnold & Meagher, 2011). A review of the literature on how to engage parents in parenting programmes (Axford, Barlow, Coad et al., 2012) identified several actions that can enhance engagement, especially with hard-to-reach families, and include a clear recruitment process, good communication and liaison with stakeholders, incentives for recruitment and retention, active and creative outreach work, investment in building relationships with parents, making programmes easily accessible, and having realistic expectations. Historically, these considerations have often been neglected, but, increasingly, their importance is recognised in parenting programme manuals and training. There is also a need for coordinated care, whereby

---

[2] http://www.gcu.ac.uk/triplep/research/currentresearch/parentingsupportforoffenders/ (accessed 25 September 2015).

the organisation delivering the intervention seeks to connect parents to other services (e.g., substance misuse clinics, mental health services, debt counselling, housing support) that address critical health and social or financial problems, some of which may underlie their poor parenting or account for their inability to attend the parenting programme.

Third, fidelity is likely to be stronger when the right people deliver the programme; however, more research on this topic is needed (see below). Providers would ideally have the appropriate traits, personal attributes, qualifications, experience, knowledge and skills. Training in the specific programme can compensate partially for deficits in any of these areas. Practitioner attitude toward and support for prevention has also been shown to be a factor in whether a programme is adopted or maintained (Dusenbury, Brannigan, Falco & Hansen, 2003). Characteristics such as confidence and animation have been linked to greater adherence, and a practitioner's own beliefs and behaviours can affect his/her delivery. For example, teachers who are teaching substance prevention are less likely to intervene with students who smoke if they themselves are smokers. Practitioners who are newly qualified professionals and have had more training are more likely to be enthusiastic about prevention programmes but may be less adept at adapting the programme for the circumstances. For example, in a study of a highly manualised intervention designed to improve literacy, two groups delivered the intervention. The group with lower adherence but with a more experienced practitioner achieved better results than the group with higher fidelity but a less experienced practitioner (Simmons, Kame'enui, Harn et al., 2007). The more experienced practitioner, being sensitive to students' progress, left out some review sections and added more time for activities. By contrast, the less experienced practitioner stuck rigidly to the manual and struggled to engage the children within the sessions. Parenting programme developers increasingly specify the qualifications, skills, background and personal qualities required of practitioners. However, some programmes have been successfully delivered, with positive outcomes, by parents for parents (Day, Michelson, Thomson et al., 2012). There is also a *realpolitik* case for designing programmes that can be delivered not by clinical psychologists, which is difficult owing to their scarcity and cost, but by children's centre staff, who tend to be less qualified but directly commissioned for this role.

Fourth, the people who deliver the programme need to have training and support to help maintain high levels of fidelity (Dusenbury, Brannigan, Falco & Hansen, 2003; Asmussen, Matthews, Weizel et al., 2012). Well-trained practitioners are more likely to understand the underlying theoretical concepts of the intervention and how each of the activities contributes to achieving the outcomes and changes the programme promotes. Also, well-trained practitioners are more likely to be confident in their delivery of material and more able to adapt the programme and respond to the needs of their participants while maintaining the core components of the model. Programmes such as Incredible Years and Triple P have intensive training and support procedures that involve several levels of responsibility and expertise and require practitioners to demonstrate their skills and knowledge before progressing to the next level of accreditation. In Incredible Years, training materials are differentiated for novice and experienced practitioners so that training can be adapted to suit the needs and previous experience of practitioners (Webster-Stratton, Newcomer, Herman & Reinke, 2011). For example, for novice practitioners, a greater amount of time is spent on discussion with a larger number of scenarios completed that involve varying contexts. Webster-Stratton, Newcomer, Herman and Reinke (2011) also highlight the value of peer coaching. Having an instructional coach embedded into delivery enables quality to be monitored and maintained (e.g., Fixsen, Louis de la Parte Florida Mental Health Institute & University of South Florida, 2005). Coaches are experienced practitioners and experienced adaptors. They conduct regular fidelity observations with feedback and identify areas for improvement. They also provide the practitioner with a means of tackling obstacles, such as difficulty engaging parents, confronting challenging behaviours, and coping with issues around culture and diversity, while maintaining the core components of the intervention.

Fifth, the organisation involved in delivering the parenting programme needs to be set up to support fidelity. Having good management structures to support an outcome-driven culture (Kam, Greenberg & Walls, 2003) is one of the factors required to promote effectiveness, even with interventions proven in trials (Scott, Carby & Rendu, 2008). Programme supervision, coaching and feedback are generally not included in standard organisation management and appraisal, so more must be done to embed the fidelity review procedures into organisational or system procedures (e.g., allowing feedback on attendance and satisfaction scores as part of line management, giving rewards for high adherence). Barriers to effective implementation include time constraints and a lack of money and other resources. In addition, organisations that are overwhelmed or structurally turbulent are likely to have more implementation issues. In advance of implementing Incredible Years, an 'Agency Readiness Questionnaire'[3] can be used (it is not always completed) to see whether various organisational aspects are in place to deliver with high quality and fidelity. It involves assessing eight areas of organisational capacity and can highlight whether the programme is a good fit for the context and whether the organisation has the necessary resources and capacity:

- The perceived need and target population;
- Whether the programme addresses the organisational goals and philosophy;
- The organisation's commitment and human resources to deliver the programme;
- The organisation's financial resources and capacity to deliver the programme;
- What organisational capacity is there for marketing and for recruiting families, working with communities and providing space and support for parent groups, daycare, food and transportation;
- Once training has been delivered, what organisational capacity there is for building a supportive infrastructure and providing external technical support, ongoing monitoring, fidelity checks and programme evaluation;
- What plans the organisation has for programme evaluation; and
- What plans the organisation has in place for long-term maintenance of the programme.

The sixth way to promote fidelity is to monitor what practitioners actually do. Fidelity tools provide a means of tracking adherence, dose, quality and participant responsiveness to programme delivery – usually week-by-week and either online or by pen and paper. The evidence linking fidelity monitoring with improved outcomes is strong. For example, a review of meta-analyses of whole-school anti-bullying programmes and mentoring programmes found that the programmes that monitored fidelity achieved up to three times the level of impact as those that did not (Durlak & DuPre, 2008). Although monitoring with feedback does place an additional administrative burden upon delivery staff, in a study of the implementation of the Family Nurse Partnership home visiting programme, researchers found that once staff understood the purpose of the fidelity forms, a high rate of completion was achieved (Barnes, Ball, Meadows et al., 2008). In this respect, the importance of administrative support should not be underestimated. In an implementation study involving evidence-based programmes, such as Incredible Years, a lack of administrative support to ease the burden of fidelity monitoring was a barrier

---

[3] www.incredibleyears.com.

to high-fidelity delivery (Hutchings, Bywater, Eames & Martin, 2008; Lindsay, Strand, Cullen et al., 2011). All parenting programmes listed on the well-respected Blueprints for Healthy Youth Development[4] database have fidelity-monitoring procedures.

Conclusions

In prevention and implementation science, fidelity refers to delivering an intervention in a way that is faithful to the original design (whether or not the intervention has been tested and found effective). Generally, studies have found a positive association between fidelity and outcomes, including for evidence-based parenting programmes.

There is increased acceptance that adaptation is needed, for instance, to adjust for culture and to increase practitioner buy-in, but that it needs to be managed. Some parenting programmes have been adapted for different populations, and developers increasingly distinguish between core and adaptable elements. Adaptation is arguably most successful when the logic model is respected, and the developer is consulted.

The most effective parenting programmes adopt strategies to increase fidelity. These include using a manual, targeting the right users, recruiting suitable practitioners, providing adequate training and support, ensuring that the implementing organisation is ready and supportive, and monitoring what practitioners actually do. The same programmes also stress aspects of adherence (e.g., the importance of role play rehearsal of new skills) and quality and user engagement (e.g., the importance of the practitioner building a reciprocal relationship with parents).

At the same time, there is much about fidelity that is not known. Studies that test the relationship between fidelity and outcomes prospectively are needed. Fidelity can be varied deliberately to help with understanding a range of issues, including: what constitutes the optimal degree of adherence and exposure; how much adaptation is permissible before an intervention becomes ineffective; what type of adaptation is most beneficial or least detrimental (e.g., modification, addition or subtraction, and concerning which dimensions of fidelity); and whether or how different dimensions of fidelity should be weighted (e.g., if high quality compensates for low exposure).

Regarding the issue of weighting, it is noticeable that most studies that measure fidelity tend to focus more on adherence and exposure than on quality of delivery. This may be because quality is harder to conceptualise and measure. But quality may be a key part of why high fidelity ensures outcomes: better therapists are able to hold core principles while adapting procedures or the form of delivery to suit clients; however, practitioners who deliver the entire programme to the letter but do it poorly may decrease engagement, and outcomes will not be achieved. Proven parenting programmes emphasise starting with the parents' own goals, building on existing strengths, and adopting a user-led and collaborative approach. This requires an interpretation of fidelity that goes beyond 'doing what the manual tells you' and ensuring high-quality delivery of the principles and protocols in order to engage and work with the individual given his/her particular circumstances and needs.

Another issue requiring more attention concerns core components. Often, the core components of an intervention – defined in terms of its *active ingredients* or mechanisms (i.e., the elements that make the intervention work) – are hypothesised only; they have not been tested (or

---

[4] www.blueprintsprograms.com.

verified) through empirical analysis. Thus, claims that adherence to these components ensures impact and that modifying them reduces impact may be unfounded. Equally, supposed non-core components may be more important than originally thought: we tamper in ignorance. While canvassing intervention designers may help with identifying what are believed to be 'essential' elements, it is preferable to conduct 'component analysis' (Carroll, Patterson, Wood et al., 2007). This requires methods such as deliberately varying what is delivered and seeing what effect this has or conducting statistical mediator analyses to trace which parts of the logic model are realised in practice.

A further research topic involves determining the optimal balance between allowing enough flexibility to promote scale-up without reducing effectiveness. While high-fidelity implementation may increase impact, it may reduce the likelihood of the intervention becoming integrated in mainstream provision. Of course, this – and other issues referred to in this concluding section – may vary depending on the subject area. Care is needed to discriminate carefully between what applies in one area, such as group-based parenting programmes, and what holds in another, such as individual therapy.

Future studies could also examine the extent to which the type of person delivering the intervention affects fidelity and outcomes. One issue is whether professionals perform better than trained volunteers. Another concerns the relative importance of experience compared with training; for instance, it may be more important to be familiar with working with struggling families and good at empathising than to have specified qualifications.

Some of these issues potentially have important cost implications. For example, if an 8-week programme achieves the same impact as the 12-week version, it makes sense to implement the shorter one and save up to a third of the delivery costs. Similarly, if using volunteers achieves, for example, 80% of the impact achieved when professionals deliver the programme, then it might be prudent to use volunteers, particularly if it makes the difference between implementing the intervention and not having enough money to do so. However, when the population concerns children and families with great need, such as those suffering neglect or abuse, programme developers advocate a more intense (longer) programme delivery by experienced, highly qualified, practitioners (Webster-Stratton & Reid, 2010).

While much about fidelity remains unknown, it is important to measure fidelity in efficacy and effectiveness studies because these fidelity constructs can help to explain the results. For instance, if a programme has no, or less than expected, impact, it may be because the intervention was not implemented properly. It is essential to study fidelity in real-life settings and not just clinical trials where additional support to boost fidelity may be available (Hasson, 2015).

When studies measure fidelity, including evaluations of parenting programmes, the studies should consider the following (Hasson, 2015). First, it is optimal to measure the core components. If these are not known (as is often the case), then all components should be measured. Second, in order to gain a full picture of fidelity, all dimensions – adherence, exposure, quality and so on – should be examined. To assist with this, when interventions are designed they should be described in terms of these dimensions. Third, it makes sense to collect fidelity data for the duration of an intervention since fidelity is likely to fluctuate over time. Adherence may be higher at the outset, for instance, when practitioners are fresh from training, enthusiastic, and reluctant to deviate from the materials; however, quality may increase over time. Finally, a multi-method approach that involves a selection of observation, self-report, interview and document review helps to gain a fuller picture. Observations are expensive and time-consuming, but they capture additions that practitioners make (practitioners often do not reflect on the adaptations they make).

References

Asmussen, K.A., Matthews, T., Weizel, K. et al. (2012). *Evaluation of the National Academy of Parenting Practitioners' Training Offer in evidence based parenting programmes.* DFE-RR186. London: Department for Education.

Axford, N., Barlow, J., Coad, J. et al. (2015). *The best start at home: What works to improve the quality of parent–child interactions from conception to age 5 years? A rapid review of interventions.* London: Early Intervention Foundation.

Axford, N., Lehtonen, M., Tobin, K. et al. (2012). Engaging parents in parenting programs: Lessons from research and practice. *Children & Youth Services Review* 34, 2061–2071.

Baker, C.N., Arnold, D.H. & Meagher, S. (2011). Enrollment and attendance in a parent training prevention program for conduct problems. *Prevention Science*, 12, 126–138.

Bandura, A. (1977). *Social Learning Theory.* Englewood Cliffs, NJ: Prentice Hall.

Barlow, J., Johnston, I., Kendrick, D. et al. (2006). Individual and group-based parenting programmes for the treatment of physical child abuse and neglect. *Cochrane Database of Systematic Reviews* 2006, Issue 3. Art. No.: CD005463.

Barlow, J., Smailagic, N., Ferriter, M. et al. (2010). Group-based parent training programmes for improving emotional and behavioural adjustment in children from birth to three years old. Cochrane Database of Systematic Reviews 2010, Issue 3. Art. No.: CD003680.

Barlow, J., Smailagic, N., Huband, N. et al. (2012). Group-based parent training programmes for improving parental psychosocial health. Cochrane Database of Systematic Reviews 2012, Issue 6. Art. No.: CD002020.

Barnes, J., Ball, M., Meadows, P. et al. (2008). *Nurse-Family Partnership Programme: First year pilot sites implementation in England: Pregnancy and the post-partum period.* Research Report DCSF-RW051. London: Department for Children, Schools and Families.

Bellg, A.J., Borrelli, B., Resnick, B. et al. (2004). Enhancing treatment fidelity in health behavior change studies: Best practices and recommendations from the NIH Behavior Change Consortium. *Health Psychology*, 23, 443.

Berman, P. & McLaughlin, M.W. (1978). *Federal programs supporting educational change, vol. VIII: Implementing and sustaining innovations.* Santa Monica, California: Rand.

Berry, V., Axford, N., Blower, S. et al. (2014). Prevention of child maltreatment. In: J. Conte (ed) *Child Abuse and Neglect Worldwide.* Santa Barbara CA: Praeger.

Blakely, C.H., Mayer, J.P., Gottschalk, R.G. et al. (1987). The fidelity-adaptation debate: Implications for the implementation of public sector social programs. *American Journal of Community Psychology*, 15, 253–268.

Bodenmann, G., Cina, A., Ledermann, T. & Sanders, M.R. (2008). The efficacy of the Triple P-Positive Parenting Program in improving parenting and child behavior: A comparison with two other treatment conditions. *Behavior Research and Therapy*, 46, 411–427.

Botvin, G.J., Baker, E., Dusenbury, L. et al. (1990). Preventing adolescent drug abuse through a multimodal cognitive-behavioral approach: Results of a 3-year study. *Journal of Consulting and Clinical Psychology*, 58, 437–446.

Botvin, G.J., Baker, E., Filazzola, A. & Botvin, E. (1990). A cognitive-behavioral approach to substance abuse prevention: One-year follow-up. *Addictive Behaviors*, 15, 47–63.

Breitenstein, S.M., Fogg, L., Garvey, C. et al. (2010). Measuring implementation fidelity in a community-based parenting intervention. *Nursing Research*, 59, 158–165.

Bumbarger, B. & Perkins, D. (2008). After randomised trials: Issues related to dissemination of evidence-based interventions. *Journal of Children's Services*, 3, 55–64.

Carroll, C., Patterson, M., Wood, S. et al. (2007). A conceptual framework for implementation fidelity. *Implementation Science*, 2, 1–9.

Castro, F.G., Barrera, M. & Martinez, C.R. (2004). The cultural adaptation of prevention interventions: Resolving tensions between fidelity and fit. *Prevention Science*, 5, 41–45.

Dane, A.V. & Schneider, B.H. (1998). Program integrity in primary and early secondary prevention: Are implementation effects out of control? *Clinical Psychology Review*, 18, 23–45.

Day, C., Michelson, D., Thomson, S. et al. (2012). Evaluation of a peer led parenting intervention for disruptive behaviour problems in children: Community based randomised controlled trial. *BMJ* 2012; 344:e1107.

Dearing, J.W. (2008). Evolution of diffusion and dissemination theory. *Journal of Public Health Management and Practice*, 14, 99–108.

Dixon, J., Biehal, N., Green, J. et al. (2014). Trials and tribulations: Challenges and prospects for randomised controlled trials of social work with children. *British Journal of Social Work*, 44, 1563–1581.

Durlak, J.A. (2010). The importance of doing well in whatever you do: A commentary on the special section, Implementation research in early childhood education. *Early Childhood Research Quarterly*, 25, 348–357.

Durlak, J.A. & DuPre, E.P. (2008). Implementation matters: A review of research on the influence of implementation on program outcomes and the factors affecting implementation. *American Journal of Community Psychology*, 41, 327–350.

Dusenbury, L., Brannigan, R., Falco, M. & Hansen, W.B. (2003). A review of research on fidelity of implementation: Implications for drug abuse prevention in school settings. *Health Education Research*, 18, 237–56.

Eames, C., Daley, D., Hutchings, J. et al. (2009). Treatment fidelity as a predictor of behaviour change in parents attending group based intervention. *Child Care Health and Development*, 35, 603–612.

Elliott, D.S. & Mihalic, S. (2004). Issues in disseminating and replicating effective prevention programs. *Prevention Science* 5, 47–53.

Fixsen, D.L., Louis de la Parte Florida Mental Health Institute & University of South Florida (2005). *Implementation research: A synthesis of the literature*. Tampa, Florida: National Implementation Research Network.

Forgatch, M.S., Patterson, G.R. & DeGarmo, D.S. (2006). Evaluating fidelity: Predictive validity for a measure of competent adherence to the Oregon model of parent management training. *Behavior Therapy*, 36, 3–13.

Forgatch, M.S. & DeGarmo, D.S. (2011). Sustaining fidelity following the nationwide PMTO™ implementation in Norway. *Prevention Science*, 12, 235–246.

Forgatch, M.S., Patterson, G.R. & Gewirtz, A.H. (2013). Looking forward: The promise of widespread implementation of parent training programs. *Perspectives on Psychological Science*, 8, 682–694.

Furlong, M., McGilloway, S., Bywater, T. et al. (2012). Behavioral and cognitive-behavioural group-based parenting interventions for early-onset conduct problems in children age 3–12 years. *Cochrane Database of Systematic Reviews*, Issue 2. Art. No.: CD008225.

Garbacz, L.L., Brown, D.M., Spee, G.A. et al. (2014). Establishing treatment fidelity in evidence-based parent training programs for externalizing disorders in children and adolescents. *Clinical Child and Family Psychology Review*, 17, 230–247.

Gardner, F., Burton, J. & Klimes, I. (2006). Randomized controlled trial of a parenting intervention in the voluntary sector for reducing conduct problems in children: Outcomes and mechanisms of change. *Journal of Child Psychology and Psychiatry*, 47, 1123–1132.

Gardner, F., Montgomery, P. & Knerr, W. (2015). Transporting evidence-based parenting programs for child problem behaviour (age 3–10) between countries: Systematic review and meta-analysis. *Journal of Clinical Child & Adolescent Psychology*, 1–14.

Gardner, F., Hutchings, J., Bywater, T. & Whitaker, C. (2010). Who benefits and how does it work? Moderators and mediators of outcome in an effectiveness trial of a parenting intervention. *Journal of Clinical Child & Adolescent Psychology*, 39, 1–13.

Gersten, R., Fuchs, L., Compton, D. et al. (2005). Quality indicators for group experimental and quasi-experimental research in special education. *Exceptional Children*, 71, 149–164.

Green, D.P., Goldman, S.L. & Salovey, P. (1993). Measurement error masks bipolarity in affect ratings. *Journal of Personality and Social Psychology*, 64, 1029–1041.

Green, J., Biehal, N., Roberts, C. et al. (2014). Multidimensional treatment foster care for adolescents in English care: Randomised trial and observational cohort evaluation. *British Journal of Psychiatry*, 204, 214–221.

Hansen, W.B., Graham, J.W., Wolkenstein, B.H. & Rohrbach, L.A. (1991). Program integrity as a moderator of prevention program effectiveness: Results for fifth-grade students in the adolescent alcohol prevention trial. *Journal of Studies on Alcohol*, 52, 568–579.

Harn, B., Parisi, D. & Stoolmiller, M. (2014). Balancing fidelity with flexibility and fit: What do we really know about fidelity of implementation in schools? *Exceptional Children*, 79, 181–193.

Hasson, H. (2015). Intervention fidelity in clinical trials. In: D.A. Richards & I.R. Hallberg (eds), *Complex Interventions in Health: An Overview if Research Methods*. London: Routledge.

Hogue, A., Henderson, C.E., Dauber, S. et al. (2008). Treatment adherence, competence and outcome in individual and family therapy for adolescent behavior problems. *Journal of Consulting and Clinical Psychology*, 76, 544.

Hutchings, J., Gardner, F. & Lane, E. (2004). Making evidence based interventions work in clinical settings: Common and specific therapy factors and implementation fidelity. In: C. Sutton, D. Utting & D. Farrington (eds), *Support from the start: Working with young children and their families to reduce the risks of crime and antisocial behaviour*. Research Report 524. London: Department for Education and Skills.

Hutchings, J., Bywater, T., Eames, C. & Martin, P. (2008). Implementing child mental health interventions in service settings: Lessons from three pragmatic randomised controlled trials in Wales. *Journal of Children's Services*, 3, 17–27.

Hutchings, J., Bywater, T., Daley, D. et al. (2007). A pragmatic randomised control trial of a parenting intervention in Sure Start services for children at risk of developing conduct disorder. *British Medical Journal*, 334, 678–682.

Johnson, R. & Wilson, H. (2012). Parents' evaluation of 'Understanding Your Child's Behaviour', a parenting group based on the Solihull Approach. *Community Practitioner*, 85, 29–33.

Kam, C., Greenberg, M.T. & Walls, C.T. (2003). Examining the role of implementation quality in school-based prevention using the PATHS curriculum. *Prevention Science*, 4, 55–63.

Kling, A., Forster, M., Sundell, K. & Melin, L. (2010). A randomised controlled effectiveness trial of parent management training with varying degrees of therapist support. *Behavior Therapy*, 41, 530–542.

Kretlow, A.G. & Bartholomew, C. (2010). Using coaching to improve the fidelity of evidence-based practices: A review of studies. *Teacher Education and Special Education*, 33, 279–299.

Lee, C.-Y., August, G., Realmuto, G. et al. (2008). Fidelity at a distance: Assessing implementation fidelity of the Early Risers prevention program in a going-to-scale intervention trial. *Prevention Science*, 9, 215–229.

Lindsay, G. Strand, S., Cullen, M.A. et al. (2011). *Parenting Early Intervention Programme evaluation*. DFE-RR121A. London: Department for Education.

Little, M., Berry, V., Morpeth, L. et al. (2012). The impact of three evidence-based programmes delivered in public systems in Birmingham, UK. *International Journal of Conflict and Violence*, 6, 260–272.

Malti, T., Ribeaud, D. & Eisner, M. (2011). The effects of two universal preventive interventions to reduce children's externalizing behavior: A cluster-randomized controlled trial. *Journal of Clinical Child and Adolescent Psychology*, 40, 677–692.

Martin, A.J. & Sanders, M.R. (2003). Balancing work and family: A controlled evaluation of the Triple P-Positive Parenting Program as a work-site intervention. *Child and Adolescent Mental Health*, 8, 161–169.

Mihalic, S. (2004). The importance of implementation fidelity. *Emotional & Behavioral Disorders in Youth*, 4, 83–86.

Mihalic, S., Fagan, A. & Argamaso, S. (2008). Implementing the LifeSkills Training drug prevention program: Factors related to implementation fidelity. *Implementation Science*, 3, 1–16.

Mihalic, S., Fagan, A., Irwin, K. et al. (2002). *Blueprints for violence prevention replications: Factors for implementation success.* Boulder, CO: University of Colorado, Center for the Study and Prevention of Violence.

Mountford, A. & Darton, S. (2013). Family Links response to: Effectiveness and cost effectiveness of a universal parenting skills programme in deprived communities: Multicentre randomised controlled trial – Simkiss et al. E-letter. *BMJ Open*, http://bmjopen.bmj.com/content/3/8/e002851.full/reply#bmjopen_el_7253 (accessed 25 September 2015).

MRC (Medical Research Council) (2008). *Developing and evaluating complex interventions: New guidance*, www.mrc.ac.uk/complexinterventionsguidance (accessed 25 September 2015).

Olds, D.L., Henderson, C.R., Chamberlin, R. & Tatelbaum, R. (1986). Preventing child abuse and neglect: A randomized trial of nurse home visitation. *Pediatrics*, 78, 65–78.

Pentz, M.A., Trebow, E., Hansen, W.B. et al. (1990). Effects of program implementation on adolescent drug use behavior: The Midwestern Prevention Project (MPP). *Evaluation Review*, 14, 264–289.

Puckering, C., Cox, A., Mills, M. et al. (2013). The impact of intensive family support on mothers and children: Mellow Parenting programme, www.mellowparenting.org (accessed 19 September 2015).

Rohrbach, L.A., Graham, J.W. & Hansen, W.B. (1993). Diffusion of a school-based substance abuse prevention program: Predictors of program implementation. *Preventive Medicine*, 22, 237–260.

Sanders, M.R. & McFarland, M. (2000). Treatment of depressed mothers with disruptive children: A controlled evaluation of cognitive behavioral family intervention. *Behavior Therapy*, 31, 89–112.

Sanders, M.R., Kirby, J.N., Tellegen, C.L. & Day, J.J. (2014). The Triple P-Positive Parenting Program: A systematic review and meta-analysis of a multi-level system of parenting support. *Clinical Psychology Review*, 34, 658.

Scott, S., Carby, A. & Rendu, A. (2008). *Impact of therapists' skill on effectiveness of parenting programmes for child antisocial behaviour.* London: Kings College London, Institute of Psychiatry, and University College London.

Scott, S., Spender, Q., Doolan, M. et al. (2001). Multicentre controlled trial of parenting groups for child antisocial behaviour in clinical practice. *British Medical Journal*, 323, 1–5.

Simkiss, D.E., Snooks, H.A., Stallard, N. et al. (2013). Effectiveness and cost-effectiveness of a universal parenting skills programme in deprived communities: Multicentre randomised controlled trial. *BMJ Open*, 3, e002851.

Simmons, D., Kame'enui, E., Harn, B. et al. (2007). Attributes of effective and efficient kindergarten reading intervention: An examination of instructional time and design specificity. *Journal of Learning Disabilities*, 40, 331–347.

Tracey, L., Bywater, T., Blower, S. et al. (2014). *Public involvement in research: Social emotional well-being in early years.* York: Institute for Effective Education, University of York.

Von Hippel, E. (2005). *Democratizing Innovation.* Cambridge, MA: The MIT Press.

Von Thiele Schwartz, U., Hasson, H. & Lindfors, P. (2015). Applying a fidelity framework to understand adaptations in an occupational health intervention. *WORK: A Journal of Prevention, Assessment & Rehabilitation*, 51, 195–203.

Webster-Stratton, C. & Hammond, M. (1997). Treating children with early-onset conduct problems: A comparison of child and parent training interventions. *Journal of Consulting and Clinical Psychology* 65, 93–109.

Webster-Stratton, C. & Reid, M. (2010). Adapting the Incredible Years, an evidence-based parenting programme, for families involved in the child welfare system. *Journal of Children's Services*, 5, 25–42.

Webster-Stratton, C., Newcomer, L.L., Herman, K.C. & Reinke, W.M. (2011). The Incredible Years Teacher Classroom Management Training: The methods and principles that support fidelity of training delivery. *School Psychology Review*, 40, 509–529.

Westermark, P.K., Hansson, K. & Olsson, M. (2011). Multidimensional Treatment Foster Care (MTFC): Results from an independent replication. *Journal of Family Therapy*, 33, 20–41.

22

School-Based Prevention of and Intervention in Child Maltreatment

Current Practice in the United States and Future Directions

Cristin M. Hall, Megan C. Runion and Daniel F. Perkins

The Pennsylvania State University

It is estimated that over 600,000 children experience physical, sexual or psychological maltreatment each year in the United States (Kids Count Data Center, 2014). Children who have experienced maltreatment are subject to a cascade of effects given that physical, psychological and behavioural development are inextricably linked together, all having an impact on the other. The US Department of Health and Human Services (2013) reports that physical consequences, specifically brain injury or stilted neurological development from abuse and neglect, will have concomitant effects on a child's ability to learn and regulate their behaviour and emotions that may have subsequent negative effects on future functioning. Although they caution that not all children who experience abuse and neglect will have these kinds of long-lasting effects, the stark reality of how children may be put at such a striking disadvantage in their development cannot be ignored.

The United Nations Convention on the Rights of the Child 1989 requires participating UN States to take legislative, administrative and other measures to protect children from abuse (Mathews, 2014). Although this convention is not yet ratified in the United States, schools are important contexts for the detection, reporting, prevention of and intervention in child maltreatment, and in the US school personnel including teachers, school psychologists, guidance counsellors and principals are bound by mandated reporting laws (Child Welfare Information Gateway, 2014). School serves as one of the most important contexts for child development in that it is in effect their primary learning environment for social skill development, academic learning and adult supervision. As such, schools may serve either as a protective environment or an environment whereby children are exposed to further stress (Hart, 1988). Specifically, schools may provide supportive environments where children at risk or who have been victims of maltreatment may be identified, referred for appropriate treatment, provided with a structured day with caring adults and exposed to pro-social peers.

Unfortunately, due to school-level policies and practices, poorly supported staff, and peer-level aggression and rejection, schools may also simply be an extension of whatever trauma children are experiencing in the home environment (Deb & Walsh, 2012; Frederick & Goddard, 2010; Hart, 1988), thus compounding their relative risk for poor outcomes later in life. Schools may struggle to support students in a variety of ways. In particular, schools may have difficulty with classroom or behaviour management, inadequate instructional materials and curricula, insufficient pre- and post-referral services for special education, and administrative or financial concerns that have a significant impact on school personnel and students. More specific to child maltreatment, schools may not have adequate resources for professional development, consultation and intervention related to children who are victims of maltreatment. Sadly, there are more concerning reports regarding school personnel-to-student sexual abuse with which local, State and Federal agencies have not adequately dealt (GAO-14-42, 2014). The prevalence of victimisation of children by school personnel is unknown, yet increases in media reports and recommendations by the US Government Accountability Office strongly indicate that current efforts at detection, prevention and intervention are inadequate at this time, putting children at risk.

School personnel at the teacher, student services and administrative levels grapple with how best to serve children at risk and are in need of guidance on issues of professional development, mandated reporting, prevention programming, their role in intervention and referral, and policy decisions. In order to address these concerns, this chapter seeks to examine the current status of school-based detection, prevention and intervention for child maltreatment. Empirical evidence and perspectives on the fields of school psychology, school-based prevention, and school and community cooperation will be discussed in an effort to clarify 'where we are' and 'where we are going' in regard to child maltreatment. Woven through the discussion, we will explore these topics using the United States' Institutes of Medicine (IOM) Protractor (Figure 22.1) as a framework to examine multi-tiered levels of prevention, treatment and maintenance initiatives that may guide conceptualisation of school-based child maltreatment efforts.

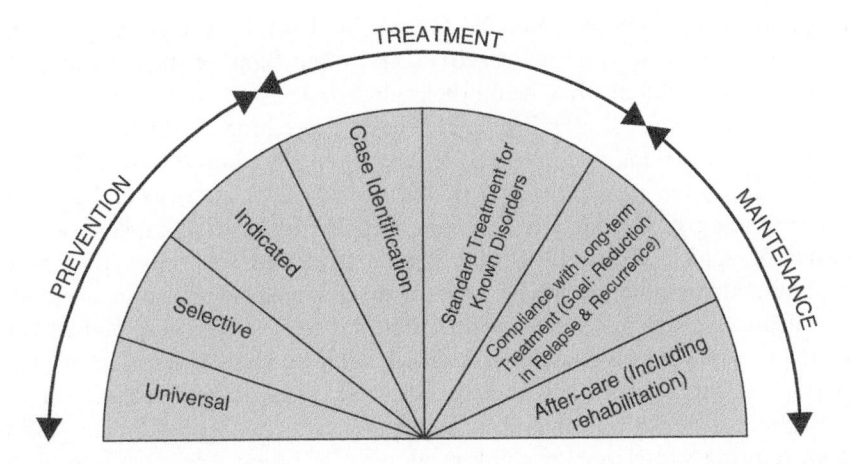

Figure 22.1 IOM Protractor. Source: Springer 2006. Reproduced with permission of Community Prevention Institute (CPI).

Perspectives on the Role of School Personnel

Serving children at risk has long been recognised as a complicated and challenging task (Fantuzzo, McWayne & Bulotsky, 2003). Several researchers have called for the adoption of collaborative public health models to serve children in school contexts. Children who are exposed to the multiple risks associated with poverty (including risk for child maltreatment) may not benefit from traditional or clinical service models, which take place away from the context of the problems they face and generally struggle with issues of cultural relevance and attrition. Specifically, Fantuzzo and colleagues proposed a population-based, child-centred framework to serve urban, low-income children in Head Start programmes. Although this model is not specifically tied to child maltreatment efforts, it provides an exemplar of current attempts to create better interdisciplinary practices and inter-agency cooperation to improve outcomes for children. The authors assert that if the whole child is recognised, collaborative efforts can become less cumbersome and make a difference to support children in their development.

Other perspectives on child maltreatment efforts in schools relate to social justice and human rights promotion (Hart & Hart, 2014). Hart and Hart's (2014) article reviews the historical and current relevance of the United Nations Convention on the Rights of the Child in school psychologist practice. School psychologists are often in a 'gate-keeper' role, which requires that they be leaders in school efforts and in promoting practices (i.e., academic, social, emotional and behavioural) that support the overall school success of children; thus, they are active and important participants in effecting school practice and change. The UN Convention on the Rights of the Child outlined international ambitions for establishing better protection and promotion of child well-being. Although the Convention outlines a variety of goals to support children that include prevention of economic exploitation and protection of civil rights, it also specifically recommends protection from a variety of sources of maltreatment to include physical violence, sexual exploitation, substance abuse, human trafficking and even self-harm. Viewing the school's efforts in child maltreatment from the perspective of social justice is not a commonly discussed perspective, yet it provides an important reminder of the broader implications and themes around prioritising child maltreatment protection. In the midst of everything that schools are charged with doing and all of the various ways in which they are accountable (e.g., US laws: No Child Left Behind Act, US Individuals with Disabilities Education Improvement Act), schools likely do not often think of their broader mission to serve as protectors of children while being their educators.

More recent work on the role of school personnel in preventing child maltreatment includes a qualitative survey of school psychologists in the United Kingdom (Woods, Bond, Tyldesley et al., 2011). The authors were able to conduct focus groups, site visits and a questionnaire with school psychologists nationwide, although they did not provide a specific description of the size or demographic composition of their sample. In their description of their findings, the authors highlighted the potential role of school psychologists in the areas of identification, procedural safeguards, evaluation of individual children, professional development and parent outreach, and advocacy for vulnerable or disabled children. Despite these critical tasks being viewed by respondents as important, there were several areas of concern, including the need for better methods of identification and further training in child maltreatment, and the need for better prioritising protection of children within the varied roles and responsibilities of school psychologists. Although arguably this study does not address the particular needs of United States school systems and child protection services, or the role of other school professionals such as school nurses, administrators, teachers or guidance counsellors, it likely outlines parallel concerns and considerations for the role of school professionals in child maltreatment prevention and intervention.

The IOM Protractor: A Conceptual Framework from Public Health

Given the serious ramifications of preventing and effectively intervening in cases of child maltreatment, it is imperative that education professionals have a guiding framework for conceptualising the design, coordination and execution of programming. Further, any attempts to put system-wide change in place must take into consideration the current needs, capacity and training of those whose role it is to carry out these endeavours, so that they might be more readily adopted and sustained within schools. Education researchers and leaders in the field have begun to adopt three-tiered service models for preventing maltreatment and supporting development of students in academic, behavioural and social–emotional domains. The advent of such initiatives such as Response to Intervention (RtI; Tilly, 2008) and School-Wide Positive Behaviour Intervention and Support (SWPBIS; Sugai & Horner, 2002) have changed the way school personnel think about supporting students, which is in some ways very similar to public health models for disease prevention and management. Models such as RtI and SWPBIS have been helpful in providing a framework with guiding principles such as universal screening, progress-monitoring, evidence-based intervention and curriculum provision at all levels, and accountability that still allows schools to choose curricula and procedures that are relevant and sustainable in their unique school district.

The adoption of a tiered service-delivery model may similarly provide the same scaffold and guiding principles for schools that are in need of a more comprehensive approach to child maltreatment. Currently, models such as RtI utilise a three-tiered model that include universal, selective and indicated levels of intervention, although some models use different descriptors for those levels. While the three tiers provide a useful framework, in the case of child maltreatment, the IOM Protractor may be an important extension (see Figure 22.1). The Protractor includes broad areas of prevention, treatment and maintenance as part of the model. The terms universal, selective and indicated are under the prevention umbrella and treatment and maintenance are distinct. The treatment section includes case identification and standard treatment for known disorders. Finally, the maintenance section includes compliance with both long-term care and after-care.

School professionals often are overwhelmed with many demands for compliance and accountability, which may make the Protractor framework seem insurmountable. However, the implementation of all levels of the framework need not be considered to be the sole responsibility of educators, but rather should occur in cooperation with other stakeholders. Universal, selective and indicated programming for students, teachers and parents to educate about warning signs, mandated reporting, and how to ask for help could be integrated into existing social–emotional learning, professional development or community outreach initiatives. Under the treatment area, case identification can be thought of as part of mandated reporting efforts, a part of health screening, or as providing resources for parents to ask for help from community or school-based professionals.

At the levels of treatment and maintenance, partnerships between home, school and community providers are essential (Herrera & Carey, 1993). In instances when children are at risk or have been abused or neglected, school personnel have a reasonable responsibility to be familiar with available community resources and to make appropriate referrals. Specifically, for maintenance of treatment to include compliance and after-care, educators could provide support in several important ways. First, if parents are agreeable to signing release of information forms, even on a limited, need-to-know basis, school professionals can provide important insight to community providers about academic and social–emotional adjustment, which may inform treatment goals and provide indicators of overall progress in children's school context. Regular updates from teachers, a guidance counsellor or other identified point of contact may inform goals in community-based services. Second, community providers, provided there is written consent from the parent or guardian, may also provide important progress updates to schools, provide information about current goals, and offer helpful suggestions about how to assist a child in need. Schools, in turn, can help with maintaining and sustaining those strategies and supports for children.

The remainder of this chapter will review current research on existing prevention and education programmes used in schools as well as current research on interventions for students who have been victimised. While it may sometimes be appropriate or feasible to provide direct service to victims, community-based providers may also be utilised for treatment.

Prevention: School- and Community-Based Educational Programming for Child Maltreatment

There are many school- and community-based programmes designed to help educate children about child physical, sexual and psychological abuse and how to ask for help (Fantuzzo, Stevenson, Weiss et al., 1997; Topping & Barron, 2009). Broadly, these programmes can be designed for:

- professionals (e.g., Child sexual abuse prevention: Teacher training workshop, Kleemeier, Webb, Hazzard & Pohl, 1988; Clearinghouse for Military Family Readiness, 2012a);
- parents (e.g., Parenting Our Children to Excellence [PACE], Begle & Dumas, 2011; Begle et al., 2012; Dumas et al., 2010; Clearinghouse for Military Family Readiness, 2014b);
- children (e.g., Safe Child Program, www.safechild.org, Fryer et al., 1987; Clearinghouse for Military Family Readiness, 2012c; Who Do You Tell?, Tutty, 1997, www.whodoyoutell.com; Clearinghouse for Military Family Readiness, 2012d); or
- families as a whole (e.g., Family Wellness: Survival Skills for Healthy Families, www.familywellness.com; Clearinghouse for Military Family Readiness, 2014d).

Some prevention programmes are geared toward a school-based audience, while others are designed for use in community settings such as recreation centres or churches. Many of the programmes are designed for universal prevention efforts, although some, such as PACE, are also designed to assist at-risk families. Selective or targeted prevention programmes (e.g., SafeCare®; Chaffin, Hecht, Bard et al., 2012) are better suited for community providers as they are typically home-visiting models for families who have been reported for possible child abuse or neglect or those identified at risk for child maltreatment.

Critical reviews and meta-analyses of the effectiveness of such psychoeducational prevention programmes have primarily focused on the impact of programmes that target child sexual abuse (Barron & Topping, 2013; Davis & Gidycz, 2000; Ko & Cosden, 2001; Topping &

Barron, 2009). Davis and Gidycz (2000) conducted a meta-analysis of child sexual abuse prevention programmes including 73 separate published and unpublished studies. Outcomes examined were prevention-related knowledge and skills but did not include actual reporting behaviour of children. Generally, higher effect sizes were found for unpublished studies and those with methodological problems. Overall, the analysis demonstrated that programmes that included sound instructional practices (e.g., modelling, practice and reinforcement) and included three or more sessions on the material had the most impact on skills and knowledge. Younger children, those in preschool and elementary school, also benefited the most from such programming. Another review of the impact of educational prevention programmes indicated similar findings for the benefits of including modelling, discussion, distributed sessions and active parent input (Topping & Barron, 2009). Unfortunately, methodological challenges across studies of these programmes include difficulty with how to reliably measure reductions in abuse and increases in reports.

Although proximal outcomes immediately after participation in a child abuse prevention programme may be promising, questions remain about long-term impact on knowledge, skills and prevention of abuse for those students who participate. In a high-school follow-up study by Ko and Cosden (2001), the authors were able to collect data from students who had completed elementary or middle school prevention programmes and those who had not been exposed to such programming (N=137). There were mixed results regarding abuse-related knowledge between groups. Specifically, there were no statistically significant differences in general abuse-related knowledge between groups, but those students who participated in a prevention programme did score higher than those who did not on a subset of knowledge questions that were specific to content taught in the prevention programme. For example, students who had participated in a prevention programme were more likely to correctly answer questions about victim-blaming but still had limited knowledge of date rape and pornography. Students who utilised learnt strategies when mistreated by a known abuser less often reported that the strategies were effective (34%) compared to those students who were abused by an unknown person (62%). The authors admitted that prevention programming may have differential impacts for students with known abusers (e.g., interfamily, neighbours, coaches and family friends) and those with unknown abusers (e.g., persons known to them more casually or strangers).

In a recent review by Brassard and Fiorvanti (2015), core components of successful school-based prevention programmes for child sexual abuse were examined. Specifically, the authors highlighted the Safe Child Program (Kraizer, Witte & Fryer, 1989), Stay Safe Program (MacIntyre, Carr, Lawlor & Flattery, 2000), Talking about Touching (Sylvester, 1997), and the Body Safety Training Program (Wurtele, Kast, Miller-Perrin & Kondrick, 1989) as those that were in line with broadly identified best practices in prevention of child sexual abuse for direct child training programmes. Generally, the review identified several strategies that have led to better outcomes including: opportunities for practice and varied presentation modalities (e.g., video, discussion and role play); longer duration of programmes and more sessions with distributed practice and learning; family involvement; and developmentally appropriate instructional techniques for young children. The authors noted that in their review there were no known child-focused prevention programmes on interpersonal violence or psychological maltreatment designed for school delivery. Although there may not be programmes specifically for these purposes that are designed for school-based delivery, there are some programmes (see Table 22.1) delivered in community contexts that address violence prevention more broadly (e.g., Green Dot) and programmes that are geared toward improved family interactions (e.g., Family Wellness: Survival Skills for Healthy Families); however, these programmes have limited empirical support at this time.

Table 22.1 Child maltreatment programmes.

Programme	Placement on Clearinghouse Continuum of Evidence[a]	Target population	Sector	Summary
Child Sexual Abuse Prevention: Teacher Training Workshop (Clearinghouse for Military Family Readiness, 2012a)	Unclear +	Providers	School-based	The Child sexual abuse prevention: Teacher training workshop (Child Sexual Abuse Prevention) is a 6-hour training for K-12 teachers. Its purpose is to increase teacher awareness of child sexual abuse, help teachers recognise signs of sexual abuse, and increase teacher reporting of suspected abuse.
Child-Parent Center (CPC) Program (Clearinghouse for Military Family Readiness, 2013a)	Promising	Children, Parents	Family-based, Medical setting, School-based	The CPC Program is for low-income families with children age 3 to 9. It aims to support academic success and parent involvement. In addition to school-related improvements compared to a control group, participating families had fewer substantiated maltreatment incidents and showed long-term positive outcomes.
Criando a Nuestros Ninos hacia el Exito (CANNE; Clearinghouse for Military Family Readiness, 2014a)	Unclear +	Parents	School-based	CANNE is the Spanish adaptation of PACE. It involves behavioural training for Latino parents of preschoolers to improve parent–child interactions and parenting practices, and to decrease child behaviour problems.
Family Wellness: Survival Skills for Healthy Families (Clearinghouse for Military Family Readiness, 2014b)	Unclear Ø	Families	Community-based, Faith-based, School-based	The Family Wellness programme is for families with children 8 years of age and older. It focuses on parenting skills, family functioning and couple relationships.
Girls Inc. Project BOLD (Clearinghouse for Military Family Readiness, 2013b)	Unclear Ø	Adolescents, Children	Community-based, School-based	The Girls Inc. Project BOLD programme is for girls age 6 to 18. It focuses on physical and personal safety, emphasising self-defence strategies and help seeking.
Green Dot etc. (Clearinghouse for Military Family Readiness, 2014c)	Unclear +	Adults, Providers, Service Members	Community-based, School-based, Work site	Green Dot etc. is a community-level programme that focuses on social norms and promotes bystander engagement in order to prevent violence and increase safe intervention.

(*Continued*)

Table 22.1 (Cont'd)

Programme	Placement on Clearinghouse Continuum of Evidence[a]	Target population	Sector	Summary
Parenting Our Children to Excellence (PACE; Clearinghouse for Military Family Readiness, 2014d)	Unclear +	Parents	School-based	PACE is a behavioural training programme for parents of children aged 3 to 6 years. Parent–child interactions are targeted through increased parental satisfaction and self-efficacy and decreased parent stress. Targets of child outcomes include improved coping skills and decreased problem behaviours.
Safe Child Program (Clearinghouse for Military Family Readiness, 2012b)	Promising	Children	School-based	The Safe Child Program is for children in preschool through third grade. It teaches young children skills for reducing risk of abuse and increasing personal safety. Participants were shown to be more likely than a comparison group to resist advances from a stranger.
TOUCH (Clearinghouse for Military Family Readiness, 2015b)	Unclear +	Children	School-based	TOUCH involves a performance by trained high-school students for elementary students, which aims to teach schoolchildren about maltreatment and how to refuse inappropriate touches.
The School Success Program (Mallett, 2012)	N/A	Adolescents, Children, Families	Family-based, Community-based, School-based	The School Success Program provides a certified teacher as a consistent tutor for a maltreated child in the home, and focuses on school-related outcomes.
The Tweenees Program (Barron & Topping, 2013)	N/A	Adolescents	School-based	The Tweenees program (Matthew & Laurie, 2002) aims to increase student awareness and disclosure of child sexual abuse.
Who Do You Tell? (Clearinghouse for Military Family Readiness, 2015a)	Unclear +	Children	Community-based, School-based	WDYT is for children in grade K-6. It aims to teach students about abuse and how to refuse inappropriate advances, in order to prevent sexual abuse.

[a] See http://militaryfamilies.psu.edu/understanding-placement-process.

Treatment: Child Maltreatment Detection and Reporting as First Steps

As part of a treatment effort in schools, both case identification or detection and mandated reports, as well as standard care that may be provided in the school or community, must be explored. Clearly, if professionals do not have adequate training or support, detection may be difficult to conduct in a way that is both sensitive and specific. Treatment efforts may become a moot point if incidents are not properly identified and reported to proper authorities. Most training programmes in education (i.e., teacher preparation and the preparation of guidance counsellors, school psychologists and other specialists) include some coverage of mandated reporting and child abuse; however, no empirical data exists that demonstrates that this training is adequate to prepare professionals for reporting child abuse (Smith, 2010).

There has long been evidence of challenges in mandated reporting behaviour to include under-reporting (Kenny, 2001; Zellman, 1990) and a lack of consensus on what meets the threshold for suspicion of abuse (Levi & Crowell, 2011). Earlier research regarding reporting behaviour of mandated reporters (Zellman, 1990) demonstrated some startling results. Although 92% of elementary school principals and 84% of secondary school principals surveyed reported making a mandated report at some time in their career, 40% of those surveyed admitted to failing to report an instance of possible child maltreatment in their careers. Reasons for failing to report included the report being difficult for the professional in question, believing that they could do better than 'the system' and not believing that the instance was reportable.

More recent data indicate that 27% of teachers made at least one mandated report in their career (Kenny, 2001). Special education teachers were more likely (35%) to have made a report compared to regular education teachers (20%). A possible explanation for increased reporting among special education teachers may be that children with special needs are at increased risk for maltreatment (Sullivan & Knutson, 2000). Female staff were more than six times more likely to make reports than males, although it was not clear if the generally greater number of women in teaching roles may account for this discrepancy. In trying to understand US teachers' attitudes about mandated reporting it was found that more than 45% of teachers 'strongly agreed' that they should *not* be mandated reporters, only 3% were aware of their school's mandated reporting policies, and 40% felt they would not get adequate administrative support in making a mandated report. When given hypothetical vignettes, teachers demonstrated adequate identification of when to report; nevertheless, their survey response indicated that their pre-service training on child abuse detection, symptoms and reporting was not adequate (Kenny, 2001).

In early childhood education settings it appears that there are similar gaps in understanding (Smith, 2010). In a study of both undergraduate majors in child development and early childhood educators (N=141), participants were asked to examine a series of vignettes depicting abusive or ambiguous instances of possible child abuse (i.e., physical, psychological, sexual, as well as neglect) and their likelihood of reporting the instance as abuse to authorities. Participants in the sample demonstrated a clear understanding of child sexual abuse and physical abuse but had more difficulty with differentiating contact with infant or child genitalia, acts of psychological abuse and neglect. Overall, participants were more likely to report when they were more certain of the instance being abuse. If certainty is a significant predictor of reporting behaviour, one may question how pre-service and in-service training efforts may scaffold mandated reporting efforts in schools.

In an effort to understand the landscape of pre-service instruction around issues of child maltreatment, Champion and colleagues (2003) examined the results of two surveys in 1992 (N=102) and 2001 (N=85) with directors of APA-accredited programmes in clinical, counselling and school psychology within the US. Many programmes offered coursework that was specifically aimed at teaching students about child maltreatment and the nuances of maltreatment. Despite more than half of programmes offering specific coursework, very few programmes, approximately 20%, offered practicum placements that were targeted at serving children who were victims of maltreatment. The majority of programmes offered students information about child maltreatment as part of their ethics or professional issues courses (80%), and exposure to mandated reporting in general practicum placements. Although clinical training programmes in allied fields that serve children in schools have specifically investigated training on child maltreatment, similar data was not immediately available about teacher preparation courses.

Research efforts on in-service training programmes have revealed less-than-encouraging results of professional development in child maltreatment. In a review article examining both reporting behaviour and professional development training, Alvarez, Kenny, Donohue and Carpin (2004) found that barriers to appropriate reporting included gaps in knowledge (e.g., signs of abuse and policies and procedures), perceived negative consequences for the child and for their own career, and negative attitudes toward child protective service agencies in general. The authors explained that in their review they found limited empirical evidence for existing professional development programmes for mandated reporting efforts. Sound professional development training should include signs of abuse, types of abuse, reporting procedures and legal information, and how to involve the child or family if appropriate. Generally, more rigorous evaluation is necessary in making better attempts to train professionals in effective detection and reporting to include evaluation of actual reporting behaviour, not just knowledge and attitudes.

In targeted efforts to ensure that children in need are identified and parents are aware of supports in the community, schools may adopt more directed efforts to find and serve children in need. Mandell (2000) described a unique effort by Baltimore City Public Schools that noted increased reports of abuse at the time of report card distribution. In response to these anecdotal reports, the district began including messages to parents with report cards containing positive parenting strategies and crisis intervention contact numbers, and coordinated these inserted messages with public campaigns that aired on radio and television. Data collected from agencies for which contact information was included in the resources list noted that when report cards were distributed they received more calls than at other times. Encouraging results also included the fact that parents were utilising Parents Anonymous for parenting help and tutoring services, and the Students Helping Students hotline for teenagers. This unique public service effort aimed at parents is another way in which schools could aid both detection and prevention, as distinct from teacher and administrator efforts for child identification and support.

Treatment: School-Based Interventions for Survivors of Child Maltreatment

Schools may provide a place where students who have been exposed to maltreatment can receive supportive or clinical intervention or coordinated care with partnerships in the community. Although schools may not always have personnel with specific training or supervised experience with trauma or counselling with victimised children, they may still provide structure and important supports that can facilitate and help to buttress intervention efforts that take place with outside providers. A potential initiative for school-based efforts is to get more information from students about their perceptions of the support they receive or do not receive at school in the wake of being abused. Schönbucher, Maier, Mohler-Kuo et al. (2014) interviewed adolescents in the US who had been sexually abused about their perceptions of supportive behaviour from a variety of professionals to include school personnel. Eighty per cent of those interviewed indicated that they needed more support from a variety of professionals and members of their social support group. The authors emphasised the importance of training teachers and school staff in how to speak to victims of sexual abuse so that they can provide adequate support in the event of student disclosures.

Child sexual abuse has been a focus in the literature on prevention of and intervention in child maltreatment, yet few studies have examined intervention related to other kinds of abuse, such as physical or psychological abuse. Brassard, Rivelis and Diaz (2009) reviewed a variety of interventions that may be used with child victims of physical and psychological abuse in school settings. Specifically, the authors outlined a series of criteria for selecting reviewed interventions including that interventions would: address relevant symptoms for children exposed to violence in the home, be appropriate for students ranging from preschool to high school, be suitable for school-based implementation, be amenable to implementation by those with skill levels comparable to school psychologists, have published empirical support, and be readily accessible to the public for implementation. From the perspective of these outlined criteria the authors reviewed a variety of interventions including Incredible Years (Webster-Stratton, 2001), Primary Mental Health Project (Cowen, Hightower, Pedro-Carroll et al., 1996), Promoting Alternative Thinking Strategies (PATHS; Kusche & Greenberg, 1994), and Cognitive Behavioural Intervention for Trauma in Schools (Jaycox, Kataoka, Stein et al., 2012) to name a few. More importantly, the authors introduced a decision tree for the selection of which students to treat and how to do so. Specifically, the decision tree indicates that in those instances where abuse is indicated, including abuse histories or symptoms that require treatment, that only in instances where a student has symptoms that are 'too severe' to be treated in schools should practitioners refer out to community-based services.

Although the recommendation for referral only arises in the case of severe symptoms, there are other important questions in relation to school-based treatment. Brassard, Rivelis and Diaz (2009) also outlined other important assumptions in their flowchart that may preclude school-based treatment or at least call into question the overall capacity for school-based service provision. In their outline the authors indicate the possibility of a family component of treatment; this is predicated on a clinician being trained for family treatment and having the required time and resources, and families being willing to participate in family treatment. Group treatment is also listed as a possible option, noting that this requires adequate training, the child having the 'emotional resources/control required', the child having the requisite social skills and having an appropriate level of symptoms for group treatment. The research information to date is not clear as to whether school psychologists and guidance counsellors have the required skills and the temporal and/or fiscal resources or support to deliver services to traumatised children in school settings. Manualised programmes included in Brassard, Rivelis and Diaz review (2009) may be an appropriate approach for some children who have experienced maltreatment, but how these more universal interventions (e.g., PATHS and Incredible Years) affect children with traumatic stress symptoms is not well understood.

Not all intervention efforts to support children who have experienced maltreatment need to be solely focused on social–emotional outcomes. Mallett (2012) described outcomes related to an examination of the School Success Program in which certified teachers are assigned to work individually with children at school or at home in order to provide consistency and instructional support. The study had methodological problems, to include lack of a comparison group, differing levels of intervention and changes in measurement over time. Despite these limitations, findings from the study indicated that students who participated had significant increases in scores on standardised measures of achievement. Research on academic outcomes for children who have experienced maltreatment are encouraging given that they are at high risk for academic failure (Mallett, 2012), yet more rigorous studies with greater control over intervention delivery and measurement are necessary to determine efficacy of programmes and services.

Maintenance: Long-Term Care and After-Care

Longer-term care for victims of child maltreatment in school settings is not often thought of as most efforts are on prevention and, to a somewhat lesser extent, on school-based intervention. Schools may serve two important roles in maintenance for victims of child maltreatment, including: (i) support with continued treatment and care coordination in the community; and (ii) reporting and prevention of future abuse. School-based personnel, outside of the special education realm, typically do not think of case management, care coordination and continuity of care as part of their responsibility in the midst of instructional responsibilities and increasing demands for academic performance. Despite the fact that case management does not seem an appropriate role for school professionals, identifying systems in schools to streamline such efforts would benefit school personnel and families by providing consistency and coordination of communication across contexts.

It stands to reason to ask who would fill the role of primary case manager for students who experience child maltreatment. Elementary school teachers are increasingly called upon to respond to multiple demands, and, as a result, it is not likely they can be made serve as case manager or point of contact in the school setting, even though they may know the student best. In middle- and high-school environments, students do not have a primary teacher, thus general education teachers serving as case managers makes little sense. Similarly, guidance counsellors, school social workers or school psychologists may not be in good positions to be case managers, depending on the unique structure of schools. School administrators would do well to systemically meet with student services personnel (e.g., guidance, social workers, school psychologists and instructional support teachers) to discuss a workflow and identify personnel to proactively handle communication and coordination of service provision for students who have experienced child maltreatment and who require monitoring, support, referral or intervention. School personnel should be aware of how these processes work for students in need.

By systemically identifying and formalising a school-based case manager, schools can then more effectively facilitate continued treatment in the community and be in a better position to help support children and families. Care coordination may include, but is not limited to, the following kinds of services:

1. Being the primary contact for providers that may be interacting with the child while on school grounds. The providers include: law enforcement, children and youth services, child advocates, mental health personnel, guardians and foster or biological parents.
2. Consolidating information about current living arrangements, progress in treatment, and progress in legal proceedings, thus being able to keep relevant school personnel informed (e.g., coaches, teachers and administrators).

3. Communicating current therapy goals and techniques so that any coping strategies or accommodations that are required in the school setting (e.g., calm-down areas, safe adults to talk to, and behavioural interventions and supports) can be appropriately implemented or supported by those that interact with the child.
4. Providing progress-monitoring updates (i.e., behavioural, emotional and academic) from school-based personnel (e.g., teachers and coaches).

When a child has been subjected to abuse once, there is no guarantee that the child will not be mistreated again (re-victimisation). Re-victimisation is a concept that originated with the sexual assault trauma field of research (Campbell, Wasco, Ahrens et al., 2001) and refers to a process by which individuals who were already sexually assaulted experience a second traumatic process when they feel they are not believed, not adequately served or not supported by those around them, to include law enforcement, medical and mental health professionals, and family and friends. Re-victimisation has not been studied in school-based child maltreatment intervention specifically; however, its occurrence seems plausible and may be probable. As such, understanding the risk associated with re-victimisation demands research attention. The literature on re-victimisation in community settings indicates that those who receive unhelpful services, a total lack of provision of needed services, and the acceptance of false beliefs about sexual assault (e.g., rape myths and belief in a 'just world') by those around them experience re-victimisation (Campbell, Wasco, Ahrens et al., 2001). Therefore, these individuals can be subjected to judgemental attitudes and are more likely to experience further victimisation by the very agencies and persons charged with their care.

If school-based personnel, through a multi-tiered service model such as that presented here, are aware of and actively participating in the support of students who are victims of maltreatment, they can be trained to look for signs of additional abuse. Specifically, those individuals identified as case managers for students in the school setting should receive both sufficient background information about the child and specialised training in recognising the signs and symptoms of maltreatment, so that they are in a better position to observe possible abuse in already identified children. Secondary prevention efforts, or those indicated to prevent re-victimisation of children, should include advanced detection efforts and implementation of supports as well as specific techniques to avoid re-victimisation by peers, teachers or other school community members. At a minimum, school professionals should not contribute to treatment that exacerbates an already painful situation for children by being ill-prepared to assist.

Conclusions: How Schools Can Help Moving Forward

For schools to begin child maltreatment prevention efforts in earnest, personnel should recognise the social justice perspective that children have a right to be protected from maltreatment by the able adults in their lives. Despite this perspective being codified into US law through mandated reporting requirements, current efforts at detecting, preventing and intervening in cases of child maltreatment continue to fall short. This chapter has identified areas of need for children and school personnel, and proposed some supports and frameworks to better prepare those at the front lines of addressing child maltreatment. In terms of need, schools require resources for professional development, consultation and intervention for working with victims or potential victims of maltreatment. While different school personnel (e.g., teachers and administrators) may be better suited for involvement with victims of maltreatment at different levels of education, there are consistent possible roles for school psychologists and community services to fill in school efforts. Specifically, school psychologists could play a major part in identification, procedural safeguards, evaluation of individual children, professional development and parent outreach, and advocacy for vulnerable or disabled children, while community services would likely be more appropriate for treatment.

These roles lend themselves to a public health approach. The IOM Protractor, as depicted in Figure 22.1, was reviewed as a particularly useful model for schools in addressing child maltreatment because it extends the three-tiered comprehensive framework (i.e., universal, selective and indicated levels of intervention) already in use by many schools to address development in academic, behavioural and social–emotional domains. Recommendations were made for each broad area within the Protractor, including a range of programmes and strategies that could be incorporated into existing initiatives such as professional development, parent outreach, health screenings or classroom accommodations. Although self-care for those taking on these roles was not discussed in the current chapter, it is important to emphasise and provide support for them in practice.

While the majority of programmes discussed within this chapter have some empirical support, the literature as a whole has apparent gaps that could be addressed in partnership with researchers and those in practice (i.e., school personnel and community providers). Research outcomes have primarily focused on participant knowledge and skill gain tied to educational programme content, which in itself has been narrowly focused on prevention of child sexual abuse. The field has made gains in specifying core components and recommended instructional practices for school-based maltreatment prevention programmes. Still, the mixed results for long-term maintenance of gains point to the need for improvement of existing programmes or creation of new programmes that more fully incorporate these best practices. In addition, outcomes of interest should be expanded to include reductions in maltreatment incidents and/or increases in rates of reporting to necessary authorities, especially by teachers, who may be in the best position to identify symptoms in their students. An initiative by Baltimore City Public Schools was described as an example whereby some of these existing gaps were addressed using a creative public health approach.

Gaps also exist in treatment for victims of maltreatment, as illustrated by a study finding that 80% of adolescents interviewed after being abused needed more support from friends and professionals (Schönbucher, Maier, Mohler-Kuo et al., 2014). Beyond this less structured form of support, schools should follow evidence-based decision trees to determine when referrals to community sources are needed for treatment; nevertheless, regardless of treatment location, schools should take and maintain a vested interest in the student across social–emotional, behavioural and academic outcomes. This extension of school services to long-term care and after-care is an area with limited research and ripe for examination. Care coordination as a secondary prevention effort requires its own consensus, infrastructure and implementation within a school for providing sustained student support. Applied research testing on care coordination models within schools is needed.

To conclude, schools that move toward a public health approach to the prevention and treatment of child maltreatment could better serve children. Schools should be aware of any State and Federal guidance related to child maltreatment, such as mandated reporting or required curricula (e.g., Erin's Laws). School personnel should look beyond requirements for existing community coalitions to join or to take a more active role in, as representatives of their school or district. Whether within a school or district or at community level, building a response to child maltreatment requires extensive planning through conducting needs assessments, documenting the problem to be addressed, involving local resources and key stakeholders, and creating processes for group collaboration. The group's vision, mission, objectives, strategies and plans should be agreed upon explicitly, before the action plan is put in place, refined and maintained (Fawcett, Claassen, Thurman et al., 1996). By taking a more holistic approach, schools can use their resources in a more impactful way, while collaborating with community resources specifically targeted to serve victims of maltreatment.

Further Resources

Centres for Disease Control and Prevention: http://www.cdc.gov/violenceprevention/childmaltreatment/prevention.html
Child Welfare Information Gateway: https://www.childwelfare.gov/topics/preventing/
The National Child Traumatic Stress Network: www.nctsn.org/resources/audiences/school-personnel
The National Data Archive on Child Abuse and Neglect (NDACAN): www.ndacan.cornell.edu
Zero to Three: http://www.zerotothree.org/maltreatment/

References

Alvarez, K.M., Kenny, M.C., Donohue, B. & Carpin, K.M. (2004). Why are professionals failing to initiate mandated reports of child maltreatment, and are there any empirically based training programs to assist professionals in the reporting process? *Aggression and Violent Behavior*, 9, 563–578.

Barron, I.G. & Topping, K.J. (2013). Exploratory evaluation of a school-based child sexual abuse prevention program. *Journal of Child Sexual Abuse*, 22, 931–948.

Begle, A.M. & Dumas, J.E. (2011). Child and parental outcomes following involvement in a preventive intervention: Efficacy of the PACE program. *The Journal of Primary Prevention*, 32, 67–81.

Begle, A.M., Lopez, C., Cappa, K. et al. (2012). Ethnicity differences in child and parental outcomes following involvement the PACE program. *Behaviour Research and Therapy*, 50, 56–64.

Brassard, M., Rivelis, E. & Diaz, V. (2009). School-based counseling of abused children. *Psychology in the Schools*, 46, 206–217.

Brassard, M.R. & Fiorvanti, C.M. (2015). Schoolbased child abuse prevention programs. *Psychology in the Schools*, 52, 40–60.

Campbell, R., Wasco, S.M., Ahrens, C.E. et al. (2001). Preventing the 'second rape': Rape survivors' experiences with community service providers. *Journal of Interpersonal Violence*, 16, 1239–1259.

Chaffin, M., Hecht, D., Bard, D. et al. (2012). A statewide trial of the SafeCare home-based services model with parents in child protective services. *Pediatrics*, 129, 509–515.

Champion, K.M., Shipman, K., Bonner, B.L. et al. (2003). Child maltreatment training in doctoral programs in clinical, counseling, and school psychology: Where do we go from here? *Child Maltreatment*, 8, 211–217.

Child Trends Data Bank (2015). *Child maltreatment: Indicators on children and youth*, www.childtrends.org/wp-content/uploads/2014/07/40_Child_Maltreatment.pdf.

Child Welfare Information Gateway (2013). *Long-term consequences of child abuse and neglect*. Washington, DC: US Department of Health and Human Services, Children's Bureau, www.childwelfare.gov/pubpdfs/long_term_consequences.pdf.

Child Welfare Information Gateway (2014). *Mandatory reporters of child abuse and neglect*. Washington, DC: US Department of Health and Human Services, Children's Bureau.

Clearinghouse for Military Family Readiness (2012a). *Child sexual abuse prevention: Teacher training workshop* [Fact Sheet], http://militaryfamilies.psu.edu/programs/child-sexual-abuse-prevention-teacher-training-workshop.

Clearinghouse for Military Family Readiness (2012b). *Safe child program* [Fact Sheet], http://militaryfamilies.psu.edu/programs/safe-child-program.

Clearinghouse for Military Family Readiness (2013a). *Child-Parent Center (CPC) Program* [Fact Sheet], http://militaryfamilies.psu.edu/programs/child-parent-center-cpc-program.

Clearinghouse for Military Family Readiness (2013b). *Girls Inc. Project BOLD* [Fact Sheet], http://militaryfamilies.psu.edu/programs/girls-inc-project-bold.

Clearinghouse for Military Family Readiness (2014a). *Criando a Nuestros Ninos hacia el Exito (CANNE)* [Fact Sheet], http://militaryfamilies.psu.edu/programs/criando-nuestros-ninos-hacia-el-exito-canne.

Clearinghouse for Military Family Readiness (2014b). *Parenting Our Children to Excellence (PACE)* [Fact Sheet], http://militaryfamilies.psu.edu/programs/parenting-our-children-excellence-pace.

Clearinghouse for Military Family Readiness (2014c). *Green Dot etc.* [Fact Sheet], http://militaryfamilies.psu.edu/programs/green-dot-etc.

Clearinghouse for Military Family Readiness (2014d). *Family wellness: Survival skills for healthy families* [Fact Sheet], http://militaryfamilies.psu.edu/programs/family-wellness-survival-skills-healthy-families.

Clearinghouse for Military Family Readiness (2015a). *Who Do You Tell? (WDYT)* [Fact Sheet], http://militaryfamilies.psu.edu/programs/who-do-you-tell-wdyt.

Clearinghouse for Military Family Readiness (2015b). *TOUCH* [Fact Sheet], http://www.militaryfamilies.psu.edu/programs/touch.

Cowen, E.L., Hightower, A.D., Pedro-Carroll, J.L. et al. (1996). *School-based prevention for children at risk: The Primary Mental Health Project*. American Psychological Association.

Davis, M.K. & Gidycz, C.A. (2000). Child sexual abuse prevention programs: A meta-analysis. *Journal of Clinical Child Psychology*, 29, 257–265.

Deb, S. & Walsh, K. (2012). Impact of physical, psychological, and sexual violence on social adjustment of school children in India. *School Psychology International*, 33, 391–415.

Dumas, J.E., Begle, A.M., French, B. & Pearl, A. (2010). Effects of monetary incentives on engagement in the PACE parenting program. *Journal of Clinical Child & Adolescent Psychology*, 39, 302–313.

Fantuzzo, J., McWayne, C. & Bulotsky, R. (2003). Forging strategic partnerships to advance mental health science and practice for vulnerable children. *School Psychology Review*, 32, 17–37.

Fantuzzo, J., Stevenson, H., Weiss, A. et al. (1997). A partnership-directed school-based intervention for child physical abuse and neglect: Beyond mandatory reporting. *School Psychology Review*, 26(2), 298–313.

Fawcett, S.B., Claassen, L., Thurman, T. et al. (1996). *Preventing child abuse and neglect: An action planning guide for building a caring community*. Work Group on Health Promotion & Community Development, University of Kansas.

Frederick, J. & Goddard, C. (2010). School was just a nightmare: Childhood abuse and neglect and school experiences. *Child & Family Social Work*, 15, 22–30.

Fryer, G.E., Kraizer, S.K. & Mlyoshi, T. (1987). Measuring actual reduction of risk to child abuse: A new approach. *Child Abuse & Neglect*, 11, 173–179.

Government Accountability Office (2014). *Child welfare: Federal agencies can better support state efforts to prevent and respond to sexual abuse by school personnel. GAO-14–42*. Washington, DC: United States Government Accountability Office.

Hart, S.N. (1988). Psychological maltreatment: Emphasis on prevention. *School Psychology International*, 9, 243–255.

Hart, S.N. & Hart, B.W. (2014). Children's rights and school psychology: Historical perspective and implications for the profession. *School Psychology International*, 35, 6–28.

Herrera, M. & Carey, K.T. (1993). Child sexual abuse: Issues and strategies for school psychologists. *School Psychology International*, 14, 69–81.

Institute of Medicine (1994). *Reducing Risks for Mental Disorders: Frontiers for Preventive Intervention Research*. P.J. Mrazek and R.J. Haggerty (eds), Committee on Prevention of Mental Disorders, Division of Biobehavorial Sciences and Mental Disorders. Washington, DC: National Academy Press.

Jaycox, L.H., Kataoka, S.H., Stein, B.D. et al. (2012). Cognitive behavioral intervention for trauma in schools. *Journal of Applied School Psychology*, 28, 239–255.

Kenny, M.C. (2001). Child abuse reporting: Teachers' perceived deterrents. *Child Abuse & Neglect*, 25, 81–92.

Kids Count Data Center (2014). *Children who are confirmed by child protective services as victims of maltreatment*, http://datacenter.kidscount.org/data/tables/6221-children-who-are-confirmed-by-child-protective-services-as-victims-of-maltreatment?loc=1&loct=1#detailed/1/any/false/868,867,133,38,35/any/12943,12942.

Kleemeier, C., Webb, C., Hazzard, A. & Pohl, J. (1988). Child sexual abuse prevention: Evaluation of a teacher training model. *Child Abuse & Neglect*, 12, 555–561.

Ko, S.F. & Cosden, M.A. (2001). Do elementary school-based child abuse prevention programs work? A high school follow up. *Psychology in the Schools*, 38, 57–66.

Kraizer, S., Witte, S.S. & Fryer, G.E. (1989). Child sexual abuse prevention programs: What makes them effective in protecting children? *Children Today*, 18(5), 23–27.

Kusche, C.A. & Greenberg, M.T. (1994). *The PATHS Curriculum*. Seattle: Developmental Research and Programs.

Levi, B.H. & Crowell, K. (2011). Child abuse experts disagree about the threshold for mandated reporting. *Clinical Pediatrics*, 50, 321–329.

MacIntyre, D., Carr, A., Lawlor, M. & Flattery, M. (2000). Development of the stay safe programme. *Child Abuse Review*, 9, 200–216.

Mallett, C.A. (2012). The school success program: Improving maltreated children's academic and school-related outcomes. *Children & Schools*, 34, 13–26.

Mandell, S. (2000). Child abuse prevention at report card time. *Journal of Community Psychology*, 28, 687–690.

Matthew, L. & Laurie, M. (2002). *Tweenees resource pack: Personal safety for children 5–13 years*. Dundee, Scotland: Young Women's Centre (Trading) Limited.

Mathews, B. (2014). Mandatory reporting laws and identification of child abuse and neglect: Consideration of differential maltreatment types, and cross-jurisdictional analysis of child sexual abuse reports. *Social Sciences*, 3, 460–482.

Schönbucher, V., Maier, T., Mohler-Kuo, M. et al. (2014). Adolescent perspectives on social support received in the aftermath of sexual abuse: A qualitative study. *Archives of Sexual Behavior*, 43, 571–586.

Smith, M.C. (2010). Early childhood educators: Perspectives on maltreatment and mandated reporting. *Children and Youth Services Review*, 32, 20–27.

Springer, F. & Phillips, J. (2006). The IOM Model: A tool for prevention planning and implementation. *Prevention Tactics*, 8, 13.

Sugai, G. & Horner, R. (2002). The evolution of discipline practices: School-wide positive behavior supports. *Child & Family Behavior Therapy*, 24, 23–50.

Sullivan, P.M. & Knutson, J.F. (2000). Maltreatment and disabilities: A population-based epidemiological study. *Child Abuse & Neglect*, 24, 1257–1273.

Sylvester, L. (1997). *Talking About Touching: Personal Safety Curriculum (1996 editions) Preschool to Grade 3 Curriculum Evaluation Summary*. Seattle, WA: Committee for Children.

Tilly, W.D. (2008). The evolution of school psychology to science-based practice: Problem solving and the three-tiered model. In: A. Thomas & J. Grimes (eds) *Best Practices in School Psychology V*, 1, 17–36. Bethesda, MD: National Association of School Psychologists.

Topping, K.J. & Barron, I.G. (2009). School-based child sexual abuse prevention programs: A review of effectiveness. *Review of Educational Research*, 79, 431–463.

Tutty, L.M. (1997). Child sexual abuse prevention programs: Evaluating Who Do You Tell. *Child Abuse & Neglect*, 21, 869–881.

Webster-Stratton, C. (2001). The Incredible Years: Parents, teachers, and children training series. *Residential Treatment for Children & Youth*, 18, 31–45.

Woods, K., Bond, C., Tyldesley, K. et al. (2011). The role of school psychologists in child protection and safeguarding. *School Psychology International*, 32, 361–376.

Wurtele, S.K., Kast, L.C., Miller-Perrin, C.L. & Kondrick, P.A. (1989). Comparison of programs for teaching personal safety skills to preschoolers. *Journal of Consulting and Clinical Psychology*, 57, 505.

Zellman, G.L. (1990). Child abuse reporting and failure to report among mandated reporters: Prevalence, incidence, and reasons. *Journal of Interpersonal Violence*, 5, 3–22.

23

Using Assessment of Attachment in Child Care Proceedings to Guide Intervention

Patricia McKinsey Crittenden[1] and Clark Baim[2]

[1] Family Relations Institute, Miami, FL
[2] Change Point Ltd, Birmingham, UK

Attachment often contributes to decision-making in child care proceedings.[1] Attachment refers to the protection and comfort that caregivers provide and these are precisely the attributes threatened in child care proceedings. Assessment of attachment can reveal family members' protective strategies, the historical experiences that have shaped the strategies, and the underlying information processing that generates self-, partner- and child-protective behaviour. Knowing the strategies, experiences and psychological processes of family members can inform both placement decisions and treatment planning.

As simple as that sounds, attachment and assessment of attachment are quite controversial. There is disagreement about the meaning of attachment, how it should be assessed, who is qualified to assess it, and whether it can yield valid evidence or only expert opinion. In this chapter we offer an approach to attachment that evolved from work with maltreating families and discuss differences between this approach and other approaches. We then describe a protocol for presenting attachment evidence to courts and discuss using the evidence for treatment planning. We close with a case example in early childhood. We propose that the approach that we offer can protect children and reduce costs.

The Dynamic-Maturational Model (DMM) of Attachment and Adaptation

Attachment theory provides a model for understanding how human beings survive danger, form protective relationships and promote the survival of their children (Bowlby, 1969, 1973, 1988; Crittenden & Ainsworth, 1989). Early work on attachment focused on how infants

---

[1] In the US, these are called 'child custody proceedings'.

The Wiley Handbook of What Works in Child Maltreatment: An Evidence-Based Approach to Assessment and Intervention in Child Protection, First Edition. Edited by Louise Dixon, Daniel F. Perkins, Catherine Hamilton-Giachritsis, and Leam A. Craig.
© 2017 John Wiley & Sons Ltd. Published 2017 by John Wiley & Sons Ltd.

elicited protection from their caregivers (Ainsworth, Blehar, Waters & Wall, 1978); that work provided a sound developmental base from which to understand later-developing individual differences in attachment (Crittenden & Ainsworth, 1989). More recent research has shown that attachment strategies are an important feature of psychosocial functioning across the lifespan (Baim & Morrison, 2011; Cicchetti & Valentino, 2006; Crittenden, 1995, 2015; George, Kaplan & Main, 1996; Howe, 2005, 2011; Thompson & Raikes, 2003).

The Dynamic-Maturational Model of Attachment and Adaptation (DMM) offers a model of attachment across the lifespan that addresses the developmental processes and clinical applications described by Bowlby and Ainsworth (Ainsworth & Bowlby, 1991). The DMM began in Ainsworth's laboratory with two samples of maltreating families with infants and young children (Crittenden, 1983, 1985, 1988) and expanded to a lifespan theory of adaptation and treatment of maladaptation (Crittenden, 2015; Crittenden & Ainsworth, 1989; Crittenden, Dallos, Landini & Kozlowska, 2014). As such, the DMM is highly relevant to professionals who work with families involved in child care proceedings.

The DMM expands Ainsworth's model of individual differences in middle-class, non-maltreating families with a wider array of strategies used in maltreating families and families with mental illness. Seen in the context of the family system, children's attachment strategies are understood as their best solution for obtaining safety and comfort from the particular caregivers on whom their lives depend. The DMM offers an alternative to symptom-based diagnoses of psychopathology by focusing instead on the function of the 'symptom' behaviour (Crittenden, 2002a; Fonagy, 2001; Wallin, 2007). It is also a strengths-based and function-based alternative to the notion of disorganised attachment (e.g., George, Chapter 14 of this text; cf., Crittenden & Ainsworth, 1989, p. 442–443).

The bases of attachment. One might ask why attachment is elevated to such a crucial role in human adaptation. It is because the attachment of infant to caregiver is where all our innate (genetic) qualities, both those that are universal to our species and those that are unique to each individual, meet experience. This experience includes our own specific experience and also the learnt 'cultural' experience of previous generations, as it is incorporated in the behaviour of our caregivers. Biology and experience meet in the infant–caregiver relationship. Put another way, attachment shapes the early development of the human brain. Later, especially after children enter community settings such as school, there will be other influences that can augment or moderate the impact of early attachment. But they do so on a base defined by what happened early in life when the infant needed protection and comfort.

Information processing is at the core of the DMM approach to attachment (see Bowlby, 1980, chapter 4). Information processing refers to the ways that the brain represents experience through activation and potentiation of neural networks that represent 'self-in-context' (Cozolino, 2002; Schacter & Tulving, 1994). An important and closely related concept is the notion of *dispositional representation*, i.e., the potential actions that are disposed by the representation (Crittenden, 2015; Crittenden & Landini, 2011; Damasio, 1994; Panksepp, 2005). Crucially, the brain produces multiple dispositional representations (DRs) concurrently that might or might not dispose the same action (Eagleman, 2011). The process of generating DRs develops as an interaction of maturation with experience, beginning at birth and continuing throughout life. Adaptation depends upon generating multiple predictive DRs of potentially protective actions and learning to enact the DR that both protects in the short term and also promotes further development in the long term.

Individual differences in attachment strategies. Ainsworth's work with middle-class families demonstrated how differences in mothers' early *sensitive responsiveness* to infant distress predicted individual differences in infant attachment at one year of age (Ainsworth, Blehar, Waters & Wall, 1978). *Sensitivity* to infant signals is important because it allows adults to attune their responses to the infant's state. *Responsiveness* reflects the temporal and affective qualities of the adult's response; responses can lessen babies' distress and help them to feel safe and comfortable or, conversely, heighten infants' distress. Either way, infants learn the relation between their behaviour and caregivers' responses and modify their behaviour accordingly.

Ainsworth identified three main patterns of attachment, labelled A, B and C, with several sub-patterns (A1–2, B1–4 and C1–2), see Figure 23.1. Type B organisation was observed when mothers were both sensitive and responsive to their infants' signals. Type A organisations arose when mothers were predictably *responsive* but *insensitive*. The Type C strategy developed when babies received care that was *unpredictably responsive* and *inconsistently sensitive*. In learning theory terms, Type B reflects the experience of predictable reinforcement of mild displays of negative affect; Type A reflects predictable punishment of expression of negative affect, and Type C reflects unpredictable and intermittent reinforcement of displays of intense negative affect.

Crittenden's expansion of Ainsworth's work includes more complex strategies used by older children and adults (Crittenden & Ainsworth, 1989, p. 442–443). These comprise compulsive Type A strategies (A3–8), coercive Type C strategies (C3–8) and A/C combinations; see Figure 23.1. These strategies reflect commonly recognised forms of maladaptive behaviour, but differ from symptom-based diagnoses in that they are seen as a functional attempt to reduce danger and increase comfort. They differ from the ABC + D model (where D denotes 'disorganisation') in finding both organisation and adaptive function in disturbed behaviour. When the function better fits the past context in which the behaviour was learnt than the current context, the behaviour can be maladaptive and even dangerous.

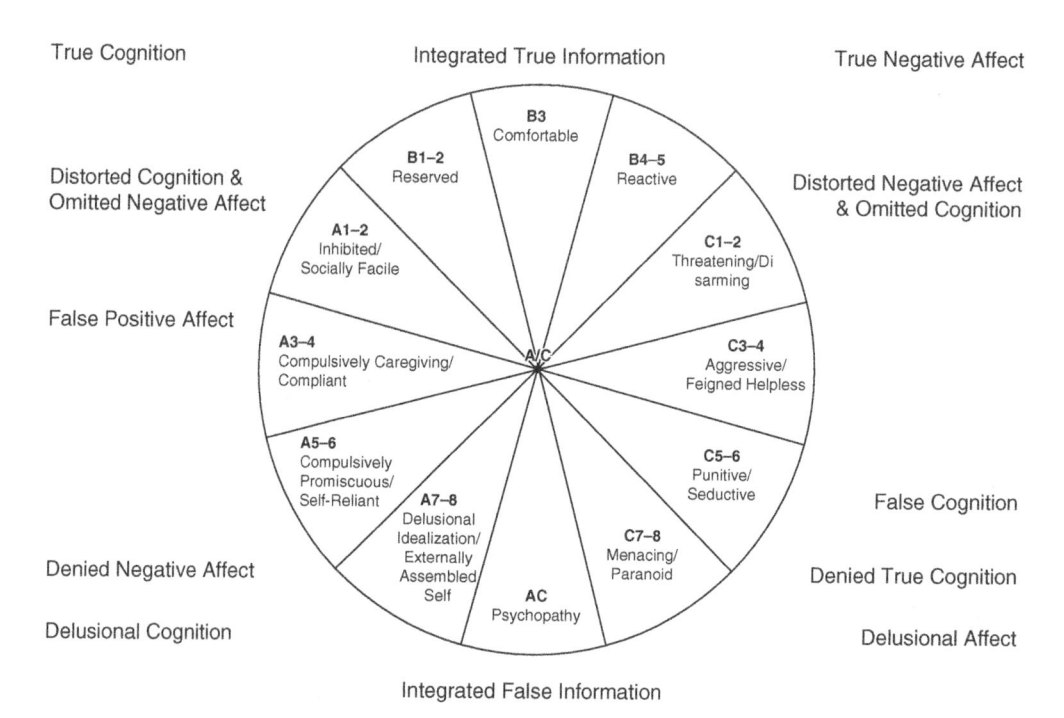

Figure 23.1 The Dynamic-Maturational Model of Attachment and Adaptation.

Within the DMM, the strategies used by many maltreated children and maltreating parents include: (i) *compulsive caregiving* toward neglectful/depressed parents (A3, Bowlby, 1980; Crittenden, 1992a), (ii) *compulsive compliance* to threatening parents (A4, Crittenden, 1985; Crittenden & DiLalla, 1988), (iii) *compulsive promiscuity and self-reliance* in response to abandoning parents (A5–6, Bowlby, 1980; Crittenden, 1995), (iv) *punitive/seductive* (C5–6, Crittenden, 1994; Crittenden 2008), and (v) *delusional idealisation* of dangerous people (A7, Crittenden, 2008; Kuleshnyk, 1984). Because maltreated children are essentially never securely attached and the use of these strategies increases maltreated children's safety and comfort, the DMM focuses more on 'adaptation' than security, as compared to other models of attachment.

Information processing and strategic attachment behaviour. In terms of information processing, individuals using a Type A strategy tend to omit negative feelings from processing and to act in accordance with expected consequences. In other words, their dispositional representations prioritise 'cognitive' information about causal contingencies. Individuals using the Type C strategy do the opposite: they act in accordance with their negative feelings, with little attention to consequences. They prioritise 'affect'. Both take psychological shortcuts that sometimes precipitate dangerous behaviour or fail to elicit protective behaviour. Individuals using the Type B strategy integrate cognitive and affective information. Such individuals have more balanced and complex DRs and, as a consequence, are more likely to demonstrate behaviour that is adaptive in the widest range of circumstances. Nevertheless, in infancy, all strategies are limited by infant's motoric immaturity and, even more, by their psychological immaturity in which all information and processing is pre-conscious.

Experience is far too complex for infants to perceive and comprehend. Therefore, the role of attachment figures is to moderate infants' experience, protecting and comforting infants when they cannot yet do so themselves, encouraging infants to regulate what they can regulate, and assisting infants to learn new psychological processes and behavioural skills in their 'zone of proximal development' (ZPD, Vygotsky, 1978). When infants must act beyond their ZPD, they employ psychological 'shortcuts' that reduce complexity (and distort the resulting DR).

As children mature, they become able to process information in more sophisticated ways that include linguistic, conscious and ultimately integrative representation. Correspondingly, caregivers need to adapt so as to promote learning in children's ever-changing ZPD. Adjustment difficulties can arise when parents or children continue to use psychological shortcuts that block out or misinterpret crucial information beyond the time when they were necessary.

Difficulties can also develop when individuals have contradictory DRs and lack integrative processes for selecting the response that best fits the current situation. An example of a maladaptive shortcut would be a parent who, with a conscious DR, wants to protect and comfort the child, but who also, in a pre-conscious DR from childhood, fears the child's aggression. If the pre-conscious DR is based on past endangerment, it might be accessed more rapidly and given priority (Mather & Sutherland, 2011). This can result in parental aggression, i.e., child abuse. In other cases, the mixed DRs yield changing and unpredictable parental behaviour. The point is that a psychological process that was adaptive in childhood can become maladaptive later in life. To understand dangerous behaviour, we must consider both the context in which it was learnt and that in which it was applied.

A dimensional model of protective attachment strategies. Figure 23.1 shows the array of DMM strategies and their associated transformations of information. The strategies on the left privilege 'cognitive' information regarding temporal contingencies whereas those on the right privilege negative affect; the centre reflects integration. Vertically, the Type A and Type C strategies with higher numbers (i.e., lower down on the circle) use more extensive transformations of information. Individuals using these strategies are likely to (i) have experienced more unprotected and uncomforted danger, (ii) have developed less conscious strategies, and, for those with the highest numbers, (iii) be dangerous to themselves or others.

Broadly speaking, there is a correlation between age when the strategy was organised and the harm experienced in childhood. Examples of age-salient dangers are separation/abandonment in early childhood; rejection, teasing, mocking and bullying in middle childhood; and deception, betrayal, romantic rejection and premature home leaving in adolescence. Endangered children are at risk for psychological problems (Gerhardt, 2004; Hertzman, 2013; Keyes, Eaton, Krueger et al., 2014; McLaughlin, Greif, Gruber et al., 2012; Perry, 2008; Read, Mosher & Bentall, 2004; de Zulueta, 1993). The most severe disturbances (e.g., the eating and personality disorders, the psychoses, and violent or sexual forms of criminality) develop in the transition to adulthood; these problems may require a series of age-salient threats to coalesce (Crittenden, 2008, 2015). By early adulthood, information can be utterly transformed: true and false, pleasure and pain, and safety and danger can become reversed. At such extremes, care or affection can be perceived as treacherous; this causes profound problems of trust in relationships – including therapeutic relationships.

It should be clarified, however, that it is not the danger itself that creates psychological and interpersonal problems. It is the shortcuts in information processing that must be made when the danger is more than the individual can understand, but must be faced without protection or comfort from a trusted caregiver. Crucially, parents who maltreat their children usually have experienced unprotected and uncomforted danger (Milaniak & Widom, 2015) and, thus, can be expected to enter adulthood and parenthood with the transformations of information and strategies associated with endangerment.

See Crittenden (2015) for fuller coverage of the DMM and the research supporting its clinical applications (see also, Brown & Elliott, 2016; Farnfield, Hautamaki, Nørbech & Sahhar, 2010; Landa & Duschinsky, 2013; Pocock, 2010).

Assessing attachment across the lifespan. Because infants' strategies are pre-conscious and aspects of strategies remain pre-conscious for everyone, identifying protective strategies requires techniques that delve below the conscious surface of behaviour or self-reports of behaviour. Like medical imagining techniques that reveal the state of bodily organs (for example, X-rays, CAT scans, fMRIs), assessments of attachment must identify non-conscious aspects of behaviour. Depending upon the age of the person, enacted or verbally represented strategies are assessed. Based on Ainsworth's enacted Strange Situation (Ainsworth, Blehar, Waters & Wall, 1978) and the representational Adult Attachment Interview (George, Kaplan & Main, 1996), an age-defined set of DMM assessments of attachment has been developed and validated (see Table 23.1).

The advantages of using this telescoping set of assessments are (i) the wide range of possible strategies, including those that are particularly relevant to maltreatment and mental illness, (ii) the attunement of each assessment to the developmental capacities and challenges of each age period, and (iii) the use of the same model across the lifespan, making it suitable for assessment of families. The DMM assessments identify individuals' strengths, the historical conditions leading to their strategies, and the types of transformations of information that underlay their strategies. Because treatment is intended to change the psychological processes that generate behaviour, identifying those processes is important.

Table 23.1 DMM assessments of protective attachment strategies.

Assessment*	Age range	Enacted or represented
Infant CARE-Index (ICI)	Birth–15 months	Enacted
Toddler CARE-Index (TCI)	16–72 months	Enacted
Strange Situation Procedure (SSP)	11–17 months	Enacted
Preschool Assessment of Attachment (PAA)	18–72 months	Enacted
School-age Assessment of Attachment (SAA)	6 years–puberty	Represented in discourse & plot
Transition to Adulthood Attachment Interview (TAAI)	16–25 years	Represented in discourse
Adult Attachment Interview (AAI)	25+ years	Represented in discourse
Parents Interview (PI)	All ages	Enacted & represented

*See Farnfield, Hautamäki, Nørbech & Sahhar, 2010 and Crittenden, 2015 for the validating studies.

In cases of maltreatment, especially cases in which a child might grow up without his/her parents and parents might lose custody of their children, the most precise and predictive assessments are needed. We think the DMM assessments offer the best methods available at this time for generating a psychological image of individual and family protective functioning.

IASA Family Attachment Court Protocol

Attachment is often invoked in child care proceedings, but is used in discrepant and sometimes contradictory ways, offered as opinion without evidence that can be examined, and assessed by professionals without formal training in attachment. To address these shortcomings, the International Association for the Study of Attachment (IASA) has developed an empirically based protocol for addressing attachment in court proceedings (Crittenden, Farnfield, Landini & Grey, 2013). The IASA Family Attachment Court Protocol defines attachment, describes how to assess attachment (together with the published studies on maltreating families that validate the assessments), designates criteria for being qualified to assess attachment, and defines three types of authorised Family Attachment Court Reports.

The central goal of the Protocol is to move from expert *opinion* on attachment to *evidence* regarding attachment that is commensurate with the standard set in *Daubert v Merrell Dow Pharmaceuticals* (1993) for criminal evidence. The evidence can range from transcribed excerpts or still photos taken from videotapes to provision of the full assessment. Reports require a certificate authorising the professional to use the assessment in court reports.

The Protocol specifies that the professional works for the court (and not for one party to the proceedings) and that all family members and potential parent figures be assessed, i.e., parents, siblings and alternate caregivers. Because the DMM has a lifespan set of compatible assessments, each coded 'blindly' (that is, without any information about the family or case), the results of the assessments can be combined with the history and other professionals' reports to the court to generate a Family Functional Formulation (FFF). The FFF specifies family members' protective strategies, the conditions that elicit use of the strategies, and the way family members' strategies work together. The strategies are extracted from the age-defined assessments, whereas family functioning is most clearly discerned in the Parents Interview.

An IASA Family Attachment Report has four parts. Part 1 provides an introduction (presentation of the problem, the source of the request for the report, a list of the questions posed by the court, the family, the qualifications of the professional and the table of contents of the report). Part 2 defines attachment at the ages of family members and includes a description of each assessment used. (These materials are 'plug-ins' that are available on www.iasa-dmm.org/familycourtprotocol.) Part 3 provides the evidence, that is, results of the 'blind' coding of each assessment, including strategy, adaptive strengths, needs/limitations, and unanswered questions about the individuals' functioning. Part 4 is the integration of the attachment evidence with the history and other professionals' reports (as revealed in the 'court bundle'), the Family Functional Formulation, recommendations for intervention, including changes that professionals could make to become more effective, and lastly, answers to the questions posed by the court. The report closes with a list of research cited in the report.

The central advantages of the IASA Family Attachment Court Protocol are (i) replacement of self-appointed experts working for one side or the other with authorised experts in attachment working for the court, (ii) use of tangible evidence that can be examined, (iii) explicit definition of attachment at different ages, (iv) use of age-defined assessments that differentiate among maltreating family members (rather than considering most to be disorganised, cannot classify, or unresolved), (v) published and validated means of interpreting the assessments, and (vi) a structure for the report, from evidence to formulation to treatment recommendations and responses to the court's questions.

DMM Integrative Treatment

The reason for developing the DMM was to improve treatment. In spite of there being more than 1000 published forms of psychological treatment, none has evidence of being superior to the others (for a review, see Crittenden, 2015, chapter 15). According to Martin Seligman, past president of the American Psychological Association, treatment efficacy has not improved in the last 25 years (Seligman, 2013). Moreover, harmful effects from treatment are estimated at 10–20% (Crittenden, 2015, p. 227). Either a new approach or a guide to matching treatment to problem – or both – are needed. DMM Integrative Treatment is an attempt to establish basic principles for delivering treatment and use the principles to implement a change process (Crittenden, 2002b, 2015; Crittenden & Dallos, 2014; Crittenden, Dallos, Landini & Kozlowska, 2014).

Basic principles of treatment. Although treatment is a huge topic that exceeds the scope of a chapter, the following ideas capture the essence of DMM Integrative Treatment.

1. **Premise.** The basic premise is that maltreating parents and maltreated children have not experienced attuned, protective and comforting family relationships, and, as a consequence, they do not expect such relationships, nor do they know how to act within them. Treatment is the process of using an informed, regulated relationship to promote family members' ability to establish and maintain adaptive relationships.
2. **Therapeutic relationship.** Establishing a therapeutic relationship is seen as crucial to all subsequent effort because the relationship with the professional functions to correct the experience of misattuned relationships. To do this, it is crucial that the professional appreciate family members as they are, particularly in terms of the non-conscious aspects of their experience. Given that most maltreating parents have problems in relationships, DMM Integrative Treatment is implemented by fewer professionals interacting directly

with the family, with the multidisciplinary team supporting these professionals (Crittenden, 1992b). This is a 'team around the professional' approach as compared to 'team around the client'.

3. **Adaptation.** DMM Integrative Treatment is a strengths-based, non-stigmatising approach that assumes that distressed individuals have learnt important things about protection from danger, but that early shortcuts in psychological processing have made it difficult for them to adapt to changing conditions. Thus, instead of focusing on maltreatment, symptoms or anxious attachment, treatment should address safety (and, for parents, reproductive safety) in the current context. For example, children's acting-out behaviour can be seen as protective when it diverts parents' attention to the child and away from parental conflict. Similarly, hypervigilance leading to inattention at school may function to keep children prepared for unexpected danger. The notion is that every strategy is the best strategy in some context, but none is best in every context. Consequently, a major goal of DMM Integrative Treatment is to increase the array of strategies that an individual can use and, then, to help the individual to discover when to use each; the latter requires a conscious, reflective process.

4. **Interpersonal problems.** A functional perspective situates maltreating behaviour and psychiatric symptoms in the interpersonal contexts of the family and the system of professionals involved with the family. This is quite different from assigning maltreatment to parents or psychiatric diagnoses to individuals. The DMM defines behaviour that occurs between people as interpersonal, meaningful and dynamic.

5. **Zone of proximal development.** The treatment itself begins with the person's existing competencies and builds on these in the zone of proximal development (Vygotsky, 1978). For maltreating parents, this is quite different from the treatment plan being based on the child's needs. When another person's needs are the basis for the plan, treatment is unlikely to fit the person's readiness and there may be no progress – or harm could be done. The goal is to establish a process of successful change such that the parent becomes increasingly able to examine their own experience so as to implement more adaptive responses.

6. **Choosing treatment strategies.** Because Types A and C reflect opposite psychological processes and the high-numbered strategies use extreme transformations of information (omitted, distorted, falsified, denied or delusional), different treatment approaches may be needed for different families and individuals within families. Generic approaches might benefit some family members while harming others. For maltreating families, that means knowing more than the type of maltreatment or that they have insecure attachment; it means knowing how each family member processes information. As with attachment strategies, each treatment strategy is right in some contexts and none is right in every context. For example, a child or parent who uses a Type A strategy might benefit from techniques that focus on somatic and psychological feelings. The challenge for professionals is to hear and work with the fearful, sad or angry person behind the positive or compliant exterior. By contrast, a person who uses a Type C strategy might need approaches focused on the contingencies that elicit and follow their own behaviour. A key for professionals is to see beyond the intensely displayed feelings to the hidden feelings and the lack of predictability. In both cases, the therapist should help the person to access omitted information and identify transformed information. While doing this, the therapist can help the person to consider alternative solutions to specific problems, that is, to use reflective integration to select occasion-specific adaptive behaviour.

7. **Family work.** The DMM conceptualisation provides a powerful rationale for working with the entire family. The idea is not to catch and treat 'bad' parents or 'dysfunctional'

children, but instead to promote positive changes in mental health and interpersonal functioning throughout the family. Working with a child in isolation, without addressing the family's functioning, can inadvertently set the child up for more severe danger as other family members struggle to re-establish the family's prior functioning. For example, a compulsively compliant child who becomes assertive as a result of therapy may find himself/herself in more danger if the parent feels their assertive communication is disrespectful (Crittenden, 2005).

8. **Treatment process.** DMM Integrative Treatment proceeds in a *recursive process* of using treatment acts as tiny experiments (Beck, Rush, Shaw & Emery, 1979) that yield feedback to guide reflection and revision. This process is precisely the process used by adaptive adults; when parents acquire it, the treatment is approaching completion because the parents are more able to notice discrepancies, make meaning from such discrepancies, apportion and accept responsibility accurately, and repair ruptures in their family interactions.

9. **Concluding a course of treatment.** Some treatment is successful: parents improve, children's symptoms dissipate and child protection services are ended. Parents should be guided to feel proud of their ability to adapt and to continue to adapt as a basic life process. In other cases, progress is made, but the children's needs are not met sufficiently or quickly enough. In these cases, a decision must be made as to whether continued or changed services can help. If not, it is important to frame this as the lack of suitable services or resources (as opposed to the limitations of the parents). Blaming parents will not help them or their children and there is much that we do not know about treatment and more that we cannot afford. In all cases, it is important to show family members what they have accomplished and how it helps them to live safer lives.

When a decision must be made to remove children, the pain to everyone should be acknowledged. Parents should not be criticised for feeling angry or resentful (because these are appropriate feelings) and children should not be encouraged to act falsely happy about out-of-home placement. When parental rights are terminated, ways should be sought for the parent to leave evidence of their desire to raise their children for a later time when their older or grown children might want this evidence.

In sum, DMM professionals treat people, not disorders. DMM Integrative Treatment is principled, not packaged. It engages parents and children with professionals, as opposed to rolling out programmes. Rather than giving people information they may be unready to use, it guides people to use information more adaptively.

Advantages of DMM Integrative Treatment. There are a number of advantages to the DMM conceptualisation. It is a *comprehensive* theory of treatment that includes and *integrates* all types of treatment (e.g., psychodynamic, family systems, cognitive, behavioural, body oriented, etc.) with *developmental processes*. Focusing treatment on protection and reproduction can streamline the treatment, thus lowering the cost. The array of DMM protective strategies gives meaning to complex and contradictory behaviour; this promotes the cooperation of parents and children.

The Real World: Case Study

We present a case study to demonstrate the value of the IASA Family Attachment Court Protocol and DMM assessments of attachment. Rather than presenting an ideal case, we chose a typical case that reflects the usual limitations of time, funding and adequately skilled personnel.

Case: Level 1 IASA Family Attachment Court Report
A multi-problem family with a toddler and young school-aged child

The presenting problem. Mr and Mrs Weary[2] had a long history of contact with social services. At the time of this Level I IASA Family Attachment Court Report, their two children (Susan aged six and Jasper aged 32 months) were in separate foster placements. Susan had originally been placed with Jasper but, when her behaviour deteriorated, she was placed separately.

The decisions before the court were whether or not to reunite the family and what services would be needed to accomplish that. A full set of DMM assessments was administered. The assessments were analysed before the history and other professionals' reports were read. After reading the court bundle, a Family Functional Formulation (FFF) was developed, and then the questions in the instructions were answered. All of this was done by an authorised DMM coder whose reliability certificates were appended to the report along with the publication of the Protocol (Crittenden, Dallos, Landini & Kozlowska, 2014).

The assessments

Jasper. At 32 months, Jasper was clearly organising an aggressive and feigned helpless (Type C3–4) strategy with his parents and, in addition, a compulsive caregiving (Type A3) strategy with his father. During the CARE-Index assessment with his mother, Jasper was disarmingly uncooperative. He pretended to be unable to draw when his mother tried to guide his hand; when she tried to get him to feed the doll, he pushed it away and smiled innocently. They struggled throughout, with Mrs Weary becoming quite stern. When Mrs Weary put the toys away (the frustration task), Jasper whined and went limp. When she returned the toys (the repair) and tried to kiss and caress him, he pulled back sharply. Overall, the interaction indicated mild risk (attachment strategy: C4) and a need to (i) address Mrs Weary's need for comfort and (ii) the use of reinforcement.

With his father, Jasper's strategy was similar, but more intensely aggressive. Jasper pulled away, shouting 'no!' several times. This made his father angry and more insistent. However, after the frustration episode, Jasper 'fed' his father with the tea set. This combination of coercive confrontation (C3) and resolution by capitulation and caregiving (A3) put the dyad in the high-risk category.

Susan. The School-aged Assessment of Attachment (SAA) involves seven picture cards about which the child should tell a fantasy story and a recalled experience. Susan, age six, began by saying her stories would be sad. In the stories that followed, it was not fully possible to differentiate fantasy from fiction. For fantasy stories, Susan told about:

1. Card 1 (Going out alone): almost getting run over while mum was in the house;
2. Card 2 (Rejected by best friend): finds a new friend immediately and everything is fine;
3. Card 3 (Moving house): moving the furniture for the adults who were not strong enough;
4. Card 4 (Bullying): calling the police who put the bullies in jail;

---

[2] All names are pseudonyms and identifying details have been changed, but without changing the psychosocial context.

5. Card 5 (Father leaving): making her own house because dad and mum went away;
6. Card 6 (Running away): being taunted by her parents and everyone laughing;
7. Card 7 (Mother to hospital): bossing the doctors who didn't know what to do and now the family doesn't live together.

In two of the fantasy stories, the girl was vulnerable and the parents did not protect her (but the police did.) In four of the stories, the girl is powerful and fills the adult role toward the adults who act like children. In all of the stories, the girl was alone, with even the professionals (the doctors) not knowing how to help.

For recalled events, Susan told ordinary stories about playing outside, moving to a house together, the teacher making the children play nicely, and her mother having a baby. These stories were told without the detail and emotion of the fantasy stories.

Susan was seen as feeling very sad and thinking her situation was hopeless, but trying very hard to be grown up and powerful so that she could protect her parents who, she thought, could not protect either her or themselves. In addition, Susan showed evidence of needing delusional/magical solutions to situations in which she was actually very vulnerable.

Susan's Family Drawing was on three separate pages that reflected the three households in which her family lived. She drew black stick figures with huge smiles that filled their faces.

Mrs Weary. The Adult Attachment Interview (AAI) is designed to assess a person's current psychological functioning in relation to parenting. The following history was drawn from Mrs Weary's AAI: Mrs Weary was abandoned repeatedly by her alcoholic mother, and lived on and off with relatives. She didn't know her father. She was 'whooped' (hit) quite often (probably meeting today's standard for child abuse) by her grandmother and sexually abused when she was 11, but she did not say by whom or in what way. She often refused to go to school because of bullying. By the time she reached age 19, three of her caregivers had died from the consequences of alcoholism. Mrs Weary married at 20 and experienced postnatal depression when Susan was born. She had recently taken half a bottle of sleeping pills.

Using the DMM-AAI discourse analysis, Mrs Weary's AAI was classified as: Dp $Utr(p)_{CSA}$ $(ds)_{abandonment,\ PA}$ $l(dp)_{GM,\ A,\ U}$ $A7_{GM}$ $C5_{M}$.

That is, Mrs Weary was depressed (Dp), delusionally idealised her abusive grandmother (A7) and derogated her mother (C5). She was aware that nothing she did changed her mother's behaviour or reduced her grandmother's punishment (futility is one marker for depression, Dp). Moreover, although she knew that many family members were alcoholic, she had not wondered why that might be. Instead, she was psychologically preoccupied (p) with the unresolved psychological trauma (Utr) of child sexual abuse $(Utr(p)_{CSA})$, attributing many things in her life to it, but refusing to talk about it. She dismissed (ds) the significance or effects of her mother's repeated abandonment of her $(Utr(ds)_{abandonment})$ and her grandmother's abusive physical punishment $(Utr(ds)_{PA})$. She treated the deaths of her caregivers as inevitable $(Ul(dp)_{GM,\ A,\ U})$. Her strength was her commitment to family relationships, even through hard times.

Mr Weary. Mr Weary said that he had had a happy childhood, but recalled almost nothing about it. His parents divorced when he was 12 because of his father's extramarital affairs. The court placed the children with their father; Mr Weary had not wondered why this had occurred. His stepmother punished them very harshly and his father taunted him as a 'sissy' when he complained. As a child, Mr Weary had been hospitalised several times, but he could not recall why.

Using the DMM-AAI discourse analysis, Mr Weary's attachment strategy was identified as $\text{Utr(dn)}_{\text{PA-F, PN-M}}$ A4, A7_M C5_F.

That is, Mr Weary obeyed powerful people (A4), including his father, the interviewer and the courts. In addition, he idealised his mother (A7_M) and derogated his father (C5_F). There were linguistic indications of unresolved psychological trauma, particularly around injury and punishment ($\text{Utr(dn)}_{\text{PA-F, PN-M}}$), but Mr Weary denied (dn) being physically abused by his father (PA-F) or physically neglected by his mother (PN-M).

Mr Weary asserted that physical punishment was wrong, but also spoke of spanking as normal and appropriate. He referred several times to the generational change in the rules about physical punishment and showed neither awareness of his own pain as a child, nor that of his children in foster care.

The contradictory evidence that Mr Weary offered suggested that he could not reflect on his experience or be considered psychologically integrated. Like his wife, he was committed to his family and wanted his children back; moreover, he took active leadership in achieving this.

Family. The Parents Interview (PI) involved the entire family and was videotaped. Each parent was asked about his/her childhood and parenthood. Mr Weary took charge and spoke at length about the misbehaviour of the children, even making sarcastic comments about them and also his wife. He used 'borrowed professional language' to espouse a non-punitive approach, but his sarcasm and inability to tell his own contribution to episodes and his omission of conclusions matched his AAI his strategies of compulsive compliance with power and attacks on weakness. Mrs Weary listened silently and Susan sat isolated, but occasionally helped Jasper. Jasper demanded attention and was yelled at, ignored and cuddled at different times.

The unexpected benefits of the PI were that Mr and Mrs Weary told each other things about their childhoods that they had not known. Their mutual experiences of harsh punishment, maternal absence, distrust of fathers and changes of household had not been known to the professionals either. The inconsistency of their responses to their children was displayed clearly as was Mrs Weary's 'emotional neglect' and Mr Weary's 'emotional abuse'. Strikingly, all the family members appeared unhealthy, particularly Mrs Weary who was pale and thin and Mr Weary who was extremely obese.

The Family Functional Formulation. The formulation of the family revolved around Mr and Mrs Weary's shared need for comfort and stability and the incompatibility of that for giving care to children. Their shared denial of the neglect and abuse they experienced as children led to withdrawal on Mrs Weary's part and 'righteous' punishment by Mr Weary. Both resented the new standards of parenting used to evaluate them. Nevertheless, both tried to show what they had been taught in parent education, but the language was not their own and their behaviour was inconsistent, leading to greater child disruptiveness and parental frustration.

It was recommended that parent education be discontinued because it required reflective skills that Mr and Mrs Weary did not yet have; as a consequence of providing it too soon, strict punishment had become inconsistent parenting, which increased Jasper's defiance. Instead, four approaches were suggested:

1. Health work for both parents that involved diet, exercise groups, and, for Mrs Weary, attention to clothing, hairstyles and cosmetics. Engaging in family and neighbourhood activities was a specific goal intended to reduce the family's isolation, increase their good times and expose them to models of normal family life.
2. Because of their shared childhood problems and Mr Weary's fear of his wife's infidelity, six couples' sessions were recommended to address making non-verbal expression of feelings explicit, developing conflict repair strategies, and enjoying marital sexuality. Particular attention was to be focused on eliminating Mr Weary's sarcasm and Mrs Weary's acceptance of it.
3. Sessions of parent–child video-feedback focused on (i) recognising the signs of impending trouble with Jasper and heading it off before it occurred (that is, being sensitively responsive) and (ii) using positive and negative consequences more systemically. The second point was important because Jasper's parents sometimes punished and sometimes rewarded his acting-out behaviour. Greater clarity and consistency regarding what was approved and what was not was needed if Jasper was to learn what he should do.
4. The professionals were asked to support the parents, using the same compassion for the parents that they hoped the parents would show for their children. It was clarified that compassion is not permission to commit harm, but is the beginning of working together to prevent harm.

The court decision and outcome. The court returned the children home, Jasper first and Susan a month later (after the recommendations had been implemented). Jasper's behaviour escalated briefly, but when his parents learnt to foresee and prevent his distress, he calmed down and became more cooperative. This pleased and engaged his parents. It took several months for Susan to begin to relax a bit at home, although she remained an anxious, inhibited child. Six months later, the family was still together, there was no emotional abuse or neglect, the intensity of both the children's disruptions and the parents' responses was lower, and Mr and Mrs Weary looked healthier and more attractive – and much less weary.

Conclusions regarding the theory and case example

In this case, the assessments of the parents revealed the extent of the parents' endangerment when they were children, their desire to give their children better experiences than they had had, and their current use of information processing that was reliant on pre-conscious processes, biased by transformed information, and affected by unresolved childhood trauma and loss. Put another way, these parents wanted to protect their children, but their psychological competencies were attuned to pre-conscious response to danger. The effects of this were visible in their children's assessments and in their parental relationship. Susan, as the first-born and older child, appeared to have tried to do as her parents wanted and even tried to care for them. When this failed to make her safer or more comfortable by attracting her parents, she both gave up and also felt very sad (states that are congruent with Seligman's (1975) notion of learnt helplessness). However, because feeling so vulnerable in the face of real threats of both aggression and abandonment was intolerable, Susan generated representations of ideal parents and denied their negative behaviour. In the context of 'good Susan', Jasper used a strategy of unpredictable aggression to try to attract attention, thereby increasing the probability of protection. The interplay of family history and children's strategies described here is not unusual. First-born children in troubled families typically receive more attention in a better-structured context than their younger siblings. It is often most adaptive for them to try to conform. Later-born siblings not only have a more complex, less focused family context, they also are less skilled at compliance than their older siblings. Aggressively increasing the chaos tends to be a better strategy for second-born children. Recognition of these family-level processes turned the professionals' attention away from the symptom behaviour of the children to resolving historical shortcuts in the parents' processing that affected their behaviour in the present.

Strikingly, the outcome of DMM assessment has moved beyond classification toward being a condensed psychological autobiography and family narrative – one that professionals can use to generate a personal treatment plan for each family member and for the family as a whole. Good assessment should promote good treatment and family functional formulations reduce costly exploration through misfitting interventions. We think the DMM assessments function to speed and focus treatment.

Summary

Since child abuse was identified in the 1960s, increasing numbers of children have been identified as maltreated and many children have been placed in foster care. While it is clear that some children must be protected from their parents, most professionals believe that too many children are removed. Further, it is clear that rehabilitative interventions sometimes cause harm.

In this chapter, we have offered three ways to reduce the number of children needing out-of-home care and to improve the functioning of the troubled families who retain their children. Specifically, we have suggested: i) redefining attachment as adaptation to danger, ii) replacing professional opinion about children's attachment with evidence regarding all family members' attachment, and iii) using Family Functional Formulations to design personalised treatment plans that are suited to individuals' patterns of information processing and readiness to learn.

Defining attachment as adaptation. Professionals need to think freshly about attachment. Describing troubled individuals as anxiously attached is not productive for professionals who already knew that the problems were severe. In this chapter, we define attachment as learnt strategies for protecting the self (and later one's partner and children) from danger. Dangerous parental behaviour is understood as misguided protective behaviour that is carried from childhood (when immaturity required psychological shortcuts) to adulthood, when it is misapplied.

Using the DMM strategies can enable professionals to make meaning of maladaptive behaviour. When professionals have informed compassion, their relationships with parents improve which, in turn, can facilitate parents' learning more adaptive ways to care for their children. Talking with maltreating parents about shortcuts that were essential in their childhood but are outdated now (a) respects parents' accomplishment of surviving adversity up to now, (b) acknowledges their intention to protect their children better than they themselves were protected, and (c) affirms their potential to continue to learn. Parents intuitively accept the DMM strategies as fitting themselves and find hope in the notion of lifelong adaptation. This is the first step in a productive plan for change.

Attachment and the courts. Attachment has often been used to argue for supporting the child–parent bond, but courts have had to rely on professionals' opinion regarding attachment. Often the opinions are contradictory without there being a way to validate any perspective. The DMM assessments offer differentiating evidence that all parties can examine. The evidence is drawn from assessments that have published validation on maltreating samples and is interpreted by authorised professionals. This permits disagreements to be resolved empirically.

The IASA Family Attachment Court Protocol offers several ways to present evidence on attachment to courts, together with clarity regarding the expertise underlying each. This facilitates decision-making by assisting the court to weigh the evidence judiciously.

Attachment and treatment. Families under child protection supervision vary greatly, but all experience anxious attachment. The DMM differentiates many psychologically different forms of anxious attachment. This differentiation can help professionals to identify treatments that can (a) correct the psychological shortcuts used by parents and children (thus, changing the behaviour that is disposed and enacted) and (b) reduce the risk of harmful interventions. Iatrogenic harm – that is, harm arising from intervention – can be generated when children's needs are used to select treatments for which parents are not yet ready, when the function of a behaviour is not understood, and when parents' needs are not addressed. A particular concern is educational interventions that require parents to adapt the ideas to their own family situation; most maltreating parents are not able to carry out such integrative processing. We think that the effectiveness of protective services will be greater and the cost lower if (i) ill-suited services are withheld and (ii) services reflect parents' needs. Our case example highlights the importance of selecting treatments that are in each individual's zone of proximal development, revealing parents' unresolved psychological traumas, and meeting parents' needs – so that they can meet their children's needs.

Conclusion

Parents are important people; they are the architects of the next generation. If we care about children, we must cherish and empower their parents (Bowlby, 1951). Although child protection services and family courts were designed to protect children from inadequate parents, too often they compound the problems that families face, turn parents into the enemy, and set children on a course to an even more uncertain future. Is it possible that professionals, too, use psychological shortcuts that over-simplify complex situations in ways that make action possible but not always effective? Moreover, if the services we offer are perceived as threatening by parents or their children, we might elicit precisely the protective strategies that we seek to change (thus strengthening these DRs) and also preclude parents having the corrective opportunity of experiencing a protective and comforting relationship that promoted their own growth.

It is striking that parents who maltreat their children almost always say that they want to raise their children better than they were raised. The problem is that they may still be highly attuned to the dangers they faced in their own childhoods, remaining unaware of the ways in which they repeat patterns from the past. To nurture their hope for the future – and the hope of their children – we must address these patterns and the information processing that underpins them. Using an empathic relationship to help parents to free themselves from their past may be the best way to help children to have a fresh future.

It has often been observed that we can only change ourselves, not others. Surely the same is true for professionals. Could changing the way we understand and respond to troubled parents change outcomes for families? If so, our best approach will be to engage compassionately with each family member, appreciating each perspective, and then following a variation of the Golden Rule; do unto parents as we would have them do unto their children.

References

Ainsworth, M.D.S. & Bowlby, J. (1991). An ethological approach to personality development. *American Psychologist*, 41, 333–341.

Ainsworth, M., Blehar, M., Waters, E. & Wall, S. (1978). *Patterns of Attachment*. Hillsdale, NJ: Erlbaum.

Baim, C. & Morrison, T. (2011). *Attachment-based Practice with Adults: Understanding Strategies and Promoting Positive Change*. Brighton: Pavilion.

Beck, A.T., Rush, A.J., Shaw, B.F. & Emery, G. (1979). *Cognitive Therapy of Depression*. New York: Guilford Press.

Bowlby, J. (1951). *Maternal Care and Mental Health*. New York: Schocken.

Bowlby, J. (1969). *Attachment and Loss, Volume 1: Attachment*. New York: Basic Books.

Bowlby, J. (1973). *Attachment and Loss, Volume II: Separation, Anxiety and Anger*. The International Psycho-Analytical Library, 95. London: The Hogarth Press and the Institute of Psycho-Analysis, 1–429.

Bowlby, J. (1980). *Attachment and Loss, Volume 3: Loss*. New York: Basic Books.

Bowlby, J. (1988/1995). *A Secure Base: Clinical Applications of Attachment Theory*. London: Routledge.

Brown, D.P. & Elliott, D.S. (2016). *Attachment Disturbances in Adults: A Treatment Manual for Comprehensive Attachment Repair*. New York: Norton & Company.

Cicchetti, D. & Valentino, K. (2006). An ecological-transactional perspective on child maltreatment: Failure of the average expectable environment and its influence upon child development. In: D. Cicchetti and D.J. Cohen (eds) *Developmental Psychopathology: Risk, Disorder, and Adaptation*, 2nd edn, vol. 3. New York: Wiley.

Cozolino, L. (2002). *The Neuroscience of Psychotherapy: Building and Rebuilding the Human Brain*. New York: Norton.

Crittenden, P.M. (1983). *Mother and infant patterns of interaction: Developmental relationships*. Dissertation presented to the University of Virginia.

Crittenden, P.M. (1985). Social networks, quality of child-rearing, and child development. *Child Development*, 56, 1299–1313.

Crittenden, P.M. (1988). Relationships at risk. In: J. Belsky & T. Nezworski (eds), *The Clinical Implications of Attachment*. Hillsdale, NJ: Lawrence Erlbaum, 136–174.

Crittenden, P.M. (1992a). Children's strategies for coping with adverse home environments. *International Journal of Child Abuse and Neglect*, 16, 329–343.

Crittenden, P.M. (1992b). The social ecology of treatment: Case study of a service system for maltreated children. *American Journal of Orthopsychiatry*, 62, 22–34.

Crittenden, P.M. (1994). Peering into the black box: An exploratory treatise on the development of self in young children. In: D. Cicchetti & S. Toth (eds), *Rochester Symposium on Developmental Psychopathology, Vol. 5. The Self and Its Disorders*. Rochester, NY: University of Rochester Press, 79–148.

Crittenden, P.M. (1995). Attachment and psychopathology. In: S. Goldberg, R. Muir, J. Kerr, (eds), *John Bowlby's Attachment Theory: Historical, Clinical, and Social Significance*. New York: The Analytic Press, 367–406.

Crittenden, P.M. (2002a). Attachment, information processing and psychiatric disorder. *World Psychiatry*, 1, 72–75.

Crittenden, P.M. (2002b). If I knew then what I know now: Integrity and fragmentation in the treatment of child abuse and neglect. In: K. Browne, H. Hanks, P. Stratton and C. Hamilton (eds), *Prediction and Prevention of Child Abuse: A Handbook*. Chichester: John Wiley and Sons, Ltd, 111–126.

Crittenden, P.M. (2005). The origins of physical punishment: An ethological/attachment perspective on the use of punishment by human parents. In: M. Donnelly & M.A. Strauss (eds), *Corporal Punishment of Children in Theoretical Perspective*. New Haven: Yale University Press, 73–90.

Crittenden, P.M. (2008). *Raising Parents: Attachment, Parenting and Child Safety*. Devon: Willan Press.

Crittenden, P.M. (2015). *Raising Parents: Attachment, Representation, and Treatment*, 2nd edn. London: Routledge.

Crittenden, P.M. & Ainsworth, M.D.S. (1989). Child maltreatment and attachment theory. In: D. Cicchetti and V. Carlson (eds), *Handbook of Child Maltreatment*. New York: Cambridge University Press, 432–463.

Crittenden, P.M. & Dallos, R.D. (2014). An attachment approach to treatment: DMM-FST integrative treatment. *Clinical Child and Family Psychology Review*, 2, 53–61.

Crittenden, P.M. & DiLalla, D.L. (1988). Compulsive compliance: The development of an inhibitory coping strategy in infancy. *Journal of Abnormal Child Psychology*, 16, 585–599.

Crittenden, P. & Landini, A. (2011). *Assessing Adult Attachment: A Dynamic-Maturational Approach to Discourse Analysis*. New York: Norton.

Crittenden, P., Dallos, R., Landini, A. & Kozlowska, K. (2014). *Attachment and Family Therapy*. Maidenhead: Open University Press.

Crittenden, P.M., Farnfield, S., Landini, A. & Grey, B. (2013). Assessing attachment for family court decision-making. *Journal of Forensic Practice*, 15, 237–248.

Damasio, A. (1994). *Descartes' Error: Emotion, Reason and the Human Brain*. New York: Avon.

Daubert v Merrell Dow Pharmaceuticals (1993) 509 US 579.

De Zulueta, F. (1993). *From Pain to Violence: The Traumatic Roots of Destructiveness*. London: Whurr Publishers.

Eagleman, D. (2011). *Incognito: The Secret Lives of the Brain*. New York: Knopf Doubleday.

Farnfield, S., Hautamaki, A., Nørbech, P. & Sahhar, N. (2010). DMM assessments of attachment and adaptation: Procedures, validity and utility. *Clinical Child Psychology and Psychiatry* 15, 313–328.

Fonagy, P. (2001). *Attachment Theory and Psychoanalysis*. New York: Other Press.

George, C., Kaplan, N. & Main, M. (1996). *The Adult Attachment Interview Protocol*, 3rd edn. Unpublished manuscript, University of California, Berkeley.

Gerhardt, S. (2004). *Why Love Matters: How Affection Shapes a Baby's Brain*. Hove: Routledge.

Hertzman, C. (2013). The significance of early childhood adversity. *Paediatric Child Health*, 18, 127.

Howe, D. (2005). *Child Abuse and Neglect: Attachment, Development and Intervention*. Basingstoke: Palgrave Macmillan.

Howe, D. (2011). *Attachment Across the Lifecourse: A Brief Introduction*. Basingstoke: Palgrave Macmillan.

Keyes, K.M., Eaton, N.R., Krueger, R.F. et al. (2014). Childhood maltreatment and the structure of common psychiatric disorders. *British Journal of Psychiatry*.

Kuleshnyk, I. (1984). The Stockholm syndrome: Toward an understanding. *Social Action and the Law*, 10, 37.

Landa, S. & Duschinsky, R. (2013). Crittenden's Dynamic-Maturational Model of Attachment and Adaptation. *Review of General Psychology*, 17, 326–338.

Mather, M. & Sutherland, M.R. (2011). Arousal-biased competition in perception and memory. *Perspectives on Psychological Science*, 6, 114–133.

McLaughlin, K.A., Greif, G.J., Gruber, M.J. et al. (2012). Childhood adversities and first onset of psychiatric disorders in a national sample of US adolescents. *Archives of General Psychiatry*, 69, 1151–1160.

Milaniak, I. & Widom, C.S. (2015). Does child abuse and neglect increase risk for perpetration of violence inside and outside the home? *Psychology of Violence*, 5, 246–255.

Panksepp, J. (2005). *Affective Neuroscience: The Foundations of Human and Animal Emotions (Series in Affective Science)*. Oxford: Oxford University Press.

Perry, B. (2008). Child maltreatment: A neurodevelopmental perspective on the role of abuse in psychopathology. In: P. Beauchaine and S.P. Hinshaw (eds), *Textbook of Child and Adolescent Psychopathology*. Hoboken: John Wiley & Sons, Inc.

Pocock, D. (2010). The DMM – Wow! But how to handle its potential strength? *Clinical Child Psychology and Psychiatry*, 15, 303–311.

Read, J., L. Mosher & R. Bentall (eds) (2004). *Models of Madness: Psychological, Social and Biological Approaches to Schizophrenia*. Hove: Brunner-Routledge.

Schacter, D.L. & Tulving, E. (1994). What are the memory systems of 1994? In: D.L. Schacter & E. Tulving (eds), *Memory Systems 1994*. Cambridge, MA: Bradford, 1–38.

Seligman, M.P.E. (1975). *Helplessness: On Depression, Development, and Death*. New York: W.H. Freeman.

Seligman, M. (2013). *Washington Post* (2013), www.washingtonpost.com/in-debating-newtoen-massacre-don't-confuse-crazy-and-evil/2013/01/03/4d12eb62-5136-11e2-8b49-64675006147f_story.html.

Thompson, A. & Raikes, H. (2003). Towards the next quarter-century: conceptual and methodological challenges for attachment theory. *Development and Psychopathology* 15, 691–718.

Vygotsky, L.S. (1978). *Mind and Society: The Development of Higher Psychological Processes*. Cambridge, MA: Harvard University Press.

Wallin, D. (2007). *Attachment in Psychotherapy*. New York: Guilford.

Part V
Novel Interventions with Families

24

Working Systemically with Families with Intimate Partner Violence

Arlene Vetere

VID Specialized University, Olso, Norway

When we know, or suspect, that violence occurs between adults who look after children, our fears and concerns for the safety of all family members are raised. So, the question of whether it can be safe to offer family and couples therapy becomes both urgent and vexed. The UK-based 'Reading Safer Families' family violence intervention project has been developed over the past 20 years. It offers assessment and therapeutic intervention to individuals, couples and families who are referred to our practice when violence is a problem. Referrals are received from health and social care professional practitioners, the probation service and women's shelters. A *minimum* of six meetings are offered to establish and review a safety plan within a no-violence contract, designed to de-escalate conflictual patterns of interaction, to manage unhelpful physiological arousal, and to help establish new patterns of problem-solving where hurt, fear and disappointment may find resolution. If it is considered unsafe to embark on relationship therapy with a couple or family, individual therapeutic work may be offered for both victims and perpetrators. The intervention project is governed by UK definitions of intimate partner violence and UK law and works with violence in all its forms: physical, psychological/emotional, sexual, neglect. It is concerned with children's exposure to adult violence and violence across the family life cycle in all intimate relationships: couples, parents and children, including grown-up children, siblings (both younger and older), older people and their carers.

Our therapeutic practice is embedded in a systemic framework, which is used to explore and support the triangular relationship between risk of future violence, responsibility for safety and for behaviour that harms others, and collaborative practice with families and the professional network (Cooper & Vetere, 2005). Indeed, systemic therapy has been demonstrated to be effective with a wide range of child and adult psychological problems and family and relationship difficulties, including violent and antisocial behaviour patterns (Carr, 2009a; Carr, 2009b). Eckhardt, Murphy, Whitaker et al. (2013) in their Findings from the Partner Abuse State of Knowledge Project conclude that a wide variety of interventions appear to reduce or eliminate interpersonal violence among perpetrators and victims, such as individual, couple and family therapy, and group therapy. In particular, they recommend that practitioners and policy-makers both consider and implement a variety of different interventions in the community to reduce interpersonal violence.

This chapter describes a safety methodology for safe therapeutic practice with individuals, couples and families in the 'Reading Safer Families' family violence intervention project. In this chapter, we will outline and explain how we use a systemic approach to help family members stop the violence, and where possible, to repair relationships. We outline our contra-indications for relationship therapy at the end of this chapter.

Setting the Scene

People are more likely to be killed, physically assaulted, hit, beaten up, slapped or spanked in their own homes by other family members than anywhere else, or by anyone else in our society (Gelles & Cornell, 1990, p. 5)

A wish for denial. When I read the above quotation, I am reminded of my wish for denial – the wish that perhaps the violence did not happen, or was not so serious, or will not happen again. There is much written about this from an individual perspective, but as a systemic practitioner, I am interested in what happens when a group collectively holds a wish for denial, such as in a family or a professional team (Hanks & Vetere, 2016). Alternately, what happens when there is fear and anxiety within the professional system, for example, how are these dynamic processes recognised, who can comment on them, and who is there to help? When working with families in the child protection system we need to pay attention to the complex relationships between professionals and family members and the unspoken role of anxiety around risks of future violence in determining whether or not we shall be allowed to settle down into working therapeutically with a family.

Entitlement to safety. We have observed that most definitions of physical and emotional abuse in the family speak of what people *do* that harms others. Very few definitions speak of what people do not do, and when thinking of safety we need to consider how people do not take steps to protect themselves and others. We meet family members who hold no sense of entitlement to be safe in their intimate relationships. Our first task is to deconstruct this lack of entitlement – what happened to you as you grew up that you did not develop the idea that you could be safe? What did people do to you? And what did they not do? Our moral position in this work is clear – we believe people are entitled to live without fear of the people they love. We recognise this is easy to say, and harder to achieve, and that it sits alongside our own complex moral dilemmas and meanings around violence in relationships and within different levels of society.

Substance use as affect regulation. Many family members we meet have an untreated substance use problem (Vetere, 2014). For some, their reliance on psychoactive substances is a form of affect regulation, for example, alcohol provides an escape from unbearable feelings of shame, fear, sadness and humiliation. To insist, as some family violence projects do, that the substance use be treated first, before entry to the project, is too much to ask of some family members if their emotional and relational context remains unchanged. Thus we insist they access treatment from our local community drugs and alcohol service alongside working with us. We attend to the relational context and problems of affect regulation, while the alcohol key worker, for example, supports the reduction of substance use. These partnerships are enabled and supported by close and careful liaison between ourselves and our colleagues in the community drugs and alcohol service, with full knowledge and participation of the affected family members.

Corrective and replicative scripts. As systemic practitioners we are interested in family culture – that collection of ideas, beliefs and practices that defines a family group – and how children learn that culture and perhaps pass it on in their own adult relationships as parents and partners. Intergenerational learning in families has been conceptualised as a process of enacting corrective and replicative scripts, for example, in relation to care giving, how we decide to continue with some caring practices (replicative – making soup for our children when they are sick, because our mother did it for us as a child, and it was comforting) and how we decide to change them (corrective – perhaps we did not like the soup as it made us nauseous, so for our children we try to find another way to offer comfort when they are sick) (Byng-Hall, 1995). Working with corrective scripts allows us to acknowledge family members' *intentions* to change and to do things better in their own turn, even if the effect is not to make things better! So, when working with family violence, we are always interested in what the children are learning; for example, how children might be learning that violence is acceptable, or not acceptable, or tolerable, or trivial, or deserved, and how the parents (and grandparents?) in their turn, when children, learnt that violence is part of family life. If the violence is observed between the adults in the household, we might ask future questions to help the parents articulate a different future for their own children. For example, John, as a father, when your daughter grows up, what do you want her to learn from you about how to keep herself safe? Mary, as a mother, when your son grows up, what do you want him to learn from you about how to keep a future partner safe? Future questions enable family members to speak with hope and aspiration for the future of their children and families, and can form the basis of growing trust between family members and practitioners. We can then use their responses to work backwards, so to say, to the present, and to begin to plan for safety, with an idea of their preferred futures.

The need for multiple theories. When working with family violence, we have two conversations simultaneously, i.e., understanding how violence comes to pass, and helping family members hold themselves accountable for their behaviour that harms others. Violence in family relationships is a complex phenomenon, with moral, legal and psychological aspects. We need to understand how violent behaviour happens in order to make a safety plan, and to help family members predict and prevent violence, often by de-escalating conflictual interactions in difficult moments and working therapeutically with their trauma histories and responses. Pregnancy provides us with a poignant and dangerous example of when multiple theories help us understand what might be happening in the partners' relationship with each other and their unborn child. Audit studies would suggest that one-third of violence from a man partner to his woman partner either starts or escalates during pregnancy (McWilliams & McKiernan, 1993). Systemic theory holds the triangle as the basic human relationship, rather than the dyad. This means that when any two people get together their relationship is influenced by each other's relationship with a third – the third might be present, absent or dead (Dallos & Vetere, 2012). For example, when two sisters go out to supper, their relationship is influenced by each other's relationship with their absent sister. With pregnancy, the presence and meaning of the unborn child has made concrete the triangular nature of the couple relationship. Similarly, attachment theory and trauma theory help us understand the powerful intersect between love, passion and unhelpful physiological arousal on the one hand, and systemic theory of control, coercion and violence on the other. Powerful emotions such as jealousy and fear of loss can be aroused for a partner during a pregnancy, so understanding the attachment significance and attachment threat can aid our safety planning with a couple. Reliance on a single model explanation for family violence, and for intervention with family violence, cannot help us explain the complexity of the history and the lived reality of violence in families.

Our Safety Methodology for Safe Practice: Risk, Responsibility and Collaboration

The management of risk of further violence

Our work is never without risk of further violence, so we think about the management of risk in some respects as separate from the assessment of risk. Whenever we are confronted with questions of safety and risk, we occupy these three positions simultaneously: we know what we know; we know what we do not know; and we do not know what we do not know. Hence our response is to take action and plan for safety within our risk management strategy. Our safety methodology is based in the systemic theory of triangles – we work for safety using three perspectives/positions as a basic minimum. The three perspectives are: the client family, ourselves and that of the 'stable third'.

When there is fear and anxiety within the professional system about the possibility of further physical violence in the family, we pay attention to this by recruiting a third perspective into our safety planning work. We are trying to create a stable triangle as a platform for safe practice. The 'stable third' can corroborate what the family members are telling us about stopping the violence, can help us think about and plan for safety, and, if children are involved, the stable third needs to know the children and to be able to visit the family home. If our referral has come from the social worker, and the family get on with the social worker, they can also be our stable third. If not, anyone can, in principle, be our stable third, as long as they are known and trusted by all members of the family/professional system. In our experience this has been faith leaders, social workers, community and youth workers, CPNs, family doctors, health visitors, grandparents, and so on. The stable third attends our first or second meeting with the family when we are drawing up the safety plan, and returns to review the safety plan with us and the family after the third or fourth meeting, and further as deemed necessary.

The safety plan is developed within a no-violence contract. The no-violence contract is either a written or a spoken undertaking to stop further physical violence. The family members' responsibility is to stop the violence and our responsibility is to help them stop. We allow a minimum of six meetings to establish the safety plan and give it a chance of working. We call these meetings 'safety planning meetings'. We do not call them relationship therapy meetings, despite the fact we are using therapeutic ideas and methods to develop and support the safety plan.

The safety plan is designed to help predict future violence, to prevent future violence, and to de-escalate conflictual, difficult interactions that have in the past led to unhelpful physiological arousal, activation of schemas of entitlement to use violence, defensive processes of self-protection against shame and humiliation, and the escalation into emotional and physical assault. Thus, we start by asking for a description of the worst or last episode of violence. We walk around in the description slowly, asking who was there, and what happened – we track what people did, what they thought, what they felt, what they said and what they intended – so that we might understand how difficult interaction escalated into violence. We are looking for the triggers for violence – internal triggers and external triggers – as well as people's resources, strengths and past experiences of coping and preventing violence.

External triggers for violence are often events, episodes and relationships outside the family that cause stress in the couple/family relationships, such as debts, gambling, job losses, hostile neighbours, difficult relationships with extended family, and so on. These external sources of stress and anxiety can prompt a difficult discussion for a couple, for example, with an accusation that one is spending too much money, or not trying hard enough to look for another job, or one partner is loyal to in-laws and not the other partner, and so on. These external stresses and how they are discussed and managed in the couple relationship have the potential to create hurt feelings, and strong emotional reactions of fear, shame and anger.

Internal triggers for violence often have attachment significance and arise out of attachment threats and attachment injuries, for example, fear of loss, rejection and abandonment, and fear of shaming and humiliation (Dallos & Vetere, 2009). Family members might be carrying forward unresolved hurts and experiences of shame from past interactions that are triggered within the current interaction. We often find we work with family members who do not repair or heal past hurts in their relationships, for fear of 'going back' and triggering further emotional upset and more violence. These unresolved hurts, disappointments and humiliations can be re-evoked in a difficult interaction, accompanied by unhelpful physiological arousal, leaving family members preoccupied with affect regulation and struggling to think clearly about choices and action. Thus, rehearsing the safety plan, many times over, is critical to help people remember the plan when they are anxious and physiologically flooded. This is why 'time out' is a useful short-term strategy in helping to manage physiological flooding. Any family member can call 'time out' and all need to agree to follow the safety plan. If we are working with a man who is in an intimate partnership and possibly has children, it is crucial that the partner consults with us about whether the safety plan can work. The stable third also informs the safety planning as described above. We also discuss and plan how people will calm themselves down, and what people will do when they calm down – whether it can be safe to return to the topic that escalated unhelpfully, or whether they take the discussion to the stable third, or wait for the next meeting with us.

As part of the safety planning and 'time out' agreements, we are also helping people develop a range of strategies to help them calm and soothe themselves when unhelpfully aroused. Many family members we work with have not had childhood experiences of being comforted when frightened and distressed and often struggle to self-soothe, to distract themselves, and to 'talk' themselves down. We seek feedback on how they calmed down, at each subsequent meeting, and whether, upon implementing new strategies of self-soothing, they could feel themselves calming down. We explore self-talk during the arousal phase of a difficult interaction. Very often people do not realise they are 'talking up' their arousal, perhaps with self-statements of entitlement and defensiveness. We slow down these processes to help people begin to recognise and track how they talk to themselves in ways that aggravate their arousal levels. In addition, we help people tune into their bodies and their physiological responses; for example, learning to recognise the early build-up of tension in the muscles, of changes in breathing and heart rate, and so on. At each subsequent meeting we seek feedback on the safety plan, make adjustments and changes where needed, and reinforce success and signs of safety. Our approach to long-term safety is to support the development of trust and emotional safety in family members' relationships, constructive problem-solving, healing and repair in relationships, and more satisfying and bonding interactions.

The assessment of risk of further violence

The assessment of risk of further violence proceeds alongside the safety planning (i.e., the management of risk). We recognise that past violence is a predictor of future violence, so assessment of risk completes the work we do on helping people take responsibility for their behaviour (see section below). We ask about the frequency, severity and duration of violence, and the contexts in which it occurs; for example, at home, at work, in the sports hall, in the pub, in the street, and so on. In our project we are concerned to help people understand and manage their emotional responses, and so we need to determine if the violence arises out of unhelpful, unregulated arousal and entitlement to treat others in certain ways, or whether the violence is primarily calculated to control and coerce in an instrumental way. We are trained to work therapeutically with the former, but not the latter, so this distinction is crucial to our work.

We explore family members' capacity for empathy and to 'stand in the emotional shoes of the other'. We are looking for a willingness to listen to others, to develop a compassionate curiosity about the other's position and experiences in interactions, and to reflect on one's own experiences and learning. Self-reflexivity may not have developed fully for some family members whose own childhoods were marred by fear and violence, when it was not safe to contemplate what was happening (van der Kolk, 2014). Self-protective strategies sometimes demand we do not dwell on others' intentions to harm us, or their failure to protect us. We are fully prepared in our work to help family members further develop their compassion for their own adverse childhood experiences, and for others' hurt and distress, often caused by them, and to develop their ability to integrate and reflect on their intentions, actions, thoughts and feelings.

As part of our assessment of the risk of future physical violence, we require some acknowledgement from family members that there is a problem, and that it needs to be addressed. Our responsibility is to help family members develop their commitment to a resolution, and their responsibility is to stop the violence. We address this further in the section immediately below.

Responsibility for safety and for behaviour that harms others

In taking responsibility for behaviour that harms others, family members need to recognise the impact their behaviour has on others, on themselves, and just as importantly, on their relationships with family members. They are required to develop a commitment to a resolution and to recognise that violent behaviour is a problem to be solved! Constant blaming of others is a contra-indication for therapeutic work with family relationships. However, initial defensiveness is to be expected when family members are told to come and work with us and sometimes we find that people believe defensiveness is the best way to protect their family life. We often ask future questions to help people soften in the face of their own defensiveness and to speak well and with aspiration for the future of their families. As an example: John, as a father, what do you hope your daughter will learn from you about how to keep herself safe in her future relationships? We then use their responses to work back to the present day and to see how we might work together to achieve these aspirations for future safety.

We do not meet with children in the company of their parents/carers until we are convinced that the parents are taking safety seriously. We might well meet the children on their own or in a sibling group (Vetere & Cooper, 2005). Their points of view are helpful in safety planning, and we can support them in thinking of their own safety. We may find that the children have been taking responsibility for safety in the family, for example, calling the police when there is violence, trying to protect their mothers, or telling extended family members. We ask where the children go when there is violence, if they know where their siblings are, who they talk to about the violence and what they 'do' with their worries and fears. We might learn that violence is an open secret within the family system so that talking with us might be the first time the children have been encouraged to be direct and straightforward about their experiences.

We meet mothers who tell us their children do not know about the violence to them. This is a difficult and poignant conversation to have with a mother who has comforted herself with the belief she has protected the children from knowing. We tell mothers we think the children always know about the violence – they may not know the details, but they are sensitive to the well-being of their parents and the people looking after them, and to the well-being of the relationship between the parents. Sometimes we talk to the mothers about the research findings on children's exposure to violence and the developmental impact for the children (Mullender, Hague, Imam et al., 2002).

Finally, in our attempts to help people take responsibility, we pay attention to the language people use to describe their violent behaviour. In particular we look for language that minimises both the violence and its impact. For example, if someone said, I just hit him, or, I only hit her – we would deconstruct the minimising words 'only' and 'just'. We would ask, if I was there, what would I see? Where did you hit her? What did you hit her with? How hard did you hit her? How many times did you hit her? What did she do when you hit her? And so on. Similarly we listen for the use of the active or passive voice (in grammatical terms) when people talk about their violent behaviour. The active voice in grammar is agentic language, whereas the passive voice in grammar can slide away from responsibility for action. For example, the sentence, 'I hit him' locates agency with the speaker, whereas the phrase 'the red mist came down' as a description of a violent rage appears to have no subject or agent. Often, family members will use the phrase, 'I lost it', when referring to an aggressive outburst. We listen for idiomatic language and try to encourage people to deconstruct their use of these 'taken for granted' phrases. So, we might ask, 'what did you lose? From the point of view of the person you hit, you might be thought to have gained it.' This approach to deconstruction can pave the way to unravelling the paradox of interpersonal power, i.e., at the moment I felt at my most helpless, I hit out at you, to shut you up, yet that is the moment when you felt me at my most powerful.

Collaborative practice

Most of the couples and families we work with in the child protection system are required to work with us as part of a wider legal agreement to either help keep the family together or to assess for and enable family re-unification following child protection proceedings. Sometimes we are asked to help a couple make a safe separation given the increased risk of violence during times of separation and divorce. This all raises the question of how we can work in cooperative and collaborative ways, with the family and with their professional network. We ask the family whether we can still have a useful and helpful conversation. For all our clients, the stakes are very high – they can lose that which is most precious to them – and this in turn can raise defensive and self-protective processes that could get in their way of achieving their goals.

The ability to trust and to form trusting relationships is central to achieving change and in taking emotional and relational risks. Thus, we aim to be as transparent as possible in our work. We achieve this in a number of ways. We identify and speak about the risks we all take in this work with the family: a) for the parents and children, any further violence could threaten the parents' ability to look after their children; b) for the stable third, who might also be their social worker, any further violence could threaten their ability to promote safety planning work; and c) for us, any further violence could threaten our reputation and ability to work with families for their future safety. We are clear about our moral position in this work – we believe all family members are entitled to live without fear of the people they love. We realise this is sometimes very hard to achieve, and we are clear about our own moral dilemmas in relation to physical and emotional violence.

We live in cultures that take up different positions around the use of violence at different levels of social structure, but what seems to be important in this work is the willingness to acknowledge these discrepancies, and the fact we are all subject to similar conflicting social discourses. We recognise that we are asking our clients to promise to never behave with violence again, and similarly we recognise that we do not actually ask the same of ourselves. Living family life in the goldfish bowl of others' critical scrutiny, and sometimes over long periods and with many changes of social worker, demands much of a family's resources and family members' willingness to stay committed and cooperative around working toward a resolution. In our experience, parents' ability to see professional practitioners as potentially helpful to their family and their ability to remain cooperative are useful predictors of good outcomes for the family. Thus much of what we do in our work with families is helping them to navigate complex professional systems and supporting and promoting cooperative working relationships. This involves us in spending as much time in liaising with the professional network as in working face-to-face with families. We fully acknowledge our role as agents of social control in our work with families. Our expressed purpose is to help them stop the violence and live safer and more fulfilling lives so they can continue to care for themselves, for each other and for their children, for now and for the future.

Our approach to transparency in our practice is embodied in our use of reflective processes. Whenever possible we work together – one of us takes the lead interviewing/practitioner role and the other acts as the in-room consultant, and we keep the same role for the duration of the work with a particular family. The in-room consultant takes the process notes during the meetings with the family and they form the basis of any report we are asked to provide. The in-room consultant might intervene two or three times during the conversation between the lead therapist and the family members, and will offer a summary of their thinking and responses to the conversational exchange near the end of the meeting. During these interventions, we invite the family members to listen to our conversation and then to offer their reflections on what they have heard. The in-room consultant's interventions might consist of offering support for difficult family experiences, for example, with a family bereavement, or providing support for what is going well for the family, or in raising questions of safety and responsibility when the lead is working to help the development of trust in the face of defensiveness and fear. We have written extensively elsewhere of our use of reflecting processes (Cooper & Vetere, 2005; Vetere & Dallos, 2009) but suffice to say here that we make a commitment to bringing our ideas into the room in our work with families and undertake to tell them what we are thinking, what we notice and appreciate about them, and, of course, what we might be worried about.

Contra-Indications for Safe Relational Therapeutic Practice with Couples and Families

In many respects, the contra-indications for safe therapeutic practice with family and couple relationships can be seen as the opposite of the signs of safety for safe practice. As explained above, we offer a minimum of six meetings to develop a safety plan within the no-violence contract and to see if the safety plan can work. If we consider it unsafe to offer relationship therapy, we can still offer individual therapy or group work.

The contra-indications are not a checklist as such, but together, in combination, inform our thinking and decision not to proceed with relationship therapy and inform our supervision of other professionals' practice (Vetere, 2012). Thus, if the person responsible for inflicting harm on others is unwilling or unable to take responsibility for their actions, and does not acknowledge that their behaviour is a problem, and has an effect on themselves, on others and in their relationships within the family, we do not offer relationship therapy. Unwillingness to take responsibility for behaviour that harms others can show as constant blaming of others, as a refusal to reflect on past experience and show empathy for the victim, as an unwillingness to listen to another point of view, and as an inability to develop a commitment to a resolution. We might also see a lack of respect for social control, seeing people as objects rather than as people, and a refusal to treat an alcohol/drug problem that is implicated in the violence.

Working in the Territory: Looking After Ourselves

In our therapeutic work with family violence we hear terrible stories and witness harm and injury, alongside powerful and heart-warming processes of reconciliation and recovery. The emotional impact on us of doing this work was summed up by Berger (2001) as an openness 'to absorbing profound loss, hurt and mistrust from our clients but also the stimulation of these human states present in all of us' (p. 189). The risks to us of secondary traumatisation are well documented and can originate from too much time spent listening to traumatic material, or a too high case load with little or no supervision or organisational support, and with a strong wish for denial (Figley, 2002). The impact of secondary traumatisation can show with symptoms of post-traumatic stress, such as difficulties with sleeping, hyper-vigilance, difficulties concentrating, and so on, or with the evocation of powerful feelings in the therapist, such as intense compassion and an intensification of efforts to be compassionate. Our unexamined and unacknowledged feelings can get in the way of our work, and, if not attended to, can lead to a feeling of 'burnout', which is characterised by cynicism, a sense of hopelessness and reduced effectiveness.

For us, it is important both to be aware of these risks to our well-being and ability to practise therapeutically, and to look for and support signs of adversity-activated growth in our personal and professional development. This 'both/and' relationship to risk, growth and well-being is best seen and supported in regular reflective supervision and consultation, in our experience. In this context we can pay attention to counter-transference issues and to any emergent signs of post-traumatic stress, and support colleagues in seeking further help if needed. Our self-care and sense of competence and confidence in our work is supported by setting and reviewing realistic expectations and goals that help us maintain our sense of appropriate interpersonal and emotional boundaries. We will always ask about our supervisees' well-being and expect those who supervise us to be similarly interested and supportive. We find that our sense of balance in life is best achieved by not always working alone, by reading the literature, by teaching others and attending conferences and further training, by taking occasional 'time outs' from therapy, by collaborating with community groups and by framing some of our work as preventative for the next generation. Fundamentally for us, good supervision helps us stay persistent in the face of disappointment, discouragement and 'not listening'.

References

Berger, H. (2001). Trauma and the therapist. In: T. Spiers (ed), *Trauma: A Practitioner's Guide to Counselling*. Hove: Brunner Routledge.

Byng-Hall, J. (1995). *Rewriting Family Scripts: Improvisations and Systems Change*. New York: Guilford Press.

Carr, A. (2009a). The effectiveness of family therapy and systemic interventions for child-focused problems. *Journal of Family Therapy*, 31, 3–45.

Carr, A. (2009b). The effectiveness of family therapy and systemic interventions for adult-focused problems. *Journal of Family Therapy*, 31, 46–74.

Cooper, J. & Vetere, A. (2005). *Domestic Violence and Family Safety: Working Systemically with Violence in the Family*. Chichester: John Wiley & Sons, Ltd.

Dallos, R. & Vetere, A., (2009). *Systemic Therapy and Attachment Narratives: Applications in a Range of Clinical Settings*. London: Routledge.

Dallos, R. & Vetere, A. (2012). Triangles and triangulation: A possible bridge between systemic theory and attachment theory. *Journal of Family Therapy*, 34, 117–137.

Eckhardt, C., Murphy, C., Whitaker, D. et al. (2013). The effectiveness of intervention programs for perpetrators and victims of interpersonal violence: Findings from the Partner Abuse State of Knowledge Project. *Partner Abuse*, 4, 175–195.

Figley, C. (2002). Compassion fatigue: Psychotherapists' chronic lack of self-care. *Journal of Clinical Psychology*, 58, 1433–1441.

Gelles, R. & Cornell, C. (1990). *Intimate Violence in Families*. Beverly Hills, CA: Sage.

Hanks, H. & Vetere, A. (2016). Working at the extremes: the impact on us of doing the work. In A. Vetere and P. Stratton (eds.), *Interacting Selves: Systemic solutions for personal and professional development in counselling and psychotherapy*, 65–84. London: Routledge.

McWilliams, M. & McKiernan, J. (1993). *Bringing It Out in the Open: Domestic violence in Northern Ireland*. Belfast: Her Majesty's Stationery Office.

Mullender, A., Hague, G., Imam, U. et al. (2002). *Children's Perspectives on Domestic Violence*. London: Sage.

van der Kolk, B. (2014). *The Body Keeps the Score: Brain, Mind and Body in the Treatment of Trauma*. New York: Viking.

Vetere, A. (2012). Supervision and consultation practice with domestic violence. *Clinical Child Psychology and Psychiatry*, 17, 181–185.

Vetere, A. (2014). Alcohol misuse, attachment dilemmas, and triangles of interaction: A systemic approach to practice. In: R. Gill (ed), *Addictions from an Attachment Perspective: Do Broken Bonds and Early Trauma Lead to Addictive Behaviours?* London: Karnac.

Vetere, A. & Cooper, J. (2005). In: A. Vetere and E. Dowling (eds), *Narrative Therapies with Children and Their Families*. London: Routledge.

Vetere, A. & Dallos, R. (2009). Family mirrors: Reflective practice in systemic therapies. In: J. Stedmon and R. Dallos (eds), *Reflective Practice in Psychotherapy and Counselling*. Maidenhead: Open University Press.

25

Working with Non-Offending Parents in Cases of Child Sexual Abuse

Isabelle V. Daignault[1], Mireille Cyr[2] and Martine Hébert[3]

[1] School of Criminology, University of Montreal
[2] Psychology Department, University of Montreal
[3] Department of Sexology, University of Quebec, Montreal

Child sexual abuse is a form of violence that often presents itself insidiously, thus leaving its young victims with the challenging task of understanding and revealing its occurrence. Once this form of abuse is out in the open, non-offending parents often describe a shocking wave of uneasiness scattered with negative feelings of great intensity. Helping families through this crisis certainly involves a systemic approach, one that takes into account the needs of the victim, of his/her family members and of the parent responsible for protecting and supporting the child through the upcoming steps leading to recovery. The challenge lies in the fact that such steps have the characteristic of being unknown to most parents and to most sources of support. In other words, very few people know what to do and how to react in cases of sexual abuse. Yet the victim needs to feel that others do. Michel Lemay (2006), child psychiatrist, addresses what he calls the role and toll of working with non-offending parents in cases of sexual abuse. He underscores how clinicians sometimes foster ambivalent feelings with regard to parents. He describes parents as the forever forgotten ones but also the often-accused ones. As Lemay outlines, we as clinicians attribute to parents' numerous roles in the presenting problem, varying from parents being fully to partly responsible, to being vulnerable and requiring therapeutic help. Yet, the implication of parents is also perceived as essential to a successful therapeutic intervention in children. We want them to take responsibility, to be involved and mobilised for change (Lemay, 2006). In this chapter, the various challenges faced by parents after their child's disclosure of sexual abuse will be examined. Our review will include the familial, social and judicial dimensions of parents' adaptation as well as the existing services that can be provided to help parents in the support and protection roles we expect them to play.

The Wiley Handbook of What Works in Child Maltreatment: An Evidence-Based Approach to Assessment and Intervention in Child Protection, First Edition. Edited by Louise Dixon, Daniel F. Perkins, Catherine Hamilton-Giachritsis, and Leam A. Craig.
© 2017 John Wiley & Sons Ltd. Published 2017 by John Wiley & Sons Ltd.

Disclosure-Related Challenges for Non-Offending Parents

For parents, learning that their child has been sexually abused can be extremely traumatic. Elliott and Carnes (2001) have compared such an experience to that of parents whose children have died tragically. In the eyes of the parent, CSA can reflect one of society's most pervert and insidious behaviours happening toward their child. Becoming aware of its occurrence often comes as a shock, to which some parents may react with great despair and helplessness, others with disgust, anger or rage, or with denial, panic or fear. These feelings are at times intensified for families confronted with other important stressors and adverse life events (Massat & Lundy, 1998) and for parents who have themselves experienced sexual abuse in childhood (Cyr, McDuff & Wright, 1999; Hiebert-Murphy, 1998). Generally, victims tend to keep the occurrence of CSA to themselves, or often hesitate for long periods of time before disclosing (Hébert, Tourigny, Cyr et al., 2009; Lamb & Edgar-Smith, 1994; Smith, Letourneau, Saunders et al., 2000). In a review of retrospective studies published since the beginning of the 90s, London, Bruck, Ceci and Shuman (2005) reported that only 32–42% of child victims disclose before reaching adulthood. Only a small proportion of cases (around 10%) disclose at the time the abuse occurs (London et al., 2005). Non-disclosure or significantly delayed disclosure may be particularly characteristic of sexual abuse cases involving boys as victims (Hébert, Tourigny, Cyr et al., 2009).

Understanding delay of disclosure represents a first challenge for parents, as they often feel the need to understand why their child has waited for so long, or has not solicited their support and protection. Parents might appreciate being reminded that children often experience feelings of shame, guilt and confusion, that they may fear disbelief and may anticipate a series of negative consequences subsequent to disclosure, such as important changes in the family (Malloy, Brubacher & Lamb, 2011; Schönbucher, Maier, Mohler-Kuo et al., 2012; Smith & Cook, 2008). These feelings also seem more likely to occur when the abuse involves an intra-familial perpetrator (Goodman-Brown, Edelstein, Goodman et al., 2003; Malloy, Brubacher & Lamb, 2011; Schaeffer, Leventhal & Asnes, 2011). One study suggested that children hesitate to disclose based on their parents' perceived or anticipated response to the abuse (Hershkowitz, Horowitz & Lamb, 2007). According to this study, 88% of children who delayed disclosure anticipated that their parents would be anxious, as they were perceived to generally react this way to stress. Understanding the motives for which children may delay disclosure can be of interest to parents, clinicians, investigators and prosecutors, and may improve their interventions. A recent qualitative study modified the standard forensic interview protocol for sexually abused children by requiring interviewers to ask questions about 'facilitators and barriers to disclosure' (Schaeffer, Leventhal & Asnes, 2011) (also see Chapter 15, Nicol, La Rooy & Lamb, this volume). The authors argued that knowing about these motives helps parents to support their children through the upcoming legal, protective and therapeutic procedures.

Non-Offending Parents Facing Their Child's Social and Judicial Experience

In the aftermath of disclosure, parents will have to face multiple challenges in accompanying their child through the various steps of the social and judicial service trajectory. Depending on parents' coping strategies and on a multitude of pre-existing factors, these challenges can feel overwhelming and lead to significant psychological distress. Concerns confronting families include: the child's investigation interview by police officers; the evaluation of the protective capacities of the parents; the possible loss of parental custody in cases of intra-familial abuse; separation or divorce that may result in a reduction of the household income; move of residence; and losses in relationships with family and friends (Massat & Lundy, 1998). In the months following the abuse, families can also be confronted with unfamiliar and distressing situations and procedures such as court proceedings and media attention (Dyb, Holen, Steinberg et al., 2003). In particular, testifying in court (especially the anticipation of this event) has been reported as a major stressor for both children and parents (Dyb, Holen, Steinberg et al., 2003; Sas, Hurley, Hatch et al., 1993). All of these events have the potential to add to the emotional tumult faced by the victims and their parents. For these reasons, researchers and clinicians (Banyard, Englund & Rozelle, 2001; Manion, McIntyre, Firestone et al., 1996; Runyan, Hunter, Everson et al., 1992) have suggested that the parental reactions following disclosure of sexual abuse may be best conceptualised as a form of secondary traumatisation.

Thus, subsequent to the allegation of sexual abuse, children and their parents begin a process involving a series of social and judicial procedures, often not knowing what to expect or what is expected of them. Although parents and professionals may appreciate the importance of these procedures for the protection of the child and the potential prosecution of sexual offenders, they are apprehensive of their potential negative impact. They may be worried about the child's capacity or willingness to talk in the videotaped investigative interview, fearful of possible actions taken by the child protection services, as well as concerned about their ability to provide appropriate support. Ideally, immediate support is provided to parents in anticipation of and preparation for the child's meeting with protection services and with the police. Parents are also worried about the physical and psychological impact of the abuse and may have unrealistic expectations regarding the conclusions of the socio-judicial medical examination, as they may perceive it as an element of proof. Yet, this examination provides physical evidence in less than 5% of cases (Allard-Dansereau & Frappier, 2011). Parents need to be well informed of the conclusions that can be drawn from these reports. If the police corroborate the allegation, a prosecutor can also meet the child or view the recording of the interview to assess whether the case should be presented in court. Non-offending parents may also need to be prepared and supported in accepting the decisions of the prosecutor.

Judicial procedures are generally not adapted for children and are both intimidating and complex (Quas & Goodman, 2012; Wiley, 2009). As it is often the case with adults (Herman, 2003; Wemmers, 2013), judicial procedures are thought to be taxing and stressful for children (Foster & Hagedorn, 2014; Quas, Goodman, Ghetti et al., 2005), and susceptible to leading to secondary victimisation. In the case of CSA, they can involve questioning and re-questioning about particularly intimate events, which took place in the context of a relationship with a perpetrator who is often known to and close to the family, or is a family member (Tavkar & Hansen, 2011). Knowing this, parents may, in certain circumstances, have to decide whether they want to take legal action or not. They often turn to professionals for advice. Yet, studies evaluating the psychological impact of such procedures are scant. The work of Goodman and Quas outlines that although most studies have found an association between testifying in court and negative psychological consequences (Goodman, Taub, Jones et al., 1992; Quas, Goodman, Ghetti et al., 2005), results remain mixed (Quas & Goodman, 2012).

The perceived negative impact of court procedures may be reinforced by the fact that only a small portion of CSA cases will in fact ever be prosecuted (Sedlak, Schultz, Wells et al., 2006; Stroud, Martens & Barker, 2000). The majority of cases sent to prosecutors are not pursued further (Stroud, Martens & Barker, 2000), as elements of proof often solely rely on the testimony of the child (London, Bruck, Ceci & Shuman, 2005), which can be severely challenged by the defence. Anticipating these procedures as well as the delay it takes to get through them, parents often feel helpless, frustrated and angry at the system. They often wonder whether it will be traumatising for the child, and may feel responsible for exposing them to such turmoil. Thus, the complexity and potential impact of these initial steps following disclosure, and the importance of the decisions that are being made, outline the importance of providing adequate interdisciplinary support to sexually abused children and their families.

Responding to the Needs of the Family: Child Advocacy Programmes

As families have to meet with various agencies as a result of sexual abuse disclosure, Tavkar and Hansen (2011) outlined the importance for children and their parents to have access to coordinated and supportive services during the initial crisis of disclosure and through the following steps. Starting in 1984, in the United States, the child advocacy model was developed expressly to better coordinate procedures following disclosure and to facilitate accessibility to services for children and their families. This model was also thought to increase the number of successful criminal prosecutions in CSA cases, while providing an investigation process in a child-friendly environment (Faller & Palusci, 2007). Child Advocacy Centres (CAC) generally provide children and their families with centralised cross-sector services under one roof. Services may include: the police investigative interview, forensic medical examination, child protection psychosocial assessment, meeting with the prosecutor, mental health assessment and therapeutic services.

Although clinically sound, very few studies have been conducted to assess the implementation and effectiveness of these models in terms of investigations, substantiation rates, arrest and prosecution, coordination and child re-victimisation (Conners-Burrow, Tempel, Sigel et al., 2012). In 2007, the University of New Hampshire Crimes Against Children Research Centre published the first quasi-experimental national evaluation of four well-established CACs in the US. Children receiving services from CACs were compared to those receiving services in comparison communities. Results generally indicated that CACs foster better outcomes in sexual abuse cases. They lead to more forensic medical examinations (Walsh, Cross, Jones et al., 2007), fewer forensic interviews with the same child (Cross, Jones, Walsh et al., 2007) and generally improved coordination of interventions (Cross, Jones, Walsh et al., 2007). However, results also indicated that successful criminal prosecution of offenders remained a challenge, as well as the regular use of child-sensitive investigations of sexual abuse allegations (Faller & Palusci, 2007). In relation to parents, the study conducted by Jones, Cross, Walsh and Simone (2007) outlined a definite interest in this model in relation to children's and non-offending parents' satisfaction. They have found that the CAC model can help parents feel less distressed, more cognisant of the process and more in tune with their children's needs. Parents receiving the services of a CAC generally felt more satisfied than parents who did not receive services from a CAC (Jones, Cross, Walsh and Simone, 2007).

With the multiplication of child and family advocacy programmes in North America, inspiring approaches have been developed to complement these CAC services to better respond to parents and children's needs. Inspired by a health care case management model, such programmes aim to optimise the coordination of interdisciplinary work and to increase emotional and practical support provided to parents from the time of initial disclosure and investigation to the end of the judicial process. In a Canadian Child Advocacy Centre situated in Montreal, Quebec, these case management services have been offered to avoid leaving the parent without resources or services for periods during which they are awaiting the next intervention. The case manager is mandated as the principal and constant source of support for parents from the beginning to the end of procedures. However, while these specific aspects of CAC programmes have been elaborated to respond to numerous clinical organisational needs in various ways, their impact has rarely been studied empirically (Elliott & Carnes, 2001).

The efficacy of this case management approach was tested in the Montreal CAC (Hébert & Séguin, 2011). Non-offending parents were offered services immediately after the initial police investigation of the child. Services included individual counselling sessions when needed, as well as ongoing on-call phone services. The objectives of these sessions were to assuage caregivers' emotional distress, provide advice on crisis management, identify potential sources of support and services and provide factual and practical information concerning sexual abuse and upcoming procedures (medical examination, role of child protection services, meeting with the prosecutor, obtaining compensation for criminal acts, etc.). The pilot study was conducted with a sample of 42 non-offending parents of children aged 2–12 years (Mean age = 6.93). Parents completed a short questionnaire measuring their level of psychological distress at the initial interview and then in a telephone follow-up interview nine weeks later. The majority of participants (86%) were mothers and 62% of cases involved intra-familial sexual abuse. Parents were living in difficult socio-demographic conditions as one out of three were without employment and close to half (45%) had a family income below the poverty line (less than £11,500). Close to a third (36%) of parents reported a history of CSA, and only 21% had disclosed and even fewer (14%) received services following the event. At initial assessment, non-offending parents were experiencing severe psychological distress including symptoms of depression, anxiety, irritability and difficulties in concentration, and 74% achieved clinical levels of distress. The results of this pilot intervention revealed that parents participated in an average of 2.83 case management meetings (ranges 1 to 7) lasting a mean of 85 minutes. A total of 28 parents also relied on the available phone services (Mean 3.79 calls; ranges 1 to 13). Cases required coordination with other agencies including child protection services and police and medical services, and practitioners also used phone contacts to coordinate the services (Mean 2.40 calls). This case management approach significantly alleviated parental psychological distress, as the rate of clinical levels dropped from 74% to 15% within the nine-week research follow-up. In turn, of course, this may increase the availability of the parent to be able to respond to their child's emotional needs appropriately.

Interpretation of the results is, however, hampered by the absence of a control group and results may be attributed to the mere passage of time. Of interest is that parents making greater use of such services (more meetings, more calls) were those experiencing higher distress. As expected, they were also parents for whom practitioners made more telephone contacts to facilitate and coordinate services. Level of satisfaction was found to be very high, as the vast majority of parents indicated that the meetings helped them identify their needs (88%), they felt better informed of the next steps involved (86%), as well as of the different resources available (83%), and developed a better understanding of the child's needs and how to be helpful to them (79%). Although these findings identify efficient ways to support parents following disclosure, this study needs to be replicated with a control group.

Parents Becoming Aware of the Consequences of Abuse on Their Child

Non-offending parents are often extremely worried about the negative impact that sexual abuse will have on the development of their child. Studies have highlighted the pervasive consequences associated with CSA; sexually abused children are more likely to present high levels of anxiety, depression, somatic complaints, social withdrawal, and anger and aggressive behaviour, compared with non-abused children (Hébert, Parent, Daignault & Tourigny, 2006; Wolfe, 2006). Post-traumatic stress symptoms including intrusive thoughts and flashbacks, avoidance, hyper arousal and hyper vigilance appear particularly salient in CSA children (Bernard-Bonnin, Hébert, Daignault & Allard-Dansereau, 2008; Wolfe, 2006). Victims are also more likely to present difficulties adapting in school (Daignault & Hébert, 2008) and to display sexual behaviour problems (Friedrich, Trane & Gully, 2005). These latter behaviours often seem particularly distressing to parents, while practitioners may feel uncomfortable in dealing with such behaviours, which adds to the worry of parents. In addition, some parents may worry that such sexualised behaviour problems will persist into adolescence and lead to pervasive behaviours in adulthood.

Highlighting the heterogeneity of profiles in sexually abused children may foster a sense of hope in non-offending parents by outlining elements on which they can exert a certain control (providing support, encouraging approach coping etc.). Considerable diversity is in fact noted in children; outcomes are associated with the characteristics of the abuse experienced and also with a host of personal (attributions, coping), familial (support, cohesion) and extra-familial (peer support, community support) factors (Hébert, Parent, Daignault & Tourigny, 2006). Some children appear to fare better as they benefit from a series of protective factors, such as a harmonious family environment, reliance on approach coping strategies and a higher level of self-esteem. Diverse profiles have also been found with preschoolers who were victims of CSA. Children rated as high in regulation capacities and attachment skills, and having mothers with high resiliency and efficient coping skills (seeking social support), fare better (Hébert, Langevin & Charest, 2014). These results highlight that parents have to expect that their child may react in various ways to the abuse and that hope for improvement or better outcomes lies in a number of factors amenable to change.

Child's Sexual Abuse and Its Impact on Non-Offending Parents

Psychological impact

Studies have documented the negative impact of CSA disclosure on the non-offending parent's psychological health (Hébert, Daigneault, Collin-Vézina & Cyr, 2007), yet few studies have distinguished between non-offending mothers and fathers (Davies, 1995; Dyb, Holen, Steinberg et al., 2003; Manion, McIntyre, Firestone et al., 1996). In one recent study, both mothers (49% vs. 23%) and fathers (30% vs. 18%) showed rates of depression that were twice as high as those of the general population (Cyr, Hébert, Frappier et al., 2014). Clinicians assessed symptoms of depression with the Structured Clinical Interview for DSM-IV (SCID; First, Spitzer, Gibbon & Williams, 1995). Their results show that 41% of mothers and 14% of fathers meet the clinical range criteria for depression as compared to 6% of women and 4% of men of the general population. Similar results were obtained by a more recent study (Runyon, Spandorfer & Schroeder, 2014). A number of studies (Cyr, McDuff & Wright, 1999; Dyb, Holen, Steinberg et al., 2003; Davies, 1995; Hubbard, 1989; Kelley, 1990) also observed the presence of post-traumatic stress disorder (PTSD) symptoms among parents of sexually abused children.

Although the percentage of parents presenting PTSD symptoms was not as high as for depression, PTSD symptoms were present in a fifth of the fathers in Davies's (1995) study and a third of the mothers in Cyr, McDuff and Wright (1999) study. Our recent study (Cyr, Hébert, Frappier et al., 2014) indicated that 13.1% of mothers and 7.1% of fathers meet the diagnostic criteria for PTSD. With respect to gender, only four studies compared fathers' and mothers' scores of psychological distress (Cyr, Hébert, Frappier et al., 2014; Davies, 1995; Kelley, 1990, Manion, McIntyre, Firestone et al., 1996), whereas other studies combined parents' scores due to small sample sizes (Dyb, Holen, Steinberg et al., 2003; Sas et al., 1993). Fathers were found to obtain lower scores of psychological distress and PTSD symptoms, and fewer of these scores reached the clinical range when compared with mothers. On the other hand, Kelley (1990) observed that perceived distress (as assessed by number of symptoms and their intensity) was significantly higher for fathers than for mothers two years following disclosure.

Evolution of symptoms

Disclosure of CSA may provoke an important commotion that can impact on parents' psychological health for a significant length of time. Only a handful of studies have explored the evolution of psychological distress in parents over time. Some have found a slight decrease in the psychological distress of mothers over a one-year period (Newberger, Gremy, Waternaux & Newberger, 1993), indicating more distress in mothers than fathers (Manion, Firestone, Cloutier et al., 1998). Others observed an increase in the intensity and number of symptoms of fathers over a two-year period, after which their distress was significantly higher than that of mothers (Kelley, 1990). This last result was also observed in a more recent study. Cyr, Hébert, Frappier et al., (2014) found that psychological distress of mothers tended to decrease over time, while that of fathers tended to increase. Indeed, at 24-month assessment time, fathers were more likely to report psychological distress than mothers were.

With regard to PTSD symptoms, Manion, Firestone, Cloutier et al. (1998) observed that mothers' as well as fathers' PTSD scores decreased over time. In Cyr, Hébert, Frappier et al.'s (2014) study, in the year following disclosure, only mothers displayed symptoms of PTSD (17.6% vs. 0%). Surprisingly, although PTSD rates decreased for mothers over the two-year assessment period, the incidence of PTSD symptoms for fathers increased at the 24-month assessment. In another study, at four-year follow-up, Dyb, Holen, Steinberg et al. (2003) noted that one-third of parents still reported high levels of PTSD intrusive symptoms and just over one-quarter reported high levels of PTSD avoidance symptoms. Levels of PTSD symptoms were in fact significantly correlated with lower scores of psychological well-being. Altogether, these results indicate that becoming aware of the sexual abuse of their child, and being more cognisant of its effect, has a significant impact on the psychological well-being of a number of parents, although not all will be as affected and develop symptoms. With the passage of time, symptoms seem to decrease in number and intensity for the majority of parents, while a small number of mothers and fathers still report difficulties.

Physical impact

Very few studies have explored the impact of CSA disclosure on the physical health of the parents. It could be expected that both the psychological and physical health of parents decreases following such a traumatic event. In a qualitative study conducted by Lafleur (2009), mothers reported physical health problems after disclosure. These problems were generally short-lived, and included headaches/migraines, gastrointestinal problems, skin conditions, weakened immune systems and exacerbation of pre-disclosure health problems.

More recently, Cyr, Hébert, Frappier et al. (2014) found that before disclosure half of the 76 mothers and 17 fathers retrospectively described their general health as good or excellent, obtaining scores similar to that of the general population. However, following disclosure, more than 10% of mothers and fathers described a decline in their current health status, with women feeling significantly more affected than men. Two years after disclosure of sexual abuse, the percentage of parents describing their physical health as very good or excellent remained significantly lower than what it was before the disclosure. In addition, two years after the disclosure, 28% of mothers and 18% of fathers still presented physical health-related limitations in their work capacity, activities and leisure.

Although these results need to be replicated with larger samples, findings suggest that the physical health of both mothers and fathers is likely to be affected after disclosure. As is often the case for psychological health problems, the major impact of the abuse is expected to occur in the first year post-disclosure. Nevertheless, a significant proportion of parents still experience physical problems and health-related limitations over longer periods of time. These consequences deserve to be addressed with parents to help improve their quality of life and to help them support their child through their own experience.

Providing Support: The Profiles of Parents of Sexually Abused Children

Theoretically speaking, support provided by non-offending mothers has been conceptualised as an important factor for the recovery of children (Elliott & Carnes, 2001). Yet, many studies conducted with children indicate that maternal support has an effect on a limited number of outcome variables. Bolen and Gergely (2015) have conducted a meta-analysis to quantify the effects of support in children. Their results indicated significant but small effect sizes (largest effect size of .17) on the relationship between caregiver support and children's functioning post-disclosure. In most of the studies, maternal support was defined by concepts such as the level of expressed affection, acceptance toward the child, quality of the relationship and general support. Support was also defined as more specific reactions to the CSA disclosure such as believing the child, giving emotional support in relation to the abuse, protecting the child from the perpetrator or ensuring that the child receives appropriate health services. Studies assessing support indicate that the majority of mothers believe their children (65% to 78%; Cyr, Wright, Toupin et al., 2002, 2003; Cyr, Hébert, Frappier et al., 2014; Pintello & Zuravin, 2001); this percentage generally increases with the passage of time (few weeks; Alaggia, 2004; Bolen & Lamb, 2004). Between 50% and 80% of mothers protect their child by distancing them from the perpetrator (Cyr et al., 2002; Cyr, Wright, Toupin et al., 2003; Heriot, 1996; Runyan et al., 1992), and two-thirds of mothers consult professional services for their child (Cyr, Wright, Toupin et al., 2003), but only half of the mothers were evaluated as being able to offer emotional support that matched the needs of their child (Cyr, Wright, Toupin et al., 2003; Runyan, Hunter, Everson et al., 1992).

These results suggest that when children make an allegation of sexual abuse, they are generally believed and that nearly half of the children receive some protection and emotional support. Nevertheless, mothers' reactions to such allegations are expected to vary greatly. In order to develop a better understanding of the characteristics of supportive mothers, we have attempted to derive profiles of supportive mothers (Cyr, McDuff & Hébert, 2013). A cluster analysis was conducted on a total of 226 non-offending mothers recruited from child protective services. Based on Belsky's model (1984) of determinants of parenting and on the stress and adaptation literature that accounts for individual vulnerability, we have taken into account the following potential determinants of maternal support: maternal developmental history, psychological and psychosocial resources, current stress and support, and mother–child relationship, in addition to the sexual abuse characteristics. The measure of maternal support was based on the Parental Reaction to Abuse Disclosure Scale (PRADS; Everson, Hunter, Runyan et al., 1989), which includes four dimensions: belief, protection, emotional support and search for services for the child and family, as well as on two dimensions of parental practice (supervision and discipline) to account for non-specific support.

Results of the cluster analysis revealed four distinct subgroups of supportive mothers that we labelled resilient (32.7%), avoidant-coping (32.7%), traumatised (19.1%) and anger-oriented reaction (15.5%) groups. The 'resilient' group of mothers believed and protected their children and provided both general and specific emotional support. The relationship with their children appeared to be adequate and mothers provided proper supervision and discipline. These mothers expressed anger at the perpetrator but not to the child. They were older than the mothers in the other groups, and they were more likely to be living in a marital relationship, which could explain their higher family income. They reported neither psychological symptoms nor a high level of life stressors.

The 'avoidant-coping' group of mothers reported a moderate level of PTSD symptoms, including avoidance symptoms and a high level of avoidant-coping. Although these mothers seemed to provide an adequate level of general support, their level of specific support was weaker than that of resilient mothers. Close to one-third of these mothers did not offer emotional support related to the abuse and did not seek psychological services for their child. About 10% did not believe their child, and 16% did not protect them from the perpetrator. The avoidant behaviours of these mothers may be linked to the increased risk that their children run of suffering other forms of maltreatment, as we observed that 20% of their children reported physical violence during the abuse.

The third group of mothers was labelled 'traumatised' because they experienced the highest levels of child maltreatment and reported negative impacts from their relations with their birth family members compared to the three other groups. This group reported a high level of stressful situations in their current life, as well as high emotional reactivity measured by the highest level of neuroticism. Although nearly half were employed (the highest level across the groups), their jobs did not bring in sufficient income, as they were characterised by the lowest income of all the groups. These mothers might represent a group marked by the intergenerational transmission of child maltreatment. Nevertheless, their response to the disclosure of the child seemed relatively adequate. This group of mothers could probably qualify for a diagnosis of complex PTSD based on their own high level of child maltreatment experience and high levels of neuroticism (Cook, Spinazzola, Ford et al., 2005; Herman, 1992; van der Kolk & Courtois, 2005).

Finally, mothers of the anger-oriented group were less supportive than mothers of other groups. They believed their children's allegations and protected them from the perpetrators, yet they reported a difficult relationship with their children and reported anger toward them. We cannot know if these relational problems were present before CSA disclosure, or if they appeared after as a consequence of it, or as a consequence of overprotection and heightened vigilance regarding their comings and goings (Davies, 1995). In addition, these mothers differed from mothers in the other groups, as they were more punitive and more inconsistent with their discipline, and offered less supervision. These mothers also presented higher psychological distress, PTSD and anger.

Such a typology might be helpful in determining mothers' needs and in designing specific interventions to best address these needs. For example, mothers in the resilient group, as well as their child, seemed to cope successfully with this stressful situation. A short-term educational approach describing the developmental consequences of the abuse and supportive interventions for the child might be sufficient. Comparatively, mothers of the anger-oriented profile may need a more intensive and lengthier intervention to sustain optimal rearing practices and a caring relationship with their child. The intense anger felt by these mothers and their level of neuroticism and avoidance-coping should be addressed specifically. The avoidance-coping group of mothers will need interventions to alleviate their PTSD symptoms, including avoidance symptoms and avoidance-coping strategies. Social interventions that help to deal with current life stressors (e.g., finding a better job, appropriate house, effective support group) as well as psychotherapy to deal with their past experience of traumatisation are required for the traumatised group of mothers. Cluster analyses reveal the heterogeneity of profiles of mothers and outline the importance of developing tailored interventions with the parents and child. By caring for the parent's specific needs professionals will ensure that they endorse the intervention and that they are motivated and mobilised to bring changes within the family.

Working with Non-Abusing Parents in Assessing the Child's Needs

Although some non-offending parents may experience more adversity than others following disclosure of the abuse, their contribution to the assessment of the child's needs is essential. Whether the sexual abuse took place within the family or not, the reactions and adaptation of the child's environment are rooted within the family and are systemic in nature (Friedrich, 1990; Spaccarelli, 1994). Thus, the quality of such assessments is of crucial importance in elaborating tailored interventions. The assessment of the child's needs is often closely linked to the parent's current life stressors. Aside from disclosure and procedural challenges, parents are confronted by a host of issues that may exert an influence on their ability to remain objective in their assessment, and to support their child through the process. Research has documented that many other stressors often concurrently challenge families confronted with CSA (Massat & Lundy, 1998). Recognising the importance of these challenges in the assessment process can serve to develop appropriate interventions. Our findings indicated that the majority of families (95%) for whom an event of sexual abuse had been confirmed concurrently experienced other stresses, such as other forms of violence, death in the family, financial problems, illness, work-related stress, pregnancy, etc., and 47% of mothers reported the presence of more than five particularly stressful events. Mothers (41%) also reported an increase in the number of conflicts within the family. Analysis of the socio-demographic characteristics of families consulting the Montreal CAC indicates that 70% of the families are struggling with financial issues (annual family income below £22,500). Also a major concern in terms of intervention is that approximately 46% of the mothers have themselves experienced sexual abuse as a child and that 58% of these mothers had never disclosed. This experience can have an impact on their capacity to be responsive and in tune with their children's needs. Parents had also been exposed to other forms of violence as a child, such as emotional abuse (67%), neglect (32%) and physical abuse (40%). Since families confronted with CSA often face several challenges, CSA can, in certain cases, arise as the event that surpasses the family's coping capacities. In this sense, it is of importance not to overlook the parent(s)' needs in the assessment process.

The assessment of the child entails the use of various sources of information: the parents and potentially other family members (e.g., siblings or grandparents), the school, the child, police, paediatricians and child protection services (Friedrich, 2002). Although the parent's assessment may be rather objective and informative, his/her opinion or perception can also be influenced by his/her own victimisation, feelings of denial or guilt, or by other judicial or familial preoccupations (Lanktree, Gilbert, Briere et al., 2008). The first priority of assessment is the family and child's sense of security (Briere & Scott, 2006). This entails whether the family or child feel threatened or in danger, whether there continues to be other concomitant forms of violence within the family and whether there are physical injuries or health issues that need to be taken care of (Briere & Scott, 2006). Also a priority of assessment is the verification of the presence of cognitive disorganisation, psychotic symptoms, and suicidal or homicidal ideation in the child or the parent, as these reactions may be aggravated by a more thorough assessment procedure (Najavits, 2002).

With regards to the needs of the child, although other sources of information may be solicited, the parents remain the main source of information by which to conduct the assessment. Going through this process of assessment often sets the stage for feelings of distress in parents. Considering the potential impact of the disclosure on their psychological and physical health (Cyr, Hébert, Frappier et al., 2014), parents' needs also have to be assessed. The purpose of the assessment of and intervention with parents is to provide means to ensure that their coping abilities are not exceeded in dealing with their child's abuse. At this point in time, parents may not have had many opportunities to talk to someone about the sexual abuse of their child and about their own reactions and feelings. Depending on the situation, and on the parent's history of victimisation, a wide range of responses can be expected, from complete denial to trivialisation, anger, fear, sadness, helplessness and intense feelings of guilt. Some parents will even consider recourse to self-justice to ensure their child's protection (Friedrich, 2002). Considering the parent's potential contribution to a child's recovery, remaining attuned to parental needs throughout the assessment and intervention process should be a priority of intervention. Encouraging parents to focus on aspects of family life over which they can exert a certain control and on factors of protection for the child's health and recovery can be beneficial. For instance, parents can introduce elements into their daily routine (e.g., more quality family time, various coping strategies for stress, a new routine) and provide more support for challenging activities. It can also be helpful to remind them of protective factors for the child's health and recovery, such as having disclosed, areas of competence, having supportive parents, receiving help, etc. A referral to supportive or therapeutic services should be considered to ensure the parent's optimal adaptation or to maintain the conjugal relationship in such period of crisis (Friedrich, 2002; Lewin & Bergin, 2001).

Among the various elements that should be considered in the assessment of the family's and the parents' needs, research outlines the importance of the following: the various sources of stress to which the child and family are exposed (Kaplow, Dodge, Amaya-Jackson & Saxe, 2005; Cyr, McDuff & Wright, 1999; Cyr, Hébert, Frappier et al., 2014; Cyr, Zuk & Payer, 2011), the parent's mental health and history of victimisation (Lewin & Bergin, 2001), the quality of the conjugal relationship, and conflict and cohesion within the family (Cyr, Wright, Toupin et al., 2002; Friedrich, 2002), the attachment relationship between the parent and the child (Friedrich, 2002), the parent's parenting skills (Friedrich, 2002), and the support offered to the child by the parent (Elliott & Carnes, 2001; Thériault, Cyr & Wright, 1997). Cyr, Zuk & Payer (2011) also suggest assessing substance abuse and personality disorders.

Conducting such a comprehensive assessment that includes the needs of the parents can have several advantages for the preparation of an effective and tailored therapeutic intervention. A common challenge to any trauma-oriented intervention is the engagement of the parents and the child in the therapeutic process (Cohen, Mannarino & Deblinger, 2012). Cohen and colleagues outline the importance of reviewing the results of the assessment with the child and non-offending parents as a process of engagement. Summarising the impact of the abuse on the child but also on the parent's adaptation while defining their strengths and areas of competence provides grounds for hope, engagement and motivation to change. It also helps to clarify the importance of treatment as a manageable solution. In doing so, the assessment also provides the necessary information to identify and address all the potential barriers to a parent's mobilisation for treatment (Cohen, Mannarino & Deblinger, 2012).

Working with Non-Abusing Parents in Therapy: How to Help Parents Play an Active Role in Providing a Secure and Understanding Environment

Right from the beginning of the intervention process, parents need to find ways to focus on the child, avoid doubting, trying to remain calm and validating that the choice to disclose was the right one. Ideally, they need to demonstrate that they are able to address this subject without minimising the child's distress and without appearing overwhelmed. Parents may also have to be able to say that they understand why it was hard to tell. In many cases, parents simply cannot reach this level of containment without benefiting from some kind of supportive intervention that will eventually help the parent become a better source of support for his/her child. With regard to their child's therapeutic process, when non-offending parents are well enough and engaged in a trusting therapeutic relationship, they can be perceived as catalysers of change. If they can stay empathic to their child's needs and difficulties, they can play a crucial role in mobilising the child to engage in treatment and to maintain motivation and interest. Mobilising the parent while caring for his/her needs is essential for successful therapy. Parents can also play a fundamental role in maintaining therapeutic gains, especially if caregivers are able to model the expression of feelings and adequately reflect the child's feelings and keep on reminding their child of effective coping skills.

Chaotic lifestyles and home environments come with multiple challenges in relation to providing the supervision, time, support and attention that are hoped for from parents (Cohen, Mannarino & Deblinger, 2012). However, because parents are so important in their children's recovery, these issues may need to be addressed with the parent before any sort of therapy can begin with the child. Referral of the non-offending parent may be necessary in certain instances such as ongoing violence, trauma or conflictual mother–child relationship.

There are also several theoretical and clinical arguments for involving non-offending caregivers in their child's therapeutic interventions. Theoretically speaking, when fear or trauma occurs, the child turns to an attachment figure for security and protection (Ainsworth & Bowlby, 1991). In the case of sexual abuse, because of its insidious nature, the child may not have instantly identified danger and turned to attachment figures, especially if the perpetrator was a family member. The particularities of this interpersonal and intimate type of abuse create misunderstandings in the relationship with the non-offending caregivers. This outlines the importance of a systemic reconstruction of the notions of trust and attachment within the family. Ideally, the non-offending caregiver reconsolidates this relationship. As proposed by Cohen, Mannarino and Deblinger (2006), as parents are advised on a plane to fit their oxygen masks before helping their children, this guideline applies very well to the disclosure and outcome of CSA, as all members of the family are boarding this trip. Clinically speaking, parents who are least supportive need to be prioritised to benefit from appropriate services and information (Mannarino & Cohen, 1996; Lewin & Bergin, 2001). Aside from taking charge of the family dynamic to get through this episode of crisis, the non-offending parent is conceptualised as a model, one that can potentially demonstrate to the child that he/she can trust other adults and professionals involved in the intervention and one that models hope and optimism. Intervention attempts to help parents find within themselves the caregiver who is skilled at dealing with stress and who can recreate a safe and comforting home.

Considering the decisive influence that parents can exert on the adaptation and ultimate recovery of their child, various therapeutic models have been developed through which parents are very much involved in consolidating the use and efficacy of therapeutic tools. For example, cognitive behavioural therapies, as well as interventions developed for children experiencing complex trauma, encourage an approach oriented toward consolidating the relationship between the parent and the child (Briere & Lanktree, 2012; Ford & Courtois, 2009). One empirically validated therapeutic model that emphasises parental involvement with regard to child abuse is Trauma-Focused Cognitive Behavioural Therapy (TF-CBT; Cohen et al., 2006). The rationale behind this approach is that as the child moves along the therapeutic components, and the parent masters supportive and communication strategies, the therapist becomes less directive and less involved in session and leaves more room for the parent to play his/her role in the relationship. The child and parent's roles gradually become more active to help develop a sense of self-efficacy (Cohen, Mannarino & Deblinger, 2012).

Conclusions

Parents confronted with the challenge of learning, accepting and coping with the sexual abuse of their child are most likely not prepared for such a potentially traumatic experience. Research has highlighted the important role that parents can play in the adaptation of their child. The key learning points that can be taken from the evidence base which can assist professionals in understanding how best to mobilise parents to provide support to their children are summarised in Table 25.1.

We have outlined some of the challenges that parents meet in learning to accept this reality and in finding ways for the child and family to move on with their lives. In doing so, parents may themselves experience significant distress and may also be dealing with other stressors that may add to already existing challenges within the family, such as conjugal conflicts and socioeconomic problems. Parents therefore need to be well supported by therapists and other professionals. In supporting parents, professionals should nourish the therapeutic relationship with the parent and be careful to avoid any forms of judgement (Alaggia, 2002). Such circumstances can help parents to minimise the impact of the abuse on their child, by feeling supported in providing a secure and understanding environment while promoting motivation for therapy and for change.

Table 25.1 Key Learning Points from the evidence base: Knowledge to assist professionals in mobilising parents to provide support to their children.

The collaboration and mobilisation of parents are crucial to efficient interventions. Parents often feel the need to be involved, consulted, informed and supported.

Understanding delay of disclosure often represents a first challenge for parents.

Non-offending parents are often in shock post-disclosure; immediate support is ideally provided in anticipation of and preparation for the child's interview with police officers and child protection services.

Parents need to be well informed of the limited conclusions that can be drawn from medical assessments conducted post-disclosure (physical evidence in less than 5% of cases).

Anticipating judicial procedures as well as the delay it takes to get through them, parents often feel helpless, frustrated and angry at the system and may feel responsible for exposing their child to such turmoil.

Coordinated and supportive services such as those provided in Child Advocacy Centres (CAC) and complementary case management services are inspiring models of client-centred care.

Highlighting the heterogeneity of profiles in sexually abused children may foster a sense of hope in non-offending parents by outlining protection factors and elements on which they can exert a certain control.

Disclosure of CSA may provoke an important commotion that can impact on parents' psychological and physical health for a significant length of time (up to two years post-disclosure), with mothers and fathers appearing to respond in distinctive ways. These consequences deserve to be addressed with parents.

The typologies are informative for tailored interventions. Four distinct subgroups of supporting mothers were identified. Only half of them were evaluated as being able to offer emotional support that matched the needs of their child.

A thorough assessment of the parents' needs considers that families confronted to CSA often face other important challenges (history of CSA, concomitant violence, financial and conjugal problems...) and includes referral to supportive services.

Summarising the impact of the abuse on the child, but also on the parent's adaptation and specific needs, while defining their strengths and areas of competence provides the grounds for hope, engagement and motivation to change.

References

Ainsworth, M.D.S. & Bowlby, J. (1991). An ethological approach to personality development. *American Psychologist*, 46, 333–341.

Alaggia, R. (2002). Balancing acts: Reconceptualizing support in maternal response to intra familial child sexual abuse. *Clinical Social Work Journal*, 30, 41–56.

Alaggia, R. (2004). Many ways of telling: Expanding conceptualization of child sexual abuse disclosure. *Child Abuse & Neglect: An International Journal*, 28, 1213–1227.

Allard-Dansereau, C. & Frappier, J.-Y. (2011). L'intervention médicale et médicolégale auprès des enfants et des adolescents victimes d'agression sexuelle. In: M. Hébert, M. Cyr & M. Tourigny (eds), *L'Agression Sexuelle envers les Enfants, Tome I*. Québec, QC: Presses de l'Université du Québec, 97–148.

Banyard, V.L., Englund, D.W. & Rozelle, D. (2001). Parenting the traumatized child: Attending to the needs of nonoffending caregivers of traumatized children. *Psychotherapy*, 38, 74–87.

Belsky, J. (1984). The determinants of parenting: A Process Model. *Child Development*, 55, 83–96.

Bernard-Bonnin, A.-C., Hébert, M., Daignault, I.V., Allard-Dansereau, C. (2008). Disclosure of sexual abuse, and personal and familial factors as predictors of post-traumatic stress disorder symptoms in school-aged girls. *Paediatrics & Child Health*, 13, 479–486.

Bolen, R.M. & Gergely, K.B. (2015). A meta-analytic review of the relationship between nonoffending caregiver support and postdisclosure functioning in sexually abused children. *Trauma, Violence & Abuse*, 16, 258–279.

Bolen, R. & Lamb, J.L. (2004). Ambivalence of nonoffending guardians after child sexual abuse disclosure. *Journal of Interpersonal Violence*, 19, 185–211.

Briere, J.N. & Lanktree, C.B. (2012). *Treating complex trauma in adolescents and young adults*. Washington, DC: Sage.

Briere, J. & Scott, C. (2006). *Principles of Trauma Therapy: A Guide to Symptoms, Evaluation, and Treatment:* Thousand Oaks, CA: Sage Publications, Inc.

Cohen, J.A., Mannarino, A.P. & Deblinger, E. (2006). *Treating Trauma and Traumatic Grief in Children and Adolescents*. New York: Guilford Press.

Cohen, J.A., Mannarino, A.P. & Deblinger, E. (2012). *Trauma-Focused CBT for Children and Adolescents: Treatment Applications*. New York: Guilford Press.

Conners-Burrow, N.A., Tempel, A.B., Sigel, B.A. et al. (2012). The development of a systematic approach to mental health screening in Child Advocacy Centers. *Children & Youth Services Review*, 34, 1675–1682.

Cook, A., Spinazzola, J., Ford, J. et al. (2005). Complex trauma in children and adolescents. *Psychiatric Annals*, 35, 390–398.

Cross, T.P., Jones, L.M., Walsh, W.A. et al. (2007). Child forensic interviewing in Children's Advocacy Centers: Empirical data on a practice model. *Child Abuse & Neglect*, 31, 1031–1052.

Cyr, M., McDuff, P. & Hébert, M. (2013). Support and profiles of non-offending mothers of sexually abused children. *Journal of Child Sexual Abuse*, 22, 209–230.

Cyr, M., McDuff, P. & Wright, J. (1999). Le profil des mères d'enfants abusés sexuellement: santé mentale, stress et adaptation. *Santé Mentale au Québec*, 2, 191–216.

Cyr, M., Zuk, S. & Payer, M. (2011). Le profil des parents dont les enfants sont agressés sexuellement. In: M. Hébert, M. Cyr & M. Tourigny (eds), *L'Agression Sexuelle envers les Enfants, Tome I*. Québec, QC: Presses de l'Université du Québec.

Cyr, M., Hébert, M., Frappier, J.-Y. et al. (2014). Parental support provided by non-offending caregivers to sexually abused children: A comparison between mothers and fathers. *Journal of Child Custody*, 11, 216–236.

Cyr, M., Wright, J., Toupin, J. et al. (2002). Les déterminants du soutien maternel offert par les mères à leurs enfants ayant vécu une agression sexuelle récente. *Revue de Psychoéducation et d'Orientation*, 31, 319–337.

Cyr, M., Wright, J., Toupin, J. et al. (2003). Predictors of maternal support: The point of view of adolescent victims of sexual abuse and their mothers. *Journal of Child Sexual Abuse: Research, Treatment & Program Innovations for Victims, Survivors & Offenders*, 12, 39–65.

Daignault, I.V. & Hébert, M. (2008). Short-term correlates of child sexual abuse: An exploratory study predicting girls' academic, cognitive, and social functioning, 1 year later. *Journal of Child & Adolescent Trauma*, 1, 301–316.

Davies, M.G. (1995). Parental distress and ability to cope following disclosure of extra-familial sexual abuse. *Child Abuse & Neglect*, 19, 399–408.

Dyb, G., Holen, A., Steinberg, A.M. et al. (2003). Alleged sexual abuse at a day care center: Impact on parents. *Child Abuse & Neglect*, 27, 939–950.

Elliott, A. & Carnes, C. (2001). Reactions of nonoffending parents to the sexual abuse of their child: A review of the literature. *Child Maltreatment*, 6, 314–331.

Everson, M.D., Hunter, W.M., Runyan, D.K. et al. (1989). Maternal support following disclosure of incest. *American Journal of Orthopsychiatry*, 59, 197–207.

Faller, K.C. & Palusci, V.J. (2007). Children's advocacy centers: Do they lead to positive case outcomes? *Child Abuse & Neglect*, 31, 1021–1029.

First, M.B., Spitzer, R.L., Gibbon, M. & Williams, J.B.W. (1995). *Structured Clinical Interview for Axis I DSM-IV Disorders – Patient Edition (SCID-I/P)*. New York: Biometrics Research Department, NY State Psychiatric Institute.

Ford, J.D. & Courtois, C.A. (2009). Treating complex traumatic stress disorders: An evidence-based guide. In: C.A. Courtois & J.D. Ford (eds), *Treating Complex Traumatic Stress Disorders: An Evidence-Based Guide*. New York: Guilford Press, 13–30.

Foster, J.M. & Hagedorn, W.B. (2014). Through the eyes of the wounded: A narrative analysis of children's sexual abuse experiences and recovery process. *Journal of Child Sexual Abuse*, 23, 538–557.

Friedrich, W.N. (1990). *Psychotherapy of Sexually Abused Children and Their Families*. New York: W.W. Norton and Company.

Friedrich, W.N. (2002). *Psychological Assessment of Sexually Abused Children and Their Families*. Thousand Oaks, CA: Sage Publications Inc.

Friedrich, W.N., Trane, S.T. & Gully, K.J. (2005). Letter to the Editor: Re: It is a mistake to conclude that sexual abuse and sexualized behaviour are not related: A reply to Drach, Wientzen, and Ricci (2001). *Child Abuse & Neglect*, 29, 297–302.

Goodman, G.S., Taub, E.P., Jones, D.P.H. et al. (1992). Testifying in criminal court. *Monographs of the Society for Research on Child Development*, 57, 1–159.

Goodman-Brown, T.B., Edelstein, R.S., Goodman, G.S. et al. (2003). Why children tell: A model of children's disclosure of sexual abuse. *Child Abuse & Neglect*, 27, 525–540.

Hébert, M. & Séguin, R. (2011). *Évaluation du programme de services personnalisés aux parents*. Rapport de recherche présenté à Condition Féminine Canada. Montréal (QC): Centre d'Expertise Marie-Vincent.

Hébert, M., Langevin, R. & Charest, F. (2014). Factors associated with resilience in preschoolers reporting sexual abuse: A typological analysis. *International Journal of Child and Adolescent Resilience*, 2, 46–58.

Hébert, M., Daignault, I., Collin-Vézina, D. & Cyr, M. (2007). Factors linked to distress in mothers of children disclosing sexual abuse. *Journal of Nervous and Mental Disease*, 195, 805–811.

Hébert, M., Parent, N., Daignault, I.V. & Tourigny, M. (2006). A typological analysis of behavioural profiles of sexually abused children. *Child Maltreatment*, 11, 203–216.

Hébert, M., Tourigny, M., Cyr, M. et al. (2009). Prevalence of childhood sexual abuse and timing of disclosure in a representative sample of adults from Quebec. *Canadian Journal of Psychiatry*, 54, 631–636.

Heriot, J. (1996). Maternal protectiveness following disclosure of intrafamilial child sexual abuse. *Journal of Interpersonal Violence*, 11, 181–194.

Herman, J.L. (1992). *Trauma and Recovery*. New York: Basic Books.

Herman, J.L. (2003). The mental health of crime victims: Impact of legal intervention. *Journal of Traumatic Stress*, 16, 159–166.

Hershkowitz, I., Horowitz, D. & Lamb, M.E. (2007). Individual and family variables associated with disclosure and nondisclosure of child abuse in Israel. In: M.-E. Pipe, M.E. Lamb, Y. Orbach and A.-C. Cederborg (eds), *Child Sexual Abuse: Disclosure, Delay, and Denial*. Mahwah, NJ: Lawrence Erlbaum Associates Publishers, 65–75.

Hiebert-Murphy, D. (1998). Emotional distress among mothers whose children have been sexually abused: The role of a history of child sexual abuse, social support, and coping, *Child Abuse & Neglect*, 22, 423–435.

Hubbard, G.B. (1989). Mother's perception of incest: Sustained disruption and turmoil. *Archives of Psychiatric Nursing*, 1, 34–40.

Jones, L.M., Cross, T.P., Walsh, W.A. & Simone, M. (2007). Do Children's Advocacy Centers improve families' experiences of child sexual abuse investigations? *Child Abuse & Neglect*, 31, 1069–1085.

Kaplow, J., Dodge, K., Amaya-Jackson, L. & Saxe, G. (2005). Pathways to PTSD, part II: Sexually abused children. *American Journal of Psychiatry*, 162, 1305–1310.

Kelley, S.J. (1990). Responsibility and management strategies in child sexual abuse: A comparison of child protective workers, nurses, and police officers. *Child Welfare*, 69, 43–51.

Lafleur, C.T. (2009). *Mother's reactions to disclosures of sibling sexual abuse (Doctoral dissertation)*. Kansas State University libraries, http://krex.k-state.edu/dspace/handle/2097/1370.

Lamb, S. & Edgar-Smith, S. (1994). Aspects of disclosure: Mediators of outcome of childhood sexual abuse. *Journal of Interpersonal Violence*, 9, 307–326.

Lanktree, C.B., Gilbert, A.M., Briere, J. et al. (2008). Multi-informant assessment of maltreated children: Convergent and discriminant validity of the TSCC and TSCYC. *Child Abuse & Neglect*, 32, 621–625.

Lemay, M. (2006). *Aveux et désaveux d'un psychiatre: dialogues*. Montréal, QC: Éditions du CHU Sainte-Justine.

Lewin, L. & Bergin, C. (2001). Attachment behaviours, depression, and anxiety in nonoffending mothers of child sexual abuse victims. *Child Maltreatment*, 6, 365–375.

London, K., Bruck, M., Ceci, S.J. & Shuman, D.W. (2005). Disclosure of child sexual abuse: What does the research tell us about the ways that children tell? *Psychology, Public Policy, and Law*, 11, 194–226.

Malloy, L.C., Brubacher, S.P. & Lamb, M.E. (2011). Expected consequences of disclosure revealed in investigative interviews with suspected victims of child sexual abuse. *Applied Developmental Science*, 15, 8–19.

Manion, I., Firestone, P., Cloutier, P. et al. (1998). Child extrafamilial sexual abuse: Predicting parent and child functioning. *Child Abuse & Neglect*, 22, 1285–1304.

Manion, I.G., McIntyre, J., Firestone, P. et al. (1996). Secondary traumatization in parents following the disclosure of extrafamilial child sexual abuse: Initial effects. *Child Abuse & Neglect*, 20, 1095–1109.

Mannarino, A.P. & Cohen, J.A. (1996). Family related variables and psychological system formation in sexually abused girls. *Journal of Child Sexual Abuse*, 5, 105–119.

Massat, C.R. & Lundy, M. (1998). 'Reporting costs' to nonoffending parents in cases of intrafamilial child sexual abuse. *Child Welfare*, 77, 371–388.

Najavits, L.M. (2002). *Seeking Safety: A Treatment Manual for PTSD and Substance Abuse*. New York: Guilford Press.

Newberger, C.M., Gremy, I.M., Waternaux, C.M. & Newberger, E.J. (1993). Mothers of sexually abused children: Trauma and repair in longitudinal perspective. *American Journal of Orthopsychiatry*, 63, 92–102.

Pintello, D. & Zuravin, S. (2001). Intrafamilial child sexual abuse: Predictors of postdisclosure maternal belief and protective action. *Child Maltreatment*, 6, 344–352.

Quas, J.A. & Goodman, G.S. (2012). Consequences of criminal court involvement for child victims. *Psychology, Public Policy, and Law*, 18, 392–414.

Quas, J.A., Goodman, G.S., Ghetti, S. et al. (2005). Childhood sexual assault victims: Long-term outcomes after testifying in criminal court. *Monographs of the Society for Research in Child Development*, 70, 118–128.

Runyon, M.K., Spandorfer, E.D. & Schroeder, C.M. (2014). Cognitions and distress in caregivers after their child's sexual abuse disclosure. *Journal of Child Sexual Abuse*, 23, 146–159.

Runyan, D.K., Hunter, W.M., Everson, M.D. et al. (1992). *Maternal support for child victims of sexual abuse: Determinants and implications*. Newton, MA: National Center on Child Abuse & Neglect.

Sas, L.D., Hurley, P., Hatch, A. et al. (1993). *Three years after the verdict: A longitudinal study of the social and psychological adjustment of child witnesses referred to the child witness project*. Ottawa, Canada: Health and Welfare Canada.

Schaeffer, P., Leventhal, J.M. & Asnes, A. G. (2011). Children's disclosures of sexual abuse: Learning from direct inquiry. *Child Abuse & Neglect*, 35, 343–352.

Schönbucher, V., Maier, T., Mohler-Kuo, M. et al. (2012). Disclosure of child sexual abuse by adolescents: A qualitative in-depth study. *Journal of Interpersonal Violence*, 27, 3486–3513.

Sedlak, S., Schultz, D., Wells, S. et al. (2006). Child protection and justice systems processing of serious child abuse and neglect cases. *Child Abuse & Neglect*, 30, 657–677.

Smith, D.W., Letourneau, E.J. Saunders, B.E. et al. (2000). Delay in disclosure of childhood rape: Results from a national survey. *Child Abuse & Neglect*, 24, 273–287.

Smith, S.G. & Cook, S.L. (2008). Disclosing sexual assault to parents. The influence of parental messages about sex. *Violence Against Women*, 14, 1326–1348.

Spaccarelli, S. (1994). Stress, appraisal and coping in child sexual abuse: A theoretical and empirical review. *Psychological Bulletin*, 116, 340–362.

Stroud, D., Martens, S. & Barker, J. (2000). Criminal investigations of child sexual abuse: A comparison of cases referred to the prosecutor to those not referred. *Child Abuse & Neglect*, 24, 689–700.

Tavkar, P. & Hansen, D.J. (2011). Interventions for families victimized by child sexual abuse: Clinical issues and approaches for child advocacy center-based services. *Aggression and Violent Behaviour*, 16, 188–199.

Thériault, C., Cyr, M. & Wright, J. (1997). Soutien maternel aux enfants victimes d'abus sexuel: Conceptualisation, effets et facteurs associés. *Revue québécoise de psychologie*, 18, 147–167.

van der Kolk, B.A. & Courtois, C.A. (2005). Editorial comments: Complex developmental trauma. *Journal of Traumatic Stress*, 18, 385–388.

Walsh, W.A., Cross, T.P., Jones, L.M. et al. (2007). Which sexual abuse victims receive a forensic medical examination? The impact of Children's Advocacy Centers. *Child Abuse & Neglect*, 31, 1053–1068.

Wemmers, J.-A. (2013). Victims' experiences in the criminal justice system and their recovery from crime. *International Review of Victimology*, 19, 221–233.

Wiley, T.R.A. (2009). Legal and social service responses to child sexual abuse: A primer and discussion of relevant research. *Journal of Child Sexual Abuse*, 18, 267–289.

Wolfe, V.V. (2006). Child sexual abuse. In: E.J. Mash & R.A. Barkley (eds), *Treatment of Childhood Disorders*. New York: Guilford Press, 647–727.

26

Working with Parents with Intellectual Disabilities in Child Care Proceedings

Beth Tarleton
School for Policy Studies, University of Bristol, UK

This chapter focuses on how to support parents with intellectual disabilities (ID) to be the best parent possible. While this chapter offers a particular focus for parents who are involved in child care proceedings, the principles discussed should be utilised when providing early, preventative support for parents with ID so that serious concerns for the welfare of their children do not arise. This chapter begins by introducing parents with ID, the issues they might face and the terms used to describe this group of parents. It also discusses the issues relating to engaging parents with support and is followed by recommendations of best practice in supporting parents with ID when they are involved in child protection.

Definition

The term 'parents with intellectual disabilities' (ID) is used to include parents with a diagnosed intellectual developmental disability (IDD). This is defined as an Intelligence Quotient (IQ) below 69, evidence of deficits in social and adaptive functioning, and onset prior to 18 years of age (DSM-V; APA, 2013). While ID is a commonly used term within the literature, the Diagnostic and Statistical Manual of Mental Disorders Fifth Edition (DSM-V: APA, 2013) refers to an 'intellectual developmental disability' (IDD). This is defined as 'a disorder with onset during the developmental period that includes both intellectual and adaptive functioning deficits in conceptual, social, and practical domains' (p. 33). Specifically, in DSM-V, intellectual disability is described as involving:

> impairments of general mental abilities that impact adaptive functioning in three domains, or areas. These domains determine how well an individual copes with everyday tasks:

- The conceptual domain includes skills in language, reading, writing, math, reasoning, knowledge and memory.
- The social domain refers to empathy, social judgement, interpersonal communication skills, the ability to make and retain friendships, and similar capacities.

The Wiley Handbook of What Works in Child Maltreatment: An Evidence-Based Approach to Assessment and Intervention in Child Protection, First Edition. Edited by Louise Dixon, Daniel F. Perkins, Catherine Hamilton-Giachritsis, and Leam A. Craig.
© 2017 John Wiley & Sons Ltd. Published 2017 by John Wiley & Sons Ltd.

- The practical domain centres on self-management in areas such as personal care, job responsibilities, money management, recreation and organising school and work tasks. (http://www.dsm5.org/documents/intellectual%20disability%20fact%20sheet.pdf)

However, a number of different terms are often used interchangeably across the world to describe intellectual disability, including 'learning disability' or 'cognitive impairment'. For example, in the UK, the term 'learning disability' is commonly used within social care policy and described as:

> A significantly reduced ability to understand new or complex information, to learn new skills (impaired intelligence); with a reduced ability to cope independently (impaired social functioning); which started before adulthood, with a lasting effect on development. (Department of Health, 2001, p. 14)

This is a similar position to that taken in Australia by Healthy Start, which supports professionals working with parents they describe as having 'learning difficulties'. As their website states:

> Healthy Start uses the term 'learning difficulties' in a specific way: as indicating a need for education (teaching) of skills that most people learn incidentally to enable them to participate fully in the community, without supervision. Other terms that are commonly used include 'learning disability' and 'intellectual disability'. (www.healthystart.net.au/index.php/about-healthy-start/our-approach)

For simplicity purposes, this chapter will refer to people with intellectual developmental disabilities (IDD) based on DSM-V criteria.

Additional Issues for Parents with IDD and Outcomes for Their Children

Parents with IDD often struggle with everyday life and with meeting the needs of their children without appropriately tailored support and teaching. Parents with IDD are also reported as facing economic hardships, having small social support networks, lacking appropriate information about parenting and facing stereotypes, such as they should not or cannot parent or learn the necessary skills (Darbyshire & Stenfert Kroese, 2012; Stenfert Kroese, Hussein, Clifford & Ahmed, 2002; Tarleton, Ward & Howarth, 2006).

Lindblad, Billstedt, Gillberg and Fernell (2013) interviewed ten adult children of parents with IDD. The interviews revealed that six of the ten children had been removed from their parents' care during childhood due to neglect or abuse. Six of these children also had mild IDD themselves while most of the adult children reported difficulties in their relations with family and in school. The adult children reported that some of their parents had received informal support from family, friends or the church, but none of the interviewees reported support from services.

A study by Emerson and Brigham (2014), which utilised a population sample across three Primary Care Trusts in England and Wales, indicated that in their model, which was adjusted for between-group differences in exposure to low socio-economic position, parental IDD was associated with an increased risk of child developmental delay and speech and language problems, but not with child behaviour problems or frequent accidents or injuries. The authors note that most of the factors that were considered to be correlates of parental IDD, such as environmental factors like poor housing and lack of support, were 'amenable to change through policy interventions' (p. 920).

The International Association for the Scientific Study of Intellectual Disabilities [IASSID], Special Interest Research Group on Parents and Parenting with Intellectual Disabilities (IASSID SIRG, 2008) and Collings and Llewellyn (2012) summarised the literature focusing on outcomes for children of parents with IDD, which has been developing since the 1970s. Collings and Llewellyn (2012) concluded that while there is evidence to suggest poorer outcomes for these children, this seems to be linked as much to poverty and poor social environments as to the parents' intellectual disability.

International research has shown that with appropriate support parents with IDD can look after their children appropriately when they and their family are provided with appropriately tailored ongoing support (DoH & DfES, 2007; Faureholm, 2010; IASSID SIRG, 2008; McGaw & Newman, 2005; Tarleton, Ward & Howarth, 2006). However, this support is frequently unavailable and many parents with learning difficulties come into contact with children's services.

Involvement of Children's Services

There are no definitive recent statistics regarding the number of parents with IDD involved with children's services, although for many years it has been cited that 40–50% of children of parents with IDD are removed from their parents' care (McConnell, Llewellyn & Ferronato, 2006). Booth, Booth and McConnell (2005) found that one-sixth of children subject to care proceedings had at least one parent with a 'learning disability', this figure rising to almost a quarter if parents with 'borderline learning disabilities' were included (Full Scale IQ 70–79). Similarly, Masson, Pearce, Bader et al. (2008) found that 12.5% of the parents involved in care proceedings in England and Wales had 'learning difficulties' (this term was not specifically defined). Similar rates have been found in other countries. For example, a Canadian study found that parental cognitive impairment (defined as parents with intellectual disabilities and borderline intellectual functioning) was noted in 10.1% of sampled cases that were opened for child maltreatment investigation and in 27.3% of sampled cases that resulted in child welfare court application (similar to judicial proceedings) in 2003 (McConnell, Feldman, Aunos & Prasad, 2011). Concerns for the children's welfare usually relate to unintentional neglect (by omission) due to a lack of awareness of the child's need and/or availability of appropriate support and education (Cleaver & Nicholson, 2008; McConnell & Llewellyn, 2002; McGaw & Newman, 2005; Tymnchuck, 1992).

There are often many issues facing parents with IDD who are in contact with social care and children's services. For example, they are often living on low or very low incomes, unemployed, living in unsatisfactory housing in difficult neighbourhoods, and are without recourse to the information they need in formats they can understand (Cleaver & Nicholson, 2008; Emerson & Brigham, 2013; SCIE, 2005). Parents with IDD often have other issues, such as poor mental and physical health, domestic violence or substance misuse, or they have grown up in care (Cleaver & Nicholson, 2008; McGaw & Newman, 2005). A study of a special parenting service for parents with IDD in Cornwall, UK, found that three-quarters of the parents involved with the service reported abuse and neglect in their own childhoods (McGaw, Shaw & Beckley, 2007).

Parental Service Engagement

Parents with IDD and the professionals who work with them sometimes report difficulties in engaging with each other (Tarleton, Ward & Howarth, 2006). Athwal (2012) suggested that parental engagement relates to the expectations of parents and professionals, parents' feelings toward agencies and their access to appropriate information. Parents with IDD are recorded as holding a number of perceptions of professionals, these include: professionals assume they cannot parent or cannot improve their parenting; have fixed ideas about what should happen to their children; assume that they will fail as parents; have too high expectations of them as parents and fail to communicate with parents in a way that they understand (Tarleton, Ward & Howarth, 2006). These issues are highlighted in research discussing child protection proceedings and the court processes (Booth & Booth, 2004; McConnell & Llewellyn, 2002). Parents with IDD have also reported not understanding the child protection system or why their child[ren] were removed from their care (McGhee & Hunter 2011; Swift, Johnson, Mason, Pearce, Bader et al., 2013).

Research has highlighted that some professionals working with parents with regard to child protection concerns may have negative biases toward parents with IDD (Proctor & Azar, 2012; Sheerin, 1998; Wilson, McKenzie, Quayle & Murray, 2013). Other studies describe the pressures professionals are working under, including short time scales, a lack of appropriate services, and having had little or no experience working with or training about parents with ID (Lewis, Stenfert Kroese & O'Brien, 2015). Jones (2013) found that professionals 'feel' for parents with IDD while Lewis, Stenfert Kroese and O'Brien (2015) reported that children's social workers in England and Wales sometimes feel 'torn' between the parents' and child's needs and the demands of the system they work within. These workers recognised the power imbalance for parents with ID and reported making extra efforts for them.

Best-Practice Guidelines in the UK

Best practice in working with parents with IDD have been summarised in McGaw and Newman (2005) and Tarleton, Ward and Howarth (2006). These studies fed into the English and Scottish Good Practice Guidance on Working with Parents with a Learning Disability (Department of Health & Department for Education and Skills [DoH & DfES], 2007; Scottish Consortium for Learning Disabilities, 2009). These best-practice guidance documents stress the need for:

1. accessible information and communication
2. clear processes and pathways
3. support to meet the need of both parents and children
4. long-term support where necessary
5. access to independent advocacy for parents.

Section 2 of the English guidance 'Good practice where safeguarding procedures are necessary' (DoH & DfES, 2007) stressed the importance of ensuring that parents understand the concerns regarding their children, that using an advocate is beneficial, and that the wider issues impacting on the family should be addressed. It also stated that support should continue to be provided, according to assessed need, even when the child is no longer the subject of a child protection plan so that improvements are maintained. The guidance indicated that this support would reduce 'revolving door' referrals and that ongoing support should involve both adult and children's services (section 2.2.11). In England, this guidance has recently been updated by the Working Together with Parents Network (2016).

This type of support fits with the early intervention agenda in the UK (HM Government, 2010), the Think Family approach (Department for Children, School and Families, 2010), the Children Act 1989's aim that all children should stay with their families whenever possible and the 2014 Care Act's emphasis on preventative support. While the Good Practice Guidance is not legally binding, it is recommended that it is followed to ensure that appropriate support is provided so that parents with IDD are able to fulfil their parenting responsibilities (Equality Act 2010). The Working Together with Parents network (WTPN) provides free support to any professional working with parents with IDD (wtpn.co.uk) in the UK and aims to promote the development of preventative early positive support for parents with IDD.

Identifying Parents with IDD

Many parents with IDD have not previously been in contact with services. If parents have a borderline intellectual disability they may have attended mainstream school and maintained employment. Many services for adults with IDD have had strict eligibility criteria meaning that parents with borderline intellectual disability would not be eligible for support in their own right (Goodringe, 2000). Often, parents' need for support is only recognised when concerns are raised about their ability to care for children. Paradoxically, these parents can be in far greater need of support than adults with an IDD who can access support services.

The English Care and Support (Eligibility Criteria) Regulations 2014 in England and Wales state that an adult's support needs should be met, in their own right, if they arise from an impairment or illness and if, as a consequence, the adult's well-being will be adversely affected. To qualify for support, the adult must be assessed as being unable to manage at least two 'specified outcomes', which include caring responsibilities for a child and maintaining a habitable home environment or engaging in work.

While many parents with IDD would fulfil at least two of these criteria and require assistance with various tasks, receiving that assistance depends on a service having the necessary resources to meet the needs.

Advice should always be sought from the local authority's adult 'learning disability' team if there are concerns as to whether a parent has a learning difficulty. There are also a number of screening tools that have been developed. One example is the Screening Tool Relating to the Assessment of Parents with suspected Learning Difficulties (STRAP-LD; Hames & English, undated; McDonnell & Hames, 2005), which was designed to enable non-psychologists to carry out a brief assessment with parents with suspected IDD to indicate whether a referral to clinical psychology services for a formal diagnosis is necessary. Developed for health visitors, midwives, social workers and other professionals, the tool includes asking the participant to read a passage. Scores are provided for the number of mistakes made. The adult is then asked eight questions about the information in the passage. Tools should be used with support from a clinical psychologist as raising this issue may be uncomfortable for both the professional and parent.

Ongoing Support for Parents with IDD

It has been increasingly recognised that parents with IDD often need ongoing support to ensure 'good enough' parenting and positive outcomes for their children (Azar, Mirella & Proctor, 2013; Conder & Mirfin-Veitch, 2010; McIntyre & Stewart, 2011; Wilson, McKenzie, Quayle & Murray, 2013; WTPN, 2009). Yet child protection services are often unable to provide ongoing support for parents. In 2011, Lightfoot and LaLiberte described the change needed within the field of child protection as a 'paradigm shift', stressing that support should compensate for the parent's disability so that they can fulfil their parenting responsibilities appropriately. Azar, Mirella and Proctor's (2013) review of the literature confirmed the need for this type of support and also called for a system change in child protection in order that long-term pro-active support could be provided to parents. Cleaver and Nicholson (2008), working from a children's social work perspective, in the UK, concluded that many of the difficulties parents faced could be ameliorated with positive support but that services struggled to meet parents' ongoing clinical and support needs. Therefore, the authors called for specialist training and support for workers (op. cit.).

Best practice also recognises that parents' learning difficulties are lifelong difficulties and although parents may respond to short-term interventions, improvements may be lost when support is withdrawn. McGaw and Newman's (2005) seminal book, *What Works for Parents with ID*, reviewed the international literature and provided examples of interventions and support. They noted that 'the main predictor of competent parenting is an adequate structure of professional and informal support' (p. 24) and that 'supporting families may require a combination of skilled support during crucial child developmental periods, more "low-level" but reliable support for lengthier periods and commitment to the family' (p. ix). McGaw and Newman (2005) argued that this is particularly necessary during the child's early years. However, it is being recognised that parents require support at all stages of their parenting career. McGaw and Newman also recognised the need for multi-agency services to work together in a standardised way in partnership with parents while undertaking assessment, intervention and long-term support of families. They called for the development of service protocols and performance indicators to raise and maintain standards of service delivery.

Similarly, Tarleton, Ward & Howarth (2006) and Tarleton and Ward (2007) drew together best-practice guidance across the UK in supporting parents with IDD and introduced the idea of 'parenting with support' whereby parents are provided with pro-active, ongoing, individualised support. This concept focused on empowering parents and supporting positive outcomes for children through: providing competency-promoting positive support to the whole family through coordinated multi-agency working; raising frontline professionals' awareness of this vulnerable group of parents; and providing frontline professionals with training so that support needs would be picked up before parents become involved with child protection services.

'Parenting with support' is similar to the idea of 'supported parenting' (Booth & Booth, 1996, www.supportedparenting.co.uk/philosophy/). Tarleton, Ward and Howarth (2006) and Tarleton and Turner (2015), however, noted that 'supported parenting' appeared to focus on supporting parents with little discussion of the child(ren)'s needs and outcomes. 'Parenting with support' recognises that it is vital to ensure that the child's needs are always paramount, while still empowering parents.

Across the world a similar approach to positive support is being taken. In Australia, Healthy Start is a national strategy for parents with IDD, which aims 'to build Australia's capacity to support the healthy and happy development of children whose parents have learning difficulties' (www.healthystart.net.au/index.php/about-healthy-start/background). The organisation states that this resource was developed because 'service providers reported feeling challenged in supporting mothers and fathers with learning difficulties and they wanted strategies that work' (www.healthystart.net.au/index.php/about-healthy-start/background). Heathy Start states that programmes are most effective when they are:

- family-centred
- involve parent participation
- focus on strength and ability
- involve parents in goal-setting and decision-making
- focus on performance rather than knowledge.

In Quebec, Aunos, Proctor and Moxness (2010), working from a rehabilitation service for adults with learning difficulties, developed positive practice in supporting parents with IDD following similar principles and standards. These include:

- Establishing clear guidelines and internal policies that support the self-determination of persons with intellectual disabilities...and promote a positive approach and timely delivery of services to parents;
- Building partnerships with all organisations involved;
- Enhancing collaboration with natural/informal networks;
- Involving staff in training, continuing education and supervision;
- Appointing a case worker (key worker) who assesses the support needs and plans appropriate services.

Empowering parents and meeting children's needs

Parents with IDD often report being scared to engage with services, fearing that their child[ren] will be removed from their care if they admit to difficulties with parenting (Tarleton, Ward & Howarth, 2006; Traustadottir & Bjorg Sigurjonsdottir, 2010). However, Traustadottir and Bjorg Sigurjonsdottir (2010) suggested that, in contrast to viewing this in the traditional way as 'resistance', which they defined as attempts to 'counter the actions or effects of someone or something' (p. 108), 'resistance' to involvement with services is actually the parents' way of protecting their family as they resist the power of professionals in their lives and behave as 'active agents' in shaping their lives (p. 115). Therefore, the way in which professionals relate to parents is vital to their engagement.

From a client perspective, parents with IDD suggest a number of strategies to ensure that professionals engage with them as positively as possible. The WTPN London Parents Advisory Group (2014) provide guidance for professionals to work positively (see Table 26.1) and to communicate effectively with parents with IDD (see Table 26.2). Professionals should ask the parents with IDD what works for them and not assume that a parent can read or that they have someone who can read things for them.

There are excellent guides from CHANGE (2009) and Department of Health (2010) that provide detailed advice regarding making information easy to understand. An assessment by a speech and language therapist regarding the parent's communication support needs or having a 'communication facilitator' in important meetings can also support professionals in communicating positively with the parents (Matthews & Stansfield, 2014).

Table 26.1 Guidance on working with parents with IDD (adapted from WTPN London Parents Advisory Group, 2014).

Positive professional practice	Explanation/example
Arrive on time	Let parents know if you are running late
If possible/appropriate, tell parents in advance if you are coming to do a home visit	If possible, confirm the time and date in a pictorial letter (see below) or a text. Ensure the parent knows who you are (include a picture) and your role
Be polite, friendly and respectful	Speak directly to the parent (rather than other professionals or supporters who may be present)
Try and build up a positive relationship	Be positive with parents whenever possible
Be straight forward – tell parents 'as it is'	Spell out exactly what needs to change: 'You need to get the dog outside, vacuum all the carpets, wash the kitchen floor…' rather than 'You need to clean up your house'
Talk slowly and clearly and explain and explain again if need be	See below regarding teaching new skills
Match body language and expressions to the information being given	Don't give bad news with a smiling face as this mean the information given may be misunderstood
Show parents you are listening to them	Try not to be looking down and writing lots of notes while talking to parents
Look 'outside the box' for the reasons for the difficulties	The issue might not be poor parenting, there might be another reason like poverty
Do not make assumptions	Try and find the reason parents are doing what we are doing

Table 26.2 Guidance on communicating with parents with IDD (adapted from WTPN London Parents Advisory Group, 2014).

Positive professional practice	Explanation/example
Use short sentences	No more than 15 words. Only one point to a sentence and no clauses or complicated grammar such as double negatives
Avoid jargon and use words that are easy to understand	Explain jargon that is used regularly within the child protection system
Be as 'concrete' as possible	Abstract concepts should be avoided or explained as clearly as possible. Avoid metaphors
In written communication also:	
Use a clear large font	Such as Arial or Century Gothic. Font size 14 at least
Use numbers in the text	Use 2 instead of two
Use clear explanatory pictures which present the key point of the text	Pictures should be preferably on the left of the text and have no distracting elements. For example, pictures of clock times, of a calendar with a date highlighted and of the venue can support parents in attending meetings

When convening a meeting involving parents with IDD, the WTPN London Parents Advisory Group (2014) also advise that parents should be:

- provided with an advocate
- told the reason for the meeting
- provided with full details regarding the meeting in advance, including new information or concerns

- provided the paperwork well in advance of the meeting in a format that they understand so that they can prepare their responses
- told where the meeting is and be provided, if necessary, with directions
- offered childcare if needed.

Meetings should have a clear focus and be as short as possible but include breaks if necessary. They should not use jargon or discuss side issues. Professionals should ensure parents are at the centre of the meeting and ask the parents what works for them. Professionals should understand that parents may be scared about losing their child[ren] and that anger and frustration could be an expression of either a lack of understanding or fear. After the meeting, parents should be provided with a record of the meeting in good time and be supported to understand its implications. An advocate can fulfil this role.

Using an advocate

Advocacy for parents with IDD is recognised as a key element of best practice with parents involved with child protection proceedings (DoH & DfES, 2007; McGhee & Hunter, 2011; Tarleton, 2013). The Care Act 2014 in England and Wales now states that if parents are struggling to engage fully with the child protection process, then all efforts should be made to ensure an advocate supports them.

The support of an advocate is seen to reduce the power imbalance between professionals and parents. An advocate can support parents to engage more positively with the concerns for their children (rather than in anger or through fear and frustration). The advocate provides the parent with support to understand the child protection process and the concerns for their child/ren's welfare, and to contribute to the process by putting forward their views (Booth & Booth, 1998; Tarleton, Ward and Howarth, 2006; Ward & Tarleton, 2010). This is often done through supporting the parents in understanding reports and thinking about their response, accompanying parents to meetings and providing ongoing emotional support.

Good advocates will have an understanding of both children and adult services and be able to explain both to the parents. They should work to standards relevant to advocacy with adults with learning disabilities, as well as those relating to child protection (Lindley & Richards, 2002; Mencap, 2007).

Tarleton (2013) showed how an advocate could be of benefit to the parent with IDD and to the children's services professionals. Professionals recognised that parents were being provided with emotional support, a role that they found difficult to fulfil when focusing on the needs of the children. The parent's understanding of the issues was also recognised as supporting their engagement with the child protection process and services provided. Advocacy for parents with IDD has been reported as cost effective in terms of reduced service use and positive outcomes for parents and children (Bauer, Wistow, Dixon & Knapp, 2013).

Assessing parents' support needs

An appropriate parenting assessment is key to providing positive support for parents with IDD. Assessments should be carried out by professionals with experience of working with parents with IDD or, at the very least, with support from services that work with adults with IDD. When conducting parenting capacity assessments, professionals should recognise that parents with IDD, like any other group, are diverse with regard to parenting skills. Parent intelligence alone is a poor predictor of parenting capacity; while parents with very low scores on intelligence tests (i.e., IQ scores below 60) tend to have more difficulties, an IQ score below 60 does not provide a sufficient basis upon which to infer incapacity or predict future harm to a child (Tymchuk & Feldman, 1991).

Parents with IDD are recognised as being at a higher risk of experiencing physical and mental health problems, which are frequently untreated, and often have experienced abuse, discrimination and hate crime. Parents' own support needs should be assessed and addressed before their parenting capacity is addressed. In England and Wales this is stipulated by: the Care Act 2014; Guidance on Eligibility Criteria for Adult Social Care England (2010); and Department for Education (2013).

Parents with IDD may also be lacking in positive parenting role models, support and relevant life experience (Tarleton, Ward & Howarth, 2006). It should be recognised that, although some parents with IDD may struggle to provide a rich stimulating home environment, particularly in relation to language development, inadequate stimulation cannot be assumed and sufficient stimulation may be being provided by other sources (grandparents, school, workers, etc.). Indeed, most studies have demonstrated that parents with IDD provide a level of stimulation that is not significantly different to non-IDD parents (see Feldman, 2002 for a review).

A contextual and functional approach to assessment should be taken that does not see parenting capacity as an individual trait, but acknowledges that parenting capacity is a changing state that is influenced by many factors including children's changing needs, available resources and supports, and socio-economic factors (Munro, 1999; Turney, Platt, Selwyn & Farmer, 2012). The assessment should cover all of the aspects of the Common Assessment Framework (see Gray, this volume Chapter 8) but be undertaken in a way that matches the parents' communication needs (i.e., using pictures and keeping discussions concrete). It should identify parental strengths as well as needs and consider whether the parent is able to provide 'good enough' parenting, recognising the interplay between individual parents and factors that impact on the family (Spencer, 2001), for example, poverty, social isolation and hate crime. It should focus on parents' current knowledge and skills, their learning ability and the circumstances under which the parents successfully learn or apply what is learnt. The supports and services currently, or previously, provided to the parents and the impact of these services should be considered. Assessors may need to consider if these services and supports are provided in the right way (i.e., are they individually tailored to parents to support their parenting?). When undertaking an assessment, the assessor should use the language and communication style the parent understands as parents with IDD will often require easy-to-read information. In addition, psychometric testing should not be the main or only source of assessment, as there are other more appropriate approaches devised specifically for parents with IDD. For example, professionals supporting parents with IDD in the Tarleton, Ward and Howarth (2006) study, and anecdotally since, reported that the Parent Assessment Manual (McGaw, 1999) was the most frequently used assessment.

Providing individualised ongoing support

Parents with IDD have identified a wide range of areas in which they may need support. These can include the practical realities of looking after a young child, such as routines, feeding/healthy eating, managing their children's behaviour and understanding how to keep them safe. They may also need support with paperwork, their finances (including weekly budgeting) and practical tasks around the home. Unfortunately, parents may also need support to deal with harassment and bullying and knowing how to protect themselves (Tarleton, Ward & Howarth, 2006; West Berkshire Mencap, 2004; WTPN London Parents Advisory Group, 2014). Given that parents with IDD are more likely than other parents to be living in socially disadvantaged circumstances, they may also need support to overcome wider problems, such as poverty, debt and poor housing (Cleaver & Nicholson; SCIE, 2005; Tarleton & Ward, 2007).

Support should be provided in a flexible way, which starts from the parent's capabilities and supports parents to build confidence and self-esteem (McGaw & Newman 2005; Tarleton, Ward & Howarth, 2006; Wilson, McKenzie, Quayle & Murray, 2013). If appropriate, support could be garnered from family, the local community or voluntary/community support services. Family group conferencing is a technique that can be used to harness family support (www.frg.org.uk/involving-families/family-group-conferences), while many advocacy organisations that work with adults with learning difficulties offer parenting groups. The benefits of parenting groups are discussed below.

As few workers as possible should provide ongoing practical support to parents in an individualised way, preferably coordinated by a key worker who can share information between professionals. Parents stress that the workers who provide ongoing support should listen to them and communicate honestly and clearly with them (see Tables 26.2 and 26.3), including showing respect, empathy and genuineness, in order to build a relationship that facilitates the parent's skill development and understanding of the child protection process (Moore, 2013). Strategies for successful multi-agency working and an example of a service providing positive support are discussed in more detail below.

Pregnant women with IDD should also be provided with support to access standard antenatal care as midwives may not be experienced in working with women with IDD and expectant mothers may be fearful of attending or may struggle with understanding what is happening. These women are increasingly being recognised as a vulnerable group, as a higher proportion of pregnant women with learning difficulties are teenagers, obese, single and smokers (Hoglund, Lindgren & Larsson, 2012b). They are also being recognised as at higher risk of pre-term birth, birth by caesarean section and at increased likelihood of having smaller babies (Hoglund, Lindgren & Larsson, 2012a), all of which may mean that the baby is harder to care for and that mothers may be in need of additional, targeted support to ensure the well-being of the baby. A multi-agency team often provides this support.

Multi-agency working

Coordinated multi-agency support is regarded as vital to providing appropriate support for parents with IDD (Aunos & Pachos, 2013; SCIE, 2006; Tarleton, Ward & Howarth, 2006). As parents with IDD are often involved with a wide range of professionals, practical ways of supporting coordinated multi-agency working with a consistent approach between workers include:

- Use of a keyworker system to coordinate support to parents
- Sharing of information between workers with parent's consent
- Common goals including clarity and agreement on what is required of the particular family to ensure positive outcomes for the children
- Honesty, openness and ongoing communication between all workers involved
- Understanding of individual professional roles and their boundaries
- Shared goals and attitudes developed within the team through joint training
- Creativity in finding appropriate solutions

- Training in understanding parents with IDD for workers whose experience is in protecting children
- Training and support in child protection for workers whose experience is in supporting adults with IDD. (Aunos & Pachos, 2013; DoH & DfES, 2007; SCIE, 2006; Tarleton, Ward & Howarth, 2006)

The development of joint protocols and care pathways between all of the services involved in working with parents with IDD is advised. These should discuss eligibility and referrals; roles, responsibilities and accountabilities; communication; and joint training and development (DoH & DfES, 2007; SCIE 2006). An example of a joint protocol is the Suffolk Accord (https://www.access-unlimited.co.uk/assets/Accord.pdf).

Skill development

Home-based, individualised parenting programmes have been shown to significantly improve the parenting skills of parents with IDD (Feldman, 1994, 2010; Wade, Llewellyn & Matthews, 2008). In 2013, Rao reported that the majority of 50 parents involved in a specifically adapted, individual, home-based parenting programme increased their skills. The best outcomes are achieved when the parent's current skills are assessed and an individual programme developed. Feldman (2010) suggest key elements of a successful programme include:

- concrete discussion
- step-by-step approach
- pictorial posters and manuals
- audio and videotapes
- modelling
- practice
- positive feedback and encouragement
- corrective feedback
- role playing
- game format
- self-monitoring.

Role play and modelling exactly how a task should be completed are particularly useful techniques which can also be applied to playing with children and interacting with babies. Some services and parenting groups use video to support parental learning as it provides information visually and can be returned to repeatedly. Video can be used in a variety of ways, for instance: videoing the steps of a practical task; providing insight into the way in which other parents interact with their child; or showing the parents a video of their own parenting, encouraging the positive aspects. Video Interaction Guidance™ is used by some professionals. This is an intervention through which a trained practitioner works with a parent to support the development of their communication and interaction and often results in improvements in their social learning and emotional well-being. A series of interactions are videoed and edited, and successful clips are watched in detail allowing the learner to see 'what works' in their interactions. This process allows the parent to notice and build on positive interactions (www.videointeractionguidance.net; Kennedy, Landor & Todd, 2011).

Parenting groups and group parenting programmes

Parents groups are valued by parents and professionals alike as a cost-effective means of supporting parents which can improve their social networks and self-esteem through peer support and provide informal access to advice from a range of professionals (Murshed, 2005; Tarleton, Ward & Howarth, 2006). In Tarleton, Ward & Howarth's (2006) study, parents and professionals involved with parenting groups stressed that they should:

- Be held at a neutral venue not associated with children and families services
- Be held on a regular day and at a regular time
- Provide transport – one service provided an escorted minibus to reduce time spent by workers picking up and dropping off parents
- Have a structure and ground rules which enable parents to share their experiences with other parents in a safe environment and to learn from and support each other
- Provide specific information for parents of school-age children, as many services only support families until children start school.

Supporting parents to organise these groups also provides them with the opportunity to develop meeting skills such as agenda development and confidence at speaking in the group.

Group-based parenting programmes have also been shown to be beneficial for parents with IDD when adapted to their needs. Glazemaker and Deboutte (2013) described the successful modification of the group-based Positive Parenting Programme (often known as Triple P; www.triplep.net/glo-en/home/) for parents with IDD. In the UK, an adapted Mellow Parenting Programme called Mellow Futures has been piloted, which utilised many of the strategies for skill development discussed above. Mellow Parenting programmes are attachment-based parenting programmes that aim to develop positive relationships in hard-to-reach families (www.mellowparenting.org/). Mellow Futures includes adapted Mellow Bumps (antenatal 6-week programme) and Mellow Babies (post-natal 14-week programme) for mothers with IDD. Mellow programmes provide a structured environment where parents can learn how to improve their relationship with their child. During the post-birth group, mothers and babies attend together and babies attend their own 'children's group' while mothers reflect on their parenting. Video feedback on the mother's positive interaction with their babies is also provided as well as mother-and-baby meals and activity sessions. As well as attending the programme each week a mentor is provided to support the mother to think about and enact their learning at home. Tarleton and Turner (2015) found that mothers really enjoyed attending Mellow Futures programmes and reported having learnt how to care for their baby while looking into the issues that impact on their parenting. Parents also had, often for the first time, developed supportive peer relationships with other mothers. Professionals involved with the families also reported, for the majority of mothers, improvements in the mother's relationship with and care for her baby and lowering of the level of concerns for the baby's welfare.

However, if attending mainstream programmes, parents with IDD will likely need specific support as they may be daunted by attending a new group and the material will need to be adapted in order to meet their communication needs. Support for attending parenting groups and other support services was provided by the workers at the Valuing People Support Service.

Case Example of a Parent Support Service: Valuing Parents Support Service

Valuing Parents Support Service (VPSS) is a venture jointly funded by the adult and children's services in Medway, England. This is a local service, not available nationally. It aims to provide holistic assessment, intervention and support to parents with IDD with children under eight years of age while also identifying 'high-risk' families where children should not be cared for by their parents. The VPSS team strives to implement the English Good Practice Guidance on Working with Parents with IDD (DoH & DfES, 2007) and the practical strategies described by McGaw and Newman (2005) and Tarleton, Ward and Howarth (2006). The team aim to provide intensive support and training to help parents care for their children appropriately and engage with children's services.

The support provided by VPSS includes supporting parents with everyday tasks such as shopping, paying bills, household organisation, safety and cleanliness, as well as specific teaching/role modelling of parenting skills. The team facilitates parents in accessing mainstream parenting groups and engages with issues that impact on their ability to parent. These include poor housing, domestic violence and the grief of having previous children removed. VPSS either directly supports parents or enables them to access specialist services, such as the Freedom Programme (for domestic violence: www.freedomprogramme.co.uk/). VPSS also provides advocacy support to parents where team members help parents to understand reports and accompany them to meetings and court. If children have been removed from their parents' care, team members support parents to move on with their lives and, when appropriate, to remain in contact with their children through supported contact or the letterbox process (keeping in contact with an adopted child by post).

The workers at VPSS are from a range of different backgrounds including learning disabilities, child protection, youth work and family support. They worked with parents in a wide range of ways, specifically to:

- Build relationships with parents based on trust and respect. Parents are allocated specific workers who communicate regularly with each other;
- Work in partnership with parents at their pace;
- Use easy-to-understand materials to enhance parental understanding;
- Enable parents to assess groups provided by children's services and in the local community;
- Support parents to engage with other services concerned with the welfare of their children;
- Engage in interdisciplinary working where they are respected for their professionalism and due respect for the welfare of the children. Strategies that support this include ongoing communication with all the other professionals involved with the family, understanding and respecting the different professional roles, and developing shared clarity around the aims of the assessment and support.

Using a Matching Needs and Services Audit (MNS; Dartington Social Research Unit, 1999), which was undertaken by an independent social work consultant, Tarleton, Porter, Brown and Davis (2011) demonstrated that the outcomes for the children of parents with IDD were improved in comparison to children and families supported by the local authority Children's Services Assessment Service (AS). The MNS audit analysed the needs of children whose parents with IDD were currently supported by the VPSS (32 children from 24 families) and a sample of parents who did not have an IDD who were being supported by the co-located AS (17 children from nine families). Child protection concerns were expressed regarding all the families in touch with the VPSS and AS. The AS undertook detailed assessment work to assist courts in deciding whether children could remain at home with their families. This assessment was carried out in the context of the provision of appropriate services to support the well-being of the children while a decision was made. Members of the VPSS provided parents with IDD with support, while the AS provided parents without IDD with support. The support offered by both services varied according to individual need, but regularly consisted of direct work with parents on a one-to-one basis, group work on specific issues and referrals to other projects for support with issues such as domestic violence or substance misuse. The AS undertook their assessment during a 12-week parenting programme, which parents attended five days per week.

As shown in Table 26.3, in the 24 VPSS families over a third had been in care themselves (38%) and had previously had children removed from their care (41%), compared to 12% and 12% respectively for the AS families. Despite this, it was considered that a similar number of their children's needs were more fully or partially met (87%) in comparison to families supported by the AS (88%). A higher number of children's needs were considered to be fully met: 50% when support was provided by the VPSS in contrast to 29% when parents were supported by the AS. Nearly two-thirds of the children in families supported by the VPSS were considered as not at risk of significant harm in comparison to only 6% of the families supported by the AS service (for more detail see Tarleton & Porter, 2012).

The qualitative evaluation showed that VPSS was regarded as 'vital' to child protection plans. A number of child protection social workers noted they had 'discharged' (closed cases) early as they were confident in the service's ability to monitor and provide ongoing support to families.

This service provides an example of positive practice in action and it is hoped that in the longer term it will be a model for specialist services which provide long-term support for parents with IDD. This would eventually reduce the number of parents with IDD involved with child protection procedures. Until this time, it is hoped that workers working with parents with IDD who are involved in the child protection process will utilise the strategies discussed in this chapter in order to improve parental engagement and understanding of the concerns regarding the welfare of their children and to be able to provide appropriately tailored support to these families in order to promote the best outcomes for their children.

Table 26.3 Comparison of needs of and outcomes for families supported by the Valuing Parents Support Service and Assessment Service.

	VPSS (N=32 children; 24 families) n%	Assessment Service (N=17 children; 9 families) n%
Parents who were looked after	12 38	2 12
Children previously removed	13 41	2 12
Children living with parents	25 78	4 24
Children not at risk of significant harm	19 62	1 6
Children's needs fully or partially met	28 87	15 88
Children's needs fully met	16 50	5 29
Children's needs partially met	12 38	10 59

Conclusion

Parents with IDD are recognised as facing a number of barriers to being the best parents possible. These factors include difficulties related to their impairment, as well as barriers related to their often poor socio-economic status and lack of community support. A substantial amount of best practice has been developed around working with parents with IDD in response to their individual support and communication needs. However, in many areas pro-active support is not available and a 'paradigm shift' (Lightfoot & LaLiberte, 2011) is required in order to ensure that these vulnerable parents are provided with support that is tailored to their needs and that reduces the likelihood of poorer outcomes for and concerns about the welfare of their children.

References

American Psychiatric Association (2013). *Diagnostic and Statistical Manual of Mental Disorders*, 5th edn. Washington, DC: APA.

Athwal, S. (2012). *Being a parent with learning difficulties: An exploratory study of parents' views and experiences of local support services.* Doctorate in Applied Educational Psychology thesis, University of Birmingham, Birmingham.

Aunos, M. & Pachos, L. (2013). Changing perspective: Workers' perception of inter-agency collaboration with parents with an intellectual disability. *Journal of Public Welfare*, 7, 658–674.

Aunos, M., Proctor, L. & Moxness, K. (2010). Turning fights into realities in Quebec, Canada. In: G. Llewellyn, R. Traustadottir, D. McConnell & H. Sigurjonsdottir (eds), *Parents with Intellectual Disabilities, Past, Present and Future*. West Sussex: Wiley Blackwell, 189–204.

Azar, S., Mirella, M. & Proctor, S. (2013). Practice changes in child protection system to address the needs of parents with cognitive disabilities. *Journal of Public Child Welfare*, 7, 610–632.

Bauer, A. & Wistow, G., Dixon, J. & Knapp, M. (2013). *Investing in advocacy interventions for parents with learning disabilities: What is the economic argument? Discussion paper, 2860*. Kent: Personal Social Services Research Unit.

Booth, T. & Booth, W. (1996). Supported parenting for people with learning difficulties: Lessons from Wisconsin. *Representing Children*, 9, 99–107.

Booth, T. & Booth, W. (1998). *Advocacy for Parents with Learning Difficulties: Developing Advocacy Support*. York: Joseph Rowntree Foundation.

Booth T. & Booth, W. (2004). *Parents with learning difficulties: Child protection and the courts, a report to the Nuffield Foundation on Grant No. CPF/00151/G*, www.supportedparenting.com/projects/NuffieldReport.pdf.

Booth, T., Booth, W. & McConnell, D. (2005). The prevalence and outcomes of care proceedings involving parents with learning difficulties in the family courts. *Journal of Intellectual Disability Research*, 18, 7–17.

Care Act 2014 (England).

CHANGE (2009). *How to make information accessible: A guide to producing easy read documents*, www.changepeople.org/downloads/CHANGE_How_to_Make_Info_Accessible_guide_2009.pdf.

Children Act 1989 (England).

Cleaver, H. & Nicholson, D. (2008). *Parental Learning Disability and Children's Needs: Family Experiences and Effective Practice*. London: Jessica Kingsley.

Collings, S. & Llewellyn, G. (2012). Children of parents with intellectual disability: Facing poor outcomes or faring okay? *Journal of Intellectual and Developmental Disabilities*, 37, 65–82.

Conder, J. & Mirfin-Veitch, B. (2010). Planned pregnancy, planned parenting: Enabling choice for adults with a learning disability. *British Journal of Learning Disabilities*, 39, 105–112.

Darbyshire, L. & Stenfert Kroese, B. (2012). Psychological well-being and social support for parents with intellectual disabilities: Risk factors and interventions. *Journal of Policy and Practice in Intellectual Disabilities*, 9, 40–52.

Dartington Social Research Unit (1999). *Matching needs and services*, 2nd edn. Dartington: DSRU.

Department for Children, School and Families (2009). *Think Family Toolkit*, http://webarchive.nationalarchives.gov.uk/20130401151715/www.education.gov.uk/publications/eOrderingDownload/Think-Family.pdf.

Department of Education (2013). Working together to safeguard children, www.gov.uk/government/publications/working-together-to-safeguard-children.

Department of Health (2001). *Valuing people: A new strategy for learning disability for the 21st century*. London: Department of Health.

Department of Health (2010). *Making written information easier to understand for people with learning disabilities: Guidance for people who commission or produce Easy Read information – Revised Edition 2010*, www.gov.uk/government/publications/making-written-information-easier-to-understand-for-people-with-learning-disabilities-guidance-for-people.

Department of Health and Department for Education and Skills (2007). *Good practice guidance on working with parents with a learning disability*. London: Department of Health and Department for Education and Skills.

Emerson, E. & Brigham, P. (2013). Health behaviours and mental health status of parents with intellectual disabilities: Cross sectional study. *Public Health*, 127, 1111–1116.

Emerson, E. & Brigham, P. (2014). The developmental health of children of parents with intellectual disabilities: Cross sectional study. *Research in Developmental Disabilities*, 35, 917–921.

Equality Act 2010 (England).

Faureholm, J. (2010). Children and their life experiences. In: G. Llewellyn, R. Traustadottir, D. McConnell & H. Sigurjonsdottir (eds), *Parents with Intellectual Disabilities, Past, Present and Future*. West Sussex: Wiley Blackwell, 63–78.

Feldman, M. (1994). Parenting education for parents with intellectual disabilities: Review of research outcome studies. *Research in Developmental Disabilities*, 15, 299–322.

Feldman, M. (2002). Children of parents with intellectual disabilities. In: R.J. McMahon & R.D. Peters (eds), *The Effects of Parental Dysfunction on Children*. New York: Kluwer Academic/Plenum, 205–223.

Feldman, M. (2010). Parent Education Programs. In: G. Llewellyn, R. Traustadottir, D. McConnell & H. Sigurjonsdottir (eds), *Parents with Intellectual Disabilities, Past, Present and Future*. West Sussex: Wiley Blackwell, 121–136.

Glazemaker, I. & Deboutte, D. (2013). Modifying the 'Positive Parenting Program' for parents with intellectual disabilities. *Journal of Intellectual Disability Research*, 57, 616–626.

Goodringe, S. (2000). *A jigsaw of services: Inspection of services to support disabled adults in their parenting role*. London: Department of Health.

Hames, A. & English, S. (undated). *Screening tool relating to the assessment of parents with suspected learning disabilities (also known as the Sanderson Screening Tool)*. Unpublished.

Hoglund, B., Lindgren, P. & Larsson, M. (2012a). Newborns of mothers with intellectual disability have a higher risk of perinatal death and being small for gestational age. *Acta Obstet Gynecol Scand*, 91, 1409–1414.

Hoglund, B., Lindgren, P. & Larsson, M. (2012b). Pregnancy and birth outcomes of women with intellectual disability in Sweden: A national register study. *Acta Obstet Gynecol Scand*, 91, 1381–1387.

HM Government Care and Support (Eligibility Criteria) Regulations 2014, www.legislation.gov.uk/ukdsi/2014/9780111124185.

IASSID Special Interest Research Group on Parents and Parenting with Intellectual Disabilities (2008). Parents labelled with intellectual disability: Position of the IASSID SIRG on parents and parenting with intellectual disabilities. *Journal of Applied Research in Intellectual Disabilities*, 21, 296–307.

Jones, N. (2013). Good Enough Parents? Exploring attitudes of family centre workers supporting and assessing parents with learning difficulties. *Practice: Social work in Action*, 25, 169–190.

Kennedy, H., Landor, M. & Todd, L. (2011). *Video Interaction Guidance: A Relationship Based Intervention to Promote Attunement, Empathy and Well-Being.* London: Jessica Kingsley.

Lewis, C., Stenfert Kroese, B. & O'Brien A. (2015) Child and family social workers' experiences of working with parents with intellectual disabilities. *Advances in Mental Health and Intellectual Disabilities*, 9, 2, 327–337.

Lightfoot, E. & LaLiberte, T. (2011). Parental supports for parents with intellectual and developmental disabilities. *Journal of Intellectual and Developmental Disabilities*, 49, 1–7.

Lindblad, I., Billstedt, E., Gillberg, C. & Fernell, E. (2013). An interview study of young adults born to mothers with mild intellectual disability. *Journal of Intellectual Disabilities*, 17, 329–338.

Lindley, B. & Richards, M. (2002). *Protocol on advice and advocacy for parents (child protection).* Cambridge: Centre for Family Research, University of Cambridge.

Masson, J., Pearce, J. & Bader, K. et al. (2008). *Care profiling study.* London: Ministry of Justice Research Series 4/08.

Matthews, A. & Stansfield, J. (2014). Supporting communication for parents with intellectual impairments: Communication facilitation in social work led parenting meetings. *British Journal of Learning Disabilities*, 42, 244–250.

McConnell, D. & Llewellyn, G. (2002). Stereotypes, parents with intellectual disability and child protection. *Journal of Social Welfare and Family Law*, 24, 297–317.

McConnell, D., Llewellyn, G. & Ferronato, L. (2006). Context-contingent decision making in child protection practice. *International Journal of Social Welfare*, 15, 230–239.

McConnell, D., Feldman, M., Aunos, M. & Prasad, N. (2011). Parental cognitive impairment and child maltreatment in Canada. *Child Abuse & Neglect*, 35, 621–632.

McDonnell, P. & Hames, A. (2005). Designing and piloting a screening tool relating to the assessment of parents with suspected learning difficulties *Clinical Psychology*, 46, 19–21.

McGaw, S. (1999). *Parent Assessment Manual.* www.pillcreekpublishing.com/.

McGaw, S. & Newman, T. (2005). *What works for parents with learning disabilities?* Ilford: Barnardos.

McGaw, S., Shaw, T. & Beckley. K. (2007). Prevalence of psychopathy across a service population of parents with intellectual disabilities and their children. *Journal of Policy and Practice in Intellectual Disabilities*, 4, 11–22.

McGhee, J. & Hunter, S. (2011). The Scottish children's hearings tribunal system: A better forum for parents with learning disabilities? *Journal of Social Welfare and Family Law*, 33, 255–266.

McIntyre, G. & Stewart, A. (2011). For the record: The lived experience of parents with a learning disability – a pilot study examining the Scottish perspective. *British Journal of Learning Disabilities*, 40, 5–14.

Mencap (2007). *Providing the right support for parents with a learning disability. Evaluating the work of the north east parents' support service and the Walsall parents' advocacy service,* www.mencap.org.uk/node/5868 Walsall parents' advocacy service.

Moore, H. (2013). *The experiences of parents with learning disabilities receiving formal support: The interpersonal context of parenting.* Unpublished clinical psychology thesis, University of Cardiff.

Munro, E. (1999). Common errors of reasoning in child protection work, *Child Abuse & Neglect*, 23, 745–758.

Murshed, M. (2005). Good practice ... parents with learning difficulties. *Disability, Pregnancy and Parenthood International*, 50, 16–17.

Proctor, S. & Azar, S. (2012). The effect of intellectual disability status on child protection worker decision-making. *Journal of Intellectual Disability Research*, 57, 1104–1116.

Rao, T. (2013). Implementation of an intensive, home-based program for parents with intellectual disabilities. *Journal of Public Child Welfare*, 7, 691–706.

Scottish Consortium for Learning Disabilities (SCLD) (2009). *Scottish good practice guidelines for supporting parents with learning disabilities.* Glasgow: SCLD.

Sheerin, F. (1998). Parents with learning disabilities: A review of the literature. *Journal of Advanced Nursing*, 28, 126–133.

Social Care Institute for Excellence (SCIE) (2005). *Helping parents with learning disabilities in their role as parents,* www.scie.org.uk/publications/briefings/briefing14/index.asp.

Social Care Institute for Excellence (SCIE) (2006). *Support for disabled parents: Knowledge review*, www.scie.org.uk/publications/knowledgereviews/kr11.pdf.

Spencer, M. (2001). Proceed with caution: The limitations of current parenting capacity assessments. *The Child, Youth and Family Work Journal*, 1, 16–24.

Stenfert Kroese, B., Hussein, H., Clifford, C. & Ahmed, N. (2002). Social support networks and psychological well-being of mothers with intellectual disabilities. *Journal of Applied Research in Intellectual Disabilities*, 15, 324–340.

Swift, P., Johnson, K., Mason, V. et al. (2013). *What happens when people with learning disabilities need advice about the law?* Bristol: Norah Fry Research Centre, University of Bristol.

Tarleton, B. (2013). Expanding the Engagement Model: The role of the specialist advocate in supporting parents with learning disabilities in child protection proceedings. *Journal of Public Child Welfare*, 7, 675–690.

Tarleton, B. (2015). A few steps along the road? Promoting support for parents with learning difficulties. *British Journal of Learning Disabilities*, 43, 114–120.

Tarleton, B. (2016). Working Together with Parents Network (WTPN) update of the DoH/DfES Good practice guidance on working with parents with a learning disability (2007). Bristol: Norah Fry Centre for Disability Studies. http://www.bristol.ac.uk/media-library/sites/sps/documents/wtpn/2016%20WTPN%20UPDATE%20OF%20THE%20GPG%20-%20finalised%20with%20cover.pdf

Tarleton, B. & Porter, S. (2012). Crossing no man's land: A specialist support service for parents with learning disabilities. *Child and Family Social Work*, 17, 233–243.

Tarleton, B. & Turner, W. (2015). Mellow Futures. *Parent pioneer pilot programme evaluation*. London: Mencap (forthcoming).

Tarleton, B. & Ward, L. (2007). 'Parenting with support': The views and experiences of parents with intellectual disabilities. *Journal of Policy and Practice in Intellectual Disabilities*, 4, 19–202.

Tarleton, B., Ward, L. & Howarth, J. (2006). *Finding the right support? A review of issues and positive practice to support parents with learning difficulties and their children*. London: Baring Foundation.

Tarleton, B., Porter, S., Brown, L. & Davis, L. (2011). *Evaluation of the Valuing Parents Support Service*. Internal report for funder. Bristol: Norah Fry Research Centre.

Traustadottir, R. & Bjorg Sigurjonsdottir, H.B. (2010). Parenting and resistance: Strategies in dealing with services and professionals. In: G. Llewellyn, R. Traustadottir, D. McConnell and H. Sigurjonsdottir (eds), *Parents with Intellectual Disabilities, Past, Present and Future*. West Sussex: Wiley Blackwell, 107–118.

Turney, D., Platt, D., Selwyn, J. & Farmer, E. (2012). *Improving Child and Family Assessments: Turning Research into Practice*. London: Jessica Kingsley.

Tymnchuck, A.J. (1992). Predicting adequacy of parenting by people with mental retardation. *Child Abuse & Neglect*, 16, 165–178.

Tymchuk, A. & Feldman, M. (1991). Parents with mental retardation and their children: Review of research relevant to professional practice, *Canadian Psychology*, 32, 486–496.

Wade, C., Llewellyn, G. & Matthews, J. (2008). Review of parent training interventions for parents with intellectual disability. *Journal of Applied Research in Intellectual Disabilities*, 21, 351–366.

Ward, L. & Tarleton, B. (2010). Advocacy for change: 'The final tool in the toolbox'. In: G. Llewellyn, R. Traustadottir, D. McConnell and H. Sigurjonsdottir (eds), *Parents with Intellectual Disabilities, Past, Present and Future*. West Sussex: Wiley Blackwell, 225–240.

West Berkshire Mencap (2004). *Partners in parenting: An audit of services for parents with learning disabilities in West Berkshire*. West Berkshire: Mencap.

Wilson, S., McKenzie, K., Quayle, E. & Murray, G. (2013). The postnatal support needs of mothers with an intellectual disability. *Midwifery*, 29, 592–598.

Working Together with Parents Network (2009). *Supporting parents with learning disabilities and difficulties – Stories of positive practice*. Bristol, Norah Fry Research, www.bristol.ac.uk/wtpn/resources/success-stories/.

WTPN London Parents Advisory Group (2014). *Good practice and parents with a learning disability*. Bristol: Norah Fry Research Centre, www.bristol.ac.uk/medialibrary/sites/sps/documents/Parents%20views%20on%20positive%20practice.pdf.

27

Working with Parents with a Diagnosis of Personality Disorder

Tanya Garrett
Independent practice and University of Birmingham

Whether one embraces the term 'personality disorder' or not,[1] it is undisputed that there are characterological traits and difficulties that can impact significantly upon parenting capacity (Adshead, 2015) and hence would benefit from intervention. Most psychosocial interventions for adults with a diagnosis of personality disorder are primarily aimed at addressing the difficulties which they may have in their psychological and interpersonal functioning (e.g., Dialectical Behaviour Therapy; Linehan, 1993). However, those clients who are parents also have to face and address the impact of their difficulties on their children, and on their interactions with their children (for instance, they may struggle with children becoming more independent). In turn, these difficulties may impact on their ability to focus on the intervention or their view of its relevance. Arguably, therefore, their role as a parent ought to be part of an intervention package addressing personality issues. The impact of personality difficulties on parenting will be addressed in more detail below. However, this issue is rarely addressed in services that are focused on adults, despite it being very important in ensuring that professionals discharge their child protection duties (e.g., Department of Health, 2003). This chapter will first define personality disorder and outline the diagnostic system before reviewing the types of difficulties faced by parents with personality disorder.

Personality Disorders

Definitions, prevalence and co-morbidity

Personality disorder is defined in the Diagnostic and Statistical Manual of Mental Disorders, Fifth Edition (DSM-V: American Psychiatric Association, 2013) as an inflexible and pervasive enduring pattern of inner experience and behaviour that deviates markedly from the expectations of the individual's culture. It is manifested in the areas of cognition, emotion, interpersonal

---

[1] There are strong objections to the term by some. Many professionals have concerns regarding the validity of diagnostic systems (e.g., British Psychological Society, 2015), and some clients object strongly due to the impact of labelling.

functioning or impulsive control, across a range of personal and social situations. Personality disorder leads to clinically significant distress or impairment in important areas of functioning. Its onset can be traced back to childhood or adolescence and the pattern is stable and of long duration. Those with personality disorders show tenuous stability under conditions of stress, are adaptively inflexible and tend to foster vicious circles which perpetuate and intensify their pre-existing difficulties.

The Diagnostic and Statistical Manual (DSM-V; APA, 2013) approach points to so-called 'cluster A' personality disorders (the 'odd or eccentric' types: Paranoid, Schizoid and Schizotypal), 'cluster B' (the 'dramatic, emotional or erratic' types: Antisocial, Borderline, Histrionic, Narcissistic) and 'cluster C' (the 'anxious and fearful' types: Avoidant, Dependent, Obsessive-Compulsive). Furthermore, so-called personality disorder not otherwise specified would include depressive or passive-aggressive types.

However, a contemporary discussion of personality disorder would not be complete without a mention of the great controversy which now surrounds it and other diagnoses in mental health. During the preparation of the fifth version of the American Psychiatric Association's Diagnostic and Statistical Manual (DMS-V; APA, 2013), there was a great deal of debate about the validity of diagnosis in the mental health field, and the apparent broadening of definitions to the extent that it was felt that 'normal' behaviour was becoming pathologised (e.g., Kinderman, Read, Moncrieff & Bentall, 2013). It is generally more helpful to think about the difficulties individual parents are trying to manage rather than the specifics of a diagnosis. Further, service users are increasingly rejecting labelling in mental health, in favour of descriptive or trauma-based models (e.g., Dillon, Johnstone & Longden, 2012; Holmes, 2012). As of 2015, clinical psychologists are required by their professional body in the UK to avoid the use of diagnostic terminology wherever possible, and to show an awareness of its inherent problems. Nonetheless, this inevitably problematic term is employed at times in this chapter as it would be extremely difficult to discuss research and service provision without doing so.

Personality disorder is relatively common in the general population, but there are variations in its severity, the degree of distress which the individual experiences, and prevalence between different age groups, with younger people being more likely to meet diagnostic criteria. The National Institute for Mental Health in England (NIMHE, 2003) noted that 10–13% of adults would meet diagnostic criteria. Maier, Lichtermann, Klingler et al. (1992) found that slightly more women (10.3%) than men (9.6%) have a personality disorder, though it is important to note that gender differences vary, depending on the type of personality disorder. The most commonly occurring types are compulsive, dependent and passive-aggressive. Among mentally ill populations, estimates of co-morbid personality disorder range between 36% and 67% and the prevalence is thought to be extremely high in the prison population (NIMHE, 2003).

Indeed, a number of studies suggest a close association between crime and personality disorder, particularly Antisocial Personality Disorder (APD). For instance, Gunn (1977) found that 20% of prisoners in the south east of England had abnormal personality features. Bluglass (1979), in a study of Scottish prisons, reported that 40% of newly convicted prisoners in a Scottish prison had psychopathic (antisocial) personality disorder. Guze (1976) reported that 70% of prisoners discharged from American prisons were classified as sociopathic. Rollin (1969) suggests that abnormal personality may contribute substantially to the causes of crime in people with other psychiatric diagnoses. For example, violent crimes are more likely among those with a diagnosis of schizophrenia who had antisocial personality traits before the onset of their mental illness. Costello (1996) describes how high levels of dependency and personality pathology in husbands are associated with increased probability of spousal physical abuse. Similarly, dependent personality disorder carries an increased probability of child abuse and elder abuse (Costello, 1996). Those who have attracted a diagnosis of personality disorder are more likely to suffer from alcohol and drug problems and are also more likely to experience adverse life events, such as relationship difficulties, housing problems and long-term unemployment (NIMHE, 2003).

Personality disorder in adults has its origins in childhood disturbance (e.g., Johnson, Cohen, Brown et al., 1999; Ryan, 1989). Adults who present with personality disorder have often been subjected to severe neglect and abuse, and are likely to have had a parent or caregiver who has significant mental health difficulties and difficulties in parenting (e.g., NIMHE, 2003). Hence, the term 'personality disorder' can be a 'shorthand' way of summarising the impact on a person's functioning of highly adverse childhood experiences which are unmitigated by positive experiences.

Parents Diagnosed with a Personality Disorder

Important issues which are likely to arise in people – and therefore parents – with personality disorder include emotional dysregulation (e.g., lability of mood and anger) and interpersonal difficulties (e.g., fear of abandonment/dependence and chaotic relationships). Furthermore, behaviours exhibited by such individuals are likely to be problematic; for instance, deliberate self-harm and impulsivity, and their thoughts (for example, dissociative responses or paranoid ideation) may be unhelpful or unusual. In addition, people who may be labelled with a personality disorder frequently have significant attachment issues, having often been raised in an invalidating environment or similar, their own parents often having had similar issues with their personality functioning themselves (Macfie, 2009).

The impact on parenting

To illustrate the kinds of specific issues which might arise for individuals with a particular type of personality disorder, Antisocial Personality Disorder, for example, is associated with a wide range of interpersonal and social disturbance. In particular, clinically significant traits of impulsivity, high negative emotionality, low conscientiousness, irresponsible and exploitative behaviour, recklessness and deceitfulness are apparent in their unstable interpersonal relationships. In addition, they exhibit disregard for the consequences of their behaviour, a failure to learn from experience, egocentricity and disregard for the feelings of others. These traits all present obvious challenges for developing effective and appropriate parenting.

Further, personality disorders can be associated with Fabricated or Induced Illness (FII). FII is extremely rare but it is also probably under-diagnosed. Parents who engage in FII, who also have a psychiatric diagnosis, are more likely to be diagnosed with a personality disorder than any other mental disorder (e.g., Sheridan, 2003). Despite that, it is likely that only a small number of adults with personality disorder come into this category; however, it is difficult to determine since the limited research that has been undertaken considers this question from the opposite perspective, that is, the proportion of those perpetrating FII who have a diagnosis of personality disorder (anything between some 20% according to Sheridan (2003) to 89%, according to Bools, Neale & Meadow (1994)).

These matters have clear links to problems in parenting capacity such as attachment issues, difficulty in helping children to develop appropriate interpersonal strategies and behaviours, and difficulty in ensuring that children are able to regulate their emotions suitably.

The impact on children

It is clear that personality disorder in a parent has a significant impact on their children – just as the early family experiences of parents themselves contributed to their own difficulties (Johnson, Cohen, Brown et al., 1999; Johnson, Cohen, Chen et al., 2006). From vulnerability to stress through attachment disorder to delinquency and even personality disorder itself, the far-reaching impact on children of a parent's personality disorder cannot be underestimated.

There are various mechanisms for this. Firstly, such parents are more *emotionally vulnerable*. Research indicates that parents with a diagnosis of personality disorder may have very limited ability to cope with the symptoms of relatively moderate mental health problems (e.g., mild anxiety or depression; Tracy, Cheng, Martens & Robins, 2011). Such parents will find it much harder to prioritise their children's needs or offer an appropriate consistency of care than some other parents. As Adshead (2015) noted, 'if a parent feels helpless and hostile, they are more likely to treat their child as an adult or peer' (p. 18). Unresolved trauma, which is associated with personality disorder, often obstructs a parent's ability to parent effectively. Parents who are unable to reflect back on their childhood history and integrate their experiences have a limited capacity for emotional availability to their children (Crandell & Hobson, 1999). This is commonly seen, for instance, in mothers with Borderline Personality Disorder (BPD), who may lack the capacity to respond appropriately to their children as a result of projecting past material into the mother–child interaction (Crandell, Fitzgerald & Whipple, 1997). For example, defensive splitting may interfere with the parent–child relationship via the mother's perception of the child as either 'all good', who needs to be saved, or 'all bad', who needs to be reprimanded (Glickauf-Hughes & Mehlman, 1998; Newman & Stevenson, 2005).

Second, individuals with significant personality difficulties tend to have *attachment styles* classified as disorganised and unresolved (Levy, 2005). These attachment styles may influence the manner in which a parent relates to his/her child; specifically, parents with unresolved trauma may relate to their child in a manner that oscillates between hostility and passivity (Main & Hesse, 1990). There is also evidence that maternal BPD impacts infant affect and early markers of self- and emotion-regulation skills (Crandell, Patrick & Hobson, 2003; Hobson, Patrick, Crandell et al., 2005; Newman, Stevenson, Bergman & Boyce, 2007; Stepp, Whalen, Pilkonis et al., 2011). Crandell, Fitzgerald and Whipple (1997) ascertained that the manner in which mothers mentally organised and accurately perceived their childhoods predicted the manner in which the mothers interacted with their children. Thus, mothers identified as having a 'secure' attachment in childhood exhibited interactions which were more natural and attuned to their children than mothers identified as 'insecure'. Mothers with BPD tend to interact with their children in an 'intrusively insensitive' manner (Hobson, Patrick & Valentine, 2005). These interactions may interfere with the child's developing ability to relate to other people within the environment and result in significant interpersonal problems for the child.

Thirdly, they may exhibit *behaviours* that place their children at risk; for instance, they are more likely to act impulsively and to be more easily overwhelmed by adversity. Hostility in personality-disordered parents increases the risk of mental disorder generally – including personality disorder – in children. Adshead (2015) pointed out that parental behaviours commonly associated with personality disorder, such as somatising behaviours, eating disorders and factitious disorders can have a significant adverse impact on children's health. Frank harm or abuse may occur; 'parental personality disorder is a risk factor for family violence and child maltreatment in certain circumstances, usually when parental cluster B disorders...occur in combination with substance misuse and environmental stress' (Adshead, 2015, p. 16). This is particularly evidenced in the increased risk of domestic abuse which can occur when two parents with personality disorder become involved in a relationship. Furthermore, it seems that mothers (on whom the majority of the research appears to have focused) with BPD in particular may engage in a greater number of negative parenting behaviours, which may increase their offspring's risk for psychopathology (e.g., Johnson, Cohen, Chen et al., 2006).

Fourth, their ability to act as a *helpful and appropriate model* may be compromised. For instance, one would expect parents to model appropriate regulation of affect, forming and maintaining of appropriate relationships, and impulse control. Indeed, they may invalidate the emotions of their children; it is likely that parents with BPD, as a result of their own difficulties understanding their feelings, lack of skills to manage their own emotions, and their own childhood history of parental invalidation, would have a hard time modelling appropriate emotion-socialisation strategies. Mothers with BPD may thus teach their children maladaptive ways of expressing and managing emotions (Stepp, Whalen, Pilkonis et al., 2011).

Fifth, parents with significant personality difficulties experience and exhibit *problematic emotions*. Hobson and colleagues (1998), for instance, demonstrated that individuals with BPD displayed dysfunctional moment-to-moment relatedness with a psychotherapist, including hostility and intense, idealising and devaluing exchanges when compared to individuals with dysthymia. If these patterns of interaction are typical between mothers with BPD and their children, then the impact on the child's social-emotional development would be substantial. Glickauf-Hughes and Mehlman (1998) suggest that 'a mother's hostility, rage and destructive behaviour may be disguised as love, making it difficult for a child to trust his/her own perceptions of reality' (p. 296).

There may be a *lack of emotional sensitivity* in such parents. Research in relation to parenting perceptions (e.g., Newman, Stevenson, Bergman & Boyce, 2007) suggests that parents with significant personality difficulties are less sensitive and demonstrate less structuring in their interaction with their infants when compared to mother–infant dyads where there is an absence of personality issues. In addition, they also tend to engage in insensitive forms of communication, such as critical, intrusive and frightening comments and behaviours. Parenting strategies characterised by oscillations between over-involvement and under-involvement may be evident in those with BPD in particular (Stepp, Whalen, Pilkonis et al., 2011). For example, mothers with BPD reported more neglectful and punishing responses to their adolescent's emotional displays, even when controlling for current depressive symptoms (Whalen, Silk & Dahl, 2010). These same mothers also reported almost equal amounts of reward, a supportive emotion-socialisation strategy compared to depressed and healthy control mothers. Stepp, Whalen, Pilkonis et al., (2011) suggest that 'over time, this inconsistency may lead their adolescents to deny or question their emotional responses increasing the potential for emotional vulnerability and further invalidation by others or self' (p. 81).

Furthermore, a mother with BPD may have reduced *capacity to adequately regulate her own emotions*, which may obstruct her ability to cope with the varying affective states of her child (Newman & Stevenson, 2005; Paris, 1999). It is common for parents with BPD to feel anxious, estranged, confused or overwhelmed by their infants (Hobson, Patrick, Crandell et al., 2005; Holman, 1985; Newman & Stevenson, 2005). When such parents become obstructed in their own 'defensive and entangled organisation of thought' (Crandell, Fitzgerald & Whipple, 1997, p. 250), they prevent their children from integrating certain affective experiences and behaviours. Parents with BPD, for instance, are characteristically volatile and have difficulty controlling intense, inappropriate anger that is often precipitated by environmental changes and/or intense abandonment fears (APA, 2013; Paris, 1999). Their strong outbursts of anger can be detrimental to the developing child, and many children of mothers with BPD are victims of verbal and/or physical abuse (Newman & Stevenson, 2005).

Finally, perhaps the sine qua non of personality disorder is the *interpersonal difficulties* that are so commonly evident. Hobson, Patrick, Hobson et al. (2009) concluded that maternal BPD is associated with dysregulated mother–infant communication. They found that women with BPD have conflictual interpersonal relations that may extend to disrupted patterns of interaction with their infants. In their study, 85% of women with BPD showed disrupted affective communication with their infants, who also exhibited frightened/disoriented behaviour, compared with women in the comparison group. Newman, Stevenson, Bergman and Boyce (2007) showed that due to poor quality interactions on the part of parents with personality disorders, their children evidenced avoidant behaviours, being less attentive, less interested and less eager to interact with their mothers.

Intergenerational transmission of PD

Aggregating all of these concerns points to an increased risk of the child of a parent with personality disorder developing the same problems. Barnow, Spitzer, Grabe et al. (2006) suggested that children of mothers with BPD are exposed to a combination of risk factors and are at greater risk of emotional, behavioural and somatic problems.

There is considerable evidence to support this (e.g., Stepp, Whalen, Pilkonis et al., 2011; Weiss, Zelkowitz, Feldman et al., 1996). Further, Stepp, Whalen, Pilkonis et al. (2011) suggested that these constructs may be related to a variety of poor psychosocial outcomes. These include difficulty in forming and maintaining stable and meaningful interactions with others, and identity disturbances which are associated with self-injurious behaviour and dissociative symptoms (Ogawa et al., 1997; Yates, 2004). Early deficits in emotion regulation have also been shown to be associated with later internalising (e.g., negative attributional style, ruminative response style, dysfunctional attitudes, self-criticism, insecure attachment style) and externalising disorders (e.g., excessive reassurance seeking, attention problems, delinquency, aggression, anxiety, depression and low self-esteem) throughout childhood (Barnow, Spitzer, Grabe et al., 2006; Eisenberg, Cumberland, Spinrad et al., 2007; Suveg, Hoffman, Zeman & Thomassin, 2009). Hence, Stepp, Whalen, Pilkonis et al. (2011) conclude 'from infancy through early adolescence, maternal BPD places children at risk for a range of emotional and behavioral problems' (p. 79).

Children of mothers with BPD show a significantly higher prevalence of 'disorganised' attachment than children of mothers without BPD (Hobson, Patrick, Crandell et al., 2005). Disorganisation in children typically arises in response to recurrent stress. In the case of children of parents with BPD, children's disorganised responses appear to develop out of what Main and Hesse (1990) describes as an 'approach-avoidant dilemma', that is, the erratic or volatile behaviours of the mother result in stress and cause children to simultaneously cling to and push away from their caregiver. There is little known about cognitive development in children whose parents have a disorder of personality, but high levels of 'disorganised' attachment status suggest that these children will face significant cognitive impairments. Attachment security with the primary caregiver is correlated with positive intellectual development and functioning of children in that responsiveness and attunement, maternal involvement, and emotional sensitivity support healthy cognitive development (Crandell & Hobson, 1999). Hence, a mother with a diagnosis of borderline personality disorder with the attendant intrusive insensitivity and unpredictability is highly likely to negatively affect a child's cognitive development. Adshead (2015) makes a powerful case for the importance of providing help to such parents, describing in detail the qualities which parents need, and arguing, essentially, that it is those very qualities (such as being able function well in relationships with others and hence to model and teach good interpersonal skills/relationship functioning) that are problematic in parents with a diagnosis of personality disorder.

Interventions

There are a variety of contexts in which a parent with personality disorder may come to the attention of intervention services. Parents may seek treatment voluntarily, usually because they are troubled by their symptoms, and may or may not have previously attracted a diagnosis of personality disorder. Sometimes they may seek assistance from professionals via, for instance, Child and Adolescent Mental Health Services (CAMHS) in relation to their parenting, or be required to undertake it in the context of local authority involvement with their children, or even in the context of legal proceedings in which the local authority has removed, is threatening to remove, or wishes to remove the child[ren]. Indeed, it is often in the context of local authority involvement or legal proceedings that a parent's difficulties with their personality functioning are first identified (Adshead, 2015). Often in such a scenario, there is some degree of compulsion on the part of the parent to seek help.

Occasionally, the parent may receive psychological intervention funded by the local authority. Personal experience suggests that there are some local authorities which may, following a favourable psychological assessment, fund psychological therapies for parents whose children have been, or may be, removed and are considered likely to benefit within reasonable timescales and be able to care for their children again. This is presumably because (notwithstanding the emotional and other consequences for children and families) some local authorities have made a cost–benefit analysis showing that the costs of legal proceedings or long-term foster care for these and any future children are likely to outweigh the relatively expensive, but shorter-term, costs of funding psychological intervention.

Service provision

Among many mental health professionals there has been a historical view that personality disorder is untreatable (Sherer, 2008). Some professionals seem to retain this view, despite considerable evidence (e.g., Kisely, 1999; McGlashan, 1993; Paris, 1993; Perry, Banon & Ianni, 1999) and government efforts to bring the treatment of personality disorder into the mainstream of National Health Service (NHS) work (e.g., NIMHE, 2003).

The report by the National Institute for Mental Health England (NIMHE, 2003) makes it clear that there is something of a 'postcode lottery' when it comes to the provision of interventions for people with personality disorder. This can only have become more problematic with the closure of specialist services, funding restrictions and priority changes which mean that there is less and less provision for those with mental health issues generally, and personality disorder specifically.

Making personality disorder the business of mainstream mental health services seemed to be gaining traction for some years after the publication of this advice, with specific personality disorder treatment services being established throughout the UK. However, more recent fiscal difficulties have led to services being closed down (e.g., the Henderson Hospital, Webb House in Crewe and Main House in the West Midlands) and, arguably, mental health services are once again focusing on severe and enduring mental illness.

However, some pockets of good practice remain. Cooper (2012), for instance, describes the Early Years Parenting Unit (EYPU), a service in North London, under a service-level agreement with Islington's children's social care. The EYPU only takes referrals from social workers who believe children are at risk of being taken into care. In the year since the unit opened 15 families have entered the programme. In four of the families, the risks have reduced to the point where children who were about to be taken into care have instead been placed on the child-in-need register. Participation in the programme requires two days per week commitment from parents. What makes the EYPU unique is that the same staff deal with all three presenting issues in one place – the parent's own problems and mental health, their parenting and the child's developmental problems. While expensive, it is suggested that significant savings are ultimately made in comparison with the cost of care proceedings. However at the time of writing, this service was threatened with closure. These developments render problematic Adshead's (2015) argument that:

> there are two compelling reasons to impose a duty on mental healthcare providers to offer services for adults with personality disorders that specifically focus on their parenting identity: first, because effective therapies for personality disorder are now available; and second, because there is a strong utilitarian and economic argument for improving parental mental health so as to reduce the economic and psychological burden of their offspring's future psychiatric morbidity. (p. 15)

Intervention issues

The type of intervention available from statutory services varies, dependent on local preferences/availability, and varying interpretations of the research literature. However, Linehan's (1993) Dialectical Behaviour Therapy (DBT) is a very influential model, with Young and Gluhoski's (1996) schema-focused therapy also finding wide favour in the UK. Cognitive therapy-based models (e.g., Beck, Freeman & Davis, 2004) are also significant in this field (NIMHE, 2003).

DBT, mainly an intervention for BPD, focuses on the dysfunction in emotional regulation which Linehan regards as central to BPD. This is seen as physiologically based and as responsible for the dramatic overreaction displayed by individuals with such difficulties to events and for their impulsive acts. Linehan suggests that during their development, these individuals are exposed to others who discount their emotional experiences and insist that they are positive despite their distress (the so-called invalidating environment). As a result, they are thought to receive inadequate training in emotional regulation skills and, at the same time, learn to take a disparaging, punitive attitude toward their own emotions. This results in an incapacity to tolerate strong emotions for long enough in order to grieve significant losses, leading to 'bereavement overload'.

A series of unrelenting crises follows as a result of this multitude of problems, with which such individuals are often unable to cope. Those with borderline personality disorder therefore learn that they must rely on others in many situations, yet are unable to ask assertively for help (because they 'know' that they need to maintain a positive attitude) or seek help by revealing their neediness. They therefore maintain a façade of confidence while trying to obtain the help of others subtly and indirectly. However, their attempts at consistent subtlety are hampered by their strong emotional responses and impulsive acts. There are four primary modes of treatment in DBT, namely individual therapy, group skills training, telephone contact with the therapist, and therapist consultation.

Young and Gluhoski's (e.g., Young & Gluhoski, 1996) schema-focused therapy postulates that early maladaptive schemas (extremely stable and enduring patterns of thinking), which develop during childhood, result in maladaptive behaviour patterns that reinforce the schemas which are elaborated throughout development and into adulthood. In the case of significant personality disorder, there are a large number of schemas, thus resulting in a wide range of symptoms and frequent crises. These schemas include: abandonment/loss, unloveability, dependence, subjugation/lack of individuation, mistrust, inadequate self-discipline, fear of losing emotional control, guilt/punishment, and emotional deprivation. Intervention can be conducted on an individual or group basis, with a dual focus on childhood origins of schemas and their current manifestation or impact in day-to-day life, in particular, interactions with others.

Cognitive therapy (e.g., Beck, Freeman & Davis, 2004) emphasises the role of the person's basic assumptions in influencing their perception and interpretation of events and in shaping behaviour and emotional responses. Dichotomous thinking and a weak or unstable sense of identity are seen as central. Therapy focuses on the individual's basic assumptions about themselves and the world around them, dichotomous thinking, and weak or unstable sense of identity, using the therapeutic relationship as a tool for illustrating and addressing interpersonal pathologies, changing unhelpful thinking so that it becomes more realistic and helpful, and controlling emotional lability and impulsivity,

In addition to therapies for personality dysfunction, parents with personality disorders need interventions that can address their relationships with their children and their parenting skills (Adshead, 2015). Hence, working with a parent with a personality disorder is different to working with an individual who is not a parent. Even if intervention is taking place in an adult mental health-type setting, all professionals have a duty to ascertain whether the service user is a parent and ensure that they are mindful of child protection issues. Arguably, this requires them to incorporate parenting issues into the intervention.

Even if, however, clinicians are not directly targeting parenting issues/behaviours, they nevertheless may be having a positive impact on parenting capacity. As parental responses to their child's emotional expression play a significant role in teaching the child how to manage his/her own emotions (Eisenberg, Fabes & Spinrad, 2006; Morris, Silk, Steinberg et al., 2007), their own natural responses to their clients' expressions of emotion will likely be having a positive impact on their clients' parenting capacity anyway. As a helpful yardstick, regardless of the specific therapeutic approach, the therapist should try to interact with the client in a way that is accepting of the client as he/she is but which encourages change; is centred and firm yet flexible when the circumstances require it; and nurturing but benevolently demanding. Thus, the importance of the therapeutic relationship itself for improving parenting has perhaps been under-explored. The therapist has a crucial role in not only meeting the personality-disordered parent's needs, for example, for empathy, unconditional positive regard, and warmth (Hovarth & Symonds, 1991), as well as consistency, but also in modelling appropriate interpersonal behaviours, such as emotional warmth, sensitivity to emotional states and concern. These qualities of good psychological therapy will have an obvious, but important, impact on the client's parenting behaviours.

However, directly addressing inappropriate parenting behaviours may be the focus in some circumstances. This is not commonly available but one can envisage a sensitive Child and

Adolescent Mental Health Service identifying a parent with personality disorder and ensuring that specific interventions are provided to address their parenting deficits. Interventions designed specifically for parents with personality disorder and their children do not exist. However, authors have made general recommendations favouring attachment therapies (cf., Macfie, Fitzpatrick, Rivas & Cox, 2008), especially during infancy through the preschool period and/or psychoeducation-based interventions (cf., Gunderson, Berkowitz & Ruiz-Sancho, 1997) for family members of those with BPD. This may also involve psychoeducation.

Case Example: Working with Narcissistic Clients

Considered by some to be among the most challenging clients to work with, those with significant narcissistic personality characteristics perhaps present some of the biggest challenges to their children. Grandiose and emotionally unavailable, arrogant, entitled, exploitative, embedded in fantasies of grandeur, self-centred, yet charming, these clients can also present with co-morbid issues such as low mood, mood swings, substance misuse and suicidal behaviours. They tend to derogate others, particularly those who give negative feedback, and struggle to forgive others, envying their successes, and feeling guilty and shameful. In general, such persons spend much time ruminating about issues of antagonism/social rank and avoid forming or thinking about attachments, thus concealing their vulnerable self (DiMaggio, 2012). Empathy dysfunction is considered central to narcissism, with cognitive empathy considered less diminished than affective empathy. Persons with significant narcissistic traits are able to understand how someone else feels, but cannot respond appropriately.

There is no consensus on the causes of Narcissistic Personality Disorder, although theories abound. It is likely that lack of parental empathy toward a child's developmental needs is a common issue. In the context of disturbed attachment, parents may fail to appropriately recognise, name and regulate the child's emotions, particularly in cases of heightened arousal, for example, when the child becomes angry or distressed. The developing child is therefore left with intense emotions that receive no appropriate recognition or appropriate responses, which leads to affect dysregulation. In children, with their basic needs unmet, attachment is therefore likely to become an issue; this translates to being attachment-avoidant in adulthood yet, at the same time, constantly striving for attention and admiration. Clinically, one can easily see how such a pattern could readily be transmitted down the generations without intervention.

Another developmental pathway may be that the child is raised in a family where status and success are of utmost importance and only qualities that lead to sustaining a grandiose self-image are valued, while other behaviours are disregarded or punished. Alternatively, overt grandiosity may be a reaction to slights and humiliation, a kind of armour used to avoid subjugation.

Often the narcissistic client has come to therapy under some kind of duress, rather than presenting as inherently motivated. Whether the motivator is a partner or a social worker, resentment must be addressed through the medium of building a strong therapeutic alliance so that the client works *with* rather than *against* the therapist. The construction of a shared therapeutic agenda, perhaps – at least initially – using the medium of the other individual/agency's concerns, in particular the interests/needs of the child, or even the client's wish to have the child remain in, or returned to, their care, as well as those (if any) of the client, can be helpful. With regard to the latter, it may be that it will take time for him/her to identify any such issues, and the therapeutic relationship may provide the vehicle for this; once a working alliance has been established, the therapist may be able to highlight his/her experience of the client's interpersonal strategies and presentation, in a tentative attempt to foster an objective stance/perspective, and thus set an agenda that will be helpful to the client's aim.

Ultimately, one would wish to see the narcissistic client addressing a dual agenda, making therapeutic gains for him/herself, as well as improving parenting capacity. Perhaps working on the latter agenda would have a positive impact on the former, as well as vice versa. It may be beneficial to start with the client's own view of the kind of adult that he/she would want the child to become. This may elicit implicit concerns that the client has about his/her own functioning, in particular the difficulties he/she has experienced in this regard, depending on the level of insight present. Sometimes, completing the Young Parenting Inventory (YPI-1; Young, 1994) can elicit useful information about the person's experiences of being parented, contributing to the development of positive insight, and can contribute to a formulation of the problem.

Supervision is a vital component in working with this population, in particular to manage negative feelings which are sometimes engendered in the therapist because of the particularly combative and critical approach that such individuals often take in the therapy room, which could if unchecked ultimately prove counter-therapeutic. Surely, if the therapist is feeling this, the child is too?

Conclusions

There has perhaps never been such a difficult time to work with parents diagnosed with a personality disorder. Specialist services are closing, mental health services are falling back on their 'core business' and demand is growing, including from the courts (Tickle, 2015). Yet never have we been so aware of the need to intervene with this population, and never so aware of the likely savings in distress and cost if we can do so effectively.

It is vital that professionals working with parents with personality disorder are mindful of the impact of their issues, difficulties and symptoms on their capacity to parent and the need to work with other professionals, especially in social care. It is also important that explicit links are made when working with these clients to ensure that they develop awareness of the impact of their difficulties on their children. Many professionals would wish that, in their specific area of expertise, more was done with school-age children to increase their awareness, and perhaps prevent later problems from developing when they become parents. In the field of personality disorder, this seems particularly relevant.

References

Adshead, G. (2015). Parenting and personality disorder: Clinical and child protection implications. *Advances in Psychiatric Treatment*, 21, 15–22.

American Psychiatric Association (2013). *Diagnostic and Statistical Manual of Mental Disorders*, 5th edn. Arlington, VA: American Psychiatric Association.

Barnow, S., Spitzer, C., Grabe, H.J. et al. (2006). Individual characteristics, familial experience, and psychopathology in children of mothers with borderline personality disorder. *Journal of the American Academy of Child & Adolescent Psychiatry*, 45, 965–972.

Beck, A.T., Freeman, A. & Davis, D.D. (2004). *Cognitive Therapy of Personality Disorders*. New York: Guilford Press.

Bluglass, R. (1979). The Psychiatric Assessment of Homicide. *British Journal of Hospital Medicine*, 22, 366–377.

Bools, C., Neale, B. & Meadow, R. (1994). Munchausen Syndrome by proxy: Unusual manifestations and disturbing sequelae. *Child Abuse & Neglect*, 18, 773–788.

British Psychological Society (Division of Clinical Psychology) (2015). *Guidelines in Relation to Language on Functional Psychiatric Diagnosis.* Leicester: British Psychological Society.

Cooper, J. (2012). Social workers pioneer new approach to personality disorders. *Community Care*, 12 December.

Costello, C.G. (1996). *Personality Characteristics of the Personality Disordered.* New York: John Wiley & Sons, Inc.

Crandell, L.E. & Hobson, R.P. (1999). Individual differences in young children's IQ: A social-developmental perspective. *Journal of Child Psychology and Psychiatry*, 40, 455–464.

Crandell, L.E., Fitzgerald, H.E. & Whipple, E.E. (1997). Dyadic synchrony in parent–child interactions: A link with maternal representations of attachment relationships. *Infant Mental Health Journal*, 18, 247–264.

Crandell, L.E., Patrick, M.P.H. & Hobson, R.P. (2003). 'Still-face' interactions between mothers with borderline personality disorder and their 2-month-old infants. *British Journal of Psychiatry*, 3, 239–247.

Department of Health (2003). *Confidentiality – NHS Code of Practice.* London: The Stationery Office.

Dillon, J., Johnstone, L. & Longden, E. (2012). Trauma, dissociation, attachment and neuroscience: A new paradigm for understanding severe mental distress. *The Journal of Critical Psychology, Counselling and Psychotherapy*, 12, 145–156.

Dimaggio, G. (2012). Narcissistic personality disorder: Rethinking what we know. *Psychiatric* Times (accessed 18 July 2012).

Eisenberg, N., Fabes, R.A. & Spinrad, T.L. (2006). Prosocial development. In: N. Eisenberg and W. Damon (eds), *Handbook of Child Psychology. Vol. 3. Social, Emotional, and Personality Development*, 6th edn. New York: John Wiley & Sons, Inc.

Eisenberg, N., Cumberland, A., Spinrad, T.L. et al. (2007). The relations of regulation and emotionality to children's externalizing and internalizing problem behavior. *Child Development*, 72, 1112–1134.

Glickauf-Hughes, C. & Mehlman, E. (1998). Non- borderline patients with mothers who manifest border- line pathology. *British Journal of Psychotherapy*, 14, 294–302.

Gunderson, J.G., Berkowitz, C. & Ruiz-Sancho, A. (1997). Families of borderline patients: A psychoeducational approach. *Bulletin of the Menninger Clinic*, 61, 446–457.

Gunn, J. (1977). Criminal behaviour and mental disorder. *British Journal of Psychiatry*, 130, 317–329.

Guze, S. (1976). *Criminality and Psychiatric Disorder.* New York: Oxford University Press.

Hobson, R.P., Patrick, M.P. & Valentine, J.D. (1998). Objectivity in psychoanalytic judgements. *British Journal of Psychiatry*, 173, 172–177.

Hobson, P.R., Patrick, M., Crandell, L. et al. (2005). Personal relatedness and attachment in infants of mothers with borderline personality disorder. *Development and Psychopathology*, 17, 329–347.

Hobson, R.P., Patrick, M.P., Hobson, J.A. et al. (2009). How mothers with borderline personality disorder relate to their year-old infants. *British Journal of Psychiatry*, 195, 325–330.

Holman, S.L. (1985). A group program for borderline mothers and their toddlers. *International Journal of Group Psychotherapy*, 35, 79–83.

Holmes, G. (2012). If we are to have mental health services, let's centre them on concepts of trauma, not illness. *The Journal of Critical Psychology, Counselling and Psychotherapy*, 12, 127–131.

Hovarth, A. & Symonds, B.D. (1991). Relation between working alliance and outcome in psychotherapy: A meta-analysis. *Journal of Counseling Psychology*, 38, 139–149.

Johnson, J.G., Cohen, P., Brown, J. et al. (1999). Childhood maltreatment increases risk for personality disorders during young adulthood: Findings of a community-based longitudinal study. *Archives of General Psychiatry*, 56, 600–606.

Johnson, J.G., Cohen, P., Chen, H. et al. (2006). Parenting behaviours associated with risk for offspring personality disorder during adulthood. *Archives of General Psychiatry*, 63, 579–587.

Kinderman, P., Read, J., Moncrieff, J. & Bentall, R.P. (2013). Drop the language of disorder. *Evidence Based Mental Health*, 16, 2–3.

Kisely, S. (1999). Psychotherapy for severe personality disorder: Exploring the limits of evidence based purchasing. *British Medical Journal*, 318, 1410–1412.

Levy, K.N. (2005). The implications of attachment theory and research for understanding borderline personality disorder. *Development and Psychopathology*, 17, 959–986.

Linehan, M.M. (1993). *Cognitive Behavioural Treatment of Borderline Personality Disorder*. New York and London: Guilford Press.

Macfie, J. (2009). Development in children and adolescents whose mothers have borderline personality disorder. *Child Development Perspectives*, 3, 66.

Macfie, J., Fitzpatrick, K.L., Rivas, E.M. & Cox, M.J. (2008). Independent influences on mother–toddler role reversal: Infant–mother attachment disorganization and role reversal in mother's childhood. *Attachment and Human Development*, 10, 29–39.

Maier, W., Lichtermann, D., Klingler, T. et al. (1992). Prevalences of personality disorders (DSM-III-R) in the community. *Journal of Personality Disorders*, 6, 187–196.

Main, M. & Hesse, E. (1990). Parents' unresolved traumatic experiences are related to infant disorganized/disoriented attachment status: Is frightened and/or frightening parental behavior the linking mechanism? In: M.T. Greenberg, D. Cicchetti and E. Cummings (eds), *Attachment in the Preschool Years: Theory, Research, and Intervention*. Chicago: University of Chicago Press.

McGlashan, T.H. (1993). Implications of outcome research for the treatment of borderline personality disorder. In: J. Paris (ed) *Borderline Personality Disorder: Etiology and Treatment*. Washington, DC: American Psychiatric Press.

Morris, A.S., Silk, J.S., Steinberg, L. et al. (2007). The role of the family context in the development of emotion regulation. *Social Development*, 16, 361–368.

National Institute for Mental Health in England (NIMHE) (2003). *Personality disorder: No longer a diagnosis of exclusion. Policy implementation guidance for the development of services for people with personality disorder*. London: Department of Health.

Newman, L. & Stevenson, C. (2005). Parenting and borderline personality disorder: Ghosts in the nursery. *Clinical Child Psychology and Psychiatry*, 10(385), 385–394.

Newman, L.K., Stevenson, C.S., Bergman, L.R. & Boyce, P. (2007). Borderline personality disorder, mother–infant interaction and parenting perceptions: preliminary findings. *Australian and New Zealand Journal of Psychiatry*, 41, 598–605.

Ogawa J., Sroufe L.A., Weinfield N.S. et al. (1997). Development and the fragmented self: A longitudinal study of dissociative symptomatology in a non-clinical sample. *Developmental Psychopathology*, 4, 855–879.

Paris, J. (1993). The treatment of borderline personality disorder in the light of the research on its long term outcome. *Canadian Journal of Psychiatry*, 38, 528–534.

Paris, J. (1999). Borderline personality disorder. In: T. Millon, P.H. Blaney & R.D. Davies (eds), *Oxford Textbook of Psychopathology*. New York: Oxford University Press, 628–652.

Perry, J.C., Banon, E. & Ianni, F. (1999). Effectiveness of psychotherapy for personality disorders. *American Journal of Psychiatry*, 156, 1312–1321.

Rollin, H. (1969). *The Mentally Abnormal Offender and the Law*. London: Pergamon Press.

Ryan, G. (1989). Victim to victimiser. *Journal of Interpersonal Violence*, 4, 325–341.

Sherer, R. (2008). Personality disorder: 'Untreatable' myth is challenged. *Psychiatric Times*.

Sheridan, M.S. (2003). The deceit continues: An updated literature review of Munchausen Syndrome by Proxy. *Child Abuse & Neglect*, 27, 431–51.

Stepp, S.D., Whalen, D.J., Pilkonis, P.A. et al. (2011). Children of mothers with borderline personality disorder: Identifying parenting behaviors as potential targets for intervention. *Personality Disorder*, 3, 76–91.

Suveg, C., Hoffman, B., Zeman, J. & Thomassin, K. (2009). Emotion related predictors of anxious and depressive symptoms in youth. *Child Psychiatry and Human Development*, 40, 223–239.

Tickle, L. (2015). Are we failing parents whose children are taken into care? *Guardian*, www.theguardian.com/society/2015/apr/25/are-we-failing-parents-whose-children-are-taken-into-care (accessed 25 April 2015).

Tracy, J.L., Cheng, J.T., Martens, J.P. & Robins, R.W. (2011). The emotional dynamics of narcissism: Inflated by pride, deflated by shame. In: W.K. Campbell & J. Miller (eds), *Handbook of Narcissism and Narcissistic Personality Disorder*. New York: John Wiley & Sons, Inc.

Weiss, M., Zelkowitz, P., Feldman, R.B. et al. (1996). Psychopathology in offspring of mothers with borderline personality disorder: A pilot study. *Canadian Journal of Psychiatry*, 41, 285–290.

Whalen, D., Silk, J.S. & Dahl, R. (2010). The effect of maternal borderline personality disorder on maternal emotion socialization and adolescent emotional vulnerability. Poster presented at the 2010 Biennial Meeting of the Society for Research on Adolescence. Philadelphia, PA: 2010.

Yates, T.M. (2004). The developmental psychopathology of self-injurious behavior: Compensatory regulation in posttraumatic adaptation. *Clinical Psychology Review*, 21, 35–74.

Young, J. (1994). *Young Parenting Inventory (YPI-I)*, www.schematherapy.com.

Young, J.E. & Gluhoski, V.L. (1996). Schema-focused diagnosis for personality disorders. In: F.W. Kaslow (ed), *Handbook of Relational Diagnosis and Dysfunctional Family Patterns*. New York: John Wiley & Sons, Inc., 300–321.

28
Working with Parents Who Misuse Alcohol and Drugs

Rebecca L. Sanford, Stephanie Haynes Ratliff and Michele Staton-Tindall

University of Kentucky, US

Introduction

Caregiver substance misuse and the impact on children has become an important area of study in recent years. In terms of prevalence, a representative population-based study has estimated that more than eight million children in the US between 2002 and 2007 were living with at least one caregiver who misused alcohol and/or used illicit substances or was dependent upon those substances (Substance Abuse and Mental Health Services Administration (SAMHSA), 2010). A UK study that involved a sample of over 160,000 participants from a national treatment monitoring system indicated that nearly half of treatment-involved drug users had dependent children; however, many of these children did not live with their drug-using parents (Meier, Donmall & McElduff, 2004). Other studies have shown that 35.6 million, approximately half of US children, live with a caregiver who uses alcohol, illicit substances or tobacco (National Center on Addiction and Substance Abuse (CASA), 2005). While tobacco is the most common substance used in many of these homes (approximately 27 million), approximately 17 million children are exposed to caregivers who engage in binge drinking, and 9.2 million children live with caregivers who use illicit substances (CASA, 2005). In addition, the recent 2013 National Survey on Drug Use and Health found that approximately one-quarter of under-age drinkers in the US indicated that they received alcohol from their parents or caregivers (National Survey on Drug Use and Health (NSDUH), 2014).

Despite the availability of nationally representative data on the prevalence of caregiver substance use and misuse, the current understanding of substance misuse among child welfare-involved caregivers is limited. This is due to the lack of a unified reporting system, definitional issues, and lack of worker training in identifying substance misuse (Young, Boles & Otero, 2007). Although the prevalence of substance misuse in the child welfare system is not clear (as described in detail below), a great deal of information about the impact of substance use on individuals in a caregiving role has recently emerged, demonstrating the impact of caregiver

---

The Wiley Handbook of What Works in Child Maltreatment: An Evidence-Based Approach to Assessment and Intervention in Child Protection, First Edition. Edited by Louise Dixon, Daniel F. Perkins, Catherine Hamilton-Giachritsis, and Leam A. Craig.
© 2017 John Wiley & Sons Ltd. Published 2017 by John Wiley & Sons Ltd.

substance misuse on child welfare. Empirical evidence demonstrates that parental substance misuse places children at increased risk for maltreatment (Famularo, Kinscherff & Fenton, 1992; Magura & Laudet, 1996; Walsh, MacMillan & Jamieson, 2003). For example, caregivers who use or misuse substances are nearly three times more likely to abuse their children and 3.2 times more likely to neglect their children (Chaffin, Kelleher & Hollenberg, 1996). A representative study with a community sample indicated that exposure to parental substance misuse was associated with a twofold increase in the risk of exposure to physical and sexual abuse in childhood (Walsh, MacMillan & Jamieson, 2003). Consequences for children of caregiver substance misuse include an increased likelihood for developing health and mental health disorders (Fellitti, Anda, Nordenberg et al., 1998), addictive behaviours as adolescents (Drapela & Mosher, 2007), and engaging in substance use and misuse as adults (Widom, White, Czaja & Marmorstein, 2007).

Such effects have been demonstrated despite measurement limitations. While advances have been made in the substance use literature to understand the distinctions associated with impact, consequences and severity of substance use, the child welfare literature has historically been limited to dichotomous measures of 'any' versus 'no' presence of substance use among families and households (Staton-Tindall, Sprang & Clark, 2012). While the field has grown in recent years and has advanced our understanding of caregiver substance use and child maltreatment, current knowledge is significantly weakened by the measurement and assessment of caregiver substance use, specifically with regard to the mechanisms of action and risk for children (Testa & Smith, 2009). In order to advance knowledge in the area of caregiver substance use and child maltreatment, definitions of caregiver substance use must be clarified along a continuum, from use to misuse, with substance use disorder describing more extreme levels of misuse. Because of the altered physical and psychological effects of drugs, 'use' and 'misuse' are often used interchangeably in the literature (World Health Organization, 2014).

In the newly revised Diagnostic and Statistical Manual for Mental Disorders-5th Edition (DSM-V; APA, 2013), criteria for substance 'abuse' and 'dependence' were combined to focus more readily on the overall indicators of severity associated with substance use 'disorder' (www.dsm5.org). Substance use disorders are defined as 'a cluster of cognitive, behavioural, and physiological symptoms indicating that the individual continues using the substance despite significant substance-related problems' (American Psychological Association (APA), 2013, p. 483). Rather than a dichotomous diagnosis of abuse or dependence, substance use disorder is now evaluated on a continuum of severity ranging from mild to severe (APA, 2013). While still a generally accepted term in the nomenclature of professionals working in the area of substance misuse, 'addiction' is no longer included in the DSM-V due to the negative connotations associated with the word (APA, 2013, p. 485). Substance use disorder is the clinically appropriate and neutral term used to describe all levels of the disorder, from mild misuse to the more chronic form of the disorder (APA, 2013). For consistency, this chapter will use the term 'substance use' to describe general use of any substances. 'Substance misuse' will be used to describe the use of illicit substances or use of legal substances to a degree deemed to be problematic or that could pose risks for child maltreatment. Additionally, the term 'substance use disorder' will be used to describe misuse that reaches the level of diagnostic consideration.

Caregiver substance misuse and child maltreatment have been associated with a number of theoretical explanations that include (i) the presence of substance use and related behaviours across generations (McCloskey & Bailey, 2000; Sheridan, 1995) and (ii) deficits in the child/caregiver attachment and bonding experiences that can be associated with neglect, abuse, or limited nurturing associated with high levels of disorganisation and avoidant behaviour

(Drapela & Mosher, 2007; Goodman, Hans & Cox, 1999; Rodning, Beckwith & Howard, 1991). This chapter moves beyond theoretical debate to examine what works in practice to address problems associated with family functioning in the child welfare system due to caregiver substance use and the impact on children. A thorough discussion follows regarding the issue of substance misuse in the child welfare system with a focus on the challenges and the impact on the system, in addition to the prospects for treatment of substance use disorders and child welfare outcomes. Although the evidence in this area is only recently emerging, several programmes have been shown to have some degree of efficacy. A focus on the child welfare response to substance misuse that includes worker-level strategies (e.g., screening for substance misuse and referring for services) and system-level strategies (e.g., training for child welfare staff and collaborative efforts for system integration) is arguably preferable considering the evidence. The chapter concludes with consideration of areas for further research and development. It is suggested that evidence-based practices should be implemented and further evaluated to advance this area of practice.

Substance Use and the Child Welfare System

Referrals and outcomes

Initial referrals. Given the increased risk of maltreatment among children of substance-misusing caregivers, it follows that maternal substance use has been shown to increase the likelihood of involvement with the child welfare system (Street, Whitlingum, Gibson et al., 2008). Rates of parental alcohol and other drug misuse cited as a reason for child removal in the US increased from 13.9% in 1992 to 30.5% in 2012 (Gardner, 2014). Furthermore, the limited research on incidents of child fatalities indicates that substance misuse is estimated to be a factor in as many as 57% of abuse or neglect cases (Brandon, 2009; Douglas, 2013). However, substance misuse issues are not more likely to occur in cases that involve a fatality (Douglas & Mohn, 2014). Despite this, substance misuse is still considered a major risk factor for a substantial percentage of fatality cases, particularly when it occurs in conjunction with other risk factors (Brandon, 2009; Douglas, 2013; Sheldon-Sherman, Wilson & Smith, 2013). For example, a third of fatalities occurred in families in which the risk factors of substance misuse, mental health issues and domestic violence were present (Brandon, 2009).

While the impact of parental substance misuse on child maltreatment is well established, the prevalence of parental substance misuse in child welfare populations is not. It is extremely difficult to ascertain accurate estimates of the occurrence of substance misuse issues in US populations involved with the child welfare system due to the fact that there is no federally mandated system for reporting this information (Young, Boles & Otero, 2007). States may vary in their collection and recording of this information, and some states do not collect this information in a meaningful, aggregated way. In addition, measures used to define the presence of substance abuse issues may vary greatly. Self-report is a common measure used to determine the presence of substance misuse issues within a family, but this strategy is fraught with challenges as many substance-misusing parents are hesitant to share this truth with child welfare workers due to fear of the consequences (Robertson & Haight, 2012; Taylor & Kroll, 2004). Definitional issues and lack of education on the topic for child welfare workers contribute to the missing data on the prevalence of substance abuse issues in child welfare (Young, Boles & Otero, 2007). For example, child welfare staff may not be aptly trained in administering basic screening tools and may only respond to substance misuse concerns that are glaringly obvious (Wolock & Magura, 1996), failing to recognise subtle indications of substance misuse. While the available data on the prevalence of substance use among child welfare populations are lacking in the US, they are even more scant in the UK (Forrester, 2000). Although estimations of the prevalence of substance abuse issues among child welfare populations range from 20% to 80% in the US (De Bortoli, Coles & Dolan, 2013; Famularo, Kinscherff & Fenton, 1992; Young, Boles & Otero, 2007), they range from only 30% to 52% in the UK (Forrester & Harwin, 2006; Forrester, 2000) and there is little recent data. This large range is likely due to inconsistent screening and reporting of substance misuse and variable sampling procedures in studies of substance-misusing caregivers.

Re-referral and long-term outcomes. Substance misuse not only increases the likelihood for maltreatment and initial referral to the child welfare system, but it may also have a detrimental impact throughout the duration of the family's involvement with the child welfare system. Data suggest that families who experience substance misuse issues are more likely to be re-referred to the child welfare system for future instances of suspected maltreatment (Brook & McDonald, 2009; Fuller & Wells, 2003; Fuller, Wells & Cotton, 2001; Laslett, Room, Dietze & Ferris, 2012; Wolock & Magura, 1996). This phenomenon may be explained, in part, by relapse, which is a common experience for those involved in changing substance misuse behaviours (Laslett, Room, Dietze & Ferris, 2012). Furthermore, parental substance misuse has also been shown to increase the likelihood of children re-entering care once reunified (Brook & McDonald, 2009), even among families where caregivers sought treatment for substance abuse issues (Barth, Gibbons & Guo, 2006; Miller, Fisher, Fetrow & Jordan, 2006). In summary, substance misuse is associated with: longer foster care stays for youth (Lloyd & Akin, 2014); permanent removal of children from the care of the biological parents (Murphy, Jellinek, Quinn et al., 1991), especially when the primary drug of misuse is cocaine (Hong, Ryan, Hernandez & Brown, 2014); and the outcome of adoption for children in long-term foster care (Cheng, 2010), which is likely due to difficulties that caregivers experience in achieving and maintaining sobriety to ensure safety of children long-term.

Further research is needed to determine if the substance of misuse impacts child welfare outcomes differentially. Studies have shown contradictory information on this topic with some research indicating that alcohol misuse and drug misuse result in similar outcomes for child welfare-involved caregivers (Laslett, Room, Dietze & Ferris, 2012). Other research indicates that outcomes differ dependent on the type of drug being used and the co-occurrence of alcohol misuse and drug misuse (Hong, Ryan, Hernandez & Brown, 2014; Lloyd & Akin, 2014). Polysubstance misuse occurs frequently among substance-abusing caregivers (De Bortoli, Coles & Dolan, 2013; Forrester & Harwin, 2006) and may have an impact on the outcomes in child welfare. Considering the nuanced nature of substance misuse and the need for interventions tailored to the type of drug used (Lloyd & Akin, 2014), additional research is arguably needed to further the development of child welfare interventions that are based on the drug of misuse.

Challenges of substance misuse for the child welfare system

The existing empirical literature consistently shows that substance misuse plays an important role in child maltreatment and child welfare outcomes, and working with substance-misusing caregivers presents challenges for child welfare workers. Challenges that arise for workers include: i) encountering engagement difficulties with caregivers; and ii) responding to legislation and policies that prioritise permanency and may run counter to substance use disorder treatment needs and trajectories.

Engagement difficulties. Engagement is vital to the success of the child welfare process (Gladstone, Dumbrill, Leslie et al., 2012; Mirick, 2014), particularly when substance misuse issues are present (Sun, 2000). However, substance misuse issues can make engagement difficult; parents are often reluctant to share information about substance use habits due to denial or due to the fear of having the children removed from their care (Klee, 1998; Taylor, Toner, Templeton & Velleman, 2008), or they are non-compliant and reject outright the services offered (De Bortoli, Coles & Dolan, 2013; Murphy, Jellinek, Quinn et al., 1991; Robertson & Haight, 2012). An authoritative stance is often employed by child welfare workers to attempt to elicit participation from the client, but this approach is not an effective way to garner engagement and collaboration (Schreiber, Fuller & Paceley, 2013; Sun, 2000). Instead, a 'nonjudgemental and nonauthoritative attitude' is preferable (Sun, 2000, p. 147), especially when caregivers do not recognise or deny the extent and impact of their substance use. Utilising relational approaches with honesty and respect can counter the difficulties in engaging substance-abusing families (Robertson & Haight, 2012). Effective relational approaches involve 'extending warmth, accepting anger and defensiveness without judgement, understanding and responding to needs in flexible ways, and focusing on strengths' (Schreiber, Fuller & Paceley, 2013, p. 713). However, engaging in discussion about substance use can be challenging for workers, particularly if training and supervision on the issue are sparse.

The complex nature of substance misuse is another challenge for child welfare workers. Substance misuse typically occurs not in isolation but in the context of and interaction with other social, psychological and environmental problems (Azzi-Lessing & Olsen, 1996; Forrester & Harwin, 2006). Parents using substances often also experience a number of other problems that must be addressed from a child welfare perspective. Mental health issues, housing stability, unemployment and poverty, involvement with the criminal justice system, and intimate partner violence are risk factors that often co-occur with substance misuse issues and make the process complicated and challenging (Choi & Ryan, 2007; Forrester & Harwin, 2006; Murphy, Jellinek, Quinn et al., 1991; Stromwall, Larson, Nieri et al., 2008). Choi and Ryan (2007) found that 75.9% of mothers faced more than four different needs, primarily in the areas of housing, mental health services, job training and transportation. Limited resources and services within communities, intergenerational patterns of substance misuse and mental health issues (Marshall, Huang & Ryan, 2011), and the culture of substance misuse within families/communities may further complicate this relationship.

Responding to legislation and policies. The process of working with substance-misusing caregivers is also complicated in the US by legislation at the Federal level enacted in policies at the level of the local jurisdiction. The US Adoption and Safe Families Act (ASFA) of 1997 was instrumental in prioritising permanency for children involved in the US child welfare system. ASFA promotes the timely achievement of permanency for youth with recognition of the importance of stability in healthy development (Green, Rockhill & Furrer, 2006; Schroeder, Lemieux & Pogue, 2008). ASFA requires that a permanency plan be established within 12 months after a child enters out-of-home care, and, in most cases, the termination of the parental rights process is initiated after the child has been in foster care for 15 out of the most recent 22 months (Adoption and Safe Families Act 1997). However, timelines for achieving permanency legislated by ASFA come in direct opposition to the difficult nature of substance use disorders (Azzi-Lessing & Olsen, 1996; Schroeder, Lemieux & Pogue, 2008), particularly those that are chronic in nature. Difficulties accessing timely and appropriate treatment and co-occurrence of substance misuse with other problems can create challenges to achieving the safety and stability necessary within the ASFA timeframes. A hypothesised reason for the documented phenomenon of re-entry in the foster care system for youth reunified with parents who have received treatment for substance use disorder is the shortened length of time that caregivers have to achieve sobriety before resuming parenting responsibilities: 'the current pressure to decrease time in out-of-home care before reunification might run counter to best practice with children of such parents' (Miller, Fisher, Fetrow & Jordan, 2006, p. 270).

Despite these challenges, prompt treatment of substance use disorder has been shown to improve child welfare outcomes. Completed treatment for substance use disorder increases the likelihood of reunification for families with children placed in out-of-home care (Grant, Huggins, Graham et al., 2011; Green, Rockhill & Furrer, 2007; Grella, Needell, Shi & Hser, 2009), and one study indicates that mothers who completed treatment for substance use disorder were more than twice as likely to reunify with their children than mothers who did not complete treatment (Choi, Huang & Ryan, 2012). Treatment has also been shown to decrease the risk of permanent removal of the child from the biological parents (Hong, Ryan, Hernandez & Brown, 2014). Those who enter treatment sooner after becoming involved with child protective services are more likely to complete treatment (Green, Rockhill & Furrer, 2006). In addition, parents entering substance use disorder treatment quickly after the beginning of child welfare involvement has been shown to reduce the time children spend in foster care and increase the likelihood of reunification (Green, Rockhill & Furrer, 2007). This emphasises the importance of early identification and treatment of substance misuse issues for child welfare outcomes.

How Should the Child Welfare System Respond?

Despite growing knowledge on the significant impact that parental substance misuse has on the healthy development of the child, general child welfare outcomes and the impact of treatment for substance use disorders, child welfare workers arguably lack training in these issues. In general they do not have extensive training in the unique nature of substance misuse, screening for substance misuse and working effectively with families in which substance misuse is occurring (Chuang, Wells, Bellettiere & Cross, 2013; Dore, Doris & Wright, 1995; Schroeder, Lemieux & Pogue, 2008; Tracy, 1994). Furthermore, child welfare systems may not be equipped at a systematic level to respond to the needs of caregivers with substance misuse issues. The child protection response must occur at two primary levels:

1. The level of the individual worker who is responsible for carrying out work with the family, and
2. The system level that is responsible for establishing standards of practice, agency priorities and programming.

The approaches to working with caregivers who misuse substances will be discussed with respect to the efficacy of each of these levels of intervention. The worker-level strategies can be implemented with relative ease at the individual level. However, the system-level interventions require systematic organisation, implementation and oversight.

Worker-level strategies

As child welfare providers investigate allegations of abuse and neglect, the provider must determine if parental substance misuse is a factor. Prompt recognition of how the role of parental substance misuse impacts child safety and/or puts the child at risk is imperative. Though substance use does not always put the child at risk for maltreatment, addressing the substance misuse issues early in the case is likely to promote positive outcomes for the family. Positive outcomes related to early identification of parental substance misuse include: using the case plan to address the substance use as a risk factor, less time in out-of-home care for children, decreased rates of re-entry into the child welfare system, and overall improved safety and well-being for the family (Green, Rockhill & Furrer, 2007). In order to promote timely interventions, workers can utilise screening techniques and provide informed and appropriate referrals for assessment and treatment.

Screening. Given what is known about the prevalence of substance misuse in child welfare populations and the impact of substance misuse on outcomes in the child welfare system, universal screening is indicated as a potential approach for promptly identifying substance misuse issues (Meyer, McWey, McKendrick & Henderson, 2010). For example, the UNCOPE screener (Brook, Yan, Lloyd & McDonald, 2014), the Alcohol Use Disorders Identification Tool (AUDIT) and Drug Abuse Screening Test (DAST) screeners (Chuang, Wells, Bellettiere & Cross, 2013) have been used with child welfare populations to identify substance misuse (see Table 28.1 for more information on these screeners).

However, screening of substance misuse issues happens inconsistently and one study indicates that less than a third (27%) of child welfare workers used formal screening or assessment procedures to identify substance misuse among caregivers (Chuang, Wells, Bellettiere & Cross, 2013). Insufficient training on substance misuse screening tools (Schroeder, Lemieux & Pogue, 2008), burdensome and overwhelming caseloads, and competing priorities are hypothesised as reasons for lack of screening (Chuang, Wells, Bellettiere & Cross, 2013). Despite these challenges, screening for substance use among parents and caregivers is often the first formal step in identifying alcohol and drug misuse as a risk factor in child abuse and neglect cases. Screening tools combined with observations of the client and additional collateral information, such as urine drug tests, assist in the identification of substance misuse and support earlier recognition of and intervention for problems (Substance Abuse and Mental Health Services Administration – Health Resources and Service Administration (SAMHSA-HRSA), 2014). Used correctly, screening tools can also reduce bias and subjectivity on the part of workers (Rapp, Dulmas, Wodarski & Feit, 1999).

The purpose of substance misuse screens is not to diagnose but to determine if more in-depth assessment is necessary. Screens for alcohol and substance misuse are easy to administer, can be accessed at little to no financial cost and usually require very little time to process (Rapp, Dulmas, Wodarski & Feit, 1999). The formats for screening tools vary depending on the specific screen, but, typically, screens are completed by provider interview or client self-report. Given the prevalence of substance misuse issues in the child welfare population, screening should be universally administered in all cases even if the reason for child welfare involvement is not caregiver substance misuse. However, if substance misuse is already a primary reason for child welfare involvement, caregivers should be referred directly to a treatment provider for assessment and possible treatment (Brook, Yan, Lloyd & McDonald, 2014).

Screening considerations must also take into account the continuum of substance misuse. Child welfare workers often categorise substance misuse dichotomously and specify that substance misuse is occurring or is not occurring (Staton-Tindall, Sprang & Clark, 2012).

Yet, substance misuse is a complex phenomenon with gradations and nuances that may impact each situation differently; screening tools can offer perspectives on the nature, frequency, scope and impact of substance misuse. Higher scores on the screening tools may indicate greater levels of need and potential risk for maltreatment (Brook, Yan, Lloyd & McDonald, 2014). Appropriate assessment of the severity of the substance misuse issue allows for allocation of scarce resources to those with the most severe needs (Brook, Yan, Lloyd & McDonald, 2014). However, screening can also help to identify those who may not be misusing drugs or alcohol, but are engaging in risky use perhaps at the mild end of the substance use disorder continuum. These screening results could help direct resources toward the prevention of the development of more serious addictive behaviour.

Of utmost concern in the process of screening for substance misuse issues is the development of an empathic, trusting relationship that promotes honesty on the part of the client (Schroeder, Lemieux & Pogue, 2008). Workers must be trained in the administration and scoring of the tool and in the requisite skills for engaging in an open, honest dialogue with the client. Without adequate skill development, workers may appear demeaning, condescending and judgemental.

Screening tools are particularly useful in the child welfare setting because time is often limited, yet objective data are necessary to accurately identify substance misuse problems and ensure adequate treatment for presenting issues. Table 28.1 provides a summary of possible screening tools but it does not provide an exhaustive list: many screening tools are available online and all should be retrieved from the online source to ensure the most current version is being used. Furthermore, child welfare professionals need to consider tools that are appropriate for the specific population or individual client with whom they are working. A list of viable, evidence-based screening tools can be found through the US National Institutes of Health, specifically the US National Institute on Drug Abuse (www.drugabuse.gov) and the US National Institute on Alcohol Abuse and Alcoholism (www.niaaa.nih.gov). The US National Center on Substance Abuse and Child Welfare, through the US Substance Abuse and Mental Health Services Administration (www.ncsacw.samhsa.gov), also maintains helpful information for child welfare professionals specifically. The resources found on these websites are accessible internationally, but the European Monitoring Centre for Drugs and Drug Addiction (www.emcdda.europa.eu) and the World Health Organization (www.who.int/substance_abuse/en/) provide additional resources for practitioners in Europe and other areas throughout the world.

Referring to services and collaborating with treatment providers. The child welfare worker does not typically provide treatment to caregivers struggling with substance misuse, but he/she should be trained to provide appropriate referrals for clients whose screening results indicate a need for further assessment and possible treatment (Young, Nakashian, Yeh & Amatetti, 2006). A positive screen and/or other collateral information (e.g., substance use mentioned in the report to child welfare services, legal problems related to substance use, past reports involving parent's substance use, or positive drug screens) that indicate a possible alcohol or drug misuse requires further assessment by a skilled counsellor or agency that provides treatment for substance use disorders. Child welfare workers can support the assessment process by inquiring about assessment techniques and tools utilised by the treatment professional. In addition, child welfare workers should obtain necessary client consent to share observations and screening results with the treatment professional in order to support a thorough and accurate assessment.

The assessment process culminates in recommendations for treatment and intervention, if deemed necessary. Typically, substance abuse treatment professionals, in conjunction with the individual receiving treatment, make decisions about appropriate treatment approaches.

Table 28.1 Selected screening and assessment tools.

Tool	Administration/ number of items	What it screens for	Access (Tools are free to access unless otherwise noted)	Citation
Addiction Severity Index (ASI)	Worker administration; training needed for administration and scoring; 200 items	Drug and alcohol use	http://www.tresearch.org/tools/download-asi-instruments-manuals/	McLellan, Kushner, Metzger et al., 1992; McLellan, Luborsky, O'Brien & Woody, 1980
Alcohol Use Disorders Identification Test (AUDIT)	Worker administration; 10 items	Alcohol use	http://whqlibdoc.who.int/hq/2001/WHO_MSD_MSB_01.6a.pdf	Babor, Higgins-Biddle, Saunders & Monteiro, 2001
CAGE/ CAGEAID Questionnaire	Self or worker administration; 4 items	CAGE: Alcohol use; CAGEAID: Alcohol and drug use	http://pubs.niaaa.nih.gov/publications/inscage.htm	Ewing, 1984
Drug Abuse Screening Test (DAST)	Self or worker administration; Several versions available: 28 item, 20 item and 10 item	Drug use	http://www.camh.net/Publications/CAMH_Publications/drug_abuse_screening_test.html	Gavin, Ross & Skinner, 1989
Drug Use Screening Inventory Revised (DUSI-R)	Self or worker administration; 159 items	Substance use, mental health issues, and functioning	Fee required for access; http://www.yourhealthcheck.org/organization/dusi	Tarter & Kirisci, 1997
Global Appraisal of Individual Need – Short Screener (GAIN-SS)	Self or worker administration; 23 items Other versions are available	Substance abuse, externalising and internalising behaviours, crime/violence	Fee required for use; http://www.gaincc.org/	Dennis, Feeney & Titus, 2013
Michigan Alcoholism Screening Test (MAST) (other versions available)	Self or worker administration; 25 items	Alcohol use	http://www.integration.samhsa.gov/clinical-practice/sbirt/Mast.pdf	Selzer, 1971

4 Ps Plus	Self or worker administration; 4 primary items with 7 follow-up items	Alcohol and drug use during pregnancy	Licensing fee required; more information available at: http://www.ntiupstream.com/4psabout/	Chasnoff, McGourty, Bailey et al., 2005; Anthony, Austin & Cormier, 2010
Risk Inventory for Substance-Affected Families	Worker administration; 8 rating scales	Addresses the impact of substance abuse on maltreatment	Fee required for access; more information available at: http://www.cfsri.org/	
Substance Abuse Subtle Screening Inventory (SASSI)	Worker administration; 93 items	Drug and alcohol abuse; subtle indications of misuse that may not be readily accessed in other screening tools	Fee required for access; find more information at: www.sassi.com	Rapp, Dulmas, Wodarski & Feit, 1999; Miller 1985, 1999
TWEAK	Self or worker administration; 5 items	Alcohol use during pregnancy	http://www.alcohol.gov.au/internet/alcohol/publishing.nsf/Content/DA90	Chang, 2001; Russell, 1994
T-ACE	Self or worker administration; 4 items	Alcohol use during pregnancy		Chang, 2001; Russell, 1994
UNCOPE	Self or worker administration; 6 items	Drug and alcohol use	http://www.evinceassessment.com/UNCOPE_for_web.pdf	Brook, Yan, Lloyd & McDonald, 2014; Hoffman, 1999

Though child welfare workers are not involved in providing treatment, they can support the ongoing treatment process by collaborating regularly with the treatment provider after obtaining client consent to discuss such matters. Child welfare workers can support the treatment process by being knowledgeable about treatment options and promoting compliance with treatment through collaboration and ongoing contact with treatment providers (Meyer, McWey, McKendrick & Henderson, 2010). Treatment delivery modalities range in frequency, duration and intensity depending on needs. Settings for treatment include detox, outpatient, inpatient, residential and intensive outpatient. In each of the service-delivery options, utilisation of evidence-based practices in addressing problems with child welfare-involved families is an important consideration (Young, Nakashian, Yeh & Amatetti, 2006).

Evidence-based practice in child welfare is defined as a combination of three factors: best research evidence, best clinical experience, and being consistent with client and family values (California Evidence-Based Clearing House for Child Welfare, 2014). The California Evidence-Based Clearinghouse for Child Welfare (www.cebc4cw.org) and the Clearinghouse for Military Family Readiness (www.militaryfamilies.psu.edu) maintain a comprehensive system of evidence-based treatment approaches for adult substance use disorder treatment. Child welfare professionals should consult these resources to learn more about evidence-based approaches to substance use disorder treatment. However, the resources available in a particular community may vary, and not all treatment options are available in all areas. Child welfare professionals must be adept at identifying treatment options available within the community served. Additional resources can be found in Table 28.2.

Promoting engagement in substance abuse treatment. Given the importance of treatment completion for child welfare outcomes, engagement in services to address substance misuse is of primary concern. Child welfare workers hold a position of considerable influence for caregivers who need treatment for substance use disorders, particularly as workers provide ongoing case management services to clients in need of treatment. Principles of motivational interviewing and a strengths-based case management approach can be used by child welfare workers to prepare substance-misusing parents for the treatment process (Schroeder, Lemieux & Pogue, 2008) and to enhance commitment to treatment. Motivational interviewing is defined as:

> A collaborative, goal-oriented style of communication with particular attention to the language of change, designed to strengthen personal motivation for and commitment to a specific goal by eliciting and exploring the person's own reasons for change within an atmosphere of acceptance and compassion (motivationalinterviewing.org, 2014).

Principles of motivational interviewing can help identify the level of the clients' readiness to change and can determine how to support the client through the change process (Breshears, Yeh & Young, 2004). Traditional approaches to practice rely on coercive techniques to motivate change. In comparison, motivational interviewing promotes the use of collaboration, honesty and empathy to encourage substance-misusing individuals to explore the extent and impact of their use to find internal motivation for change. Motivational interviewing techniques recognise the ambivalence that most people experience through the change process and seek to explore this ambivalence to help clients internalise the motivation to change (Miller & Rollnick, 2002).

Motivational interviewing has demonstrated effectiveness with substance-misusing populations (Miller & Rollnick, 2002), but only a limited number of studies explore the effectiveness

Table 28.2 Selected resources for more information.

Resource	Information provided	To learn more
US National Institute of Drug Abuse	• Fact sheets with information about commonly abused substances and pertinent information for professionals • Educational resources for professionals about drug use • Screening tools relevant to drug use • Assessment and treatment information	www.drugabuse.gov
US National Institute of Alcohol Abuse and Alcoholism	• Fact sheets about alcohol use and misuse • Educational resources for professionals about alcohol misuse • Screening tools for alcohol use • Assessment and treatment information	www.niaaa.nih.gov
California Evidence-Based Clearinghouse for Child Welfare	• Information about evidence-based approaches to addressing a variety of issues, including substance abuse • Provides details about the current level of support for treatment options as well as the relevance of each option for the child welfare system	www.ceb4cw.org
US National Center on Substance Abuse and Child Welfare	• Resources and information about hot topics in the field of substance abuse and child welfare • Information about collaboration between systems and strategies for enhancing collaboration • Training resources and online tutorials for professionals • Downloadable resource specifically about substance abuse in the child welfare field: *Understanding Substance Abuse and Facilitating Recovery: A Guide for Child Welfare Workers*	www.ncsacw.samhsa.gov
Screening Assessment for Family Engagement, Retention, and Recovery (SAFERR) (through the NCSACW)	• Screening tools • Information about collaboration between the substance abuse and child welfare systems	https://www.ncsacw.samhsa.gov/resources/SAFERR.aspx

(*Continued*)

Table 28.2 (Cont'd)

Resource	Information provided	To learn more
US SAMHSA Treatment Locator	• Provides information about treatment facilities and options available in a community or area (available only in the US)	https://findtreatment.samhsa.gov
US SAMHSA's National Registry of Evidence-based Programs and Practices	• Searchable database of evidence-based substance abuse and mental health treatment programmes	www.nrepp.samhsa.gov
European Monitoring Centre for Drugs and Drug Addiction	• Information about the prevalence of substance use in European countries • Provides information about best practice approaches for assessment and treatment of substance use-related disorders • Includes repository of screening and assessment tools	www.emcdda.europa.eu
World Health Organization – Substance Abuse	• Provides current research and information about worldwide substance use prevalence • Includes a limited number of tools for assessment and screening of substance use	www.who.int/substance_abuse/en/
Clearinghouse for Military Family Readiness	• Includes a Continuum of Evidence with a variety of programmes for addressing the needs of military personnel and families, including substance use needs	www.militaryfamilies.psu.edu

of motivational interviewing as a strategy to improve linkage to services and treatment entry for child welfare-involved caregivers, and none offer positive results (Mullins, Suarez, Ondersma & Page, 2004; Rapp, Otto, Lane et al., 2008). Motivational interviewing has been demonstrated as an evidence-based practice for working with substance-misusing adults in general. However, additional research is needed to better understand the utility of motivational interviewing with the child welfare population, particularly as motivational interviewing has not shown positive results with coerced populations (Mullins et al., 2004).

Another approach gaining support in the literature is strengths-based case management (Rapp, Otto, Lane et al., 2008). Foundationally, social work is built on the principles of strengths-based practice. Implementing strengths-based principles in practice with the child welfare population may be challenging for some workers especially if their educational background is not in social work. However, a strengths-based case management approach may be effective in helping caregivers access treatment for substance misuse (Rapp, Otto, Lane et al., 2008). One study found that substance-misusing caregivers who received strengths-based case management were 18% more likely to engage in treatment than those receiving the usual standard of care (Rapp, Otto, Lane et al., 2008). Strengths-based case management employs the traditional case management functions of 'assessment, planning, linking, monitoring, and advocacy' with strengths-based principles of building on client strengths, encouraging client involvement and choice in treatment and the use of informal supports, and emphasising the importance of the worker–client relationship (Rapp, Otto, Lane et al., 2008, p. 175). Strengths-based approaches to practice have been shown to predict buy-in from substance-misusing families (Kemp, Marcenko, Lyons & Kruzich, 2014), with substance-misusing parents more likely to engage in services when they perceive that the worker utilises strengths-based practices (Kemp, Marcenko, Lyons & Kruzich, 2014). Strengths-based approaches can be easily implemented in work with families; however, this approach should be supported through training, supervision and modelling.

Case management services should also be fairly proactive in nature so as to respond to the comprehensive needs of families involved in the child welfare system (Rockhill, Green & Newton-Curtis, 2008). Families in the child welfare system often experience practical, financial and emotional barriers to completing substance abuse treatment (Rockhill, Green & Newton-Curtis, 2008), and case management can be implemented to help reduce barriers and increase access to and involvement with services. Intensive case management has shown promise in promoting engagement in treatment, an area of utmost importance for substance-misusing parents. However, the implications for child welfare outcomes need to be further investigated (Dauber, Neighbors, Dasaro et al., 2012).

System-level strategies

Worker-level strategies can help increase the effectiveness of services provided to individual families served, but system-level strategies are intended to shape the culture of the service-delivery system so that similar approaches are applied universally. System-level interventions present additional challenges for the child welfare field as they often require significant commitments of time and financial resources and implementation of new processes, such as regular meetings with other service providers and agencies, development of memorandums of agreement, and updating forms to allow for better collaboration and sharing of information. System-level strategies can include straightforward approaches to enhancing training for child welfare staff and more complex approaches designed to support greater integration of the child welfare system and treatment system for substance use disorders.

Table 28.3 Training for child welfare staff.

Suggested content for training:
- Substance use/misuse definitions
- Impact of substance use on child safety, permanency and well-being
- Worker perceptions and biases related to substance misuse and child welfare issues
- Techniques to engage with clients, particularly clients who are ambivalent about change
- Screening tools
- Assessment and treatment options, especially those relevant to the community served by the staff
- Responding holistically to clients with substance misuse issues to meet concrete needs as well as treatment needs
- Effective collaboration strategies for working with substance misuse treatment service providers, specifically confidentiality and communication requirements and strategies for communicating with treatment providers in substance misuse treatment programmes

Training for child welfare staff. Given the unique challenges of working with caregivers struggling with substance misuse, training for child welfare staff is essential. A suggested list of training topics based on literature in this area is summarised in Table 28.3. At a minimum, training should address the following topics: i) general information about substance misuse and its impact on child development and maltreatment; ii) worker perceptions and biases about substance misuse and working with caregivers who misuse substances; iii) engagement techniques; iv) screening tools to utilise in practice; v) assessment and treatment options, specifically those that are available and relevant locally; and vi) strategies to promote effective collaboration with treatment providers (Young, Nakashian, Yeh & Amatetti, 2006).

In order to effectively meet the needs of caregivers who have substance misuse issues, child welfare workers must be able to accurately identify the issue and treatment needs (Tracy & Farkas, 1994). Training has been shown to positively impact workers' knowledge of substance use disorder issues and confidence in addressing substance misuse problems (Gregoire, 1994). Despite this, implementation of such training remains limited. Training should increase worker knowledge of how to assess the impact of parental substance misuse on the care of the child (Howell, 2008). Substance use does not necessarily lead to child maltreatment and workers must be able to conduct differential assessments to determine misuse that is a concern for child welfare (Howell, 2008). Training for child welfare staff in the identification of possible substance misuse issues is essential, especially when considering that many cases that come to the attention of the child welfare agency do not have involvement with a substance misuse treatment provider:

> Social workers are working with large numbers of serious cases involving substance misuse and it is rare for there to be a specialist professional involved. They need the knowledge and skills, backed up by research-based guidance, to work effectively with *this issue* (Forrester & Harwin, 2006, p. 332)

Staff should be trained in general information about substance misuse, such as emotional, behavioural and environmental indicators of misuse, as well as the reasons why people develop substance use disorders (Young, Nakashian, Yeh & Amatetti, 2006). Staff must also know specific information about the types of drugs most commonly misused, the impact of these substances on caregiver functioning, child welfare implications and the range of treatment options available for addressing misuse (Lloyd & Akin, 2014). The primary drug of misuse may impact treatment completion and child welfare workers must be able to tailor case plans based on the primary type of substance misused (Choi & Ryan, 2006). For example, methadone treatment referrals are rarely made in child welfare services (Choi & Ryan, 2006) despite the effectiveness that this approach has for the treatment of substance use disorders involving heroin. Matching services to meet the unique needs of the family has been shown to increase rates of reunification (Chuang, Moore, Barrett & Young, 2012). For example, families who received services matched to their needs were over four times more likely to be reunified (Choi & Ryan, 2007). Training should assist workers in developing knowledge about the range of available treatments for different types of drug misuse (Choi & Ryan, 2006). In addition, given the complex nature of substance misuse, workers should be trained to enable them to respond effectively to the holistic needs of the client in an integrated and comprehensive manner and to provide specialised services, including assistance with transportation or access to education to improve outcomes (Chuang, Moore, Barrett & Young, 2012).

Research indicates a misalignment between worker perception and parent perception of treatment needs, especially when substance misuse occurs with other issues, which suggests that workers underestimate the need for treatment (Stromwall, Larson, Nieri et al., 2008). In addition, many caregivers in need of treatment for substance use disorder do not receive necessary referrals and services (Berger, Slack, Waldfogel & Bruch, 2010; Choi & Ryan, 2007) due in part to the unique issues and responsibilities of parents with substance misuse issues (Stewart, Gossop & Trakada, 2007). Training should help workers develop skills to screen for substance misuse issues and co-occurring issues that may require specialised treatment (Stromwall, Larson, Nieri et al., 2008).

Worker perception of substance misuse can influence the child welfare response to the caregiver even if the substance misuse does not pose a safety risk to the child (Howell, 2008; Berger, Slack, Waldfogel & Bruch, 2010). Thus, discussion of the worker's personal perceptions and biases regarding substance misuse should be included in training (Howell, 2008), with opportunities to discuss strategies for addressing perceptions that may interfere with practice and impede effective engagement with substance-misusing caregivers (Tracy & Farkas, 1994).

Workers may feel torn between the sometimes-conflicting responsibilities to ensure the safety of the child and to assist the family through the change process (Schreiber, Fuller & Paceley, 2013). Good training will help workers develop an awareness of this conflict and increase skills to effectively engage caregivers in the change process while also ensuring the safety of the child (Schreiber, Fuller & Paceley, 2013). Compassion, respect and empathy can be difficult for workers to muster and convey, particularly when working with parents who have harmed a child. Workers may also require, implicitly or explicitly, assumption of responsibility and compliance from parents in order to proceed with efforts to engage them in services (Altman, 2008). However, the importance of engagement is well documented, and both trust in the worker and engagement in services are strong predictors for parental change (Gladstone, Dumbrill, Leslie et al., 2012; Altman, 2008). Therefore, training should focus on helping workers develop skill in strengths-based and relational approaches to practice with substance-misusing caregivers. It should support workers as they develop skills to facilitate engagement and trust, and to manage difficult emotions of their own or their clients (Schreiber, Fuller & Paceley, 2013). In summary, strengths-based approaches must be taught in training, modelled in supervision and supported with encouraging oversight to ensure positive engagement and trust in the worker. A further need is to emphasise the ambivalent feelings inherent in the change process. As Altman (2008) states:

> Change is difficult. For clients not asking for services in a cooperative arrangement, it can be an antagonistic experience. Many child welfare clients perceive themselves as being forced to see workers against their will, believe that the system is not just or fair, see the agency and its workers as unwanted intrusions into their lives, and view the remedies recommended to them as meaningless or harmful. (p. 58)

Principles of motivational interviewing can be helpful to workers as they make sense of the difficult nature of change and determine how to best support this process (Miller & Rollnick, 2002). Although child welfare services are typically reactive in nature, occurring only after the development of problems that necessitate intervention, preventative programmes offer promise for reducing risk factors that lead to child welfare involvement. For example, the Family Check-Up is a family-based intervention that emphasises strengths and individualised approaches to prevention of problematic behaviour in youth (Gill, Hyde, Shaw et al., 2008). Principles of the Family Check-Up model could be modified to train child welfare staff on strategies to increase motivation for change and engagement in treatment while also emphasising strengths and prevention.

Collaboration and system integration. Child welfare workers often indicate on caregiver case plans that there is a need for substance use assessment and treatment, and the need for a follow-up to a positive screen or report of substance use described in the allegations of abuse or neglect. The caregiver's successful engagement with assessment and treatment is often dependent on the collaboration and information sharing that occurs between child welfare workers and treatment providers (Young & Gardner, 2002, p. 103). Numerous factors provide barriers to collaboration between child welfare services and substance use disorder treatment providers. These include: confidentiality policies and concerns; differing measures of success; conflicting values and philosophies regarding response to substance-using parents; mistrust and misunderstanding about other agencies; identification of the primary client as the child or parent; and timeliness and accessibility of services (Drabble, 2007; Green, Rockhill & Burrus, 2008; He, Traube & Young, 2014; Mcalpine, Marshall & Doran, 2001; Marsh & Smith, 2011). These professional silos often serve as barriers to successful collaboration and systems integration (Staton-Tindall, Sprang & Clark, 2012).

Successful collaboration has been conceptualised as incorporating three functions 'building shared values systems, improving communication, and providing a "team" of support' (Green, Rockhill & Burrus, 2008, p. 29). Collaboration typically requires that a deliberate effort is made by involved systems and partners, and must be cultivated over time and repeated experiences. Even when values differ, typically child welfare and substance use disorder treatment services share a mutual purpose of addressing substance misuse issues and child welfare concerns simultaneously (Drabble, 2007). Though the two systems may differ in their perspectives on how to accomplish this purpose, building on these commonalities is important in the process of developing shared values systems (Drabble, 2007). Cross-training of staff is a suggested strategy for developing shared values systems (Green, Rockhill & Burrus, 2008; He, Traube & Young, 2014; Kerwin, 2005).

An important component of collaboration is communication among treatment providers, court personnel and case workers. Regular communication between treatment providers and case workers facilitates case progression and prevents families being overlooked or forgotten. However, communication needs to be in-depth, timely and consistent to be effective. Expectations of case plans, treatment goals and court requirements should also be clearly conveyed to families. All providers involved with the family should be aware of the requirements of the other agencies involved in the case. Hence, information sharing and collaboration results in improved case monitoring, knowledge of progress, and quicker and more comprehensive access to resources (Young, Nakashian, Yeh & Amatetti, 2006).

However, effective collaboration is dependent on information sharing between the worker and treatment provider. This is impacted upon by confidentiality legislation and professional regulations, which may differ between countries, but also there may be different legislation for different elements of concern. For example, in the US, confidentiality laws (42 USC.§ 290dd-2; Title 42 The Public Health and Welfare, 1994) and regulations (42 C.F.R., Part 2; Confidentiality of Alcohol and Drug Abuse Patient Records, 2015) apply to most *substance use disorder treatment programmes* in the US, aiming to protect the rights of all clients seeking substance use treatment. In addition, the child welfare worker must abide by *confidentiality of child abuse and neglect information*-mandated national laws, such as the Child Abuse Prevention and Treatment Act (CAPTA), originally enacted in 1974 (42 USC.§ 67; Child Abuse Prevention and Treatment Act, 1974). Both child welfare workers and treatment providers must work with caregivers to obtain written caregiver consent to release and share confidential information (US Department of Health and Human Services, 1999). Thus, child welfare workers and treatment providers need to receive practical training regarding effective ways to communicate within the parameters of these laws and regulations.

Organisational culture also impacts the degree and nature of inter-agency collaboration (Smith & Mogro-Wilson, 2007). Agencies can support inter-agency collaboration by instituting policies that support this and providing training to staff on the benefits and techniques of effective collaboration (Smith & Mogro-Wilson, 2007). As with any skill, staff are more likely to employ inter-agency collaboration if they feel confident in their ability to do so and perceive the benefits of it.

Agencies and workers can implement collaboration, but system integration requires a more advanced level of cross-system organisation. Innovative approaches to cross-system integration are gaining appeal and support. Team approaches to integrative practice are built on the foundations of shared values and effective communication. Co-location of staff, recovery coaches, Sobriety Treatment and Recovery Teams (START) and family drug courts represent innovative approaches to system integration.

Co-location of staff. Co-location models place service providers from different social service systems within the same physical working space, which creates regular opportunities for open communication among service providers (Lee, Esaki & Greene, 2009). Regular communication and collaboration allow for early identification of substance use disorder treatment needs and afford a team approach to linking families to necessary services (Lee, Esaki & Greene, 2009). Studies of the effectiveness of staff co-location are limited but offer insights into a promising approach to system integration (Lee, Esaki & Greene, 2009). For example, preliminary findings suggest that simply placing a substance use disorder treatment provider or professional in a child welfare office is not enough. Rather, the co-location process must be approached carefully with ample planning and delineated procedures to ensure engagement and buy-in from all service providers (Lee, Esaki & Greene, 2009).

Recovery coaches, parent mentors and START. One promising practice is the use of recovery coaches. Recovery coaches connect caregivers to services, conduct home visits, provide advocacy and assist in case management. Families who receive recovery coach services and support are more likely to access substance use disorder treatment and achieve family reunification (Ryan, Marsh, Testa & Louderman, 2006), as well as have decreased risk for a new substance-exposed birth after completing services (Ryan, Choi, Hong et al., 2008). While there are some differences, providers (known as peer mentors, recovery specialists, or family advocates) provide similar approaches in supporting families involved in child welfare. The innovative recovery coach approach is becoming more widespread; however, research regarding its effectiveness is limited (Berrick, Cohen & Anthony, 2011) and needed.

Family-centred programmes are increasing in number and focus on addressing substance use and incorporating other family members in the treatment services. Examples of family-centred programmes range from residential substance use disorder treatment that enables children to reside with the parent while treatment is being sought to evidence-based programmes, such as Celebrating Families and Strengthening Families, that address parenting and incorporate substance misuse education (Gardner, 2014).

The Sobriety Treatment and Recovery Teams (START) is another model for incorporating peer mentors as an essential part of the child welfare service-delivery process. START is an integrated approach to practice. This model combines the child welfare system and substance misuse system by using family mentors who have sustained sobriety and have personal knowledge of the child welfare system to assist families as they navigate both systems (Huebner, Willauer & Posze, 2012). START programmes have been shown to improve rates of sobriety, decrease rates of out-of-home care placement and produce cost savings for the child welfare agency (Huebner, Willauer & Posze, 2012).

Family drug courts. Modelled after traditional drug courts, family drug courts provide accountability while 'helping the parent to become drug free and to develop adequate parenting and "coping" skills to be able to serve as an effective parent on a day-to-day basis' (Choi, 2012, p. 448). The court system provides an additional level of oversight, which is conveyed with compassion and support for the caregivers, as the goal of family drug courts is to provide accountability, not punishment, as parents address serious substance use disorders and provide safety and permanency for their children (Choi, 2012).

Family drug courts are a relatively new innovation in the child welfare system, and they represent a unique partnership between the child welfare and legal systems. Family drug courts have been gaining attention as an innovative approach in the US (Choi, 2012; Gifford, Eldred, Vernerey & Sloan, 2014) and the UK (Bambrough, Shaw & Kershaw, 2014; Harwin, Alrouh, Ryan & Tunnard, 2013). The family drug court system presents an opportunity for less adversarial relationships and greater collaboration among all team members who work with the family. In addition, it supports increased family involvement in the development of the case plan and the resulting recommendations and treatments (Bambrough, Shaw & Kershaw, 2014). Emerging data suggest that this may be a promising approach and results suggest 'improved screening and assessment, increased access to treatment services, and improved accountability of parents' (Choi, 2012, p. 456). A preliminary study of a Family Drug and Alcohol Court in the UK indicated that caregivers involved in the drug court programme received treatment sooner, received a broader range of services, and were more successful at remaining engaged in treatment over time (Bambrough, Shaw & Kershaw, 2014). Further, US studies have indicated that for those who fully complete family drug treatment court, reunification rates were higher (Chuang, Moore, Barrett & Young, 2012; Gifford, Eldred, Vernerey & Sloan, 2014), children spent less time in foster care (Gifford, Eldred, Vernerey & Sloan, 2014), and re-entry to care was lower (Chuang, Moore, Barrett & Young, 2012). One study suggests that full completion of the programme is most important in achieving positive outcomes (Gifford, Eldred, Vernerey & Sloan, 2014). However, time to permanency has been shown to be greater for those who do complete the programme (Chuang, Moore, Barrett & Young, 2012), which is possibly due to the length of time necessary for treatment completion.

Thus, further research is needed to determine if this is a viable and effective approach to working with substance-misusing caregivers particularly given the long-term nature of substance misuse issues (Gifford, Eldred, Vernerey & Sloan, 2014; Twomey, Miller-Loncar, Hinckley & Lester, 2010).

Looking Ahead

Although the prevalence of substance misuse in the child welfare system remains unclear, the impact of caregiver substance misuse on child welfare outcomes is well established. Looking forward, the child welfare system needs to respond to the challenge of substance misuse among caregivers, even though this issue has traditionally been thought of as outside the domain, or silo, of child welfare (Staton-Tindall, Sprang & Clark, 2012). In order to address the complex needs of families served by the child welfare system, emerging from silos to build collaboration and consensus is essential. Three recommendations are offered as integral in accomplishing this goal:

1. Develop a better understanding of the prevalence and differential impact of substance misuse;
2. Enhance substance misuse education for child welfare professionals; and
3. Increase cross-system collaboration and integration to address complex needs of substance-misusing caregivers.

First, there must be a greater effort to understand the prevalence of substance use and misuse in the child welfare system (Young, Boles & Otero, 2007). An appropriate response to the problem first depends on appropriate identification of the scope and magnitude of the problem. Thus, child welfare agencies need to increase accurate identification of substance use and misuse among caregivers, with a system for collecting, reporting and disseminating the data on national and global levels developed to better understand the magnitude of the problem. In addition, the impact of substance use on families and the differential impact of various types of drugs need to be better understood. Emerging data suggest that the substance of misuse may differentially impact child welfare outcomes; additional research is needed to better understand the complexity of substance misuse and how the child welfare system can best respond.

Second, there is a clear need for more practical education for child welfare professionals regarding effective strategies that can be used to work with substance-misusing caregivers with an emphasis on the impact of substance abuse and treatment on child welfare outcomes (Tracy & Farkas, 1994). Research demonstrates the importance of early identification and intervention to treat substance misuse. In addition, holistic interventions that address co-occurring issues should be developed and used to better meet the needs of substance-misusing caregivers.

Third, caregivers with substance misuse issues present with complex and challenging needs that require collaboration and system integration (Marsh & Smith, 2011; Osterling & Austin, 2008). Emerging from silos to implement promising practices and evidence-based approaches is a necessity (Staton-Tindall, Sprang & Clark, 2012). Although the child welfare system has traditionally relied on treatment professionals to bear the responsibility of addressing substance misuse issues, the child welfare system cannot abdicate responsibility in this area. The child welfare system must recognise the influence it has to ensure caregivers receive timely, adequate and effective intervention for substance use disorders. Child welfare professionals have considerable influence in determining referrals for services and they can use this influence to ensure clients have access to evidence-based and individualised approaches (Marsh & Smith, 2011). Substance misuse clearly has significant implications for child welfare systems, and caregivers would be best served by an agency response that honours this connection. Programmes with emerging evidence of efficacy, such as co-location of staff, family drug treatment courts and recovery coaches, need to be implemented and further evaluated (Osterling & Austin, 2008).

Conclusion

In conclusion, although the evidence in the area of interventions for parents who misuse substances is only recently emerging, several programmes have been shown to have some degree of efficacy. A focus on the child welfare response to substance misuse should include worker-level strategies, such as screening, and system-level strategies, such as training and collaboration. Therefore, three recommendations are suggested, whereby the way forward is to consider identification of parents in need of support, additional training of staff and cross-system collaboration. Addressing these areas may present a way forward in working with these parents with complex needs that can be overlooked.

Disclaimer: Reference in this text to any specific commercial products, services, companies or manufacturers does not constitute endorsement or recommendation by the authors.

References

Adoption and Safe Families Act 1997. P.L. 105–189 (1997).
Altman, J.C. (2008). Engaging families in child welfare services: Worker versus client perspectives. *Child Welfare*, 87, 41–61.
American Psychological Association (2013). *Diagnostic and Statistical Manual of Mental Disorders*, 5th edn. Washington, DC: American Psychological Association.
Anthony, E.K., Austin, M.J. & Cormier, D.R. (2010). Early detection of prenatal substance exposure and the role of child welfare. *Children and Youth Services Review*, 32, 6–12.
Azzi-Lessing, L. & Olsen, L.J. (1996). Substance abuse-affected families in the child welfare system: New challenges, new alliances. *Social Work*, 41, 15–23.
Babor, T.F., Higgins-Biddle, J.C., Saunders, J.B. & Monteiro, M.G. (2001). *The alcohol use disorders identification test: Guidelines for use in primary care*, 2nd edn. Geneva: World Health Organization, Department of Mental Health and Substance Dependence.
Bambrough, S., Shaw, M. & Kershaw, S. (2014). The Family Drug and Alcohol Court Service in London: A new way of doing care proceedings. *Journal of Social Work Practice*, 28, 357–370.
Barth, R.P., Gibbons, C. & Guo, S. (2006). Substance abuse treatment and the recurrence of maltreatment among caregivers with children living at home: A propensity score analysis. *Journal of Substance Abuse Treatment*, 30, 93–104.
Berger, L.M., Slack, K.S., Waldfogel, J. & Bruch, S.K. (2010). Caseworker-perceived caregiver substance abuse and child protective services outcomes. *Child Maltreatment*, 15, 199–210.
Berrick, J.D., Cohen, E. & Anthony, E. (2011). Partnering with parents: Promising approaches to improve reunification outcomes for children in foster care. *Journal of Family Strengths*, 11, 14.
Brandon, M. (2009). Child fatality or serious injury through maltreatment: Making sense of outcomes. *Children and Youth Services Review*, 31, 1107–1112.

Breshears, E.M., Yeh, S. & Young, N.K. (2004). *Understanding substance abuse and facilitating recovery: A guide for child welfare workers.* US Department of Health and Human Services. Rockville, MD: Substance Abuse and Mental Health Services Administration.

Brook, J. & McDonald, T. (2009). The impact of parental substance abuse on the stability of the family reunifications from foster care. *Children and Youth Services Review*, 31, 193–198.

Brook, J., Yan, Y., Lloyd, M.H. & McDonald, T.P. (2014). Screening for substance use disorders as a supplement to caseworker assessment among foster care-involved families. *Journal of Public Child Welfare*, 8, 239–259.

California Evidence-Based Clearinghouse of Child Welfare (2014), www.cebc4cw.org/what-is-evidence-based-practice/.

Chaffin, M., Kelleher, K. & Hollenberg, J. (1996). Onset of physical abuse and neglect: Psychiatric, substance abuse, and social risk factors from prospective community data. *Child Abuse & Neglect*, 20, 191–203.

Chang, G. (2001). Alcohol-screening instruments for pregnant women. *Alcohol Research & Health*, 25, 204–209.

Chasnoff, I.J., McGourty, R.F., Bailey, G.W. et al. (2005). The 4Ps Plus© screen for substance use in pregnancy: Clinical application and outcomes. *Journal of Perinatology*, 25, 368–374.

Cheng, T.C. (2010). Factors associated with reunification: A longitudinal analysis of long-term foster care. *Children and Youth Services Review*, 32, 1311–1316.

Child Abuse Prevention and Treatment Act. P.L. 93–247 (1974).

Child Welfare Information Gateway (2014). *Parental substance use and the child welfare system.* Washington, DC: Department of Health and Human Services, Children's Bureau, www.childwelfare.gov.

Choi, S. (2012). Family drug courts in child welfare. *Child and Adolescent Social Work Journal*, 29, 447–461.

Choi, S. & Ryan, J.P. (2006). Completing substance abuse treatment in child welfare: The role of co-occurring problems and primary drug of choice. *Child Maltreatment*, 11, 313–325.

Choi, S. & Ryan, J.P. (2007). Co-occurring problems for substance abusing mothers in child welfare: Matching services to improve family reunification. *Children and Youth Services Review*, 29, 1395–1410.

Choi, S., Huang, H. & Ryan, J.P. (2012). Substance abuse treatment completion in child welfare: Does substance abuse treatment completion matter in the decision to reunify families? *Children and Youth Services Review*, 34, 1639–1645.

Chuang, E., Moore, K., Barrett, B. & Young, M.S. (2012). Effect of an integrated family dependency treatment court on child welfare reunification, time to permanency and re-entry rates. *Children and Youth Services Review*, 34, 1896–1902.

Chuang, E., Wells, R., Bellettiere, J. & Cross, T.P. (2013). Identifying the substance abuse treatment needs of caregivers involved with child welfare. *Journal of Substance Abuse Treatment*, 45, 118–125.

Confidentiality of Alcohol and Drug Abuse Patient Records, 42 C.F.R. Part 2 (2015).

Dauber, S., Neighbors, C., Dasaro, C. et al. (2012). Impact of intensive case management on child welfare system involvement for substance-dependent parenting women on public assistance. *Children and Youth Services Review*, 34, 1359–1366.

De Bortoli, L., Coles, J. & Dolan, M. (2013). Parental substance misuse and compliance as factors determining child removal: A sample from the Victorian Children's Court in Australia. *Children and Youth Services Review*, 35, 1319–1326.

Dennis, M.L., Feeney, T. & Titus, J.C. (2013). *Global Appraisal of Individual Needs-Short Screener (GAIN-SS): Administration and scoring manual, version 3.* Bloomington, IL: Chestnut Health Systems.

Dore, M.M., Doris, J.M. & Wright, P. (1995). Identifying substance abuse in maltreating families: A child welfare challenge. *Child Abuse & Neglect*, 19, 531–543.

Douglas, E.M. (2013). Case, service, and family characteristics of households that experience a child maltreatment fatality in the United States. *Child Abuse Review*, 22, 311–326.

Douglas, E.M. & Mohn, B.L. (2014). Fatal and non-fatal child maltreatment in the US: An analysis of child, caregiver, and service utilization with the National Child Abuse and Neglect Data Set. *Child Abuse & Neglect*, 38, 42–51.

Drabble, L. (2007). Pathways to collaboration: Exploring values and collaborative practice between child welfare and substance abuse treatment fields. *Child Maltreatment*, 12, 31–42.

Drapela, L.A. & Mosher, C. (2007). The conditional effect of *parental drug use* on *parental* attachment and adolescent *drug use*: Social control and social development model perspectives. *Journal of Child & Adolescent Substance Abuse*, 16, 63–87.

Ewing, J.A. (1984). Detecting alcoholism: The CAGE questionnaire. *JAMA: Journal of the American Medical Association*, 252, 1905–1907.

Famularo, R., Kinscherff, R. & Fenton, T. (1992). Parental substance abuse and the nature of child maltreatment. *Child Abuse & Neglect*, 16, 475–483.

Fellitti, V.J., Anda, R.F., Nordenberg, D. et al. (1998). Relationship of childhood abuse and household dysfunction to many of the leading causes of death in adults: The Adverse Childhood Experiences (ACE) Study. *American Journal of Preventative Medicine*, 14, 245–258.

Forrester, D. (2000). Parental substance misuse and child protection in a British sample: A survey of children on the Child Protection Register in an inner London district office. *Child Abuse Review*, 9, 235–246.

Forrester, D. & Harwin, J. (2006). Parental substance misuse and child care social work: Findings from the first stage of a study of 100 families. *Child and Family Social Work*, 11, 325–335.

Fuller, T.L. & Wells, S.J. (2003). Predicting maltreatment recurrence among CPS cases with alcohol and other drug involvement. *Children and Youth Services Review*, 25, 553–569.

Fuller, T.L., Wells, S.J. & Cotton, E.E. (2001). Predictors of maltreatment recurrence at two milestones in the life of a case. *Children and Youth Services Review*, 23, 49–78.

Gardner, S. (2014). State-level policy advocacy for children affected by parental substance use. *Children and Family Futures*, www.childwelfaresparc.org on 22 November 2014.

Gavin, D.R., Ross, H.E. & Skinner, H.A. (1989). Diagnostic validity of the Drug Abuse Screening Test in the assessment of DSM-III drug disorders. *British Journal of Addiction*, 84, 301–307.

Gifford, E.J., Eldred, L.M., Vernerey, A. & Sloan, F.A. (2014). How does family drug treatment court participation affect child welfare outcomes? *Child Abuse & Neglect*, 38, 1659–1670.

Gill, A.M., Hyde, L.W., Shaw, D.S. et al. (2008). The Family Check-Up in early childhood: A case study of intervention process and change. *Journal of Clinical Child and Adolescent Psychology*, 37, 893–904.

Gladstone, J., Dumbrill, G., Leslie, B. et al. (2012). Looking at engagement and outcome from the perspectives of child protection workers and parents. *Children and Youth Services Review*, 34, 112–118.

Goodman, G., Hans, S.L. & Cox, S.M. (1999). Attachment behavior and its antecedents in offspring born to methadone-maintained women. *Journal of Clinical Child Psychology*, 28, 58–69.

Grant, T., Huggins, J., Graham, C. et al. (2011). Maternal substance abuse and disrupted parenting: Distinguishing mothers who keep their children from those who do not. *Children and Youth Services Review*, 33, 2176–2185.

Green, B.L., Rockhill, A. & Burrus, S. (2008). The role of interagency collaboration for substance-abusing families involved with child welfare. *Child Welfare*, 87, 29–61.

Green, B.L., Rockhill, A. & Furrer, C. (2006). Understanding patterns of substance abuse treatment for women involved with child welfare: The influence of the Adoption and Safe Families Act (ASFA). *American Journal of Drug and Alcohol Abuse*, 32, 149–176.

Green, B.L., Rockhill, A. & Furrer, C. (2007). Does substance abuse treatment make a difference for child welfare case outcomes? A statewide longitudinal analysis. *Children and Youth Services Review*, 29, 460–473.

Gregoire, T.K. (1994). Assessing the benefits and increasing the utility of addiction training for public child welfare workers: A pilot study. *Child Welfare*, 73, 69–81.

Grella, C.E., Needell, B., Shi, Y. & Hser, Y.I. (2009). Do drug treatment services predict reunification outcomes of mothers and their children in child welfare? *Journal of Substance Abuse Treatment*, 36, 278–293.

Harwin, J., Alrouh, B., Ryan, M. & Tunnard, J. (2013). Strengthening prospects for safe and lasting family reunification: Can a Family Drug and Alcohol Court make a contribution? *Journal of Social Welfare & Family Law*, 35, 459–474.

He, A.S., Traube, D.E. & Young, N.K. (2014). Perceptions of parental substance use disorders in cross-system collaboration among child welfare, alcohol and other drugs, and dependency court organizations. *Child Abuse & Neglect*, 38, 939–951.

Hoffmann, N.G. (1999). *UNCOPE*. Smithfield, RI: Hoffmann.

Hong, J.S., Ryan, J.P., Hernandez, P.M. & Brown, S. (2014). Termination of parental rights for parents with substance use disorder: For whom and then what? *Social Work in Public Health*, 29, 503–517.

Howell, M.L. (2008). Decisions with good intentions: Substance use allegations and child protective services screening decisions. *Journal of Public Child Welfare*, 2, 293–316.

Huebner, R.A., Willauer, T. & Posze, L. (2012). The impact of Sobriety Treatment and Recovery Teams (START) on family outcomes. *Families in Society*, 93, 196–203.

Kemp, S.P., Marcenko, M.O., Lyons, S.J. & Kruzich, J.M. (2014). Strength-based practice and parental engagement in child welfare services: An empirical examination. *Children and Youth Services Review*, 47, 27–35.

Kerwin, M.L.E. (2005). Collaboration between child welfare and substance-abuse fields: Combined treatment programs for mothers. *Journal of Pediatric Psychiatry*, 30, 581–597.

Klee, H. (1998). Drug-using parents: Analyzing the stereotypes. *International Journal of Drug Policy*, 9, 437–448.

Laslett, A.M., Room, R., Dietze, P. & Ferris, J. (2012). Alcohol's involvement in recurrent child abuse and neglect cases. *Addiction*, 107, 1786–1793.

Lee, E., Esaki, N. & Greene, R. (2009). Collocation: Integration child welfare and substance abuse services. *Journal of Social Work Practice in the Addictions*, 9, 55–70.

Lloyd, M.H. & Akin, B.A. (2014). The disparate impact of alcohol, methamphetamine, and other drugs on family reunification. *Children and Youth Services Review*, 44, 72–81.

Magura, S. & Laudet, A.B. (1996). Parental substance abuse and child maltreatment: Review and implications for intervention. *Children and Youth Services Review*, 18, 193–220.

Marsh, J.C. & Smith, B.D. (2011). Integrated substance abuse and child welfare services for women: A progress review. *Child and Youth Service Review*, 33, 466–472.

Marshall, J.M., Huang, H. & Ryan, J.P. (2011). Intergenerational families in child welfare: Assessing needs and estimating permanency. *Children and Youth Services Review*, 33, 1024–1030.

McAlpine, C., Marshall, C. & Doran, N.H. (2001). Combining child welfare and substance abuse services: A blended model of intervention. *Child Welfare*, 80, 129–149.

McCloskey, L.A. & Bailey, J.A. (2000). The intergenerational transmission of risk for child sexual abuse. *Journal of Interpersonal Violence*, 15, 1019–1035.

McLellan, A.T., Luborsky, L., O'Brien, C.P. & Woody, G.E. (1980). An improved instrument for substance abuse patients: The Addiction Severity Index. *Journal of Nervous & Mental Diseases*, 168, 26–33.

McLellan, A.T., Kushner, H., Metzger, D. et al. (1992). The fifth edition of the Addiction Severity Index. *Journal of Substance Abuse Treatment*, 9, 199–213.

Meier, P.S., Donmall, M.C. & McElduff, P. (2004). Characteristics of drug users who do or do not have care of their children. *Addiction*, 99, 955–961.

Meyer, A.S., McWey, L.M., McKendrick, W. & Henderson, T.L. (2010). Substance using parents, foster care, and termination of parental rights: The importance of risk factors for legal outcomes. *Children and Youth Services Review*, 32, 639–649.

Miller, G.A. (1985, 1999). *The Substance Abuse Subtle Screening Inventory (SASSI) manual*, 2nd edn. Springville, IN: The SASSI Institute.

Miller, K.A., Fisher, P.A., Fetrow, B. & Jordan, K. (2006). Trouble on the journey home: Reunification failures in foster care. *Children and Youth Services Review*, 28, 260–274.

Miller, W.R. & Rollnick, S. (2002). *Motivational Interviewing: Preparing People for Change*. New York: Guilford Press.

Mirick, R.G. (2014). Engagement in child protective services: The role of substance abuse, intimate partner violence and race. *Child and Adolescents: Social Work Journal*, 31, 267–279. Motivational Interviewing (n.d.), www.motivationalinterviewing.org/sites/default/files/glossary_of_mi_terms-1.pdf.

Mullins, S.M., Suarez, M., Ondersma, S.J. & Page, M.C. (2004). The impact of motivational interviewing on substance abuse treatment retention: A randomized control trial of women involved with child welfare. *Journal of Substance Abuse Treatment*, 27, 51–58.

Murphy, J.M., Jellinek, M., Quinn, D. et al. (1991). Substance abuse and serious child maltreatment: Prevalence, risk, and outcome in a court sample. *Child Abuse & Neglect*, 15, 197–211.

National Center on Addiction and Substance Abuse (CASA). (2005) *Family matters: Substance abuse and the American family*. New York: CASA.

Osterling, K.L. & Austin, M.J. (2008). Substance abuse interventions for parents involved in the child welfare system. *Journal of Evidence-Based Social Work*, 5(1–2), 157–189.

Rapp, L.A., Dulmas, C.N., Wodarski, J.S. & Feit, M.D. (1999). Screening of substance abuse in public welfare and child protective service clients. *Journal of Addictive Diseases*, 18, 83–88.

Rapp, R.C., Otto, A.L., Lane, D.T. et al. (2008). Improving linkage with substance abuse treatment using brief case management and motivational interviewing. *Drug and Alcohol Dependence*, 94, 172–182.

Robertson, A.S. & Haight, W. (2012). Engaging child welfare-involved families impacted by substance misuse: Scottish policies and practices. *Children and Youth Services Review*, 34, 1992–2001.

Rockhill, A., Green, B.L. & Furrer, C. (2007). Is the Adoption and Safe Families Act influencing child welfare outcomes for families with substance abuse issues. *Child Maltreatment*, 12, 7–19.

Rockhill, A., Green, B.L. & Newton-Curtis, L. (2008). Accessing substance abuse treatment: Issues for parents involved with child welfare services. *Child Welfare*, 87, 63–93.

Rodning, C., Beckwith, L. & Howard, J. (1991). Quality of attachment and home environments in children prenatally exposed to PCP and cocaine. *Development and Psychopathology*, 3, 351–366.

Russell, M. (1994). New assessment tools for drinking in pregnancy: T-ACE, TWEAK, and others. *Alcohol and Health Research World*, 18, 55–61.

Ryan, J.P., Marsh, J.C., Testa, M.F. & Louderman, R. (2006). Integrating substance abuse treatment and child welfare services: Findings from the Illinois alcohol and other drug abuse waiver demonstration. *Social Work Research*, 30, 95–107.

Ryan, J.P., Choi, S., Hong, J.S. et al. (2008). Recovery coaches and substance exposed births: An experiment in child welfare. *Child Abuse & Neglect*, 32, 1072–1079.

Schreiber, J.C., Fuller, T. & Paceley, M.S. (2013). Engagement in child protective services: Parent perception of worker skills. *Children and Youth Services Review*, 35, 707–715.

Schroeder, J., Lemieux, C. & Pogue, R. (2008). The collision of the Adoption and Safe Families Act and substance abuse: Research-based education and training priorities for child welfare professionals. *Journal of Teaching in Social Work*, 28, 227–246.

Selzer, M.L. (1971). The Michigan Alcoholism Screening Test (MAST): The quest for a new diagnostic instrument. *American Journal of Psychiatry*, 127, 1653–1658.

Sheldon-Sherman, J., Wilson, D. & Smith, S. (2013). Extent and nature of child maltreatment- related fatalities: Implications for policy and practice. *Child Welfare*, 92, 41–58.

Sheridan, M.J. (1995). A proposed intergenerational model of substance abuse, family functioning, and abuse/neglect. *Child Abuse & Neglect*, 5, 519–530.

Smith, B.D. & Mogro-Wilson, C. (2007). Multi-level influences on the practice of inter-agency collaboration in child welfare and substance abuse treatment. *Children and Youth Services Review*, 29, 545–556.

Staton-Tindall, M., Sprang, G. & Clark, J. (2012). Caregiver drug use and arrest as correlates of child trauma exposure. *Journal of Evidence-Based Social Work*, 9, 265–282.

Stewart, D., Gossop, M. & Trakada, K. (2007). Drug dependent parents: Childcare responsibilities, involvement with treatment services, and treatment outcomes. *Addictive Behaviors*, 32, 1657–1668.

Street, K., Whitlingum, G., Gibson, P. et al. (2008). Is adequate parenting compatible with maternal drug use? A 5-year follow-up. *Child: Care, Health & Development*, 34, 204–206.

Stromwall, L.K., Larson, N.C., Nieri, T. et al. (2008). Parents with co-occurring mental health and substance abuse conditions involved in child protective services: Clinical profile and treatment needs. *Child Welfare*, 87, 95–113.

Substance Abuse and Mental Health Services Administration (2010). *Results from the 2009 National Survey on Drug Use and Health: Volume I. Summary of National Findings (Office of Applied Studies, NSDUH Series H-38A, HHS Publication No. SMA 10–4856Findings)*. Rockville, MD.

Substance Abuse and Mental Health Services Administration (2014). *Results from the 2013 National Survey on Drug Use and Health: Summary of National Findings (NSDUH Series H-48, HHS Publication No. (SMA) 14-4863)*. Rockville, MD: Substance Abuse and Mental Health Services Administration.

Sun, A. (2000). Helping substance-abusing mothers in the child-welfare system: Turning crisis into opportunity. *Families in Society: The Journal of Contemporary Human Services*, 81, 142–151.

Tarter, R. & Karisci, L. (1997). The Drug Use Screening Inventory for Adults: Psychometric structure and discriminative sensitivity. *American Journal of Drug and Alcohol Abuse*, 23, 207–219.

Taylor, A. & Kroll, B. (2004). Working with parental substance misuse: Dilemmas for practice. *British Journal of Social Work*, 34, 1115–1132.

Taylor, A., Toner, P., Templeton, L. & Velleman, R. (2008). Parental alcohol misuse in complex families: The implications for engagement. *British Journal of Social Work*, 38, 843–864.

Testa, M.F. & Smith, B. (2009). Prevention and drug treatment. *The Future of Children*, 19(2), 147–167.

Title 42 The Public Health and Welfare of 1994, P.L. 102–321, §290dd-2. (1992).

Tracy, E.M. (1994). Maternal substance abuse: Protecting the child, preserving the family. *Social Work*, 39, 534–540.

Tracy, E.M. & Farkas, K.J. (1994). Preparing practitioners for child welfare practice with substance-abusing families. *Child Welfare*, 73, 57–68.

Twomey, J.E., Miller-Loncar, C., Hinckley, M. & Lester, B.M. (2010). After family treatment drug court: Maternal, infant, and permanency outcomes. *Child Welfare*, 89, 23–41.

US Department of Health and Human Services (1999). *Blending perspectives and building common ground. A report to Congress on substance abuse and child protection*. Washington, DC: US Government Printing Office.

US Department of Health and Human Services (2008). *Alcohol Alert*. National Institute on Alcohol Abuse and Alcoholism, http://pubs.niaaa.nih.gov/publications/AA76/AA76.htm.

US Department of Health and Human Services (2012). *Principles of Drug Addiction Treatment: A research-based guide*, 3rd edn. National Institute on Drug Abuse, www.drugabuse.gov/sites/default/files/podat_1.pdf.

US Department of Health and Human Services, Substance Abuse and Mental Health Services Administration (2013). *Seeking Safety*. National Registry of Evidence-based Programs and Practices, www.nrepp.samhsa.gov/ViewIntervention.aspx?id=139.

Walsh, C., MacMillan, H.L. & Jamieson, E. (2003). The relationship between parental substance abuse and child maltreatment: Findings from the Ontario Health Supplement. *Child Abuse & Neglect*, 27, 1409–1425.

Widom, C.S., White, H. R, Czaja, S.J. & Marmorstein, N.R. (2007). Long-term effects of child abuse and neglect on alcohol use and excessive drinking in middle adulthood. *Journal of Studies on Alcohol and Drugs*, 68, 317–326.

Wolock, I. & Magura, S. (1996). Parental substance abuse as a predictor of child maltreatment re-reports. *Child Abuse & Neglect*, 20, 1183–1193.

Young, N.K. & Gardner, S.L. (2002). *Navigating the pathways: lessons and promising practices in linking alcohol and drug services with child welfare*, 2002. SAMHSA Publication No. SMA 02-3752. Rockville, MD: Center for Substance Abuse Treatment, Substance Abuse and Mental Health Services Administration.

Young, N.K., Boles, S.M. & Otero, C. (2007). Parental substance use disorders and child maltreatment: Overlap, gaps, and opportunities. *Child Maltreatment*, 12, 137–149.

Young, N.K., Nakashian, M., Yeh, S. & Amatetti, S. (2006). *Screening and Assessment for Family Engagement, Retention, and Recovery (SAFERR)*. DHHS Pub. No. 0000. Rockville, MD: Substance Abuse and Mental Health Services Administration.

Index

Page references in *italics* refer to Figures, those in **bold** refer to Tables

4 Ps Plus, **475**

Re A [2015], 160
abandonment, 51, 65, 76, 388, 389
 case study, 395, 397
abdication, parental, 228–229
abuse *see* child maltreatment
abusive imagery, 176, 180
access of perpetrator to child, 29, 139, 181, 183–184
 CSEM, 260, 264, 270, 271
accidental death, **53**, 54–55
adaptation, 354–355, 427
 case study, 393–398
 DMM, 385–387, *387*, 388–390, **390**, 398–400
 DMM Integrative Treatment, 391–393
 non-offending parents, 415, 422, 424–426, **428**
 parenting programmes, 354–355, 358, 359, 361
Addiction Severity Index (ASI), **474**
adherence, 352–353, 354–356, 358–360, 361–362
adolescence, 20, 24, 54, 99, 300, 316, 420
 attachment, 224, 230, **232**, 389
 brain development, 4, 36, 87, 89
 homicide, **19**, 19–20, 48–49
 memory, 240
 negative outcomes of abuse, 4, 9, 29, 42
 parental substance abuse, 467
 parenting programmes, 164, 172, 333, 334, 356–357
 risk factors, 24, 36, 39
 risk-taking behaviour, 4, 36, 55–56
 school-based interventions, **373–374**, 376–377, 380
 sexual exploitation, 178–180, 182, 187, 189
adoption, 119, 142, 150, 171, 291, 446
 babies of single mothers, 132
 looked-after children, 116–117, 470–471
Adoption and Children Act (2002), 116
adoption orders, 116–117
Adoption and Safe Families Act (1997)(USA), 470–471
Adult Attachment Interview (AAI), 389, **390**, 395–396
ADVANCE parenting programme, 342, 344
Adverse Childhood Experiences (ACEs), 77, 313
advocacy, 440–441, 443
affective disorders, 85
African Charter on the Rights and Welfare of the Child (1999), 188
age, 35, 73, 99, 303, 329
 alcohol, 466
 attachment assessment, 386, 389, **390**, 391

The Wiley Handbook of What Works in Child Maltreatment: An Evidence-Based Approach to Assessment and Intervention in Child Protection, First Edition. Edited by Louise Dixon, Daniel F. Perkins, Catherine Hamilton-Giachritsis, and Leam A. Craig.
© 2017 John Wiley & Sons Ltd. Published 2017 by John Wiley & Sons Ltd.

age (cont'd)
  CSEM, 259
  fatal child maltreatment, 31, 34, 48–49, **50**, 53, 55–56, **56**
  forensic interviewing, 7, 240–249, 252
  homicide, **19**, 19–20, 48–49, 51
  Incredible Years, 342–343
  language, 7, 242–243, 246
  memory, 7, 240–242, 252
  parenting programmes, 329–335, **337–341**, 345–346, 351
  personality disorder, 453
  previous abuse, 18, 19–21, **22–23**, 24–25
  removal of children, 141
  school-based interventions, 372, **373–374**
  sexual abuse, **23**, 24, 35, 419
  therapy for sexual abuse, 314, 315, 317, 320
Aid to Families with Dependent Children, **58**
alcohol, 11, 55, 77, 454, 466, 468–469, 472–473
  assessments in child care proceedings, 284, 290
  CSEM, 269, **269**
  fatal child maltreatment, **50**, 59, *59*, **60**, 61
  IPV, 406–407
  neglect, 329
  removal of children, 139, 140
  SAAF, *214*, *215*
  screening, 472–473, **474–475**, **477–478**
Alcohol Use Disorders Identification Tool (AUDIT), 472, **474**
alternative care, 157–158, 160
Alternatives for Families: A Cognitive Behavioural Therapy (AF-CBT), 298, 300–301
altruistic filicide, 49, 51, 61
ambivalent-resistant attachment, 228, **232**
amygdala, 86–87, 88, 90, *91*, 298
anamnestic risk assessment, 285–286
anger, 441, 457
  attachment, 223, 227, 228, 229, 231
  non-offending parents, 416, 420, 423–424, **428**
  parenting programmes, 164–165, 167, **168**, 354
anger management, 169, 308, 330, 336
Anna Freud Centre Parent Infant Project (PIP), **338**
anterior cingulate cortex (ACC), 88, 90
anterior insula, 90
anterior temporal lobe, 88
anti-social behaviour, 75, 92, 103
anti-sociality, 260, 264, 268, 273

anti-social personality disorder (APD), 453, 454
anxiety disorders, *60*, 208, 409, 419, 456
  attachment, 227, 228
  brain development, 90
  consequence of emotional abuse, 73, 329
  consequence of maltreatment, 72, 85, 87, 298
  consequence of neglect, 74
  consequence of sexual abuse, 72–73, 420
  interventions, 315, 319
  parental substance abuse, 75
assaults on child protection staff, 143–155
Assessment Framework, 7, 284–285, **285**, 286–287, **290**
  child care proceedings, 282, 284–287
  SAAF, 202, 204, *205*, 205–206, 209, 219
Assessment Service (AS), 447
Association of Directors of Children's Services (ADCS), 122
attachment, 16, 30–33, 224–225
  across the lifespan, 389–390
  assessment in child care proceedings, 9–10, 385–400
  bases, 386
  case study, 393–398
  component in evaluating parenting, 231, **232–233**
  CPP, 314
  definition, 222–224
  dimensional model, 388–389
  DMM, 385–387, *387*, 388–390, **390**, 399–400
  DMM Integrative treatment, 391–393
  IASA court protocol, 390–391
  Incredible Years, 342
  individual differences, 386–388
  IPV, 407–408, 409
  non-offending parents, 420, 425, 426–427
  parental substance abuse, 467
  parenting assessment, 7, 222–234
  parenting programmes, 332, 334, 342, 350, 354
  parents with IDD, 445
  patterns of caregiving, 225–231
  personality disorder, 454, 455, 457, 461
  strategic behaviour, 388
  TF-CBT, 316, 318
attachment behavioural system, 223
attention deficit hyperactivity disorder (ADHD), 354
Attentive Parenting Programme, 342–343
Audio CASI, 18

autism, 57, 354
avoidant attachment, 227–228, 229, **232**

Re B [2013], 116, 119
babysitters, 53
Baltimore City Public Schools, 376, 380
Barnardo's, 179
behavioural parenting programmes, 5–6, 163–172
    assessments, **232**, 234
    group-based, 335–336, 344, 350
behaviour as risk factor, 36, **50**, 56–57, 79
Better Start, 331
birthing difficulties, 35
Blueprints for Healthy Youth Development, 336, 361
Body Safety Training Program, 372
borderline personality disorder (BPD), 453, 455–457, 459, 461
Borders, Citizenship and Immigration Act (2009), 118
Boy Scouts of America (BSA), 183–184
Bradford Trident, 331
brain development, 85–93, 164, 386
    activation, *91*
    adolescence, 4, 36, 87, 89
    consequences of maltreatment, 85–93, 120, 298, 310, 367
    functional differences after maltreatment, 89–93
    imaging, 85–86, **86**
    memory, 240–241
    structural differences after maltreatment, 85–93
    TF-CBT, 316, 318
Re B-S [2013], 116, 119, 160
bullying, 31, **37**, 180, 306, 360, 443
    adolescent suicide, 55
    case study, 394–395
    prevalence and incidence, 17, 25

Re CA [2012], 157
CAGE, **474**
CAGEAID, **474**
California Evidence-Based Clearinghouse for Child Welfare (CEBC), 313–315, 476, **477**
Care Act (2014), 437, 442
caregivers *see* parenting
care orders, 116
Care Placement Evaluation (CaPE), 332
care plans, 203, 209
Care and Support (Eligibility Criteria) Regulations (2014), 437

case management, 418–419, 476, 479
'cause no further harm', 142
Celebrating Families, 484
Centres for Disease Control and Prevention (CDC), 176, 183, 189–190
    National Intimate Partner and Sexual Violence Survey, 97
child abduction, 54
child abuse *see* child maltreatment; child physical abuse (CPA); child sexual abuse (CSA)
Child Abuse Prevention and Treatment Act (CAPTA) (1974), 483
Child and Adolescent Mental Health Services (CAMHS), 335, 458, 460–461
Child and Adolescent Welfare Assessment Checklist, 280–281
Child Advocacy Centers (CACs), 10, 418–419, 424, **428**
child advocacy programmes, 418–419
Child Behaviour Checklist, 333
child care proceedings, 5–6, 10–11, 150
    assessment, 7–8, 278–292
    assessment of attachment, 9–10, 385–400
    Family Court protocol, 390–391
    framework, 284–285, **285**, 286–287, **290**
    legislation, 150–151, 159–160, 279
    parents with IDD, 10, 433–448
    use of pre-proceedings, 10, 151–152, 153–160
child characteristics, 55, **56**, 56–57, **58**, 59
    ecological model, 32, *33*
child custody evaluation cases, 258–273
child deaths in England, **114**
    non-accidental, 19
    see also fatal child maltreatment
child demographics in the UK, **114**, 114–115
child-directed interaction (CDI), 299, 301
Child and Family Training UK, 125
ChildLine, 18
child maltreatment, 2, 6, 8–10, 15–25
    aetiology, 4, 29–42
    approaches to prevention, 41–42
    attachment, 224, 231, 385–400
    behavioural parenting interventions, 5–6, 163–172
    brain development, 85–86, 120, 298, 310, 367
    cases known to services, **19**, 19–21
    child care proceedings, 150, 287, 288, 290–292
    Children's Services, 113
    chronic, 138, 139
    community surveys, 21, **22–23**, 24–25

child maltreatment (*cont'd*)
  consequences, 4, 71–80, 87, 91, 92
  co-occurrence with IPV, 2, 5, 97, 98–101, 103–106, 405, 412
  cost, 42, 122, 330
  definitions, 71, **72**
  detection and reporting, 375–376
  developmental theories, 30–32
  DMM, 385–386
  EBTs, 297–310
  emotional health consequences, 76
  family preservation, 133, 134
  forensic interviewing, 239, 242–243, 245–246, 248, 250–252
  legislation, 117
  long-term care and aftercare, 378–379
  mandated reporting, 9, 367–368, 370, 375–376, 380
  multi-factor model, 32, *33*, 34–35, *35*
  parental substance abuse, 467, 468–469, 472–473, 480, 485
  parenting programmes, 164–165, 167, 169, 328–331, 344, 350, 354, 362
  parents with IDD, 434, 435
  personality disorder, 454, 456
  physical health consequences, 77
  prevalence and incidence, 3–4, 15–25
  psychological health consequences, 71–76, 85, 87, 298
  reasons for non-disclosure, 16–17
  related deaths, **53**, 54–55
  removal of children, 136, 138–141
  risk and protection factors, 35–36, **37–38**, 38–41, 328–346
  SAAF, 201–220
  school-based interventions, 367–372, **373–374**, 375–381
  severity, 139
  single-factor approaches, 29–30
  treatment of survivors, 376–378
  Triple P, 165–167, *166*, **168**, 169, 170
  see also fatal child maltreatment
Child-Parent Center (CPC) Program, **373**
Child-Parent Psychotherapy (CPP), 8, 314
child physical abuse (CPA), 8, 121, 124, 297–310, 423, 424
  consequences, 4, 72, 76, 77, 297–298
  child protection plans, 115, **116**
  co-occurrence with IPV, 5, 97, 98–101, 103–106, 405, 412
  CPC-CBT, 301–310
  definition, 72
  forensic interviewing, 246
  parental substance abuse, 467
  parenting programmes, 329–330, 334, 345
  prevalence and incidence, 97, 297
  school-based interventions, 367, 369, 371–372, 375, 377
child pornography, **72**, 188
child protection agencies, 15–17, 20–21, 25
child protection plans (CPPs), 2, 31, 78, 115, **116**, 121
  fatal maltreatment, **56**, 56–57
  neglect, 115, **116**, 328
  numbers, 2, **114**, 115, **116**, 121
  parents with IDD, 436-438, 441, 443, 447
  pre-proceedings, 153, 159–160
Child Protection Register, 328
Child Protection Services (CPS), **58**, 75, 76, 78, 419
  CPC-CBT, 303–304, 306
  MST-CAN, 300
  parental substance abuse, 471
  parents with IDD, 437–438, 441, 443, 447
  SAAF, 201–202
Children Act (1989), 115–117, 120, 150–151, 201, 279, 437
Children Act (2004), 117–118, 120, 151
Children and Families Act (2014), 118, 119, 151, 159–160, 279
Children and Family Court Advisory and Support Services (CAFCASS), 2, 150, 153, 280
Children and Family Court Advisory and Support Services (CAFCASS) Cymru, 280–281
Children (Northern Ireland) Order (1995), 151
Children's Centres, 124, 154, 335, 350
  funding, 122
Children's Commissioner in England, 118, 119, 121
Children's Services, 5, 113–126, 131–145
  Assessment Service, 447
  child protection plans, 115, **116**
  demographics, **114**, 114–115
  family preservation, 133–136
  partnerships with parents, 142–145
  public health approach, *123*, 123–125
  removal of children, 136–142
Children Youth and Families Act (Victoria) (2005), 136, 141
child sexual abuse (CSA), 121, 176–190
  adolescent suicide, 55
  age, **23**, 24, 35, 419

by school personnel, 368
case study, 395
consequences, 4, 72–73, 76, 77, 177, 419–420
CPC-CBT, 303
custody evaluation cases, 7–8, 258–273
definition, 16, **72**
delay of disclosure, 416, **428**
effective therapies, 8, 313–325
exploitation, 176–179, 181–190
fatal, 56
forensic interviewing, 239, 246, 248, 249, 416, 418
gender, 21, 24, 35, 73, 176, 181, 416
homicide, **52**, 54
Internet and online, 36, **37–38**, 40
IPV, 405
non-offending parents, 10, 415–427, **428**
parental substance abuse, 467
prevalence and incidence, 17–18, 20–21, **22–23**, 24–25
protection plans, 115, **116**
removal of children, 138, 139–140
re-victimisation, 379
risk and protective factors, 35–36, **37–38**, 40, 56, 420, 425
school-based interventions, 367–369, 371–372, 375, 377, 379
TF-CBT, 316–325
YSOs, 183–185
Child Sexual Abuse Prevention Teacher Training Workshop, 371, **373**
child sexual exploitation material (CSEM), 7, 258–273
  case studies, 265–272
  re-offending, 260, 263–265, 273
child welfare order, 202
child welfare services, 121–122, 468–471, 485–486
  parental substance abuse, 466–473, 476, 479–485
  prevalence of reported cases, 16, 19–20
  referrals, 468–469
  training for staff, **480**, 480–482
Clearinghouse for Military Family Readiness, 476, **478**
Climbié, Victoria, 117, 120
cocaine, 469
Cochrane System, 1–2
cognitive appraisal, 34, *35*, 36
Cognitive Behavioural Intervention for Trauma in Schools, 377

cognitive behavioural therapy (CBT), 9, 315, 427
  EBTs, 298, 300–310
  parenting programmes, 169, 170, 335–336, 344, 350–351
Cognitive Behaviour Therapy, 125
cognitive functioning, 86–89, 90–91, 240–246
  interviewing strategies, 246–247
cognitive impairment *see* intellectual disability
cognitive therapy, 11, 459, 460
collaboration, 470, 473, 476, **477**, **479–480**, 480, 482–486
co-location of staff, 483, 486
Combined Parent-Child Cognitive Behavioural Therapy (CPC-CBT), 298, 301–303
  summary of components, 303–310
commercial sexual exploitation of children (CSEC), 176, 179–180, 182, 186–189
Commissioning Toolkit, 345
Common Assessment Framework, 442
communication, 457, 476, **480**, 482–483
  lessons learnt, 62, **63**, 64
  parents with IDD, 433, 436, 439, **440**, 442–445, 448
communities, 23, **38**, 39–40, 41–42
  interventions, 371–372, **373–374**, 375–376, 377–378, 380
  surveys, 3, 15, 18, 21, **22–23**, 24, 25
Communities That Care, 9, 330, 331
Community Youth Development Study, 330
comprehensive monitoring (CMT), 243
Computer Assisted Self Interviewing (CASI), 18
conduct disorder, 122, 343, 350, 351
confidentiality, 482–483
Confidentiality of Alcohol and Drug Abuse Parent Records (2015), 483
confirmation bias, 132
constricted caregiving, 230–231
contact sexual offences, 8, 258, 260, 262–264, 272–273
  case studies, 265–272
  prevalence and incidence, **23**, 24
controlling caregiving, 230–231
controlling-punitive attachment, 229, 230–231
controlling strategies, 229–230
COPINE Scale, 259
Coroners and Justice Act (2009), 259
corpus callosum (CC), 89, 298
cortical hypoactivation, 89
cortisol, 89
counter-transference, 413
court proceedings, 416–418, **428**

covert filicide, *50*, 51, 55
  risk factors, 56, 61, 62
Criando a Nuestros Ninos hacia el Exito (CANNE), **373**
Criminal Justice Act (1988), 259
crying, 54, 56–57, 64
culture, 5, 32, *33*, 61–62, 125, 369
  assessments, 279, 285, 288
  IPV, 407, 412
  parenting programmes, 354, 355, 361
  physical punishment, 16
  risk and protection factors, 40–41
  sexual abuse, 181–182, 186
cyberspace, 25, 177, 179, 180, 182, 190
  see also Internet and online abuse

Darkness to Light, 184
Daubert v Merrell Dow Pharmaceuticals (1993), 390
deafness, 36, 179
decision-making, 62, **63**, 64
declarative memory, 240
delay, 243–245
  disclosure, 416, **428**
  forensic interviewing, 241–242, 243–245, 246, 252
depression, 18, 92, 298, 315–316
  attachment, 223, 229
  consequence of emotional abuse, 329
  consequence of maltreatment, 85, 87, 91, 92
  consequence of neglect, 74, 75
  consequence of sexual abuse, 72–73, 313
  CSEM, 261, 263
  EBTs, 300, 303, 304
  IPV, 100, 102–103
  non-offending parents, 419, 420
  parental, 60, 61
  parenting programmes, 334, 344
  postnatal, 211, 218
  TF-CBT, 317, 319, 321
deprivational abuse, 51, **53**, 53, 56
  see also neglect
development of children, 15, 30–32, 215–217
  SAAF, 203–204, *205*, 205–209, *210–211*, 211–213, 216–218
  see also brain development
Dialectical Behaviour Therapy (DBT), 11, 459–460
differentiation, 352
Diffusion Tensor Imaging (DTI), **86**, 88–89

disability, 18, 115, 120, 164, 369
  attachment, **233**
  fatal child maltreatment, **50**, 55
  parental, 131, 136
  removal of children, 140–141
  risk factor, 35, 36, 57, 79
  SAAF, 204–205, 211
  sexual abuse, 179
discipline, 17, 24, 54, 165
  see also punishment
discouraging closeness, 227
dispositional representations (DRs), 386, 388, 399
distress, 416, 418–421, 423, 425, 427, 453
domestic violence, 2, 24, 97–106
  case study, 153, 156
  consequence of child maltreatment, 71, 75–78
  CPC-CBT, 303
  CPP, 314
  emotional abuse, 329
  fatal child maltreatment, **50**, 51, 59, *59*, **60**, 468
  gender, 24
  MARAC, 280
  overt filicide, **52**
  parenting programmes, 331, 334–335, 344, 358
  parents with IDD, 435, 445, 447
  personality disorder, 454, 456, 457
  SAAF, 206
  school-based interventions, 377
  witnessed by children, **23**, 24, 35, 75–78, 206, 281
  see also intimate partner violence (IPV)
Domestic Violence Toolkit, 280
drug abuse *see* substance abuse
Drug Abuse Screening Test (DAST), 472, **474**
Drug Use Screening Inventory Revised (DUSI-R), **474**
Dynamic-Maturational Model of Attachment (DMM), 9–10, 385–387, *387*, 388–390, **390**, 398–399
  case study, 393–398
  Integrative Treatment, 391–393
dysregulated caregiving and attachment, 224, 228–231, **232**, 234

Early Intervention Foundation, 336
Early Years Parenting Unit (EYPU), 11, 459
ecological model, 4, 32, *32*, 34, 42
  risk and protective factors, 35–36, **37–38**, 38–41
ecological theory of child maltreatment, 39–42

ecological-transactional model, 32, *33*, 34, 41
Economic and Social Research Council (ESRC), 151, 152
Education Act (2002), 118
educational attainment, 4, 76, 79, 343, 344
efficacy of interventions, 299, 314, 378, 391
　parental substance abuse, 468, 471
　parenting programmes, 344, 353, 354, 358, 362
　TF-CBT, 316, 317, 318, 321
emotional (psychological) abuse, 99, 115, **116**, 424
　case study, 396–397
　consequences, 73, 76, 77, 78, 329
　definition, **72**, 73, 329
　IPV, 405, 412
　parenting programmes, 328–330, 332, 345
　prevalence and incidence, 20–21, **22–23**, 24–25
　removal of children, 138
　school-based interventions, 367, 371–372, **373**, 375, 377
emotional dysregulation, 454, 456, 457, 459, 461
emotional impact of CSA, 420–421
emotional neglect, 71, **72**, 76
emotional regulation as protective factor, 36
emotion processing, 86–91
enduring protective factors, *33*, 34
engagement, 36, 426
　AF-CBT, 301
　CPC-CBT, 301, 304–305, 307
　FFT, 333
　parental substance abuse, 470, 476, 479, 481
　parenting programmes, 350, 352–353, 355, 357–358, 360
　parents with IDD, 436, 441, 446
　TF-CBT, 316, 317
Enhanced Outpatient Treatment (EOT), 300
Enough Abuse Campaign, 186
episodic memory, 240–241, 242, 244
Equality Act (2010), 437
ethnicity or race, 57, 61–62
European Convention on Human Rights (ECHR), 150
European Monitoring Centre for Drugs and Drug Addiction, 473, **478**
evaluation and decision in assessment, 289
Event Related Potential (ERP), **86**, 89–90
Every Child Matters, 117–118, 120, 124
Evidence2Success (E2S), 9, 330–331

evidence-based therapies (EBTs), 297–310
　case illustration, 303–310
evolutionary theory, 30, 31
exosystem, 32, *33*
expert witnesses, 283
exposure, 352–353, 356, 360–362
external triggers, 409
Eye Movement Desensitisation and Reprocessing for Children and Adolescents (EMDR), 8, 314, 315

Fabricated or Induced Illness (FII), 454
facilitation, 260, *261*, 262
failed protection attachment, 228–229
false memories, 245
Families and Schools Together (FAST), 334, 336, **340**
Family Check-Up, 482
family circumstances, **50**
Family Drug and Alcohol Court, 484
family drug courts, 484–485, 486
family and environmental factors, 61–62
　SAAF, 203–204, *205*, 205–206, 207–209, *210*, *214*, *215*, 217
Family Functional Formulation (FFF), 390, 391, 398
　case study, 394, 396
family justice, 119
Family Justice Review, 159
Family Links, 331, 351, 356–357
Family Links Nurturing Programme (FLNP), **340**, 356–357
Family Nurse Partnership, 350, 360
family preservation, 5, 132, 133–136
family support programmes, 2, 5, 20, 132–133
　fatal child maltreatment, 62, **63**, 64
Family Violence Surveys, 2, 98, 99, 102
Family Wellness, 371, 372, **373**
　Survival Skills for Healthy Families, 371, 372, **373**
fatal assaults, *50*, 51, **52**, 53–54
fatal child maltreatment, 4, 32, 48–65
　age, 31, 35, 48–49, **50**, 53, 55–56, **56**
　causes of death, 35, 51, **52–53**, 53–55
　classification, **52–53**
　covert filicide, *50*, 51, 55, 56, 61, 62
　learning from, 62, **63**, 64
　nature, 49, **50**, *50*, 51–55
　neglect, 19, 329
　overt filicide, *50*, 51, **52**
　parental substance abuse, 468

fatal child maltreatment (cont'd)
  prevalence and incidence, 2, 19, 48–49, 56, 121
  prevention, 64–65
  risk factors, 4, 39, 49, 55–57, **58**, *59*, 59, **60**, 61–62, 64–65
fathers, 30, 182, 350
  fatal child maltreatment, 51, 53, 62, **63**, 64
  non-offending parents, 420–422, **428**
  overt filicide, 51
female genital mutilation, 40, 120
fidelity, 9, 349, 351–354, 355–358
  adaptation, 354–355
  definition, 351–353
  MST, 333
  parenting programmes, 331, 333, 344–345, 350–362
financing, 121, 122–123
Findings from the Partner Abuse State of Knowledge Project, 405
First World Congress against Commercial Sexual Exploitation of Children, 188
'fixed thinking', **63**
flexibility of parenting programmes, 331, 353, 355, 358, 362
flexible caregiving, 225–226, 234
forensic interviewing, 7, 239–252
  cognitive competencies, 240–246
  sexual abuse, 239, 246, 248, 249, 416, 418
  training, 250–252
formulation model, *261*, 261–262
foster care, 76, 89, 119, 291, 317, 458
  attachment assessment, 394, 398
  case studies, 154, 394
  fatal child maltreatment, **58**
  Incredible Years, 343
  parental substance abuse, 469, 470–471, 484
  parenting programmes, 170, 171, 332, 343, 346
  pre-proceedings, 151, 154, 158, 160
Fostering Changes, **339**
Four Pre-Conditions of Abuse, 262
fractional anisotropy (FA), 88
Framework for Assessment *see* Assessment Framework
Freedom Programme, 446
free-recall narrative accounts, 247–248, 252
fronto-cingulate circuits, 91
fronto-limbic circuits, 89, 90–91
fronto-striatal pathways, 88
Functional Family Therapy (FFT), 332, 333

functional Magnetic Resonance Imaging (fMRI), **86**, 90, 90–92
functioning and intensions of parents, 139

gang violence, **52**, 54
gender, 20–21, **22–23**, 24–25, 35, 73
  adolescent suicide, 55
  CSA, 21, 24, 35, 73, 176, 181, 416
  fatal child maltreatment, 48, **50**, 53, 55–56, **56**
  homicides, 2, 19, 20, 48
  IPV, 98–100, 103, 105–106
  neonatal deaths, 56
  online abuse, 40
  overt filicide, 51
  personality disorder, 453
  sexual exploitation, 24, 180
genetics, 79, 85, 92, 163
genetic variants and adverse environments (GXE), 92
Girls Inc.Project BOLD, 373
Global Appraisal of Individual Need – Short Screener (GAIN-SS), **474**
government secrecy in Australia, 134–135
Green Dot etc., 372, **373**
grooming, 16, 180–182, 184, 188, 320
  CSEM, 263, 265, 267, 270, **271**, 272–273
  risk and protective factors, 36, **37–38**

Head Start, 369
Healthy Child Programme (HCP), 124
Healthy Start, 434, 438–439
heightened caregiving, 228
helpless parenting, 229, 230, **232**
heroin, 481
hierarchical violence, 99–100
hippocampus, 87, 88, 241, 298
home visiting, 125, 133, 134
homicide, **19**, 19–20, 48–49
  adolescence, **19**, 19–20, 48–49
  age, **19**, 19–20, 48–49, 51
  child victims, 2, **52**, 54, 61, 121, 297
  fatal child maltreatment, 48–49, *50*, 51
  gender, 2, 19, 20, 48
  infancy, 19–20, 48–49, 297
  overt filicide, 51
hypotheses in assessment, 287

ill-health as risk factor, 36
impairment of child's health and development, 203, 204, *205*, 205–206

implementation of intervention plan, 203, 215–217
impulsivity, 454, 455, 460
incest, **268**, **269**, 270
Incredible Years (IY), 331, 336, **339**, 342–344, 351, 377
  BASIC, 342, 343, 344
  fidelity, 356, 358, 359–360
  training, 359–360
indecent photographs, 259–260, **266**
infancy, 24, 35, 141,
  abandonment, 65
  attachment, 222, 224, 229–230, **232**, 386–388
  brain development, 90
  consequences of neglect, 74
  covert filicide, 51, **52**
  fatal child maltreatment, 49, **53**, 55–57, 61
  homicide, 19–20, 48–49, 297
  overt filicide, 51
  risk factor, 56–57, 61
Infant CARE-Index (ICI), **390**, 394
Infant-Child Psychotherapy (IPP), 314
inflexible caregiving, 226–228
information gathering, 287–288, **290**, 291
information testing, 288–289
informed consent, 158
insecure attachment, 31, 226–228, **232**
Institutes of Medicine (IOM) Protractor, 9, 368, *368*, 370–371, 380
institutional care, 87, 88, 89, 90
integrity of interventions, 349
intellectual developmental disability (IDD), 433–448
  definition, 433–434
  ongoing support, 438–439, **440**, 440–443, **447**, 444–446
intellectual disabilities (ID), 10, 433–448
  definition, 433–434
Intelligence Quotient (IQ), 433, 442
inter-agency co-operation, 62, **63**
intergenerational cycle of maltreatment (ICM), 30, 35, 38–39, 61
internal triggers, 409
International Association for the Scientific Study of Intellectual Disabilities (Special Interest Research Group on Parents and Parenting with Intellectual Disabilities) (IASSID SIRG), 435
International Association for the Study of Attachment (IASA), 9–10, 31, 390–398
  Family Attachment Report, 390–391

International Society for the Prevention of Child Abuse and Neglect (ISPCAN), 113
Internet-based interventions (IBIs), 182
Internet and online abuse, 31, 36, **37**–**38**, 40–42
  case studies, 265–272
  CSEM, 258–261, *261*, 262–273
  grooming, 36, **37–38**
  risk and protective factors, 36, **37–38**, 39–41
  sexual exploitation, 176–177, 180, 182, 184–185, 188
interpersonal difficulties, 454, 457
interpersonal variables, 35–36, **37**
Intervention Fidelity Assessment Checklist (IFAC), 357
intervention plan for SAAF, 203, 215–220
  outcome measurement, 217–219
intimate partner violence (IPV), 10, 25, 32, 97–106, 131, 405–414
  co-occurrence with child maltreatment, 2, 5, 97, 98–101, 103–106, 405, 412
  parental substance abuse, 102, 406–407, 470
  prevalence, 17, **23**, 97–98
  removal of children, 136, 139
  risk factors, 5, 39, 101–104
  witnessed by children, 99, 100–101, 104–106, 407, 411
  see also domestic violence
invisibility of children, 62, **63**

Re J [2015], 160
Re J (a child) [2013], 281
Jack, Judge Simon, 281

language, 242–243
  forensic interviewing, 15, 241–243, 246, 250, 252
Lanzarote Convention (2010), 188
latent vulnerability, 93
learning difficulties or disability, 154, 18, 204, 209
  definition, 434
  wife of man in CSEM case, **267**, 271
  see also intellectual developmental disability (IDD); intellectual disability (ID)
legal advice in pre-proceedings, 152, 154–160
legislation, 5, 6, 113, 126, 131, 259
  Australia, 136, 141, 145
  ban on chastisement, 124
  care proceedings, 150–151, 159–160, 279
  confidentiality, 483
  pre-proceedings, 159–160

legislation (cont'd)
  SAAF, 201–202
  sexual exploitation, 187–188
  substance use, 470–471
  UK, 117–120
  UNCRC, 117
letter before proceedings (LbP), 151, 154–155
Lloyd-Jones, Edward, 279
local authorities, 115, 118–119, 123, 458
  looked-after children, 20, 116, 119, 343
  MASH, 104–105
  parents with IDD, 437, 447
  pre-proceedings, 6, 150–160
Local Authority Social Services Act (1970), 119
Local Safeguarding Board Regulations (2006), 119
Local Safeguarding Children Boards (LSCBs), 118
lone parents, 38, **60**, 62, 114, **114**, 132
looked-after children (LACs), 20, 116–117, 119, 121, 343

Re M [2003], 282
macrosystem, 32, *33*
magnetic resonance imaging (MRI), 85
maltreatment research, 77–79
mandated reporting, 9, 367–368, 370, 375–376, 380
Maryland Scale of Scientific Methods, 2
masturbation, 261, 265, 267, **268**, **269**, 270, 270
Matching Needs and Services Audit (MNS), 447
Mellow Babies, 445
Mellow Bumps, 445
Mellow Futures, 445-446
Mellow Parenting, **338**, 351, 445
memory, 240–242
  brain development, 85, 86, 87
  forensic interviewing, 240–249, 250, 252
mental health, 18, 29, 92, 177, 280
  attachment, 223–225, 229–230, 234, 386, 393
  case study, 395
  consequence of child maltreatment, 18, 71–76, 79, 85, 89, 91–93, 330
  consequence of CPA, 297–298
  consequence of CSA, 177, 420
  covert filicide, 51, **52**, 53
  CPC-CBT, 302
  CSEM, 263, 264, 269, **269**
  EBTs, 300, 302
  fatal child maltreatment, 49, **50**, 59, *59*, **60**, 61, 468

  IPV, 102–103
  non-offending parents, 419–423, 425–426
  overt filicide, 51
  parental, 10–11, 61, 79, 131, 136, 154, 298, 329, 468
  parental and SAAF, 211, 213, 218
  parental substance abuse, 467, 470
  parenting programmes, 332, 335–336, 344–345, 351
  parents with IDD, 435, 442
  parents with personality disorder, 452–462
  risk factor, 18, 38–39, 79
  SAAF, 211, 213, *214*, *215*, 218
  screening, **474**
  TF-CBT, 317–318
mesosystem, 32, *33*
meta-analyses, 21, 72–74, 86–88, 422
  CSEM, 260, 265
  parenting programmes, 351, 360
  school-based interventions, 371–372
  sexual abuse, 176, 177
methadone, 481
Michigan Alcoholism Screening Test (MAST), **474**
microsystem, 32, *33*
Minnesota Multiphasic Personality Inventory, 260
mothers, 100, 419–422, **428**, 455–456
  covert filicide, 51, 53, 62
  fatal child maltreatment, 62, **63**, 64
  overt filicide, 51, 62
  postnatal depression, 211, 218
motivation, 49, **50**, 51, 265, 267, **268**
  CSEM, 260–261, *261*, 262, 265, 267, 278, **268**, 272
motivational interviewing, 476, 479, 482
Motivation-Facilitation Model (M-F Model), 260, *261*, 262
Multi Agency Risk Assessment Conference (MARAC), system, 280
Multi Agency Safeguarding Hubs (MASH), 104–105
Multidimensional Treatment Foster Care (MTFC), 123, 125, 332, 345
multi-factorial models, 32, *33*, 34–35, *35*
multisystemic therapy (MST), 300, 332, 333–334
Multisystemic Therapy for Child Abuse and Neglect (MST-CAN), 125, 298, 300
Multi-Treatment Foster Care (MTFC), 350, 356
Munby, Lord Justice James, 281
Munro Report of Child Protection (2011), 279

narcissistic personality disorder, 453, 461–462
National Adoption Leadership Board, 116
National Center for Missing and Exploited Children, 182
National Center on Substance Abuse and Child Welfare, 473, **477**
National Child Protection Authority (Sri Lanka), 189
National Coalition to Prevent Child Sexual Abuse and Exploitation, 189
National Institute of Alcohol Abuse and Alcoholism, 473, **477**
National Institute of Child Health and Human Development (NICHD), 246, 248, 251, 252
National Institute of Drug Abuse, 473, **477**
National Institute of Health, 473
National Institute of Mental Health (NIMH), 302
National Offender Management Service, 263
National Study of Child and Adolescent Well-Being, 102
National Survey on Drug Use and Health, 466
neglect, 3–4, 6, 113, 396–397, 424
   aetiology, 4, 29–42
   care proceedings, 150, 288, 292
   cases known to services, **19**, 19–21
   child protection plans, 115, **116**, 328
   community surveys, 21, **22–23**, 24–25
   consequences, 4, 71–80, 93, 120
   cost, 42, 122, 330
   definition, **72**, 328–329
   EBTs, 298, 300
   ecological perspectives, 29–42
   family preservation, 133, 134
   fatal child maltreatment, 49, 51, **52**, **53**, 53, 54–55
   forensic interviewing, 246
   IPV, 100, 405
   legislation, 117
   parental substance abuse, 467, 468, 472
   parenting programmes, 167, 328–330, 332, 334–335, 345
   parenting programmes and fidelity, 350, 354, 362
   parents with IDD, 434, 435
   personality disorder, 454
   pre-proceedings, 159
   prevalence and incidence, 15–25
   removal of children, 136, 138, 140–141
   risk and protective factors, 35-36, **37–38**, 38–41, 56, 62

SAAF, 202
school-based interventions, 367, 370, 375
sexual exploitation, 183
NESTA, 336
neurocognitive systems, 5, 93
neuroimaging, 4–5, 85, **86**, 86–89, 90–92, 93
New Beginnings, **337**
New South Wales Department of Family and Community Services, 135
non-offending parents, 10, 313–325
non-resident adults, 17, **23**
Northampton CC v S [2015], 158, 160
no-violence contract, 408
NSPCC, 121, 124, 329–330
nurse family partnerships, 125

Obama, President Barack, 189
Obscene Publication Act (1959), 259
Office for Standards in Education, Children's Services and Skill (Ofsted), 281
online abuse *see* Internet and online abuse
orbitofrontal cortex (OFC), 88
outcomes and measures of SAAF, 203, 217–219
out-of-control parenting, 229, 230
out-of-home care, 132, 134, 142, 170
   attachment, 393, 398
   parental substance abuse, 470–471, 472, 484
   pre-proceedings, 151
overt filicide, *50*, 51, **52**

parental change, 137–138
parental characteristics, *59*, 59, **60**, 61
parental cooperation, 140
parental education, 133
Parental Reaction to Abuse Disclosure Scale (PRADS), 423
Parent Assessment Manual, 442
parent-child interaction, 234, 298, 426
   attachment, 3, 223–231, **232**
   CPC-CBT, 298, 301–310
   Incredible Years, 342
   mental health, 211
   parenting programmes, 330, 332, 334, 357
   personality disorder, 455, 456–457
   pre-proceedings, 151
   Triple P, **168**, 169–170
Parent-Child Interaction, Therapy (PCIT), 125, 298, 299–300, 304

parent-directed interaction (PDI), 299, 301
parenting, 74–75, 78–80, 284, 328–346,
    349–362
  attachment, 7, 31, 222–231, **232–233**, 234
  behavioural intervention, 5–6, 163–172
  capacity, 6, 120, 137–138, 203–204, *205*,
    205–213, 441–442
  case studies, 265, **266–267**, 267, **268**,
    268–269, **269–270**, 270–271, **271**, 272
  children's ill health, 36, 57
  Children's Services, 132, 137–138, 140,
    142–145
  coercive, 167, 298, 301–303
  cost of programmes, 170–171, 331, 333–334,
    344–345
  EBTs, 298–307
  evidence-based programmes, 349-362
  group programmes, 9, 165–167, **168**, 169,
    328–336, **337–341**, 342–346
  IDD, 433–448
  interaction measures, 234
  investigative and legal context, 259–261,
    261, 262
  mental health, 10–11, 61, 79, 131, 136, 154,
    298, 329, 468
  non-offenders, 415–427, **428**
  personality disorders, 452–462
  pre-proceedings, 151, 153, 157, 159
  prevalence and incidence of maltreatment, 17,
    22–23, 24–25
  programmes, 6–10, 41, 124–125, 163–172,
    328–346, 349–362
  risk assessment, 7, 258–273
  sexual exploitation, 180–183
  substance abuse, 466–473, **474–475**, **477–478**,
    479, **480**, 480–486
  Sweden, 25, 124
  TF-CBT, 317–322
  Triple P, 124–125, 163, 165–167, *166*, **168**,
    169, 170
  variables, 37, 38–39
Parenting Our Children to Excellence (PACE),
  371, **373**, **374**
Parenting Programme Evaluation Tool (PPET),
  336, **337–341**
Parenting Scale, 167
Parent mentors, 483, 484
Parents Anonymous, 376
Parent's Attributions for Child's Behaviour
  Measure, 167
Parents Interview (PI), **390**, 390, 396

Parents Plus Early Years (PPEY), **339**
Parents Under Pressure, 125
parent traps, **168**, 169
partnerships with parents, 133, 142–145
Pathfinders Early Intervention Programme, 344
Pathways Triple P (PTP), 6, 167, **168**, 169, 170
patterns of harm and protection, 203, 206–207,
    207, 208–209
PEACE interviewing model, 251
peers, 31, 39–40, 90, 368
  homicide, 19–20, **52**, 54
  prevalence of abuse, 17, 19–20, **22–23**, 25
  risk and protective factors, 36, **37**, 39–40
Period of PURPLE Crying Program, 64
personality disorder, 10–11, 209, 452–462
  definitions, 452–454
  intergenerational transmission, 457–458
personal salience, 7, 243, 245
physical abuse *see* child physical abuse (CPA)
physical health of maltreated children, 71, 77, 79
physical neglect, **72**, 74
placement order, 116
planning in care proceedings assessment, 287
police, 15, 16, 19, 118, 145, 239
  care proceedings, 280, 281
  CSEM, 264, **266–268**
  homicide data, 49
  sexual abuse, 321–322, 324, 416–419, 425, **428**
poly-victimisation, 15, 24, 39
pornography, **266**, **268**, **269**, **270**, 270–271
  CSEM, 258–259, 264
Positive Parenting Programme *see* Triple P
post-traumatic stress disorder (PTSD), 30,
    91–92, 100, 297, 314–316, 413
  consequence of child maltreatment, 87, 91, 92
  CSA, 314–316, 420
  CPC-CBT, 298, 302–304
  EMDR, 315
  MST-CAN, 300
  parents of CSA victims, 420–421, 423–424
  PEA, 316
  TF-CBT, 317–319, 321, 325
potentiating factors, *33*, 34
poverty, **114**, 115, 164, 331, 369
  consequence of maltreatment, 76, 79
  CSA, 419, 424
  neglect, 74, 329
  parental substance abuse, 470
  parents with IDD, 435, 442, 443
  risk factors, 17, 25, 39, 79
  sexual exploitation, 189

PRACTICE, 318–320
pre-birth child protection, 153, 154, 157
prefrontal cortex (PFC), 87–88, 90, 241
pregnancy, 331–332, 336, **337–338**, 345, 350, 445
　IPV, 407–408
　parents with IDD, 443
　screening for substance abuse, **475**
pre-proceedings meeting (PPM), 152–158
pre-proceedings process, 6, 150–160
　cost, 151
Preschool Assessment of Attachment (PAA), **390**
prevalence of maltreatment, 15–25
prevention of maltreatment, 5–6, 41–42, 163–172
　Children's Services, 5, 113–126
　Fatal child maltreatment, 62, **63**, 64–65
　pre-proceedings, 150–160
　public health, 5–6, *123*, 123–125, 126, 163–172
　sexual exploitation, 6, 176–190
Prevention Project Dunkelfeld, 187
previous maltreatment, 34, 38, 93, 292, 442
　abusers, 29–30, 34, 38–39, 61, 136, 292, 306
　domestic violence, 2, 102
　evidence-based assessment, *210*, *211*, 213, *214*, *215*
　non-offending parents, 416, 423, 424, 427
　parental, 30, 35, 38–39
　removal of children, 139–140, 153, **443**, 446–447, **447**
　risk factor, 30, **53**, 54–57, **58**, 59, 62
　sexual exploitation, 177, 263–264
　suicide, 55
Primary Mental Health Project, 377
primary prevention, 41, *123*, 123
privacy, 279, 281, 285
procedural memory, 240
Prolonged Exposure for Adolescents (PE-A), 8, 314, 315–316
Promoting Alternative Thinking Strategies (PATHS), 377
proportionate universalism, 163, 166, 170
prostitution, 176, 182, 188
Protecting Children Is Everyone's Business, 189
Protecting Victoria's Vulnerable Children Inquiry, 133, 135
Protection of Children Act (1978), 259
protective attachment strategies, 388–389, **390**

protective factors, 4, 31, 35–36, **37–38**, 38–42, 291
　CSA, 420, 425
　IPV and child maltreatment, 5, 105
　multi-factor models, *33*, 34–35, *35*
　parenting programmes, 9, 329–330, 331, 334–335
　removal of children, 141
　SAAF, 207, 208
　sexual exploitation, 181, 183
Protocol to Prevent, Suppress, and Punish Trafficking in Persons, Especially Women and Children (2003), 188
pseudo-photographs, 259
psychoeducation, 301, 314, 315, 371, 461
　CPC-CBT, 304, 306, 307
　TF-CBT, 316, 318–32433
psychoeducational parenting intervention (PPI), 314
psychological consequences of maltreatment, 4, 71–76, 79, 100
psychometric assessment, 262, 263, **267**, 267, 442
psychopathology, 29–30, 35, 453, 456
　attachment, 229, 230, 386, *387*
　consequence of child maltreatment, 4–5, 89, 91–92, 93
public health, 2–6, 41, 170, 335, 345, 369
　CPA, 8, 297
　CSA, 177, 186
　family preservation, 133, 136
　fatal child maltreatment, 64–65
　IOM Protractor, 370–371, 380
　prevention of child maltreatment, 5–6, *123*, 123–125, 126, 163–172
Public Law Outline (PLO), 279, 283
punishment, 15–16, 72, 78, 118, 297, 301
　case study, 395–397
　CPC-CBT, 302, 304–307, 309
　see also discipline

quality in parenting programmes, 352, 353, 357, 358–361, 362
questioning, 248–249
　forensic interviewing, 240, 242–249, 252
　training, 250–252

R v Oliver [2003] 259
rapport, 246–247, 250
Reading Safer Families, 10, 405, 406
reciprocal violence, 99–100, 101

recovery coaches, 483–484, 486
religion, 51
removal of children, 5, 131–133, 136–142, 150, 155, 393
  parental substance abuse, 136, 139, 141–142, 468–471
  parents with IDD, 434–436, 439, 441, 446
  personality disorder, 458, 459
  SAAF, 202, 203
representational parenting, **232–233**, 234
re-referrals, 2, 20, 469
resilience model, 34–35, *35*
respite care, 151
Response to Intervention (RtI), 370
responsiveness, 352, 386–387, 392
re-victimisation, 379, 418
reward cues, 91
risk factors, 30, 35–36, **37–38**, 38–42, 61–62, 101–104
  assessments in care proceedings, 289–292
  attachment, 228, 234
  child characteristics, 55, **56**, 56–57, **58**, 59
  fatal child maltreatment, 4, 39, 49, 55–57, **58**, *59*, 59, **60**, 61–62, 64–65
  insecure attachment, 31
  IPV and CPA, 5, 101–106
  multi-factor models, 32, *33*, 34–35, *35*
  parental characteristics, *59*, 59, **60**, 61
  parental substance use, 39, 468, 472
  parenting programmes, 9, 329–329, 331, 334–335, 345
  personality disorder, 457
  removal of children, 141
  SAAF, 207, 208
  sexual exploitation, 181, 182–183, 185, 189–190
Risk Inventory for Substance-Affected Families, **475**
'rule of optimism', **63**, 131, 140

SafeCare, 298–299
Safe Child Program, 371, 372, **374**
Safeguarding Children Assessment and Analysis Framework (SAAF), 7, 201–220
  example rating scale table, *214–215*
  Framework for Assessment, *205*
  linear and circular processes, *207*
  seven stage model, 203–219
  severity of impairment of child's health, *210*, *211*
  systemic analysis of identified factors, *212*

Safeguarding Vulnerable Groups Act (2006), 183
Safeguarding Vulnerable Groups Order (Northern Ireland)(2007), 183
'safe haven' laws, 65
Safer Internet Centre, 182
safety plans, 405–407, 408–412
  contraindications, 406, 410, 413
schema-focused therapy, 11, 459–460
schizophrenia, 85, 453
school, 17–18, 24, 371–372, **373–374**
  corporal punishment, 15
  intervention, 9, 367–372, **373–374**, 375–381
  IOM Protractor, *368*, 368, 370–371
  long-term care and aftercare 469
  mandated reporting, 9, 367–368, 370, 375–376, 380
  personnel, 368, 369–370
  programmes to avoid sexual abuse, 177–181, 184, 378–379
  risk and protective factors, **37–38**, 40
  survivors of child maltreatment, 376–378
School-Age Assessment of Attachment (SAA), **390**, 394–395
school psychologists, 367–369, 375–378, 380
School Readiness Programme, 342
School Success Program, **374**, 377–378
School-Wide Positive Behaviour Intervention and Support (SWPBIS), 370
Scientist-Practitioner approach, 262, 264–265, 272–273
Screening Assessment for Family Engagement, Retention, and Recovery (SAFERR), **477**
screening for substance use, 469, 472–475, **480**, 480, 482, 484, 486
  selected resources, **477–478**
  selected tools, **474–475**
  training, 479, **480**, 480–483, 486
secondary prevention, 41, 57, *123*, 123
secondary traumatisation, 413, 417
secondary victimisation, 417
secure attachment, 225–226, **232**
self-harm, 20, 55, 369, 454, 457
self-relevance, 243–245, 252
self-report surveys, 3, 16–17, 21, 25
semantic memory, 240
sensitivity, 386–387, 392, 456, 457
Sentencing Advisory Panel, 259
sentimentality, 228
Serious Case Reviews, 51, 53, 54, 56–57, 59
  lessons learnt, 62, **63**, 64
service provision in fatal child maltreatment, **50**

Sex Offender Registry, 183
sex tourism, 176, 187–188
sexual abuse *see* child sexual abuse (CSA)
sexual exploitation, 6, 7–8, 120, 121, 176–190
   case studies, 265, **266–267**, 267, **268**, 268–272
   child-focused strategies, 177–180
   child homicide, **52**
   gender, 24, 180
   motivation, 261, 262, 265, 267, **268**
   overcoming external inhibitions, 262, **270**, 270–271
   overcoming internal inhibitions, 262, 268–269, **269**, 270
   overcoming victim resistance, 262, **271**, 271–272
   parent-focused strategies, 180–183
   parenting and child custody, 258–273
   prevalence and incidence, 17, 24
   societal-level strategies, 185–189
   youth serving organizations, 183–185
Sexual Interests Domain, 263
Sexual Offences Act (2003), 259
shaking, **52**, 56–57, 65
siblings as perpetrators, 17, 21, **23**, 25
situational prevention theory, 183
smacking, 118, 124, 329
smoking, 77, 466
Sobriety Treatment and Recovery Teams (START), 483–484
social justice, 369, 379
social learning, 30, 299, 335–336, 350, 444
social media, 31, 40, 184–185
Social Media Guidelines, 184
social networking sites (SNSs), 184
social workers, 120, 283–284, 459
   assessments in care proceedings, 8, 279–89, **290**, 290–292
   Children's Services, 142, 143–144
   forensic interviewing, 239
   IPV, 408, 412
   named publicly, 281
   parents with IDD, 436, 437, 438, 447
   pre-proceedings, 150–159
   SAAF, 202, 219
societal variables, 40–41
socio-economics, 2, 10, 17–18, 39, 97, 131, 344
   consequences of child maltreatment, 4, 71, 76, 79
   fatal child maltreatment, 61–62
   homicide, 19

parents with IDD, 434–435, 442, 448
physical neglect, 74
Solihull Approach Parenting Group (SAPG), **341**, 351
spanking, 396
special educational needs, 119, 375
Stable 2007, 264
'start-again syndrome', **63**
Static-99, 264
Stay Safe Program, 372
Step Change, 332–333
stepfamilies, 30, **114**, 115
stigma, 24, 123, 177, 267
   parenting programmes, 6, 166, 170, 171
'Stop It Now!', 41, 186–187
Strange Situation Procedure, 389, **390**
STRAP-LD, 437
Strengthening Families, 484
Strengthening Families Strengthening Communities (SFSC), **341**
Strengths and Difficulties Questionnaire, 218
stress, 92, 310, 354, 409, 417
   brain development, 87, 89, 93
   consequences of CPA, 297–298
   covert filicide, 53
   fatal child maltreatment, **52**, 54
   hormone secretion, 89
   personality disorder, 453, 455, 456, 457
   risk factor, 39
   see also post-traumatic stress disorder (PTSD)
Structured Assessment of Risk and Need: Treatment Needs Analysis (SARN:TNA), 263
Students Helping Students, 376
Study of Adolescents' Family Experiences (SAFE) project, 333
subjective units of distress scale (SUDS), 323–324
substance abuse, adolescent, 55
substance abuse, parental, 11, 38–39, 71, 75–77, 125, 466–486
   assessment in child care proceedings, 284
   child welfare, 466–479, **480**, 480–482
   CSEM, 260, 269, **269**
   disorder definition, 467
   effective child protection, 131, 144
   fatal child maltreatment, **50**, **53**, 59, 59, **60**, 61, 468
   IDD, 435, 447
   IPV, 102, 406–407, 470
   neglect, 75–76, 329
   parenting programmes, 334, 344

substance abuse, parental (cont'd)
  personality disorder, 454
  physical health consequences, 77, 79
  pre-proceedings, 154, 158
  prevalence, 466, 469, 485
  removal of children, 136, 139, 141–142, 468–471
  resources for information, **477–478**
  risk factor, 38, 468, 472
  SAAF, *214*, *215*
  screening and assessment tools, 469, 472, **474–475**
substance abuse by victims, 313, 369
  consequence of maltreatment, **53**, 55, 73, 75–77, 79, 85, 91
Substance Abuse and Mental Health Services Administration (SAMHSA), 466, 472–473, **474**, 477, 478
  National Registry of Evidence-Based Programs and Practices, **478**
  Treatment Locator, **478**
Substance Abuse Subtle Screening Inventory (SASSI), **475**
sudden infant death syndrome (SIDS), 55
suggestibility, 7, 245–246, 250
suicide, 51, **52**, 55
supervision neglect, **53**, 54, 75–76, 77
  definition, 71, **72**
Supported by Research Evidence, 313, 314–316
Sure Start Children's Centres, 124
Sustainable Development Goals (SDGs), 126
systemic analysis, 209, 211, *212*
Systemic Therapy for At Risk Teens (START), 334

T-ACE, **475**
Talking About Touching, 372
task demand training (TDT), 243
Teaching and Reaching Using Students and Theater (TRUST), **374**
temperament and behaviour as risk factors, 36, 50, 56–57, 79
tertiary prevention, 41, *123*, 123
Think Family, 437
threat cues, 86, 90, *91*, 93
thresholds, 63
time-limited psychodynamic psychotherapy (TLDP-A), 316
'time out' agreements, 409
Toddler CARE-Index (TCI), **390**
trafficking, 120, 126, 369
  CSEC, 176, 179, 182, 186–189

Trafficking Victims Protection Act (TVPA) (2000), 187–188
training, 278, **480**, 480–482
  parenting programmes, 359–360, 361, 362
  reporting child maltreatment, 375–376, 380
  substance abuse, 466, 468–473, 479, **480**, 480–482, 486
  working with parents with IDD, 436, 438, 444–445
transient buffers, *33*, 34
transient challengers, *33*, 34
Transition to Adulthood Attachment Interview (TAAI), **390**
transparency, 135–136, 142, 145, 281, 412
trauma, 30, 407
Trauma-Focused Cognitive Behavioural Theory (TF-CBT), 8, 10, 302, 313, 314, 315–325, 427
  case study, 320–325
  description, 328–320
  review of research, 316–318
treatment as usual (TAU), 299, 301, 303, 317
Triple A Driver, 262, 269
Triple P (Positive Parenting Programme), 6, 124–125, 336, **337**, 344, 351
  costs, 170
  fidelity, 356, 358, 359
  parents with IDD, 445
  prevention of child maltreatment, 163, 165–167, *166*, **168**, 169–172
TWEAK, **475**
Tweenees Program, The, **374**

Re U [2012], 157
unborn children, 206, 209, 211
uncinate fasciculus, 88
UNCOPE screener, 472, **475**
unemployment, 260, 329, 435, 454, 470
  risk factor, 34, 39, 57, 62
United Kingdom Border Agency, 118
United Nations Committee on the Rights of the Child, 113, 117
United Nations Convention on the Rights of the Child (UNCRC), 40, 113, 117, 118, 126, 297
  care proceedings, 150
  removal of children, 141
  school-based interventions, 367, 369
  sexual exploitation, 180, 188
United Nations Study on Violence against Children, 113

Valuing Parents Support Service (VPSS), **443**, 446–447, **447**
Valuing Parents Support Service and Assessment Service, **447**
Vetting and Barring Scheme, 183
victimisation, 29–30, 31, 259, 368
    prevention of abuse and neglect, 15, 17–18, 21, **22–23**, 24–25
    sexual exploitation, 177–180, 182, 186
voluntary agreements, 116

wait-list control (WLC) groups, 315
Webster-Stratton Incredible Years programme, 125
Well-Supported by Research Evidence, 313, 314–316
What Works, 1–2, 3
white matter tracts, 88–89
Who Do You Tell?, 371, **374**
William Wilberforce Trafficking Victims Protection Reauthorization Act (2008), 187

wishes of the child, 141, 286, 288
'Words Not Said' programme, 41
working memory, 240
Working Together, 118, 119–120
Working Together with Parents Network (WTPN), 437, 439–440, **440**
    London Parents Advisory Group, 439, 440
World Health Organisation, 177, 473, **478**
    definition of child maltreatment, 16
    Multi-Country Study on Women's Health and Violence Against Women, 98
    Regional Committee for Europe, 188
World Report on Violence and Health (2002), 48

Young Parenting Inventory, 462
youth-serving organizations (YSOs), 176, 177, 183–185

zone of proximal development (ZPD), 388, 392, 399

Printed and bound by CPI Group (UK) Ltd, Croydon, CR0 4YY